Sanctioning Saddam

Sanctioning Saddam

The Politics of Intervention in Iraq

Sarah Graham-Brown

I.B.Tauris *Publishers*
LONDON • NEW YORK
in association with
MERIP

Published in 1999 by I.B.Tauris & Co Ltd
Victoria House, Bloomsbury Square, London WC1B 4DZ
175 Fifth Avenue, New York NY 10010
in association with Middle East Research and Information Project
1500 Massachusetts Avenue, NW, Suite 119, Washington DC 20005

In the United States and Canada distributed by St. Martin's Press
175 Fifth Avenue, New York NY 10010

ISBN 1 86064 473 2

A full CIP record for this book is available from the British Library
A full CIP record for this book is available from the Library of Congress

Library of Congress catalog card: available

Typeset in Caslon by Dexter Haven, London
Printed and bound in Great Britain by WBC Book Manufacturers, Bridgend

CONTENTS

ACKNOWLEDGEMENTS

The writing of this book was made possible by a grant for research and writing from the John D. and Catherine T. MacArthur Foundation. It is being published in association with the Middle East Research and Information Project in Washington DC, and I thank its staff and editorial committee for their encouragement and support. Finally, I thank Christian Aid in London, both for the support and encouragement given to me by its Middle East team when I was in the last stages of completing the book and for its help with promotion in the UK.

I have used a large number of libraries in the course of research, and I would particularly like to thank all the staff at the Documentation Unit, Centre for Arab Gulf Studies, University of Exeter, who helped me gather together material on several flying visits to Exeter, and Paul Auchterlonie, Librarian for Middle Eastern Studies, University of Exeter for his help in tracing more obscure titles. Thanks also to Kendal Nezan and Akil Marceau who kindly helped me with sources at the Kurdish Institute in Paris.

My job as coordinator of the Gulf Information Project, based at the Refugee Council in London, gave me the impetus to write this book. Although many of my collegues in the aid agencies concerned – CAFOD, Christian Aid, Oxfam, Quaker Peace and Service and Save the Children Fund, as well as the Refugee Council – have now moved on to other jobs, their ideas, experience and concerns provided the basis for this book. I also benefitted greatly from the fund of information within the NGO community, including both humanitarian and human rights organisations in Europe and the US, as well as Iraqi ones set up since 1991. Thanks are especially due to the staff responsible for Iraq over a number of years at Amnesty International in London and Human Rights Watch in New York.

I interviewed a large number of people for this book. Some of the interviewees are cited in the footnotes, where they are quoted or provided specific information. However, many others contributed valuable background and analysis, and I would particularly like to thank the following people for taking the time to help: Dr Shaul Bahkash, Frederic Charillon, Dr Shahram Chubin, Chris Dammers, Terry Giles, Karim Ghezraoui, Amanda Harding, Joost Hilterman, Yousif al-Khoei, Michiel Leezenberg, Bronwyn Lewis, David McDowall, Dr Kamil Mahdi, Dr Phebe Marr, Sir John Moberly, Dr David Nabarro, Roger Normand, Dr Soli Ozel, John Packer, Monica Press, Dr William Quandt, Laith Qubba, Dr Philip Robins, Gary Sick, Dr Stefan Sperl, Victor Tanner, Dr Charles Tripp, David Weaver, Valerie Yorke and Sarah Zaidy.

A substantial number of government, UN and ICRC officials and diplomats were also interviewed off the record. My thanks to all of them for their assistance.

On a more informal level, a number of people helped me by suggesting sources of information or contacts, providing ideas and analysis in informal discussions, and giving me the opportunity to attend seminars and debates. In particular, I thank Patrick Costello, Jeff Crisp, Dr Richard Garfield, Haris Gazdar, Falih A. Jabbar, Isam al-Khafaji, Larry Minear, Kamran Qaradaghi, Robert Rossborough, Barbara Stapleton, David Styan and Michael Yorke.

My thanks also to Baudouin Koenig and Maysoon Pachachi for allowing me to consult the interview material gathered for their films. Thanks also to ABC News, BBC Radio 4 and Roberts and Wykenham Films for the use of transcript material.

Many friends and colleagues came to my aid at various stages of the project, and put up with my complaints and doubts. David Cortright, Deniz Kandiyoti, Chris Johnson supported my application for funds to write the book, and Anna Enayat commissioned me to write the book and waited patiently for the manuscript. She joined Joe Stork and Nels Johnson in reading at least two drafts of the book. Particular thanks are due for their stamina as well as their insights. Barbara Harlow, Ann Lesch, Hania Mufti, Sami Zubaida also read all or part of the manuscript and provided valuable comments. Michele Cohen and Barbara Smith kindly gave their time at short notice to help with reading the proofs. Finally, thanks to all at I.B. Tauris who have been involved in production, and Robert Hastings who had the task of copy editing.

A NOTE ON THE TEXT

In this book, I have used the spelling 'Saddam Hussein', which does not conform with the system of Arabic transliteration otherwise used, as this is the spelling most familiar to Western readers.

GLOSSARY

UNITED NATIONS AND OTHER MULTILATERAL
ORGANISATIONS MENTIONED IN THE TEXT

ECHO: European Community Humanitarian Office
ICRC: International Committee of the Red Cross
IFRCS: International Federation of Red Cross and Red Crescent Societies
IOM: International Organisation for Migration
OSCE: Organisation for Security and Cooperation in Europe
UNDHA: United Nations Department of Humanitarian Affairs
   SUI: Special Unit for Iraq (Geneva)
   OIP: Office of the Iraq Programme (New York)
   IRCU: Inter-Agency Relief Coordination Unit (Baghdad)
UNDP: United Nations Development Programme
UNDRO: United Nations Disaster Relief Organisation
(UN)FAO: United Nations Food and Agriculture Organisation
UNHCR: United Nations High Commission for Refugees
UNICEF: United Nations Children's Fund
UNIFIL: United Nations Interim Force in Lebanon
UNIKOM: United Nations Iraq-Kuwait Observer Mission
UNOCHA: United Nations Office for the Coordination of Humanitarian Affairs
UNOHCI: United Nations Humanitarian Coordinator for Iraq
UNPROFOR: United Nations Protection Forces in Former Yugoslavia
UNSCOM: United Nations Special Commission
UNTAF: United Nations Transitional Assistance Force
(UN)WFP: United Nations World Food Programme

THE MAIN IRAQI POLITICAL GROUPS
(only the groups and parties mentioned frequently in the text are included)

The Ba'th Party
The Ba'th Arab Socialist Party was founded in 1944 in Syria by Michel Aflaq.
Ba'thist ideas were introduced to Iraq in 1949, but the party remained a small political
group until the overthrow of the Iraqi monarchy in 1958. The Iraqi Ba'th Party split
with the Syrian party in 1966. Iraq has been ruled by the Ba'th Party since 1968. In
September 1977, all members of the party's Regional Command became members of
the Revolutionary Command Council, which meant that the party and the state
became virtually indistinguishable.

Iraqi National Congress (INC)
Formed in June 1992 at a conference of Iraqi opposition groups and individuals in Vienna. INC subsequently established an office in Iraqi Kurdistan It is a pro-Western coalition whose primary objective is the removal of Saddam Hussein's regime.

Iraqi Communist Party (ICP)
Founded in 1934, this originally pro-Soviet party was admitted in 1973 to the National Progressive Patriotic Front formed by the Ba'th Party. A series of disagreements with the government over Kurdish autonomy and the Iran-Iraq War led to its withdrawal from the NPPF and exile of many of its members. Its Kurdish branch remained in existence, and in 1993, a separate Kurdish Communist Party (KCP) was formed, though closely linked to the ICP.

Da'wa Party
A Shi'i Muslim movement founded in the late 1950s. The most influential figure in the early period of its existence was Sayyid Muhammad Baqr al-Sadr who was executed by the Ba'thist government in 1980, as the culmination in a government campaign against the party after it had conducted attacks against government leaders. Its base shifted to Iran but since the 1980s, the relationship between the party and the Government of the Islamic Republic became increasingly tense, and some of its members moved to Syria.

Islamic Movement of Iraqi Kurdistan (IMIK)
Formed in 1986 or 1987, a Sunni Muslim movement inheriting some of the organisational structures of the Muslim Brotherhood which was founded Iraqi Kurdistan in the 1950s. With a strong base in Halabja, it developed links with Saudi Arabia as well as with Iran. Some of its members had fought in Afghanistan.

Iraqi National Accord (al-Wifaq)
An opposition group established since the 1991 Gulf War, said to include a number of former army officers and government officials.

Kurdistan Democratic Party (KDP)
Founded in 1946 by Mullah Mustapha Barzani, and since 1979 led by his son, Masud Barzani. The party sided with Iran during the Iran-Iraq War. The party is dominant in the north-western part of the Kurdish region.

Kurdistan Front
Established in May 1988 as an umbrella organisation for Kurdish political groups.

Patriotic Union of Kurdistan (PUK)
Founded in 1975 and led since that time by Jalal Talabani. The KDP's main competitor, its base of support is the south-eastern region, where the Surani dialect is spoken.

Supreme Council of the Islamic Revolution of Iraq (SCIRI)
Founded in Teheran in November 1982, and led by Hojatolislam Sayyid Muhammad Bakr al-Hakim , it was intended as a representative organisation of Iraqi Shi'i Islamic parties based in Iran. However, at the end of the Iran-Iraq War, a rift developed between SCIRI and the Da'wa Party, which froze its participation. In 1983, SCIRI also established a military unit, the Badr Corps.

INTRODUCTION

I n early February 1999, on the eighth anniversary of the 1991 Gulf War, US planes were again in action against Iraqi targets over the no-fly zones, the economic embargo was still in place, and the permanent Security Council members were looking for ways to break the deadlock between them.

The sense of *déjà vu* is familiar to anyone who has followed the twists and turns of international policy on Iraq since 1990, and whatever view of the arguments is taken, it is deeply frustrating. This book is an attempt to explain how this *impasse* was reached. I decided to write it after working between 1991 and 1994 with a group of British aid agencies which had been running aid programmes in Iraq from the time of the Gulf War. My work was primarily to pull together information relating to international policy on Iraq, UN activities and the work of the many other NGOs and human rights organisations which were addressing various aspects of the ongoing crisis.

The practical difficulties of working in Iraq rapidly became evident. What, after the initial emergency, were NGOs supposed to be doing in Iraq? Were they, as some people felt, merely providing crutches for a population of 19 million or more, most of whose lives had been disrupted by sanctions and war? Most felt this was anyway a task beyond their capacities. Aid workers were also frequently perturbed by the confused – or deliberately obscured – goals of post-war sanctions. Who really was deciding what the rationale of sanctions was? Was it some impersonal force of international law? As unanimity in the Security Council on the goals of sanctions began to break down, whose version was valid?

Taking these questions as a starting point, the book explores the history of political, economic and humanitarian intervention in Iraq by the international community since 1991. Both my colleagues and I were constantly aware of how wider political developments – inside Iraq, in neighbouring states and in the international community – constantly affected, and often foiled, our attempts to develop any coherent strategy on aid to Iraq. For this reason, I felt that in order to discuss the dilemmas of delivering humanitarian aid in a crisis, it was important to understand and confront these broader issues.

I decided to try and pull together the disparate themes in this complex picture, rather than focusing on particular aspects such as the impact of economic sanctions or the use of military force. This is very much 'history' in the making, and consequently its conclusions have to be provisional. Much information remains to be unearthed, and may lead to different conclusions than those reached here. But it seemed worth attempting such an exploration, on which other work may be able to build.

It examines the decisions made by external forces – the UN Security Council, national governments, UN humanitarian agencies and international NGOs – and how the state and the people of Iraq have responded. In 1991, humanitarian intervention was in fact an afterthought to war, a short-term response to civil conflict and a refugee crisis of unanticipated magnitude. It has left a legacy of ideas about the potential of international intervention to both coerce and protect. Some of the questions raised by this story therefore have resonances with other major humanitarian crises which have occurred at regular intervals since 1991 – including Somalia, Bosnia and Rwanda – where the basic problems have equally remained unresolved.

I have used the term 'international intervention' rather broadly to cover a variety of actions, from bombing raids and ground attacks to economic sanctions and humanitarian aid. I understand all these to be either coercive actions or at least actions which were not initiated or requested by the target government. In Iraq, humanitarian aid comes in this last category since prior to 1990 it was not a recipient of aid. Most academic analysts use the term intervention in a narrower sense. For some commentators, 'intervention' would not include measures agreed through international bodies such as the Security Council which formally recognise the sovereignty of the target state. Another authority defines humanitarian intervention 'as military intervention in a state without the approval of the authorities, and with the purpose of preventing widespread suffering or death among the inhabitants'.[1]

The book is organised in three sections which offer different perspectives on events in Iraq since 1991 – essentially three different places to stand when viewing events. The reason for taking this approach – at the risk of a degree of repetition – is to try and express the complex relationships between local, regional and international developments, and to understand the dynamics of each set of relationships.

Discussions with diplomats or foreign ministry officials from various states sometimes revealed perspectives so much at variance as to give the impression that quite different situations were under scrutiny. Furthermore, comparing these predominantly Western perspectives with those of Iraqis, either living in their country or outside it, revealed a further divergence, whatever their political views. I have endeavoured to give some sense of these diverging perspectives, although the conclusions drawn are my own.

The first section examines the standpoint of governments and the UN in formulating policy towards Iraq, and how Iraq responded. It argues that many of the decisions made by the UN and leading Western governments under the pressure of a humanitarian crisis in the months after the Gulf War set a pattern for future relations with the Iraqi Government, with the Kurds and Iraq's neighbours. It then examines in some detail how the economic embargo has worked in practice, and its outcomes. Finally it asks what were the practical effects of the measures taken in 1991 and 1992 to protect and provide aid for vulnerable sections of the Iraqi population.

The second section examines the situation inside Iraq: what the effects of the embargo have been and how the Government and population have responded. The situation in Iraqi Kurdistan is discussed separately since the experience of this region since 1992 has been somewhat different from that of the rest of Iraq.

Not only have many external forces been involved in the process of intervention, but the process itself has brought changes in Iraq. The Government has responded to external pressures with alternate defiance and acquiescence. Internally, the priority of survival has enhanced levels of political and social manipulation and conflict. The country's citizens are not simply passive victims, as often portrayed. As individuals, families and communities they respond to shortages, coercion and deprivation in a variety of ways which are not always predictable.

All this may seem far from the minutiae of aid programmes, but from the beginning, both UN agencies and NGOs working in Iraq and in surrounding states found the political questions hard to avoid. The third section therefore takes the first two as the context in which to discuss the politics of the UN humanitarian aid programme and the influence and effectiveness of NGOs working in different parts of the country.

The book covers a wide range of subjects and issues. It is obviously impossible to treat all of them in the same depth, and it therefore focuses particularly on issues relating to humanitarian aid and human rights, with less emphasis on military action and arms control issues. The work of the weapons inspectorate, UNSCOM, is discussed only in the more general context of political and military relations with Iraq. Occasions since 1991 when military force was used by members of the Gulf War Coalition are only referred to if they affected decision-making in the Security Council. These confrontations have usually been widely covered in the Western and Arab press, and are summarised chronologically in an appendix. A glossary is also provided, in which is listed the array of international organisations and political parties mentioned.

This book does not in any sense pretend to be a history of Iraq, but it seemed impossible to understand what happened after 1991 without some understanding of the previous decade – of how the regime had operated, how it had previously survived defeat, and how Iraq's people had reacted to the strange combination of rapidly rising and then falling living standards, repression and prolonged war. Hence some aspects of the history of the previous decade are discussed, based on studies produced in the 1970s and 1980s, hopefully to contribute to an understanding of why events turned out so differently to how many people expected or imagined in April 1991.

Several important issues are not included in the scope of the book. The many environmental outcomes of the Gulf War are only briefly discussed. Regional aspects of war-induced pollution are not included. Finally, while the fate of Iraqi refugees who have remained outside the country is treated in some detail, the fate of the many people of other nationalities – third-country nationals who were migrant workers in Iraq and Kuwait at the time of the invasion, Kuwaiti prisoners of war and others still missing since 1991 and, in Kuwait, the Palestinian community and the *bidouns* (stateless inhabitants of Kuwait) – are not dealt with.[2]

THE POLITICS OF INFORMATION

One of the difficulties of writing this book has been the dubious reliability of many sources of information. The issue of politicised information will frequently be referred to because it has been a major difficulty in assessing events in Iraq since 1991. In a society which has been heavily controlled since the 1960s, information is inevitably shaped by the political pressures exerted by the regime and by the hopes and wishes of its opponents. Into this situation came another element: after the Gulf War, information became a weapon in the confrontation between Iraq and some members of the Security Council. Also caught up in this are UN organisations, non-government agencies, human rights and commercial organisations, all of which have particular perspectives and cultures of information and concealment.

Information on events and trends within Iraq has become a political commodity. On one side, the Iraqi Government encourages the view that responsibility for all the country's misfortunes lies at the door of the '30-nation conspiracy'. The US Government's view of events, on the other hand, is coloured by its wish to emphasise the weakening or imminent collapse of Saddam's regime. Meanwhile, Iraqi opposition groups inevitably highlight the ills caused by the Government and the disasters it has inflicted on the Iraqi people. Rumours and theories abound on all sides, but serious analysis is hampered by these narrow political agendas, and by the lack of access for independent observers with the opportunity to move about freely and have open discussions with different sections of the population.

Both the Government and its adversaries in the international community have attempted to simplify the outcomes of sanctions for their own ends. Those in the international community who wish, for a variety of reasons – most of which have little to do with humanitarian needs or human rights – to see sanctions remain in place, stress the political responsibility of the regime for all the outcomes of sanctions, whether foreseen or not. The regime, on the other hand, continues to use civilian suffering to call for the lifting of sanctions, and to blame on those sanctions all the ills of society.

Since Western press interest in Iraq, even in the Kurds, began to fade in 1992, the only events which have hit the headlines for more than a day or so have been the increasingly frequent confrontations between Iraq and the UN or coalition forces, and periodic bouts of mayhem within Saddam Hussein's inner circle of relatives and supporters. Many column inches were consumed by the defection of Saddam Hussein's sons-in-law Hussein Kamil al-Majid and Saddam Kamil al-Majid in August 1995 – and their gruesome end when they decided to return to Iraq in January 1996 – and the assassination attempt on Uday Hussein in December 1996.

From August 1990 onwards, most public attention has been focused on Saddam Hussein himself. For Americans especially, the portrayal of Saddam shifted from promising ally who could be made 'to see sense' to the Middle Eastern equivalent of Hitler. The continued focus of political rhetoric and press reports on Saddam and some of the brutal personalities surrounding him has largely precluded discussion of why the regime has survived through two wars and an economic embargo.

The paucity of knowledge about how Iraqi society works is not limited to the period after 1990. The limited access outsiders have to information, and the difficulties Iraqis have had in speaking freely – except in exile – is a problem which goes back to the 1970s. Some very important economic and political studies were researched and written in the 1970s and 1980s, but mostly by people who were not living in Iraq at that time (see Bibliography, Part II). Even for the best informed of these observers, both Iraqis and Westerners, post-1990 analysis has to be based more on interviews and anecdote than on any systematic gathering of information. Before 1990, it is now evident that businessmen and arms dealers, and the more enterprising members of the diplomatic community, did develop knowledge of aspects of Iraq's economy and society, but only insofar as it suited their needs. They too were constrained by the limits placed on them by the regime. Therefore the question of what has changed since 1990, and how much has it changed, is still very difficult to answer.

From April 1991, a flood of journalists, UN officials and aid workers entered Iraq, and for about six months there was relative freedom to move around and meet people, sometimes without 'minders'. At that time many Iraqis seemed willing to speak much more openly to outsiders than they had been before the war. However, the majority of those who came to work or visit had no prior experience of Iraq, and therefore no means of comparing what they saw and heard with conditions before the war. As the Government progressively reasserted control, especially through its security services, the channels of information again began to narrow. By late 1992, few aid workers were operating outside Baghdad, and the opportunities for unimpeded travel were reduced.

After October 1991, the three northern governorates, no longer under Iraqi government control, became open to aid agencies, human rights workers and journalists. For the first year after the war, there was a great deal of interest in this region, which attracted Western politicians as well as other foreign visitors. However, as time passed with no clear resolution to the overall situation in Iraq, interest diminished. By 1994, in the US at least, government policy did not encourage discussion of the effect of prolonged economic sanctions, while the growing internal conflict in the Kurdish-controlled areas received little coverage in the Western media. An additional problem since 1994 has been the growing restrictions imposed by the Turkish authorities on journalists, human rights workers and latterly aid agencies which wished to enter northern Iraq through Turkey.

The reports of humanitarian agencies focus on emergency aid priorities such as food, healthcare, water and sanitation, for which they need to raise funds from the international community. Since 1991 a number of official reports have appeared on the humanitarian situation in Iraq, although sometimes their contents have been contentious.

Another source of information on conditions inside Iraq comes from those who have left the country since 1990: the relatively small number who have obtained visas to other countries, and many more who have left as refugees. Since human rights organisations are denied access to government-controlled Iraq, most of their information comes from refugees and others leaving the country, or fleeing to the Kurdish-controlled areas of the north. Again most of this information is individual and anecdotal.

The media in Iraq are tightly controlled, and information from these sources has to be understood in this light. In similar fashion, information from the official media of surrounding countries – Turkey, Iran, Kuwait, Syria and even Jordan – is subject to the specific interests of the governments concerned. Opposition groups also produce large amounts of information, but share a tendency common among such groups to magnify the importance of their actions, and on occasion to exaggerate the threat from government forces. However, since some of this material has proved reasonably accurate, it cannot be dismissed as unreliable out of hand.

Information from Western governments may depend on their intelligence sources, which they jealously guard, and what is released to the public may be selected to support their position at the time – whether on arms control, human rights or the impact of sanctions. Furthermore, it seems that 'human' intelligence on the ground is lacking, except as filtered through opposition groups. Aerial surveillance has been intense since the Gulf War, and undoubtedly has revealed the progress of many events, most notably the draining of sections of the southern marshes, though such information is not necessarily released to the public.

As much as possible of what follows is based on information which is corroborated by more than one source, but it cannot pretend to tell the whole story or to be wholly accurate. The aim is to ask what happens inside an authoritarian society when it is placed under acute pressures by international intervention, and to sketch out some of the trends which may be developing as a result.

As far as possible, sources of information – published material and on-the-record interviews – are either cited or discussed in the relevant chapters. Books and major articles or reports are also included in the bibliography. However, there are instances where no references are given. There are several reasons for this.

First, between 1991 and 1994, as part of my work, I produced a newsletter on events in Iraq and decision-making in the international community relating to Iraq and neighbouring states. This relied to a considerable extent on off-the-record briefings, and information which came from meetings and discussions which were not in the public domain. Consequently, I felt that when using this information as background in the book, I should respect the confidentiality of these sources. At times the *Gulf Newsletter* is cited when it summarises information from these interviews or discussions.

Secondly, because Iraqis both inside and outside the country often feel vulnerable or at risk, I have decided not to use any names of Iraqis quoted in the text, except where they are political figures, academics whose work is published or have agreed to be named. Where stories gathered from refugees and others who have left the country are used, no references are given except their place of origin and their country of refuge or immigration.

Many people from outside Iraq who have been involved in political or humanitarian aspects of intervention since 1991 have not wanted to be quoted directly, especially if they are still active, and I have respected that wish. This includes government officials, diplomats, UN and ICRC officials. Iraqi government and opposition sources are both used, with some attempt where the information is controversial to assess its credibility.

In such a contentious climate, it is difficult to rely entirely on single sources of information. Where possible, facts and interpretations of events have been checked with more than one source. Where this has not been possible, the story is either used only as a footnote, or words such as reportedly or allegedly are used to indicate that its status.

NOTES ON INTRODUCTION

1   Roberts (1996), p 19.
2   On war deaths and environmental damage, see Middle East Watch (1991), *Needless Deaths in the Gulf War: Civilian Casualties During the Air Campaign and Violations of the Laws of War* (New York); Saul Bloom, John M. Miller and Philippa Winkler (eds) *(1994), Hidden Casualties: Environmental, Health and Political Consequences of the Persian Gulf War* (Arms Control Research Center (ARC)/London, Earthscan). On displaced and vulnerable populations after the Gulf War, see Nicholas Van Hear (1993), 'Mass flight in the Middle East: involuntary migration and the Gulf conflict 1990–91' in R. Black and V. Robinson (eds), *Geography and refugees: patterns and processes of change* (London); Amnesty International (1993), *Iraq: Secret Detention of Kuwaitis and Third Country Nationals* (London); Middle East Watch (1991), *Nowhere to Go: The Tragedy of the Remaining Palestinian Families in Kuwait* (New York); Ann M. Lesch (1991), 'Palestinian in Kuwait', *Journal of Palestine Studies*, vol. 20, no. 4 (Summer), pp 42–54; Human Rights Watch/Middle East (1995), *The Bedoons of Kuwait: Citizens without Citizenship* (New York).

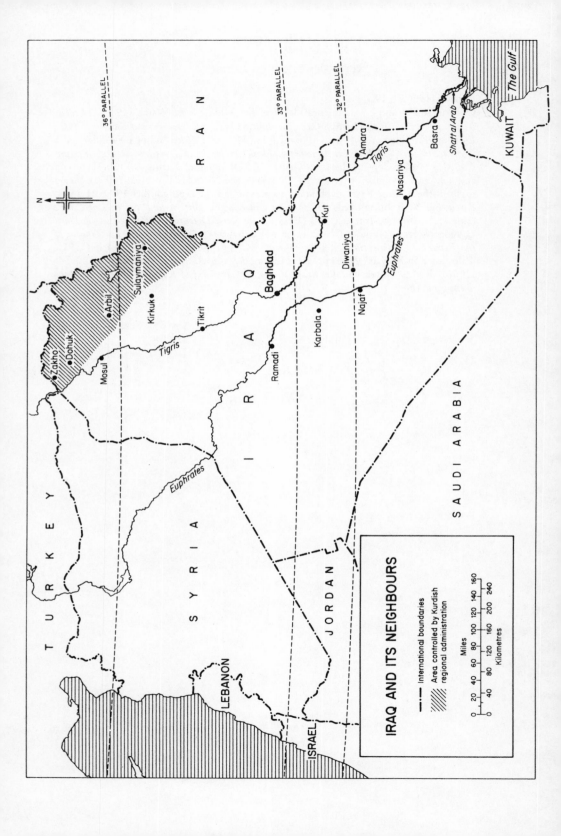

IRAQ AND ITS NEIGHBOURS

International boundaries
Area controlled by Kurdish regional administration

Miles
0   20   40   60   80   100 120 140 160
0   40   80   120 160 200 240
Kilometres

TURKEY

IRAN

SYRIA

LEBANON

ISRAEL

JORDAN

SAUDI ARABIA

KUWAIT

The Gulf

IRAQ

Baghdad

Zakho
Dohuk
Mosul
Arbil
Sulaymaniya
Kirkuk
Tikrit
Ramadi
Karbala
Najaf
Diwaniya
Kut
Amara
Nasariya
Basra

Tigris
Euphrates
Shatt al Arab

36° PARALLEL
33° PARALLEL
32° PARALLEL

N

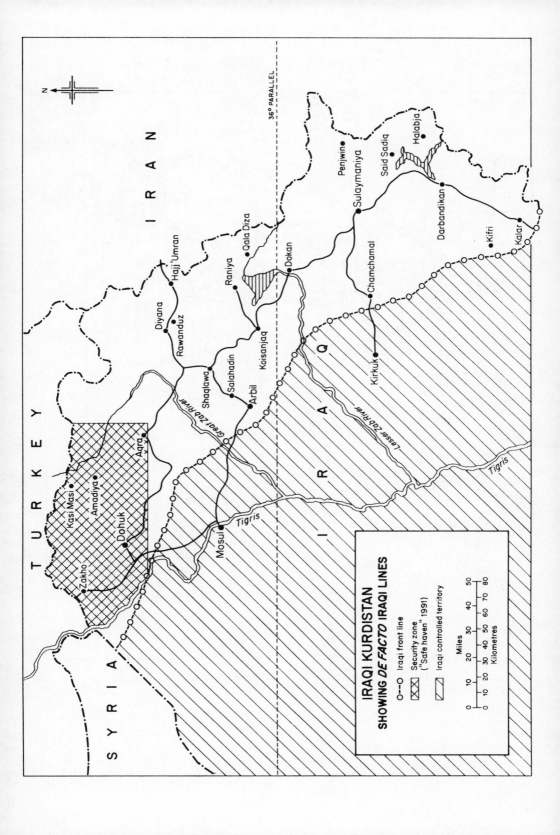

IRAQI KURDISTAN
SHOWING *DE FACTO* IRAQI LINES

O—O Iraqi front line
▨ Security zone ("Safe haven" 1991)
▨ Iraqi controlled territory

Miles
0   10   20   30   40   50
0 10 20 30 40 50 60 70 80
Kilometres

36° PARALLEL

I R A N

T U R K E Y

S Y R I A

I R A Q

Penjwin
Halabja
Said Sadiq
Sulaymaniya
Darbandikan
Kifri
Kalar
Chamchamal
Qala Diza
Raniya
Dokan
Hajj 'Umran
Diyana
Rawanduz
Koisanjaq
Kirkuk
Shaqlawa
Salahadin
Arbil
Aqra
Kasi Masi
Amadiya
Dohuk
Zakho
Mosul

Great Zab River
Lesser Zab River
Tigris
Tigris

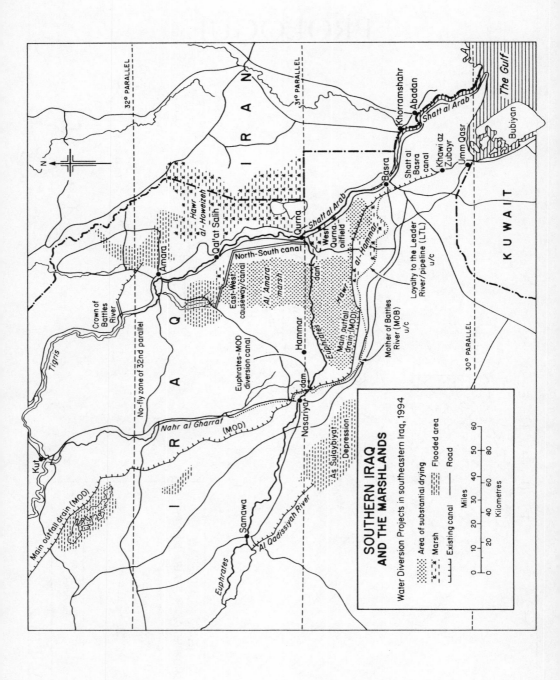

SOUTHERN IRAQ AND THE MARSHLANDS

Water Diversion Projects in southeastern Iraq, 1994

Area of substantial drying

~x~x~ Marsh   Flooded area

——— Existing canal   Road

Miles
0   10   20   30   40   50   60

Kilometres
0   20   40   60   80

Labels on map:

The Gulf

KUWAIT

IRAN

IRAQ

32° PARALLEL

31° PARALLEL

30° PARALLEL

No-fly zone of 32nd parallel

N

Khorramshahr

Abadan

Shatt al Arab

Basra

Shatt al Basra canal

Khawi az Zubayr

Umm Qasr

Bubiyan

Qurna

Shatt al Arab

West Qurna oilfield

Hawr al-Hammar

Loyalty to the Leader River/pipeline (LTL) u/c

Amara

Hawr al-Howeizeh

Qal'at Salih

North-South canal

East-West causeway/canal

Al Amara marsh

Euphrates

dam

dam

Main outfall drain (MOD)

Mother of Battles River (MOB) u/c

Crown of Battles River

Tigris

Euphrates-MOD diversion canal

Nahr al Gharraf (MOD)

Hammar

Nasariya

As Sulaybiyat Depression

Kut

Main outfall drain (MOD)

Samawa

Al Qadissiyah River

Euphrates

PROLOGUE

IRAQ AND THE INTERNATIONAL COMMUNITY BEFORE AUGUST 1990

A remarkable feature of the 1990 crisis over Iraq's invasion of Kuwait was the reversal of attitudes to Iraq among the Security Council's permanent members. In the case of the US and UK the change was abrupt. For Russia and France, Iraq's main allies and trading partners over a long period, the shift was more hesitant. In the 1980s, Iraq was viewed as of strategic importance in the Gulf region, while its purchasing power from oil revenues made it an attractive market for arms sales and consumer exports as well as for civil contracts – whether for new projects, or to restore what had been destroyed during the Iran-Iraq War. Although the extent of Iraq's military expansion after the Iran-Iraq War was well known, the main preoccupation was to secure a share in this lucrative market. An economic climate in which European governments increasingly supported export competition in defence and other sectors further encouraged this trend.

The shift in Western policy only came because the Iraqi regime, feeling the pressures created by its war economy, decided to challenge Kuwait and, if only indirectly, Saudi Arabia. After the invasion of Kuwait, the US and British Governments in particular projected a stridently critical position which belied the policies of the previous decade, emphasising what had previously been played down: the Iraqi Government's propensity for aggression towards its neighbours and repression of its own people.

Many of the issues which featured in the post-1991 conflict with Iraq – from weapons of mass destruction to human rights – had their roots in the 1980s. Revelations on the extent of dealings with Iraq among leading coalition states in the pre-war period began to appear in the media soon after the 1991 war ended, mainly as a result of US congressional investigations and the Scott enquiry in the UK.

US policy in the Gulf region since the 1970s had given priority to the stability of Saudi Arabia and, to a lesser extent, the other oil-rich states in the Gulf. This influenced its view of the balance of power between Saudi Arabia and the other two major states in the region, Iraq and Iran. Relations with Iraq during the 1970s were cool,

1

given its alliance with the Soviet Union and superpower competition in the region. Its policy at that time rested on the 'twin pillars' of the Shah's Iran and Saudi Arabia.

In 1979, Pentagon analysts, led by Paul D. Wolfowitz and including Dennis Ross, who became Secretary of State James Baker's director of policy in the Bush administration, wrote a secret paper which discussed the possibility of an Iraqi invasion of Kuwait. It discussed the threat this would pose to Saudi Arabia, and possible US military responses. However, this scenario was largely ignored by the Carter and Reagan administrations.

During the 1980s, US policy-makers became increasingly preoccupied with containing Iran which, after the establishment of the Islamic Republic, was perceived as the main threat in the region. 'Iraq's decision to launch a... war with Iran was seen by top officials in both administrations, not as a confirmation of the expansionist and aggressive nature of the Ba'thist regime, but as a move that could check the power of revolutionary Iran.'[1] Diplomatic relations with Iraq, broken in 1967, were restored in 1984. Iraq was also taken off the US list of 'states supporting terrorism' in 1982. It was only reinstated on this list after the invasion of Kuwait. During the Iran-Iraq War, the US reportedly went so far as to give Iraq satellite pictures of Iran's military positions and operations.[2]

The balance of international opinion generally tilted against Iran and in favour of Iraq, which at the time was promoting itself as the protector of the Arabs against the 'Persians'. By 1982, it became evident that Iraq would not win the war easily, and the regime became increasingly dependent on the Gulf states, particularly Saudi Arabia and Kuwait, to finance its war effort. Efforts by some Gulf states to mediate an end to the war were a matter of concern in Baghdad. However, since they were unable to find much common ground with Iran, they continued to finance Iraq.[3]

The Soviet Union developed close ties with Iraq in the 1970s. The relationship began as that of Cold War patron and client, but Iraq increasingly slipped from Soviet political control, to the extent that in 1980 Saddam Hussein declared war on Iran without even notifying Moscow in advance.[4] The Soviets' domination of Iraq's foreign trade diminished as Western competition increased, but despite a brief Soviet embargo on supplying weapons to Iraq between 1980 and 1982, it still remained Iraq's main source of military equipment. As of 1989, the Soviet Union accounted for 47 percent of Iraq's major weapons systems and France 28 percent.[5]

France, like the UK, had historical links with Iraq, gaining a quarter share in the Iraq Petroleum Company in the settlement which followed World War I. Iraq nationalised IPC in 1972, but France was guaranteed the same level of oil supplies as before nationalisation, helping it to weather the 1973 crisis. Its military co-operation with Iraq subsequently increased, including the supply of inputs for the Osirak nuclear reactor, bombed by the Israelis in 1981. Under Socialist governments in the 1980s, France moved closer to Iraq during the Iran-Iraq War, as relations with Teheran had soured soon after Ayatollah Khomeini took power.

Indeed, much Western policy towards Iraq during the Iran-Iraq War was based on the notion that Iraq presented a lesser danger than Iran. With the exception of France, most major Western states passed legislation to control the transfer of lethal weapons to both Iran and Iraq. However, there were numerous loopholes which in practice allowed suppliers to 'tilt' in favour of Iraq. The extent of this tilt only became publicly apparent after 1990 in investigations into arms sales and sales of military-related equipment to Iraq, particularly during the latter part of the war. In the view of some analysts, 'If Iran had not been severed from its main arms suppliers and if Saddam had not enjoyed the massive military support of almost the entire international community, he would undoubtedly have lost the [Iran-Iraq] war'.[6]

British guidelines on defence equipment called for a ban on supplies of lethal equipment to either side in the Iran-Iraq War. However the Scott enquiry concluded that although up to 1987 the guidelines may have been followed as far as weapons were concerned, 'the DTI [Department of Trade and Industry] did not regard dual-use equipment as being subject to the guidelines'. Additionally, it was found that the defence allocations made to Iraq under successive financial protocols, allowing it to purchase defence-related materials, were 'not consistent with the government policy of strict impartiality or even-handedness towards the combatants in the Iran/Iraq war'.[7] During the 1980s, the UK, along with Jordan, also became an important base for Iraqi front companies, mainly concerned with military purchases.[8]

During the Iran-Iraq War, US policy was to prohibit sales of military equipment to both belligerents, and prior to 1982 such sales to Iraq had anyway been banned because Iraq was on the list of 'terrorist-supporting states'. Ironically, the only exception to this ban on commercial sales of defence items was 'if the items were for the protection of the head of state. As a result of the exception, license applications valued at $48 million were approved.'[9]

However, the value of such exports was small compared with the other major category of dual-use items which, once Iraq was removed from the terrorist list, was not subject to restrictions. These items included aircraft, helicopters, machine tools, computers and other electronic equipment. It was in transfers of high technology items that the US probably contributed significantly to Iraq's military and weapons programme. According to Department of Commerce data, licences in this category valued at $1.5 billion were approved for Iraq between 1985 and 1990, though not all the transactions were actually completed.[10]

The report also suggested that several Middle Eastern states, including Saudi Arabia, Kuwait and possibly the United Arab Emirates (UAE), had supplied Iraq with defence materials sold to them by the US.[11] Other investigations have alleged that substantial amounts of defence material was transferred from Jordan to Iraq.[12]

Evidence has also emerged since 1991 of lax enforcement of rules on defence and dual-use exports to Iraq in a number of other European countries. Germany in particular had pursued a liberal trade policy since the 1960s which had allowed German firms to become involved in arms and chemical sales to Iraq and Libya. This was not tightened up until February 1991.[13]

After the war ended in 1988, the commercial possibilities of reconstruction and Iraq's continued development of its military industries were seen as opportunities too good to miss. However, from the mid-1980s Iraq experienced increasing problems in paying for what it had ordered. Its response was to put pressure on its suppliers to provide new credits. During the war, Tariq Aziz reportedly used the argument that if Iraq did not receive more weapons it would lose the war, and then it would not be able to pay back its debts. For France, and more particularly the Soviet Union, to which Iraq had the largest debts, this issue of repayment became a consideration in their post-1990 policies.

In 1989–90, disputes arose with France over payment for materials already received. The French Ministry of Finance objected to further credits in view of Iraq's poor record of payment. However, the Iraqis continued to bargain new contracts against payment of arrears. Iraq's debt to France by 1990 was said to be some FF24 billion, of which an estimated 15 billion were guaranteed by COFACE, France's official export guarantee agency. Arrears to COFACE were financed in a triangular deal with the oil companies Elf Aquitaine and Total.[14]

The British Export Credit Guarantee Department (ECGD) encountered a similar problem with Iraqi arrears, though on a smaller scale. As the Scott Report noted: 'The basic problem regarding the continuing credit arrangements with Iraq was that in order to induce Iraq to continue to make the interest payments and capital payments due in respect of existing indebtedness, it was judged necessary to offer some quantity of new credit'. As of June 1990, the ECGD's exposure in Iraq was given as £1 billion.[15]

After the Iran-Iraq War, the British Government's public position on defence sales to Iraq remained the same, but in practice the guidelines were further relaxed to favour expanded trade – both civilian and military – with Iraq. It was not until late July 1990 that the Prime Minister Margaret Thatcher and the Foreign Secretary agreed in principle that there should be a publicly announced relaxation in the UK's position on military trade with Iraq. This decision was overtaken by the Iraqi invasion of Kuwait.

The scale of Iraqi military procurement and its development of strategic weapons were discussed in an inter-departmental review on defence sales policy towards Iraq in July 1990. However, it was noted that 'Iraq is an important export market for the UK, though she continues to experience severe payment difficulties. UK visible exports to Iraq totalled £450 million in 1989. Invisible exports were also important. The trade balance has been consistently in the UK's favour in recent years.'[16]

The end of the Iran-Iraq War provided the Bush administration with a natural opportunity to reassess Washington's tilt towards Iraq. But despite the urging of some officials in the State Department, the Bush administration did not challenge the assumptions behind the Reagan adminstration's approach. Indeed, not only did commercial relations and trade credits increase after the end of the war, but Secretary of State James Baker reportedly even sought to enlist Iraq's assistance in its attempt to launch a Palestinian-Israeli dialogue in 1989.[17]

Since 1982, Iraq had became a major market for US agricultural goods, which supplied about 30 percent of its needs, creating some domestic pressure in the US for continued trade relations. Almost $1 billion a year in agricultural credits continued after the war ended in 1988. Annual trade between the US and Iraq grew from around $500 million in the early 1980s to $3.5 billion in 1990.[18]

It seems that both commercial gain and concerns about the regional balance of power allowed all the leading players to watch Iraq's military expansion without analysing its possible political consequences. This was despite growing difficulties in relations with Iraq, and not only over payment of bills. Revelations about the Iran-Contra affair, in which the US also sold military equipment to Iran during the war, created mistrust of American intentions on the Iraqi side. By March 1990, the execution of the Iranian-born British journalist Farzad Bazoft on charges of spying for Israel and the discovery by British customs officials of electronic capacitators for nuclear weapons and of components of a suspected 'supergun' had raised the tensions. Yet the US, along with Britain and other European states, continued to pursue basically conciliatory policies.[19]

According to one analysis, 'the Bush adminstration's reluctance to cast Iraq as an adversary actually stemmed from more deep-seated intelligence assumptions and foreign policy calculations. Intelligence analysts later conceded that the fundamental mistake in US dealings with Baghdad was the failure to understand the explosive relationship between the deteriorating Iraqi economy and its outsize military.'[20]

HUMAN RIGHTS ISSUES

From August 1990, Iraq's human rights record became a subject of indignant attack from politicians in leading coalition states. For more than a decade before that date, Amnesty International and other human rights organisations had highlighted the extent of human rights abuses in Iraq. This stirred some criticism in the West but little practical response. Even those states which did criticise the abuses continued political, military and commercial relations with Iraq. As one observer noted, 'Prewar Iraq provides a striking example of the insignificance of human rights questions in international relations'.[21] It took the Iraqi threat to Kuwait, and potentially to Saudi Arabia, to galvanise international attention.

A further consequence of the long period of repressive government in Iraq was even less widely acknowledged: the large number of Iraqis living in exile. After the majority of the two million people who fled in 1991 had returned, there were still estimated to be about some four million Iraqis living outside their country. For the majority, exile began in the 1960s and 1970s. Academics and journalists, writers, painters and architects chose to leave when they found the mixture of coercion and cooptation characteristic of Ba'thist rule too much to take. The era of the Iran-Iraq War led many young men to leave in an attempt to avoid military service in that brutal conflict.

Others fled because of their political affiliations, or were forced out by ethnic or religious persecution. In the 1970s, an estimated 200,000 Shi'i Fayli Kurds were deported to Iran because of their presumed 'Iranian origin' (see page 215). Some 30,000 members of the Barzan clan, Sunni Kurds from north-western Iraq, also became refugees in Iran following the Algiers agreement of 1975 which ended Iranian support for the Iraqi Kurds. In the early 1970s and again in the early 1980s, hundreds of thousands of Shi'i Iraqis were deported to Iran as 'Iranians and Iraqis of Iranian origin'.[22] Soon afterwards, the leadership of clandestine Islamist groups in Iraq, particularly followers of Ayatollah Baqr al-Sadr (executed in 1980) and of the Shi'i Da'wa party, fled to Iran.

In 1988 and 1989, well over 100,000 Iraqi Kurds fled from Iraq during the Anfal campaigns (see Chapter 6), especially after the chemical bombing of Halabja in which some 5000 people were killed and many more injured.[23] Reports that Iraq was engaging in massive destruction, killings, use of chemical weapons and forcible deportation of the Kurdish population in the north of the country did arouse shock and public protest in the West. The US State Department issued a condemnation of the use of chemical weapons at Halabja.[24] But even abuses on this scale did not weigh too heavily against the growing scale of trade interests.

An argument recently used by the Clinton administration over relations with China was deployed by both the US and UK – that it was better to maintain a dialogue (and trade) with the offending state rather than to cut it off. Sanctions, it was argued, were ineffective while at the same time damaging to national interests.

In the US Congress, the Senate Foreign Relations Committee in 1988 sponsored a resolution calling for sanctions to be imposed on Iraq which would have affected $800 million in guaranteed loans. A resolution proposing more limited measures was also approved by the House of Representatives Foreign Affairs Committee. However, both measures became bogged down by congressional special interests, as did a general measure from the Senate to impose sanctions on countries using chemical weapons.[25] Any form of sanctions was opposed by the administration on the grounds that they were against the national interest. The White House called the sanctions proposed after Halabja 'terribly premature' and counterproductive for 'billions of dollars' of business for US companies.[26]

The British Government was well aware of the scale of the abuse. In June 1988 its Defence Attache in Baghdad reported 'Iraq's widespread razing of Kurdish villages, expulsion of Kurdish people from the mountains [sic] guerrilla areas in the North East, including extermination by chemical weapons of those who refuse to leave'.[27] It was also acutely conscious of public sensitivities about defence sales to Iraq. These were being stepped up at the end of the Iran-Iraq War, without any public announcement of the change in policy. According to a note by his Private Secretary, Foreign Secretary Lord Howe was reluctant to make the changes public because 'it could look very cynical if so soon after expressing outrage over Iraqi treatment of the Kurds we were to adopt a more flexible approach on arms sales'. Howe later said he did not regard this as cynical but rather as reflecting the importance of Iraqi defence sales to British trade.[28]

In the UN Commission for Human Rights (UNHCR) in Geneva, draft resolutions on the human rights situation in Iraq were voted down in 1989 and 1990, mainly because of opposition from non-aligned states. In 1989 the draft resolution was sponsored by 15 states – not including either the US or France – though they voted for the resolution.[29] In 1990, a resolution proposing to send a mission to Iraq was rejected. This time the US was among the sponsors.

The French decision not to sponsor the 1989 resolution might seem surprising since there was considerable public interest in the Kurdish issue in France at this time, generated mainly through the Kurdish Institute in Paris. With France Liberté, the Institute organised an international Kurdish conference on human rights in October 1989, with French Government financial support.[30] However, the pro-Iraq lobby was still powerful, and had been able to limit government criticism of Iraq for its use of chemical gas, both against Iranian troops during the Iran-Iraq War and at Halabja. The French Government was reportedly active in preventing Iraq being singled out for condemnation over its chemical attacks at an international conference in early 1989 on preventing the proliferation of chemical weapons.[31]

The Iraqi invasion of Kuwait, rather like the British Falklands campaign in regard to Argentina, provoked a sudden surge of concern about human rights in the aggressor state. Suddenly the brutalities of the Iraqi regime became part of the justification for going to war, when previously even relatively minor sanctions or resolutions of censure were not regarded with great enthusiasm. This *volte face* was most clearly evident in the US, where President Bush became vocal over these abuses.

The irony was not lost on Iraqis in the opposition. A Kurdish spokesman commented that Saddam's invasion of Kuwait achieved, at a stroke, what many years of campaigning by the Iraqi opposition, Arab and Kurd, and of exposing massive human rights abuses had failed to achieve. It made the Iraqi regime a focus of hostility for major Western governments, convincing them that Saddam Hussein was dangerous and had to be punished.[32]

THE INVASION OF KUWAIT: AUGUST 1990–FEBRUARY 1991[33]

Iraq's invasion of Kuwait in August 1990 seems to have been motivated mainly by its growing economic crisis following the Iran-Iraq War. Requiring an immediate injection of funds, Iraq had demanded that the Gulf states, especially Kuwait and Saudi Arabia, should 'forgive' the loans they had made in support of Iraq during the war. The Iraqi Government was also among several oil states to demand that Kuwait and the UAE cease to overstep their oil quotas, a demand which was finally accepted under pressure from Saudi Arabia, Iraq and Iran at a July 1990 Gulf oil ministers meeting in Jeddah. Finally, the Iraqi Government charged Kuwait with 'stealing' from the Rumailia oilfield which spanned their border, over which the two states had a long-standing dispute.[34]

The speed and extent of the international response to the Iraqi invasion came as a surprise – and not only to the Iraqi regime. The unanimity of response within the UN Security Council was unprecedented. Within a few weeks not only was a comprehensive economic embargo on Iraq agreed (under Resolution 661) but it had been implemented by most of Iraq's main trading partners. Furthermore, Iraq's key oil pipelines, controlled by Turkey and Saudi Arabia, had been shut down.

The Gulf crisis signalled the end of the logjam imposed on the Security Council by the Cold War, during which the two superpowers had systematically blocked each others' initiatives. With the Soviet Union largely absorbed in its own problems, the US, as militarily the most powerful member of the Council, found a new hegemony in a situation where it regarded its vital interests to be at stake. If the 1990 crisis had involved the invasion of a state which was not the focus of US interests, the latter might have been less eager to assume a leadership role.

The US attitude towards the UN, especially where the Middle East was concerned, had generally been negative prior to August 1990. US governments had devoted considerable effort to defending Israel against Security Council resolutions, using its veto 27 times between 1973 and 1990 on issues related to the Arab-Israeli conflict.[35] This negative position was obviously reinforced by its rivalries with the Soviet Union over the Middle East. The first cooperative action was Resolution 598 (20 July 1987) which aimed to end the Iran-Iraq War. It was adopted unanimously under Chapter VII of the UN Charter, which allows the Security Council to take action to enforce the resolution.[36]

For the smaller, less powerful states on the Security Council, action to help a small state which had been invaded by a larger neighbour was viewed as an important principle. However, defence of oil supplies was certainly a key issue. Many observers have pointed to numerous small states which have had their borders infringed without provoking such a unanimous international response.

For most of the major players, however, it was not so much the sovereignty of Kuwait which was at stake, but Saudi Arabia, as the largest oil producer, a major trading partner and the linchpin of US policy in the region. Correctly or not, it was believed that Iraq intended to threaten Saudi Arabia, if not to invade it. This was the guiding concern of US policy-making from the beginning of the crisis.

This concern explained the scale of early military mobilisation on the part of the US and UK, and to a lesser extent France.[37] The British Secretary of State for Defence, Tom King, told the House of Commons on 7 September 1990, 'We are not there to attack Kuwait or Iraq. We are there to defend Saudi Arabia and to ensure that the United Nations embargo is effectively implemented'.[38]

The refusal of the Iraqi regime to back down, even in the face of such strong international pressure, also took many of the participants by surprise. The Iraqi Government resorted to various kinds of bargaining. On the political level it tried to establish a link with the Palestine issue, arguing that Saddam Hussein's goal was to see the Palestine issue resolved as part of an overall regional settlement before dealing with the question of Kuwait. This was presumably intended both to enhance Iraq's political role in the region and to delay pressure for withdrawal from Kuwait. Despite international rejection of this proposal, what did emerge was the idea of an international conference on Palestine, originally proposed years before by the Soviet Union. This proposal was taken up by France and the US during the run-up to the 1991 war.[39]

A far more direct provocation was the taking of foreign hostages to fend off international military action. Saddam Hussein seems to have only finally accepted the likelihood of war at the end of 1990.[40] Even then, the conviction that the US would shy away from the casualties which a major war might bring seems to have encouraged continued brinkmanship. He may have estimated that the chances of international military action were small in view of the fact that when Iraq had attacked Iran in 1980, the Security Council had simply sat on its hands.[41]

It seems that not all Saddam's circle necessarily approved of the extent of his brinkmanship. Tariq Aziz was later quoted as saying that he had not agreed with Saddam in holding onto Kuwait even in the face of the 'terrible fire-power of the allies'. However, he described – presumably in justification of his own role – a sense of fatalism which prevailed about the likelihood of war: 'we found ourselves in a position where we could do nothing to avoid it'.[42]

A greater surprise for the Iraqi Government was the unfavourable response in the Arab world to the invasion. Despite increasingly tense relations with the Gulf states after the Iran-Iraq War, and the fact that both Egypt and Syria joined the Western Coalition, the image of Iraq as defender of the Arab World against Iran seemed to persist in Iraqi thinking. In 1990, Iraq was not exactly surrounded by friendly states. Almost two decades of hostility with Syria persisted, while the latter's alliance with Iran continued. Consequently the trans-Syrian pipeline, closed in 1982, remained inaccessible. Once Turkey and Saudi Arabia had decided to close their oil pipelines from Iraq, all bulk export of oil by land was cut off, while the naval blockade prevented any large-scale use of its port of Umm Qasr.[43] Jordan alone among Iraq's neighbours was not hostile, and was reluctant for its own economic and political reasons to join the embargo.

Negotiations on a peace treaty between Iran and Iraq had been deadlocked since fighting ended in 1988. They were resumed in June 1990, largely at Saddam Hussein's initiative. As one commentator suggests, 'In retrospect, it seems clear that when he reopened talks with Iran, Saddam Hussein was already planning the invasion of Kuwait and desired to secure his eastern flank before moving his army southward'.[44] On 14 August, Saddam wrote to President Rafsanjani announcing a unilateral withdrawal of Iraqi troops from Iranian territory. He offered to begin an immediate exchange of prisoners, and – although his wording seemed deliberately imprecise – implied he would settle the Shatt al-Arab issue (the ostensible cause of the Iran-Iraq War) on Iran's terms. Iraqi forces did withdraw from Iranian territory, many, though not all, the prisoners were exchanged, and diplomatic relations were resumed.[45] Iran did not, however, go so far as to support Iraq during the war. It observed the embargo, with the exception of accepting Iraqi planes (which subsequently remained impounded) and gave no military assistance.

Differences of opinion emerged within the Security Council, not on the question of whether Iraq should withdraw from Kuwait but on how this should be achieved. The initial consensus on the imposition of sanctions was undoubtedly solid but the subsequent movement towards the use of force raised more doubts. The positions taken by France and the Soviet Union, previously strong allies of Iraq, were critical to the outcome. Soviet policy vacillated between support for the US position and attempts to establish a separate diplomatic role for the Soviet Union both in regard to Iraq and a possible peace conference on the Palestinian-Israeli conflict. In France, as in the rest of the European Union, the imposition of the economic embargo was quick and decisive, but there was greater reluctance than in the UK to send troops in support of a US-dominated operation to defend Saudi Arabia. There was more emphasis on finding a diplomatic solution and more willingness to let sanctions work than was evident in either the US or UK. In September, President Mitterand made a speech to the UN General Assembly which, while insisting that Iraq should agree to withdraw from Kuwait, held out the possibility of an international conference on Middle East regional problems, including Palestine and elections in Kuwait, rather than the automatic restoration to power of the ruling al-Sabah family.

French policy was, however, split between supporters of the pro-Arab view and those who, like Foreign Minister Roland Dumas, a close associate of President Mitterand, spoke against 'appeasement' of aggression.[46] Within the French Government pressures for a more pro-Iraqi policy came particularly from Jean-Pierre Chévènement in the Defence Ministry. Similar pressures came from the French arms industry, where it was argued, 'que Koweit ne vaut pas la perte du marché irakien. Et ils avancent un argument qu'ils estiment indiscutable: en case de conflit, les sociétés françaises ne recuperont jamais ce que Baghdad leur doit pour les contrats civils et militaires.'[47]

The efforts at mediation and negotiation by both French and Russian officials, and by prominent individuals from other countries, were undermined from two directions: first, the refusal of the Iraqi Government to make sufficient concessions for any credible settlement; and second, from October 1990 onwards the signals from Washington that it viewed the use of force as the most likely outcome.

The threat of military force was developed in parallel to economic sanctions, rather than after they had been tried and found wanting. By September 1990, a major force of 265,000 American and 8000 British troops was being built up to 'defend' Saudi Arabia. This was despite Saudi Arabia's initial hesitation to accept foreign troops.[48] By late October, President Bush and some members of his adminstration had come close to deciding that the war option was preferable. However, prior to that date opinions seemed divided, with President Bush's National Security Advisor, Brent Scowcroft, and Secretary of State, James Baker, arguing that sanctions could still work and collective action could achieve a peaceful solution.[49] The British Prime Minister, Margaret Thatcher, on the other hand, constantly pressed Bush to take a hard line.[50]

The Bush administration's decision, announced on 8 November, to almost double the number of its troops in Saudi Arabia, gave a strong indication that the US was moving to an offensive military posture, apparently fearing that international cohesion was weakening. It was in this context that Resolution 678 was adopted on 29 November, calling for 'all necessary means' to be used to end the occupation of Kuwait. This was understood to include the use of force, but the US agreed to drop any explicit reference to force which allowed the Soviet Union to vote for the motion and China to abstain, rather than using its veto.[51]

Aside from bargaining on the contents of the resolution, the US twisted arms and offered inducements to those Security Council members whose acceptance was not guaranteed. China, the main objector to a war strategy among the permanent members, was induced to abstain by what Secretary of State Baker described as 'subtle peer pressure'.[52] Only Yemen joined Cuba to vote against the resolution.[53] Other Security Council states which had been uneasy about the actions taken against Iraq, including Zimbabwe and Ecuador, did not vote against it. Leverage could be exerted on more vulnerable countries the more easily because the bargaining counter previously available – to turn to the Soviet Union – was no longer a practical option.[54] The only concession which the US was obliged to make was to accept the French and Russian proposal for a 'grace' period up to 15 January 1991, before which no military action would be taken, and during which attempts would be made to negotiate a settlement.

Ironically, the US public and Congress at this stage seemed less convinced by the war option than the administration. James Baker in his memoirs argues that the administration got international support for the war before it had domestic support from Congress and public opinion. President Bush was acutely conscious that the war option commanded less than 50 percent public support, according to opinion polls. 'Much as the November 8 force augmentation announcement had been the turning point in the military build-up, and Resolution 678 the key to cementing the international coalition, my meeting with Tariq Aziz [on 12 January 1991] became the turning point in building domestic consensus'.[55] Meanwhile, Mrs Thatcher's resignation at the end of November 1990 did not significantly alter British policy on Iraq. The UK Government continued to support the US view that the 15 January deadline must be met, even after all foreign hostages were released in early December.

In making the decision to use force rather than rely solely on the economic embargo to change Iraq's policy, there was no process to ascertain whether sanctions were 'working', and therefore whether they should be pursued. No serious attempt was made in the Security Council to evaluate their likely outcome. Essentially the argument among those in favour of using force was that the economic embargo was expected to take at least a year to have sufficient impact on Iraq to make it change its policy. In that time, the political difficulties of maintaining a large military force in Saudi Arabia would increase. There were fears that existing fault lines within the coalition against Iraq would deepen. Particular strains would emerge over the US relationship with Israel and the economic problems of Iraq's main trading partners. From the US point of view, the possibility of an 'Arab solution' or a deal brokered by a third party was regarded as unlikely to meet American interests. Having used leverage to get the other major international powers to agree to the use of force, the US administration had therefore essentially constructed a *fait accompli*, unless it made a major policy reversal.[56]

Although Resolution 678, adopted under Chapter VII of the UN Charter, was taken as the basis for the subsequent use of massive force, control of military action passed to leading members of the Coalition, not, as intended in the UN Charter, to a collective command directly controlled by the Security Council.[57] Once the use of force was accepted as the likely outcome, the US, with the preponderance of military strength, inevitably led military operations. The states which sent contingents accepted that they were going to war 'draped in the UN flag' but were essentially under US command.

The initial Gulf crisis dramatically raised the profile of the Security Council, but it was marginalised during the period of armed conflict. The Council did not reconvene in public session until the fighting was over, three months later.[58] Another effect of the crisis was to marginalise the role of the UN Secretary General.

> If the Charter had left him in any doubt on that score, it was resolved by unambiguous communications from Permanent Members of the Council. According to several of his staff, the Secretary General was also actively discouraged from going to Baghdad until after the failure of US Secretary of State James Baker's own mission, by which time it was far too late.[59]

Outside government circles, there still remained a groundswell of opinion in most Western states that sanctions should have been allowed time to work. This was probably more generalised in most continental European states, where governments, with the exception of the Netherlands, took a less hard-line position than that of the US and UK. The scale of the air war in January also raised concerns about civilian casualties. However, intensive news management by the military during the war stressing that this was a 'clean' war, and the low rate of coalition casualties once ground troops were committed probably tipped popular opinion in favour of the war.

The domination of military decision-making by the US was not only evident in the conduct of the war but also in the timing of the ceasefire. The decision to stop fighting was dictated formally by Iraq's withdrawal from Kuwait. However, it was also driven by US military concerns that extending the campaign risked more casualties and the danger of becoming trapped in a political quagmire. The military essentially 'wanted to quit while they were ahead'. The US administration, conscious that public support was fragile, feared bad publicity and a 'turkey shoot' image after the rout of Iraqi soldiers on the road from Kuwait.[60] There were also concerns about holding the Coalition together – especially its Arab members – and avoiding getting 'bogged down' in divisive Iraqi politics.

The rifts and fault-lines which were evident in Security Council debates before the war re-emerged in the following years. The issue was no longer Iraq's invasion of a sovereign state – albeit a very particular one with strategic and economic importance – but how Iraq could be coerced into accepting arms control and a variety of other measures under the ceasefire agreement. A consensus on how to do this was achieved in the major resolutions passed by the Council soon after the war, but at the cost of a good deal of ambiguity. Under pressure of subsequent events, not least Iraq's continued refusal to accept all these terms, the apparently united international front of early 1991 gradually began to unravel.

NOTES ON PROLOGUE

1   Gordon and Trainor (1995), p 8. Herrman (1991) points out that 'even analysts who typically took a hard-line position towards the Soviet Union and a very pro-Israeli stance advocated the tilt towards Iraq' (p 47), citing the examples of Daniel Pipes and Laurie Mylroie who, since 1991, have become among the strongest advocates of a hard line against Saddam Hussein.

2   Rubin (1994), pp 257

3   Chubin and Tripp (1988), pp 152–4.

4   Smolansky (1991), p 288.

5   Campaign Against the Arms Trade (1991), p 2.

6   Karsh and Rautsi (1991), p 247.

7   Scott (1996), vol. 1, p 367.

8   *New York Times*, 2 April 1991, 'Iraqi Agents and Fronts Listed by the Treasury'.

9   US General Accounting Office (1994), p 1.

10 *Ibid.*, pp 4–5. According to the *New York Times*, an under-secretary at the Department of Commerce, Dennis E. Kloske, said in evidence to a House Foreign Affairs subcommittee that the administration and the State Department, still intent on encouraging better relations with Iraq, had ignored his recommendations in early 1990 that the flow of advanced technology to Iraq should be reduced. ('Official Reported to Face Ouster after his Dissent on Iraqi Exports', 10 April 1991).

11 The published version of the General Accounting Office report referred only to Saudi Arabia and the UAE (where the allegations could not be verified because of 'political sensitivities'). Kuwait was not named. However, a *Los Angeles Times* article on 12 September 1992 quoted the original, classified, version of the report, identifying Kuwait as the 'Middle East country' (referred to on p 6 of the published report) which transferred US TOW missiles to Iraq in 1984 ('Kuwaitis, Saudis Supplied Iraq With US Arms').

12 The so-called Iraq Note prepared by various UK government departments and distributed to ministers on 13 July 1990 stated in paragraph 7: 'It appears that Iraq systematically uses Jordan as a cover for her procurement activities, almost certainly with the connivance of senior figures in the Jordanian administration' (Scott [1996], vol. 1, p 444). Scott himself commented: 'Knowledge of the risk that military exports to Jordan would find their way to Iraq did not, in practice, result in the refusal of licences for the export of defence equipment to Jordan' (Scott [1996], vol. 2, p 833).

13 Hubel (1994), pp 280–1.

14 Angeli and Mesnier (1992), pp 193–5; Hubel (1994), p 278.

15 Scott (1996), vol. 1, pp 463, 465.

16 *Ibid.*, p 441.

17 The message, sent in November 1989 via the US Ambassador in Iraq, April Glaspie, reportedly asked for Iraqi support for Egypt's efforts to persuade the Palestinians to agree to US plans for a dialogue with Israel (*New York Times*, 26 October 1992, 'Baker, Telling Iraqis of Loan Aid Asked Help on Palestinian Talks').

18 Freedman and Karsh (1993), pp 25–26. The use of agricultural credits formed the basis of a series of allegations from 1990 onwards concerning the abuse of these funds by the Iraqis for military purposes. These were the subject of several congressional investigations.

19 Dannreuther (1991), p 21.

20 Gordon and Trainor (1994), p 9.

21 Dammers (1994), p 406.

22 UNHCR in Teheran estimated the total number of expellees and refugees to have reached 400,000 by 1985. The majority of those who were expelled still live in cities in Iran. Those who can identify an Iranian grandparent have been able to become Iranian citizens, but most others live in a kind of legal limbo, neither Iranians nor refugees. There is considerable poverty in some sections of this Iraqi population.

23   During 1988, 46,500 Iraqi Kurdish refugees from the earlier period were repatriated from Iran to Iraq under an Iraqi amnesty which ended in October 1988, according to UNHCR.

24   Randal (1997), p 81.

25   Aruri (1992), pp 318–21.

26   Freedman and Karsh (1993), pp 25–6; Rubin (1994), p 261.

27   Quoted in Scott (1996), vol. 1, p 236.

28   *Ibid.*, p 379.

29   The sponsors were Australia, Belgium, Canada, Denmark, Germany (Federal Republic), Greece, Ireland, Italy, Luxembourg, Netherlands, Norway, Portugal, Spain, Sweden and UK (UN Commission on Human Rights, Report on the 45th Session, 30 January–10 March 1989 [Economic and Social Council Official Records 1989 Supplement 2 E/1989/20; E/CN.4/1989/86]).

30   Kendal Nezan, Director of the Kurdish Institute, Paris (Interview with author, 20 October 1997).

31   Angeli and Mesnier (1992), pp 196–98. According to Jonathan Randal, Baghdad agreed to attend the conference only after France had promised that the Kurds could not attend (Randal [1997], p 81).

32   Kutschera (1997), p 85, quoting Hoshyar Zibari, Kurdistan Democratic Party spokesman in Europe.

33   A good deal has been written about this period (see bibliography for details). This section only highlights issues which set the scene for post-war developments.

34   Karsh and Rautsi (1991), pp 204–211. For details of the border dispute, see Richard Schofield (1991).

35   Parsons (1991) notes that most Security Council resolutions before 1990, including Resolution 242 at the end of the 1967 war, were adopted under Chapter VI, where the Council has only recommendatory powers. In the Arab-Israeli conflict, he argues that the pattern was for Arab states and their allies to put forward a draft resolution 'pointing towards a Chapter VII mandatory action, say, sanctions against Israel. Western delegations would reject it.' Then there was the choice of forcing a vote, leading to a veto – usually by the US – or having the draft watered down, with the Western powers trying to substitute 'Chapter VI words' for 'Chapter VII words' (p 267).

36   Parsons (1991), p 268.

37   Freedman and Karsh (1993), pp 114–118.

38   Hansard, House of Commons, 7 September 1990, vol. 177, Column 842.

39   Karsh and Rautsi (1991), pp 229–231.

40   *Ibid.*, pp 240–1.

41   Urquhart (1993), p 84.

42   *Le Monde*, 9 May 1991, 'M. Tarek Aziz: Nous ne pouvions rien faire pour éviter la guerre', quoting the *Washington Post*, 8 May 1991.

43   Chubin (1987), pp 17–19.

44   Bakhash (1993), p 66.

45   Although the Iranian Government did not say so publicly, the exchange of letters in August 1991 had not constituted a formal agreement on the border. 'A close reading of Saddam Hussein's August 14, 1990 offer to Iran suggests that the Iraqi president did not intend to revert to the arrangements for shared sovereignty over the Shatt al-Arab agreed under the 1975 Algiers accord. Rather, he was only offering Iran shared administration of the Shatt in exchange for a recognition of full Iraqi sovereignty over the waterway.' (Bakhash [1993], p 70).

46   Heisbourg (1992), p 26.

47   Angeli and Mesnier (1992), p 15.

48   Freedman and Karsh (1993), pp 86–7.

49   Dannreuther (1991), p 33. According to Gordon and Trainor, 'By late October [1990],

the weight of opinion within the administration was against waiting for sanctions to work'. (p 153).

50   Gordon and Trainor (1994), pp 153, 167; Jim Wurst (1991), p 543, interviewing Stephen Lewis, former Canadian Ambassador to the UN. Lewis's view was that from September 1990, Bush had decided on the war option. Later, 'when troop levels jumped from 250,000 to nearly 500,000 and when the decision was made to set a January 15 deadline for Iraq to comply with UN resolutions… there was no longer any possibility for reversing course'.

51   Taylor and Groom (1992), p 16.

52   Baker (1995), pp 346–7.

53   US Secretary of State James Baker observed that Yemen's vote against Resolution 678 was 'the most expensive' its UN ambassador had ever made (Freedman and Karsh [1993], p 234).

54   The United States was said to have courted non-aligned Security Council members: Ethiopia with promises to broker peace talks between the Government and rebel groups, Malaysia with hints of foreign aid (Wurst [1991], p 541).

55   Baker (1995), pp 346–7.

56   Aspin (1991), pp 25–9 summarises an evaluation conducted by the House Armed Services Committee in early December 1990. From their study of previous economic embargoes, Kimberly Elliott, Gary Hufbauer and Jeffery Schott anticipated that sanctions would take one to two years to 'work', ie to change Iraqi policy. This also appears to have been the US intelligence assessment.

57   A Military Staff Committee of the Security Council was the intended vehicle of command, but this committee had never actually functioned (Johansen [1991], p 563). 'Under Article 42, the [UN] Charter provides the authorisation for the resort to collective force to terminate breaches of international peace… Operation Desert Storm did not fall precisely within the framework of Article 42, which would have required the command of the relevant forces to function through the Security Council' (Smith [1994], p 6).

58   Parsons (1991), p 271.

59   Francke and Nolte (1993), pp 161–2.

60   Talbott (1992), p 59. The US appears to have been taken by surprise at the speed of victory: 'There was an initial miscalculation about the strength and morale of the Iraqis'. It was only after large numbers of troops surrendered that the scale of the Iraqi collapse became evident to the US commanders (Marine General Walt Boomer quoted in the *Washington Post*, 12 March 1998, 'Victory Revisited'). It seems that at least in retrospect, even the UK Government was not entirely happy about the timing of the ceasefire. For example, former Minister of Defence Tom King later said, 'I thought [the advance] stopped too soon – this was an American decision, the idea of the hundred-hour war', speaking in the BBC programme 'What if…? The Gulf War', broadcast on 20 July 1996 (BBC Bristol).

PART I

International Policy on Iraq and its Consequences 1991–8

CHAPTER 1

Unforeseen Circumstances

Iraq's retreat from Kuwait marked the end of the 1991 Gulf War, but it triggered a succession of events that few would have predicted. In the months following the war, both the international community and the Government of Iraq took decisions which influenced the course of events in the tense and conflict-ridden years which followed.

Leading Security Council members took an essentially short-term view of the rapidly developing humanitarian crisis, often responding as much to domestic pressures as to events in Iraq. Few of the key decision-makers in the West had sufficient knowledge of Iraq to weigh the longer-term impact of their actions. For its part, the Iraqi regime made decisions which would enable it to survive. It also sought to test the boundaries of international tolerance.

Immediately after the Coalition's ceasefire, on 28 February, the US made clear that it intended to impose harsh terms on Iraq, emphasising the scale of its defeat. Having ruled out a military advance on Baghdad, the leading coalition states wanted to impose sufficiently draconian conditions on the Iraqi regime that, whether or not Saddam Hussein stayed in power, Iraq's ambitions beyond its borders would be quashed. It was widely believed, particularly by the US administration, that Saddam Hussein could not long survive such a humiliating defeat.

On 2 March, the Security Council passed Resolution 686, which demanded that Iraq cease hostile actions. As originally drafted by the US, the resolution had included an explicit threat 'to resume offensive combat operations if Iraq does not comply with all demands'. This was apparently dropped after Soviet objections.[1] In its final form, Resolution 686 demanded that Iraq accept all 12 UN resolutions passed since 2 August

1990; rescind the annexation of Kuwait; accept liability for damage and loss during the occupation; cease all hostile acts against any member states, including missile attacks and flights of combat aircraft; and release all prisoners and detainees.[2] President Bush also signalled that the US would not be prepared to assist with reconstruction: 'At this point, I don't want to see one single dime of the United States' taxpayers' money go into the reconstruction of Iraq.'[3]

However, on the ground, events were taking a new turn. As coalition forces halted their advance in southern Iraq, Iraqi soldiers retreating from Kuwait triggered a civil insurrection in the Basra area. The uprising spread rapidly through the south of the country, drawing in Iraqi Shi'i opposition groups based in Iran. Another uprising, this time involving the predominantly Kurdish population, followed in the north of Iraq (for details of the uprisings see Chapter 4).

At this stage, the US administration and the military establishment had one common and immediate goal: to get their troops home and declare a 'victory'.[4] However, hopes for a clear-cut victory and a rapid troop withdrawal were foiled by the uprisings. The US went to war to protect its strategic interests in the Gulf region, but the administration had no long-term political strategy to replace its previous policy of cooperation with Iraq. The war was perceived as being about protecting Saudi Arabia and Kuwait, not about Iraq's governance. Essentially the same problem faced other leading Western coalition members which had cultivated relations with Iraq during the 1980s.

Furthermore, once the war was over, the main focus of US interest in the Middle East turned towards an initiative to settle the Israeli-Palestinian conflict, taking advantage of the new balance of power in the region created by the Gulf crisis. In early March, Secretary of State James Baker began the first of a series of tours of Europe, the Soviet Union and the Middle East with the primary purpose of initiating peace negotiations between Israel, the Palestinians and the Arab states.[5]

On 3 March, coalition military leaders met Iraqi commanders in Safwan, southern Iraq, to agree the practical aspects of the ceasefire. The discussions were said to have focused on the risk that Iraqi forces posed to the allies. General Schwarzkopf, leading the coalition delegation, appeared to have little interest in the civil unrest engulfing southern Iraq. In fact he explicitly agreed, to the surprise of the Iraqi commanders, that Iraq could fly military helicopters – but not fighters or bombers – in areas where there were no coalition forces.[6] This effectively allowed Iraq to use helicopter gun-ships, along with artillery and ground forces, to crush the rebellions.[7]

During March, while the uprisings were in progress, several members of Congress, administration officials and many outside experts argued that the United States should prohibit Iraq from using helicopters. Two Iraqi fighter-bombers were shot down by US forces during March, and President Bush once claimed that the use of helicopters infringed the ceasefire terms. However, after a series of ambiguous statements, White House Spokesman Marlin Fitzwater finally clarified on 26 March that the US would not interfere with the operations of Iraqi helicopters unless they posed a threat to US forces. He added that the US would not assist the rebels.[8]

The mixed signals from the US Government over the rebellions highlighted continuing disagreements within the administration on the future of Iraq. At that time, according to one Bush administration official, 'There was no consensus within the administration on the importance of removing Saddam Hussein'.[9] US forces were occupying some 15 percent of Iraqi territory in the south of the country and the administration apparently feared that its troops might become involved in the fighting taking place only a few miles from their lines. Its only 'tough' statement was in response to an allegation from opposition groups that Iraqi forces were using chemical weapons against the rebels in Najaf and Karbala.[10] The Iraqi representative at the UN was warned that the US would not tolerate such attacks. Action by US ground forces was not, however, envisaged.[11]

The US Adminstration thus opted for 'neutrality' in the internal conflict, while warning Iran not to intervene in the south.[12] Neither the British nor the French dissented from the US view that the uprisings were an internal affair, though President Mitterand did leave open the possibility that coalition forces could intervene if asked to do so by the Security Council.

The absence of US assistance to the rebels, either in the north or the south, appeared particularly ironic. During the ground war, President Bush, against the counsel of some of his advisors, had urged 'the Iraqi military and the Iraqi people' to 'take matters into their own hands' and 'force Saddam Hussein, the dictator, to step aside'.[13] British Prime Minister John Major made more guarded remarks in a similar vein a few days later.[14] The President apparently intended his message for anti-Saddam elements in the military and the ruling Ba'th Party, whom he was hoping would seize power and maintain a strong central government in Baghdad. A *Washington Post* article in which Bush's statement appeared noted that his comments 'reflected a belief that Iraq's military forces and governing elite are increasingly desperate to stop the allied destruction of their country'.[15]

Brent Scowcroft, the President's National Security Advisor, later confirmed 'we clearly would have preferred a coup. There's no question about that.'[16] Some observers say that the US was influenced by Saudi claims to have an 'inside' candidate, a Sunni general. At the end of the war, Saudi leaders had promoted the view that the Iraqi army would remove Saddam as a result of the military defeat. Prince Bandar bin Sultan, the Saudi Ambassador in Washington, expressed this expectation to John Major after the ceasefire. His view seems to have been shared by other Arab leaders, and by President Ozal of Turkey.[17] It was later suggested that a potential coup at the height of the Kurdish uprising never materialised because the officers concerned concluded that the US would not back the rebellion.[18]

While a coup might have met the political goals of a number of Western and Arab coalition members, the post-war uprisings did not. Their character, particularly when the populations of Baghdad and the central provinces did not join in, was regarded as too threatening to Iraq's unity and too open to Iranian influence. These were both issues which preoccupied Saudi Arabia and Turkey as well as Western members of the Coalition.[19] It is notable, however, that despite these fears Iran did not intervene directly. It provided arms and assistance to Iranian-based Iraqi opposition groups, but even when the Iraqi army attacked the holiest Shi'i shrines in Najaf and Karbala, Iranian regular forces made no move. In fact, the uprising in the south proved short-lived, and by mid-March it was virtually crushed, with brutal retribution by Iraqi security services and Republican Guard troops. In the north, the Kurdish uprising soon came under attack from regrouped Iraqi forces.

The suppression of the uprisings coincided with a Security Council decision to impose permanent ceasefire terms on the defeated Iraq. This was seen as an urgent priority because Saudi Arabia and Kuwait wanted coalition forces to remain in place until a permanent ceasefire was secured. The coalition states which had prosecuted the war on behalf of the UN, but not under its direct control, therefore returned to the Security Council to frame the ceasefire. UNSC Resolution 687, finally approved on 3 April, was long and unprecedentedly complex, described in one account as a 'Christmas tree' because so much was hung on it.[20]

The draconian nature of the resolution reflected the view of Saudi Arabia and Kuwait, supported by the US and UK, that harsh conditions should be imposed on Iraq. It provided that the economic embargo on Iraq would be continued to enforce the eradication of Iraq's weapons of mass destruction, and an open-ended embargo on weapons acquisition. A UN commission was to delineate Iraq's border with Kuwait and Iraq was to accept Kuwait's sovereignty, return prisoners-of-war, and pay compensation for war damage. (For an analysis of how this resolution has been implemented, see Chapter 2.)

From the beginning, there were clear differences of interpretation within the Security Council on the goals of the continued economic sanctions: whether they were designed to change the Government of Iraq's behaviour or, as the US and UK Governments suggested, to change the regime. Initially, these governments believed sanctions would hasten its fall. The UK's UN Ambassador, Sir David Hannay, stated during discussions on Resolution 687, 'My Government believes that it will in fact prove impossible for Iraq to rejoin the community of civilised nations while Saddam Hussein remains in power'.[21] President Bush shared this view. At a press conference on 16 April he said, 'Do I think the answer is now for Saddam Hussein to be kicked out? Absolutely... There will not be normalised relations with the US until Saddam Hussein is out of there. And we will continue economic sanctions.'[22]

At this point, the Iraqi Government was in too weak a position to challenge the resolution, and had little option but to accept its onerous terms. On 10 April, the Security Council received the text of an Iraq National Assembly decision adopted on 6 April 'to agree to UNSC resolution 687' (1991). Iraq's acceptance of the resolution cleared the way for US troops to begin their withdrawal from southern Iraq.

THE REFUGEE CRISIS

As the Security Council was framing Resolution 687 in late March and the first days of April, reports began arriving of a rapidly-growing exodus of refugees both in the south and the north of Iraq, as the uprisings were crushed. If the coalition states had not anticipated the uprisings as an outcome of Iraq's military defeat, neither did they expect that the suppression of the rebellions would create so great a tide of refugees and displaced people. Least of all did they want a role in dealing with this crisis.[23]

Until March 1991, the exodus from Iraq and Kuwait had consisted mainly of third-country nationals, migrant workers displaced since August 1990.[24] This affected several of the surrounding countries, including Jordan, Syria, Turkey and Iran. In January 1991, only small numbers of Iraqi refugees, including some 2000 deserting soldiers, were reported to be arriving in Turkey. But by March, the UN High Commission for Refugees (UNHCR) was reporting that Iraqis were fleeing to Iran, Turkey and to a lesser extent Syria. The UN had made some contingency plans for a refugee outflow during the war, and one of their representatives in the region anti-cipated the possibility of a large scale post-war refugee crisis.[25] However, the warning was discounted, and certainly nobody expected movements of people on the scale which occurred in March and April 1991.

The refugee crisis developed on several fronts in the course of a few weeks. It created an unexpected obstacle for the major coalition states, whose immediate aim was to bring the Gulf War to a successful close. In retrospect, a US official admitted that there was, at the time, an almost indecent haste to get the troops home. The extent of the international community's willingness to respond to this new crisis depended largely on the potential for fleeing Iraqis to cross borders, thus internationalising the problem. The main actual or potential recipients of refugees were Turkey, Iran, Saudi Arabia and Kuwait. The Western coalition members responded to the concerns of their allies – Turkey, Saudi Arabia and Kuwait – none of which were eager to accept refugees from Iraq. However, the outcomes were different in each case.

Refugees in the south

Many of those who fled their homes when the uprising in the south was crushed went either to the extensive marshes of southern Iraq (long a refuge for deserters and dissidents) or directly to south-western Iran, where UNHCR reported that 68,000 Iraqi refugees had arrived by 1 May.[26] The refugees included urban and rural dwellers, the poor and the affluent, professionals and farmers.

Desperate Iraqis also sought protection from US troops stationed in Safwan and on the ceasefire line running just to the south of Suq al-Shuyukh, Nasariya and Samawa. They included soldiers wanting to surrender and families seeking refuge from the retribution of the Republican Guard and security services. By early April, a temporary camp established in the former Iraqi customs compound near Safwan (in the disputed Iraq-Kuwait border zone) housed some 10,000 people. The US army was providing food, water and medical care. A further 20,000 people congregated around the town of Sadah close to the Saudi border.

The approaching US military pull-out from Iraq highlighted the vulnerability of displaced civilians to retaliation from Iraqi troops. The International Committee of the Red Cross (ICRC) pointed out that, as the occupying power in southern Iraq, the US was responsible for Iraqi nationals who had fled to territory under its control. They could not therefore just be abandoned when the troops withdrew.[27]

US forces were to be replaced by the UN Iraq-Kuwait Observation Mission (UNIKOM), an unarmed observer force whose task was confined to supervising the demilitarised zone (DMZ) between the two countries.[28] The possibility was briefly mooted of using this zone as a 'safe haven' for displaced Iraqis.[29] However, the Iraqi authorities, not UNIKOM, were to be in control of law and order and basic services in the Iraqi sector of the DMZ. Therefore, as a representative of ICRC pointed out, the zone could not be turned into a 'mini-state' or a haven for the displaced.[30] Neither ICRC nor UNHCR had any way of protecting Iraqi civilians once the Government re-established its authority in the areas from which the coalition forces had withdrawn.[31] UNIKOM was given no civil administration or humanitarian functions. As one author noted, 'The UN did not want to make UNIKOM a magnet for political refugees'. Its mandate was 'carefully limited by the UN Secretariat to avoid humanitarian entanglements and to tightly constrain the operation's geographic scope'.[32]

By 14 April, US troops were beginning their withdrawal and the problem of what to do with displaced civilians was becoming urgent. Nonetheless, at his news conference on 16 April announcing US participation in the 'safe haven' in the north (see below, p 28), President Bush did not admit that there was any problem with the protection of civilians in the southern occupied zone once US troops withdrew:

> The United Nations [ie UNIKOM] will be there soon and we think that will be very good assurance that they [civilians in the south] will not be attacked. People forget that the United States has been doing a wonderful job for those refugees for a long time... So what we want to do is see – in that neutral zone – see the Blue Helmets come in there, and then I will continue to keep moving our people out as rapidly as possible. I want to bring them home.[33]

The UN Secretary General had placed the onus of finding a solution to the problem of displaced people in the south on the UN system.[34] This task fell to UNHCR – exceptionally, because its mandate did not formally cover persons displaced within their own country. UN headquarters staff in New York and the UN High Commissioner for Refugees, Sadako Ogata, initially envisaged 'humanitarian support' for the displaced inside Iraq. However, because of the protection problems posed by this option, a UNHCR mission to Saudi Arabia and Kuwait subsequently succeeded in redefining the problem 'as one of asylum, rather than the need for expeditious practical arrangements by UNHCR for continued assistance' inside Iraq.

Having established this point, the question was where the refugees could go. It rapidly became evident that the Kuwaitis were not willing to take any Iraqi refugees, and they were not pressed to do so.[35] However, after what was described as 'intense diplomatic pressure' from the US, and appeals from the UK and other parties, the Saudi Ministry of Defence, with the approval of King Fahd, agreed on 24 April to admit both the 20,000 Iraqis who were close to the Saudi border at Rafha and some 10,000 who had been in the temporary camp at Safwan. They were to be housed in a closed camp at Rafha near the Iraqi border, built and paid for by Saudi Arabia. A further 15,000 Iraqi POWs were admitted and placed in a separate camp at Artawiya. Iran also agreed to take 2000 of these refugees[36] (for further details see Chapter 3).

Despite the continuing reports of displacement, military attacks and human rights abuses in southern Iraq, no further serious consideration was given to any kind of 'haven' in the south once coalition forces had withdrawn. Fear of Iranian influence within any haven in southern Iraq appears to have been the main reason for this inaction. The relatively small size of the refugee problem in the south and the fact that the receiving state was Iran (which, in contrast to Turkey, had little leverage with Western coalition members) also influenced decision-making.

Meanwhile, as the US pulled its soldiers out of southern Iraq on schedule, its forces and those of its coalition allies were being drawn into another, much larger humanitarian crisis in the north.

The northern crisis

The failure of the rebellion in the north resulted in mass flight on a much larger scale, creating new and more intense pressures for military and humanitarian action. In a three-week period from late March, the number of Iraqi refugees fleeing to the

Turkish border grew from 4700 (27 March) to over 400,000, while by mid-May, some 1.5 million people had taken refuge in Iran or on the Iranian border. An estimated 760,000 crossed into Iran in six days at the end of March and beginning of April.[37]

The magnitude of the refugee flow in the north can only be understood in the light of the region's history in the 1980s. The Iraqi Anfal operations in 1988 had involved not only chemical attacks on Kurdish populations but had systematically razed villages and towns, destroyed the agricultural economy of the mountain regions and displaced much of the rural population. People's past experiences – and the stories and videos circulating about the Anfal operations during the 1991 uprisings – did not dispose them to wait and see what would happen when Iraqi troops crushed the rebellion and pushed back into the north.[38] Fears were increased by reports of ferocious Iraqi retribution in recaptured areas. There were reports of summary executions and hostage-taking. In Kirkuk, some 5000 people were said to have been arrested. Those Kurds remaining in the city, mainly women and children, were reportedly ordered to leave by the Iraqi forces.[39]

The panic was not confined to civilians: Kurdish fighters (*peshmergas*) also feared for the safety of their families if government forces overran their homes. Many of the Kurds recruited into the Iraqi forces as auxiliaries (*jash*) during the 1980s had defected during the uprisings and therefore had all the more to fear from the returning government forces. All but a hard core of *peshmergas* fled northwards as successive cities – Kirkuk, Arbil, Sulaymaniya – fell to Iraqi forces. Only the region along the northern and eastern borders remained in Kurdish hands.[40]

As in the south, the poor and the rich alike fled the advancing Iraqis towards the mountainous borders, using any form of transport they could lay their hands on. On the roads, refugees were reportedly strafed by Iraqi military helicopters.[41] The Kurdish Front leaders' pleas to the Coalition to stop the Iraqis from using helicopters had gone unheard.[42]

The Iranian authorities closed the border with Iraq for a day or two (7–8 April) but, for the most part, refugees were allowed to cross into Iran. The Iranians also dropped some supplies on the road to the border. UNHCR found that about half the refugees fleeing to Iran either had cars or some kind of farm transport. But those who went on foot had arduous journeys, up to two weeks on the road.

The profile of the refugees both in Iran and on the Turkish border was in one sense the classic one: almost half were said to be children and the majority of the adults (30 percent) were women. However, unusually, they included a significant number of relatively affluent city-dwellers and urban professionals. The refugees who fled to Iran from northern Iraq were reported to be 55–60 percent urban, including professors and members of the business community, mostly, in all probability, from the largest city in the region, Sulaymaniya. In other circumstances, more affluent people would have left by air for Europe, but since there was no possibility of doing so they fled across land borders with everyone else.

World attention, however, became focused on the somewhat smaller but still formidable flow of people towards the Turkish border. This flight was better publicised, mainly because at the beginning of April the Turkish Government made it known that it was averse to accepting these refugees and closed its border.

In 1988, 55,000–60,000 Iraqi Kurds, fleeing the Anfal operations following Iraqi chemical attacks, had eventually been allowed into Turkey after being held at the border. In 1989, a large number of Bulgarian Turks were accepted in Turkey, which argued therefore that it could not accept a further inflow of refugees.[43] This time, the Government made clear that it would refuse to allow the new refugees to cross the border. Even in February 1991, before more than a handful of refugees had arrived in Turkey, the Foreign Ministry made several representations to the UN Disaster Relief Organisation (UNDRO) warning that the Turkish Government would find 'serious difficulties' in accepting further refugees if the international community failed to provide financial assistance.[44] However, the main concern of the Turkish Government and military establishment over the Kurdish exodus from Iraq was less financial than political. Since 1984, the war being waged between the Turkish army and Partiya Karkari Kurdistan (PKK, the Kurdistan Workers Party) involved Turkey's own Kurdish population, and was taking place in the region adjacent to the Iraqi border. In 1991, the prospect of a further large inflow of Iraqi Kurds was therefore patently unwelcome.

The Turkish National Security Council, on which the military has strong representation, dealt with the crisis from Ankara. The Council considered the mass of refugees on the border a threat to Turkey's security, and claims were made that PKK members would be able to cross with the refugees.[45] The border was therefore closed on 2 April. Up to 250,000 refugees did subsequently manage to enter Turkish territory, but they were kept in the mountainous border zone until 15 April. After that, the Turkish army began to move some of the remaining refugees (about 20,000 to start with) to a camp near Silopi.[46] The only other exception was apparently made for Turcomans, also fleeing from northern Iraq. They were initially put in a camp at Semdinli, further from the border, and later some 30,000 were reportedly transferred to Kayseri in central Turkey.[47]

The flight of the Kurds occurred at the end of a severe winter. There was snow on the mountains, temperatures dropped to below freezing at night and there were no local sources of food. The refugees were spread out along 165 miles of mountain border, in 17 locations, and in a region made dangerous by large numbers of anti-personnel mines. Even those who were able to cross the border found themselves in terrain that was little more hospitable. Many were kept alive by help from Kurds living on the Turkish side of the border. The Turkish Red Crescent gave limited assistance, but the numbers – estimated by early April at more than 400,000 – were far beyond the capacity of any local organisation to deal with.

In the worst period in early April, the US State Department and relief agencies reported that from 500 to 1000 deaths were occurring daily.[48] As the camera crews arrived and the photographs of desperate people appeared in Western newspapers and on TV, public opinion in Western capitals, combined with the pressure already being exerted politically by the Turkish Government, began to impel the international community to take action.

Ironically, as a congressional report noted soon afterwards, if the refugees had been permitted to cross the border and move out of the high mountain areas, mortality levels would probably have been lower.[49] Thus the Coalition and the UN had to find a way of 'saving' those who were being put in further jeopardy by the Turkish Government's policy.

PROTECTING REFUGEES? RESOLUTION 688
AND THE 'SAFE HAVEN' PROPOSALS

It is little exaggeration to say that the leading members of the Gulf War Coalition were pushed into creating the 'safe haven'. The pressure to respond to the immediate humanitarian crisis was increasing, but no ready-made formula existed in international humanitarian action to prevent a refugee outflow to a particular country.

Three key factors shaped the events which followed. First, the over-riding wish of the US administration, and particularly President Bush, to get US troops home; secondly, Turkey's resistance to accepting Kurdish refugees; and finally, the strong public reaction in France, the UK and some other European states to the Kurdish humanitarian crisis.

On 2 April, President Ozal sought President Bush's support for urgent action in the Security Council, telling his Western NATO allies that Turkey would not accept the refugees.[50] Under other circumstances, strong pressure might have been brought to bear on the state in question to keep its borders open. But Turkey, as an important member of the Coalition against Iraq, was not subject to this pressure.

On the same day, a letter from the Government of Turkey to the Security Council said that Iraq's actions in driving people towards the Turkish border 'constitute an excessive use of force and a threat to the region's peace and security'.[51] Iran also addressed a letter to the Council expressing its concern at the refugee crisis on its border.[52]

Although the French Government had shown reluctance to act during the uprisings, a strong lobby sympathetic to the Kurds led by Danielle Mitterand, wife of the President, and by a group around Bernard Kouchner, Secretary of State for Humanitarian Affairs, sought an active policy of humanitarian intervention. Invoking 'le devoir d'ingérence', they pressed for cross-border action, if necessary, to secure the refugees' safety.[53]

The French Government tried to persuade the other four permanent members of the Security Council to include a call for an end to repression of the Kurds in northern Iraq in Resolution 687. Fear of a Chinese veto prevented the US and UK from supporting this proposal. The final text, therefore, did not allude to human rights, or the safety and protection of any population within Iraq. In their statements on the resolution's adoption, the representatives of France, Austria, the UK and Belgium all called for a Security Council response to the plight of the Kurds but did not explicitly suggest the use of force.[54] The British Ambassador to the UN, Sir David Hannay, wrote in a letter to the Security Council, 'There is a very long tradition of not interfering in the internal affairs of a member state, and that is a tradition based on the [UN] Charter, so there is a very difficult path to tread'.[55]

Two days later, further lobbying by France resulted in the adoption of UNSC Resolution 688 at a meeting requested by France and Turkey.[56] The draft resolution was reportedly shown to the Turkish Government in Ankara by its Western allies, though Turkey was not a Security Council member.[57] The final version focused on the cross-border, and therefore international, dimension of the crisis, which overcame objections from some Security Council members that the resolution was addressing a purely internal Iraqi affair. This point was stressed not only by nonaligned states and the Soviet Union, but also by the US.[58]

However, the formula did not satisfy all the members: Cuba, Yemen and Zimbabwe voted against and China and India abstained. The 10–3 vote contrasted with the unanimous, or near-unanimous, votes on other Iraq resolutions. The final resolution also 'insisted... that Iraq allow immediate access by international humanitarian organisations to all those in need of assistance in all parts of Iraq...' It did not explicitly authorise action under Chapter VII of the UN Charter and did not specify any means of enforcement (see Chapter 3).

After the Security Council had adopted Resolution 688, President Ozal suggested the idea of a 'safe haven' within Iraq. His argument was that the refugees ought to be brought out of the mountains to the plains – in Iraq rather than in Turkey – where aid agencies could have easier access to them.[59]

In the UK, there was initially some reluctance on the part of both the Government and the opposition leadership to intervene directly in the refugee crisis. However, at the beginning of April, former Prime Minster Margaret Thatcher issued an impassioned appeal on behalf of the Kurds. While she did not call for military intervention, she urged humanitarian aid, and said this was not a time for 'legal niceties'.[60]

The heightened public profile which these statements gave to the plight of the Kurds may have spurred Prime Minister John Major to make his proposal for a 'safe haven' in the north. The plan, outlined to a European Council foreign ministers' meeting on 8 April, envisaged 'the establishment of a safe haven in northern Iraq under United Nations control where refugees... would be safe from attack and able to receive relief supplies in a regular and ordered way.' Major further clarified that this was to be an 'enclave' which might at a later stage include some larger towns in the north. He did not set any time-frame but said, 'I do not necessarily envisage it as a short-term option'. The safe haven 'would need to be there for so long as it was necessary to ensure that the Kurds and the other refugees were safe'. The European Council recorded 'its support for the move to establish in Iraq a United Nations protected zone for minorities'.[61]

Major also urged support for a humanitarian aid effort, emphasising that there was no intention of partitioning Iraq. He envisaged that the safe haven could be set up 'under the rubric of Resolution 688' and that no further Security Council resolution would be required. Sir David Hannay, Britain's Ambassador to the UN, stressed that the safe zone was 'a purely humanitarian concept', not 'a juridical or political one'.[62]

The US response during the critical week following Major's proposal appeared confused. The administration at first seemed positive towards the safe haven idea, then backed away from it, emphasising instead the need to deliver humanitarian aid to the border area. The reasons for the confusion seem to have been several. First, as one senior official put it, there were 'a lot of hands' involved in making these decisions. Secondly, President Bush's first priority was to get the troops home. Neither he nor the Pentagon wanted to commit US forces to further involvement in Iraq. Thirdly, the response to Resolution 688 and to the proposed safe havens made it clear that not all members of the Security Council were happy with international intervention in Iraq's internal conflicts, while the Iraqi Government predictably voiced strong objections to the proposal.

Finally, combined with 'great reluctance to get involved', according to the same official, 'it seemed to us in Washington that there was an unusual degree of interest in the UK and France [in the Kurdish crisis] perhaps because of Kurdish interest groups we did not have in the US'.[63] The US administration therefore seemed to assume that the UK and France would provide the 'lion's share' of the inputs for humanitarian aid. It was certainly evident that in France, and to a lesser extent in the UK, there was more sympathy and a somewhat better grasp of the situation. However, the US administration had also resisted the efforts of Kurdish leaders to meet with senior officials to put their case when a Kurdish delegation visited the US at the end of February 1991.[64]

From 7 April, the US began air drops of supplies to refugees on the Turkish/Iraqi border, flown from Incirlik air base in Turkey by US planes, which were soon joined by aircraft from the UK and France.[65] This military relief effort was named Operation Provide Comfort. Secretary of State Baker's visit to Çukurca refugee camp on the Turkish border on 8 April seems to have shifted views in the US adminstration on the scope of needs. After a meeting with European leaders on 12 April, President Bush said that there was 'total agreement' on providing humanitarian aid to the Kurds, and accepted the idea of 'safe havens' where the refugees could be taken care of. However, the White House Press Secretary, Marlin Fitzwater, later emphasised that such safe areas would be temporary: 'No one wants a demarcation that says this is a permanent area or new country.'[66]

In Turkey the pressure, and the message, were certainly clear. On 13 April, at a meeting with US Generals Jamerson and Potter, Hayri Kozakcioglu, 'supergovernor' of the south-eastern region of Turkey, made it clear that he wanted to see the Kurds return to Iraq. He suggested as suitable the area around Zakho, near the Habur border crossing from Turkey.[67] This view was strongly pressed by the US Ambassador to Turkey, Morton Abramowitz, who was reportedly convinced that if Turkey was pushed by the international community to accept the refugees, the Government of Turgut Özal would be undermined. Abramowitz also believed that Iraq, not Turkey, should be forced to deal with the problem.[68]

After a week of intense discussion between the US, the EC and Turkey, agreement was reached to secure an area of northern Iraq adjacent to the Turkish border to which refugees could return. It became clear that in order to make this in any sense a safe area it would have to be policed by coalition forces. No UN force existed for such a purpose, but coalition ground troops were still in the region, located in Saudi Arabia, Kuwait and southern Iraq.

Nonetheless, on 14 April President Bush was still asserting that not one American soldier would become embroiled in Iraq's internal conflict. It took two more days for the President to yield publicly to increasing pressure from Congress and domestic as well as international public opinion. On 16 April he agreed to send US ground troops into northern Iraq to allow humanitarian assistance to be provided to the refugees on Iraqi territory. But, in contrast to John Major, he expressed the hope that this would not be 'a long term effort', and asserted that it was 'not intended as a permanent solution to the plight of the Iraqi Kurds'.[69]

In France, a different initiative had been developed by the Department of Humanitarian Affairs. Bernard Kouchner and his director of operations, Michel Bonnot, had the idea of using French troops in a 'relais humanitaire' to secure safe corridors through which the refugees could pass back into Iraq. They had gained the support of senior UN officials for this initiative. However, it was overtaken by President Bush's decision to commit US ground troops to 'Operation Safe Haven'.[70]

OPERATION SAFE HAVEN

Once President Bush had decided to commit US troops to northern Iraq, events moved swiftly. The US had already ordered Iraq not to fly aircraft (this time including helicopters), or undertake military operations north of the 36th parallel of latitude, as soon as coalition aircraft began airdrops of aid to refugees on the border from 7 April.[71] The no-fly zone served to protect coalition air operations, and later, allied ground forces in the safe haven. The no-fly zone covered a far larger area than the safe haven. Some reservations were expressed at the fact that the zone excluded two major centres of Kurdish population – Kirkuk and Sulaymaniya – which are close to the Iranian border.[72]

After the uprisings, Iraqi forces had retaken most of the main towns in the northern governorates, but some districts, particularly in the mountainous areas near the Turkish and Iranian borders, remained in the hands of one or other of the Kurdish parties (eight in all) which made up the Kurdistan Front. The Kurdistan Democratic Party (KDP) and the Patriotic Union of Kurdistan (PUK) and their *peshmergas* dominated the Front, with the KDP located mainly in the north-west and PUK based in the south-east around Sulaymaniya. The area in which coalition forces were to establish the safe haven, around the town of Zakho, was under Iraqi control.

Chronology of Operation Provide Comfort/Operation Safe Haven

March 28	Iraqi troops retake Kirkuk.
April 2	Fall of Sulaymaniya to Iraqi forces.
April 2	Letter from the Government of Turkey to the Security Council concerning the Iraqi refugees massing along the Turkish border.
April 3	UN Security Council passes Resolution 687.
April 5	UN Security Council passes Resolution 688.
April 7	Air drops of humanitarian aid begin on Turkish-Iraqi border. US orders Iraq to cease all military activity north of the 36th parallel.
April 8	EC leaders endorse John Major's plan for 'safe haven' in northern Iraq.
April 9	US Secretary of State James Baker visits Çukurca camp on the Turkish border.
April 14	US begins pulling troops out of southern Iraq.
April 16	US agrees to send ground troops to northern Iraq.
April 18	Sadruddin Aga Khan signs Memorandum of Understanding in Baghdad.
April 20	US and British troops arrive in Zakho.
May 23	US and coalition forces reach agreement with Iraqi Government that non-combatant soldiers and aid workers can enter Dohuk.
end May	US announces troops will be out of northern Iraq in June.
June 7	UN scheduled to take over US camps and relief programme. Only 60 UN Guards in place.
June 11	In the first full-scale review, the Security Council votes to maintain sanctions.
June 21	Scheduled withdrawal of ground forces from safe haven delayed.
July 15	Allied forces complete their withdrawal from northern Iraq to Turkey.
October 10	Last coalition ground troops leave Turkey.

The US administration did not demand the withdrawal of Iraqi forces from the whole area covered by the no-fly zone. Consideration had been given to the idea of establishing a 'no-drive' zone, to exclude Iraqi troops and officials, but in the end a more ad hoc arrangement was pursued. Iraqi forces were simply warned to stay away from areas in which coalition troops were located.[73]

The initial stage of Operation Safe Haven was to secure Zakho town, where the US and British ground troops arrived on 20 April. They were followed by two Disaster Assistance Response Teams (DARTs) from the USAID's Office of Foreign Disaster Assistance (OFDA), which were to set up camps for the returning refugees. Iraqi regular troops withdrew from the town but a group of 300 Iraqi 'police' remained. They were said to have intimidated both Kurdish leaders brought by coalition forces for an exploratory visit and the civilians still living in Zakho. These security personnel withdrew after negotiations and a show of force by British Marines.[74] The US and UK forces were joined by contingents from 13 nations, including France, the Netherlands, Spain and Italy, involving at its peak 23,000 troops.[75]

Although the original idea of US policy-makers was to confine the safe haven to the vicinity of Zakho, pressure to cover the main areas from which the majority of the refugees had originated – which included Dohuk and villages all along the Turkish border – led to the *de facto* expansion eastwards of the area secured by ground troops along the Turkish border. British Marines pushed as far as Amadiya and, by the end of April, French paratroopers had reached Suri, further east. However, the area secured was kept within the confines of the region adjacent to the Turkish border and stopped short of the point where the Iran-Iraq border began.

Although some refugees did return once Zakho was in coalition hands, there was pressure from the Kurdish leadership for coalition forces to gain control of Dohuk, the nearest large town to the Turkish border.[76] By early May, a bottleneck was also developing in the increasingly overcrowded transit camp set up in Zakho, as its inhabitants were reluctant to go home.[77] A large proportion of the refugees were thought to have come from Dohuk and its environs, and it was argued that a coalition presence in the city would induce more people to return.

The evident enthusiasm among many of the participants in Operation Safe Haven was tempered by greater caution in Western capitals, especially Washington. This was particularly evident in the manoeuvres which ensued over Dohuk.[78]

After an initial advance towards Dohuk by coalition forces, Washington and Major General John M. Shalikashvili, the general commanding the whole operation, intervened to preempt a battle for the city. It seems that the US administration wanted a softer approach in the hope that negotiations taking place between the Kurds and Baghdad would succeed. There was also nervousness over the implications of a full military occupation of a major city. The Iraqis tried to re-enter Dohuk once the allied advance stopped, but finally an arrangement was negotiated whereby only a handful of US soldiers – along with civilian personnel – moved in, in return for withdrawal of Iraqi troops from the city. By the end of May, the flow of returning refugees increased dramatically.[79]

The Iraqis did not in fact attempt any serious challenge to the coalition ground troops. Indeed the higher-ranking Iraqi officers who dealt with the Military Coordination Centre (MCC, a unit set up in Zakho to maintain direct liaison with the Iraqi forces), were relatively cooperative. Some local commanders were more resistant, and there were difficulties in controlling the activities of Iraqi security services – whose operatives apparently killed or arrested some civilians – but few serious military incidents occurred. Where fighting did break out it was generally the result of Kurdish *peshmergas* challenging Iraqi forces.

In fact, there was an ironic coincidence of interests between US goals, with the military command's concern over casualties and the need for a rapid exit, and the Iraqi Government's wish to get coalition forces out of Iraq as soon as possible. Neither wanted confrontations.[80] US participants were perceived by their UK and French colleagues as stressing their self-containment, and this was confirmed by instructions from the Pentagon to avoid clashes with Iraqis.

Another source of unease in Washington was the cooperation which developed between military and aid personnel in Iraq and the Kurdistan Front (KF). The perceived need to achieve the refugees' rapid return meant that on the ground the military and the DART teams found it necessary to enlist the KF in the process. However, the State Department apparently tried to discourage this on the grounds that it meant the US was dealing directly with 'rebels'. This reflected the general concerns in Washington about contacts with the Iraqi opposition, and in particular fears of offending Turkey by working with the KF.[81]

Thus the concept of the 'safe haven' emerged in a climate of confusion and, on the part of the US in particular, reluctance to act. There were fears about the possible political consequences of creating even a small enclave by force of arms, mainly because of the implications this might have for the independence or even autonomy of the Kurds. However, in the press of events, the full humanitarian consequences were not worked out in advance.[82]

UNHCR and the issue of protection

For UNCHR, the state of confusion which prevailed was even greater. In early April, UNHCR had been designated the lead UN agency to assist refugees in Iran and Turkey. But it was rapidly relegated to the sidelines as key coalition states moved to manage the refugee crisis. This was in part a result of the very rapid movement of events, and the strong political pressures which shaped developments. However, internal institutional failures played their role. UNHCR's work frequently involves emergency responses, but in this case it was slow to react and bureaucratically inept. Its conspicuous absence in the field in the early days of the relief operation was noted in Western capitals.

UNHCR's poor performance in this crisis has been widely acknowledged within, as well as outside, the organisation. The scale of the crisis and its political ramifications was one reason for the failure. The shortage of funds from the international community, which would have enabled UNHCR to meet the emergency, created further practical and logistical obstacles. In the circumstances, it is unreasonable to compare its performance to that of a coalition military force of more than 20,000 troops with full transport and logistical backup.

However, it was political as much as bureaucratic or financial difficulties which virtually paralysed the organisation during those critical weeks in April. The coalition states were essentially thrusting the political difficulties which had arisen after the war back in UNHCR's direction. UNHCR was under pressure to respond to the various crises which were developing in the north and south of Iraq, all of which created problems relating to its mandate. The tension between its formal mandate and the demands being made upon it by the international community paralysed its decision-making. As a consequence, UNHCR's presence in the field was delayed, which weakened its position when it questioned some of the assumptions behind the safe haven policy.[83]

In the period up to early May, the unfortunate UNHCR officials who arrived, first in Turkey and later in Zakho, were often without equipment, instructions or even a roof over their heads.[84] The attempt to play UNHCR's intended role as coordinator of relief work was ludicrous in the face of the formidable military organisation of Operations Provide Comfort and Safe Haven. In common with most others involved in this relief effort, few UN officials had any experience in the region, of its culture or its politics. Their mandate was unclear, and lines of responsibility were muddled. It is not surprising that other participants tended to view UNHCR staff, and UN officials generally – with some notable exceptions – as arrogant and rule-bound.

The Western coalition powers agreed that the refugees in Turkey must be returned to Iraq as soon as possible, not just for their own good or protection, but because the Turkish Government had made clear it would not provide asylum. For UNHCR this raised the question of whether the refugees were being forced to return to their country, contravening the principles of the 1951 UN Convention on Refugees.[85] Turkey, though a signatory to this convention, had opted to confine its ratification to refugees of European origin. The fact that the Kurds were therefore not recognised as refugees obviously weakened UNHCR's position in demanding that they be allowed to remain in Turkey, but in fact the political decisions were taken by coalition governments without UNHCR's participation: 'The battle over asylum in Turkey was over in 48 hours, and UNHCR wasn't even in there'.[86]

UNHCR's protection mandate is to prevent any forcible return (*refoulement*) of refugees to their own country if the situation still threatens their safety. Clearly in April 1991 the situation in Iraq could not be described as 'safe'. However UNHCR's role in ensuring that refugees in Turkey were not subject to undue pressure to return to Iraq never really got off the ground. Protection officers were sent in, but too late to do much in the face of mass returns. There were some allegations of forced repatriation and of killings of refugees by Turkish soldiers. But for most the pressure was indirect, though no less telling.

Conditions in the border camps remained harsh even with coalition aid, while refugees also had to contend with the unwelcoming and sometimes brutal behaviour of the Turkish military.[87] Those in charge of Operation Provide Comfort made no secret of their goal to get the refugees back to Iraq as fast as possible. The team from the US Psychological Operations battalion 'distributed informational leaflets, used loud speakers, made radio announcements, conducted informational briefings, held meetings with Kurdish elders and contacted Christian and Muslim religious leaders at Zakho. These teams sought to inspire Kurdish self-reliance...'[88] Helicopters were provided to ferry Iraqi Kurdish leaders to border areas inside Iraq to demonstrate their safety. Some refugees were brought down to Zakho to help build refugee camps, while the BBC's Kurdish language broadcasts reported on the situation in Zakho.[89]

Some NGOs working on the border were said to be unhappy that when the political decision was made to move the refugees back to northern Iraq the military put all its efforts into this task, rather than focusing on stabilising conditions in the existing camps. Some military personnel were also concerned at the 'push' mentality of allied Joint Task Force Alpha (responsible for the border mountain camps), which was trying to get the Kurds to return even before the 'pull' structures – accommodation in the Zakho camps – were in place.[90]

UNHCR protection officers found themselves for the most part explaining to refugees what they could not expect – in particular that there would be no asylum in Turkey and no guarantee of third country resettlement. One refugee made the point forcefully: 'You ask me whether I take responsibility for my choice to return home… My reply then, is yes, I return home of my free will but my choice is not free – since such a choice in reality does not exist'.[91]

The argument used by some of the participants in Operation Provide Comfort was that the longer the Kurds stayed in the mountains, the more of them would die. They would be 'better off at home', even if the security situation could not be guaranteed in the longer term.[92] This difference of view also contributed to strained relations between the military and UNHCR, which was viewed as obstructionist.

There were also differences of approach between the US contingent, which focused on establishing a large camp in Zakho to which refugees were channelled, and the British and French military and civilian teams, which established themselves further to the north and east. The British and French strategy was to establish routes and way stations from the Turkish border areas into Iraq. Their aim, according to the head of the British Overseas Development Administration (ODA) team, was to get people resettled where they wanted to go, whether to the less damaged of the mountain villages or to the towns. Refugees who came from the mountains of Badinan, to the north and east of Zakho, or from Arbil governorate did not want to go to the Zakho camps, which were the focus of US activity.

Iran: unwelcome guests

The situation in Iran, to which almost three times as many refugees had fled, presented another set of contradictions. The scale of the international response was much smaller, and any thought of establishing a 'safe haven' along the Iranian border was ruled out by the mutual distrust and hostility between the Islamic Republic and the US. Evidently no military bases would be at the disposal of the coalition forces, as they were in Turkey. The Iranians themselves considered the whole idea of the safe haven 'controversial' and an Iranian diplomat was quoted as saying that a Kurdish enclave could lead to new demands for a Kurdish homeland.[93]

Iran had expressed a preference for the creation of 'a credible alternative to exodus' to enable the 'voluntary return of the refugees… under active and effective United Nations supervision and with United Nations guarantees for the safety and honour of the affected population, with the necessary safeguards to preclude any hampering – however temporary – of Iraq's territorial integrity'.[94]

Those working with international organisations at the time noted the marked difference in Iranian attitudes to southern Iraqi refugees in the south-west province of Khuzestan and those in the Kurdish areas. In the north, 'the Iranians weren't nice to the refugees, but they did the right thing [by letting them in]'.[95] Most of those involved were nevertheless clear that the authorities wanted the Iraqi Kurds to go home as soon as possible. This obviously raised protection concerns for UNHCR which, despite its presence in Teheran, was not permitted by the Government to move freely. Its staff did not have unrestricted access to the refugee camps, nor could they supervise repatriation, though the International Organisation for Migration (IOM) was able to provide transport. Soldiers guarded the refugee camps. Most of the Iraqi Kurdish refugees were located in areas still under heavy military control, where the Government was in conflict with its own Kurdish population.

In Khuzestan, by contrast, the atmosphere was much more supportive of the refugees, and a public welcome was allowed for leaders of the uprising who had escaped from Iraq. Iraqi opposition groups based in Iran, especially the Supreme Council for the Islamic Revolution in Iraq (SCIRI), were allowed easy access to the refugees.[96]

By the end of April, many of the refugees in north-western Iran were still without proper shelter, and epidemics threatened. Iran received only a fraction of the aid and none of the political effort which the Western coalition members invested in dealing with Turkey's difficulties. President Bush, while expressing 'acute concern' about Iraqi refugees in Iran and on the Iranian border, merely commended European Community efforts and said the US had 'offered to contribute to international efforts to meet this humanitarian challenge'.[97]

It is also true to say that such US assistance as did arrive was treated with great suspicion, and individuals from US organisations did not have an easy time in Iran, to the point of being suspected of spying.[98] States which had somewhat better relations with Iran – Germany, Belgium, France and Canada – mounted more extensive relief efforts. Germany sent some troops to help with humanitarian needs, and there was an unusual stream of European visitors to Teheran, including West German Foreign Minister Hans-Dietrich Genscher, Danielle Mitterand and the British Minister of Overseas Development, Lynda Chalker. However, the provision of European assistance was not free of problems and mutual suspicions.[99]

The amounts of assistance given to Iran were dwarfed by the effort on the Turkish border. At the height of the Iraqi refugee crisis, up until 17 May 1991, it was estimated that UNDRO received from governments, the Red Cross and private sources seven times as much funding per refugee for those on the Turkish border as for those in Iran. The US spent only $20 million in Iran, out of a total of $207.6 million allocated for Iraqi refugees by that date. The EU in the course of the year did try to rectify this balance somewhat, providing 60 percent of its ECU111 million in humanitarian aid for this crisis to Iran and the Iranian border.[100]

However, despite the Iranian Government's suspicion of coalition intentions, the establishment of the safe haven did have the desired effect of encouraging Kurdish refugees to return home. By June 1991, some 500,000, just under half the total number who had fled to Iran, had returned.

By June, with the large-scale return of refugees from Turkey and Iran, the delivery of aid and absence of armed clashes with the Iraqis, the military operation was hailed as a great success. However, behind the scenes, a series of difficult questions loomed. On what basis were the refugees returning? Who would guarantee their protection in their own country and how long would external protection remain? Linked to all these questions, what was to be the relationship between the Kurds and the Iraqi Government in future?

FINDING THE EXIT

By late April, despite the criticism heaped on the UN humanitarian agencies for their poor performance, they were under pressure to play a larger role. The US wanted UNHCR to take over the relief operation being run by DART and NGOs in the safe haven area. As early as 21 April, the Iraqi Government had also written to the Secretary General asking the UN to take over 'humanitarian centres throughout Iraq', including the camps being set up in the Zakho area.[101]

As a UN organisation which usually works with the consent of host governments, UNHCR had resisted the idea of working in northern Iraq without Baghdad's consent. However, by 16 April, it was virtually alone in its resistance to cross-border operations. The signing of the Memorandum of Understanding between the UN and the Iraqi Government soon afterwards (see below) met this object and made it difficult for UNHCR to resist working in the safe haven areas. Nonetheless, basic issues about protection from forced return and the safety of returnees were not resolved.[102]

UNHCR feared the creation of a situation similar to that in the Gaza Strip. It therefore did not want the camps to be more than transit sites, and initially objected to taking them over without assurances that some form of protection would be available to allow the full resettlement of the refugees. Under the pressure of events, however, UNHCR took formal control of Zakho camp from coalition forces on 13 May, though the final handover of relief operations did not occur until June. Even by then, the issue of how the population in the north was to be protected had not been clarified.

The MoU and UN Guards

On 18 April, the day before General Shalikashvili met with Iraqi General Nashwan to inform him that coalition troops were moving into northern Iraq, the UN Secretary General's Executive Delegate, Prince Sadruddin Aga Khan, signed a Memorandum of Understanding (MoU) which would allow the UN to carry out humanitarian assistance in all parts of Iraq, including the north.[103] Negotiations had begun less than a week after Resolution 688 had 'insisted' that aid organisations be allowed to work in Iraq. The MoU required all UN operations to be carried out with Iraqi government consent and acknowledged explicitly in its preamble that Iraq did not accept Resolution 688.[104]

From the coalition point of view, the MoU represented a necessary compromise so that aid workers could operate safely in the north. Since allied troops were going to leave, the presence of the UN and aid workers from NGOs was seen as part of the protection of the Kurds. At the time, therefore, the US 'strongly welcomed the UN plan devised by Sadruddin'.[105] Furthermore, as reports appeared describing the plight of the Iraqi population, there was increasing pressure to give assistance to civilians throughout the country, not only in the small area covered by the safe haven. It was evident that the UN could not run a humanitarian programme in Iraq without the consent of the Government which still controlled most of the country.

The states supplying troops for Operation Safe Haven wanted to withdraw them as soon as possible, but the end of the unilateral military operation was contingent on the establishment of the UN humanitarian programme, with a measure of Iraqi government consent. Once the MoU was in place, the problem of security remained.

The relief organisations needed protection from harassment throughout Iraq. In the north, the Kurdish and other minority populations needed protection from possible government attacks, whether or not they were direct recipients of assistance.

The Western coalition governments therefore needed the UN to agree some kind of protection force which would allow their military forces to withdraw. However, they were aware that it would be difficult to get a new resolution through the Security Council – Resolution 688 had already raised sharp questions about the infringement of sovereignty – with China and perhaps the Soviet Union likely to object to any further proposals of this kind.

At the end of April, John Major obtained EC and US backing for a UN 'police force' (not a fully fledged peacekeeping force) which he considered could be sent under the auspices of Resolution 688. Iraq, however, very clearly rejected this idea.[106] The result was an *impasse*, since UN Secretary General Perez de Cuellar resisted suggestions to go ahead without Iraqi approval, insisting that this would require a further Security Council resolution.

The compromise which finally emerged had little to do with protecting the Kurds. Sadruddin proposed that the 'police force' be linked to the MoU rather than directly to Resolution 688. In order to speed the exit of coalition forces, Iraq accepted this option.[107] Some commentators, and UNHCR personnel, criticised Sadruddin and his officials for not taking the issue of protection of the Kurds sufficiently seriously. Certainly some UN officials in Iraq, believing that the Government wanted to facilitate returns, appeared convinced that returning refugees were in no danger.

Sadruddin believed that the humanitarian 'umbrella' could be used to achieve some measure of security for the population in the north. He reportedly said, 'We had to improvise. The aim was a degree of security without the Security Council, of peace without peace-keeping, of international action without intervention.'[108] A less favourable judgement was that the UN Guards were 'a lowest-common denominator

---

The Memorandum of Understanding

The Memorandum of Understanding signed on 18 April 1991 allowed for the UN to establish a 'humanitarian presence in Iraq wherever such a presence may be needed'; the establishment and staffing by UN personnel of UN sub-offices and Humanitarian Centres 'in agreement and cooperation' with the Government of Iraq; the establishment by the Government, together with the UN, of 'a relief distribution and monitoring structure to permit access to all civilians covered by the relief programme, as soon as possible'; and measures for the benefit of displaced persons, 'based primarily on their personal safety and the provision of humanitarian assistance and relief for their return and normalisation of their lives in their places of origin'.[109]

The UN Guards unit – a maximum of 500 guards for the whole country – had a limited mandate: to protect UN personnel, assets and operations, including transit camps, UN humanitarian centres' relay stations, the UN coordination office in Baghdad, and sub-offices in the governorates. It was not mandated to intervene in law enforcement issues that did not involve UN resources. It could, however, report incidents which did not have a bearing on UN resources, given their possible impact on the overall security situation. Side-arms were to be provided by the Iraqi authorities with UN approval, and the numbers of guards in each area were to be decided in consultation with Government of Iraq. The agreement on the deployment of the Guards was signed on 25 May 1991.

solution to the dilemma of establishing a UN security presence in northern Iraq'.[110] The Secretary General and Sadruddin were under considerable pressure from the major coalition states to come up with a solution, even if they were criticised for giving too much leeway to Baghdad. Coalition states have subsequently criticised the expense and ineffectiveness of the UN Guards, but at the time even the US was unwilling to insist on a more 'muscular' force against objections from Iraq and some Security Council members. The UN was essentially saving coalition governments from the prospect of a prolonged and costly military presence by providing a symbolic token of security.

As the initially high hopes for a negotiated agreement between the Kurds and the Iraqi Government faded, and it became evident that coalition ground troops would leave without waiting for a political solution, increasing prominence was given to the role of UN humanitarian organisations, NGOs and the UN Guards in creating what was vaguely described as 'a climate of security' for the Kurds.

Kurdish negotiations

The other major factor in coalition calculations on withdrawing their troops was the progress of negotiations between the Kurdistan Front and the Iraqi Government which had opened in April. In view of the Iraqi regime's record in dealing with the Kurds, and the general international distrust of the Iraqi Government at that time, in retrospect it seems that a surprising degree of hope was pinned on an agreement.[111] For the coalition states, the main benefit would have been an end to any involvement in Iraq's internal affairs and to the need to protect the Kurds. UN agencies, for their part, hoped that a settlement would resolve the refugee problem. For the refugees themselves, it offered the chance of a more peaceful future.

Among the Kurdish leaders, feelings were more mixed, despite bursts of optimism. During the uprising, the leaders were described by one observer as 'supremely overconfident'.[112] After its collapse and the mass flight, refugees and their leaders were in a state of shock, deepened by the reversal of their initial heady victory.[113] Masud Barzani had apparently pleaded vainly for the Kurds 'to stay in Kurdistan and not become refugees, like the Armenians'.[114] But once the exodus had occurred, the leaders all wanted a solution that would get the refugees home. They were well aware of Turkey's determination not to host a large new Kurdish population, and feared that if they did not cooperate with the Iraqi Government, it would not allow the refugees to return at all. Initially, therefore, most of the political groups within the KF saw no option but to negotiate.[115]

The Iraqi Government had proposed negotiations with the Kurdish leadership almost immediately after the fall of Kirkuk, and the Kurds had sent an 'exploratory mission' to Baghdad on 10 April, after which they announced a ceasefire. Talks between the KF and the Government began officially on 18 April 1991, as coalition forces were about to arrive in Zakho. At the first meeting, the Iraqi stand was relatively conciliatory, possibly intended to stave off the intervention of coalition troops. Some observers have expressed surprise that the Kurds did not attempt to hold the talks on neutral ground, rather than in Baghdad, but this probably reflected the degree of insecurity felt by the Kurdish leaders and their need, like the Iraqi regime, to 'buy time'.[116]

Despite an initial agreement in principle on democracy in Iraq and autonomy for the Kurdish areas, a key point of disagreement remained, as in 1970, the future status of Kirkuk and its environs. A second round of talks in Baghdad started on 6 May, and on 18 May, Barzani announced euphorically that an agreement was imminent. He seemed to believe at this stage that some agreement on Kirkuk was possible, involving Kurdish control of the administration of Kirkuk, if not control of its oilfields, though this proved to be a chimera. Kurdish demands for free elections and a new constitution were rejected, as were proposals for international guarantees of the Kurds' autonomous status.[117]

At the same time a break in the logjam over access to Dohuk encouraged the mass return of most of the remaining refugees in Turkey. By 30 May, General Colin Powell reported to Washington that Operation Provide Comfort should be terminated as soon as the diplomatic situation allowed.[118] As the Iraqi Government became aware of the coalition forces' intention to withdraw from the north, the incentive to accept Kurdish demands diminished. During June its stance toughened. There were new demands for the surrender of all heavy weapons, the closure of Front radio stations and severance of all the KF's foreign relations.[119] It became clear that Kirkuk would remain entirely in Iraqi Government hands.

There were growing disagreements within the KF, especially between the PUK and KDP, on how much should be conceded. The KDP was willing to defer the Kirkuk issue, but the PUK resisted this.[120] The differences between the party leaders sharpened with Jalal Talabani of the PUK said to be sceptical of a successful outcome to the negotiations. Masud Barzani (KDP) was more inclined to accept an agreement because he doubted coalition assurances of protection.[121] In June, Talabani went on a visit to Turkey and constantly delayed his return.[122] When the KF leaders finally met at the end of June, the majority refused to accept the Iraqi terms.

The withdrawal of coalition forces

The coalition states themselves were not entirely in agreement on how to ensure the safety of the returning refugees. They all intended to pull their troops out of Iraq as soon as possible, but it came as something of a shock when the US announced in late May that its forces would begin pulling out on 21 June.[123] This decision was based on the view at that time that an agreement on autonomy discussions was 'imminent'; that humanitarian workers remaining in the north would create a climate of safety; and that the UN Guards would provide security. Furthermore, there was pressure from Turkey that the operation should be brought to a speedy close because the PKK was stepping up its cross-border activities.

The US and its allies were discussing with the Turkish Government the establishment of a rapid reaction force in eastern Turkey – which became known as 'Operation Poised Hammer' – as an 'over the horizon' threat if the Iraqi Government were to attack the Kurds. The British and French contingents nonetheless objected to the early US withdrawal.[124] The Kurdish leaders, especially Masud Barzani, who had the closer relations with the UK Government, prevailed upon it to call for a delay in the US withdrawal. They wanted to link it to the conclusion of an agreement with the Government. US officials argued that such a linkage would make the coalition states hostages to the negotiators.

On 25 June, John Major told the British parliament that UK forces would remain in northern Iraq until the Kurdish population received assurances on their safety and an effective UN force was on the ground, along with a continuing military deterrent presence in the region. The US troop withdrawal was delayed until mid-July.

Coalition commanders on the ground tried to reassure the Kurds, while at the same time keeping the Iraqis in the dark about the exact withdrawal date, because it was thought that this too would affect the course of negotiations. The US military made clear that the security zone was not going to be expanded and that coalition forces were going to leave. The UN, they assured, would keep the peace, and they urged the Kurds 'to settle their differences with Baghdad through negotiations'.[125]

This message was conveyed to the KF leadership at meetings between PUK and KDP representatives, General Jay Garner and General Shalikashvili on 17 and 19 June. The latter stressed that the Kurds had world opinion behind them. By this time, the Kurdish representatives seemed less sanguine about the progress of talks and pointed out that they still saw Saddam Hussein as a threat. But General Shalikashvili, while acknowledging this, said that they would have to come to an accommodation with the Iraqi Government. The generals apparently thought the Kurds had detected divisions within the Coalition over withdrawal, though in fact the Kurdish leadership was unable to do much to exploit them. Further meetings with Barzani and Talabani in early July formalised the message that the coalition forces were leaving.[126]

Meanwhile, the Kurdish leadership was given to understand that the US had signalled unofficially to Baghdad that the no-fly zone above the 36th parallel would remain in place. Around the end of June, the allies issued a *démarche* to the Iraqis, the terms of which were not made public. It outlined 'how the allies expected them to behave after allied forces had withdrawn'. Its terms were said to include staying clear of the former 'safe haven' area (subsequently referred to as 'the security zone') and a warning that Iraqi conduct would be monitored in the whole Kurdish region, not just in the security zone. It also laid terms for the Military Coordination Centre (MCC) to retain a presence in Zakho and to monitor Iraqi compliance. Iraqi army and secret police were instructed not to enter the security zone.[127]

The US had convinced the British to drop the proposal to link withdrawal of forces to the outcome of the autonomy negotiations, and redeployment resumed in July. However, according to one account, as result of this disagreement, 'the allies were compelled to publicise the presence of the Poised Hammer force in Turkey and toughen the *démarche* to the Iraqis, two things the United States did not want to do'.[128]

Coalition forces completed their withdrawal from northern Iraq in mid-July, despite the fact that no agreement had been reached in the autonomy negotiations. When all the troops had left, a total of 271 UN Guards were stationed in the north.[129] Operation Poised Hammer allowed a force of about 3000 troops to remain in south-eastern Turkey, in addition to the US F-16s based at Incirlik air base. However, the Turkish Government limited the duration of the ground troops' deployment to three months ending in September 1991.[130]

If the arrival of coalition troops had an immediate political impact, so did their departure. Both Kurdish and Iraqi forces began 'testing the waters'. Control in the three northern governorates at this stage was a patchwork. KF forces held the former security zone and a swathe of territory along the northern and eastern borders, including the town of Shaqlawa, the Rawanduz region and the strategic Hamilton road leading towards Arbil.[131] Iraqi troops remained in areas adjacent to the 'security zone' and held the cities of Arbil and Sulaymaniya and most of the 'collective settlements'.[132] In some areas there was a degree of cooperation between *peshmerga* and government forces, while in others a stand-off or intermittent clashes ensued.

In July, just after the last allied troops withdrew, fighting in Arbil and Sulaymaniya led to the withdrawal of Iraqi forces from the two city centres, leaving the *peshmergas* in control, though Iraqi troops remained encamped on the outskirts.[133] Not all the clashes were thought to be initiated by Iraqi forces: sometimes they were provoked by the *peshmergas*.[134] The Western allies reportedly warned the Kurds that if they engaged in confrontations with the Iraqis they would be on their own.[135] Certainly no response from 'Poised Hammer' resulted. The MCC seems to have viewed these episodes as insignificant: coalition forces based in Turkey 'had not been required to engage any Iraqi incursion against Kurds or NGOs'.[136]

By the end of the summer, despite continued uncertainty about the future, the majority of the refugees had returned to Iraq, not only from Turkey but also from Iran. On this border the pace of returns was much less intense, but Operation Provide Comfort had created a greater climate of confidence, which was communicated to those in Iran. A UN official in Iran suggested that an added incentive for rural dwellers was to return for the period of harvest between May and July and to plant crops between September and November.

However, the autonomy talks remained stalled. An Iraqi official reportedly offered the Kurdish negotiators a package deal which included government services but also a strong security presence – 'from aspirin to *mukhabarat*' (secret police), as one participant, Dr Mahmud Uthman, has described it. They could 'take it or leave it'. Nonetheless, on 17 September Major General James Jamerson, American commander of the rapid reaction force in Turkey, warned Iraqi Kurdish leaders that the ground force would leave in two weeks. On 10 October the last coalition ground troops left Turkey. The Turkish military were said to be unhappy with foreign troops based on their soil. 'Furthermore, it did not want allied observers around when it began to execute punitive raids on areas in northern Iraq that allegedly harboured [the PKK]'.[137]

Coalition air patrols over northern Iraq continued policing the air exclusion zone. The French and British each sent eight tactical fighters to join the US aircraft stationed at Incirlik. Agreement to use this base has since been renewed every six months by the Turkish parliament[138] (for further discussion of Turkey's role in the north, see Chapter 3).

In October, as coalition troops departed from Turkey, serious fighting broke out between Kurdistan Front *peshmerga* and government forces in Sulaymaniya, Kifri and Kalar. In a change of tactics, Iraq began to withdraw its forces from the three northern governorates of Arbil, Dohuk and Sulaymaniya in late October 1991. Fighting and shelling continued into November, causing a further 200,000 people to be displaced.

The regime also withdrew central government funds and Arab personnel from the civil administration of the three governorates. They gave an ultimatum to Kurdish officials and civil servants: either they could relocate to government-controlled territory, or they would cease to be paid. Most stayed in the Kurdish areas. The main entry point for goods to the northern governorates, at Fayda on the road from Mosul, was closed early in November, and the Government imposed an economic embargo on the north which continued until late 1996. An agreement between the Kurdish leadership and the Government to lift the embargo in return for the withdrawal of Kurdish forces from the main towns was not implemented.[139]

In ceding control of the north, the Iraqi regime lost little of immediate strategic importance. It retained full control of the oilfields of Kirkuk, and at that time its oil pipeline to Turkey, which crossed the edge of the Kurdish-controlled region, was not in operation. The withdrawal avoided the potential embarrassment of having demoralised troops either defeated by the *peshmergas* or surrendering *en masse*. It sent the Iraqi Kurds a message, re-enforced by the onset of winter, that the KF could bring them no material benefit, and emphasised the region's dependence on Baghdad.[140] Finally, it saved central government funds and dumped the humanitarian problem back into the international community's lap.

EXPANDING HUMANITARIAN AID

Both Resolution 688 and the MoU had specified that the Iraqi Government should allow access for humanitarian aid to all sections of the population needing it. However, outside the small area in the north where coalition forces were physically present, this proved difficult to implement consistently. The Iraq regime avoided head-on confrontation with coalition governments in the safe haven area, but consolidated its power in the areas it could control. In the course of 1991 this caused increasing problems for the UN humanitarian agencies and NGOs working in Iraq.

UN attempts to establish what were described as 'humanitarian centres' outside Baghdad met with limited success. In two key instances, they failed altogether. Kirkuk was the first focus of contention. While negotiations were in progress with the KF, the Iraqi authorities were already reported to be discouraging Kurds from returning to their homes there. The fact that Kirkuk was firmly under the control of Baghdad was a further deterrent.[141]

A UN official who worked in Baghdad at that time said that the Government's policy was to repopulate Kirkuk with Arabs. Those Kurds and Turcomans who had fled were therefore not encouraged to return. Certainly in the following years, the Government's policy of expelling the remaining Kurds and Turcomans reinforces this view (see Chapter 5). The main purpose of UNHCR's presence – to ensure the safe resettlement of those Kurds and Turcomans who had fled – therefore ran directly counter to government plans.

The refugees themselves were not willing to return to Kirkuk and other areas wholly under Iraqi government control without international protection, and they were supported in this by the KF. This reluctance was not surprising in view of the events which followed the uprising and the conduct of Iraqi police and special forces, which had remained in parts of the security zone. Little faith was placed in the series of amnesties declared by the authorities.[142]

UNHCR apparently raised the matter of access to Kirkuk with an Iraqi official in early June. However, there seemed to have been some crossing of wires with UN headquarters in Baghdad, which was said still to be trying to 'gather first hand evidence'. In early August a formal request from the UN Executive Delegate's office in Baghdad to establish a sub-office in Kirkuk was refused by the Government. In early September, Baghdad also refused permission for UN Guards to accompany a convoy of 3417 returnees from Penjwin to Kirkuk, as negotiated between the KF and the

Governor of Sulaymaniya. The KF at this time was still pressing for a UN presence in Kirkuk.

Other efforts to return refugees to areas under full government control also ran into problems. In August an attempt by UNHCR to encourage the return of refugees from the Zakho transit camp to Nineveh governorate collapsed when potential returnees were frightened by demands from Iraqi officials for a list of their names and destinations.

The failure to establish a humanitarian centre in Kirkuk meant that its refugees (at that time estimated to be about 30,000 in the Arbil area and 100,000 in the Sulaymaniya area) remained displaced and dependent on humanitarian assistance for food and shelter.[143] The *impasse* was never resolved, and the Kirkuki refugees, along with people from other areas under government control, were still in Kurdish-controlled northern Iraq in 1998.

A foretaste of the future constraints on unfettered aid agency action was the fate of an EU initiative to assist refugees returning from Iran. The plan, announced in June by the French Minister of Humanitarian Affairs, Bernard Kouchner, envisaged a civilian aid programme involving some 60 European aid workers providing electricity and water supplies, agricultural rehabilitation and medical services to returning refugees in Sulaymaniya governorate, which was still under partial Iraqi control. They were not to be backed by troops, and originally some members of the group, certainly the French, had wanted to operate cross-border without seeking Iraqi consent. It was subsequently agreed with the UN Executive Delegate, Sadruddin Aga Khan, that the aid work would be carried out under the terms of the MoU.

In August, the Iraqi authorities, when told of the programme by the UN, rejected it. Bernt Bernander, the Executive Delegate's representative in Baghdad, argued that it would have been impossible to conceal a programme of that size from the Iraqis.[144] Eventually some of the funding was disbursed through European NGOs which were working under the terms of the MoU, but the incident resulted in angry exchanges between UN and EU officials.

This incident demonstrated, as one observer put it, that there was a very strong element within the UN humanitarian agencies in Baghdad whose main priority was to maintain harmonious relations with the Iraqi Government. They viewed such initiatives as making a difficult situation impossible. The increasing evidence by mid-1991 that the humanitarian situation in the south required a UN presence and assistance also seemed a persuasive reason not to jeopardise access by challenging the Government over aid to the north.

In the south, the Government's pursuit of those involved in the uprising did not end once the insurrections had been crushed, but instead became part of a long campaign to seek out its participants. The security sweeps and arrests in towns and villages were reported to be intense during June and July 1991. The marsh regions between the Tigris and Euphrates became the particular target of a fierce government campaign to eradicate opposition.

After a flurry of international concern in June, little was done. On 11 June, Iran called on the UN to protect the Shi'a trapped in the southern marshes and surrounded by Iraqi troops. In a letter to the Security Council, the Islamic Republic stated that it was unable to meet the needs of another influx of Iraqi refugees. On 12 June, UK Foreign Secretary Douglas Hurd phoned Iranian Foreign Minister Ali Akbar Veliyati – a rare direct contact – for information on the situation.

The German Foreign Minister Hans-Dietrich Genscher wrote to the UN Secretary General on 13 June that his Government was dismayed by reports of brutal acts of repression against the Shi'a, and would provide further support if necessary. He suggested that the UN establish humanitarian centres in southern Iraq. The UN in Baghdad believed that there was a large concentration of Iraqi troops in the marsh area active in harassing fugitives, and officials attempted to persuade the Government to remove them and allow humanitarian access. There were, however, disagreements on the scale of the problem. In July the UN estimated the numbers in the marshes at 40,000–100,000, while the Iranian Government and Iraqi opposition sources were citing 500,000–700,000.[145]

As a result of these expressions of concern, and a certain amount of press coverage, on 11 July a UN mission headed by Sadruddin travelled to Nasariya and to villages along the edge of the marshes. 'Prior to the visit the Iraqi military withdrew its forces which had previously been firing into the marsh area.'[146] In the village of Hammar the mission met up with a UN convoy carrying food and other supplies, part of a UN attempt to set up a feeding station to assist displaced people and get some idea of their numbers.

Sadruddin wrote to Iraqi Foreign Minister Ahmed Hussein Khudayer on 15 July expressing his 'deep concern and dismay' on learning that:

> … as soon as our mission had left the area, and in particular on the 12th and 13th of July, a heavy military presence was redeployed to take up the same positions which had obviously been vacated mainly for the duration of our visit… Furthermore, my United Nations staff, which had remained in Hammar together with United Nations Guards to assist the local authorities in distributing the contents of our convoy to those in need, were summarily requested to leave the area. They complied with these instructions but not before noting carefully that military checkpoints and gun emplacements had been reinstalled every 50 meters along the lakeside and that checkpoints had also been reinstated every 500 meters along the main road to Hammar.

He warned that Iraqi actions 'will constitute a further negative element when the Security Council came to consider lifting sanctions'.[147]

This visit was part of Sadruddin's mission to assess overall humanitarian needs in Iraq, and his letter bears the same date as his formal report to the Secretary General recommending that Iraq be allowed to sell limited amounts of oil (see Chapter 2). The five permanent members of the Security Council responded rapidly to Sadruddin's account of his frustrated efforts. They called on the Iraqi Government to withdraw its forces from the marshes and allow UN representatives access to the region, asserting that Iraq was violating Resolution 688, which required that humanitarian organisations have access to the civilian population.[148]

Despite the Security Council's fast reaction, its warning carried no threat of action and did not induce the Iraqi Government to change its policy. The UN was finally able to establish small contingents of UN Guards in Basra and Amara (though not in Nasariya), along with local offices in those cities. But its agencies were never allowed to work in the marsh areas. The UN Guards in Iraq finally reached their full complement of 500 in October 1991. However, in September 1991, when a total of 420 guards were in place, only 20 were stationed in the south.[149]

Controlling and limiting UN humanitarian access was important to the Iraqi Government, and on the whole its obstruction was not seriously challenged. 'The

Government of Iraq', as one UN official put it, 'was very firm on wanting the UN out of certain areas and had more resolve than senior UN people'. Nonetheless, he observed that sometimes the Government was forced to make concessions when pressure was put on it.

The issue of access remained low on the list of Security Council priorities, and the pressure when it came to humanitarian issues was not very strong. The UN humanitarian organisations themselves, accustomed to work in cooperation with governments, were loath to challenge the Government. A more 'hands on' and force-ful UN system which could have overridden the Iraqi Government would have required more money, personnel and commitment than the international community was ready to provide. Also there was little taste for deeper involvement in the humanitarian problems within Iraq.

The sharp contrast between the standards of enforcement applied to upholding UNSCOM's mandate, and to ensuring humanitarian access, was 'justified in the eyes of most Security Council members who saw a qualitative difference between enforcing access for a UN humanitarian programme, compared with UNSCOM priorities'.[150] The issue seemed a comparatively minor one at the time, but the contrast between the sweeping claims made for humanitarian intervention, and its limitations in practice, stored up difficulties for the future.

OUTCOMES OF 'THE DRAMA IN THE MOUNTAINS'

The events of early 1991 were very dramatic and much reported. What is often for-gotten with the passage of time is that most people involved, whether on the political or humanitarian side, were only thinking of short-term goals. The civilian and military personnel responsible for the delivery of aid were trying to get their job done and the refugees down from the mountains. It was not only the military which wanted and expected a quick exit: UNHCR's initial planning only extended until the summer of 1991. The World Food Programme (WFP) expected to close its Iraqi programme in September.

Most political decision-makers, trying to avoid public embarrassment, responded to the strongest and most immediate pressures, which did not necessarily spring directly from the situation in Iraq. The limited understanding of Iraqi and Kurdish politics on the part of the majority of participants, the new and unfamiliar initiatives taken in humanitarian assistance, and the unpredictability of the Iraqi Government all made longer-term planning difficult.

Almost everything which happened in the wake of the Gulf War was unforeseen: the uprisings, the refugee outflow, the fact that the Iraqi regime remained in power and continued from time to time to resist demands made by UN agencies and UNSCOM, and Iraq's withdrawal of its forces from the northern governorates. These developments were not predicted by military or political planners, nor were they foreseen by UN agencies. Consequently, many of the decisions taken soon after the war, beginning with General Schwarzkopf's ceasefire terms, looked inappropriate a few months later.

Operation Provide Comfort, said to have been the largest and most complex humanitarian operation attempted by the military since World War II,[151] created an image of heroic rescue which has influenced public understanding of the situation in northern Iraq ever since. The images of Kurdish suffering and of soldiers and aid workers providing relief aid were real enough. According to the US Office of Foreign Disaster Assistance (OFDA), 'the two primary objectives of Operation Provide Comfort, to reduce mortality rates among the refugee population and to create conditions so that the refugees could return to their homes safely, have been accomplished'.[152] By December 1991, more than 90 percent of those who had fled in March and April had returned to Iraq, 'the fastest rate of return in UNHCR's experience'.[153]

A British participant took the view that it was a high cost, 'high tech' operation 'but it was the right thing to do – people needed protection'. He added that the goals could only be short-term because it was clear that the troops would leave quickly. Despite the limited area covered by the safe haven – roughly one-sixth of the area in which Kurds predominate – the coalition military presence had been effective in checking offensive actions by the Iraqi army in other parts of this region. This in turn contributed to the willingness of refugees to return.[154]

However, the political message – that the international community would continue to provide protection for those who had returned from the mountains – was more questionable. Looked at in a longer-term perspective, Operations Provide Comfort and Safe Haven had some serious weaknesses. First, the motives for intervention were complex. A US military commentator observed that 'humanitarian operations are the pursuit of policy by other means'.[155] In this case humanitarian action certainly masked political goals, and these did not consist solely or even mainly of saving the Kurds.

Major Western governments decided to act only when other political pressures from domestic critics and regional allies, particularly Turkey, had triggered a response. The international media played an important role in achieving this: 'The attention devoted by the Western media to the plight of the Kurds along the Turkish border threatened the political dividends that Western governments had secured from the conduct of the war itself'.[156]

The initial reluctance to become involved, especially on the part of the US, also coloured policy. One of the leading US advisors on the relief effort concluded:

> The desire to disengage eventually drove the decision-making process and shaped discussion of every option. As a result, the United States never developed a comprehensive, long-term plan for responding to the crisis. Most decisions were ad hoc, and policy guidance was often contradictory and unrealistic. At the field level, decisions were made in response to the situation and the needs of the Kurds. Inevitably, their needs came into conflict with the desire to withdraw as soon as possible.[157]

A UNHCR official put it more bluntly. It was not so much a case of having an exit strategy, but that 'exit was the strategy'.[158]

The metaphor of the mire, getting bogged down in internal politics, was a powerful legacy of the Vietnam period which influenced the US military and the civilian administration during and after the Gulf War. Part of good tactics was to have a limited goal. This was quite understandable from a military perspective, and the short duration of military intervention also reassured critics that the intention was not to 'take over' part of Iraq. But the political consequences – both of sending in troops and of pulling them out – were not effectively addressed. The British and French showed less nervousness about involvement, but the physical and political dominance of US forces, here as during the war, meant that its decisions effectively determined the course of events.

A warning note was sounded by the Lawyers Committee for Human Rights in its 1992 report reviewing the effectiveness of protection for refugees from the Gulf War:

> The international community must fully appreciate the enduring commitment necessary to undertake arrangements such as those that have been made for displaced persons and returned refugees in northern Iraq... There are no easy or inexpensive solutions to the needs of refugees and displaced persons for new permanent homes.[159]

The inherent 'short-termism' of the emergency humanitarian response concealed the fact that it was addressing the result, not the cause, of the problem. The issues of safety and protection continue to this day, in relation not only to the Kurds, but to large sections of the Iraqi population. However, the West's political establishment did not intend to address directly the underlying problem of political conflict between communities within Iraq.

The political signals given to the Kurds, both during Operation Provide Comfort and afterwards, were very mixed, and the Kurdish leaders were well aware of this. However, the very act of launching such a large and impressive military operation suggested a level of commitment which it was not intended to suggest.

For the Kurdish political leadership, the events of 1991, despite their traumatic nature, did represent a kind of triumph in that they put the Kurds on the political map. Even ordinary people felt that their plight had finally been acknowledged by the rest of the world, which had actually intervened on their behalf and 'seen' their suffering.[160] In this sense, something had indeed changed, but the hopes and expectations of action were not fulfilled by subsequent events.

The intervention set up, for the most part unintentionally, new political dynamics within Kurdish political circles, between the Kurds and the Iraqi Government, and between this region and neighbouring states. As one analyst noted, 'even purportedly humanitarian efforts have significant political consequences for the division of power between the contending parties, especially if the international presence is long-term'.[161] At the end of 1991, the Iraqi Government's decision to withdraw from the northern governorates lifted the threat of a further refugee crisis, but it created a further set of political and economic problems to which humanitarian aid could not be a sufficient response.

By focusing on the relief of immediate suffering, the coalition states also backed themselves into a corner. Because they had emphasised their 'humanitarian' commitment to the Kurds they could not entirely escape the pressures to respond to further crises as they unfolded. Thus the US and UK, and other members of the EU, have continued to find themselves embroiled in attempts to provide aid and ever-less-credible protection. Meanwhile, the root political problems have not been resolved, but have taken new forms.

There was also a political subtext to this humanitarian operation, namely the consideration given to Turkey's concerns. This meant – as a US official noted – that Turkey's cooperation, not just its acquiescence, was essential for both military and humanitarian activity in northern Iraq. In practice this has meant the progressive encroachment of Turkey's battle with its own Kurdish population into Iraqi Kurdistan, further complicating the political and humanitarian situation.

The humanitarian aid effort – even in the north – was always seen as a necessary but inconvenient addition to the coercive and punitive measures being taken against Iraq. Sadruddin had wanted to separate UN humanitarian operations in Iraq from the political measures being taken by the Security Council in order to make the UN's humanitarian presence acceptable to the Iraqi Government, and to maintain a position of neutrality in the ongoing battles between the Council and the Government. While this was understandable, it meant that the UN humanitarian agencies had little leverage when the Iraqi Government decided to deny them access or to limit a particular programme.

Despite its relative weakness, the Government was therefore able to resist many of the strictures imposed upon it. This applied particularly to humanitarian and human rights issues, on which the collective political will of the international community, and of its leading members in this conflict, was not at its strongest.

However, as UN officials have pointed out, it is not feasible to carry out aid programmes by force, especially if they involve an entire population, not only the distribution of food and medicine to refugee camps. Working in health care, water and sanitation as well as food distribution on a national level entails working with government agencies. Therefore, short of taking over the running of the state, other forms of pressure would have to be found. In the case of Iraq, neither the UN agencies nor the Security Council ever came to grips with this issue.

The Security Council came out of the Gulf crisis of 1991 with its prestige strengthened, having proved that it could take collective action. In contrast, the UN humanitarian agencies were shown in a poor light, assailed with criticisms of inefficiency, bureaucracy and too much attachment to the rules and norms of state power. In particular, they were compared unfavourably with the military in an emergency situation. While many of the complaints were justified, this ignores the responsibility of member states for monitoring and influencing UN agencies, as well as providing them with funds to do their work (see Chapter 7).

Security Council Resolution 688 gave legitimacy to the idea that sovereignty is a relative concept, allowing the UN to step in where a state's treatment of its own people is deemed to threaten international peace and security. However, even by the end of 1991, the principles it laid down – protection of civilians in Iraq, an end to state persecution and the provision of humanitarian aid and access for humanitarian agencies – were either ignored, contradicted or diluted, particularly in areas under Iraqi government control.

The 'safe haven' concept which was justified under the rubric of Resolution 688 had been applied in northern Iraq but not in the south, despite ongoing persecution of civilians there. The degree to which sovereignty might be infringed appeared to vary with the political considerations involved. Saudi Arabia and Iran had let the US off the hook by accepting Iraqis stranded in areas under US control in April 1991. But the basic problem which caused them to flee – repression by the Ba'thist state – not only remained, but in many respects got worse, causing further displacement and refugee flight.

NOTES ON CHAPTER 1

1   *Daily Telegraph*, 2 March 1991, 'UN Resolution Designed to Tighten Noose on Dictator'.
2   United Nations (1996i), Document 26.
3   *International Herald Tribune*, 2 March 1991, 'Bush Pledges Renewed Effort on Mideast Pact'.
4   For a discussion of the political views which informed the US decision to stop the war when it did, and not to attempt any advance on Baghdad, see Freedman and Karsh (1993), pp 412–4.
5   Baker (1995), pp 411–429.
6   Schwarzkopf (1992); Gordon and Trainor (1995), pp 444–7.
7   General Sir Peter de la Billiere, the commander of the British contingent in the Gulf War, has since been reported as saying that he felt Schwarzkopf was right to agree to the Iraqis flying helicopters. 'The Iraqis were responsible for establishing law and order. You could not administer the country without using the helicopters.' This suggests that the potential uses of the helicopters were well understood by the negotiators. Sir Peter further alleged that one of the battle objectives was to leave Iraq with enough forces 'to defend its borders' against Iran (*Washington Post*, 12 March 1998, 'Victory Revisited').
8   *Washington Post*, 27 March 1991, 'Neutrality in Iraq Reaffirmed by US'.
9   Wolfowitz (1997), p 108.
10 Foreign Broadcast Information Service, 'Opposition Claim on Use of Chemical Weapons Cited', 11 March 1991, quoting Damascus Radio.
11 *New York Times*, 18 March 1991, 'US Said To Plan Bombing Of Iraqis If They Gas Rebels'.
12 *Washington Post*, 14 March 1991, 'Bush Issues Warnings to Iran, Iraq in Turmoil'.
13 *New York Times*, 16 February 1991, 'Iraqi Revolt Urged'.
14 In an oral answer to Sir George Gardiner on 22 February, the Prime Minister said 'I strongly suspect that Saddam Hussein may yet become a target for his own people… He is a man without pity and, whatever his fate may be, I for one will not weep for him.' Hansard, House of Commons, vol. 184, col. 161, 22 February 1991.
15 *Washington Post*, 16 February 1991, 'Only "Shreds" of Data Feed Hope for Coup'.
16 ABC News, 26 June 1997, 'Peter Jennings Reporting: Unfinished Business – The CIA and Saddam Hussein'.
17 Munro (1996), pp 324–5; Ozel (1995), p 178. Syria appeared to share the view that Saddam would fall. During the war both the Saudis and the Syrians had been working to bring together disparate Iraqi opposition groups in the hope of forming an alternative regime to Saddam's. It was later claimed that in response to the uprisings the Governments of Egypt, Iran, Saudi Arabia and Syria sent arms and money to the rebels, with the knowledge of the US (Talbott [1992], p 62). A Saudi-funded and CIA backed radio station broadcast messages of support (*New York Times*, 6 April 1991, 'Kurd Gives Account of Broadcasts to Iraq Linked to CIA'). However, Jonathan Randal alleges that a visit by the KDP's Hoshyar Zibari to Riyadh in the third week in March – at the height of the Kurdish uprising – was abruptly terminated after Brent Scowcroft and Richard Haas arrived for talks with Saudi officials (Randal [1997], p 99).
18 The allegations came from a report to the Senate Foreign Relations Committee by staffer Peter W. Galbraith. Congress, Senate, Committee on Foreign Relations, Civil War in Iraq: A Staff Report to the Committee on Foreign Relations, May 1991, p 15.
19 *Washington Post*, 8 March 1991, 'Arabs Fear Breakup or Fundamentalist Takeover of Iraq'.
20 Munro (1996), p 340. The first text was formulated in bilateral consultations between the US and UK. On 20 March a draft text was circulated, and on 22 March a revised draft became the basis for negotiations between the five permanent members of the

Security Council (P5). Non-permanent members received a draft on 28 March, by which time a consensus had essentially been reached among the P5. Kuwait and Saudi Arabia also had an input into the discussions. The non-aligned caucus put forward some amendments but they were not officially tabled and few were adopted. The non-aligned states objected particularly that the resolution did not provide for direct negotiation between Iraq and Kuwait to determine their boundary. This was the reason for Cuba's vote against Resolution 687 and Yemen's abstention. Ecuador and other Latin American countries also objected to the Security Council purporting to determine a disputed national boundary. In the end, Cuba and Zaire voted against the resolution, with Ecuador and Yemen abstaining (Johnstone [1994], pp 14–18; Taylor and Groom [1992], p 26).

21   S/PV 2981, p 116, quoted in Sur (1992), p 42.

22   Weller (1993), p 718. Bush re-affirmed this view on several occasions during the next year: for example, on the anniversary of the start of military operations against Iraq (Sur [1992], p 42, note 138).

23   Jonathan Randal argues that the US must have been aware by late March or the first days of April that a major movement of people was occurring in the north since it was flying reconnaissance missions over the region (interview with the author, 22 October 1997).

24   All Iraqis had been subject to a travel ban since the invasion of Kuwait.

25   UNHCR's representative in Ankara suggested in late February 1991 that if the Iraqi Government survived the war there might be attacks on minority groups such as the Kurds, leading to 'an exodus of unknown proportions into Turkey' (UNHCR [1992ii], p 33). Jonathan Randal reported that in December 1990 that Frederick Cuny, who became an advisor with Operation Provide Comfort, had given the State Department's Bureau of Refugee Affairs 'the likely scenario' of a defeated Kurdish uprising and refugee exodus (Randal [1997], p 97).

26   Lawyers Committee for Human Rights (1992), p 41. USAID gave a figure of 71,000 by 18 April (USAID Fact Sheet, 18 April 1991).

27   Iraqis who sought the protection of coalition forces on Iraqi territory became protected persons in accordance with Article 4 of the Fourth Geneva Convention: 'Persons protected by the Convention are those who, at a given moment and in any manner whatsoever, find themselves, in case of conflict or occupation, in the hands of a Party to the conflict or Occupying Power of which they are not nationals'.

28   By 6 May, UNIKOM was deployed in the demilitarised zone along the Iraq-Kuwait border, just before the last US troops left the area. UNIKOM was established under Security Council Resolution 689. Its presence was to deter boundary violations and 'to observe any hostile or potentially hostile action mounted from the territory of one state to the other' (Resolution 687, para. 5). Only in 1993 was it converted into an armed force to prevent small-scale violations of the DMZ and Iraq/Kuwait border. Its mandate was expanded under Resolution 806 (1993) (UN Information Centre, 5 February 1993, 'Security Council Expands UNIKOM's Mandate to Armed Force Capable of Preventing Small Scale Violations of the DMZ and Iraq/Kuwait Boundary').

29   US officials claimed that the suggestion had originally come from Sadruddin Aga Khan, who was appointed Executive Delegate to the UN Secretary General on 9 April (*Washington Post*, 9 April 1991, 'US, Allies Want Refugee Havens Established in Iraq').

30   *Ibid.*

31   *Washington Post*, 10 April 1991, 'US Shifts on Refugee Enclaves'.

32   Durch (1993), pp 261, 268. The Secretariat wanted to avoid UNIKOM becoming, like UNIFIL in Lebanon, 'a largely humanitarian effort' (p 261). UNIKOM's terms of reference had been drawn up on 5 April, when it was already evident that large numbers of Iraqis were seeking refuge with US forces.

33   Weller (1993), p 719.

34 'Report of the Secretary General proposing terms of reference for an observer unit to be known as the United Nations Iraq-Kuwait Observation Mission (UNIKOM)', United Nations (1996i), Document 38, para. 10.

35 Ironically, at the same time Kuwait was expelling Palestinians, Jordanians and Iraqis over the border into Iraq, and refusing to allow *bidouns* (Kuwaitis without nationality) who were in Iraq to return to Kuwait. This was part of the violent Kuwaiti response to communities such as the Palestinians, who were branded traitors after the Iraqi occupation. Forced deportations from Kuwait to Iraq continued for several months after the war. Subsequently, the majority of Palestinians were unable to renew their residence permits. As a result, by the end of 1993, the Palestinian community in Kuwait was reduced from an estimated 400,000 in 1990 to about 30,000.

36 David L. Mack, Deputy Assistant Secretary of State for the Eastern Arab States and Iran (May 1990–1993), interview with the author, 12 May 1997; Munro (1996), p 341; *International Herald Tribune*, 26 April 1991, 'Saudis to Shelter Refugees From Iraq'.

37 United Nations (1996i), p 57; Lawyers Committee for Human Rights (1992), p 41, quoting UNHCR.

38 Lawyers Committee for Human Rights (1992), p 6.

39 Middle East Watch (1992), p 65; Amnesty International (1991).

40 Kutschera (1997), p 99; Randal (1997), p 51.

41 McDowall (1997), p 373; Middle East Watch (1992), pp 65–6.

42 Randal (1997), pp 49, 52; Dr Michel Bonnot, in 1991 Director of Operations in Bernard Kouchner's Department of Humanitarian Affairs and Chairman of the inter-departmental 'cellule d'ingérence humanitaire', interview with the author, 23 October 1997. These observers say that the use of helicopters also caused panic among civilians, who feared chemical attacks. In fact, at Halabja and other sites attacked during 1988, most of chemical 'cocktails' were delivered by plane or artillery, not by helicopters, though the latter were used for 'aerial harassment' (Human Rights Watch/Middle East [1995i]). But undoubtedly any aerial attack would be associated with chemical weapons in the minds of many people in the region.

43 There had been international complaints since 1988 at Turkish treatment of these Iraqi Kurdish refugees. For details see Bill Frelick (1992), pp 25–6. In turn, Turkey complained that it had neither received financial assistance to support the refugees nor had Western states been willing to resettle more than a handful of them (Zieck [1997], p 192).

44 Jordan's problems in recouping what it spent in assisting third-country nationals during the 1990–1 Gulf crisis suggest that concern over reimbursement was not altogether a spurious argument. At a UN inter-agency meeting on 11 January 1991 it was pointed out that the international community owed Jordan about $40 million for its assistance since August 1990. Jordanian and Iranian perceptions at the time were that 'the amount of UN aid received closely mirrored the political-military objectives of the Allied Coalition' (Minear *et al* [1992], pp 22–3).

45 Kirisci (1993), p 231; Aykan (1996), p 346.

46 Freedman and Boren (1992), p 50.

47 Zieck (1997), p 189, footnote 100.

48 *New York Times*, 18 April 1991, 'US Scouting Refugee Sites Well Inside Iraq's Borders, Aiming to Lure Kurds Home'. Surveys by the US Centers for Disease Control (CDC) estimated total deaths between 29 March and 25 May on the Turkish border at 6700 out of an affected population of 400,000 (USAID Fact Sheet, 7 June 1991, Situation Report no. 24). CDC reported that the Crude Mortality Rate in the main camps during the first half of April was in the range of 4.0–10.4 per 10,000 population per day. By early May death rates in the four main camps were down to less than 2.0 per 10,000. Some 60 percent of the deaths occurred in children under five years, who comprised approximately 18 percent of the refugee population (Centers for Disease Control,

'Public Health Consequences of Acute Displacement of Iraqi Citizens – March–May 1991', *Journal of the American Medical Association*, 7 August 1991, vol. 266. no. 6, p 633).

49   Staff Report, Subcommittee on Immigration and Refugee Affairs, US Senate Committee on the Judiciary, 102nd Congress, First Session, 20 May 1991, pp 36–37.

50   *Washington Post*, 3 April 1991, 'UN Action Urged on Crisis in Iraq'.

51   S/22435, Letter from the Permanent Representative of Turkey to the United Nations addressed to the President of the Security Council, 2 April 1991 (Weller [1993], p 604).

52   S/222447, Letter from the Permanent Representative of the Islamic Republic of Iran to the United Nations addressed to the Secretary General, 4 April 1991 (Weller [1993], p 606).

53   For a detailed account of French humanitarian assistance in April–May 1991, see Kouchner (1991).

54   *Le Monde*, 4 April 1991, 'L'initiative français est fraîchement accueillie au Conseil de securité'; Johnstone (1994), p 18; S/PV 2981, 3 April 1991 (Weller, pp 115–122).

55   *The Times*, 3 April 1991, 'UN plea on fleeing Kurdish refugees'.

56   United Nations (1996i), p 40.

57   Kirisci (1993), p 239, quoting *Turkish Daily News*, 6/7 April 1991.

58   The US Ambassador to the UN, Thomas Pickering, stressing that the Security Council's role was not to interfere in the internal affairs of states, added, 'The transboundary impact of Iraq's treatment of its civilian population threatens regional stability. That is what the Council has addressed today'. Proceedings of the Security Council, S/PV 2982, 5 April 1991 (Weller [1993], p 132).

59   He made the suggestion in interview on ABC television on 7 April, reported in *Le Monde*, 9 April 1991, 'Washington et Ankara suggèrent la création en Iraq de zones de securité placées sous le contrôle de l'ONU'; Kirisci (1993), p 240.

60   *Financial Times*, 4 April 1991, 'Thatcher Joins Calls for Humanitarian Aid'.

61   Press conference by John Major after a meeting of the European Council, 8 April 1991 (Weller [1993], pp 714–6); European Commission, *Bulletin of the European Union*, Brussels, EC 3-1991 para. 1.3.17.

62   *New York Times*, 10 April 1991, 'After the War: Europeans Back Off Plan to Help Kurds'.

63   David L. Mack, interview, *op. cit.*

64   Randal (1997), pp 95–6.

65   Dr Michel Bonnot says that at the end of March, as the exodus began, he had asked the French Ministry of Defence to consider air drops of supplies to the refugees on the Iraqi side of the border with Turkey. However, the Ministry was not keen on the idea and only became involved after the US initiative on 7 April created rivalry over providing assistance to these refugees (interview, *op. cit.*).

66   US Information Agency, 11 April 1991, 'US, Europe agree on refugee policy'.

67   Rudd (1993), p 150.

68   Brilliant *et al* (1995), pp 11–12.

69   Weller (1993), p 717.

70   According to Dr Michel Bonnot, the plan had the backing of Stefan di Mistura of UNHCR and Sadruddin Aga Khan, the UN Executive Delegate, but that US generals at Incirlik would not provide helicopter support for the mission (interview, *op. cit.*). A US analysis, on the other hand, claimed that the French did not have enough troops to carry out the plan immediately (Brilliant *et al* (1995), p 12, footnote 5).

71   Rudd (1993), p 125.

72   Some observers, particularly among Kurds, drew the conclusion that the exclusion of Kirkuk from the no-fly zone was a deliberate political move.

73   According to the Commander of the British forces in Operation Safe Haven, one of the major problems facing military commanders on the ground in northern Iraq was the 'virtually non-existent' sources of 'human intelligence', as opposed to aerial photographs

and intercepted signals traffic, on the degree of threat posed by remaining Iraqi forces, or by the PKK (Ross [1991], p 23).

74 R.J. Brown (1995), p 65.

75 Ross (1991), p 19.

76 At a meeting in Kani Masi on 12 May (attended by Colonel Naab of the Military Coordination Commission, along with the Iraqi representative, General Nashwan Danun, and PUK and KDP representatives) local Kurdish leaders reportedly insisted that a political settlement and security arrangements in Dohuk were needed before they would return (*New York Times*, 13 May 1991, 'Kurds Spurn Rebel Advice; Reject Plan to Return to City').

77 Dayton Maxwell, who was in charge of the DART teams, said he made a 'big pitch' for US troops to enter Dohuk. He pointed out the costs of 'winterising' Zakho camps if refugees had stayed there. Interview with the author, 14 May 1997.

78 According to Dayton Maxwell, the chain of information from the field to Incirlik and then to Washington was weaker than he had assumed at the time. He thought that what was being done in Zakho was being conveyed to Incirlik and on to Washington, but found this was not always the case (interview, *op. cit*).

79 Rudd (1993), p 342; Brilliant *et al* (1995), pp 21–24.

80 Rudd (1993), pp 343–6.

81 Brilliant *et al* (1995), p 16. Dayton Maxwell said the DART teams were told by the State Department not to talk to the *peshmergas*, probably because of the constant concerns over the legal aspect of what the US was doing – talking to rebels against the Government. They did in fact work with members of the Kurdistan Front who helped them to communicate with community leaders (interview, *op. cit.*). Rudd (1993) notes that throughout the period up to the end of the 1991 Gulf War, 'soldiers and airmen were told to avoid "the K-word"' (p 117).

82 *Washington Post*, 19 April 1991, 'US Just Now Assessing Relief Plan's Implications'.

83 Eric E. Morris (nd), p 54. For an internal review of UNHCR's performance in this crisis see UNHCR (1992ii), 'Review of UNHCR Emergency Preparedness and Response in the Persian Gulf Crisis'.

84 UNHCR (1992ii), p 37.

85 The 1951 Convention relating to the Status of Refugees prohibits expulsion or return ('refoulement') of a refugee 'in any manner whatsoever to the frontiers of territories where his life would be threatened on account of his race, religion, nationality, membership of a particular social group or political opinion' (Article 33).

86 UNHCR official, interview with the author, April 1997.

87 The presence of US Special Operations personnel in the mountain camps allegedly prevented human rights abuses by the Turkish authorities - whose conduct was causing a major Gulf War ally to get 'a bad international reputation' (Brilliant *et al* [1995], p 77).

88 R.J. Brown (1995), p 54.

89 Brilliant *et al* (1995), p 78.

90 Seiple (1996), pp 45, 193 note 71; Ross (1991), p 23.

91 UNHCR, 'Mission to monitor voluntary repatriation of Iraqi refugees from Turkey' (May 1991), Final Report.

92 Brilliant *et al* (1995), p 81; Rudd (1993), pp 332–3.

93 *Washington Post*, 10 April 1991, US 'Shifts on Refugee Enclaves'; *Financial Times*, 22 April 1991, 'Iran refuses to have safe havens near its border', quoted in Freedman and Boren (1992), note 16.

94 S/22482, Letter from the Permanent Representative of the Islamic Republic of Iran to the United Nations addressed to the Secretary General, 11 April 1991 (Weller [1993], p 613).

95 Bill Frelick, US Committee for Refugees, interview with author, 15 May 1997; Frelick, statement to the Senate Committee on the Judiciary, Subcommittee on Immigration and Refugee Affairs, 102nd Congress, 1st session, 20 May 1991.

96 Interview with an IOM official who worked on the Iran-Iraq border in the north and the south, April 1997.
97 Weller (1993), p 717.
98 Frelick, interview, *op. cit.* Dayton Maxwell said OFDA had made arrangements for supplies to Iran and the Iranians had refused (interview, *op. cit.*). One consignment of blankets donated by US private relief agencies was sent at the end of April and the US was also said to be contributing through its donations to UNHCR and ICRC (*New York Times*, 30 April 1991, 'US May Send More Aid to Kurds in Iran').
99 Danielle Mitterand recalled her attempt to set up a vaccination programme and cold chain for the refugees, which foundered on the Iranian refusal to allow French military doctors to administer the programme. In her view, this was not because these were army doctors, but because the Iranian authorities wanted to control the programme themselves. This was a common source of tension with donors and aid organisations, some of which also accused the Iranian Government of diverting aid goods for other purposes, while fobbing the refugees off with 'fifth rate' materials and equipment. (Danielle Mitterand, interview with the author, 23 October 1997; Jonathan Randal, interview, *op. cit.*).
100 *Christian Science Monitor*, 30 May 1991, 'Gulf Relief Efforts Must Include Refugees in Iran'; Commission of the European Community, Humanitarian Aid from the European Community: Emergency Aid, Food Aid, Refugee Aid, DE 70, Brussels, January 1992. The disproportionate attention given to Turkey's problems with the refugees repeated, on a larger scale, the pattern of events in 1988, when Western media attention also focused on the smaller number of refugees from the Anfal who fled to Turkey (55,000–60,000) and gave less coverage to those fleeing to Iran – up to 100,000 in 1988 alone, and probably 150,000 Iraqi Kurds in the previous decade (McDowall [1997], p 360).
101 Freedman and Boren (1992), p 61; Letter from the Minister of Foreign Affairs of Iraq addressed to the Secretary General, 21 April 1991, S/225.13 (Weller [1993], pp 720–1).
102 Zieck (1997), pp 206, 209.
103 Rudd (1993), pp 228–9.
104 The rider to the MoU in which the Iraqi Government rejected Resolution 688 was apparently accepted by the Security Council as the price of getting the Iraqis to accept the whole arrangement (Dr Juergen Dedring, interview with the author, 31 July 1998).
105 Thomas Pickering, US Ambassador to the UN, stated on 23 April, 'We strongly welcome the UN plan devised by Sadruddin and accepted by Baghdad and we expect to do our part to support it. Furthermore it is clearly compatible with the approach – the establishment of secure areas for protection and humanitarian relief – on which we and our allies have already embarked in the far north of the country. The US plans gradually to turn over control of the camps to the United Nations as the Kurds' legitimate security concerns are satisfied through the actions and verifiable commitments of the Iraqi Government' (US Congress, House of Representatives, Committee on Foreign Affairs, UN Role in the Persian Gulf and Iraqi Compliance with UN Resolutions: Hearing before the Subcommittees on Europe and the Middle East and on Human Rights and International Organisations of the Committee on Foreign Affairs, April 23 1991, p 23).
106 After negotiations with Under Secretary General Marrack Goulding in the second week in May (*Washington Post*, 10 May 1991 'Iraq Rejects UN Force to Police Refugee Havens'). President Ozal was unhappy with the police force proposal, calling rather for a continued Western military presence. Although the Soviet Union was giving somewhat mixed signals on the issue of coalition troops in Iraq, even those officials sympathetic to Western aims indicated they would like to see the troops leave northern Iraq. (*The Times*, 30 April 1991, 'Pravda denounces presence of troops').
107 *Guardian*, 11 May 1991, 'Allies insist Iraq admits UN police'. The agreement on the UN Guards appears as an annex to the MoU, dated 25 May 1991 (United Nations [1996i] Document 57).

108 Zieck (1997), p 220, footnote 239, quoting a UN Department of Humanitarian Affairs leaflet on the UN Guards Contingent.

109 United Nations (1996i), Document 44.

110 Brilliant *et al* (1995), p 56.

111 One explanation for this over-optimism was suggested by the former *jash* leader Omar Aga al-Surchi who later told *Le Monde*: 'La coalition ne parle pas à ceux qui refusent Saddam Hussein. Les allies ne sont proches que de ceux qui sont disposés à signer un accord.' *Le Monde*, 16 October 1991, 'Les Kurdes s'attendent à de nouveaux affrontements'.

112 Johnathan Randal, *Washington Post*, 3 April 1991, 'Spring of Hope Collapses Amid Feeling of Betrayal'.

113 Dr Fuad Hussein, interview with the author, 1 July 1997.

114 Randal (1997), p 55.

115 Dr. Fouad Hussein, interview, *op. cit.*

116 Kutschera (1997), pp 102–3; Randal (1997), pp 105–6.

117 McDowall (1997), p 376; R.J. Brown (1995), p 84.

118 R.J. Brown (1995), p 86.

119 McDowall (1997), p 378.

120 *Ibid.*, pp 377–8.

121 However, early on in Operation Safe Haven Barzani seems to have hoped for some form of allied protection for the whole region. In a meeting with Danielle Mitterand, one of the most sympathetic interlocutors, he reportedly called for the extension of international protection to the whole of Iraqi Kurdistan and international guarantees (*International Herald Tribune*, 23 April 1991, 'Rebels Seek to Shield all Kurdistan').

122 *Guardian*, 24 June 1991, 'Kurdish Leaders Seem at Odds Over Draft Pact with Baghdad'.

123 According to a UNHCR source, this was first announced at a meeting in Diyarbekir in late May 1991.

124 On the ground, Major-General Robin Ross, commander of the British Marines, was said to have played an important part in negotiating for the troops to remain for another month. On 10 June, British Foreign Minister Douglas Hurd was urging Washington to halt the withdrawals (*Financial Times*, 11 June 1991, 'Save Haven') while the French Foreign Minister Roland Dumas raised the issue with Secretary of State James Baker (*Le Monde*, 21 June 1991, 'Paris voudrait des guaranties avant le retrait des troupes alliées du Kurdistan'). A particular problem for all the other military contingents was their dependence on US logistics capacity. It was therefore difficult for them to operate effectively once US forces withdrew (*Guardian*, 18 June 1991, 'US urged to slow pull-out as fears for Kurds grow').

125 R.J. Brown (1995), p 91.

126 Rudd (1993), pp 399–402. He was present at some of these meetings and made notes.

127 Brilliant *et al* (1995), p 35; Zieck (1997), p 242. According to the understanding of John Bolton, Assistant Secretary, Bureau of International Organisation Affairs, this *demarche* was made 'pursuant to [Resolution] 688, which required that Iraq not interfere with various UN and other international relief efforts. And it was on that basis that all of the actions of Operation Provide Comfort were undertaken'. (Congress, House of Representatives, Committee on Foreign Affairs, UN Role in the Persian Gulf and Iraqi Compliance with UN Resolutions: Hearing before the Subcommittees on Europe and the Middle East and on Human Rights and International Organisations of the Committee on Foreign Affairs, July 18 1991, p 145).

128 Brilliant *et al* (1995), p 60.

129 Rudd (1993), p 384.

130 *International Herald Tribune*, 26 July 1991, 'Near Iraq, Tough Force With Soft Name'.

131 A small core of *peshmergas* had managed to make a stand against the Iraqis at the end of the uprisings and retained control of this region (Kutschera [1997], p 99).

132 UNHCR (1992i), p 3.

133 McDowall (1997), p 378.
134 Lawyers Committee for Human Rights (1992), pp 8–9. One interpretation of these clashes was that they were started by a Kurdish faction or factions opposed to the autonomy negotiations.
135 Randal (1997), p 107.
136 Rudd (1993), p 413.
137 Brilliant *et al* (1995), p 58.
138 Cook (1995), p 45; McDowall (1997), pp 373–9.
139 Keen (1993), pp 31–32.
140 McDowall (1997), p 378–9; Kutschera (1997), p 116.
141 During April and May, some confusion remained about the Government's intentions towards returnees to Kirkuk. At the end of April, Lamis Andoni wrote that Kurds were 'trickling back to Kirkuk and do not hide their sympathy for the opposition or fear of the government' (*Financial Times*, 23 April 1991). Middle East Watch, however, reported that during April road blocks outside the city had prevented Kurds from returning, though this policy was later eased (Middle East Watch [1992], p 65).
142 The Iraqi Government had announced a series of amnesties for deserters, and on 10 April issued an amnesty specifically for Kurds in the 'Autonomy Area' to last until the end of May. On 21 July, two general amnesties were declared. However, little faith was placed in such amnesties either by the Kurds or UNHCR, whose staff considered they should be treated 'with the greatest reservation' (Zieck [1997], p 223).
143 According to the Lawyers Committee for Human Rights (1992) 120,000 people from Kirkuk remained displaced in northern Iraq (p 15).
144 *Independent*, 30 August 1991, 'EC Plan to Assist Kurds 'Scuppered' by UN Officials'; Dr Michel Bonnot, interview, *op. cit.*
145 US Agency for International Development, Office of US Foreign Disaster Assistance, Situation Report No. 25, 17 July 1991, p 2.
146 *Ibid.*
147 *Washington Post*, 19 July 1991, 'UN Says Iraq "Tricked" Aid Mission'.
148 *New York Times*, 20 July 1991, 'Security Council Members Tell Iraq to Evacuate Region'. In a written answer to Congressman Lee Hamilton in the House Committee on Foreign Affairs, the State Department, represented at the hearing by John H. Kelly, Assistant Secretary, Bureau of Near Eastern and South Asian Affairs, reiterated this position: 'Last month's [response given after the hearing] expulsion of UN officials who were establishing a UN humanitarian center in the southern marshes was an outrageous example of Iraq's failure to meet its UN mandated obligation to facilitate humanitarian aid throughout the country. We favor the establishment of UN humanitarian centers wherever they are needed, including the south.' The statement also recalled both Resolution 688 and the MoU on the provision of humanitarian assistance and noted that it had 'strongly supported' Sadruddin and the relief agencies in carrying out their humanitarian mandate (Congress, House of Representatives, Committee on Foreign Affairs, United States Policy Toward the Middle East and Persian Gulf: Hearings before the Subcommittee on Europe and the Middle East of the Committee on Foreign Affairs, 102nd Congress, 1st session, 17 and 26 June 1991, p 63).
149 United Nations (1996i), p 58; information from UN headquarters in Baghdad, September 1991.
150 David L. Mack, interview, *op. cit.*
151 Seiple (1996), p 33.
152 US Agency for International Development, Office of US Foreign Disaster Assistance Situation Report no. 25, 17 July 1991, p 1.
153 UNHCR (1992i), p 2.
154 US Agency for International Development, Office of US Foreign Disaster Assistance (1991), Section on 'Operational Lessons', p 5.

155   Seiple (1996), p 13.
156   Mayall (1991), p 426.
157   Brilliant *et al* (1995), p 62. An OFDA assessment of Operation Provide Comfort also noted: 'At a time when the major objective was getting people home, actions that could have accelerated the repatriation and reintegration process, such as economic incentives, assistance with harvest… were often restricted or discouraged by Washington' (US Agency for International Development, Office of US Foreign Disaster Assistance [1991] Section on 'Lessons learned from Operation Provide Comfort', p 3).
158   Interview with the author, April 1997.
159   Lawyers Committee for Human Rights (1992), p 5.
160   Randal (1997), p 109.
161   Stromseth (1993), p 99.

CHAPTER 2

The Politics of
Economic Sanctions
1991–8

The invasion of Kuwait provoked a rapid and dramatic reversal in the international community's attitude towards the Ba'thist Government, in sharp contrast to the low-key international response to Iraq's attack on Iran in 1980. Iraqi representatives abroad, previously welcome in many diplomatic and business circles, suddenly found themselves cold-shouldered by their former friends. The major Western powers feared a threat to Saudi Arabia and Gulf oil supplies. Some smaller states were concerned that if the invasion went unchecked, their own more powerful neighbours might some day follow Iraq's example.

Iraq's infringement of international law produced a consensus which over-rode the usual political divisions, allowing the creation of a coalition in which permanent members of the Security Council were allied with Turkey and key Arab states, including Syria. Only days after Iraqi troops crossed the border into Kuwait, the US and a number of European states had imposed their own economic embargoes on Iraq. By 6 August, the Security Council had adopted Resolution 661 (with Cuba and Yemen abstaining), imposing a wide-ranging UN economic embargo on Iraq and occupied Kuwait and creating a Sanctions Committee to review its operation. This was the first time since the economic embargo against Southern Rhodesia in the 1960s that the UN, rather than a single state or group of states, had imposed mandatory and comprehensive economic sanctions against any member state.[1]

Resolution 661, whose principal architect was the US, was modelled on the Rhodesian resolution. It froze Iraqi financial assets abroad and banned imports and exports, allowing only medical supplies to be imported without restrictions, and, 'in humanitarian circumstances, foodstuffs'.[2] The provisions embodied in Resolution 661 were expanded in September 1990 by Resolution 665, which imposed a shipping blockade, and Resolution 670, which extended the blockade to other forms of transport, including aircraft. Resolution 666 entrusted the UN Sanctions Committee with determining when 'humanitarian circumstances' applied, allowing for food shipments. Some members, including Yemen, Cuba and Ethiopia, opposed these additional provisions. Yemen and Cuba voted against Resolution 666, arguing that despite disclaimers, these resolutions amounted to using the starvation of civilians as a weapon of war, banned under Protocol 1 of the Geneva Conventions.

Despite these reservations, the use of economic sanctions to force an Iraqi withdrawal from Kuwait attracted wide support as an alternative to military action. However, leading Security Council members, particularly the US and UK, were not willing to wait and see if the embargo would induce Iraq to leave Kuwait. The original goal of the economic embargo was finally achieved by going to war. At the end of the war, it might therefore have been expected that sanctions would be lifted.

In fact, the Security Council chose to retain economic sanctions against Iraq, but with a new and quite different set of goals. UNSC Resolution 687 (see box below), which embodied the terms of the formal ceasefire, continued the embargo on Iraqi oil exports and a ban on all imports to Iraq with certain 'humanitarian' exceptions. Immediately after the war the food blockade was lifted, allowing, in addition to medicines and health supplies, the 'simple notification' to the Sanctions Committee of the delivery of foodstuffs. Under Resolution 687, 'materials and supplies essential for civilian needs' could also be supplied with the approval of the Committee under a 'simplified and accelerated no-objection procedure' (Paragraph 20).

The embargo was now intended to enforce Iraq's compliance with a long list of requirements under Resolution 687. If Resolution 661 had been a coercive measure, the new post-war resolution could also be regarded as punitive.[3] Furthermore, as one commentator noted, measures which affected the well-being of the civilian population were combined with those which resemble 'the process of disarming a conquered country generally imposed by contemporary peace treaties'.[4] This was also the first time such a draconian UN embargo had been imposed on a state which had just suffered severe infrastructural damage in the course of a war.

Iraq was an unusually vulnerable target for economic sanctions. Most of its revenue derived from one export commodity, oil. Its ability to export depended to a considerable extent on pipelines through neighbouring countries. Its access to the sea was limited, and its port capacity further diminished by damage during the Iran-Iraq War. Hence the potential for large-scale evasion of an embargo on its oil exports appeared small.

This vulnerability, the formidable coercive force of these resolutions, and the relative cohesion of the international community in imposing them led to the belief that Iraq would comply fairly rapidly. The period which began with the adoption of Resolution 687 'was expected to be a short transition of less than one year beyond which Iraq would be subject to a permanent arms control embargo and would make payments to a compensation fund from its oil revenues'.[5] In 1991 no-one envisaged the embargo remaining in place for more than seven years.

Although the economic embargo on Rhodesia had remained in force until 1979, the policies of the South African Government, which was sympathetic to the regime of Ian Smith, did much to cushion its impact. UN economic sanctions imposed on Serbia and Montenegro in 1992 were of comparable severity but shorter duration.

Iraq had accepted Resolution 687 only because it had no alternative at the time. It soon became clear that the Government did not intend to acquiesce in its terms any further than it perceived to be necessary. 'One has the impression that in its leaders' minds, the war is not over and that it is being continued through political means.'[6] The Iraqi Government was in fact able to resist a significant number of the UN's demands.

A number of methods were used to 'test the boundaries' of the Security Council's tolerance. The Iraqi Government frequently challenged UNSCOM inspectors'

The Provisions of Resolution 687

The provisions of Resolution 661, imposing an international economic embargo on Iraq, were retained in Resolution 687. The embargo on Iraqi exports remained unchanged but modifications allowed Iraq to import foodstuffs notified to the Sanctions Committee (often referred to as the 661 Committee) and 'materials and supplies for essential civilian needs' 'under the simplified and accelerated "no-objection" procedure'.

Under Resolution 687 (3 April 1991) Iraq had to comply with the following demands:
• The identification and destruction of Iraq's weapons of mass destruction (WMD): nuclear, chemical and biological. Long-term monitoring of its WMD capacity was to be in place and tested.
• The Kuwait/Iraq border was to be demarcated by a UN Commission and Iraq was to accept Kuwait's sovereignty. Both countries were to agree their common border.
• Kuwaiti and third-country nationals held in Iraq since the war were to be repatriated, and stolen Kuwaiti property returned.
• A Compensation Commission was to be established to handle claims for war damage and injury, to be funded from the deduction of 30 percent of all Iraqi oil revenues until all claims approved by the commission were met.

Conditions for lifting the embargo:
• Under Paragraph 21, the provisions of the import ban and its humanitarian exceptions were to be reviewed every 60 days 'in the light of the policies and practices of the Government of Iraq including the implementation of all relevant resolutions of the [Security] Council, for the purpose of determining whether to reduce or lift the prohibitions referred to therein' (ie in Paragraph 20).
• Under Paragraph 22, the embargo on Iraqi exports was to 'have no further force or effect' once Iraq had complied with all the requirements under the paragraphs relating to weapons of mass destruction (Paragraphs 8–13) and the Compensation Commission was in operation (Paragraph 19).

In addition, Iraq was subject to a comprehensive ban on all imports of weapons and weapons technologies, conventional as well as nuclear, biological and chemical weapons 'until [the Security Council] takes a further decision' (Paragraphs 24 and 25). This part of the resolution is open-ended, with no time-scale attached.

The resolution provided for the setting up of two bodies to fulfil particular roles: the Compensation Commission and the UN weapons inspectorate (UNSCOM). Further resolutions spelled out their terms of reference and implementation (Resolutions 692, 699 and 715).

access to facilities or curtailed their freedom of movement, and occasionally created incidents on the disputed Iraq-Kuwait boundary. This strategy of brinkmanship led to confrontations, in response to which the US, Britain and, for a time, France threatened, and sometimes used, force. Usually the response was a rapid climbdown followed by acceptance of previously rejected Security Council demands. The Government also demonstrated a tendency to 'bargain', to try and trade off acceptance of parts of Resolution 687 for the easing of the sanctions regime.

Baghdad actively attempted to exploit the growing disagreements between permanent Security Council members on the definition and limits of sanctions. By the end of 1998, a measure of agreement remained that Iraq had not fully complied with the requirements for the elimination of weapons of mass destruction, though the consensus had become, at best, threadbare.

The passing of time and the tenacity of the Iraqi regime has nonetheless eroded the international political consensus achieved before and during the Gulf War. It has also raised a variety of uncomfortable political and moral dilemmas about the responsibilities of all parties when sanctions appeared to be contributing to the erosion of a society, while still failing to achieve compliance with all the UN's requirements.

The effectiveness of sanctions in practice has depended to a significant extent on concerns beyond Iraq itself – on the regional and domestic policies of leading Security Council members and of Iraq's neighbours, which arguably became among the most significant players in this protracted saga.

THE INTERNATIONAL POLITICAL CONTEXT

Security Council resolutions may have international legal force, but they are also political documents, indicating the degree of consensus that can be achieved among its most powerful members at any one time. 'The Security Council and its subsidiary organs are not judicial bodies and, in deciding matters initiated by parties, do not employ judicial procedures or rely on arguments generated by opposing parties. Instead, the Council is "subject to the vagaries of political consensus".'[7] Consequently, understanding the goals of the key players is important in following the mass of apparently legalistic arguments which ensued over the next seven years.

Over time, divergences of opinion over the goals of sanctions, always implicit, have become more evident. On the whole, the five permanent members of the Council – and most proactively the US, Britain and France – have dominated decision-making on Iraq, with other members playing only a limited role in modifying decisions. However, the growing disagreements between Security Council members, and the absence of a clear policy on the part of the US in the post-Gulf-War period have meant that, despite the weight of their influence in the Council, the permanent members often appeared to react rather than take the initiative in their responses to Iraq's frequent attempts to undermine, evade or end the sanctions regime.

Three potential goals of sanctions against Iraq could be identified.[8] The first, generally accepted by France, Russia and China, was that sanctions are designed to change the Government of Iraq's behaviour in the ways defined by the main requirements of Resolution 687: the elimination of Iraq's weapons of mass destruction, acceptance of Kuwait's sovereignty and its border and return of Kuwaiti property. Resolution 687 'did not include measures which sought to effect changes of the Iraqi constitution or the politico-legal structure of Iraqi society'.[9] Nor is there any 'provision to deal with the leadership of Iraq'.[10]

A second goal, implicit and sometimes explicit in American and British policies, was the downfall of the Iraqi regime. Economic sanctions did not, in the course of seven years, achieve this outcome.

A third goal was a modification of the second: the regime of Saddam Hussein could not comply with all the requirements for the lifting of the economic embargo, and by implication, therefore, sanctions would remain in force until the regime collapsed. In the meantime, they constituted a form of 'containment' (the Clinton administration's formulation) and a means of 'maintaining pressure' on Saddam Hussein.

These were not simply academic or legal disagreements but were based on differing political priorities within the Security Council. Underlying the debates about sanctions was the question of whether it was necessary to accept Saddam Hussein if he remained in power or whether, if sanctions proved ineffective, active attempts should be made to change the regime.

Living with Saddam

France, Russia and China have taken the view that if Saddam Hussein remained in power, this was a 'fact of life' to be dealt with and, if possible, used to national advantage. These states have espoused a strictly limited legal interpretation of the coercive international measures against Iraq, and the conditions under which an easing of the embargo could occur. However, they have sometimes differed in their attitudes to military intervention.

Until 1993, the French Government was willing to go along with the use or threat of force to ensure freedom of action for UNSCOM inspectors, and joined the US and UK in taking a hard line in the Sanctions Committee. France also participated in enforcing the no-fly zones. Russia and China have tended to regard US-led military action with suspicion. However, despite its strong stand on the issue of the Kurds in 1991 as the main architect of Resolution 688, French policy towards Iraq soon shifted back towards its more accustomed pragmatic position of dealing with the regime in power. In recent years, French officials and commentators have argued that the policy favoured by the US – keeping sanctions in place at any cost – has in fact strengthened the Iraqi regime.[11]

The election of Jacques Chirac as President in 1995 gave the French 're-opening' towards Iraq a further push. The new president wanted to raise France's profile in the Arab world and create a Middle Eastern policy that was distinct from that of the US. Jacques Chirac, like Yevgeny Primakov, Russian Foreign Minister between 1996 and 1998, had a long acquaintance with Saddam Hussein and his circle. In France a well-established group of politicians and businessmen who could be considered 'pro-Iraqi' have lobbied to achieve Iraq's rehabilitation since the war.[12]

The 'cohabitation' between the Socialist Government of Lionel Jospin and President Chirac did not lead to any major change in the French position. However, since 1997, the *impasse* between the international community and Iraq, Baghdad's refusal to offer gestures of 'good will', and the fading prospect of a rapid lifting of the embargo has frustrated the efforts of both the French and Russian Governments to achieve the normalisation of relations.

The major focus of French policy in the Middle East in 1996/7 was on how the EU could offer an alternative path to deal with the Palestinian-Israeli conflict, and an emphasis on good relations with Syria.[13] As far as the issue of Iraq is concerned, the EU cannot be said to have adopted any coherent position. At various times, most of its members have been critical of the US for its lack of consultation over military action, and its tendency to personalise its policy on Saddam Hussein. However, there have been frequent differences of opinion between France, with some support from Italy and Spain, on the one hand, and the UK, usually a strong supporter of the US, on the other, with more muted backing from Germany and the Netherlands.

Russia has taken an active diplomatic role over Iraq, particularly since 1994, seeking on a number of occasions to persuade Baghdad to comply with requirements under Resolution 687. As Foreign Minister and then as Prime Minister, Yevgeny Primakov appeared to view Iraq as a key to developing a new Russian role in the Middle East. However, the counterbalancing pressure is Russia's economic dependence on the US, which may limit its willingness to challenge the latter's policy.

China has played a low-key role on this issue, though as a permanent member of the Council has taken a negative view of resolutions which call for further infringements of Iraq's sovereignty. It has been dubious about support for minorities, including the Kurds, because of its own attitude towards Tibet. Talk of human rights is therefore unwelcome. However, the importance of its relations with the US has proved greater than its interest in Iraq, so far curtailing any propensity to veto Security Council resolutions.

Commercial and economic interests have played an important role in French and Russian policy. Both had long-standing economic ties with Iraq, especially in the oil industry and defence procurement. Lifting of sanctions would allow them to restore these valuable economic relations. The first post-war discussions between Iraqi officials and French oil firms were said to have started as early as mid-1991.[14] However, there are some contrasts between France and Russia. While French companies are interested in oil deals and the Government is keen to see the Iraqi debt of some £5 billion repaid whenever sanctions are lifted, there is no critical urgency to achieve these goals. Iraqi oil is not a vital need for France, and though a return to Iraq would be profitable for its leading oil companies, their future does not depend on it. Hence pursuit of these interests is always balanced against how far the French Government wishes to challenge US hegemony in the Gulf.[15]

The Russian response to economic sanctions against Iraq has been partly conditioned by domestic power struggles, but its economic difficulties give greater urgency to its efforts to recoup its debts from Iraq, build trade and secure oil deals. These debts, according to an official source in 1997, amount to about $7 billion, mainly for military deliveries in the 1980s. It is likely, however, that lucrative oil exploration contracts are the most attractive prospect.

Under Resolution 661, contracts were banned while sanctions remained in force, but different interpretations have been put on this clause. Several important 'agreements in principle' for long-term development of major oilfields have been made, including by the French Total for the Nahr 'Umar field and Elf Aquitaine for the Majnun field. These companies have not signed formal contracts but the Iraqi Government apparently considers these fields reserved for Total and Elf. Lukoil (a consortium of Russian companies) signed a contract for the West Qurna field in early 1997.[16]

The Russians claimed, in the face of US accusations, that they were close to breaching sanctions, that until the embargo was lifted only Iraqi firms would be commissioned to do preliminary work and no importation of equipment or drilling of wells would commence. However, like the French, they have pre-positioned themselves for considerable involvement in Iraq after sanctions are lifted. The French Government merely indicated that it did not 'recognise' the Elf and Total agreements.

Changing the regime?

The US and UK Governments pursued the second possible goal of post-war sanctions. Both President Bush and British officials and politicians had predicted from the outset that sanctions would remain while Saddam was in power, on the assumption that he would not be there for long and that sanctions would help to promote his downfall.[17] While this hope lingered in some minds for several years, others had increasing doubts. By August 1991, one US official said he began to feel that 'this assessment was based on an underestimate of the economic resources which the Iraqi Government was able to squeeze out, including the degree to which the regime was willing to make its people suffer'.[18]

Domestic considerations also affected policy. Post-war investigations revealed that in the 1980s the Bush administration and the British Government, its firm ally on Iraq, along with several European states (including France and Germany) had joined in building up Iraq's military power, as well as helping to rebuild its infrastructure after the Iran-Iraq War. In the UK, the Matrix Churchill trial revealed the degree of British firms' involvement in Iraqi arms deals.

During the election year of 1992, the *Washington Post* and the *New York Times* carried numerous reports on the Bush administration's pre-war dealings with Iraq.[19] While it seems unlikely that this issue was in any way decisive in Bush's defeat, the Democrats, who had not strenuously objected to Republican policies on Iraq since 1990, began to use these revelations against Bush, putting him on the defensive. After Clinton's victory, the Democrats therefore feared a backlash from the Republicans if the administration showed any leniency towards the Iraqi regime. Meanwhile, the imperatives of oil and Gulf security, which impelled the US to go to war in the first place, continued to dominate its thinking. Iraq continued to loom as a negative and potentially dangerous factor in US Gulf policy.

The first Clinton administration shifted the focus of its Iraq policy towards the third goal. The notion of 'dual containment' was developed in part to address the problem that the regime of Saddam Hussein was still in place despite the Bush adminstration's rhetoric. But in a broad perspective it was seen 'as a way of temporarily isolating the two chief opponents of the American-sponsored regional order', especially of the Palestinian and Arab-Israeli peace process.[20] The formula was launched in a speech by Martin Indyk, the National Security Council's Middle East advisor on 18 May 1993 at the Washington Institute for Near East Policy.

According to former Assistant Secretary of State Robert H. Pelletreau, 'the motivating thinking was that balance of power tactics used in 1980s had not worked and there was an ongoing threat from Iraq and Iran, both of which had ambitions in the region'.[21] With the end of bipolar era of the Cold War, Iran and Iraq could no longer play one superpower off against the other.[22] Indyk later stated, 'Our basic purpose…

is to maintain a favorable balance in the region – favorable to our interests, favorable to the interests of our regional friends in the Gulf and beyond in the Middle East'. These he identified as Egypt, Turkey, Israel and Saudi Arabia.[23]

In Pelletreau's view, during the Clinton administration's first term, dual containment achieved its major objective, which was to prevent these regimes from being a threat, not to remove them. Within US policy circles, criticism of the policy focused mainly on the approach to Iran and on the 'duality' of containment which lumped together two very different states.[24] The US had imposed a unilateral embargo on Iran and there was far less consensus with Europe and other major powers on economic sanctions of any kind.

The British Government seems to have regarded the notion of dual containment with some scepticism, but did not necessarily disagree with its Iraq component. Russian Foreign Minister Primakov's view was that to make pariahs of regimes such as Iran and Iraq was totally counterproductive, while French officials made it clear that their Government wished to distance itself from the dual containment policy in regard to both Iran and Iraq.

As far as Iraq was concerned, the formula of containment – its critics have described it as more of a slogan than a strategy – can be seen as an attempt to manage a dilemma for which successive US administrations have found no solution: a strong centralised Iraqi state threatens to become too powerful and pursue regional ambitions to the detriment of US allies; but an Iraq too weakened might fall prey to disintegrative tendencies and interference from US regional foes, especially Iran.

In the mid-1990s, some US officials evidently tried to get policy-makers to address the longer-term issues: what kind of regional power balance might realistically be expected in the Gulf in the longer term; the possible disintegrative effects of the 'containment' policy itself; and the impact of a protracted economic embargo on Iraq's social structure. However, they observed that there was a tendency in the administration to deal only with crises. This was reinforced, particularly his first term, by President Clinton's episodic attention to foreign policy issues.

Containment or coup?

If containment pursued the third goal of preventing Saddam Hussein from 'breaking out of his box', the second goal had not entirely disappeared from the US agenda. US offical contacts with the Iraqi opposition as well as clandestine attempts to destabilise, if not to overthrow, Saddam Hussein have continued. The British, too, have dealt with the external opposition, though apparently without any firm conviction that it could form the next Iraqi Government. In contrast, French governments have increasingly distanced themselves from the Kurds and avoided Iraqi opposition groups, as have the Russians. France, said one official, 'has never regarded the Iraqi National Congress as a credible option'.

The ambivalence of the US approach to changing Iraq's rulers was evident in its response to the post-war uprisings and was not resolved by either the Bush or Clinton administrations. One view is that options for change in Iraq currently on offer are liable to lead to destabilisation, and therefore the prospect of a weakened and 'contained' Saddam is the least worst option. This has effectively been the prevailing policy, but it has always had its critics. Among those who have wanted to encourage the opposition politically, two main schools of thought developed: those who believe that 'the Sunni centre' is the only possible source of a stable alternative to Saddam Hussein; and those who look to the 'periphery' – including the Kurds and Shi'a, mainly as represented by external opposition groups such as the Iraqi National Congress – to bring about change.

The first position has involved contemplating the possibility that the future leader would be part of the current ruling group, and might be complicit in many of its abuses. The second involves supporting the 'out' groups in Iraqi politics, both the Kurds and Shi'a, perhaps including Shi'i groups based in Iran. In neither scenario was change likely to come without violence. 'The present [Iraqi] regime has organised things in such a way that its removal can only be contemplated by those who are psychologically prepared and actually equipped to use considerable force'.[25]

During much of 1991, the State Department was reluctant to initiate any high-level official discussions with the Iraqi opposition despite lobbying by supporters of the Kurds. The notorious lack of unity among Iraqi opposition groups contributed to scepticism of their effectiveness. The administration's attitude seems also to have been coloured by advice from Arab allies to 'stay out of Iraqi politics' and their belief that Saddam Hussein would be rapidly ousted by a coup.[26]

However, by the end of the year, with Saddam still in place, the new Assistant Secretary of State for the region, Edward Djerejian, was calling for broader contacts with the Iraqi opposition 'to support the emergence of an Iraqi Government representative of Iraq's pluralistic society including the Shiites, Sunnis and Kurds'.[27]

The establishment of the Iraqi National Congress (INC) in June 1992 created an umbrella opposition alliance which attracted support and finance in varying degrees from London and Washington. At its initial conference in Geneva in June 1992 it encompassed only a small number of opposition groups, but in October 1992 it took the significant step of holding a congress on Iraqi soil – in Salahadin, in Iraqi Kurdistan – and significantly expanded its membership.[28] This enhanced its credibility in international circles. The INC retained its main external base in London, where the British Foreign Office was initially more open to contacts with the external opposition.

While there remained mixed feelings in the US about openly promoting the external opposition, both Bush and Clinton administrations gave money and encouragement to the CIA to engage with opposition groups and to promote clandestine contacts inside Iraq. CIA involvement began in 1991 when Bush signed a 'presidential finding' authorising covert actions against Iraq.[29] By mid-1992, the administration was asking Congress to agree $40 million to help overthrow Saddam. According to press reports, Congress, and particularly the Senate Intelligence Committee, played a significant role in the following years in encouraging this more 'pro-active' strategy against the Iraqi regime.[30]

Unlike its predecessor, the first Clinton administration – not wanting to risk failure – avoided setting the fall of Saddam Hussein as an explicit policy target. Nonetheless, from 1994 onwards, in parallel with the adminstration's 'containment' strategy, the CIA was pursuing more active clandestine efforts to destabilise the regime in Baghdad. However, its bungled interventions in 1995 and 1996 (see Chapter 3) gave further credence to the suggestion that its operations were not 'serious'.

The apparently ambiguous US attitude towards the prospect of a change of regime in Iraq has encouraged the view, widespread in the Arab world and in some Iraqi opposition circles, that the US would rather see Saddam Hussein remain in power. Paul Wolfowitz, a leading Republican advocate of building relations with the

Iraqi opposition, argues that the preference for clandestine action between 1991 and 1996 in fact weakened the possibility of a consensus among the competing opposition factions, which would have required a more open engagement.[31]

An advocate of overthrowing Saddam Hussein remarked in 1996:

> If there were a specific plan to make this happen then one would have to conclude that, at best, the plan has not worked, and that, at worst, it may have backfired. If the United States is primarily relying on UN sanctions to achieve its objective, the emerging picture from Iraq reveals injury to the Iraqi people but no clear indication that Saddam Hussein has become more vulnerable politically.[32]

Another vexed issue was whether to offer incentives to any prospective new rulers in Iraq by holding out the prospect that sanctions might be lifted or eased. In 1994, senior officials expressed caution about offering any kind of inducement without knowing what such a government's policies might be. But by 1997, after further failed coup attempts, including some sponsored by the US, the State Department adopted a more positive tone, apparently designed to encourage potential dissidents within the Iraqi ruling group to take action.

After a period during which one congressional aide described US policy on the Gulf as 'on automatic pilot', the new Secretary of State, Madeleine Albright, stated in a major policy speech on Iraq at Georgetown University in March 1997: 'Clearly, a change in Iraq's government could lead to a change in US policy. Should that occur, we would stand ready, in coordination with our allies and friends, to enter rapidly into a dialogue with the successor regime.' If a new government cooperated with UNSCOM and complied with UN resolutions, she added, 'the international community, including the United States, would look for ways to ease Iraq's reintegration'. The caveat was that Iraq should be 'independent, unified and free from undue external influence for example, from Iran'.[33] On the prospects for political pluralism and an end to human rights abuses under a new government, a National Security Council official later commented that 'even modest steps would be in the right direction'.[34]

By 1998, the goal of removing Saddam Hussein from office was put more explicitly on the agenda. In October, the Republican-dominated Congress, promoting the INC and other opposition groups, passed the Iraq Liberation Act which allocated $97 million to finance and train an Iraqi opposition militia.[35] The decision in Congress to allocate these funds appeared to be driven as much by American domestic politics as by any immediate hope of changing the Iraqi government. The Clinton administration initially responded with caution, but gave the external opposition a higher profile after the December 1998 bombing of Iraq by US and UK forces. This seemed to be part of the shift in US policy, toward making the goal of toppling Saddam Hussein once again a publicly acknowledged priority. In January 1999, the State Department appointed a special representative to work with the Iraqi opposition.[36] The groups to benefit from the Congressional funds were named as the Iraqi National Congress, the Iraqi National Accord, the Islamic Movement of Iraqi Kurdistan, the Movement for Constitutional Monarchy, the Kurdistan Democratic Party and the Patriotic Union of Kurdistan. The Supreme Council for the Islamic Revolution in Iraq (SCIRI) was also included in the list but was reported to have rejected the possibility of US military support. However given the deep divisions between these groups, the prospects of forging a united opposition seemed slight.

Regional politics and sanctions compliance

Sanctions do not prevent the target country from conducting normal diplomatic activities. The image purveyed by US official commentators of Iraq 'in a box', in isolation, is less than accurate, both economically and politically. Iraq has been prevented from making further military incursions across borders, but economic needs and political self-defence have required the Government to maintain its relations with neighbouring states.

Aside from some cross-border smuggling,[37] Iraqi relations with Kuwait and Saudi Arabia – the staunchest supporters of the US view of containment – have remained at a stand-off. Apart from recognition of the Iraq-Kuwait boundary, other outstanding issues between the two countries have yet to be resolved. Saudi Arabia and Kuwait have benefitted most from the removal of Iraq from the oil market, and have most to lose from a resurgence of Iraqi military strength. The Gulf oil-producing states also profited from the absence of Iraqi competition in the burgeoning Asian market of the mid-1990s.[38]

Three of Iraq's immediate neighbours – Turkey, Jordan and Iran – retained very significant, through ambiguous relations with Iraq. All three states have played an important part in the Iraqi Government's attempts to manage its post-war economic and political situation. Since 1991, although Iraq's overall external trade has dropped dramatically, both legal trade and smuggling have been substantial across all its borders – both those under Iraqi government and Kurdish control – mostly with Jordan and Turkey, but also on a smaller scale with Iran.

'Leakage' and infringements of the embargo on Iraq have undoubtedly been on a smaller scale than those in the Rhodesian case, or following the imposition of UN sanctions on Serbia and Montenegro. However, an embargo creates new economic dynamics. According to one analyst, 'To the extent that sanctions have an impact they create price differentials, raising the price of imports to the target country and lowering the price of its exports. The greater the impact, the greater the incentive to private interests elsewhere to trade illegally'.[39]

Of these three states, Jordan, wedged between Iraq, Israel/Palestine and Syria, has had the least room to manoeuvre, politically and economically. For a decade prior to 1990, Iraq was Jordan's main trading partner. Sanctions and the Gulf War greatly diminished both direct trade with Iraq and transit trade via Aqaba port. Already in difficulties over its external debt by the end of the 1980s, Jordan suffered the temporary withdrawal of US aid when it refused to join the Coalition against Iraq.

Jordan's gradual rehabilitation with the US since the Gulf War – the restoration of external aid and the implementation of IMF loan facilities under a structural adjustment programme – created pressures on King Hussein to distance himself politically from Iraq, despite popular sympathy among many Jordanians.[40] After the signing of the Israel-Jordan peace treaty in 1994, the US emphasised Jordan's changed role, forgiving almost all Jordan's official debts, providing new defence assistance, including the supply of 16 F-16 aircraft and, for a few months in 1996, using Azraq in Jordan as a base for US aircraft patrolling the southern Iraqi no-fly zone.[41]

Political relations with Iraq became still less cordial after Jordan temporarily gave asylum to Saddam Hussein's brother-in-law Hussein Kamil al-Majid when he defected in August 1995. For the next year Jordan hosted elements of the Iraqi opposition, in particular the Iraqi National Accord (al-Wifaq) whose planned coup attempt with CIA assistance was foiled in June 1996. In late 1995, King Hussein floated the idea of an Iraqi-Jordanian federation, though this proposal was quickly withdrawn.

It has always seemed unlikely that King Hussein would see it as in Jordan's interest to break all ties with Iraq. After Iraq's acceptance of Resolution 986, allowing limited sales of Iraqi oil (see below), there were signs that the King was trying to mend fences. He was also said to feel that the peace process could not be effective in the long run if Iraq remained excluded. With the Oslo agreements stalled, he found it expedient to continue dealings with Iraq, whatever regime was in power.

Iraq remained Jordan's largest trading partner (in 1996 it was reported to account for 19 percent of Jordan's exports and some 12 percent of its imports). With air travel halted by sanctions, the main route to Baghdad was via Amman. After the 1991 war, Zarqa free zone, through which goods passed in transit to Iraq, was reported to be overflowing with stocks. Amman became the main centre for Iraqi commercial activity, since there was more freedom to trade and make financial arrangements.[42]

In some respects, Jordan has been subjected to more pressure than Turkey to comply with sanctions. Until 1994, the US-led Maritime Interception Force (MIF) conducted inspections outside Aqaba port. They were strongly resented by the Jordanians because they caused delays for ships entering the port.[43] In 1992, US pressure forced tighter controls on the Jordanian-Iraqi border, stopping some of the large-scale evasions of the embargo, for example the export to Iraq of vehicles, spare parts and tyres.[44]

On the other hand, in the case of Jordan's oil imports from Iraq, a *de facto* waiver of sanctions rules was allowed. In 1990, Iraq had a substantial trade debt to Jordan which was being paid off by allowing Jordan to import Iraqi oil very cheaply. Jordan was reluctant to return to purchasing more expensive oil on the open market, and in September 1990 it applied to the UN Sanctions Committee to be allowed to continue importing Iraqi oil on concessionary terms in repayment of the latter's debt.

Jordan's request received no clear response from the Sanctions Committee, but in May 1991 it seems that an informal agreement was reached between Jordan and the US, the UK and France which allowed the arrangement with Iraq to continue. This 'understanding' was never made public or formally ratified by the Sanctions Committee, though its members were probably consulted. It became a semi-formalised exception to the sanctions regime.[45]

Since 1991, Iraq has been Jordan's only oil supplier, and export protocols have continued to be signed each year allowing the export of permitted goods from Jordan in exchange for oil.[46] As far as the Sanctions Committee was concerned, acceptance of these protocols was simply based on an exchange of letters and Jordan's undertaking to report on the transactions.[47] Nonetheless, these arrangements have continued long after most analysts estimate that the pre-war debt was paid off. The level of trade has been such that a further debt appears to be accumulating.[48] This perception has generated a number of complaints in the US Congress and the media about 'infringements' of sanctions by Jordan.[49]

Jordan's economic problems with sanctions were handled differently to those of Turkey, which has played a more complex role in the sanctions equation. As a member of the Gulf War Coalition and a close NATO ally of the US, it has been under pressure to conform with the economic embargo against Iraq. However, Iraq was a major trading partner in the 1980s when Turkey became a major overland trade route for both sides in the Iran-Iraq War.[50]

During the 1991 war, President Ozal, as a strong supporter of the Coalition, went so far as to welcome the idea of Saddam Hussein's fall from power. However, since the war, Turkish governments of different political colours have been keen to maintain relations with Iraq, despite an underlying mistrust between the two states. In July 1991, Prime Minister Mesut Yilmaz announced the resumption of Turkish diplomatic representation in Baghdad, signalling that some members of the Government took a less harsh line against Iraq than President Ozal.[51] In early 1992, Prime Minister Suleiman Demirel said that Iraq would remain 'a regional problem' until Saddam Hussein left power but 'it is very wrong' to seek his ouster by force.[52]

Between 1993 and 1995 there was a marked warming of relations with Baghdad, and Turkey joined Russia and France in calling for sanctions to be lifted as soon as compliance with Paragraph 22 of Resolution 687 was achieved (see below). However, Turkey's relationship with both Iraq and other coalition governments has been greatly complicated by the Kurdish issue, which currently dominates much political thinking in Turkey, and by the continuation of coalition air surveillance of northern Iraq from Turkey (see Chapter 3).

Despite Turkey's support for the Gulf War Coalition, the 'spoils of victory' have eluded it. By 1996, official sources estimated Turkey's losses of revenue since 1990 from the oil pipeline closure and reduced trade flows at $27.3 billion.[53] Turkish governments have on several occasions argued that, like Jordan, it should benefit from an arrangement allowing it to purchase oil from Iraq, but this was refused.[54]

Asked about the possibility of such an arrangement, former US Assistant Secretary of State Robert Pelletreau responded that Turkey's needs and its losses were much greater than Jordan's, so that to include it in the 'exception' granted to Jordan would have undermined the sanctions regime to a much greater extent. It was viewed as preferable 'to close our eyes to leakage via Turkey'.[55] A Russian source put it more bluntly: 'It seems the US has closed its eyes to infringements of sanctions – because it needs things from Turkey'.

Trade across Iraq's northern border has therefore continued despite the embargo. During 1991, it benefited from the large-scale movement of humanitarian supplies, as lines of Turkish trucks, fitted with extra tanks, rolled into northern Iraq, filled up with cheap fuel and returned to Turkey. 'The Turkish Government, hungry to regain revenues lost by the embargo, turned a blind eye on smuggling, first to the Kurds then to the rest of Iraq'.[56]

A Turkish truck driver explained the economics: 'In the northern Iraqi oil town of Mosul, diesel costs only pennies a gallon. In Turkey it retails for about $2.70 a gallon.' After paying odd, informal 'taxes' to Iraqi Kurdish *peshmergas* and Turkish border policemen, he could make a profit of 30 to 40 times his outlay.[57]

Since south-eastern Turkey was hit economically by the effects of sanctions, this trade allowed some sections of the population to recoup their losses. It continued until 1993 when, following the collapse of a PKK ceasefire, the Government clamped down, apparently intending to prevent the PKK profiting from this traffic. From September 1994, Turkish trucks again began to carry extra tanks to purchase fuel in Iraq to transport back to Turkey. By 1996/7 the volume of trade had swelled to an estimated 1000 trucks a day, with truck drivers making $600-700 a trip. In 1997 it was estimated that 50,000 barrels a day of diesel fuel, gasoline and kerosene was being illicitly traded into Turkey.[58]

In 1994 the Turkish Government held discussions with Iraq and the permanent members of the Security Council on 'flushing out' the oil which had remained in the Iraq-Turkey pipeline since 1990. The potential deal, from which Turkey would have obtained oil for domestic use, and humanitarian goods would have been provided for Iraq, foundered on disagreements about the distribution of humanitarian goods in northern Iraq.[59]

The only other step which Turkey's Western coalition allies were willing to take was to insist on the use of the Turkish pipeline for the proposed UN-controlled Iraqi oil sales, allowing Turkey to resume receipt of transit fees. Under the terms of Resolution 986, finally implemented in December 1996, the bulk of oil exported from Iraq under the resolution was to flow through Turkey, thereby making it a significant beneficiary.

By late 1996 Turkey was also pushing the limits of the embargo by signing a deal to buy natural gas from fields in north-eastern Iraq over a 20-year period and to construct a pipeline to transport it. While officials said Turkey would only undertake 'pre-construction' work before the embargo on Iraq was lifted, it seems that in common with a number of other countries Turkey was lining up deals in anticipation of sanctions being lifted.[60] Iraq for its part seemed eager to consolidate its economic ties with Turkey, despite tensions over border issues.[61]

Iran benefitted from economic sanctions and the military constraints on Iraq after the 1991 war, though the fact that the US played a leading role in their imposition was less welcome. The activities of UNSCOM cut down the potential for aggressive acts by Iraq, while the embargo on oil sales removed it from the oil market, to the advantage of Iran as well as the Gulf States.

Moves to improve previously frosty relations with Iraq since the Gulf War seem to have been primarily a means for Iran to demonstrate defiance of the US, particularly since the dual-containment policy came into effect. So far an open alliance between the two subjects of 'containment', predicted by some observers, has not materialised, and a legacy of distrust remains. Iraq has sporadically attempted to foster better relations, since it has needed all the allies it could find. By late 1997, after a number of false starts, some prisoner-of-war exchanges were underway, and Iraq announced that it would allow Iranian pilgrims to visit the Shi'i shrines in Najaf and Karbala, which they had been prevented from doing since the 1991 war.

Most non-US observers see Iran's main goal in regard to its immediate neighbours as achieving security and control on its borders. Its main 'destabilising' activities seem focused further afield, though it has been increasingly involved in events in northern Iraq (see Chapter 3). Both Iraq and Iran have continued to use and support each other's opposition groups. Iran has periodically bombed the bases of the Kurdistan Democratic Party of Iran (KDPI), based in northern Iraq and the Mujahedin-e Khalq (MKO), based in Iraq since the Iran-Iraq War and used since 1991 to supplement Iraq's security forces. Iraqi Shi'i opposition groups based in Iran have also received arms and support to carry out operations inside southern Iraq.

According to Iraqi Deputy Prime Minister Tariq Aziz, the Iranian Government rebuffed an Iraqi request after the Gulf War to engage in significant bilateral trade which would have breached the UN embargo.[62] Nonetheless, allegations of oil smuggling across the Iran-Iraq land border have appeared from time to time, though the quantities are not thought to be very large. Consumer goods smuggled into the Kurdish north also tend to leak down into government-controlled areas. At the very least the Iranian authorities frequently 'look the other way' when sanction-breaking takes place, allowing opportunities for parastatal organisations and the Revolutionary Guards to make money. In addition, the US has on a number of occasions quoted the Maritime Interception Force (MIF), enforcing sanctions in the Gulf, as having intercepted ships smuggling Iraqi oil and other goods for which the Iranian authorities have provided false papers through Iranian territorial waters.[63]

Iraq's limited return to the oil market since the end of 1996 under UNSC Resolution 986 has given it more leverage with its neighbours. In 1998, President Clinton described Iraq's land borders as 'extremely porous'.[64] Meanwhile, the Iraqi Government has tested the economic barriers created by the embargo as increasing numbers of private and state companies positioned themselves for post-sanctions contracts. The creation of a commercial momentum has its own logic: a significant number of major companies, whether from Europe, Asia or the Middle East, see lucrative future opportunities in Iraq, though no large or reputable organisations are likely openly to infringe embargo. Therefore the Iraqi Government has increased its efforts to use the international business community to lobby governments to lift sanctions so that contracts can be implemented.

ECONOMIC SANCTIONS AND HUMANITARIAN NEEDS 1991–3

Visitors to Iraq in the aftermath of the war judged the humanitarian situation in Iraq to be dire, if not catastrophic. During the war, the embargo had cut off most food supplies, while infrastructural damage caused by the bombing campaign severely disrupted basic civilian services, especially electricity supplies. Industry and agriculture ground to a halt. The publicity given to early UN reports on conditions in Iraq, first by Under Secretary General Martti Ahtisaari in March and then by the UN's special envoy Sadruddin Aga Khan in July, and to reports from aid agencies present in Iraq at this period, created pressure to mitigate the suffering caused to the civilian population.

For the Security Council, this created a tension between sustaining and enforcing sanctions on one hand, and on the other preventing starvation or a complete collapse of services. Even those states which took a hard line on maintaining sanctions did not want to be seen as responsible for severe civilian suffering. However, for all the protagonists, moral and humanitarian concerns had to compete with other priorities.

There were several ways in which 'humanitarian mitigation' could occur in practice. The first, built into the terms of the economic embargo, allowed Iraq to purchase some humanitarian goods for civilian needs. The second consisted of humanitarian assistance delivered by UN organisations or NGOs. The third was the possibility, envisaged in Resolution 687, of a controlled and limited lifting of the embargo on Iraqi oil exports, or the use of its assets frozen abroad to pay for humanitarian goods. Because of the highly politicised nature of the international community's relations with Iraq, all these forms of mitigation were subject not only to practical difficulties, but also to political pressures.

The Sanctions Committee played a key role in the first form of exemption from the embargo. It determined whether applications for waivers of the import ban fell under the definitions of humanitarian exceptions.[65] The work of the Committee takes place behind closed doors. Until 1995, no record of its discussions or decisions was made public or even circulated to interested parties such as UN humanitarian organisations, Security Council members, or the sanctioned state, Iraq. Only the state which made the application for a waiver was informed of the Committee's decision. Since that time, some procedural changes have been made to make the Committee's work more 'transparent'.[66]

Medicine and food were to be passed on 'simple notification', and these have rarely been challenged. However, the ambiguous category of 'materials and supplies for essential civilian needs' is subject to Committee scrutiny under 'the simplified and accelerated "no objection" procedure'. Applications for the waivers required for all goods apart from food and medicine are made by states on behalf of the companies providing the goods. UN and other humanitarian agencies are not exempt from this procedure. Iraq cannot make applications directly, nor does it have any direct access to the Committee. Decisions are by consensus in the Committee. In contrast to the Security Council, where only the permanent members have vetoes, all 15 members of the Sanctions Committee have a veto. Under the 'no objection procedure', any item which attracts suspicion – for example, as having potentially dual use – can be vetoed or put on hold while further enquiries are made.

The definition of 'essential civilian needs' in Resolution 687 was based on the findings of Martti Ahtisaari in his mission to Iraq immediately after the war. However, the needs he identified went well beyond emergency relief food and medicine. He pointed out that the power grid and communications had been seriously damaged in the war, concluding: 'The far-reaching implications of this energy and communications vacuum as regards urgent humanitarian support are of crucial significance for the nature and effectiveness of the international response'. In practice, however, the definition of these needs remained a matter of contention within the Committee.[67]

The secrecy of proceedings, and disputes over the definition of 'essential civilian needs', have raised many questions about the way the Committee has done its work. It has certainly not operated as a politically neutral body. Both harshness and leniency have been exercised, frequently in pursuit of specific members' political goals. One close observer characterised the role of the Sanctions Committee in supervising both the trade embargo and humanitarian exceptions as a 'Jekyll and Hyde situation'.

> On one hand, the sanctions regime as modified by Resolution 687 was a trade control regime designed to pressure a government to comply with other demands by restricting its access to goods and revenue. On the other, it was a humanitarian exemption regime designed to ensure that civilian households had access to a modicum of necessary goods. Various members stressed one role or another. This inherent dichotomy of functions ensured that decisions [in the Sanctions Committee] were often made through intense exchanges of divergent views.[68]

One of the chairpersons of the Committee confirmed this impression. 'One school of thinking says… we should be rather open minded as far as humanitarian needs are concerned. We should interpret the possibilities of facilitating such deliveries rather generously. But there is another school of thinking… [which] says the pressure on Iraq should be maintained as long as there is not full compliance with the resolutions.'[69]

In December 1991, the Sanctions Committee accepted a 'gentleman's agreement' that members would 'generally look favourably on requests' within certain categories of humanitarian items under the no-objection categories, for example civilian clothing, supplies for babies and infants, spare parts and materials for water treatment and sewage disposal plants. This arose from a proposal by the Ambassador for Zimbabwe on behalf of non-aligned members, suggesting that certain sectorally defined groups of items – for example educational materials – be transferred to notification status. However, the hardline members of the Committee would not accept this, and the informal understanding was a compromise.[70]

Another area of ambiguity was created by the status of Iraq's three northern governorates which, after October 1991, were outside government control. Despite appeals from the Kurdish administration and leadership, international sanctions have been maintained. The main argument against lifting the embargo on the north was that its recognition as a distinct entity would encourage the 'break-up of Iraq' and particularly upset the Turkish Government. Concern was also expressed that if sanctions were lifted on the north, imports would 'leak' to government-controlled areas, seriously weakening the embargo.[71]

Those states most consistently taking a hard line were the US, UK and France in the first years of sanctions, with occasional queries from other non-permanent members, such as Japan and Germany. Most public attention has focused on contentions by the Government of Iraq and others that patently 'civilian goods', such as pencils and paper, have been stopped or delayed by the Committee. But perhaps a more crucial and less recognised problem is that the Committee has in practice refused to give waivers for any goods which could be construed as industrial inputs. Only finished products are permitted. 'Products which are inputs to Iraqi industry, rather than finished products for domestic consumption, are generally declined, as are "dual use" items.'[72]

In a similar vein, Western permanent members wanted to limit the reconstruction of strategic Iraqi industries, including its power grid and petroleum industries.[73] Only in 1998 was any significant modification of this policy considered, and the need to restore electrical power was accepted by all Sanctions Committee members under proposals to increase the value of Iraq's UN-controlled oil sales (see Chapter 7).

This policy was evolved within the Committee, mainly at the behest of the US, UK and France. It is not anywhere embodied in Security Council resolutions. Finished goods may be easier to monitor, with less chance of dual use, but such a policy clearly has a major impact on the production of goods which are purely for civilian needs. Some observers have argued that this constitutes an 'economic warfare' strategy towards Iraq, not envisaged under the UN Charter, and designed to weaken the country's economic structure in the long term.[74] The Government of Iraq has complained about many such Sanctions Committee decisions, but the lack of access to Committee discussions makes it very difficult to either substantiate or discount any specific allegation.[75]

A striking feature of the humanitarian waiver system, in the Iraqi case as in other recent economic embargoes, was the very large volume of applications which it generated. For the most part, these were wholly commercial transactions – in 1994, applications from UN humanitarian organisations and NGOs amounted to only about 1.3 percent of the total value of applications approved. In that year, the value of applications had reached $8.4 billion. This included notifications for food ($1.2 billion, and medicine ($215 million). Under the no objection procedure $2.4 billion of requests were approved, $3.3 billion rejected and $925 million still undecided in early 1995. In 1995 the volume of applications in the 'no objection' category alone had risen to an estimated $8.8 billion.[76]

Another notable point was the prominence of the UK – a strong protagonist of a restrictive interpretation of humanitarian exemptions – among the states applying for large numbers of waivers. Although the UK Government has not generally encouraged British companies to join the many European and Asian firms positioning them-selves for contracts in Iraq once sanctions are lifted, the Department of Trade and Industry (DTI) did see its role as facilitating trade that was permitted under sanctions. At times this appeared to lead to laxity in vetting the applications put forward.[77] Several other European states followed the same line. The US, in contrast, refused, with very few exceptions, to trade with Iraq at all, even in goods exempted from the embargo.[78]

Since sanctions were unexpectedly prolonged, the dramatic decline in the living standards of the Iraqi population created pressure to find more direct ways of relieving the most acute forms of suffering. It is not clear that coalition governments initially envisaged continuing humanitarian assistance once the refugees were resettled. However, a humanitarian programme did remain in place until 1996, though on a diminishing scale.

Aid agencies constantly stressed that, faced with the effects of war damage and sanctions, meeting the needs of 19–20 million Iraqis was beyond their capacity. Iraq, they pointed out, had been a relatively wealthy country, and aid agencies could not pour in the billions of dollars required to sustain it. Certainly it was clear to aid agencies working in Iraq after the war that their efforts were little more than 'sticking plasters'. Many questioned the appropriateness of an embargo which severely undermined the civilian economy and services.

The absence of oil revenues, on which the Iraqi state had depended for over 90 percent of its foreign currency earnings, was the main impediment to Iraq's post-war recovery. Since 1991, the international community has constantly sought ways of using Iraq's oil revenues to pay for humanitarian needs without lifting sanctions. Iraq, too, sought to resume its oil sales. The main problem was to agree on the terms of the sale and the purposes for which the funds would be used. From the beginning, Security Council members had in mind to use the funds not just for Iraq's humani-tarian needs but to meet other commitments under Resolution 687, in particular to contribute to the UN Compensation Fund and to pay for the work of UNSCOM and other UN operations in Iraq.

Discussions began as early as May 1991, when the Sanctions Committee clarified that states could, if they chose, unfreeze Iraqi assets for humanitarian purposes detailed under Paragraph 20 of Resolution 687. Iraq was consequently able to make use of assets which several countries agreed to unfreeze. For example, the UK unfroze £70 million of Iraqi assets after Iraq freed the detained British businessman Ian Richter in late 1991. The funds were used to pay British firms to fulfil orders placed by Iraq for food and humanitarian goods.[79] The US, on the other hand, did not agree to unfreeze any assets.

The Iraqi Government proposed that it should be allowed to export $1.5 billion of oil to meet humanitarian needs under the terms of Paragraphs 23 of Resolution 687, which provided that the Council could permit an exceptional sale to finance such goods. France, the UK and the US opposed this.[80] But further pressure to find funds for humanitarian needs came from Sadruddin Aga Khan's July 1991 report on humani-tarian conditions in Iraq, which estimated that it would cost $22 billion to restore the power, oil, water, sanitation, food, agriculture and health sectors to pre-war levels.[81]

Sadruddin argued strongly that, since Iraq was a rich country, it could use its own oil revenues to pay for reconstruction. The Security Council evidently had no intention of lifting sanctions in the short term – the UN weapons inspectors were already involved in confrontations over searches for weapons of mass destruction – so Sadruddin argued that humanitarian needs should be met by a UN-controlled sale of oil.

Aware that it was unrealistic to suggest selling oil on a scale sufficient to meet the full amount needed to restore the civilian economy and services, Sadruddin produced an estimate covering full restoration of health services, 50 percent of pre-war electrical capacity, 40 percent of water and sanitation services, enough food for subsistence rations for the whole population and the rehabilitation of agriculture, with limited repairs to northern oil facilities, at a total cost of $6.9 billion over one year. He suggested an initial sale of $2.65 billion worth of oil over four months (a third of the total amount plus a small sum for start-up costs) to address immediate emergency needs. If the arrangement worked satisfactorily, it could be renewed.[82]

Discussions in Baghdad during Sadruddin's mission made it clear that Iraqi government officials regarded the proposal as an infringement of sovereignty. To accommodate these sensitivities, Sadruddin proposed that Iraq be allowed to use its bank accounts in the US, through which oil revenues had previously been channelled, for funds generated by the limited oil sales. This special SOMO (Iraqi State Oil and Marketing Organisation) account, from which payments would be made only for humanitarian goods approved by the Sanctions Committee, would be transparent and open to scrutiny by the Committee. He felt that Iraq was more likely to accept such an arrangement.

The Executive Delegate's office in Baghdad prepared proposals to monitor the oil sales, the purchase of supplies and distribution within the country. The monitoring of distribution was to be carried out by UN humanitarian agencies in Iraq, which could be 'further developed and strengthened' for the purpose. This proposal received support from UN humanitarian agencies and NGOs working in Iraq.[83]

Selling oil to pay for food?

The Sanctions Committee discussed Sadruddin's proposal in July without achieving a consensus. Three weeks of debate among Security Council members ensued. France, which favoured easing the embargo, circulated two draft versions of a resolution on the oil sale. The Soviet Union and China were said to have reservations but were induced to accept the idea. The oil sale was characterised as exceptional – not signifying any general easing of sanctions – and France, as well as the US and UK, reportedly objected to the ceiling of $2.65 billion for the initial sale proposed by Sadruddin.

Some of the pressure to allow an oil sale came from Kuwait and other Arab members of the Gulf War Coalition which wanted Iraq to start paying war reparations, a move which would only be possible once oil started flowing. The intention was that a proportion of the proceeds from any limited Iraqi oil sale would go into the Compensation Fund.[84]

Security Council Resolutions 706 and 712 (adopted in August and September 1991 respectively) modified and toughened up the original proposal in several crucial ways. Iraq was allowed to sell only $1.6 billion of oil over six months, with the possibility of further limited sales if the Security Council renewed the arrangement. Instead of earmarking the oil revenues solely for humanitarian use, a package was created, designating 30 percent of each tranche for the UN Compensation Fund (for individual, corporate and government claims for loss, damage or injury as a result of Iraq's invasion of Kuwait) and additional amounts for UN expenses in Iraq, particularly for the work of UNSCOM.[85]

Some Security Council members, including China and Yemen, expressed reservations over the level of intrusion on Iraq's sovereignty and there were concerns about mixing UN expenses, especially for UNSCOM and humanitarian aid, in the provisions of the same resolution. Zimbabwe and India pointed to earlier non-aligned country proposals to address the humanitarian issue which had not been taken up by the Council.[86]

Before Resolution 712 was passed in September 1991, the UN Secretary General unsuccessfully argued that the six-monthly ceiling should be raised to $2.4 billion, which would have brought the sum available for humanitarian relief closer to that proposed by Sadruddin.[87] In practice, the resolutions reduced the sum available for humanitarian aid to approximately $930 million over six months, from $2.65 billion over four months, as originally proposed. The oil revenues were to be deposited in an escrow account directly controlled by the UN, not in the SOMO account as Sadruddin had wanted.

UN officials in Baghdad indicated that the Secretary General viewed the figure of $1.6 billion as based on 'political considerations' while the $2.4 billion figure was based on 'technical considerations'. A further concern among UN officials was that an oil sale at the lower figure might cut off or severely limit international aid to Iraq, while the funds generated would not be sufficient to allow reconstruction. This would effectively defeat Sadruddin's argument that the country could afford to pay for itself.

It seems likely that these less attractive conditions reduced the chances of Iraq accepting the resolution. According to an aid agency staff member involved in the discussions in Baghdad, even by late July 'UN officials were convinced... that the US intention was to present Saddam Hussein with so unattractive a package that Iraq would reject it and thus take on the blame, at least in Western eyes, for continued civilian suffering'.[88]

Another observer closely involved in the discussions suggested that the main preoccupation of the US and UK was to ensure that the pressure on Iraq was maintained. Sadruddin's report on humanitarian conditions in Iraq made it difficult to resist some easing of the embargo. A US official was quoted as saying that the proposal for an oil sale was 'a good way to maintain the bulk of sanctions and not be on the wrong side of a potentially emotive issue'.[89] British Foreign Secretary Douglas Hurd stressed, however, that any arrangement had to be 'limited and water-tight'.[90]

For the Western members of the Council, these resolutions seem to have represented the least bad option. 'The scheme was accepted by Western Security Council members as a lesser evil to having the Committee grant Iraq export ban exemptions under Resolution 687 and was also welcomed as a trial run for certain aspects of the long term regime under which Iraq would divert a percentage of its oil revenues to the UN Compensation Fund.'

It was believed that if an exemption from the export ban had been agreed, as Iraq had originally proposed, it would not have been possible to monitor how the purchased goods were distributed in Iraq. This was one of the main principles of the scheme established by Resolutions 706 and 712, and was probably one of the main reasons that Iraq rejected them.[91]

Whatever the scheme, in-country monitoring would probably have met with Iraqi objections, and in the light of his experiences in the southern marshes Sadruddin himself cannot have been assured that the Iraqi Government would allow monitoring. Effective monitoring would also have required a level of international backing which, given the Security Council's record on such matters, might not have been forthcoming. In the event, these concerns turned out to be academic, as Iraq continued to reject the resolutions. Although both resolutions were adopted under Chapter VII of the UN Charter in line with Resolution 687, there was no way of forcing Iraq to accept them.

Between January and June 1992, there were three rounds of talks in Vienna between UN teams and Iraqi representatives. The first round in January, led by Kofi Annan for the UN, was said to have made progress on the question of allowing Iraq to use both its northern and southern export facilities (the Kirkuk-Yumurtalik pipeline through Turkey and the Mina al-Bakr terminal on the Gulf).[92] This contradicted the UN Secretary General's recommendations, embodied in Resolution 712, which specified that the oil would be exported via the pipeline.[93] Aside from the benefit to Turkey from using this route, Security Council members were said to consider Mina al-Bakr impractical because it required extensive repairs.

Discussions also touched on the possibility of using the UN escrow account only to deposit funds for the Compensation Fund and UN expenses, while allowing an account under Iraqi control for the purchase of humanitarian supplies.[94] According to a UN source, it was accepted that in-country monitoring of humanitarian supplies should be 'light'.

In January, the British Government had indicated to the new UN Secretary General Boutros Boutros-Ghali that it was willing to see minor 'face-saving' adjustments if Iraq agreed the resolutions as a whole.[95] Other Security Council members, and the UN Secretariat, were keen for agreement to be reached so that funds would be available for UN operations and for the Compensation Fund.

However, the modifications proposed at the January meetings proved too drastic for the US Government, which refused to accept them. The second round of talks, led for the UN by Giandomenico Picco, therefore started virtually from square one. The negotiations in March and June 1992 appear to have foundered mainly on Iraq's insistence on exporting at least part of its oil via Mina al-Bakr. Its resistance to exclusive use of the Turkish pipeline was probably increased by Turkish demands for back-payments for maintenance of the pipeline and a much increased level of transit fee for the new oil exports. A further problem had been created by the fact that since the end of 1991 an 80-kilometre stretch of the pipeline north of Mosul was under Iraqi Kurdish control.

The separation of the northern governorates also complicated the question of distribution of humanitarian goods inside Iraq, although the issue did not appear to be a major point of discussion in the talks. The Iraqi Government continued to object to the resolution's provision for UN monitoring of distribution, and it seemed increasingly unlikely that the resolution could be implemented while Iraq maintained its internal economic embargo against the Kurdish-controlled areas.

On 11 July 1992, the Iraqi Ministry of Foreign Affairs wrote to the UN Secretary General saying that Resolutions 706 and 712 raised issues of sovereignty and Iraq could not accept them, thus ending this cycle of negotiations.

While the talks were still in progress, the US had raised in the Security Council the alternative of compulsorily using Iraq's assets frozen abroad to pay for humanitarian supplies, the Compensation Fund and UN expenses. European Security Council members showed little enthusiasm, envisaging numerous legal complications from such a procedure.[96] However, the failure of the oil sales negotiations made the idea of re-freezing Iraq's overseas assets seem more attractive. Resolution 778 was passed on 2 October, despite Iraqi government efforts to head off its adoption.[97] Under this resolution, some $4–5 billion in frozen assets, held in 30 countries, were effectively re-frozen. Iraq lost the possibility of drawing on any of these assets by persuading individual states to unfreeze them. Oil-related assets were to be placed in a UN escrow account.[98]

President Bush announced that the US agreed to use $200 million of assets frozen in the US to match voluntary donor contributions passed through the escrow account to the humanitarian assistance programme. This mechanism did alleviate the periodic cash crises in the UN assistance programme from 1993 until Iraq accepted Resolution 986 in 1996, although the chronic shortage of funds persisted[99] (see Chapter 7).

Iraq's resistance to a limited oil sale may well have hardened after the unilateral freezing of its assets, but the Government kept the door ajar, returning to the negotiating table in mid-1993, presumably in the hope of finding greater flexibility. But no progress was made, and by September it became clear that Iraqi policy had shifted toward seeking the full lifting of the oil embargo.[100] In early October, Foreign Minister Muhammad al-Sahhaf indicated to the UN during a visit to New York that Iraq did not wish to pursue limited sales.

Throughout the two years of stalemate over these resolutions, Western governments took the opportunity to turn continuing reports of civilian suffering back onto the Iraqi regime, arguing that it could alleviate suffering and chose not to do so. The UN Special Rapporteur on human rights in Iraq, Max van der Stoel, emphasised Saddam Hussein's responsibility for the humanitarian crisis, especially because of his rejection of Resolutions 706 and 712. He pointed to the absurdity of Iraq's argument that its sovereignty was infringed by these resolutions in the light of its acceptance, albeit reluctant, of UNSCOM weapons inspectors.

But this approach caused unease among many humanitarian observers who felt that the 'package' deal offered under Resolutions 706 and 712 was one which it could have been anticipated Iraq would refuse. They argued that humanitarian needs should have been entirely separated from questions of compensation and payment for the work of UN weapons inspectors. The latter were issues for the Iraqi state alone, and civilians should not be penalised for a government decision to resist paying for these items.

If a purely humanitarian deal such as that proposed by Sadruddin had been offered, albeit with controls and monitoring, and the Iraqi Government had refused it, the regime's indifference to humanitarian need would have been incontrovertible. The mixing of humanitarian exemptions with matters such as compensation and enforcement activities of UNSCOM muddied the waters, allowing the Iraqi Government to object on other political or technical grounds. This made Western condemnation of its callousness less credible.[101]

Protagonists of the resolutions argued that if the humanitarian situation in Iraq was desperate enough, the Iraqi Government would agree to the terms. But although some of its people may have been desperate, at that stage the Government had not reached that point. The regime continued to place greater weight on not ceding control of its funds by allowing the UN to administer them, and on limiting, as far as it could, the UN's activities in the country.

MOVING THE GOALPOSTS? 1994-7

In early 1994, a close observer of US policy on Iraq characterised the continuation of the sanctions regime as 'the lowest common denominator on which everyone can agree'.[102] By the end of the year, not even this was clear.

From the end of 1993, the Iraqi Government had ceased to toy with acceptance of Resolutions 706 and 712 and began to press explicitly for full lifting of the oil sale embargo under Paragraph 22 of Resolution 687. In November 1993, it tried, unsuccessfully, to trade acceptance of Resolution 715 (which provided for long-term monitoring to prevent the rebuilding of weapons of mass destruction) for a guarantee that the embargo would be lifted once the monitoring systems were in place. It also began a concerted campaign to woo leading members of the Security Council which were most amenable to seeing the oil embargo lifted – France, Russia and China – and to highlight the growing differences of opinion among the permanent members. In March 1993, Russia, France and China had wanted to issue a Security Council presidential statement reflecting Iraq's cooperation on UN Resolutions. This was rejected by the US and UK. These disagreements became evident when, from March 1994, presidential statements ceased to be issued after the 60-day reviews of sanctions, indicating that there was no consensus.[103]

The arguments focused on ambiguities in Resolution 687 which allowed different readings of what was required of Iraq before the economic embargo could be lifted. A move to lift any part of the embargo depends on a consensus among the permanent members. Although all five major powers voted to accept the terms of Resolution 687, a negative vote (though not an abstention) by one permanent member would veto any proposal before the Council to lift the embargo as specified in the resolution.

Divergent views were expressed on whether paragraphs 21 and 22 of Resolution 687 could be implemented separately. Paragraph 22 specifies that the embargo on imports from Iraq – primarily oil – and related financial transactions 'shall have no further force or effect' once Iraq has complied with the requirements in the resolution relating to the destruction and monitoring of its weapons of mass destruction and related manufacturing capacity, and the establishment of the UN Compensation Fund.

Paragraph 22 appears to stand alone, in that it does not suggest that the lifting of the oil export ban depends on compliance with any part of the resolution other than those paragraphs relating to weapons of mass destruction. Russia and France accepted this interpretation. In the Russian view, 'As soon as the chairman of UNSCOM reports favourably, then paragraph 22 is engaged, allowing oil sales without limits'.

The French Government argued that sanctions had three main goals in order to restore regional peace and stability: that Iraq pose no threat to its neighbours; the destruction of weapons of mass destruction and imposition of a monitoring system;

and respect for Kuwait's border and its sovereignty. Once these were complied with, Chapter 22 of Resolution 687 could be regarded as implemented.

The instruments framed in 1991 had not been intended for an extended shelf life, and did not necessarily suit the purposes of all the key players over the longer term. Discussions on the US role in formulating Resolution 687 in 1991 indicate that, when it was framed, there was still a belief that Saddam Hussein would either show willingness to comply or that he would be overthrown. At that time it was apparently argued that there should be an incentive to comply – the possibility that the most onerous part of the embargo, the ban on oil exports, would be lifted – if the key parts of the resolution were implemented.[104]

By 1994, this interpretation of the resolution did not sit well with US strategy on Iraq. The US and UK adamantly opposed any 'staged' lifting of sanctions. They believed sanctions should remain in place until 'all relevant resolutions' were complied with, choosing to ignore or play down the separate requirements of Paragraph 22.

These states chose to emphasise Paragraph 21 of Resolution 687 which deals with the terms for lifting the embargo on exports to Iraq. A decision 'to reduce or lift' the prohibition is dependent on the 60-day review 'in the light of the policies and practices of the Government of Iraq, including the implementation of all relevant resolutions of the Security Council'. Two phrases are ambiguous and open to different interpretations: first, the 'policies and practices' of the Iraqi Government; and second, the question of which resolutions are 'relevant'. The French, for example, contended that Iraq could only be expected to comply with Chapter VII resolutions, which in their view excluded Resolution 688.[105] The formal status of this resolution – whether it could be considered mandatory – has never been clarified (see Chapter 3).

The US and UK nonetheless insisted that Resolution 688 should be taken into account in the reviews because it had a bearing on the 'policies and practices' of the Iraqi Government.[106] These governments further argued 'that as long as Iraq continues its flagrant disregard of its other obligations under Council resolutions and international law, the Government cannot be trusted to comply in good faith with the weapons monitoring mechanism'.[107]

Once Iraq had accepted Resolution 715 and UNSCOM had installed its monitoring system, France, Russia and China appeared to believe that if the six-month test period for the monitors was successful, full compliance on weapons of mass destruction could be achieved sometime in 1995. This would be followed by the lifting of the oil embargo.

One other key issue remained: Iraq's acceptance of Kuwaiti sovereignty and the Iraq-Kuwait boundary as defined by the UN Boundary Demarcation Commission. In November 1994, after active diplomatic initiatives by Russia, Iraq recognised the boundaries and sovereignty of Kuwait under the conditions laid down by the Security Council. However, this recognition only came after a major confrontation with coalition forces, when Iraqi troops were reported to be massing near the Kuwaiti border.

The outcome of this crisis was, predictably, used for different purposes by permanent members of the Council. President Clinton stressed that the events of October 1994 showed Iraq still threatening its neighbours, and insisted on an extended understanding of compliance. The US and UK both emphasised their continuing distrust of Iraq's 'peaceful intentions'.[108]

By this time, the US administration had made it clear that it wanted to maintain sanctions even if it was obvious that this involved 'moving the goal posts'.[109] By late

1994 there was a strong consensus among policy-makers and close observers of the Clinton administration that the basic US strategy was to keep sanctions in place and try to avoid public debate or discussion which might challenge the assumptions on which this position was based.

There was, as one congressional aide put it, no willingness to offer any 'carrots' to Iraq and no trust in Saddam Hussein. This view seems to be shared in the administration and Congress on a bipartisan basis. There was 'more inflexibility than is sensible' on the sanctions issue in the National Security Council and the State Department. There were some voices in the US which challenged this wish to move the goal posts, arguing that raising the stakes would be a disincentive to compliance by Iraq, but they made little impact on the administration.[110] Any wavering on this issue was ended by the Iraqi troop movements toward the Kuwait border.

Russia and France, on the other hand, emphasised that the crisis had resulted in Iraq's recognition of Kuwait's border and sovereignty. In previous years, France had generally accepted and indeed participated in military actions when Iraq was seen to have infringed the terms of Resolution 687. On this occasion, while acknowledging that the troop movements were 'a mistake on the part of Saddam Hussein', French officials asserted that the scale of the confrontation was based on an over-reaction by the US, and questioned the accuracy of US data on troop movements.

All had agreed that the recognition of Kuwait was a key prerequisite for further movement on lifting sanctions. In the view of some observers it also marked an important break in the international consensus on retaining the full economic embargo. Those states on the Security Council and outside it which themselves had powerful neighbours and had felt threatened by Iraq's invasion of Kuwait viewed Iraq's acceptance of Kuwait's sovereignty as the main issue which sanctions had been designed to address.[111] Other aspects of Iraq's conduct were considered less relevant. Furthermore, attitudes towards sanctions within the Middle East region were much less positive than they had been in 1991.

There appeared to be a real chance of a challenge to the US/UK position in early 1995. France further signalled its wish to see normalisation of relations by resuming low-level diplomatic relations with Baghdad in January.[112] In December 1994, as UNSCOM reported progress in installing long-term weapons monitoring in Iraq, Russia was pressing for a mandatory resolution which 'should talk about lifting or first suspending' the oil embargo once a six-month test period for the monitoring system (described as 'provisionally operational' in October 1994) was completed.[113]

Before the March 1995 sanctions review, the US administration was sufficiently concerned about the shifting climate of opinion for the UN Ambassador Madeleine Albright to tour Security Council states including the UK, Czech Republic, Italy, Oman, Argentina and Honduras, to shore up support.[114] At the end of March, Russia, France and China circulated a joint draft resolution in the UN to lift the oil embargo.[115]

Resolution 986: humanitarian relief
or the key to retaining sanctions?

During 1994, reports from Iraq indicated a rapid deterioration in humanitarian conditions in government-controlled areas, compounded by a reduction of monthly government rations in September (see Chapter 5). With declining donor contributions to the UN humanitarian programme, there was again pressure to alleviate these conditions. By this time, even the US administration accepted that the suffering among the ordinary people of Iraq was not just a figment of Iraqi government propaganda. However, their strategy was to blame the Iraqi Government rather than sanctions, focusing on its refusal to implement Resolutions 706 and 712.

At the end of 1994 there were hints that these resolutions might be revived in some form. Several motives, in addition to humanitarian concerns, encouraged this initiative. Some observers maintain that the US promoted a new resolution for a limited sale of oil for humanitarian purposes in order to lessen the pressure for sanctions to be lifted. This was borne out by subsequent comments from senior US officials. Robert Pelletreau told a congressional committee in 1996: 'Implementation of the resolution is not a precursor to lifting sanctions. It is a humanitarian exception that preserves and even reinforces the sanctions regime.'[116] Madeleine Albright's remark on 16 April

---

Resolution 986: Modifying the Rules

Resolution 986, adopted on 14 April 1995, allowed Iraq to sell $2 billion worth of oil over six months, renewable every 180 days. The framework followed UNSC Resolutions 706 and 712 of 1991 in general terms. However, there were significant modifications, partly in response to changed circumstances, but also in an apparent attempt to deal with earlier Iraqi objections.

The ceiling on six monthly sales was raised from $1.6 to $2 billion, still not reaching the amount proposed by Sadruddin in 1991. The proportional deductions for the Compensation Commission and for the expenses of UN operations in Iraq (including UNSCOM) remained the same. Iraq could export oil through its southern Mina al-Bakr terminal as well as through the Turkish pipeline, a major sticking point in previous negotiations.

Acknowledging the *de facto* separation of Iraqi Kurdistan from government-controlled Iraq (which had not yet occurred when Resolutions 706 and 712 were passed), a portion of the total revenue ($130–150 million every 90 days) was assigned directly to the UN Humanitarian Programme operating in the three northern governorates. Humanitarian goods were to be distributed in the north through the UN, not through Iraqi government channels as they would be within government-controlled areas. The resolution affirmed, however, that 'nothing in this resolution should be construed as infringing the sovereignty and territorial integrity of Iraq'.

Provisions were made for UN-appointed officials to 'observe' the distribution of humanitarian goods on the basis of the Iraqi Government's distribution plan, and their impact on the humanitarian situation. In Resolutions 706 and 712 UN, agents from the various UN organisations (UNICEF, WHO, WFP and FAO) were to 'monitor' in-country distribution. This was another area in which Iraq had raised objections in the earlier negotiations.

Iraq was to be kept fully informed on the status of the escrow account, which was to have external auditors. Iraq was allowed to import spare parts and equipment to refurbish the Kirkuk-Yumurtalik oil pipeline and to finance these costs through the escrow account.

1996 also confirms this view: 'Frankly it is the best of all possible ways to make sure that the sanctions regime remains in place so that Saddam Hussein is not entitled to pretend he is concerned for his people and shed a lot of crocodile tears'.[117]

Other incentives for the US and other Security Council members to press for a limited oil sale included Turkey's persistent demands that the international community recompense its economic losses from sanctions and the increasing pressure to proceed with UN Compensation Funds payments, since claims were being adjudicated without sufficient funds to pay them.

Resolution 986 was drafted by the US, which this time was interested in getting Iraq to accept. Tariq Aziz was in New York and was consulted. According to Assistant Secretary of State Robert Pelletreau, 'We designed Resolution 986 with a lot of help from the Government of Oman which was the Arab state on the Security Council at that time – to fashion a resolution which Iraq would accept and that would have the potential benefit to Turkey'. The use of the Mina al-Bakr outlet was accepted because this was something Iraq had wanted, though it gave less to Turkey. Although one UN source described the US as 'fragile' on Turkey's behalf, Pelletreau said that this was a change that the Arab states 'very much supported'.[118] The final version in fact raised little dissent in the Security Council. Although France and Russia wanted to see the oil embargo lifted, the strong resistance from the US made this the next best option.

Although some of the sticking points in negotiations on Resolutions 706 and 712 had been eliminated or modified (see box), Iraq nonetheless rejected the resolution. At a joint meeting of the RCC and the Ba'th Party command on 14 April, Resolution 986 was described as 'worse and more dangerous than the previous UN Security Council resolutions 706 and 712'.[119] However, social and economic conditions in Iraq continued to deteriorate and Iraq's refusal to accept the sale strengthened the argument that the regime was entirely to blame for the suffering of its people.

In January 1996, in an abrupt reversal of policy, the Iraqi Government agreed to negotiate, and finally accepted Resolution 986 in May. Its acceptance, after more than a year of resistance, appears to have been caused in part by worsening economic conditions and fears that these could create dangerous internal dissent. Humanitarian concerns were unlikely to have been a major consideration.

The pressures which built up in regard to weapons issues finally pushed Iraq to accept this resolution. Revelations in the summer of 1995 that Iraq had concealed significant parts of its chemical and biological weapons programmes from UNSCOM (see below) must finally have convinced the Iraqi leadership that there was little immediate prospect of splitting the Security Council over implementation of Paragraph 22 of Resolution 687.

The leadership was probably also influenced by the urging of France, Russia, Egypt and some other Arab states to agree to the resolution, in the absence of any prospect of a full lifting of the oil embargo. There were evidently divisions inside the Government, with Saddam Hussein reportedly the most unbending opponent of acceptance. By October 1995, however, several senior Iraqi officials were said to be advocating its acceptance.[120] Some officials, including Tariq Aziz, were reportedly convinced by the argument put forward by France that the resolution offered Iraq a way back into the oil market. Iraq may also have received some informal indication from the US that the resolution would be withdrawn if Iraq did not accept it.

The Government rationalised its acceptance by presenting the resolution as the 'thin end of the wedge' towards the full lifting of sanctions, while its opponents in the Security Council constantly reiterated that the resolution was a temporary measure and did not imply any change to the overall embargo.

Once the resolution was accepted, there were differing approaches to implementation. The US and UK directly intervened in negotiations between the UN Secretariat and the Iraqi Government, prolonging the process of agreeing to a memorandum of understanding for its implementation. The Secretariat and other Security Council members did not conceal their annoyance at this approach. Yet again there appeared to be tension between a consensual approach taken by the Secretariat and accepted by most Security Council members, and the confrontational approach of the US and UK. There were further delays after the Secretary General decided to halt preparations for the pumping of oil following Iraq's incursion into Arbil in September 1996. Oil did not flow from Iraq until December 1996.

Once implemented, the so-called oil-for-food deal suffered from both technical and political problems. It proved vulnerable to declining prices on the international oil market, which progressively diminished the value of the oil sold, and its operation was affected by the continued struggle with the Security Council over Iraq's weapons of mass destruction (see Chapter 7 for discussion of its implementation).

Finally, neither Iraq nor the international community has clearly separated this struggle over Iraq's weapons from issues of humanitarian mitigation. This was again evident in the crises of 1997 and early 1998, when both sides used the humanitarian card in the struggle to gain support. During the crisis over UNSCOM inspectors' access to presidential sites in January and February 1998 the UN Secretary General proposed, with strong backing from the US and UK, to double permitted oil sales. This was evidently intended to send a signal that the Security Council was not targeting the Iraqi people, so retaining the moral high ground for hard-line states and ensuring that sanctions remained in place.

The latter consideration meant that the Iraqi Government accepted the proposal only with reluctance, and once an agreement had been signed on inspections of presidential sites it returned to demanding the full lifting of sanctions. Meanwhile, the US continued to support the oil-for-food resolutions as the best means to retain sanctions. In May 1998, Thomas Pickering, Under Secretary for Political Affairs and formerly US Ambassador to the UN, asserted, 'In a very real sense, the "oil-for-food" program is the key to sustaining the sanctions regime until Iraq complies with its obligations'. The current Iraqi regime, he considered, was unlikely to comply. 'That means, as far as the US is concerned, that sanctions will be a fact of life for the foreseeable future.'[121]

The battle over weapons of mass destruction

UNSCOM's six-monthly report of December 1994 had a more than usually positive tone. It confirmed that long-term monitoring mechanisms were in place and being tested, though it questioned the completeness of Iraq's responses to enquiries on past programmes, particularly on biological and chemical weapons. This allowed both sides in the sanctions debate to argue that UNSCOM's findings justified their opposing positions.[122]

However, revelations by Iraqi defectors raised further doubts about the eradication of some types of weapons proscribed under UN resolutions. General Wafiq Sammara'i, a former head of Iraqi military intelligence who had defected in late 1994, alleged that Iraq was still concealing Scud R-17s and Al-Hussein missiles and had failed to acknowledge possession of biological weapons.[123] Further information came from an Iraqi nuclear scientist, Khidhir Abdul Abbas Hamza, who defected to the US in 1994.[124]

In July 1995, Iraq admitted for the first time having developed biological weapons, after four years of denial. At the same time, the Government was threatening to end cooperation with UNSCOM if no progress was made in the Security Council towards lifting the oil embargo. In August – following the defection of the former Defence and Military Industries Minister, General Hussein Kamil al-Majid, who

---

The Role of UNSCOM

The United Nations Special Commission (UNSCOM) was set up in 1991 under the terms of Resolution 687 to implement the non-nuclear aspects of the elimination of Iraq's weapons of mass destruction (WMD), and to establish the long-term monitoring programme called for by Section C of this resolution. UNSCOM was also to assist the International Atomic Energy Agency (IAEA) inspections in the nuclear field.

UNSCOM's mandate was: 'to carry out on-site inspection of Iraq's biological, chemical and missile capabilities; to take possession for destruction, removal or rendering harmless of all chemical and biological weapons and stocks of agents and all related sub-systems and components and all research, development, support and manufacturing localities; to supervise the destruction by Iraq of all its ballistic missiles with a range greater than 150kms and related major parts, and repair and production facilities; to monitor and verify Iraq's compliance with its undertaking not to use, develop, construct or acquire any of the items specified above'.

Under the terms of an exchange of letters between the UN Secretary General and the Iraqi Foreign Minister in May 1991, UNSCOM was to be granted unimpeded movement and communications facilities within Iraq, and access to all sites and facilities which UNSCOM deemed it necessary to inspect.

As part of the long-term monitoring operation set up under Resolution 715 (1991), and accepted by Iraq in 1993, Resolution 1051 (1996) established a mechanism under which the Government of Iraq and the government of the supplying country must notify a UN monitoring group of the import of potential dual-use items (ie those which might be used to manufacture weapons of mass destruction, but also have a legitimate civilian use).[125]

UNSCOM has presided over the most rigorous surveillance regime ever imposed, and has had the backing of all major Security Council states for its work. Its task was larger than at first supposed, even though it did not touch most of Iraq's conventional weaponry, with the exception of long-range missiles. The US military seems to have overestimated the amount of damage done to Iraq's WMD capacity by air attacks during the 1991 Gulf War. Most biological weapons capacity, for example, was apparently moved before the air strikes.[126]

A study based on interviews with a number of UNSCOM inspectors on their experiences during the first 29 inspections (1991–92) characterised Iraqi behaviour as 'defiant and crafty'. Despite Security Council insistence on anywhere/anytime inspections and with the constant threat of renewed hostilities in the event of non-compliance, the Iraqis managed to avoid full and detailed disclosure. The inspectors alleged there were outright

had previously been in charge of nuclear and biological weapons programmes – the Government claimed to have 'discovered' over half a million pages of documents and other evidence related to its weapons programmes. They were 'concealed' on a chicken farm said to have belonged to Hussein Kamil.

This new information, and Hussein Kamil's revelations after his defection, raised further questions about how much the Iraqis were still concealing from UNSCOM. In his October 1995 report, the Chairman of UNSCOM, Rolf Ekeus, alleged that Iraq had misled UNSCOM over aspects of its long-range missile programme; and that it had attempted to conceal its biological warfare programme and the fact that the biological agents had been 'weaponised'. It had also concealed 'its chemical missile warhead flight tests and work on the development of a missile for the delivery of a nuclear device'. The report concluded that 'in the coming months, the Government

---

attempts at concealment of evidence, hiding of equipment, and limiting or denying access to inspectors.

Furthermore, since each inspection tour was limited in time, officials would delay giving information and waste time in other ways. The number of Iraqi personnel with whom the inspectors interacted has always been limited and highly controlled.[127]

Once Iraq had accepted Resolution 715, UNSCOM put in place an 'unprecedented technical surveillance capability' – including overflights and cameras which can transmit real-time photographs to New York. Nonetheless, one author concluded:

> Perhaps one of the ultimate lessons of UNSCOM will be the realisation that there are limits on perfectly assured arms control/non-proliferation, even when verification and enforcement are carried out in highly favourable coercive/intrusive circumstances. Even in conditions that are tantamount to unconditional surrender, Iraq continues to resist, with varying degrees of success, the total imposition of an external arms control/non-proliferation system.[128]

This was written in 1992, well before the revelations in 1995 of how much Iraq had managed to conceal.

Disputes on the nature and quality of UNSCOM's data result from the highly unequal intelligence gathering capacities of the participating states. The variety of surveillance techniques available to the US, for example, increased its ability to exert pressure on UNSCOM. UNSCOM also has to depend on US facilities to analyse and interpret photographs taken by the U-2 surveillance missions over Iraq carried out under UN auspices.[129] Additionally, from 1995, according to the former US weapons inspector Scott Ritter, UNSCOM had increasingly close links with Israeli intelligence services, which both assisted with interpreting the U-2 photographs and provided information on Iraq's efforts to conceal aspects of its WMD programmes.[130]

Political tensions have developed over UNSCOM's composition and ways of working. Russian Vice Minister of Foreign Affairs Victor Passouvaliouk complained that the commission and groups of inspectors were not evenly balanced between nationalities. 'The Anglo-Saxons hold all the key positions.'[131] Differences of opinion have also developed over how comprehensive the inspectors' findings can be. Some inspectors apparently take the view that pursuing every last item in Iraq's WMD inventory is a 'bottomless pit'.[132] Richard Butler, the second Chairman of UNSCOM, attracted criticism, especially from France and Russia, over his confrontational style. Finally, the increasingly confrontational style of inspection developed by Scott Ritter and some of his associates in UNSCOM in response to Iraqi evasions seems to have contributed significantly to the build-up of tensions between Iraq and the weapons inspectors from 1996 onwards.

of Iraq needed to present three new declarations comprising full final and complete disclosures of all its proscribed capabilities' before full compliance with the relevant sections of Resolution 687 could be achieved.[133]

Until he left his post in mid-1997, Ekeus continued to stress that Iraq's biological weapons programme, along with the chemical VX precursors thought to be unaccounted for, represented an ongoing threat. This view was reiterated in UNSCOM reports under the new Chairman, Richard Butler, who took over in July 1997. The US and UK have emphasised these continuing problems, while the other members of the permanent five stressed the substantial progress that has been made towards eradicating Iraq's weapons of mass destruction. By April 1998, the International Atomic Energy Agency (IAEA) was close to ending its investigations into Iraq's nuclear weapons programme and the Security Council agreed that, subject to receiving some further clarifications from Iraq, it would move to ongoing monitoring and verification under Resolution 715.[134]

Tensions over UNSCOM's access to sites in Iraq mounted in 1997.[135] Its October report conceded that progress had been made on chemical and missile issues, but characterised biological weapons as an area 'unredeemed by progress or any approximation of the known facts of Iraq's program'.[136] The rift within the Security Council also widened and became public when, for the first time, three permanent members – France, China and Russia – joined Kenya and Egypt to abstain on a resolution drafted by the US which threatened a travel ban on some Iraqi officials if the Government continued to obstruct UNSCOM inspectors' access to sites.[137] Iraq responded by calling for the removal of all US citizens from UNSCOM, which subsequently suspended its operations in Iraq.

Russian mediation in November defused the confrontation but did not resolve the underlying crisis. A dispute over weapons inspectors' access to presidential palace sites began in December, and by February 1998, the US and UK had gone to the brink of attacking Iraq, moving large forces back into the Gulf region. The UN Secretary General, Kofi Annan, went to Baghdad and negotiated an agreement with Saddam Hussein on access for UNSCOM. However, his mission only expressed the collective will of the Security Council to the extent that they could not agree to do anything else.

Once the crisis was ended, the Council passed a resolution threatening the 'severest consequences' if Iraq reneged on the agreement.[138] This avoided giving an explicit mandate to use force, but was interpreted by the US and UK as allowing this. Fundamentally, therefore, there was still no consensus on how to deal with Iraq. On 4 August, Iraq announced the suspension of cooperation with UNSCOM and by November 1998 a second major crisis again brought the parties to the brink of conflict, only avoided by a last minute climbdown on Iraq's part.

Kofi Annan's offer of a comprehensive review of sanctions was intended to act as a 'carrot' which would bring Iraqi compliance. In fact, not only was this brushed aside by Iraq, but it opened the old rifts within the Council about the terms for lifting sanctions.[139]

The threat of air strikes caused Iraq to draw back from the brink on several occasions, but finally in December 1988, the US and UK launched massive air strikes, the most intensive since 1991. As had been predicted, one consequence of these attacks was Iraq's refusal to allow UNSCOM inspectors to return. By January 1999, this and several other factors had combined to make the continuation of

UNSCOM's work in its previous form appear impossible. In 1998, the US and UK, in an effort to maintain the Security Council consensus had blocked several 'intrusive' UNSCOM inspections.[140] This drew criticism from hardliners and from within UNSCOM itself while not satisfying those who wanted to see more rapid movement towards lifting sanctions. By the end of the year, some commentators speculated that the US administration had virtually given up on the prospect that UNSCOM could achieve the disarmament of Iraq. Finally, in January 1999 there was a wave of press allegations that the US and UK had not only used their own and other states' intelligence services to feed information to UNSCOM (see box above), but had also used UNSCOM for their own intelligence gathering purposes. Whatever the precise truth of these revelations, their political import was as evidence of the partisan uses to which UNSCOM had been put. France and Russia which, along with China, had strongly opposed the bombing raids, began to demand the lifting of the trade embargo, combined with a new type of arms control regime. France circulated proposals to this effect in the Security Council in mid-January.[141]

By the end of January 1999, the Security Council remained deadlocked on the same set of fundamental issues which had dogged their deliberations on Iraq since the mid-1990s. Meanwhile Iraq, seeing this widened split as a new opportunity, took a belligerent position, aggressively challenging the continuation of the no-fly zones (see Chapter 3) and making threatening speeches about the role of Kuwait and Saudi Arabia in supporting the US. This stance has caused some unease both in the Arab world and among the Security Council members seeking to get sanctions lifted.

The position of the US appears to have shifted towards a more explicit claim that it seeks to topple Saddam Hussein, while maintaining sanctions for the purposes of containment.[142] To counter attempts to have sanctions lifted, it has suggested in the Security Council that the ceiling on oil sales under the oil-for-food resolutions should be further raised.

The Labour Government in the UK insisted that Iraq must be allowed to see 'light at the end of the tunnel', but it has not fundamentally shifted away from the US position on sanctions and supports the use of force. At the same time, it strongly supported the expanded oil sale as proposed by Kofi Annan, indicating that it envisaged sanctions remaining in place for some time to come.

For Iraq, on the other hand, retaining at least some part of its WMD capacity has apparently remained a priority, even though it has meant forfeiting some $25 billion a year in oil export revenues for the time being. According to UNSCOM sources, Iraqi officials have stressed that in their view, chemical weapons had an important political and psychological effect during the Iran-Iraq War. The regime apparently views these capabilities as important in regaining a significant regional role.

The limitations on weapons control

The confrontations of 1997 and 1998 revealed the limits of US leverage on the weapons issue. If Iraq had expelled the UNSCOM inspectors, the only option for enforcement was seen to be a military one. Given the unacceptable risk of troop losses entailed by any ground action, air strikes were the expected response. These were acknowledged to be inappropriate, especially for targeting biological agents, since these are portable and can be stored in small amounts. In addition to the risk of numerous civilian casualties from the agent escaping into the atmosphere as a result of bombing, there would be no way of verifying the destruction of agents whose exact volume and location were unknown.

Furthermore, such action risked the permanent exclusion of UNSCOM inspectors from Iraq. As a Defense Department official, speaking at an off-the-record briefing in November 1997, admitted:

> In my view, it is not logical to believe that we can, by indirect means [ie using air strikes], attack and destroy every facility. This is a very difficult circumstance, and the only way to physically assure ourselves of the control of these facilities is to go to them, control them physically with people on the scene and monitor them... That's the vital nature of UNSCOM.[143]

There has also been a certain tension underlying UNSCOM's role. The head of UNSCOM has played a role which is more political than technical. The Iraqi Government undoubtedly played a part in 'politicising' this work. However, it seems that UNSCOM has also been subject to intense political pressures from within the Security Council, especially at times of crisis when the permanent members cannot agree on a strategy.

UNSCOM has clearly revealed the extent of Iraq's potential to wage nuclear, chemical and biological warfare. However, even in the face of such a large arsenal of weapons of mass destruction, no attempt has been made to place any responsibility on the suppliers of these weapons.

Some of Iraq's weapons capacity is the result of local production – for example, of some chemical agents and delivery systems – but most of the basic components and the technology come from the very countries which are now imposing these severe controls. During their investigations, the IAEA and UNSCOM have evidently added to the list of suppliers of components, precursors and technical expertise revealed by the Scott Report in the UK, congressional enquiries in the US and more limited investigations in other European countries. Letters of credit found in the Central Bank of Iraq further identified companies which had been selling military equipment to Iraq. All this information has been kept confidential.

The former Chairman of UNSCOM, Rolf Ekeus, explained that this decision was not a result of any 'deal' with Iraq.

> It was to do with the major governments which were the supplier countries... If we had told about... [a] major company in country X, in western Europe, I can assure you that government would never forgive us. Because what would happen was the name would be published, legislation would be taken [sic], one-sided sanctions against that company, that would hurt national economic interest and they would cut us off from information.[144]

UNSCOM, therefore, while trying to force Iraq to come clean, has taken a different attitude to its suppliers and has not demanded any public acknowledgement of their role in creating this threat.

THE EFFECTIVENESS OF POST-WAR SANCTIONS

The political effectiveness of economic sanctions as a means to coerce governments has been much studied,[145] but until recently there has been less effort to understand and document the impact of prolonged economic sanctions on the target society, whether or not the policy is successful in its coercive goals. The prolonged embargo against Iraq has brought this question into sharper focus.

According to one group of researchers:

> It is important to distinguish the *impact* of sanctions – that is, their success in economic terms – from their *effectiveness*, meaning their success in producing the desired political response... In order to be effective, sanctions must first have an impact, but this does not guarantee their success politically. It is a necessary but not a sufficient condition.[146]

In order to have an impact, an embargo needs to be fully and consistently implemented. The embargo on Iraq has been more comprehensive than most others, including that against former Yugoslavia. But how systematically it has been enforced is not altogether clear. The policy on 'leakage' over borders has, as described, varied according to the standing of Iraq's neighbours with leading Security Council states. However, the Sanctions Committee receives no systematic reporting on the movement of goods across Iraq's land borders, except that which individual states choose to submit as evidence of sanction-breaking.[147] Until 1994, the Sanctions Committee also had very limited information on maritime infringements.[148]

The views of leading Security Council members on the effectiveness of economic sanctions as an instrument of coercion have changed according to their particular interests. Following the invasion of Kuwait, policy makers in the US concluded, after only four months, that sanctions would not be effective in removing Iraqi forces from Kuwait. Those in the opposite camp argued that sanctions should be given a chance to work and that they were a viable substitute for the use of force.

After the war, the roles were reversed. The damage to Iraq's infrastructure by the bombing campaign, and the military defeat inflicted on the regime, led the pro-war camp to infer that a continuing economic embargo would be a viable way to enforce the ceasefire terms and probably to bring down the regime. Those who prior to the war had favoured sanctions found their use in the context of destruction and disruption of civilian life after the war of great concern.

A number of states have also adjusted their view of sanctions according to the target state in question. For example, the British, who had argued for leniency regarding dual-use items in discussions on the South African embargo, have taken a hard line in the Iraq Sanctions Committee, while several Muslim states which argued for leniency to Iraq were said to take a hard line on the Yugoslav (Serbia/Montenegro) Committee.[149]

The doubts about the post-war use of sanctions were compounded by questions about the motives of those imposing the embargo. There were concerns that the embargo became an instrument as much of national as international policy, as the Iraqi regime confronted those Western governments, in particular the US and UK, which wanted to remove or contain it.[150] Since this was not the stated goal of sanctions, it led to rifts in the Security Council, and gave the Iraqi Government room to argue that it was being unjustly targeted.

Since economic sanctions were employed as a political instrument, the various forms of humanitarian mitigation – whether waivers on humanitarian goods, humanitarian aid or the sale of oil – became entangled with other battles being fought, in the Security Council and outside it, over the extent of Iraq's compliance with UN resolutions. Whatever the public rhetoric, the record suggests that the humanitarian needs of the Iraqi population have never been more than a secondary concern for any of the major protagonists. The way in which the first oil-for-food resolutions were formulated demonstrated this problem. Resolution 986 sprang from a concern that the Security Council could be embarrassed by the scale of civilian suffering, but was also designed to keep sanctions in place. Equally, Iraq's decision to accept it was probably based on calculations which had little to do with the well-being of the population.

The impact of the embargo

The difficulty of obtaining reliable, independent information on the impact of the embargo has been a feature of the Iraqi case. Discussions in the Sanctions Committee during the early days of sanctions in 1990 already indicated the way information was becoming a political weapon.[151]

These early debates centred around the uncertain definition of 'humanitarian circumstances' in which food shipments were to be allowed. The chairperson indicated that 'defining "humanitarian circumstances" was a political more than a legal matter'. In the period from August 1990 until the war started in January 1991 there were sporadic confrontations on this issue. While the point made on a number of occasions by Cuba and Yemen, that 'humanitarian circumstances' should not mean that the Iraqi people starved, was generally accepted, the US and UK invoked the lack of information on the situation in Iraq, as well as allegations that the Iraqis had a lot of food stocks, to block approval of any shipments under this rubric. According to one source 'the Sanctions Committee, and in particular its British and American members, took a restrictive view of the humanitarian exception, demanding 'clear evidence' collected by an international organisation before any shipment was approved'.[152]

In September 1990 the UN Secretary General was requested by the Committee to obtain information on the food situation. However, UN agencies apparently had neither the capacity nor permission from the Iraqi Government to carry out nationwide assessments, while ICRC likewise was not allowed officially to assess nutritional or medical needs. The Secretary General also requested information direct from the Iraqi Government. Only in February 1991, once the war was in progress, did the Government agree to allow a joint UNICEF/WHO mission into Iraq.[153]

In mid-1991, two surveys, one by a UN team led by Sadruddin Aga Khan, and a second, by the International Study Team, a group of researchers based at Harvard University, provided a country-wide and multi-sectoral picture of conditions.[154] However, from 1992 until 1996, only limited surveys were possible (see Chapter 8).

There was no provision for systematic monitoring of what goods approved under the humanitarian exceptions actually reached Iraq. In 1996, the Committee conceded that 'in the absence of a verifying mechanism, the Committee has no way of confirming how much of the supplies for which authorisations were issued [under the no objection procedure] actually arrived in Iraq'.[155]

After the war, the World Food Programme (WFP) was able to monitor to some extent the state food supplies inside Iraq, but this information could not be used to assess whether, for example, unfrozen Iraqi assets had been used for food purchases, unless it could be matched with regular data on food shipments which had been approved by the Sanctions Committee.[156]

Only under Resolution 986 was there established a system of 'observers' to track the distribution of goods purchased with oil revenues, though its scope is reportedly limited. Obviously the permanent members receive information on economic and political conditions in Iraq from intelligence sources whose information is not publicly disclosed. Even if it were available, it would be no substitute for systematic surveys.

A further issue is the way information is interpreted. A realistic assessment of the impact of sanctions on the population cannot isolate the embargo as the sole cause of hardship or disruption of civilian life, as the Iraqi Government frequently claims it to be. However, this should not allow the protagonists of continued sanctions simply to discount international responsibility for the negative outcomes which the embargo has created.

International responsibility?

In 1991, a string of Security Council resolutions were composed in haste to address the post-Gulf-War crisis. Their provisions, which seemed clear enough at the time, soon became open to a variety of interpretations, depending on the political goals of the protagonists.

There are no clear external legal standards governing the application of economic sanctions. While, in general, the Security Council is bound under the UN Charter to uphold human rights, there are no guidelines as to how this principle should specifically be applied to the impact on innocent parties of a prolonged economic embargo.[157] This has so far been a very poorly developed area of international law. Rules established under the Geneva Conventions to protect civilians in time of war and populations under occupation after a war do not appear to fit the current Iraqi situation. The victors stopped short of occupation, allowing the previous regime to survive, while using economic sanctions and actual or threatened military action to enforce a ceasefire, a border settlement and disarmament. Exactly how responsibility for the humanitarian needs and human rights of the population can be assigned under these conditions is a matter for debate.

The international community arguably continues to bear some responsibility for the the unintended and unforeseen consequences of its decisions, however intransigent the sanctioned party may be. One commentator argues that responsibility lies with both parties:

> The State under sanction ('target State') is considered a recalcitrant that must suffer some infringement of its sovereignty in that its right to trade is restricted, but it otherwise retains full legitimacy as the bearer of national sovereignty and is treated in most other respects as a full-fledged (ie equal) member of the community of sovereign states. It thus remains the legitimate representative in international fora of its own civilian population. Both the sanctioning party (the Security Council) and the sanctioned party (the target State's government) are thus supposed to bear responsibility for the necessary protection of civilians in the target State.[158]

In his letter to Congress announcing the initiation of military measures in 1990, President Bush stated, 'economic hardship alone is highly unlikely to compel Saddam to retreat from Kuwait or cause regime-threatening popular discontent... Saddam Hussein has made clear his willingness to divert supplies to his military forces, even at the cost of severe deprivation of his civilian population'.[159] It could be argued that in prolonging the economic embargo after the war, against the same Iraqi regime which was being accused of 'diverting supplies', Security Council members knowingly allowed that deprivation to continue.

Equally ill-defined, but pertinent in this case, is the extent of suffering which can legitimately be imposed by the international community on a civilian population which lacks mechanisms to influence what its government decides to do. The original intention of sanctions under the UN Charter was not to create long-term social damage but to deliver a sharp shock to a recalcitrant regime.

The unique experience in the Iraqi case, when a prolonged embargo was imposed following a war, raises questions as to what level and duration of civilian suffering is acceptable in implementing a form of coercion which is being ostensibly used as a substitute for armed force. How is this to be measured? In the number of deaths in excess of normal peacetime levels, or in the less easily measurable long-term costs to the society?

The number of deaths which have occurred as a result of the embargo has certainly exceeded those which resulted from military action in 1991.[160] The experience of Iraq calls into question how far a prolonged economic embargo can be considered more 'humane' than a conventional war.

Some criteria for examining the impact of sanctions on a target society have been suggested. A professor of law, Lori Fisler Damrosch, uses two absolute criteria: first, 'a programme of economic sanctions should not diminish the standard of living of a significant segment of society below subsistence level'; second, 'a program of sanctions should target those in whom a change of behaviour is sought, and should either diminish their capacity to continue the wrongful behaviour or penalise them so that they are induced to desist from the wrongful behaviour'.

A third, relative, criterion is added: 'to the maximum feasible extent, a program of economic sanctions should be designed and implemented so as to avoid enriching the perpetrators of wrongdoing at the expense of their victims'.

However, in the case of Iraq, Damrosch herself regards the continuation of sanctions as 'the least bad alternative in moral terms...' In her view, 'Conflict containment is... a hierarchically superior value' when the alternative is the remilitarisation of Iraq.[161]

Under Damrosch's first criterion, the moment when a 'significant' number of people had fallen below 'subsistence level' would have to be decided by the international community. Close monitoring by independent observers would be needed in order to decide when such a point had been reached. As already noted, both the process of monitoring and the baseline from which social and economic decline would be measured could pose problems when political and humanitarian motives are in conflict.[162] In the Iraqi case, the UN's institutional weakness in monitoring the effects of sanctions has yet to be addressed effectively.[163]

The Iraqi embargo also fails on Damrosch's second and third criteria. It is now widely accepted that Iraqi society has been seriously damaged by the embargo and that its leadership, supposedly the target of sanctions, has suffered least, despite refusals to comply with various demands imposed by the Security Council. Some of the 'perpetrators of wrongdoing' have certainly enriched themselves with impunity.

The argument for the 'superior value' of retaining sanctions regardless of humanitarian criteria can easily shade into a form of economic warfare. Sanctions, if maintained over a long period, can undermine the overall capacity of the economy, both in terms of its production capacity and of skill levels, scientific and technical expertise and general education. Iraq's long-term capacity to threaten its neighbours, or to be a major power in the region, might then be reduced. Yet even from the perspective of *realpolitik*, this approach may prove to be short-sighted. It takes little account of the internal political forces which may develop as a result of prolonged isolation, economic decline and manipulation by a regime determined to survive at all costs.

It could be argued that the oil-for-food resolutions were a means of avoiding this economic warfare approach, while still retaining sanctions. In the Iraqi case, this formula was made possible by the fact that the Iraqi economy depended on a single high-value export commodity. However, the very mixed motives behind these proposals, combined with the weak commitment of the international community to implementation and monitoring of humanitarian programmes in Iraq, arguably undermine their credibility as an effective instrument for relieving civilian suffering.

In 1997, the UN Human Rights Committee issued a comment on the relationship between economic sanctions and respect for economic, social and cultural rights. It emphasised that, whatever the circumstances, economic sanctions should always take full account of the provisions of the International Covenant on Economic Social and Cultural Rights and those provisions of the UN Charter relating to human rights (Articles 1, 55 and 56). It also stresses that 'The imposition of sanctions does not in any way nullify or diminish the relevant obligations of the state party. As in other comparable situations, those obligations assume greater practical import in times of particular hardship.'[164]

The leading members of the international community, while not ignoring the humanitarian needs created by sanctions, have frequently put their own strategic or tactical concerns above those of ensuring the welfare of the Iraqi population.

There is no denying that this is a particularly intractable case. Even those who are critical of the hard-line approach to sanctions have concerns about what would happen if the embargo were lifted unconditionally. The Iraq sanctions thus have raised in a very stark form the tensions between national policy goals based on regional strategic interests and a multilateral consensus on humane alternatives to war.

NOTES ON CHAPTER 2

1   The first of a series of Security Council resolutions establishing the Rhodesian embargo was Resolution 232 of 12 December 1966. The only other instance of mandatory UN sanctions at that time was the arms embargo on South Africa, Resolution 418, imposed in 4 November 1977, but this did not cover other economic activities.

2   The original draft of Resolution 661 had used the even more restrictive formula 'in special humanitarian circumstances', copying the Rhodesia resolution UNSCR 253. It was modified after protests from some Security Council members, though the US, using

its naval forces in the Gulf, unilaterally stopped vessels carrying food for Iraq until mid-September 1990 (Provost [1992], pp 578–581).

3   Bethlehem (1991), vol. I, p xxxv.
4   Sur (1992), p 24.
5   Conlon (1995), p 634.
6   Sur (1992), p 56.
7   Conlon (1995), p 652.
8   Dr Phebe Marr in 'Symposium on dual containment' (1994), pp 17–18.
9   Zieck (1997), p 213–214.
10   Ambassador Peter Hohenfellner, Chairman of the Iraq Sanctions Committee 1991–2, interview in *World Chronicle*, 20 May 1992, p 3.
11   Rouleau (1995), p 68.
12   Among the politicians were Claude Cheysson, Jean Pierre Chévènement and, on the far right, Jean Marie Le Pen.
13   Ploquin and Lamchichi (1997), p 11.
14   Elf Aquitaine was said to have initiated talks with the Iraqi authorities on the development of the Majnun field in May 1991 (*Middle East Economic Survey*, 31 March 1997, 'Award of Iraq's West Qurna Oilfield Development Contract to Russian Group Could Create Precedent for Similar Deals with Other Foreign Firms'). According to its President, Total's office in Baghdad never actually closed down, even during the 1991 war (Chatelus [1997], p 45).
15   See, for example, the argument of a French commentator, Michel Chatelus, *ibid.*; Eric Rouleau, interview with the author, 21 October 1997.
16   *Middle East Economic Survey*, 31 March 1997, *op. cit.* There was considerable resentment among European companies that US companies scooped up the lions' share of Kuwait reconstruction and privatisation deals after the war, and they saw no reason not to get in line for the profits that eventually might be on offer in Iraq. For an account of how the US cornered Kuwait contracts see Seymour M. Hersch, 'The Spoils of the Gulf War', *New Yorker*, 6 September 1993, pp 70–81.
17   For example, *New York Times*, 21 May 1991, 'Bush Links End of Trading Ban to Hussein Exit'. During discussions on Resolution 687, Britain's UN Ambassador, Sir David Hannay also took this line (see Chapter 1, p 20).
18   David L. Mack, Deputy Assistant Secretary of State for the Eastern Arab States and Iran, May 1990–1993, interview with the author, 12 May 1997. Another dissenting view, expressed during the Gulf War, came from James A. Placke, former Deputy Assistant Secretary of State for Near Eastern Affairs (*Washington Post*, 24 February 1991, 'Iraq after the Crisis').
19   Investigations into these dealings with Iraq had been ongoing since 1990 under the auspices of the House of Representatives Committee on Housing, Banking, Finance and Urban Affairs, and the House Energy and Commerce Committee.
20   Brzezinski and Scowcroft (1997), p 5.
21   Robert H. Pelletreau, Assistant Secretary of State for Near Eastern Affairs, 1994–6, telephone interview with the author, 11 June 1997.
22   *Middle East International*, 25 August 1995, 'Dual Containment: origins, aims and limits'.
23   Symposium on Dual Containment (1994), pp 2, 3. See also Anthony Lake (1994) (Assistant to the President for National Security Affairs).
24   Some State Department officials were always uneasy with this formulation. Edward P. Djerejian, Assistant Secretary of State for Near Eastern and South Asian Affairs, for example, avoided its use when describing administration policy on Iran and Iraq to a Congressional hearing (US Congress, House of Representatives, Committee on Foreign Affairs, Developments in the Middle East, October 1993: Hearing before the Subcommittee on Europe and the Middle East of the Committee on Foreign Affairs, 103rd Congress, 1st session, October 21 1993, p 37). Pelletreau said he had never liked

the term dual containment, which is open to misinterpretation. 'It is not duplicated but two containment strategies to meet different threats' (interview *op. cit.*). Some criticisms of the policy from senior members of previous administrations, including Richard W. Murphy, Zbigniew Brzezinski and Brent Scowcroft, were aired in a publication from the Council on Foreign Relations (Zbigniew Brzezinski and Brent Scowcroft [1997]). For a discussion on US policy towards Iran reflecting various views, see 'Symposium: US Policy toward Iran' (1995). For an argument in favour of the 'containment' of Iran, see Clawson (1993).

25   Charles Tripp (1995), p 137.

26   David L. Mack, interview, *op. cit.* James Baker III in his memoirs reported the same view: 'All our Arab coalition partners believed that Saddam would be ousted by a coup within six to eight months' (Baker [1995], pp 441–2).

27   Statement by Edward P. Djerejian, Assistant Secretary, Bureau of Near Eastern and South Asian Affairs, Department of State, US Congress, House of Representatives, Committee on Foreign Affairs, Developments in the Middle East, November 1991: Hearing before the Subcommittee on Europe and the Middle East of the Committee on Foreign Affairs, 102nd Congress, 1st session, November 20, 1991, p 15.

28   The membership of the INC has fluctuated since 1992. Initially it included the KDP and PUK, smaller Islamist groups, some Arab nationalist groups (with the exception of those based in Syria), as well as a number of unaffiliated individuals living outside Iraq. The Salahadin conference was also attended by some Communists (excluding the Da'wa Party [which withdrew again in 1993] and SCIRI, whose subsequent relationship with the INC leadership has frequently seemed uneasy. Damascus-based nationalists and some Communists based in Syria or in Europe have remained outside the INC. Its president since 1992 has been Dr Ahmad Chalabi.

29   The CIA's mandate to act against the Iraqi regime was said to have been authorised by President Bush in May 1991 (ABC News, 'Peter Jennings Reporting: Unfinished Business – The CIA and Saddam Hussein', 26 June 1997). However, Associated Press, quoting 'intelligence sources', reported that Bush had signed secret orders authorising the CIA to aid rebel factions inside Iraq in January 1991. *New York Times*, 4 April 1991, 'Baker aide talks with Iraqi dissidents in the US'.

30   *Washington Post*, 26 June 1997, 'How the CIA's Secret War on Saddam Collapsed'. This view was supported by some active members of Washington think tanks, including the Washington Near East Policy Institute.

31   Paul Wolfowitz (Under Secretary for Policy, Department of Defence, 1991–2), interview with the author, July 1997.

32   Ben Meir (1996), p 66.

33   Secretary of State Madeleine K. Albright, Remarks at Georgetown University, Washington DC, 26 March 1997. Some senior officials were said to have wanted the former Secretary of State, Warren Christopher, to deliver such a speech two or three years earlier, but it was not regarded as appropriate at that time, when the view that 'Saddam is in a box – if it ain't broke, don't fix it' still prevailed. Furthermore, Christopher personally took a low profile on Iraq, while Madeleine Albright, as former US Ambassador at the UN, had taken a strong interest.

34   Riedel (1997), p 130.

35   *Guardian*, 21 October 1998, 'Pentagon balks at "idiotic" law urging Bay of Pigs-type invasion of Iraq'.

36   Frank Ricciardone (*Washington Post*, 22 January 1999, 'US Names New Representative For Iraqi Anti-Saddam Groups').

37   *New Yorker*, 1 November 1993, 'A Case Not Closed', pp 80–92. Discussing evidence of an Iraqi plot to assassinate former President George Bush during a visit to Kuwait in April 1993, Seymour Hersh described some of the types of smuggling alleged to take place over the 'surprisingly open' Iraq-Kuwait border.

38   Mohamedi (1997), p 4.
39   Dowty (1994), p 191.
40   Assistant Secretary of State Edward Djerejian said in 1993 that he would recommend the release of $50 million in military aid, held up in 1992, to support Jordan's positive role in the Middle East peace negotiations and because Jordan had recently been implementing sanctions more strictly (*Middle East Economic Digest*, 19 March 1993).
41   Statement by Robert H. Pelletreau, Assistant Secretary of State for Near Eastern Affairs, before the House Appropriations Committee, Subcommittee on Foreign Operations, Washington DC, March 6, 1996; *Independent*, 8 April 1996, 'US to Monitor Iraq From Base in Jordan'.
42   Statement of Julius Kroll, Kroll Associates, Congress, House of Representatives, Committee on Foreign Affairs, Iraq's Nuclear Weapons Capability and IAEA Inspections in Iraq: Joint Hearing of the Subcommittees on Europe and the Middle East and International Security, International Organisations and Human Rights of the Committee on Foreign Affairs, 103rd Congress, 1st session June 29, 1993, pp 51–52.
43   On 25 August 1994 Lloyd's Register of London began its onshore inspections of goods passing through Aqaba in Jordan bound for Iraq. At the same time the inspection of ships at sea, previously undertaken by US naval ships of the Maritime Interception Force (MIF), ceased, though its interceptions in the Gulf and Arabian Sea continued (*Middle East Economic Survey*, 29 August 1994, 'Lloyds Starts Cargo Inspection at Aqaba; Naval Blockade Lifted').
44   Dr Paul Conlon, formerly deputy secretary to the Iraq Sanctions Committee, interview with the author, 29 September 1997; *Middle East Economic Survey*, 29 June 1992, 'Jordan Rejects UN Inspectors'. However, smuggling evidently did persist on a considerable scale. In a speech to Jordanian Desert Forces and Border Guards reported on Jordanian TV on 9 January 1997, King Hussein described various types of smuggling: from sheep bought cheaply in Iraq, reared and sold on for a profit in Jordan, to drugs. 'There are also weapons and explosives involved.' He added that smugglers used advanced equipment: bullet-proof vests, night vision equipment and satellite communications (BBC Summary of World Broadcasts, 11 January 1997, 'King Hussein Promises Arms, Equipment to Stop Smuggling to Iraq', p 11).
45   Another anomaly in the operation of sanctions related to Sudan. The Iraqi Government has maintained good relations with Sudan, whose commercial traders have been a source of imports. The first commercial flight direct to Iraq since the 1991 war landed at Habbaniya airport on 22 October 1992 from Khartoum bringing 35 tonnes of fresh meat, the first consignment of an order for 20,000 tonnes of meat which Iraq had contracted with a Sudanese investment company. In 1997 Sudan Airways was still landing and taking off from Saddam International Airport in Baghdad once a week, 'clearly a violation of sanctions', according to an UNSCOM inspector (interview with Dr Koos Ooms, a Dutch member of UNSCOM, in *NRC Handelsblad*, 24 May 1997, 'VN – Onderzoeker Koos Ooms over de ontwapening van Irak').
46   Brand (1994), pp 232, 241. According to UN Statistical Yearbooks, Iraq's exports of all types of oil to Jordan were equivalent to an average of 52,362b/d in 1989, falling to 49,715 b/d in 1991 and rising again to just over 77,000b/d in 1992 and 1993 (quoted in *Middle East Economic Survey*, 11 July 1994, 'Iraq's 1993 Crude Oil and Product Exports to Jordan average 77,000B/D').
47   Dr Paul Conlon, interview, *op. cit.*
48   *Jordan Economic Monitor* (Amman), monthly newsletter published by Dr Fahed al-Fanek, February 1996, no. 2, p 5.
49   See, for example, Congress, House of Representatives, Committee on Foreign Affairs Developments in the Middle East: Hearing before the Subcommittee on Europe and the Middle East of the Committee on Foreign Affairs, 102nd Congress, 2nd session, 17 March 1992, pp 22–25. In 1994 there was a challenge to the continuation of this trade

in the House of Representatives by Congressman Lantos. He claimed that the US had been party to an agreement between the US, UK, France and Jordan to allow these oil exports to continue. It seems the UN Secretary General had not been informed and no Sanctions Committee member admitted to seeing any documentation of such an agreement (Dr Paul Conlon, interview, *op. cit.*).

50 Robins (1991), p 102. Fuller (1993) noted 'a nearly five-fold growth in trade with the Middle East from 1982 to 1987, mostly with Iran and Iraq' (p 59). By 1988, the Iraqi debt to Turkey was around $2 billion. In 1989, Iraq paid $600 million in debt service in return for the provision of new credits. But this was undermined by the Gulf crisis, after which Iraq announced that it would cease to service its foreign debt (Robins [1991], p 110).

51 *Le Monde*, 12 July 1991, 'Le Turquie a decidé de rouvrir son ambassade à Baghdad'.

52 *Washington Post*, 14 February 1992, 'Turk Warns Against Force to Oust Saddam'.

53 *Middle East Economic Survey*, 12 August 1996, 'Turkey Formally Requests Iraqi Oil Sanctions Exemption from UN'. Among the claims were annual losses of $400 million incurred by Botas, the state pipeline operator, and deprivation of potential exports to Iraq worth $2 billion annually.

54 The issue was raised in October 1993, when Prime Minister Tansu Ciller visited Washington, and again in mid-1996, soon after Iraq accepted Resolution 986. This time Turkey requested permission to import Iraqi oil outside the terms of both Resolution 687 and 986. Among the reasons for not agreeing to this was that revenue from sales outside the UN escrow account would be lost to the UN Compensation Commission (which receives 30 percent of the total), a concern already voiced in relation to Jordan (*Middle East Economic Survey*, 25 October 1993, 'Turkey Wants to Import Iraqi Oil for Domestic Use as in Jordan'; *Middle East Economic Survey*, 5 August 1996, 'Turkey to Ask UN for Special Permission to Buy Iraqi Oil').

55 Robert Pelletreau, interview, *op. cit.*

56 Brilliant *et al* (1995), p 32. For details of the trade in mid-1992, see *Guardian*, 3 August 1992 'UN loophole lets through Iraqi oil'.

57 *New York Times*, 13 September 1992, 'Where Friends of Money are the Best of Enemies'.

58 *Gulf Newsletter* (Refugee Council, London), November/December 1994, no. 11, p 4; *Middle East Economic Survey*, 29 September 1997, 'US Accuses Iraq of Smuggling Over 150,000T/M of Gas Oil to Gulf; Turkey Regulates Contraband Iraqi Petroleum Products'. In August 1997, the Turkish National Security Council recommended that the Government should tighten up on the illegal fuel trade, which continued via Habur. In 1998, further protests at Iraq's illicit oil trade appeared in the American press, for example, Reuters, 19 June 1998, 'US Reportedly Ignores Iraqi Oil-Smuggling – *New York Times*'.

59 *Middle East Economic Survey*, 12 September 1994, 'Iraqi-Turkish Talks on Pipeline Flushing Suspended Because of Differences on Distribution of Supplies to Kurdish Areas'.

60 *Middle East Economic Survey*, 13 January 1997, 'Text of Iraq-Turkey Gas Export Agreement'.

61 In the midst of a major Turkish incursion into northern Iraq in May 1997, the Iraqi representative at the UN, Nizar Hamdun, emphasised that disputes over this operation would not interfere with other aspects of bilateral relations (BBC Summary of World Broadcasts, 'UN Envoy Hamdun on Attempts to Normalise Ties with Syria, Turkish Moves' quoting Radio Monte Carlo – Middle East, Paris, 20 May 1997).

62 *Washington Post*, 16 April 1992, 'Iran Pushes Postwar Reconstruction While Seeking Stable Ties with Iraq', citing an interview with Tariq Aziz in a Jordanian newspaper.

63 In mid-1996, an MIF spokesman said since the beginning of the year it had been 'diverting' one vessel from Iraq every 3–4 days. Characteristic cargoes were diesel fuel, dates and fertiliser (*Financial Times*, '"Steady Flow" of Iraq Smugglers'). In September

1997, President Clinton, in his periodic report to Congress on Iraq's compliance with UNSC resolutions, reiterated charges of Iranian complicity in allowing the smugglers to use its territorial waters, alleging that the smuggling of Iraq gas oil from the Shatt al-Arab waterway 'continues to increase at an alarming rate'. *Middle East Economic Survey*, 29 September 1997, 'US Accuses Iraq of Smuggling Over 150,000T/M of Gas Oil to Gulf; Turkey Regulates Contraband Iraqi Petroleum Products'. The article confirmed the rise in the trade, adding that most of the products were destined for UAE ports, with some going as far as Pakistan and India.

64   The White House, Office of the Press Secretary, Text of a Letter from the President to Congress: Status of Efforts to Obtain Iraq's Compliance with UN Resolutions, Washington DC, Report to Congress, June 24, 1998 (http://www.state.gov).

65   In original conception, the Iraq Sanctions Committee was to take a role in monitoring in the implementation of the economic embargo, but its main task was envisaged as the long-term monitoring of disarmament provisions. Because this stage had yet to be reached by 1998, a major part of committee's work has in fact been assessing applications for humanitarian waivers.

66   The changes included periodically issuing press releases, providing an oral briefing after committee meetings and making available to members lists of applications under the 'no objection' procedure (Report of the Security Council Committee established by Resolution 661 [1990] concerning the situation between Iraq and Kuwait. S/1996/700 26 August 1996, hereafter United Nations [1996ii]).

67   Report on humanitarian needs in Iraq in the immediate post-crisis environment by a mission to the area led by Under Secretary General for Administration and Management, 10–17 March 1991, hereafter United Nations (1991i).

68   Conlon (1995), pp 638, 661.

69   Ambassador Peter Hohenfellner, Chairman of the Iraq Sanctions Committee 1991–2, interview in *World Chronicle*, 20 May 1992, p 9.

70   Conlon (1997), p 260; Ambassador Peter Hohenfellner, *op. cit.*, pp 5–7; United Nations (1996ii), p 11. This decision followed a statement from the President of the Security Council on 20 December 1991 (S/23305) calling for the establishment of such a list of items, to be transferred from 'no-objection' to 'simple notification' status.

71   See, for example, a State Department written reply to the House of Representatives, Committee on Foreign Affairs, Developments in the Middle East, October 1993: Hearing before the Subcommittee on Europe and the Middle East of the Committee on Foreign Affairs, October 21, 1993: 'Our policy toward the local administration of northern Iraq is part of our overall policy toward Iraq, and includes the maintenance of sanctions. This policy is not intended to denigrate the aspirations of the people of northern Iraq to live in a democratic Iraq. However, we cannot put ourselves in the position of favoring selective enforcement of sanctions in the north, which could jeopardise the sanctions regime' (p 68). Fred Cuny claimed in 1995, 'The Turks have done the most to prevent the Kurds from being granted an exemption from sanctions...' (Cuny [1995], p 21.

72   New Zealand Ministry of Foreign Affairs and Trade (1995), p 36.

73   Conlon (1997), pp 259, 278–9; von Braunmuhl and Kulessa (1995), p 48.

74   Conlon (1997), pp 278–9.

75   For example, letters from the Permanent Representative of Iraq to the United Nations addressed to the Secretary General, 22 July 1992 (S/24338), and from the Minister of Foreign Affairs of Iraq addressed to the Secretary General, 5 July 1993 (S/26204), challenging a number of refusals of orders on the grounds that they were inputs to industry.

76   Conlon (1997), p 261. According to a 1996 report from the UN Sanctions Committee, 2794 applications, amounting to 35 percent of the total of 8004 applications, were approved by the Committee in 1995 (United Nations [1996ii], p 12).

77   Conlon (1997), p 261. In 1994, for example, the UK was among the top five legitimate trade partners with Iraq, along with Jordan, the Republic of Korea, Turkey and Finland.

However, in late 1993 complaints of dubious companies making applications from the UK for waivers led the DTI to halt all applications under the humanitarian waiver, and institute a new procedure for applicants. One reason for the action was said to be the discovery of fraudulent changes to licence applications. Nonetheless, in 1995 the DTI continued to encourage legitimate trade under sanctions. It hosted a conference on 5 April 1995 'to increase awareness of export controls and assist companies in managing their business in relation to the controls'. Once Resolution 986 came into operation, the DTI loosened the licence requirements on companies dealing with Iraq, and actively encouraged companies to seek contracts for goods allowed under the resolution (*Financial Times*, 30 January 1997, 'Companies Urged to Bid for $1.3bn Iraq Orders').

78   'The extended US sanctions have generally had the same scope as the international sanctions provisions, although the Sanctions Committee of the UN Security Council has been somewhat less restrictive in permitting "humanitarian" shipments to Iraq than the United States'. The US trade embargo also applies to exports from third countries to Iraq of US-origin products, technologies and services, and to foreign exports of products and technologies with significant (greater than 10 percent) US-origin content (John Ellicott [1996], pp 558–9). In a rare exception, a US subcontractor was allowed to provide piping to a Swedish firm doing water and sanitation work in Basra (Dr Paul Conlon, interview with the author, 29 September 1997).

79   *Financial Times*, 25 November 1991, 'UK To Move on Exporting Food to Iraq'. The British Foreign Office insisted that this was a one-off deal. In a written answer on 9 July 1992 to a parliamentary question in the House of Lords, the Government gave the total of Iraqi assets held by UK banks as £580 million (Hansard, House of Lords, Fifth Series, vol. 538, col. WA 79).

80   'Iraq has a request pending before the Sanctions Committee to be allowed to sell $1.5 billion of oil in order to pay for food, medicine and other humanitarian items. The Sanctions Committee had deferred consideration of that request pending a full disclosure from Iraq of its present foreign exchange holdings and other relevant financial information' (Prepared Statement of John Bolton, Assistant Secretary for International Organisation Affairs, Department of State to Congress, House of Representatives, Committee on Foreign Affairs, UN Role in the Persian Gulf and Iraqi Compliance with UN Resolutions: Hearing before the Subcommittees on Europe and the Middle East and on Human Rights and International Organisations of the Committee on Foreign Affairs, July 18, 1991, p 72).

81   Report to the Secretary-General on Humanitarian Needs in Iraq by a Mission led by Sadruddin Aga Khan, Executive Delegate of the Secretary-General 15 July 1991 (hereafter United Nations [1991ii]). The CIA's estimate was said to be at least $30 billion (*New York Times*, 3 June 1991, 'Iraq Said to Face Many Years of Effort to Rebuild Its Economy').

82   United Nations (1991ii), p 8.

83   Fine (1992), p 36.

84   A further point of dispute had been the proportion of Iraq's oil revenues which should go to the UN Compensation Fund once oil sales resumed. On 20 May, UNSC Resolution 692 (passed 14-0 with Cuba abstaining) established the UN Compensation Fund to be financed from Iraq's oil exports. The resolution authorised a governing body consisting of all 15 Security Council members which would decide how much would be paid annually. The US had initially pressed for 40–50 percent of revenues to be taken annually for this purpose, a view supported by Kuwait. The figure finally decided upon was 30 percent. This decision determined the proportion of funds from limited oil sales via the UN escrow account which would go to the Compensation Fund.

85   Sadruddin's suggestion that oil sales should be used for humanitarian needs had, in fact, paralleled a proposal from the UN Secretary General that the sale of Iraqi oil could be used to meet the expenses of UNSCOM. The Security Council had already determined

that Iraq should pay for its activities under Resolution 699 of 17 June 1991. See 'Report of the Secretary General recommending the sale of some Iraqi petroleum and petroleum products to finance the destruction or removal of weapons systems stipulated in Security Council Resolution 687' (1991), S/22792, 15 July 1991. He had proposed that this should be done by lifting the sanctions imposed under Resolution 661 'for a limited period and under clearly defined conditions' (United Nations [1996i] Document 65).

86 S/PV.3004, 15 August 1991 (Weller [1993], pp 147–162, passim.)

87 Report of the Secretary General recommending procedures for the sale of Iraqi oil and transmitting estimates of humanitarian requirements in Iraq, S/23006, 4 September 1991 (United Nations [1996i], Document 78). The larger sum was supported by some aid agencies: for example, see Oxfam UK's Overseas Director, David Bryer, writing in the *Observer*, 15 September 1991, 'A Nation That Can Pay For Its Own Aid'.

88 Fine (1992), p 39.

89 *Independent*, 24 July 1991, 'US and Britain edge away from ban on Iraqi oil'.

90 *Guardian*, 24 July 1991, 'UN to start easing sanctions on Iraq'.

91 Conlon (1995), pp 349–50 and note 80. Thomas Pickering, the US Ambassador to the UN, in his remarks to the Security Council on Resolution 706 (16 August 1991), stressed the importance of careful monitoring 'to deter diversion of food and other humanitarian assistance to privileged sections of Iraqi society or the misuse of this assistance at the expense of those most in need'. The French representative noted the short-term nature of the resolution and the absence of trust in the Government of Iraq, which had been trying to circumvent UN resolutions by refusing UN representatives access to territory and not allowing UNHCR to set up humanitarian centres as required (S/PV.3004, 15 August 1991 in Weller [1993], pp 157–158).

92 *Middle East Economic Survey*, 16 November 1992, 'Iraqi Oil Exports and the New US Administration'.

93 Report of the Secretary General recommending procedures for the sale of Iraqi oil and transmitting estimates of humanitarian requirements in Iraq S/23006, 4 September 1991, paragraph 58 (United Nations [1996i], Document 78).

94 *Middle East Economic Survey*, 16 November 1992, *op cit*.

95 *Guardian*, 14 January 1992, 'Britain endorses United Nations Compromise on oil sales by Iraq'.

96 *Middle East Economic Survey*, 9 March 1992, 'UN Security Council Debates Use of Confiscated Iraqi Financial Assets Abroad'. The article added that there was no unanimity even within the US administration on the subject. The Treasury Department considered that such a move would entail a great deal of litigation worldwide, though the State Department favoured this option as a way of tightening sanctions.

97 Iraqi Foreign Minister Muhammad al-Sahhaf proposed to non-aligned members of the Security Council an alternative way to finance UN operations: allowing Iraq to sell $4 billion of oil, a proportion of which would go to the Compensation Commission and humanitarian activities, 5 percent to be donated for relief supplies to Bosnia and Somalia (Inter Press Service, 2 October 1992, 'United Nations: Part of Iraq's Frozen Assets Appropriated'; *New York Times*, 29 September 1992, 'Iraq, assets at risk, asks to reopen oil talks').

98 Conlon (1995), p 639. The resolution divided Iraq's frozen assets into two main categories, subject to different requirements. First, it called for the transfer to a UN escrow account (as proposed for Resolutions 706 and 712) of the proceeds of oil sales frozen on 6 August 1990, and on which there were no prior legal claims; and the proceeds of sale of stocks of Iraqi oil still held by other states. Second, states were invited to 'contribute funds from other sources to the escrow account as soon as possible' (paragraph 3). These would not incur the deductions for the Compensation Fund which would be applied to oil-related assets. Finally it stipulated that any Iraqi assets released to meet 'essential civilian needs' would henceforth have to be channelled

through the UN escrow account. They could not be paid direct to exporters, as had happened since 1991.

99 A *note verbale* from the US Government to the Security Council (S/24902) of 30 November 1992 indicated that the US held a total of $637.4 million subject to the provisions of Resolution 778. The US was thought to hold some $1.2 billion in Iraqi frozen assets, including oil delivered by Iraq but not paid for when sanctions were imposed (*Middle East Economic Survey*, 9 March 1992, 'UN Security Council Debates Use of Confiscated Iraqi Financial Assets Abroad'). As of January 1996, $421.74 million had been deposited in the escrow account, including the $200 million from the US. Only the US put any of its oil-related frozen assets into the escrow account. Other countries holding Iraqi oil stocks did not put their proceeds into the escrow account, though Saudi Arabia, Kuwait and Japan provided voluntary contributions.

100 Conlon (1995), pp 638–9. On 29 June 1993 the UN Legal Counsel was asked to lead a new round of talks with Iraq. After a meeting between Deputy Prime Minister Tariq Aziz and the UN Secretary General on 21 June, talks began on 7 July. The disagreements seemed again to centre on the Mina al-Bakr question. The Secretary General, according to one UN source, 'kept these talks very much under his hand' and very much wanted to achieve agreement. However, a further meeting with Aziz in Geneva on 1 September seems to have brought Boutros-Ghali's efforts to a fruitless end.

101 Fine (1992), p 39; interview with the author, 25 October 1996.

102 Dr Phebe Marr, Symposium on Dual Containment (1994), p 17.

103 The last presidential statement from the Security Council following the regular 60-day reviews of the sanctions regime was delivered on 18 January 1994.

104 In the discussions on framing Resolution 687, the US Ambassador to the UN said the conditions for the removal of the economic embargo must be 'an incentive to implement fully the resolution as soon as possible' (S/PV.2981, p 88, quoted in Sur [1992], p 42). At a congressional hearing in 1994, Laurie Mylroie noted: 'the way the resolution was written it linked that sale of oil to the weapons of mass destruction because the Bush administration thought we will give Saddam or the guy who will follow him the incentive to comply with what the most important parts of the resolution were judged at that time to be. I do not think anyone imagined that Saddam was going to continue and continue in this very defiant style' (Congress, House of Representatives, Committee on Foreign Affairs, US Policy toward Iraq 3 Years after the Gulf War: Hearing before the Subcommittee on Europe and the Middle East of the Committee on Foreign Affairs, February 23, 1994, p 20).

105 In June 1991, however, the European Council of Ministers made a declaration on the situation in Iraq which appeared to support the inclusion of Resolution 688 in considerations over lifting sanctions. 'The European Council considers that as long as the Iraqi authorities fail to comply with their obligations fully and unequivocally to observe all the provisions of Resolutions 687 and 688 the Security Council should not envisage lifting the sanctions imposed on Iraq' (European Commission, *Bulletin of the European Union*, Brussels, EC 6-1991, p 16, annex 3).

106 In his report on Iraqi compliance with Security Council resolutions in January 1992, the UN Secretary General did not include Resolution 688 under 'relevant resolutions which place mandatory obligations on Iraq', but after a request made in informal Security Council consultations, information on Iraq's compliance with Resolution 688 was included in his second report in March 1992 (Johnstone [1994], p 37). The practice of including material relating to Resolution 688 in papers for the 60-day review of 'all relevant resolutions' eventually became routine, despite resistance from within the UN system.

107 Cook (1995), p 92. In 1998, Bill Richardson, the US Ambassador to the UN, was still insisting that Iraq had to comply with 'all relevant resolutions', including those which deal with human rights, Kuwait property and Kuwaiti prisoners of war, although he

stressed the particular importance of the POW issue (press briefing, Palais de Nations, Geneva, 26 March 1998).

108 Hashim (1996), p 11.
109 See, for example, the discussion by a panel of 'specialists', Congress, House of Representatives, Committee on Foreign Affairs, US Policy toward Iraq 3 Years after the Gulf War: Hearing before the Subcommittee on Europe and the Middle East of the Committee on Foreign Affairs, February 23, 1994, pp 16–22.
110 See, for example, *New York Times*, 18 February 1994, 'Incentives Can Work for Iraq, Too'.
111 Dr Paul Conlon, interview, *op. cit.*
112 By mid-1997, Spain and Italy had also reopened their Baghdad embassies.
113 Sergei Lavrov, Russian Ambassador to the United Nations, quoted in *Middle East Economic Survey*, 26 December 1994/2 January 1995, 'Russia Wants Iraqi Oil Sanctions to be Lifted Next Spring'.
114 *Middle East International*, 3 March 1995, 'Show-down at the UN?'.
115 Foreign Broadcast Information Service, 'Draft UN Initiative to Lift Iraqi Oil Embargo', quoting ITAR-TASS Moscow (in English), 31 March 1995.
116 Statement by Robert H. Pelletreau, Assistant Secretary for Near Eastern Affairs, US Congress, House of Representatives, Committee on International Affairs, Developments in the Middle East: Hearing before the Committee on International Relations, 104th Congress 2nd session, 12 June 1996.
117 US Information Agency, 'US Looking Forward to Iraqi Oil Sale Agreement', 16 April 1996.
118 Robert H. Pelletreau, interview *op. cit.*
119 BBC Summary of World Broadcasts, 17 April 1995, 'RCC and Ba'th Party Say New UN Resolution More Dangerous than Previous Ones', quoting INA news agency, Baghdad, 14 April 1995.
120 *Middle East Economic Survey*, 2 October 1995, 'Security Council Asks Iraq to Reconsider its Rejection of UN Plan for Limited Oil Sales'.
121 Thomas Pickering, Under Secretary for Political Affairs, Testimony before the Senate Foreign Relations Committee, Washington DC, May 21 1998.
122 Eighth Report of the Executive Chairman of UNSCOM, 15 December 1994, (United Nations [1996i], Document 200).
123 Iraqi Broadcasting Corporation, 'Open Letter from General Wafiq al-Sammara'i in Salahadin to Rolf Ekeus, Head of the Disarmament Committee, in Baghdad', 21 February 1995.
124 *New York Times*, 15 August 1998, 'An Iraqi Defector Warns of Iraq's Nuclear Weapons Research'.
125 United Nations, 'United Nations Special Commission/Mandate' (http://www.un.org/Depts/unscom/unscom.htm).
126 Anthony Cordesman in Symposium on Dual Containment (1994), p 11.
127 Bailey (1995), pp 107–9.
128 Jacovy (1992), p 78.
129 Interview with Dr Koos Ooms, a Dutch member of UNSCOM, in *NRC Handelsblad*, 24 May 1997, *op. cit.*
130 *New Yorker*, 9 November 1998, 'Scott Ritter's Private War'; *Le Monde*, 30 September 1998, 'Israël a contribué au désarmement de l'Irak', quoting *Ha'aretz* (Tel Aviv), 28 September 1998.
131 Gresh (1998).
132 Eric Rouleau, interview, *op. cit.*
133 UN Security Council, Eighth Report of the Secretary-General on the Status of the Implementation of the Plan for the Ongoing Monitoring and Verification of Iraq's Compliance with Relevant Parts of Section C of Security Council Resolution 687 (1991). S/1995/864, 11 October 1995 (United Nations [1996i] Document 214).

134 Statement by the President of the Security Council, 'Implementation of Security Council Resolution 986 (1995) and the Memorandum of Understanding', 14 May 1998. S/PRST/1998/11.

135 UNSC Resolution 1060 (12 June 1996) and Resolution 1115 (21 June 1997) called for full access for UNSCOM. The latter also suspended the 60-day reviews of sanctions until UNSCOM's October 1997 report.

136 Report submitted by the Executive Chairman of the Special Commission established by the Secretary General pursuant to paragraph 9 (b) (i) of Security Council resolution 687 of 3 April 1991, para. 125.

137 UN Security Council Resolution 1134 (23 October 1997).

138 UN Security Council Resolution 1154 (2 March 1998).

139 *Washington Post*, 31 October 1998, 'UN Council Agrees on Nature of Iraq Review'.

140 *New Yorker, op. cit.*; *Washington Post*, 27 August 1998, 'US has been blocking UNSCOM searches since last November'.

141 Agence France Presse, 13 January 1999, 'France presents Iraq proposals to UN "big five"'.

142 The December bombing raids were ostensibly designed to control Iraq's weapons of mass destruction, but by January, William Arkin, an influential defence commentator, was suggesting that the goal was primarily to target Saddam Hussein's internal security apparatus using the intelligence gathered through UNSCOM. He noted that almost half the targets of Operation Desert Fox were focused on the regime rather than WMD targets (*Washington Post*, 17 January 1999, 'The Difference Was in the Details').

143 Department of Defense, Transcript of Background Briefing by senior Defense officials, 14 November 1997 'Iraq's Chemical and Biological Weapons Capability' (http://www.defenselink.mil/news/Nov1997/x11171997_x114iraq.html).

144 Channel 4 Television (London), 'Dispatches Special: Saddam's Secret Timebomb', 23 February 1998, Roberts and Wykeham Films.

145 One of the most definitive studies is found in Hufbauer, Schott and Elliott (1990).

146 Findings of a conference on 'Economic Sanctions and International Relations' at the University of Notre Dame in April 1993, quoted in Dowty (1994), p 190.

147 United Nations (1996ii), pp 23–26.

148 Maritime inspections were not considered to fall within the Sanctions Committee's mandate. Therefore information on infringements discovered by the multilateral Maritime Interception Force (MIF) at Aqaba port appears not to have been routinely passed to the Committee. In recent years, communications between the MIF and the committee on surveillance in the Gulf seem to have improved, and Lloyds Register, which now runs on-shore monitoring at Aqaba port, undertook to provide regular reports to the Committee.

149 Information from a UN official.

150 Weiss *et al* (1997), p 21.

151 The provisional summary records of the first 25 meetings of the Sanctions Committee (9 August–23 January 1992) were published, although the proceedings were intended to be confidential and no further record has been published (Bethlehem [1991], vol. II, pp 773–976).

152 Provost (1992), p 585.

153 Bethlehem (1991), vol. II, Sanctions Committee meetings 2, 5, 6 and 9, 19, 24.

154 Under Secretary General Martti Ahtisaari, the UN official who went to Iraq soon after its defeat in the war, was not given permission to visit Kirkuk, or cities in the south of the country (United Nations [1991i]).

155 United Nations (1996ii), p 12. The commercialisation of humanitarian waivers added to the confusion because there were increasingly large discrepancies between the scale of applications to the Sanctions Committee and orders actually fulfilled. The evidence suggests that as the number of applications increased over the years, the percentage

fulfilled fell – from about 50 percent in 1991/2 to approximately 10 percent of the total by 1994. Some orders were probably cancelled when funds for the purchase were not forthcoming. Other waivers were traded for use in smuggling goods not approved by the Sanctions Committee, or passed on by front companies to third parties, often in other parts of the world (Conlon [1997], p 262).

156 Minear *et al* (1992), p 22.
157 Normand (1996), p 42.
158 Conlon (1997), p 254.
159 Quoted in Dowty (1994), p 183.
160 Garfield (1999).
161 Damrosch (1993), pp 281–3, 306.
162 Patterson (1995), pp 91–2. Weiss *et al* (1997), p 39 outlines a range of proposed baselines. One suggestion was to monitor over time whether sanctions drove particular groups of people below the poverty line according to a set of social and economic indicators. Another was the much more general criteria based on international legal norms which should govern the implementation of a sanctions regime from its inception.
163 Weiss *et al* (1997), p 20.
164 General Comment no. 8 E/C.12/1997/8 quoted in United Nations Economic and Social Council, Commission on Human Rights (1998), Section IIIC (electronic copy: http://www.unhcr.ch).

CHAPTER 3

Protecting the Vulnerable?

The action taken in 1991 stretched the existing parameters of politically acceptable intervention virtually to the limit… [but] Emergency responses, however bold and far-reaching, cannot be more than temporary first aid if they are not underpinned by wider objectives. Without a commitment to such objectives, a crisis response offers only a brief respite from an endless cycle of violence and repression. It creates a dangerous illusion of security which, at best, raises expectations that will not be met and, at worst, encourages social and political change that invites even greater repression when emergency protection is withdrawn.[1]

During the refugee crisis which followed the Gulf War, coalition forces engaged in cross-border actions in northern Iraq to protect returning refugees and deliver humanitarian aid. The Security Council passed Resolution 688, asserting that Iraqi treatment of its civilian population was unacceptable. When the ground troops withdrew, a no-fly zone was maintained over northern Iraq, which, it was claimed, would protect the Kurdish population. These measures were seen as new and innovative ways of dealing with conflict and states' abuse of human rights, and linked together the issue of threats to human rights with the provision of humanitarian aid. Subsequent experience suggests that these bold steps were easier to initiate than to sustain.

Resolution 688 was adopted to deal with a crisis which was partly of the international community's making. As one international legal commentator argued, the fact that the internal strife was a consequence of the international military action placed 'responsibility of a political and humanitarian character' on the Coalition to prevent massive attacks by Iraqi forces against non-combatants belonging to particular ethnic and religious communities.[2]

The original draft was inspired by an ideology of humanitarian intervention which had a particularly strong voice in France at that time. Its protagonists argued that in the event of such severe abuses, the international community had a duty to put aside considerations of sovereignty to help the civilian population. This could also mean, according to some interpretations, that national armies could intervene when the UN itself did not have the capacity to act.[3]

The resolution apparently addressed human rights and humanitarian conditions throughout Iraq, but it singled out the Kurds 'in particular' and it was specifically intended to deal with the refugee crisis in the north. The original French draft had spelt out more clearly that the Iraqi Government should respect the rights of its citizens. It 'demanded that Iraq immediately end this repression and engage in a dialogue without exclusion on the respect of the rights and the realisation of the legitimate aspirations of all the peoples in Iraq'. This rang alarm bells with member states which were sensitive to infringements of sovereignty, and to the implicit reference to the status of minorities. It was amended to read: 'Demands that Iraq, as a contribution to removing the threat to international peace and security in the region,

---

Interpretations of Resolution 688

Legal authorities have differed on whether Resolution 688 can be understood to justify the use of force. Human rights activists, and the UN Special Rapporteur on human rights in Iraq, have argued that the resolution could and should be enforced because Iraq's human rights abuses continued to threaten international peace and security. Those who hold that Resolution 688 does not authorise the use of force argue that unlike the Council's earlier resolutions authorising the trade embargo or the armed attack against Iraq 'nothing in Resolution 688 even hints at the use of armed force to protect the civilian population of Iraq'.[4]

In practice, international law as created and interpreted through the Security Council is an approximate process. The fact that there was no direct challenge to the use of force, some argue, constitutes *de facto* international acceptance that the terms of the resolution allow for it. Essentially, as one informed source put it, by dint of political power the main coalition states (the US, UK and France) won the day and established a precedent. But if this consensus can be said to have legitimised the establishment of the no-fly zones, more recent military actions, initiated by only one or two Security Council members – namely the US and UK – have found much less support, throwing the previous consensus into doubt.

From the beginning, the UN establishment was not in favour of military action under Resolution 688. The view of UN Secretary General Perez de Cuellar was that Resolution 688 was not 'put in the framework of Chapter VII'.[5] The next Secretary General, Boutros Boutros-Ghali, was also careful to distance the UN from coalition countries which invoked Resolution 688 to justify the no-fly zones, though he did not openly reject their reasoning. In his account of UN actions in Iraq since 1991, he wrote that these coalition countries imposed the two no-fly zones 'in what they stated was an effort to enforce and monitor compliance with Resolution 688 (1991)'. Noting that Iraq rejected both the no-fly zones as interference in its internal affairs, he cites the coalition countries' assertion that 'the ceasefire agreement ending the war empowered them to impose such controls over Iraqi military flights'.[6]

immediately end this repression, and in the *same context* [italics added] expresses the hope that an open dialogue will take place to ensure that the human and political rights of all Iraqi citizens are respected'.[7] A reference to Article 2(7) in Chapter I of the UN Charter, which prohibits interference in the internal affairs of states, was also added.

The resolution would probably not have been passed at all had it included a reference to Chapter VII of the UN Charter, which makes a resolution mandatory and potentially permits the use of force to ensure compliance.[8] According to one analyst, some Security Council members wanted the resolution to be 'close to Chapter VII' while others did not. The outcome was 'a creative ambiguity' which has caused legal and conceptual complications ever since.[9]

Confusion arose almost immediately, as coalition troops moved into northern Iraq in April, two weeks after the resolution was passed. The US, UK and France considered that they were 'acting under' Resolution 688 in entering northern Iraq to create the safe haven. But since the resolution made no reference to the use of force, and the protagonists had not returned to seek endorsement for military action from the Security Council, this view was not universally accepted (see box).

The absence of any political settlement between the Iraqi Government and the Kurds, the continuation of economic sanctions and of Iraqi government repression, meant that large sections of the civilian population remained at risk. However, the emphasis had been on saving lives and protecting refugees from immediate harm. Once this was achieved, it was not clear how a recalcitrant government was to be persuaded to cease its abuses.

The resolution was subsequently used to justify the continued existence of the northern no-fly zone and the imposition of a second air exclusion zone in the south. It was also invoked when force was used to protect aircraft involved in policing the zones.

PROTECTION FROM ABOVE – THE NO-FLY ZONES 1992–8

In the years after the Gulf War, the sight of military aircraft on daily patrol over the no-fly zone of northern Iraq seemed a reassuring one. It had been initiated by the US as a means of securing airspace to allow coalition forces and aid workers to operate in safety. Once ground troops withdrew from the safe haven area, the no-fly zone took on new significance, demonstrating, it seemed, that the Kurds were still being protected.

From 1991 until 1998, this operation – known to the Coalition as Operation Provide Comfort II until 1997 (after which it was renamed Operation Northern Watch), and to the Turks as Operation Poised Hammer – became an institutionalised arrangement under which military aircraft flew daily surveillance missions above the 36th parallel over northern Iraq from Incirlik airbase in south-eastern Turkey. Permission for this operation had to be renewed by the Turkish Government every six months.

Although civilians in southern Iraq were also known to be at risk in 1991, there was no move to establish any comparable form of exclusion zone. One US official commented that 'a no-fly zone in the south was not thought of at that time'. Only in 1992 was this issue revisited.

'Gesture politics': the southern no-fly zone

In mid-1992, a cluster of events raised tensions and encouraged the international community to send a strong message to Iraq. In June 1992, the Memorandum of Understanding (MoU) between the Iraqi Government and the UN had expired and negotiations were not progressing well, with the Iraqis making demands for changes in the terms of UN humanitarian involvement. Security problems for UN and NGO aid staff had also increased. In July, a major confrontation took place when UNSCOM inspectors were refused access to a Ministry of Agriculture building suspected of housing documents relating to weapons of mass destruction.

At this time there were reports of increased Iraqi military activity in the southern marshes, including shelling and air attacks, and allegations that the marshes were being drained. A delegation from the Iraqi opposition which met with Secretary of State James Baker in late July lobbied for some form of safe area in southern Iraq.

On 10 August, the UN Special Rapporteur on human rights in Iraq, Max van der Stoel, was invited on an exceptional basis by Belgium, France, the UK and the US to present his report on the situation in the marshes to the Security Council. He emphasised the need for urgent action to respond to grave human rights violations there, and to send in monitors to obtain independent and reliable information.[10] The US Ambassador Edward Perkins said the situation in the south 'appeared to require a similar response [to that in the north]', suggesting that some action might be taken on the ground.[11]

However, President Bush and Brent Scowcroft decided to opt for a no-fly zone. There were some voices in Washington calling for monitors or some kind of ground intervention. But the administration's main concern was to 'punish' the Iraqis for their challenge to UNSCOM. The imposition of a no-fly zone offered the possibility of a quick response. In the view of one US official, if it had not been for the UNSCOM clash, the US 'would not have done anything' in the south.[12]

After an informal meeting of the Security Council, Britain and France appeared in broad agreement with the US proposal.[13] The rationale for the no-fly zone was spelled out on 19 August by the British Defence Minister, Malcolm Rifkind:

> The purpose of the exercise that has been approved by the British Government and which clearly is in the mind of the United States and French governments as well, is essentially to impose a 'no-fly' zone to prevent the attacks on the Shias which have been taking place from fixed wing aircraft. That's been the primary escalation that we've seen in recent weeks and therefore there is reason to be confident that the imposition of the 'no-fly' zone will be as effective in southern Iraq as it has already been in the northern part of the country, where the Kurds were similarly threatened until similar introduction of restrictions were introduced. So far as other possible conflicts on the ground are concerned, we obviously hope that these will also be with drawn, will be reduced [sic]. They're not so significant at the present time and, without the support of air cover, then there is reason to hope that there they also will be removed.[14]

Meanwhile, the threat to impose a no-fly zone further jeopardised the access of UN humanitarian agencies to the south. The Iraqis used the imminent imposition of the no-fly zone to demand the withdrawal of UN humanitarian personnel to Baghdad (see Chapter 7). A *Washington Post* article on 22 August suggested that the failure of UN Undersecretary Jan Eliasson's negotiations to renew the Memorandum of

Understanding with the Iraqi Government had 'scuttled a compromise being discussed here that would have seen the UN presence in Iraq expanded...' A Western official said that had Iraq permitted an expanded UN presence in the area 'to care for the embattled Shiites', it would have caused states involved in the proposed no-fly zone 'to reconsider their operations'.[15]

On 26 August, members of the Coalition announced the imposition of an air exclusion zone below the 32nd parallel, banning the use of helicopters and fixed-wing aircraft, and citing as justification Iraqi contraventions of Resolution 688 and the need, therefore, to monitor Iraqi compliance.[16] US, British and French planes, backed up by US AWACS surveillance aircraft, were to patrol the zone. There was no ultimatum or *démarche* to Iraq from the Security Council, which had not formally debated the imposition of the zone since the 11 August meeting to hear van der Stoel's report. On 1 September the Iraqi Government instructed its air and ground forces not to breach the no-fly zone.

There was opposition to the imposition of the zone from a number of Arab and non-aligned states. Even staunch coalition members – Egypt, Saudi Arabia and other Gulf Cooperation Council states with the exception of Kuwait – expressed their doubts.

The formulation used in announcing the no-fly zone made no mention of defending or protecting Iraqi civilians. According to a Pentagon spokesman, 'The purpose of establishing the no-fly zone – and I would emphasise it's a no-fly zone, not a security zone – is to ensure the safety of coalition aircraft monitoring compliance with United Nations Security Council Resolution 688'.[17]

The motives for choosing to impose a no-fly zone while avoiding involvement on the ground were evidently not confined to concerns over human rights or humanitarian aid. The persistent reports of Iraqi attacks on the southern marshes, including the use of fixed-wing aircraft and helicopter gunships, was certainly a trigger for action. As one US official put it, the issue of the marshes best met the need to mobilise public opinion. However, a more important concern, especially for the US, was the sense that Iraq was taking the offensive on a number of fronts against the UN. What was needed was a political gesture, a signal to the Iraqis to show that the international community could respond. In the UK Dennis Healey, Labour's Shadow Foreign Secretary, called it 'gesture politics on a grand scale'.[18]

A US State Department response to questions from the House Foreign Affairs Committee in 1993 revealed the limits of what was intended, and achieved, as regards protection in the southern no-fly zone. Noting that the circumstances leading to the creation of the northern 'safe haven' were 'unique', the statement continued:

> The creation of a security zone [in the south] would require that we significantly increase our military assets in this region, and be prepared to use them to force the Iraqi military out of the area, to keep it secure and to maintain an open ended relief operation to the area. At present there is no international support for the creation of such a security zone in southern Iraq.
>
> Iraq's attacks on the marshes to date have stayed below the threshold set by coalition forces. The Iraqi military continues to fight a war of attrition through ground attacks on the small insurgent forces in the marshes.[19]

The State Department's 1994 Human Rights report on Iraq further conceded, '[the no-fly zone over southern Iraq] continues to deter aerial attacks on the marsh dwellers but does not prevent artillery attacks or the military's large scale burning operations [in the marshes]'.[20] The evidence that the marshes were being drained, derived from satellite pictures and overflights, did not lead to any action beyond the occasional statement of condemnation.

Behind the reluctance to intervene on the ground were undoubtedly concerns about getting involved in Iraq's internal conflicts and fears that an enclave in the south would cause Saddam to lose control and lead to a breakup of the state. The proposal put forward at that time by some members of the Iraqi opposition – that the establishment of some form of allied protection would weaken Saddam's hold on the south – was therefore regarded with ambivalence in the US.

While both the Bush and Clinton administrations wanted Saddam at the very least 'under pressure' and 'in a box', there was also concern that weakening the Iraqi state's hold on the south would allow the Iranians more influence. When asked at a congressional hearing in early 1994 about the possibility of establishing a safe haven for the marsh Arabs, the Assistant Secretary of State for the Middle East, Robert Pelletreau, described the fact that they live close to the border with Iran as 'a very big complicating factor'.[21]

The northern no-fly zone: safe from whom?

The measures taken by leading coalition members during the 1991 crisis created the impression for the Western public that there was a high degree of commitment to protect the Kurds. For the Kurdish leadership, too, Operation Safe Haven appeared to symbolise a measure of political recognition. Resolution 688 made direct reference to the Kurds for the first time in an internationally agreed document. The no-fly zone was also viewed as a sign of commitment, at least to the extent that terminating it would be difficult for the coalition members without an agreement between the Kurdish leadership and Baghdad.

The withdrawal of Iraqi forces from the three northern governorates in October and November 1991 provided a breathing space for the Kurds. Saddam Hussein's calculations were undoubtedly influenced by the existence of the no-fly zone, but he also wanted to put pressure on the Kurds after the failure of the autonomy talks. He probably assumed that sooner or later one, or both, of the key Kurdish leaders would decide to negotiate.

The absence of Iraqi control in the three northern governorates (Iraqi Kurdistan) lessened the chances of another refugee crisis, which might have developed if Iraqi forces had remained in the north without any political settlement. But it also forced the leading protagonists of Operations Provide Comfort and Safe Haven to continue providing humanitarian aid and a measure of protection.

When Iraq cut trade and central government finance, compounding the impact of international economic sanctions on the welfare of the population, the response was to emphasise the provision of humanitarian aid to counter the embargo's effects. Despite its commitment to protect this population, the international community made no direct challenge to Iraq's action.

Western governments were faced with a conundrum: if the internal embargo was ended, Iraqi authority in the region would inevitably increase – something which, at that stage, neither they nor most of the inhabitants wanted to see happen. However, they had no wish to see the country break up and certainly did not want to see a separate Kurdish entity in northern Iraq. Maintaining the boundaries of Iraq as a sovereign state remained a priority. Therefore, although humanitarian assistance was provided, the Kurdish-controlled region received no formal international recognition.

Until 1996, the press and some politicians in the West continued to assert that the no-fly zones were 'protecting the Kurds and Shi'a'. The term 'safe haven' was still used on occasion when describing coalition protection in the north. For example, Martin Indyk, special assistant to the US President on the National Security Council, spoke in 1994 of 'operating the no-fly zone and the safe haven' in the north.[22] In reality the scale of protection has been much less comprehensive than this implies. The area within Dohuk governorate which had constituted the 'safe haven' held by coalition ground forces in 1991 was subsequently known as the 'security zone'. Within this zone, all that remained of the 'safe haven' was the Military Coordination Centre (MCC), based in Zakho. Its role was to 'continue to monitor the security zone and report Iraqi compliance with the stated terms'.[23] It was initially composed of military representatives of the US, UK and France. From 1993, Turkey was also represented. Any Iraqi troop movement into this security zone was expected to trigger some form of military response, at least from the US and UK, although even the extent of this commitment remained vague.

There was certainly never any commitment to keep Iraqi ground troops out of the much larger area covered by the no-fly zone.[24] In 1996, the former Secretary of State James Baker, recalling the decisions made in 1991, stated, 'We went for the no-fly zone and Resolution 688 which said he [Saddam Hussein] had to respect the human rights of his own citizens. But there was never any effort to put a specific prohibition against [Iraqi] forces moving north of the 36th parallel'.[25]

The Iraqis continued to maintain troops in Mosul, a city which lies within the no-fly zone but which has remained under full Iraqi control throughout the period since 1991. Furthermore, setting the limits of the no-fly zone at the 36th parallel had excluded the major Kurdish city of Sulaymaniya – and the part of that governorate which lies to the south of the 36th parallel – from any form of external protection.

The establishment of Kurdish control inside and beyond the no-fly zone (see map for *de facto* line between Kurdish and Iraqi forces) did not stop Iraqi security agents, or those paid by them, from causing death and injury, both to international aid workers and journalists, and to the local population. Areas close to the *de facto* border with Iraq have suffered chronic insecurity, particularly in the south-east – Kifri, Kalar, Chamchamal and Khanaqin – where frequent shelling and periodic incursions since 1991 have led to temporary displacement of the inhabitants, injury and disruption of their lives.[26] Finally, the zone offered no protection whatever from air or ground attacks on northern Iraq from the neighbouring states of Turkey and Iran.

The Regional Dimension

The events of 1991 inadvertently created a military and political vacuum in Iraqi Kurdistan in which a variety of political forces have since operated. This 'space' has generated new political problems without solving the pre-existing ones. It has encouraged Iraq's neighbours – Turkey and Iran – to intervene militarily and politically. The conflict between Kurdish nationalist movements and the Iraqi

Government has always had a regional dimension, with alliances of convenience across borders being formed and broken, encouraged by the rivalries between the main Iraqi Kurdish parties. The emergence of a Kurdish-controlled region in northern Iraq, with its attendant economic problems and lack of international status, served to intensify this interference from surrounding states.

For successive Turkish governments since 1991, the need to maintain control over developments in northern Iraq became part of the Turkish state's preoccupation with the status of its own Kurdish population. During the Gulf War, as a *quid pro quo* for agreeing to participate in the Coalition, Turkish leaders were thought to have received some kind of guarantee that the Coalition would not permit the emergence of an autonomous Iraqi Kurdistan.[27] In March 1991, President Ozal took the unprecedented step of inviting Iraqi Kurdish leaders to Ankara to receive their assurances that they did not seek separation from Iraq. At the same time, he eased somewhat the restrictions on cultural life for the Turkish Kurds.[28]

The Turkish Government's main motive in promoting the safe havens policy during the crisis of 1991 was to prevent Iraqi Kurdish refugees from remaining in Turkey, or on the Turkish border, where their presence might have fuelled the Turkish Kurds' conflict with the state. However, there were unlooked-for consequences. The PKK rapidly took advantage of the cross-border possibilities created by coalition action and by the withdrawal of Iraqi forces from the north.[29]

Despite numerous changes in government since 1991, there was little fundamental change in Turkish conduct of the war against the PKK.[30] The military command has remained firmly in control of operations in south-eastern Turkey, and has developed a proactive security policy in northern Iraq. In the meantime, Iraqi Kurdistan has fallen victim both to Turkey's failure to find a peaceful political solution to its own Kurdish problem and to the inability of the Iraqi Kurdish leaders to resolve their differences (see Chapter 6).

De facto Kurdish control in northern Iraq raised two concerns for the Turkish state. First, it created the possibility that a successful experiment in local democracy, and even limited autonomy in northern Iraq, could provide a model for the Turkish Kurds. However, the more pressing concern was the freedom of action which the PKK had gained in northern Iraq. A factor in the PKK's survival has been continued support from Syria, and to a lesser extent Iran. But arguably it was the existence of a vacuum in northern Iraq which extended the PKK's importance, even when it had suffered serious setbacks within Turkey.

All the states in the region with Kurdish minorities – Iran and Syria as well as Turkey – have regarded post-1991 developments in northern Iraq with suspicion, fearing that the Iraqi state might break up. In 1990, President Ozal reportedly said that he had received guarantees from Syria and Iran that they would not allow a Kurdish state to emerge. This followed suggestions that the Kurdish issue might be linked to a general Middle East peace settlement.[31] In August 1991 the foreign ministers of the three states discussed Kurdish issues and the implications of developments in Iraq during a meeting of the Islamic Conference Organisation in Istanbul.[32]

In November 1992, Turkey convened a meeting with Iranian and Turkish foreign ministers to discuss Iraq and the Kurdish question. Saudi Arabia declined to attend, and neither the Iraqi Government nor the Iraqi Kurds were invited.[33] After that, a trilateral coordination commission, comprising the foreign ministers of Turkey, Iran and Syria, met periodically to monitor developments in Iraq, particularly focusing on

Kurdish issues.[34] The foreign ministers have frequently reiterated their determination 'to resist all attempts to break up Iraq under any pretext'.[35]

Nonetheless, distrust and rivalry between these states persisted. Syria has periodically used its support for the PKK 'as an instrument of pressure against Turkey, its support waxing and waning with the political environment'.[36] The particular subject for leverage in the 1990s has been the issue of riparian rights to the waters of the Euphrates, on which Turkey has built a series of large dams, limiting Syria's (and Iraq's) water supply downstream.[37] In 1992 and 1994 protocols were signed in which Syria undertook to prevent hostile action against Turkey from Syrian territory and to reduce the PKK's presence in Lebanon.[38] Nonetheless, the PKK retained its base in Syria until late in 1998.

Turkey's relations with Iran have been similarly uneasy. Despite security protocols, Turkey has periodically accused the Iranian Government of allowing the PKK to operate from its territory.[39] For its part, the Iranian Government became increasingly involved in the Iraqi Kurdish internal conflict as well as attempting to crush Iranian Kurdish opposition groups based in Iraqi Kurdistan though cross-border bombardments and periodic ground incursions. It has also been concerned to prevent Turkey acquiring too much influence in northern Iraq.

The idea of some form of security zone on Turkey's border with Iraq has twice been mooted, but in both cases the Turkish Government backed away from any formal proposal to change the border for lack of international support. On 1 May 1995 President Demirel caused a diplomatic furore by calling for a 're-drawing' of the Iraq-Turkish border to make Turkey more defensible against the PKK. In September 1996, a similar proposal received backing only from the US. The Iraqi Government made clear its strong opposition to such a move, as did the Gulf Cooperation Council states. In the Arab world, such a zone was compared with the Israeli security zone in southern Lebanon. Nonetheless by 1997, the scale and duration of Turkish military operations inside Iraqi Kurdistan was creating something close to a *de facto* security zone.[40]

Maintaining the no-fly zone

From 1991, Turkey exercised a double veto on international action in northern Iraq: its permission was needed to use Incirlik airbase, from which the no-fly zone was patrolled, and it controlled access by land to Iraqi Kurdistan. Its border post at Habur was the entry point for humanitarian supplies, aid workers and all visitors to the region not wishing to enter Iraq officially via Baghdad.

Turkey has taken an increasingly active role in Operation Provide Comfort II, becoming a co-commander in the Combined Task Force at Incirlik and in the MCC in Zakho.[41] The MCC, although only a minimal presence, played an active role in contacts both with the Iraqi military and the Kurdish leadership until late 1992. Its activities were then reduced, apparently reflecting US official concerns that its representative was often making rather than implementing policy.[42] Its role was further weakened after an incident in April 1994 when US fighters patrolling the no-fly zone mistakenly shot down two US helicopters carrying MCC staff on a routine flight to see the Kurdish leadership in Salahadin, killing all on board.

Since that time, the Turkish representatives were said to have wrested the initiative from the US and British representatives. Turkish officials apparently began to refuse permission for helicopter flights outside the security zone, and to insist that meetings with Kurdish leaders only take place with all four MCC states' representatives present. This made it difficult for MCC staff to meet regularly with Kurdish leaders, who were based outside the zone, and weakened the MCC's political contacts.[43] Turkish representatives were also said to be sensitive about any challenge to the conduct of their military forces and their infringements of the rights of the local population during frequent military incursions. The embattled mood in the MCC was apparently heightened in 1996 by growing fears on the part of the Americans that there was an Iranian threat to US personnel in the MCC and OFDA.

The need to renew the airbase agreement with the Turkish Government every six months was often a source of anxiety for the Iraqi Kurds. In this increasingly painful six-monthly ritual of manoeuvring and arm-twisting, the Turkish Government had a good deal of leverage, since it was difficult to see from where else the overflights could be conducted.

Since the US and UK could not, without considerable embarrassment, abandon the Iraqi Kurds entirely, Turkey has been in a position to influence the conditions under which both the no-fly zone and humanitarian aid continued. On the other hand, as one British official suggested in 1994, when the continued use of Incirlik was becoming increasingly difficult, renewal was generally expected because of the 'degree of leverage the EU and US have over Turkey'. This of course included Turkey's ongoing interest in joining the EU.

The Turkish military command was generally in favour of retaining Operation Provide Comfort II, apparently fearing that if Saddam Hussein returned to the region he would support the PKK, in revenge for Turkey's Gulf War stance. However, some Turkish politicians have argued the economic and political advantages of a good relationship with Baghdad. There have therefore always been voices within the political establishment against continuing the airbase agreement. It also provided a symbolic target for Turkish politicians – for example, Mumtaz Soysal, who was Foreign Minister between 1994 and 1995 – who wanted to distance themselves from the US alliance.[44] To the surprise of many observers, the Government led by Necmettin Erbakan's Refah Party and the National Assembly agreed in August 1996 to renew Operation Provide Comfort (OPC) until December 1996, though those involved said the negotiations were even more difficult than usual.

Turkey's strategic importance in the region, and its strong relationship with the US, has allowed it to act in ways which in other circumstances might attract serious international censure – including cross-border military actions deploying up to 50,000 troops, and in October and November 1997 openly taking sides in the internal fighting between Iraqi Kurdish parties (see Chapter 6).

These moves to assert military control over a swathe of territory within northern Iraq are undoubtedly infringements of an international border, a border which the international community is not willing to see changed, despite the ambiguous situation in northern Iraq. Turkey's room to manoeuvre has depended on the reluctance of its Western allies to challenge the widely-held view within the Turkish establishment that the Kurdish question has to be solved by military means.

Until the mid-1990s, the United States had rarely raised the issue of human rights violations within Turkey.[45] The US State Department now openly criticises Turkey's domestic policy in regard to the Kurds, and its human rights record more generally. But this does not extend to Turkish military operations in northern Iraq, where the US response has consistently been to express 'understanding' that these actions are intended 'to hunt terrorists'. Turkey is simply urged not to stay too long.[46] As one European diplomatic source put it, 'the US is beholden to Turkey, so these things are not on the agenda'.

The EU has strongly criticised Turkey's human rights record, especially in internal military actions against the Kurdish population, but it has not taken a strong position on the injury or harassment of civilians during Turkish incursions in northern Iraq. The Council of Ministers has issued statements on border violations, but it has no capacity for enforcement.[47] The EU sees Turkey as an important member of NATO which has a role in the stability of this 'turbulent region' of the Middle East and the Gulf. Therefore, despite the increased tensions over Turkey's bid for EU membership, the response to Turkey's actions within the Middle East region is still muted.[48]

Fading commitment

The question of what policy to follow towards the Kurds created sharp differences of opinion among members of the Gulf War Coalition. The Iraqi Kurdish leaders did not promote the notion of a separate state and, being well aware of Western and regional sensitivities, were careful to avoid any suggestion that they intended to detach themselves from Iraq.

However, in the Arab world there has been little sympathy for the Kurds, or for any movement which might lead to the breakup of established states. Among the five permanent Security Council members, China made clear its objections to intervention in Iraq's internal affairs in 1991, and generally avoided involvement with the Kurds. The Soviet Union had played no role in initiating or enforcing the no-fly zone. However, Russian connections with a number of Kurdish leaders, especially those from parties of the left which in the past had strong relations with Moscow, has given it some 'behind the scenes' influence in the inter-party conflict since 1994.

French policy has moved away from its sympathetic stand towards the Kurds during 1990–1 when it had welcomed Kurdish delegations to Paris and was active in advocating international intervention in the north.[49] The strength and influence of the Kurdish lobby, closely linked to the advocates of 'le devoir d'ingerence' in 1991, had been somewhat deceptive. It had depended on a few key people, in particular on the President's wife, Danielle Mitterand, Bernard Kouchner, the Minister for Humanitarian Affairs, and on the Kurdish Institute in Paris. In March 1992, when President Mitterand received Masud Barzani in Paris, he still appeared sympathetic towards the Kurds but was offering little in the way of concrete support. He emphasised the need to seek an agreement on autonomy with the Iraqi Government to avoid the break up of Iraq. A month later, on a visit to Turkey he made clear his opposition to an independent Kurdish state.[50]

During the period of 'cohabitation' between President Mitterand and the Gaullist coalition (1993–5), which coincided with the revival of the pro-Iraq lobby in France, enthusiasm for the Kurdish cause further waned. This was compounded by the outbreak of inter-Kurdish fighting. Paris was the venue for the first round of negotiations between the warring parties in 1994, but the Government was careful to distance itself from the proceedings (see Chapter 6).

By 1996, the French Government was advocating that the Kurdish parties negotiate a settlement with Baghdad – something that the US in particular was trying to prevent – and viewed with unease the increasingly 'uninhibited' actions of Turkey. As one official commented, 'It became obvious to us that the future of the region could not be organised without agreement with Baghdad'. France became inclined to express, 'but not too loudly', in diplomatic forums that the future of Iraqi Kurdistan would be with Iraq, whoever its leader was.[51] In early 1998, French and Russian diplomats based in Baghdad were reportedly supporting efforts to broker an agreement between the Kurdish parties and the Baghdad Government.[52]

Since 1991, the US cannot be said to have developed a clear policy towards the Kurds in northern Iraq, aside from the maintenance of the no-fly zone. The political vacuum created by the Iraqi withdrawal had not been anticipated. After the withdrawal of coalition troops, US interest in encouraging the Kurds to negotiate with Baghdad seemed to diminish.[53] Concern that they would seek greater independence apparently dampened US enthusiasm for the 1992 elections for a Kurdish assembly in the north.[54] This contrasted with the rather more positive view of the elections taken by the British Government.[55]

From 1992 until 1995, US official involvement was largely confined to giving humanitarian assistance, while trying to stay out of Kurdish internal affairs. Events in the Kurdish region received little attention at the higher levels of government, which concerned itself mainly with direct Iraqi threats to the northern no-fly zone. The British Government generally took a more sympathetic line, although, like the US administration, it was particularly sensitive to Turkish concerns. In common with the US and other European states the UK did not extend any form of international recognition to the Kurdish administration.

The conflict which erupted into fighting between the KDP and PUK in 1994 eroded support for the Iraqi Kurds. Even European governments sympathetic to the Kurds felt they had no counterparts to deal with, and did not want to 'take sides' between the two parties. Active Kurdish lobbies in Europe and the US were increasingly silenced by the strident and competing rhetoric of the two parties, which devoted most of their energies to accusing and denigrating each other in public.

In 1995, the US and UK became drawn into attempts to achieve a settlement to the conflict. Concern at the apparent growth of Iran's influence in northern Iraq was reportedly one reason for US efforts to end the fighting. Meanwhile, by 1995 the US administration tended to stress that it was providing humanitarian assistance in the north, and references to 'protecting the Kurds' were avoided.[56]

Safe haven or opposition base?

Another strand of US thinking on Iraqi Kurdistan had little to do with the Kurds, but a good deal to do with the notion of containment, in which the no-fly zones were seen as a key component.[57] The Iraqi National Congress (INC) decision to establish a base in northern Iraq in late 1992 created a further opportunity for 'putting pressure on Saddam'. The US Government, through the CIA, began to channel funds to the INC to beam broadcasts and propaganda into Iraq, gather intelligence from army deserters fleeing to north, and even launch attacks into Iraq.

However, the INC's role in using the north as a 'liberated area' from which to undermine the Iraqi Government was eroded by the collapse of the Kurdish consensus in 1994. As the region slid into internal conflict, the INC found itself mediating fruitlessly between two of its leading members, the PUK and the KDP. This, along with other disputes between the INC's constituent groups, undermined its potential role as a unified opposition movement.

The US official presence in northern Iraq since 1991 had been confined to the military staff at the MCC and humanitarian aid officials working for OFDA. In late 1994, however, a small CIA team moved into offices near the INC's base in Salahadin. Their role was both to gather intelligence from army personnel who deserted to the north and to promote a more active policy of encouraging the INC to use the north as a launch pad for the overthrow of Saddam Hussein. At that time, the INC was attracting substantial numbers of Iraqi army deserters, including some senior officers. The most significant of these was General Wafiq Samara'i, a former head of military intelligence, who arrived in northern Iraq in November 1994, just as the CIA operatives were settling in.

In March 1995, the INC, with the support of General Samara'i, planned an attack on Iraq military forces, which included Republican Guard units stationed on the *de facto* line with government-controlled Iraq. The CIA officers reportedly encouraged the protagonists to believe that the US would back the attack,[58] though State Department officials denied this. On the eve of the attack the National Security Council in Washington sent a message that the US Government would have no part in the operation. As a result the KDP refused to participate. The PUK and INC went ahead with the operation but failed to trigger any mass defection or challenge to the regime.[59]

During this period, the CIA was also diversifying its support to include the Iraqi National Accord (Wifaq), which by the beginning of 1996 had a base in Amman as well as in northern Iraq. This group proved to be heavily infiltrated by Iraqi intelligence, which, combined with the group's own indiscretions, allowed the Iraqis to uncover its plans for a coup, and resulted in widespread arrests inside Iraq in June 1996.

These bungled CIA initiatives highlighted a new and dangerous role for the Kurdish-controlled region – as a base for US-directed efforts not just to contain, but to attack, the Iraqi regime – while the US and its coalition partners were supposedly protecting its population. In fact, these manoeuvres made the region more vulnerable to Iraqi attack.

WHAT PROTECTION REMAINS?

In late August 1996, as the US and UK were hosting yet another round of negotiations between the PUK and KDP in London, news came in that the KDP was cooperating with Iraqi government forces in an advance on Arbil, at that time under PUK control.[60]

The Iraqi army's first major incursion into the area covered by the northern no-fly zone since Iraqi troops were withdrawn from the region in late October 1991 was a considerable embarrassment for the US. Since it was undertaken at the invitation of one of the Kurdish parties, it could not easily be portrayed as a hostile action. Arbil lies within the no-fly zone but not in the 'security zone', while much of Sulaymaniya governorate, heartland of the PUK – the party which was still opposing the Iraqi Government – lies outside both zones. A further dilemma for the US was that any military action in support of the PUK would also appear to help the latter's main backer, Iran.

The Iraqi leadership probably had more than one motive for moving when they did. The first goal was evidently to clear out the CIA-backed opposition from northern Iraq. The timing, soon after Iraq had accepted Resolution 986, may also have reflected its wish to ensure security of the section of the oil pipeline running through KDP-controlled areas to the Turkish border, and to smooth the path for increased imports into Iraq via the Habur crossing. Greater control over the KDP's economic as well as military activities may also have been a consideration, along with the well-tried Iraqi government tradition of keeping opposition forces divided.

After a couple of days, the Iraqis withdrew most of their forces south from Arbil. In this sense, the challenge to coalition protection was limited, but it had major repercussions. The US launched punitive cruise missile attacks on southern Iraq on 3 and 4 September 1996, and announced that it was extending the southern no-fly zone northwards to the 33rd parallel of latitude, just south of Baghdad. This change was accepted by Britain but not by France, which refused to patrol beyond the 32nd parallel though it continued to operate in Southern Watch below the 32nd parallel.[61]

The US received little support for these actions. Saudi Arabia and Jordan would not allow attacks from their territory. The Turkish Government had indicated 'before we even asked' that it would not allow Incirlik to be used as a base for air action, according to one US administration official. Nor would it entertain any extension of the northern no-fly zone to cover Sulaymaniya, the PUK stronghold south of the 36th parallel.[62]

The events of September 1996 drew public attention to the weakness of the 'protection' afforded to the Kurds by the no-fly zone. Before that time, the many small breaches had gone largely unnoticed, and it could be argued that overall safety in the region had been maintained. However, the international community could not or would not deal with the inter-Kurdish fighting, and this had contributed to the alliance between the KDP and the Iraqi Government. The presence of the CIA-backed Iraqi opposition in the north allowed the Iraqis to argue that what was being 'protected' was externally-backed opposition to the regime, not the humanitarian needs of the Kurds.

Meanwhile, the removal of the MCC from Zakho (including US, British, French and Turkish military personnel), and the evacuation of all international and local staff in US and US-related aid organisations, though initially said to be a 'temporary' withdrawal, suggested to all parties a diminution of US and international commitment to the region (see Chapter 8).

The northern no-fly zone agreement was renewed by the Turkish Government on 25 December 1996, but MCC staff did not return to Zakho, thus ending the symbolic military representation of the coalition partners in northern Iraq. The Turkish Government made it clear that it did not wish to see this presence renewed.

France announced in December 1996 that it was ending its participation in the northern no-fly zone, since the MCC and US aid organisations had been withdrawn, and the 'humanitarian component' of the operation no longer existed. The French view was that there was no point in providing protection so that the Kurds could fight each other.

The French withdrawal was later characterised by a senior US official as 'of no military significance', but it did have political significance, in that it indicated a further thinning of the consensus on international policy toward Iraq. Operation Provide Comfort, as it had operated since 1991, came to an end on 31 December 1996, according to the US State Department, though American and British planes continued to fly above the northern no-fly zone as 'Operation Northern Watch'. It signalled the end of the phase in which the US could emphasise its 'humanitarian commitment' to the Kurds. 'Because of the changes in its mission as a result of the closing last fall of the Military Command Center in Zakho and the shift of humanitarian assistance in the north under UNSCR 986 to international organisations, the designation "Provide Comfort" will no longer be used.'[63]

As further Kurdish inter-party fighting erupted in 1997, the French Government produced an interpretation of Resolution 688 which was quite different to the one which the coalition had offered to justify the no-fly zones. It placed most emphasis on Iraq's sovereignty and argued that dialogue with Baghdad was the best way of establishing stability in the north.

> La France est particulièrement attachée au respect de la résolution 688 du Conseil de sécurité, qui réaffirme la souveraineté, l'integrité territoriale et l'indépendance politique de l'Iraq et appelle à l'ouverture d'un large dialogue entre les Kurdes et Bagdad. La mise en oeuvre de cette résolution constitue le seul moyen de rétablir la stabilité dans le nord de l'Iraq et d'assurer la sécurité des populations civiles. Nous appelons constamment au respect de se texte dans toutes ses dispositions.[64]

A matter of priorities

The absence of a US response in the north in September 1996, and the extension of the southern no-fly zone, sent a clear signal, elaborated under pressure by several official spokesmen, that US strategic interests lay in the south of Iraq, not the north.[65] It appeared to confirm the view that protection of the Kurds and other minorities in northern Iraq was regarded by the Clinton adminstration as a low priority. The US State Department Human Rights Report for 1996 conceded that neither of the no-fly zones offered any protection on the ground for their populations.[66]

An exchange in a congressional hearing at the time between Assistant Secretary of State Pelletreau and Representative Lee Hamilton, one of the most tenacious questioners on the Iraq issue, makes the administration's position clear:

Hamilton: We have no commitment to protect them [the Kurds] against Saddam Hussein?

Pelletreau: We have no commitment to protect them against their own bad judgement if one party invites Saddam Hussein. When he uses his military force in repression of his people, that, we feel is an action that requires a response and we did make a response, but it was not out of some commitment to the Kurds.

Hamilton: Has our policy ever said that we would create a safe haven in the north?

Pelletreau: That has not been the policy of this administration. There may have been some statements in the previous one.[67]

By the end of 1997, the increasing inclination of the Kurdish parties to deal with Baghdad, and their doubts over what future backing they might receive from the US and UK, spurred the US administration into renewed action. Considerable symbolic significance was therefore read into Acting Assistant Secretary of State David Welch's visit to Sulaymaniya in July 1998, as the first senior US official to venture beyond the no-fly zone. In September, Secretary of State Madeleine Albright orchestrated an agreement between Barzani and Talabani, signed in Washington (see Chapter 6).

The bombing raids by the US and UK in December 1998 brought a further thinning of support for the zones. France, which had already withdrawn from the northern zone and limited its participation in the southern zone, announced after the raids that it was 'suspending' its participation in the southern zone. Although in January 1999 its aircraft remained in Saudi Arabia, the French Ministry of Defence did not foresee a resumption of flights over the no-fly zone.[68]

The roles of the no-fly zones

The northern and southern no-fly zones have had contrasting histories, and the utility of the two zones, from a military and strategic point of view, has also evolved quite differently. From the point of view of the US European Command which ran Operation Provide Comfort II from Stuttgart (in concert with the British and French military commands), its strategic significance was marginal, and its practical value limited. Operation Provide Comfort was therefore not said to be a popular mission at Eurcom. Since it has been run on a 'temporary basis', it involved time-consuming and expensive rotation of personnel, and cost the US alone about $100 million per year.[69]

Turkey has constantly kept the future of the operation in doubt, and, as already noted, restricted the military actions it would tolerate.[70] There have also been allegations that the Turkish military used coalition intelligence for their own purposes in Iraqi Kurdistan, while withholding from the MCC their own information on the PKK and Turkish security operations against it.[71]

In contrast, Centcom Command has viewed Operation Southern Watch as an important strategic tool. Saudi Arabia, while not always welcoming military attacks from its bases, has not challenged the continuation of Operation Southern Watch. In the southern zone, the Saudi Government pays the in-country expenses of aircraft flying out of Saudi bases, including billets and most importantly fuel, a major item of expenditure.

In 1992, an Iraqi threat to the Kuwait border or the Gulf states was not a primary factor in US thinking because Iraq had only just begun to rebuild its forces, but the no-fly zone was regarded as important as a means of early warning, while denying Iraq airspace for its airforce to train and manoeuvre. The confrontation between Iraq and the coalition in late 1994 confirmed, from the US point of view, the strategic value of the southern zone, linked to the US troops based in the region and naval forces in the Gulf.

US Secretary of Defence William J. Perry noted that in 1994 the US had in the theatre, as a result of the no-fly zone, 70 combat aircraft; a forward based headquarters;

'enough equipment pre-positioned in Kuwait for an entire army brigade of tanks and mechanised infantry'; US air, sea and ground troops in exercises over four years in the Gulf; and ready and prepared forces to back up diplomacy.[72]

When Iraqi troop movements advanced towards the Kuwaiti border in late 1994, other Security Council members shied away from an American suggestion at the height of the crisis that some form of ground exclusion zone should be considered in southern Iraq. Security Council Resolution 949, adopted during this crisis, demanded that Iraq return troops deployed in the south to their previous positions, not enhance its military capacity there, and not use its military forces in a hostile or provocative manner against its neighbours or UN operations in Iraq. The intention was to protect the Kuwaiti border, not the Iraqi population.[73]

The perception that the southern no-fly zone had importance in political relations with the Gulf was shared by Britain and by France. The latter emphasised the importance to French policy of relations with the Gulf states, and the reassurance which the southern no-fly zone afforded them.

Speaking in early 1997, a senior Clinton administration source asserted that 'all serious challenges [by Iraq] over the six years have been met with sufficient resolve by the international community'. The no-fly zones were increasingly seen by the Bush and subsequently by the Clinton administration as part of the dual containment strategy, as ways of putting pressure on Saddam Hussein and keeping him 'in a box'.

Viewed from this perspective, Iraqi challenges to the no-fly zones have certainly received a response. However, measured in terms of Resolution 688, used to justify their imposition, they appear far less effective. Military action has almost always related to infringements of the no-fly zones themselves. Iraqi infringements of Resolution 688, whether abuses of human rights or restrictions on delivery of humanitarian aid, have been routinely reported. But the existence of the no-fly zones has proved of limited value in preventing or checking abuses.

After the Gulf War, expectations were raised that international intervention would result in new forms of protection for peoples facing brutal rulers and that the external world would come to the aid of those who were starving or freezing on mountainsides. This at least was the public message of the major Western powers. In practice, these 'path-breaking' actions were embarked upon with very mixed motives and their outcomes were extremely uneven.

The northern safe haven did help refugees to return. From 1992 to 1996, the northern no-fly zone did deter Iraqi forces from launching major attacks on Iraqi Kurdistan. It did not, however prevent the economic embargo or all the other forms of violence to which the zone has been subject. The safety of the population in Iraqi Kurdistan became increasingly compromised both by the actions of its own political leadership and the use of the region by the US to 'put pressure' on Saddam Hussein. For the rest of the Iraqi population, 'protection' against abuses has not even been on the agenda and the southern no-fly zone has come to serve an entirely different purpose.

THE ENFORCEMENT OF HUMAN RIGHTS

If the establishment of the no-fly zones had little impact on the human rights situation in Iraq, the human rights machinery of the UN has been equally unable to bring about any modification of the regime's conduct. The history of the UN Special

Rapporteur on Human Rights in Iraq illustrates both the real difficulties of enforcing the requirements of Resolution 688 and raises questions about the extent of international commitment to enforcement.

The political shocks of the Gulf War broke the logjam which had previously prevented a resolution being passed in the UN Commission on Human Rights after the events of the Anfal. On 6 March 1991 the Commission passed a resolution calling for the appointment of a UN Special Rapporteur on Human Rights for Iraq.[74] On 25 June 1991 the Commission's Chairman announced the appointment of Max van der Stoel, a former foreign minister of the Netherlands, the candidate supported by the Western group of countries, as Special Rapporteur for Iraq.

The institutional framework within which special rapporteurs work is that of the UN Economic and Social Council and the General Assembly, which, unlike the Security Council, do not have any binding powers over their members. Hence states may vote to support rapporteurs when they detail human rights abuses but there is no mechanism to insist that the offending state should change its conduct. Van der Stoel has taken an unusually active role, establishing a number of precedents within the UN system, but he has encountered serious difficulties in carrying out his mandate.

After producing a preliminary report for the UN General Assembly in November 1991, the special rapporteur travelled to Iraq on 3–9 January 1992. The visit was rushed, the Iraqi authorities having much delayed his permission to enter the country, and ran close to the deadline for presentation of his report to the Human Rights Commission in February 1992. Van der Stoel did manage to visit Baghdad, the three northern governorates (by that time effectively under Kurdish control) and, briefly, the shrine cities of Najaf and Karbala and the notorious Abu Ghraib prison west of Baghdad.[75]

The report he wrote on his return was 'very strong'. It included a good deal of material on abuses in the 1980s, especially during the Anfal, as well as on more recent events. The result was that the Government of Iraq has never again agreed to allow the Special Rapporteur or any of his representatives to visit Iraq. Consequently all information gathered since February 1992 has been obtained outside Iraq's borders.

In late 1991, Amnesty International had proposed to Security Council members and to van der Stoel that human rights monitors should be placed in Iraq, but had met with non-committal or cautious responses. However, the visit to Iraq changed van der Stoel's view. At the session of the UN Human Rights Commission in February 1992, the Special Rapporteur broke new ground by requesting that the UN should deploy human rights monitors in Iraq, insisting that 'this exceptionally grave situation requires an exceptional response'. The UN Centre for Human Rights[76] had only recently begun to consider having a field presence. Human rights monitors had only been employed in situations where a peace settlement was already agreed as, for example, in El Salvador and Cambodia.

Van der Stoel invoked Resolution 688, calling on Iraq to 'immediately end its repression of its civilian population', and proposing that a team of monitors should remain in Iraq until the human rights situation had 'drastically improved'. Van der Stoel took the view that since the repression continued, so did the threat to international peace and security, and that this justified the stationing of monitors.

This proposal was reportedly received with 'worry' within the commission. Van der Stoel persuaded the Human Rights Commission Chairman to leave the proposal for monitors in the resolution to allow for further study and reporting. As a result, the wording of the resolution was convoluted, to avoid committing the Commission to any immediate action. In Article 9, the Commission 'Strongly deplores the exceptionally grave human rights violations by the Government of Iraq in recent years, which in the Special Rapporteur's view demand an exceptional response in the form of sending to Iraq a team of human rights monitors'. The following paragraph called on the Special Rapporteur to 'develop further his recommendation for an exceptional response'.[77]

On a subsequent visit to New York, van der Stoel discussed the idea of human rights monitors further with Security Council members.[78] The reactions were still cautious. However, by July 1992, reports indicated that the situation in the southern Iraqi marshes was worsening. Van der Stoel took the unprecedented step, made possible by his long-standing diplomatic status and contacts, of having the first part of his report for the UN General Assembly laid before the Security Council. It covered the situation in the marshes and his detailed proposals for human rights monitors.[79] Over the objections of China, India and Zimbabwe, he was also invited to address the Council on its contents, something no special rapporteur had done before.[80] Before he made his presentation on 10 August, the US and UK Ambassadors reportedly asked him not to mention the proposal for monitors. In the event, the three leading coalition members – the US, France and the UK – opted for a no-fly zone rather than the use of monitors or any other action on the ground.

At the next General Assembly session on human rights in Iraq in December 1992, a resolution welcoming the proposal for monitors was passed. Predictably, the Iraqi Government 'peremptorily' rejected the idea, calling the monitors 'something resembling the political agents of the colonialist States'.[81] The human rights card has been played politically on many occasions since 1992, but there has been no further commitment to action.

In January 1994, four of the permanent members of the Security Council – France, Russia, the US and the UK – issued a *démarche* again invoking Resolution 688. It condemned human rights violations and obstruction of access to food, medicine and other humanitarian goods and explicitly called on Iraq to allow human rights monitors 'throughout the country'. This appears to have been a rhetorical gesture to make a political point: the Iraqi Government had made clear that it would not allow the monitors in and the Security Council did not propose any action to back up its censure.[82]

A senior US official admitted in 1997 that human rights policy on Iraq had not come up with 'sufficient instruments to be effective'. Another explanation is that the international will to use the instruments available has been lacking.

The scepticism of many non-aligned countries about the Western powers' use of human rights as a stick to beat enemies meant that support within the UN for the work of the special rapporteurs has been ambivalent at best. This has been compounded by the reluctance in many such states to countenance discussion of human rights issues which challenge their own domestic policies.

The result has been bureaucratic logjams and difficulties in finding funds to continue the special rapporteurs' work. In the Iraqi case, it seems that this included resistance by the Secretary General to allocating funds for monitoring. In 1994, van der Stoel stated:

> ... it must be said that these very modest activities [sending missions to surrounding countries] have not been achieved owing to the scarcity of resources allocated for the purpose and the very slow decision-making process within the United Nations. Consequently the

Special Rapporteur must record his disappointment that to date no staff have been assigned for specific monitoring purposes nor, so far as he knows, has any discernible and secure budget been allocated for the mandate.[83]

Additional funds were subsequently allocated, but the operation continued to run on a shoestring.

The resolution, with its call for monitors, has continued to be renewed each year, but has proved to be a largely rhetorical gesture. From 1993, the annual General Assembly resolution on human rights in Iraq was modified to reflect the refusal of Iraq to allow human rights monitors into the country. Although the resolution still called on Iraq to allow the monitors access to all parts of the country, it welcomed the sending of monitors to the neighbouring states: 'to such locations as would facilitate improved information flows and assessment and would help in the independent verification of reports on the situation of human rights in Iraq'.

Since 1992, staff attached to the Special Rapporteur's office have visited neighbouring countries including Iran, Kuwait, Jordan and Lebanon. They have also gone to the Habur crossing – on the border between Turkey and northern Iraq – to meet with Iraqis living in Iraqi Kurdistan.

It might seem that the Special Rapporteur could have visited the areas under Kurdish control since 1992 without Iraqi consent. This would have made it possible to monitor Iraqi government abuses in the areas which remained under its control by interviewing those who had moved to the north from these areas. It would also have allowed direct investigation of abuses – including assassinations and sabotage – carried out by Iraqi government agents inside the Kurdish-controlled areas.

The UN has continued to treat Iraq as one country, and all UN staff have to seek visas from the Baghdad Government (see Chapter 7). The Special Rapporteur took a different view of the status of Iraqi Kurdistan as far as the UN's humanitarian obligations were concerned. He argued that although Iraq retains sovereignty over the region, its withdrawal from this territory meant that it had ceded responsibility for fulfilling the population's needs. In his view, the international community was obliged to take up this responsibility. This, he argued, meant that the UN humanitarian agencies were not obliged to carry out their work in the north under the aegis of Baghdad, as they have in fact done.

In his role as Special Rapporteur on human rights, however, he did not believe that the anomalous situation in Iraqi Kurdistan gave him the right to monitor the Iraqi Government's human rights abuses from Kurdish-controlled areas. The UN Secretary General Boutros Boutros-Ghali was also said to be completely opposed to any such course.

The Special Rapporteur's mandate is also confined to monitoring the actions of the Government of Iraq. Events in Iraqi Kurdistan since 1992 – both incursions by other states (Turkey and Iran) and inter-party fighting with its attendant human rights abuses – raised the question as to whether his mandate should have been widened to include abuses by parties other than the Iraqi Government. Van der Stoel apparently believed that proposals to include either of these categories in a revised mandate were unlikely to be accepted by the Human Rights Commission. As a consequence, the Special Rapporteur has not dealt with these categories of abuse.[84]

There have been various suggestions for other forms of human rights monitoring. One was that the UN Guards could play a role in monitoring human rights, though they certainly had no powers of enforcement. In June 1991, the UN Secretary General described the Guards as 'a contingent of veritable "humanitarian witnesses"' who as necessary would prepare reports on any incidents affecting the beneficiaries of UN programmes. Sadruddin also mentioned this reporting role.[85] After September 1992, the Guards' activities were confined to the Kurdish-controlled areas. Van der Stoel continued to stress the 'relevancy and usefulness' of stationing UN human rights monitors in government-controlled areas in the light of 'the absence of a United Nations presence in the South'.[86]

Such proposals for the Guards' role in monitoring abuses or protecting civilians mostly reflected the failure of other human rights initiatives, and were not seriously thought out. The Guards' activities have focused mainly on convoy protection and guarding property, which were certainly necessary tasks. However, even in this limited role the Guards came in for a lot of criticism of their performance (see Chapter 7). They were not trained or prepared for a human rights reporting role, arriving for short tours of duty with no knowledge of the country or the language.[87] They were certainly not equipped or in a position to intervene in any abuse or conflict.

Another suggestion was that other international organisations or NGOs working in Iraq might play some monitoring role, but nothing came of this, mainly because of the difficulties and potential dangers which could be incurred by staff working in Iraq (see Chapter 8).

The main form of international leverage on Iraq, aside from the no-fly zones and periodical air strikes (which demonstrably did not prevent the Iraqis acting as they wished in areas under their control on the ground), has remained the economic embargo. In practice, the effects of the embargo generally worsened the internal human rights situation, adding impoverishment, illness and rising crime to the abuses already suffered by the population.

Indeed the Iraqi Government has even tried to use the embargo to justify its abuses. Van der Stoel reported Tariq Aziz's argument that Iraq's respect for human rights would improve if sanctions were to be lifted, suggesting that the existence of sanctions caused Iraq to violate human rights. Van der Stoel's riposte was that 'shortage of spare parts for car engines cannot be said to cause government forces to carry out acts of torture'.[88]

A similar line of argument came from Baghdad when the Government was challenged on the introduction in 1994 of amputation and branding as punishment for theft and desertion (see Chapter 5). According to Human Rights Watch/Middle East:

> The RCC [Revolutionary Command Council] has explained that these decrees are based on Islamic law and intended to combat rising crime in Iraq. Despite the government's arguments that the decrees are based on religious law and necessitated by rampant crime, Iraq is bound by its international obligations not to institute cruel, inhuman, or degrading treatment or punishment. Ambassador Hamdoon said that 'the measures were not human rights abuses... They are temporary measures that have to do with the current circumstances... When the economic sanctions are lifted (by the United Nations), there will be no need for such measures.'

Human Rights Watch/Middle East concluded, 'Difficult economic conditions that have caused a rise in crime and military desertion cannot justify Iraq's violation of its citizens' basic human rights'.[89]

The issue of economic and social rights and the impact of sanctions has been a controversial one. The Special Rapporteur on Iraq was the first among his peers to include routinely the question of economic and social rights in his analyses (though this was subsequently done to some extent in reports on former Yugoslavia). However, he has focused for the most part on the Iraqi Government's responses to sanctions, mapping out reported inequities in the rationing system and condemning the Government for refusing to accept UNSC Resolutions 706 and 712 and, until 1996, Resolution 986. This approach was reflected in the annual General Assembly resolutions on human rights in Iraq.

The scope of his work has not included the mechanisms and application of the sanctions themselves, nor has he examined directly the more contentious issue of how the international community has dealt with the impact of sanctions on the civilian population of Iraq, particularly when no other form of human rights protection was available. Other human rights organisations have touched on this issue, though most have avoided tackling it head on.[90] They have generally viewed this difficult area as outside their mandates.

War crimes and genocide: pursuing the culprits

Little progress has been made on various proposals since 1990 to bring charges of war crimes and/or genocide against the Iraqi regime. Immediately after the Gulf War, President Bush promoted the idea of a war crimes tribunal which would lead to the prosecution of named individuals. Such a tribunal, on the lines of those now established for former Yugoslavia and Rwanda, has to be approved by the Security Council.[91]

However, it was reported that 'lawyers in the State Department and Justice Department have warned that any attempt to bring Saddam before an international court would be an immensely complicated and arduous task, with no guarantee of eventual success'.[92] After the war the Bush administration did not take the matter further.[93] It even delayed the release of a judge advocate general's report on Iraqi war crimes that might have created greater pressure to act. This was eventually released in the early days of the Clinton administration.[94] Despite the urging of the Iraqi opposition and occasional expressions of interest from the Clinton administration, no form of tribunal had been initiated by the end of 1998. According to the US State Department's ambassador-at-large on war crimes issues, the Clinton administration's work thus far on Iraqi 'war crimes' had focused on gathering information for such a charge, presumably with a view to convincing other Security Council members that such a case should be brought. He spoke of 'focusing renewed attention on Saddam Hussein and the senior members of his regime'.[95] However, a further problem facing those who wish to see Saddam Hussein overthrown is that a number of the potential candidates to replace him might be subject to prosecution by such a tribunal.

A second proposal was for states to bring a case of genocide (relating to the Anfal campaign against the Kurds) in the International Court of Justice. The case was to be based on documents collated by Middle East Watch from materials seized by the Kurdish political parties from Iraqi security facilities in northern Iraq after the Iraqi forces withdrew in 1991. The difficulty in pursuing this course of action was that it has not proved possible to muster a large enough group of states to bring such a case. While the US and UK do not oppose this initiative, it was seen as preferable to find more 'neutral' parties to bring the case. The states which expressed interest have been reluctant to proceed without a larger coalition, which has not been achieved.

The establishment of a permanent International Criminal Court would provide an avenue to prosecute individual regime members against whom there is strong evidence of crimes against humanity or genocide in the future. However, the court would not deal with crimes retrospectively. Hence it would not provide an avenue to pursue charges against members of the Iraqi regime for either genocide committed in the 1980s or war crimes during the 1991 Gulf War.

IRAQI REFUGEES IN THE MIDDLE EAST SINCE 1991

After the refugee crisis of 1991, most people outside the region forgot that by no means all the refugees were able to return home, since the regime from which they had fled was still in place. They have been added to those Iraqis who became refugees before 1991. The majority of remaining refugees who fled in 1991 are concentrated in the countries surrounding Iraq: in Iran, Saudi Arabia and Turkey, with smaller numbers in Syria and Jordan. It is these countries which, willingly or not, have had to deal with the aftermath of the crisis. Protection of these refugees' rights has not generally been a high priority for the international community.

There have been some programmes of third-country resettlement from Turkey, Saudi Arabia, and Jordan, though not from Iran, but the number of refugees has risen since 1991 as more Iraqis seek refuge from the combined effects of the economic embargo, continuing human rights abuses, internecine fighting in the north, and the failing hope of any imminent improvement in the situation.

The extent to which these refugees have been given assistance and protection varies. The host countries with the largest groups of Iraqi refugees from 1991 – Iran and Saudi Arabia – have spent substantial sums on sustaining them, but they could hardly be described as welcome guests. Of the main host countries, Iran is a state party to the 1951 UN Convention relating to the status of refugees, which sets international norms for asylum and treatment of refugees. Turkey is a signatory to the convention but restricts its application to refugees from Europe. Saudi Arabia, Syria and Jordan are not signatories. In these countries UNHCR is not given access to refugees as of right. Even in Iran, its role is restricted both in terms of aid to refugees and their protection. Other aid agencies face considerable restrictions working in Iran or Turkey, and are not able to work with Iraqi refugees in Saudi Arabia.

Iran

The largest Iraqi refugee community remains in Iran. It is diverse in make-up, circumstances and geographic location. The majority of the 1.2–1.4 million Kurds who fled to Iran in March and April 1991 had returned to Iraqi Kurdistan by the end of summer 1991, and there were some further returns in 1992. Those Kurds who remained joined a large Iraqi refugee and exile community. Estimates vary, but some 600,000 Iraqis in a 'refugee-like situation' are thought to remain in Iran.[96]

The Iranians did not encourage the Kurds who arrived in 1991 to remain. There seem to have been some forced returns, but the main disincentive to stay was that the Iranian authorities stated their intention to move the 1991 refugees to camps away from the border and away from cities where there were services and opportunities to work.

At the beginning of 1994, the Iranian authorities announced their hope that it would be possible to repatriate the majority of the Iraqi Kurdish refugees (both from 1991 and earlier exoduses) into Iraqi Kurdistan. However, subsequent inter-Kurdish fighting and the difficult economic conditions have slowed voluntary repatriation, with just under 20,000 Kurds returning between 1994 and late 1998.[97]

When the PUK precipitately withdrew from Sulaymaniya in September 1996, Iran was faced with another refugee crisis as a large number of Iraqi Kurdish civilians fled the advancing KDP forces along with the PUK fighters and party cadres. Some 40,000 people crossed into Iran in September.[98] The Iranian Government repeatedly called for international aid, and permitted some aid agencies to visit the camps on the border to assess conditions.[99] Once the PUK retook Sulaymaniya, the Iranians wanted the refugees to return as fast as possible and to close the camps. UNHCR was not involved in the repatriations and therefore could not confirm that they were voluntary. By January 1997 most of those who fled in September and October had returned.[100]

Since 1991, an Iraqi Shi'i refugee community has remained in Khuzestan province in the south-west. Of the 65–70,000 refugees from southern Iraq who fled after the uprisings of March/April 1991, some 15,000 are thought to have returned during the amnesty which lasted until December 1991.[101] They were escorted to their homes by officials of the International Organisation for Migration, but neither UNHCR nor ICRC were able to keep track of what happened to them. Some refugees remaining in Iran alleged that people who returned were subsequently arrested. This was not unlikely, given the Government's persistent searches for those involved in the uprisings and the record of arrests, disappearances and killings of people returning under government amnesties during the 1980s.

Certainly fear of retribution by the Iraqi authorities, the harsh economic conditions in southern Iraq and discouragement by the Iraqi political groups present among the refugees in Iran have deterred further returns on any scale. In 1991 and 1992/3, Iran also accepted two groups of Iraqi refugees – a total of 2630 people – who had initially been housed in camps in Saudi Arabia. At the end of 1993 there were estimated to be 30,000 refugees from 1991 remaining in Khuzestan, of whom some 19,000 were living in five refugee camps. Others had settled in local communities or had gone to live in Teheran or Qom. Those living outside the camps had to be sponsored by Iranian citizens, Iraqi relatives or one of the Iraqi political groups in Iran.

The Iranian attitude to this Shi'i group was more welcoming than to the Kurds, but life has not been easy, either for those in the camps or in surrounding communities. Khuzestan was still recovering from extensive damage and depopulation during the Iran-Iraq War, and for the local population, let alone for the refugees, employment was scarce. By 1993, rations provided in the refugee camps through the over-taxed Iranian Red Crescent became increasingly erratic.

From the summer of 1993 until 1995, a new wave of refugees from southern Iraq began to arrive, totalling more than 10,000 people. In contrast to the 1991 refugees from the south, who came from all parts of the region and all walks of life, this group consisted mainly of people from the marshes, driven from their homes by the systematic draining of the marshes by the Iraqi authorities. The draining of the marshes had also facilitated army movement, allowing troops to enter villages and round up inhabitants. The journey to Iran was difficult and dangerous, and some who attempted it died or were killed by soldiers on the way.

Most of the new arrivals were gathered in a makeshift camp at Himmet, on the Iran-Iraq border in the Howeizeh marshes, from where the Iranian authorities gradually dispersed them to other camps. Some were sent to camps outside Khuzestan, at Asna in Lorestan province and Jahrom in Fars province. Further camps were also created in Khuzestan.

There were indications by 1994/5 that the Iranians were making efforts to discourage further new arrivals. The Government also tightened its grip on the camps. Until March 1994, the Iranian Red Crescent Society ran the camps in Khuzestan and provided a basic ration, though since 1993 its resources had been severely stretched. From March 1994, the Iranian refugee authority, the Bureau for Aliens and Foreign Immigrants Affairs, BAFIA (part of the Ministry of the Interior), took responsibility from the Iranian Red Crescent Society for the management of most of the refugee camps in Khuzestan.

The Government has been vocal in its complaints about the lack of international assistance which, given the number of refugees in Iran, are justified. It nonetheless has not made it easy for external organisations to work in the country. A number of aid agencies had worked in Iran during the crisis of early 1991, but all had withdrawn by the end of the year. While some international NGOs revisited Iran and agreed that there were needs among Iraqi refugees, most found difficulties in agreeing on terms of work with the Iranian authorities. Aside from arranging voluntary repatriation since 1991, UNHCR has had a relatively limited role in assisting the remaining Kurdish and Shi'i Iraqi refugees. Neither the US nor European states have accepted more than a handful of refugees from Iran. In the US case, this is explained by the absence of diplomatic relations but, in general, there has been little international support for these refugees.

Since 1992, organisations wholly or partly run and staffed by expatriate Iraqis (some based in London, others in Iran) contributed significantly to helping refugees in Khuzestan, providing assistance in the five main refugee camps (including building schools and clinics), and relief aid and medical care to the new arrivals in 1993/4. Some of these organisations had their difficulties with the Iranian authorities, while personal and political rivalries resulted in lack of coordination between their programmes. They received funds from a few donor governments and international NGOs, most of which had no presence in the area.[102]

Saudi Arabia

Under pressure from its Western allies, Saudi Arabia accepted its first ever group of refugees – 37,768 Iraqis in all: 24,000 civilians, the remainder former prisoners of war (ex-soldiers and rebels who fought in the 1991 uprising in the south) – who had sought the protection of US forces in southern Iraq. From March 1991 until December 1992, civilian refugees were accommodated in a camp at Rafha, near the Iraqi border, while former POWs and rebel fighters were held at Artawiya in 'harsh, prison-like conditions'. At the end of 1992, all the refugees were brought together in

Rafha camp. According to the US Committee for Refugees, about 4000 Iraqi refugees from both Rafha and Artawiya 'were forcibly repatriated before UNHCR was able to establish a presence in the camps'.[103]

Saudi Arabia refused to accept any of the Iraqi refugees on a permanent basis or allow any form of integration. Rafha has therefore remained a closed camp from which refugees cannot move without permission. Given continuing insecurity in Iraq, UNHCR considers resettlement in third countries to be their only option. UNHCR reported that by early 1997 nearly two-thirds of these refugees had been resettled. More than half of the total were admitted to the United States, which has therefore gone some way to discharge the obligation incurred in early 1991 when the refugees sought its army's protection. The other countries which resettled significant numbers from Saudi Arabia were Iran, Sweden, Australia and the Netherlands.[104]

However, those who do remain in Rafha camp probably have less chance of resettlement and face more years in isolation, until the situation in Iraq changes. Although UNHCR has advised Iraqi refugees that it cannot do anything to guarantee their safety if they return to Iraq, an estimated 3000 Iraqis have reportedly repatriated voluntarily from Rafha since it opened.[105]

The Saudi Arabian Government spent considerable sums on the establishment of facilities in Rafha camp, controlled by the Ministry of Defence with services provided by the Government in conjunction with the International Islamic Relief Organisation, an officially sanctioned charitable organisation. Physical conditions and facilities are therefore relatively good. However, relations between the refugees and the Saudi authorities, particularly the camp guards, became very tense. After a violent clash in March 1993, in which four Saudis and at least nine refugees were reported to have been killed and as many as 140 injured, some 400 refugees were detained. A year later, 31 refugees remained in detention in 'A'rar without trial.[106]

In May 1994 Amnesty International issued a report expressing concern at the treatment of Iraqi refugees in Rafha camp. Amnesty had 'received numerous reports of widespread human rights violations perpetrated with total impunity by the camp authorities. These include the arbitrary detention of refugees, their torture and ill-treatment... possible extrajudicial executions and forcible return to Iraq'.[107]

The Saudi authorities clearly resented criticism or enquiry on this subject. ICRC was excluded from the kingdom from the end of 1993. UNHCR itself has to operate on sufferance and has played a very low-key role. Western states are beholden to Saudi Arabia for solving a potentially embarrassing problem by accepting the refugees. They also have strong economic and strategic interests in the kingdom, and hence have not taken any strong or open stand on alleged abuses.

Turkey

After the rapid return of refugees while coalition forces were still in place, the Turkish authorities concentrated the remaining Iraqi refugees in a camp near Silopi. In late 1992, UNHCR arranged the repatriation to northern Iraq of some 17,000 Iraqi refugees who had been in Turkey since 1988, most of whom came from Dohuk governorate.[108] The remaining refugees refused to return and sought third-country resettlement – a long and often difficult process. However, by the beginning of 1994 only some 2000 Iraqi refugees from the groups which fled Iraq in 1988 and 1991 remained in Turkey.

During 1994, UNHCR determined that 634 of these refugees were to be given refugee status, and countries of resettlement were to be sought for them. The remaining 1400 were told they should return to northern Iraq. At the end of 1993, UNHCR had decided that improved security conditions in Iraqi Kurdistan would allow returns. However, internal fighting flared up from May 1994 onwards. In October 1994, 500 residents of the Silopi Haj camp went on hunger strike, demanding 'that UNHCR protect them from forced return to Iraq and resettle them in third countries'. The local Turkish governor had allegedly informed the refugees that if UNHCR did not provide another solution for them, he would deport them to Iraq. By the end of 1994, most residents decided to repatriate, leaving only 444 Iraqi residents in the camp.[109]

Seeking asylum

The prospect of any further mass movement of people out of Iraq has met with an increasingly hardline response in neighbouring states. Iran's initial response to the flight of Kurds from Sulaymaniya in 1996 indicated a hardening of its attitude compared with 1991. Initially it closed one of the main border crossings at Siran Band when large-scale movement began, and appeared to propose that the refugees be helped within Iraqi territory and not cross the border. It subsequently relented when the offensive came close to the border, but located all the camps in the border zone.[110]

During the confrontation with Iraq over UNSCOM inspections during February 1998, Turkey again signalled very clearly that it would not allow any access to its territory for Iraqi Kurds if the crisis were to trigger an exodus. Turkish Interior Minister Murat Basesgioglu announced on 7 February that if an emergency refugee situation developed, Turkey's border with Iraq would not be opened, but humanitarian aid would be provided on the Iraqi side of the border.[111] During the same crisis, Crown Prince Hassan of Jordan announced that his country would close its borders to Iraqi refugees if the US resorted to military strikes against Iraq.[112]

Increasing numbers of individuals and families have tried to leave Iraq during the years since 1991. Among those leaving via Jordan, few received visas or asylum in the West, though families who already have relatives in Western countries tend to fare better (see Chapter 5).

Those passing through Turkey faced a general hardening of Turkey's position on non-European refugees, including an explicit statement on stopping mass movements of refugees at the border, thus codifying its 1991 practice.[113] In September 1994 regulations came into force requiring that all non-European asylum seekers first present themselves to the Turkish authorities, who screen them before they approach UNHCR for refugee status.[114] Relatively few applications – a few hundred a year – were being accepted for asylum. Iraqis living in Turkey outside refugee camps were also said to be vulnerable to forcible repatriation.[115]

Most of those leaving northern Iraq have travelled through Turkey *en route* for Europe. The trade in refugee transport is expensive and dangerous: to Greece via mine-filled waters, often in ramshackle boats, to Italy or Russia and Eastern European countries. Reports from Turkey, Europe and the countries of the CIS in

1993/4 suggested that growing numbers of Iraqi Kurds were trying to seek asylum, particularly in Nordic countries.[116]

Many such 'illegal' refugees became stranded in countries which do not have adequate reception facilities for refugees, and often encountered indifference or hostility. In 1994, there were reportedly some 1500 Iraqis in Russia, many of them in difficult economic straits, and with few facilities to assist them. Some were being looked after by the Red Cross. The Russian Federation does have laws relating to refugees,[117] but some of the Baltic states, for example Latvia and Estonia, where a number of Iraqis ended up, did not even have a legal framework to deal with refugees. In 1993/4, some 86 Iraqis, including women, children and old people, spent a year or more in Estonian detention centres before finally being transferred to Finland.[118]

By 1997, the number of people leaving Iraq, particularly from Iraqi Kurdistan, and trying to reach Europe, was causing alarm in the EU.

According to the US Department of State:

> Several European governments reported that the number of [illegal immigrants and asylum seekers], especially Turkish and Iraqi Kurds, who had arrived in their countries from Turkey increased dramatically in 1997. While many travelled in small groups utilising land routes across the Turkish-Greek border, increasing numbers departed via boat and ship. There were several tragic cases of overloaded small boats sinking in the Aegean, resulting in dozens of drownings. There were also, at the end of 1997, a number of high profile cases where large vessels, carrying hundreds of people each, arrived in Italy after having departed from Turkish ports.[119]

Smuggling of migrants and refugees from and via Turkey is nothing new, but the scale of operations appeared to grow markedly in 1997, with ships being chartered to carry refugees. Illegal migrants reportedly pay $1500 or more per person in advance to smugglers for the journey to Greece or Italy by sea, often in dangerous vessels. Clearly, for a shipload of 800 or more people there are significant profits to be made by smugglers.[120]

The alarm was raised when some 1200 people, the majority of them Kurds from Turkey and Iraq, arrived in Italian ports by sea in the first week in January 1998.[121] There was pressure on Italy and Greece to tighten their hitherto liberal asylum policies. This had already happened in other European states which had previously had liberal policies on asylum: Germany, Sweden and Denmark. There were fears that if these countries allowed the refugees to remain, the refugees would find their way to other EU states, particularly Germany. Most countries in the region have tightened criteria for accepting asylum seekers and insist that the Schengen rules of free movement within the EU were predicated on strong external border controls.[122]

NOTES ON CHAPTER 3

1   Cook (1995), p 4.
2   Schachter (1991), p 469.
3   Bettati (1996i), pp 186–7.
4   Murphy (1995), pp 290–91.
5   Remarks made by the Secretary General on Entering the Building, 10 May 1991, quoted in Johnstone (1994), p 69, note 20. On the other hand, the US Ambassador to the UN, Thomas Pickering, told a congressional hearing that in implementing Operation Provide Comfort, the US was 'in our view, operating under the general authority' of Resolution 688. Asked if the UN Secretary General had approved the action, he replied, 'The Secretary General has been closely consulted and been quite supportive'. US Congress, House of Representatives, Committee on Foreign Affairs, UN Role in the Persian Gulf and Iraqi Compliance with UN Resolutions: Hearing before the Subcommittees on Europe and the Middle East and on Human Rights and International Organisations of the Committee on Foreign Affairs, April 23, 1991, p 52.
6   United Nations (1996i), p 41.
7   Zieck (1997), p 195–6, footnote 135; United Nations (1996i) UNSC Resolution 688 para. 2, Document 37.
8   Zieck (1997), p 213 notes the insertion of reference to Article 2 (7) of the Charter expressly 'to highlight and emphasise the inadmissibility of intervention in the internal affairs ("domestic jurisdiction") of Iraq either by the United Nations or individual states rather than enforcement measures based on Chapter VII of the Charter'.
9   This compromise has not proved very satisfactory either for the protagonists of intervention or their opponents: 'Both sides see the Council's resolution as legally incoherent: it bows to the principle of noninterference in domestic jurisdiction in article 2(7) but then proceeds to interfere, without making an explicit determination that the situation constitutes a breach of the international peace' (Jose E. Alvarez [1995], p 8).
10   United Nations Security Council (1992). China, India and Zimbabwe expressed reservations about this invitation (United Nations [1996i] p 106).
11   *Washington Post*, 12 August 1992, 'US Warns Iraq on Shiites'.
12   Paul Wolfowitz, Under Secretary for Policy, Department of Defense 1991–2, interview with the author, 28 May 1997.
13   *Washington Post*, 18 August 1992, 'US Plan to Bar Iraqi Flights in South Follows Stepped-Up Attacks on Shiites'.
14   BBC Radio 4 transcript ref. no. 1897, BBC Radio 4 'The World at One', Wednesday 19 August 1992.
15   *Washington Post*, 22 August 1992, 'Iraq Refuses to Renew Accord That Permits UN Role There'.
16   Statement issued by the Members of the Coalition, New York, 26 August 1992 (Weller [1993], p 725).
17   Marine Lt-Gen. Martin Brandtner, Director of Operations for the Joint Staff, quoted in *Washington Post*, 27 August 1992, 'Allies Declare "No-Fly Zone" in Iraq'.
18   InterPress Service, 19 August 1992.
19   Written response from the Department of State, US Congress, House of Representatives, Committee on Foreign Affairs, Developments in the Middle East October 1993: Hearing before the Subcommittee on Europe and the Middle East of the Committee on Foreign Affairs, October 21, 1993, p 71.
20   US Department of State (1995), p 1088.
21   US Congress, House of Representatives, Committee on Foreign Affairs, Developments in the Middle East March 1994: Hearing before the Sub-Committee on Europe and the Middle East of the Committee on Foreign Affairs, March 1, 1994, p 25.
22   Symposium on Dual Containment (1994), p 22.

23   R.J. Brown (1995), p 93; Lawyers Committee for Human Rights (1992), p 14.

24   In August 1991, when coalition forces were still based in Turkey, Britain's Armed Forces Minister Archie Hamilton stated that the allied force was intended to cover only those areas which were part of the allied enclave. 'The rest of the Kurdish-held zone, which stretches east and south-east across Iraq, was not covered, though the allies would certainly condemn any offensive action there' (Keen [1993], p 15).

25   US Congress, Senate, Committee on Armed Services, The Situation in Iraq: Hearing before the Committee on Armed Services, September 12, 1996, p 8.

26   Lawyers Committee for Human Rights (1992), p 3.

27   McDowall (1997), p 370.

28   McDowall (1997), p 371. For a personal account of behind-the-scenes discussions which preceded President Ozal's decision, see Randal (1997), pp 90–95.

29   Robins (1993), p 674.

30   By 1994, the war was estimated to cost between 7.5 and 15 billion a year. Since 1984 some 15,000 people had died in the conflict (Ozel [1995], p 183). The army itself is not unanimous in its view on tactics in regard to the Kurds, and some elements within the military apparently blame the Government for not improving economic conditions in the south-east. However, neither the military nor the civilian political establishment appear yet to have found a way to deal with Kurdish identity as an issue, or to engage with political as opposed to military forces among the Kurds. Discussion of this sensitive topic has been left to non-government bodies, for example human rights organisations, the Turkish Association of Industrialists and Businessmen (TUSIAD) and sections of the press. The war, and the widespread destruction of villages which might act as bases for the PKK, forced most of the rural population of the south-east into towns, and triggered a major wave of out-migration from the region. Although certain companies and individuals have flourished in Turkey as a result of the international embargo against Iraq – having 'cornered the trade' or cashed in on transport needs – economic activity based on cross-border trade is said to have declined, affecting income and employment in south-eastern Turkey, already an economically depressed region.

31   Turkey Briefing (London), December 1990, vol. 4, no. 6, p 3.

32   Kamran Qaradaghi, 'Iraq, the Kurds and the "big four"', al-Hayat, 8 August 1991, translated in Middle East International, 16 August 1991.

33   Gulf Newsletter, January 1993, no. 5, 'Turkey and the Iraqi Kurds', p 4.

34   Agha and Khalidi (1995), p 85.

35   See, for example, their statement after the fifth tripartite meeting, BBC Summary of World Broadcasts, 8 February 1994, 'Syrian, Iranian and Turkish Foreign Ministers Make Joint Statement after Talks', quoting Syrian Arab Republic Radio, 6 February 1994.

36   Fuller (1993), p 56.

37   Turkey Briefing, Winter 1993, vol. 7, no. 4, p 5.

38   Agha and Khalidi (1995), p 84.

39   Chubin (1994), pp 8–9.

40   Middle East International, 21 November 1997, 'Deep into Iraq'.

41   Cuny (1995), pp 21–2.

42   Ibid., p 38.

43   Ibid., p 25.

44   Ozel (1995), p 177.

45   Ibid.

46   The US position on Turkish operations in northern Iraq has remained constant since 1991. 'The United States has consistently condemned PKK terrorism and acknowledges Turkey's legitimate right to self defense. We have also expressed to the Turkish Government our view that Turkish forces should swiftly conclude any cross-border attack against suspected PKK positions and avoid death or injury to innocent civilians'

(State Department reply to supplemental question no. 2. Congress, House of Representatives, Committee on Foreign Affairs, Developments in the Middle East, November 1991: Hearing before the Subcommittee on Europe and the Middle East of the Committee on Foreign Affairs, November 20, 1991, p 69). On 21 May 1997, at a State Department Press Briefing, spokesman Nicholas Burns reiterated the same points: 'The Turkish Government has been clear. It does not seek to occupy northern Iraq. It seeks to destroy the base of a terrorist organisation that threatens Turkey – particularly the civilian population in the southeast. We believe that Turkey has a right to defend itself against terrorism. We also believe that this incursion should be short, brief in time as well as scope.'

47 During the Turkish incursion of May 1997 the EU called on Turkey to 'withdraw its military forces from Iraqi territory as soon as possible'. UN Secretary General Kofi Annan said the violation of the territorial integrity of any state was unacceptable (*Le Monde*, 22 May 1997, 'L'imbroglio des alliances au Kurdistan irakien').

48 Piet Dankert, member of the European Parliament, interview with the author, 30 September 1997.

49 France had officially invited a Kurdish delegation to France in September 1990 (Kutschera [1997], pp 86–7).

50 Kutschera (1997), p 117 and footnote 60.

51 A source in Quai D'Orsay in 1997 criticised UK and US policy as having sent a message to the Iraqi Kurds which 'encouraged ideas of independence'.

52 BBC Summary of World Broadcasts, 23 April 1998, 'Russian and French envoys mediating between Kurdish leaders and Baghdad', quoting *al-Hayat*, 18 April 1998.

53 According to Kutschera (1997), Edward Djerejian, Assistant Secretary of State, Bureau of Near Eastern and South Asian Affairs, during a meeting in October 1991 with a Kurdish delegation, would not say whether autonomy negotiations should continue or not, adding that this was a matter for the Kurds to judge (p 114).

54 David L. Mack asserts that he consistently emphasised that the US did not support an independent Kurdish state. He recalls telling Kurdish leaders, 'We want you to be in the government in Baghdad not to have a government in Arbil' (interview, *op. cit.*)

55 Kutschera (1997), p 117. In answer to a written parliamentary question from Sir David Steel asking what support the British Government would give to the KF in preparing for the elections, and what recognition Britain would give to the elections and their result, the Minister of State at the Foreign Office, Douglas Hogg, gave the following reply (15 May 1992): 'We have told the Kurdish political leaders that it is in their own interests to work together in opposing Saddam Hussein's repression and in bringing an end to the economic blockade which he has imposed on northern Iraq. We hope that regional elections will help achieve this. We support the Kurds' aim of autonomy, not independence, within Iraq's existing borders. Kurdish leaders have told us that this is what they want' (Hansard, House of Commons, vol. 207, 27 April–15 May 1992, Written Answers, col. 242.)

56 In mid-1994 Assistant Secretary of State Pelletreau stated, 'Our commitment to provide protection and humanitarian assistance to the peoples of northern Iraq and to support the continuation of Operation Provide Comfort remains absolutely firm...' (Congress, House of Representatives, Foreign Affairs Committee, Developments in the Middle East June 1994: Hearing before the Subcommittee on Europe and the Middle East of the Foreign Affairs Committee, June 14, 1994, p 49). On 2 March 1995, in a Senate Foreign Relations Committee hearing, Pelletreau stressed the humanitarian assistance provided under Operation Provide Comfort, without using the word 'protection' (US Congress, Senate, Foreign Relations Committee, US Policy Toward Iran and Iraq: Hearing before the Subcommittee on Near Eastern and South Asian Affairs, March 2, 1995, p 36). President Clinton's Letter to Congressional Leaders on Iraq dated November 4 1996 spoke of continuing to provide humanitarian assistance to the people

of northern Iraq, despite the 'temporary' withdrawal of the MCC. He did not allude to Operation Provide Comfort or any form of 'protection' (*Weekly Compilation of Presidential Documents*, vol. 32, no. 45, 11 November 1996, p 2339).

57 See, for example, Assistant Secretary of State Pelletreau's Statement to the House Committee on International Relations, September 25 1996 (electronic copy, http://www.state.gov).

58 Ahmad Chalabi, President of the INC, alleges that he was asked by one of the CIA operatives to contact with the Iranians, to suggest that Iran move troops to the border to 'distract' the Iraqis once the opposition attack began (*Washington Post*, 26 June 1997, 'How CIA's Secret War on Saddam Collapsed').

59 Details of this convoluted affair can be found in: *Washington Post*, 15 September 1996, 'Anti-Saddam Operation Cost $100 million'; ABC News, 'Peter Jenning Reporting: Unfinished Business – The CIA and Saddam Hussein', 26 June 1997; *Washington Post*, 26 June 1997, 'How CIA's Secret War on Saddam Collapsed'.

60 US intelligence was aware of Iraqi troop movements some days before the attack (see Chapter 6). According to Ahmad Chalabi, the CIA operatives disappeared from Salahadin some days before the Iraqi attack (ABC News *op. cit.*).

61 Communiqué issued by the Ministry of Foreign Affairs, Paris, 5 September 1996, SAC/96/185 – France/US/Iraq (issued in English by French Embassy in London).

62 *Washington Post*, 4 September 1996, 'Why Clinton's Response Fell Far From Site of Saddam's Aggression'; *Le Monde Diplomatique*, October 1996, 'Le Malheur kurde'; French Embassy, London, 'Interview with M. Hervé de Charette, Minister of Foreign Affairs, Broadcast on Europe 1", 8 September 1996.

63 US Department of State, Press Statement, 25 December 1996, 'Extension of Coalition Air Operations Over Northern Iraq'. In this document the MCC is referred to as the 'Military Command Centre' but it had previously been known as the 'Military Coordination Centre'.

64 Ministry of Foreign Affairs, 'La politique française à l'égard de l'Iraq', Paris, November 1997. Eric Rouleau suggested, a few weeks before this statement was issued, that the US had been infringing the terms of Resolution 688 by trying to discourage negotiations between the Kurdish parties and Baghdad (interview with the author, 22 October 1997).

65 *Washington Post*, 11 September 1996, 'US Redefines Interests to Fit Iraq Scenario'; *Daily Telegraph*, 11 September 1996, 'The Post-Heroic West'.

66 US Department of State (1997), Section IG (electronic copy, http://www.state.gov): 'The no-fly zones continue to deter aerial attacks on the marsh dwellers in southern Iraq and residents of northern Iraq, but they do not prevent artillery attacks in either areas, nor the military's large scale burning operations in the south'.

67 US Congress, House of Representatives, Committee on International Affairs, US Policy in the Persian Gulf: Hearing before the Committee on International Relations, 104th Congress 2nd session, September 25, 1996, p 19.

68 Information from the Press Section, French Embassy, London, 22 January 1999.

69 Joseph S. Nye, Assistant Secretary of Defense for International Security Affairs. US Congress, Senate, Foreign Relations Committee, US Policy Toward Iran and Iraq: Hearing before the Subcommittee on Near Eastern and South Asian Affairs, March 2, 1995, p 37. The French and British Ministries of Defence also paid towards this operation.

70 During the January 1993 confrontation with Iraq, for example, Turkey made it clear that allied planes should not be used for pre-planned bombing raids and should only strike in self-defence (Keen [1993], p 16). In 1996, it was evident that Turkey would not allow US air strikes from the Incirlik base.

71 Turkish officials at Incirlik had access to the film taken on coalition flights over northern Iraq, which they were able to use for their own purposes. Fred Cuny, writing in 1995, cited the following examples of concerns on the part of American, French and British officers about the influence of Turkey within Operation Provide Comfort:

'The Turks receive information via the MCC, the... AWACS and NATO intelligence channels about the security situation in Iraqi Kurdistan, all of which they can use in planning their attacks on Kurds on both sides of the border.

'Officers [in the MCC and CTF] report that they are under pressure to self-censor reports to make them acceptable to the Turks and information that could be important for US policy inputs is routinely watered down and in some cases, not sent up the chain-of-command.

'There are reports that Turkish officers have withheld key information about the PKK and their own security operations in northern Iraq from their allied counterparts which could endanger some MCC missions.'

On an operational level, 'the Turks have restricted the allied overflights and forced cancellation of OPC flying missions. They do not permit the allies to fly when Turkish planes are on missions in northern Iraq...' Finally, 'they have restricted AWACS flights with bureaucratic procedures' (Cuny [1995], pp 36–7).

72   'Gulf Security and US Policy', *Middle East Policy*, vol. 3, no. 4, April 1995, pp 10–11.

73   UNSC Resolution 949, 15 October 1994 (United Nations 1996i), Document 196.

74   Resolution 1991/74.

75   United Nations Economic and Social Council, Commission on Human Rights (1992), para. 13.

76   As of September 1997, the Centre became part of the Office of the High Commissioner for Human Rights.

77   Resolution 1992/71, 'Situation of Human Rights in Iraq', UN Commission on Human Rights, 55th meeting, 5 March 1992, E/CN.4/1992/94.

78   The lack of enthusiasm on the part of the UK Government was illustrated by a parliamentary answer given by the Foreign Secretary Douglas Hurd on 4 March 1992. In reply to a question by Emma Nicholson as to whether Britain would ensure human rights monitors were placed in southern Iraq, he only confirmed that the Government was 'worried' about human rights abuses, and that the Minister for Overseas Development was trying to arrange a donor conference to bring further aid. 'The best relief of human rights,' he added, would be Iraqi compliance with Resolutions 706 and 712. He did not respond directly on the issue of monitors (Hansard House of Commons, Vol. 205, 2–16 March 1992, col. 300).

79   United Nations Security Council (1992).

80   Human rights rapporteurs usually report only to the Human Rights Commission of the UN Economic and Social Council and the UN General Assembly. However, since 1992 the Special Rapporteur on former Yugoslavia has reported to both the Security Council and the General Assembly.

81   'Situation of human rights in Iraq', Note by the UN Secretary General, 13 November 1992.

82   In August 1993, the US State Department had issued a public statement condemning Iraq's 'campaign of destruction and repression in the marshes' and its infringements of Resolution 688. It supported a call from the UN Sub-Commission on Prevention of Discrimination and Protection of Minorities that the Special Rapporteur should visit the region and interview refugees, but it did not allude to the placing of monitors in Iraq.

83   United Nations Economic and Social Council, Commission on Human Rights (1994), para. 9. The US State Department of State (1995) noted in its human rights report that during 1994 another part-time employee was added to the Special Rapporteur's staff but the latter 'nevertheless asserted that he needs further resources to carry out his mandate' (p 1093).

84   Amnesty International was the only organisation to produce a major report on human rights abuses since 1991 in Iraqi Kurdistan. Human Rights Watch now includes Iraqi Kurdistan as a separate section in its annual report on Iraq. Until 1996, the US State Department's annual Human Reports gave limited coverage to Kurdish abuses, or external states' actions in Iraqi Kurdistan. Its 1997 report includes more detail.

85   Cook (1995), pp 46–7.

86 United Nations General Assembly (1992), para. 56(e).

87 Cook (1995), p 47.

88 United Nations, Economic and Social Council, Commission on Human Rights (1992), para. 28.

89 Human Rights Watch/Middle East (1995ii), pp 3–4. The Government of Iraq reiterated this argument in its fourth periodic report on its implementation of the International Covenant on Civil and Political Rights (UN Special Rapporteur, 1998i, Section IIC).

90 An exception is the Center for Economic and Social Rights in New York. However, its reports have for the most part confined themselves to these 'second generation' issues, and have not dealt with civil or political abuses.

91 The International Criminal Tribunals on former Yugoslavia and Rwanda can prosecute named individuals for four types of crime: the crime of genocide, crimes against humanity, grave breaches of the 1949 Geneva Conventions, and violations of the laws and customs of war (David J. Scheffer, Ambassador-at-Large for War Crimes Issues, US Department of State, Address before the Washington Institute for Near East Policy, Washington DC, May 21, 1998).

92 *The Sunday Times*, 3 March 1991, 'A Bit of Unfinished Agenda'.

93 Senator Claiborne Pell, who was an advocate of such a tribunal, speaking as chairman of a hearing before the Senate Foreign Relations Committee in April 1991, noted: '... last month the Senate unanimously adopted a resolution calling on the President to confer with our coalition partners in the UN to establish an international court or tribunal to prosecute the responsible Iraqi parties for crimes against international law. It is unclear what the administration's intentions are with respect to this question. Representatives of the Executive Branch were invited but declined to testify at today's hearing. This, I regret' (Congress, Senate, Committee on Foreign Relations, Persian Gulf: the Question of War Crimes: Hearing before the Committee on Foreign Relations, April 9, 1991, pp 1–2).

94 Dowty (1994), p 181. According to Martin Indyk, 'As an administration we did seek a Crimes-Against-Humanity War-Crimes Commission to be established at the UN to investigate Iraqi behaviour... We have not yet succeeded, partly because of a lack of support from coalition partners for an effort to investigate Iraqi war crimes. It's unfortunate that it had to wait until the Clinton administration came to power for the Defense Department's report on Iraqi war crimes to be published... But the Crimes Against Humanity Commission is a very real option and one which we are planning to pursue with vigor at the UN.' (Symposium on Dual Containment [1994], p 25).

95 David J. Scheffer, *op cit*.

96 Of this total, at the end of 1993 over 100,000 Iraqi refugees were being assisted by UNHCR. About 60 percent of this group were housed in camps, 17 camps in the western provinces for the Kurds, and 10 camps in the central and southern provinces for those from southern Iraq (US Committee for Refugees [1997], p 149). According to the Iranian authorities, there is a total of 645,000 Iraqis in Iran, the majority of whom arrived before 1991.

97 According to the International Organisation for Migration, up to the end of 1996, 6319 Iraqi refugees returned to Iraqi Kurdistan under the auspices of the Kurdish Repatriation Programme, funded by UNHCR. In 1997, 4913 people returned and in 1998, 8735, reflecting the improved security conditions ('IOM News: Kurds return to northern Iraq', 5 October 1998, http://www.reliefweb.int).

98 UNHCR, 'Northern Iraq Briefing Notes', 15 October 1996, http://www.reliefweb.int.

99 *Financial Times*, 13 September 1996, 'Iran Pleads For Refugee Aid'.

100 US Committee for Refugees (1997), p 149; BBC Summary of World Broadcasts, 4 December 1996, 'Some 23,000 Iraqi Kurdish Refugees Return Home From Iran', quoting IRNA news agency (Teheran), 2 December 1996; BBC Summary of World Broadcasts, 6 January 1996, 'Kurdish Refugees Return to Iraq', quoting IRNA news agency, Teheran, 4 January 1996.

101 This seems to have been the end date for two Iraqi government amnesties announced on 21 July 1991. They covered Iraqis who had left the country for political reasons, political prisoners, those in public service against whom legal measures had been taken, and deserters who were arrested or gave themselves up from 20 March 1991 onwards. They were published in *al-Thawra* and *al-Jumhuriyah* on 22 July 1991.

102 Among these organisations (the names and groups have changed over time) are the Amar Appeal (headed by Emma Nicholson MP, but run in Iran by Iraqi staff), Iraqi Civilian Aid, Iraqi Refugee Aid Committee, Relief International, and the humanitarian aid organisation of the Supreme Council for the Islamic Revolution in Iraq (SCIRI).

103 US Committee for Refugees (1995), p 121. See also the mission of the US-based Lawyers Committee for Human Rights in April 1992. On the basis of its findings, the Committee appealed to the Saudi Government to end the virtual detention regime in Artawiya.

104 UNHCR (1997), p 88.

105 US Committee for Refugees (1997), p 162.

106 Amnesty International, (1994), p 21; US Committee for Refugees (1995), p 121.

107 Amnesty International (1994), Summary.

108 US Committee for Refugees (1994), p 152.

109 Zeick (1997), p 240; US Committee for Refugees (1995), p 167.

110 US Committee for Refugees (1997), p 148. As fears of a new refugee flow increased in early September, the Director-General of BAFIA stated 'The Islamic Republic of Iran's policy in this respect is that no more refugees should be accepted. However, facilities will be provided to deliver any aid from other governments and international organisations along the border regions and the camps [already set up] in these regions' (BBC Summary of World Broadcasts, 11 September 1996, 'Iranian Interior Ministry says Kurdish refugees cannot cross Iran's border', quoting Voice of the Islamic Republic of Iran, Teheran, 9 September 1996). The Foreign Ministry issued a more conciliatory statement, saying that if faced with a situation similar to that of 1991, the Islamic Republic 'will undertake this humanitarian/Islamic task' of accepting Kurdish refugees, but emphasised the need for international assistance (BBC Summary of World Broadcasts, 11 September 1996, 'Spokesman says Iran will admit Iraqi refugees but needs help', quoting Voice of the Islamic Republic of Iran, Teheran, 10 September 1996).

111 BBC Summary of World Broadcasts, 11 February 1998, 'Turkey Ready for Buffer Zone Against Possible Influx of Refugees from Iraq', quoting Kanal-7 TV, Istanbul, 9 February 1998.

112 US Committee for Refugees, 18 February 1998, press release: 'Iraqi refugees may have no place to run'.

113 For details see Bill Frelick, 'Barriers to Protection Turkey's Asylum Regulations', Issue Brief, US Committee for Refugees, July 1996.

114 In practice, applicants are reportedly interviewed first by the police. Persons with valid visas and passports can file for asylum in the governorate where they are located, but those entering 'without proper documents' must apply at the point where they entered 'illegally' (US Committee for Refugees [1995], p 166).

115 *Ibid.*, 167–8. Non governmental organisations alleged that 'Turkey forcibly repatriated hundreds of Iraqis during the year'. UNHCR was said to have recorded 63 cases of Iraqis who were of concern to UNHCR being forcibly repatriated in 1994. According to the US Committee for Refugees, 'increasingly, Turkish authorities seemed to consider only the passport/visa status of Iraqis in Turkey, disregarding their status relative to UNHCR's mandate'. Kurdish-controlled northern Iraq is considered by Turkey to be safe for Iraqi Kurds.

116 *Gulf Newsletter*, November/December 1994, no. 11, 'Iraqi Refugees in Europe', p 7.

117 UNHCR (1997), pp 200–201.

118 *Gulf Newsletter*, no. 11, *op. cit.*
119 US Department of State (1998i), Section 2D (electronic copy, http://www.state.gov).
120 *Middle East International*, 16 January 1998, 'Human Traffic'; *Daily Telegraph*, 8 January 1998, 'Istanbul Becomes Launch Pad for Exodus to West'.
121 *Middle East International*, 16 January 1998, *op. cit.*
122 *Guardian*, 5 January 1998, 'EU Pulls Down the Shutters'; *Financial Times*, 9 January 1998 , 'Fears Mount Over Italy's Back Door'.

PART I
OVERVIEW

INTERNATIONAL COERCION AND ITS CONSTRAINTS

In the initial phase of the Gulf crisis, the strength of US involvement, as well as the sharply negative international reaction to Iraq's invasion of Kuwait, contributed to the unusually decisive action taken in establishing a comprehensive sanctions regime. This contrasted with the paralysis which overtook the Council during the Cold War and in subsequent crises during the 1990s, when not only was there no consensus for action, but no power had sufficient interest to drive forward decisions.

In the longer term, however, US interest in playing the leading role on the Iraq issue detracted from the multilateral consensus which was evident in the initial response to Iraq's invasion of Kuwait. Until 1994 the US, with British support, effectively dominated Security Council decision-making on the implementation of sanctions and weapons inspections, with few major challenges from other members. Subsequently, the diverging interests of other permanent members limited its freedom of action.

The US position was also weakened by the failure of both the Bush and Clinton administration to establish a clear or consistent strategy on the future of Iraq. Successive US administrations have seen their strategic goal as supporting their 'friends' in the Middle East region, while the Clinton administration, for want of a better alternative, added the attempt to 'contain' Iraq and Iran as 'rogue' states.

The fading international consensus and the lack of clarity over the goals of sanctions eroded even the limited common ground among the permanent five members of the Security Council, allowing the Government of Iraq to exploit the growing differences of opinion. It also blurred the extent to which the embargo could be said to be succeeding or failing. The 'dividends' of economic sanctions on Iraq could only be judged according to the intended goals. In public at least the Clinton administration continues to argue that sanctions are 'effective' because they are still in place and impose a degree of constraint on Iraq's scope for action. Those who regard sanctions as designed to meet the specific goals laid down in Resolution 687 view the embargo's achievements in a different light.

After the Gulf War, the economic embargo was no longer a substitute for the use of force, but an adjunct to it. The US in particular saw economic pressure and military force as part of a package of measures to force Iraq to comply with UN resolutions. However, the embargo did not result either in full compliance or the emergence of a new regime which would accept UN terms. The experience of UNSCOM in Iraq suggested how difficult it can be to ferret out chemical and biological weapons in a state which does not want them to be found. Iraqi resistance justified the maintenance of sanctions, but this was not how the system set up in 1991 was supposed to work.

The other option, to use military force, was also seen to have limitations. The US was willing to launch air strikes and periodically move troops to the Gulf, but it faced domestic pressure to avoid casualties. The military option has therefore, like sanctions, proved a double-edged sword. US officials frequently talk of keeping Saddam Hussein in a box, but in many respects they have fashioned a box for themselves in the pursuit of this policy.

The unexpected staying-power of the Iraqi regime and its continued resistance to the eradication of all weapons of mass destruction (WMD) indicated the extent to which an authoritarian regime can resist international instruments of coercion. When common purpose ceased to be sustained among leading Security Council members, coherent responses to Iraq's defiance became increasingly difficult.

In March 1998, Kofi Annan was welcomed back at UN Plaza from his mission to Baghdad by cheering UN staff. For once it seemed that the UN, through its Secretary General, had pulled off a deal even when the Security Council could find no real consensus on what to do about Iraq. This was a passing moment, but the token celebration suggested how low morale in the UN had become. It followed some disastrous experiences in the 1990s when UN peace-keeping and humanitarian missions were hampered both by UN internal weakness and the inability of the Security Council to provide firm backing. Ironically, in the case of Iraq, one of the few instances when the Security Council had taken a strong role, the certainties of 1991 had faded away. Within the UN system there was increasing resentment at the way US policy was seen to drive decisions, and at the high-handedness of some of the Security Council's permanent members, along with frustration with Iraqi intransigence.

The Secretary General's role in negotiating with Baghdad temporarily enhanced the UN's failing prestige and briefly rescued the US from the deficiencies of its own policy. The weapons crises of 1997 and 1998 clearly revealed the limitations of US policy, especially since confidence within the Arab region was simultaneously being undermined by US failure to advance the Palestinian-Israeli peace process.

The crisis also revealed the limits to the willingness of those powers eager to see sanctions lifted – France, Russia and China – to press the issue in the face of US opposition and Iraq's refusal to reveal the extent of its WMD activities. On the other hand, US decision-making was increasingly hemmed in by its failure to maintain a consensus in the Council.

Selective intervention

In 1991, the international response to the Kurdish refugee crisis was undoubtedly an exceptional event: the leading members of the Gulf War Coalition had troops in the region and strategic interests there. At their back was popular and media pressure to 'do something'. Despite the exceptional circumstances, the success of Operation Provide Comfort in its immediate goals suggested that such international actions, which used military force and infringed state sovereignty were both feasible and justifiable.

UNSC Resolution 688 undoubtedly represented a major step in breaking the 'sanctity' of sovereign state control. But the following years revealed how much these 'path-breaking' measures had been based on short-term expediency rather than well-thought-out principles. Later attempts at humanitarian and military intervention indicated that the underlying attitudes in the international community towards involvement in internal national conflicts had not undergone any major transformation.

The initial success in returning Kurdish refugees and maintaining an international consensus masked ongoing disagreements and ambiguities about how and when to intervene. Even in Iraq, the first response of the major powers to the uprisings and the refugee crisis was inaction. Only in the face of overwhelming pressure from a number of sources did this change. The idea of intervention against the will of a state did indeed gain currency, but the example of Iraq stopped short of providing an effective formula to implement it. Whether presented as a principled refusal to infringe another state's sovereignty or a wish not to become 'bogged down' in internal politics, the enforcement of the international community's policies on Iraq was highly selective.

Security Council members differed considerably in their willingness to infringe Iraq's sovereignty in the name of human rights and humanitarian aid, or through the use of economic sanctions. Non-aligned states were generally reluctant on principle to see the erosion of sovereignty. They viewed such interventions as little more than a tool for powerful states to impose their own priorities. France, which had been at the forefront of the movement to cross borders without state consent during the Kurdish crisis, retreated to asserting that the Kurdish problem had to be solved in the context of the whole of Iraq, even if Saddam Hussein stayed in power. Russia and China had from the beginning been reluctant to accept military interventions.

The protection afforded by both the 'safe haven' and the no-fly zone depended on the credible threat of external force to sustain it. There was no mutual consent by the warring parties to preserve the safety of civilians. Hence protection had to depend on the continued commitment by external powers to sustain the threat, and on the credibility of that threat. As one analyst noted, such a 'credible threat' can in turn 'compromise the safety of the zone, politicise its existence, and complicate humanitarian access to it'.[1]

Furthermore, the areas designated 'protected' were not demilitarised, the only prohibitions being on Iraqi flights above the 36th parallel and, less clearly stated, on Iraqi troops entering the 'security zone' in Dohuk governorate. By 1998, the supposed prohibition on Iraqi troops entering this small area had never been tested. Hence the potential for conflict remained.

Theoretically at least, these steps should have been part of a package which included a settlement of the political conflicts which had led to the crisis. However, because the Iraqi regime which had perpetrated the attacks remained in power and became involved in a long-running conflict with the international community, the resolution of the conflict did not occur. Iraqi Kurdistan became stranded between its status as part of Iraq and its separateness as a zone in which Kurds *de facto* ruled but with no recognised status and where the international community, regional powers and the Iraqi opposition had relatively free play.

Underlying the ambiguous approach of all the major powers was the problem of minorities and how to deal with them. Providing humanitarian aid to such minorities is one thing, abetting demands for independence or even autonomy is another. The hostility of the US and UK to the Government of Iraq has not led to support for any kind of separate Kurdish entity because of the pressures of another sovereign state with a Kurdish minority, Turkey. The situation is further complicated by the fact that several states in the region have large Kurdish populations, all with violent and conflictive relations with their respective states. Among the Kurds themselves there are also differing demands, ranging from independence to cultural rights to full political participation as citizens.

In northern Iraq, the policy of protection was sustained to a limited extent, but it exacerbated the disagreements and confusions with the international community on the status of the Iraqi Kurdish minority. The fears that Iraq might break up, and the priority given – particularly by the US – to accommodating Turkey's concerns and thwarting Iranian influence contributed to the complex regional embroglio.

Whatever the advantages of coalition intervention in 1991, it led to significant changes in the balance of forces inside Iraqi Kurdistan and among neighbouring states in the region. The efforts of various external powers to 'manage' this changing situation while avoiding direct involvement in Kurdish internal politics met with limited success.

Popular responses in the West

The wave of popular sympathy for the Kurds which swept the West in 1991 rapidly faded, as did more general interest in the Iraqi issue, except when the images of Stealth bombers and arrays of weaponry reappeared in the media during each successive crisis. Governments faced few real challenges to the justifications they provided for their policies. There has been little serious public debate either on the validity of sanctions or other aspects of international policy.

In the US, press attention – and criticism – revived briefly in September–October 1996 following the Iraqi incursion into Arbil, with revelations about the CIA's activities, and during the weapons confrontations of late 1997 and early 1998. Secretary of State Madeleine Albright and her team faced some hostile public audiences in early 1998, suggesting some scepticism among the US public over the administration's sabre-rattling. This came not just from the perspective of activists on the Iraq issue, but also from the political right, pursuing a non-interventionist agenda. Since 1991, the US Congress has been proactive on some issues – including enforcement of sanctions in neighbouring states – and has shown sporadic support for the Iraqi opposition. However in recent years, there has been little attention to the tougher questions on the use and impact of economic sanctions against Iraq.

The humanitarian costs of sanctions has elicited criticism in Europe and the Middle East, but little action by governments to come to grips with the problem beyond support for the oil-for-food resolutions. The EU, though a major aid donor, has no common policy on the situation in Iraq. In the US, the Government spent several years attempting to avoid discussion of humanitarian costs of sanctions, before finding in Resolution 986 and its successors a means to deflect criticism of these costs.

A public constituency which has persistently voiced concern over the impact of sanctions on the Iraqi population does exist, both in Europe and the US. It has variously consisted of a range of church organisations,[2] aid agencies working in Iraq and a handful of politicians and other leading public figures, mostly outside the structures of government. However, the efforts of these groups have been largely stymied, particularly in the US and UK, by the hard-line position of their own Governments, as well as the intransigence and appalling human rights record of the Iraqi Government. Furthermore, Iraq's problems have been eclipsed, in terms of humanitarian disasters, by other terrible and dramatic events such as the war in Bosnia and genocide in Rwanda.

There has also been a difference in focus between organisations and political groups whose primary goal has been the lifting of sanctions and those who regard sanctions as a necessary evil to control Saddam Hussein. The first group argue that the human costs are too great and the embargo is doing nothing to influence the conduct of the regime, let alone bringing about its downfall. The second group includes the main external Iraqi opposition, as well as Kurdish organisations and their supporters. While they admit the humanitarian cost of sanctions and the possible political implications for the opposition of taking over a disintegrating society, they have argued for the retention of sanctions for want of a better alternative. In contrast to South Africa, there are no opposition political forces inside Iraq which could, even if they wished, openly express support for sanctions.

The issue least addressed or discussed, whether by Western governments, the public media or the Iraqi opposition, is what the long-term effects of the past eight years will be on Iraq. Whether the horizon is 'after sanctions' or 'after Saddam', these outcomes are a subject mostly avoided in public by official analysts, academics (with the exception of a handful of Iraqi economists) and journalists. Nonetheless, the future political and economic complexion of Iraq will affect the very strategic interests which current Western policies purport to protect. What is more important, they will affect the future of more than 22 million people in Iraq and potentially the populations of neighbouring states.

Regional fallout of confrontation with Iraq

After the 1991 war it seemed that US hegemony in the Middle East, following the demise of the Soviet Union and the defeat and 'containment' of Iraq, would give the US the opportunity to intervene in other regional conflicts. But the picture has not developed as either the Bush or Clinton administrations had hoped.

The predictions of regional revolution and cataclysm from some opponents of the 1991 war proved unfounded. The 'street' did not rise up against rulers who had joined the Coalition. Neither the Gulf states nor the rest of the Middle East has seen changes in rulers either as a direct or indirect result of the Gulf War. As one observer remarked in relation to the upheavals in former Yugoslavia, wars do not necessarily overthrow rulers. However, the upbeat post-war mood promoted by the Bush administration also proved illusory. The US remained the dominant power in the region, but it is a region characterised by political stagnation, deadlock and conflict.

Not only was the situation in Iraq not resolved by the removal of Saddam Hussein or by the regime's compliance with the Security Council's post-war demands, but the

'peace process', the other pillar of US regional policy, has not produced the anticipated results. Although Jordan signed a peace treaty with Israel, by the beginning of
1999, there had been no settlement with Syria, while Israel continued to occupy a
so-called 'security zone' in southern Lebanon. Nor is there agreement with the
Palestinians on most of the key issues which would allow real peace in the region.

One of the intentions of 'dual containment', in addition to protecting Saudi
Arabia and the Gulf states, was to 'enable Israel and the moderate Arab states to
move towards peace, while the burgeoning Arab-Israeli detente would demonstrate
that the attitudes of the "rejectionist front" were costly and obsolete'.[3]

By 1997, the problem was that the *detente* with Israel was not 'burgeoning' and
various forms of rejectionism, not of the left but mainly from Islamist groups, had
gained ground. Martin Indyk, newly appointed as Assistant Secretary of State for
Near Eastern Affairs, admitted in November 1997 to 'a symbiotic link between what
happens in the peace process and what happens in the Gulf. We have long believed
that the more progress we could make in the peace process, the more effective we
would be in containing the threats from Iraq and Iran.' He also conceded that the
reverse was true: 'a stalled peace process makes it more difficult to rally support
against those who would threaten the peace of the region'.[4]

In the Gulf, the focus of US policy has remained on preventing Iraq 'threatening
its neighbours'. This has proved relatively successful, although costly because of the
repeated need to mobilise troops to send to the region. However, the late 1990s have
seen a prevailing mood of scepticism in the Middle East about US motives and goals.
For people brought up in a strong climate of nationalism, suspicious of the motives
of the Western powers, the equivocal attitude of the US Government toward Iraq has
made it hard to believe that it really wanted to see Saddam fall. By 1998, political
changes in Iran and shifts in the energy market probably ended even the rhetoric of
'dual' containment as the US made cautious moves to mend fences with Iran.

Attitudes to sanctions in the Arab world have grown increasingly ambivalent.
Most of the Arab coalition allies, with the exception of Kuwait, have slipped away
from the hardline position of the US and UK. Some of the smaller Gulf states have
joined other Arab states in expressing concern at the humanitarian effects of sanctions,
while Qatar and the UAE have restored relations with Baghdad.

The US views Egypt as an important political player in the region, and continues
to rely on it for the quick transit of military assets to and from the Gulf region, necessary on a number of occasions since 1991.[5] Yet despite this close alliance, as a
member of the Security Council in 1996–7 Egypt opposed the US position on
sanctions, while at the same time seeking to persuade Iraq to comply with UN
resolutions.

Another factor which has proved beyond US control has been the shifts in the
regional balance of power since the early 1990s, partly in response to events in the
Gulf but also because of the difficulties over an Israeli-Arab-Palestinian peace. In
particular, Syria's role has been important in undermining US strategies through its
resistance to peace with Israel, its sympathetic attitude to the PKK, its alliance with
Iran and the role of both Iran and Syria in Lebanon. Syria's continued rejection of
any agreement with Israel has been combined with a cautious re-opening of relations
with Iraq. Despite sanctions, Iraq has achieved some measure of reintegration in the
region, symbolised by Iran's invitation for it to attend the summit conference of the
Islamic Conference Organisation in Teheran at the end of 1997.

While most regional leaders may neither like nor trust the regime of Saddam Hussein, there has been an increasing tendency to measure Western treatment of Iraq against other cases: primarily the leeway given to Israel to ignore Security Council resolutions without punishment and the years spent by the Council in dithering over Bosnia. Western, and especially US, observers tend to scoff at these complaints as political rhetoric but the inconsistencies in approach undoubtedly confirm much opinion in the region in its view of Western hypocrisy.[6]

While regional states voice concern about the infringement of the economic and social rights of Iraqis, they generally give a low priority to protection of their civil and political rights. Many governments view 'human rights' as a Western-constructed political tool, a way of making other states look bad. Many in the non-aligned movement dislike both interventionism (which could be used against them by powerful states) and campaigns for the rights of minorities. There is general agreement that Iraq should remain one country, and most harbour suspicions over Western support, however equivocal, for the Kurds.

During 1991 and 1992 several factors contributed to the belief that some changes might occur in the long-running conflicts between the Governments of Iran, Turkey, Iraq and Syria on the one hand and their Kurdish populations on the other. In Iraq, allied intervention resulted, unintentionally, in a Kurdish-run administration in the north. As a result, Iraq's neighbours, Turkey, Syria and Iran, became involved, each for their own reasons, in the internal politics of the Iraqi Kurds, and the leading powers find it difficult to ignore this. As one analyst observed:

> The Allied-run Operation Provide Comfort is an apt example of the regionalisation and internationalisation of the Kurdish problem. The Kurdish rebellion and the GAP project have brought Turkey back into the Middle East. Given the unprecendented interaction between domestic and external security concerns, presently these two issues of vital importance to Turkey defy simple solutions.[7]

Turkey has not been discouraged in its view of Iraqi Kurdistan as its 'backyard', in which it could intervene at will. The army's focus on the war with the PKK, and the PKK's continued ability to find support and bases outside Turkey, meant an intensification of conflict during the 1990s. Only in 1997 and 1998 was there renewed questioning of successive governments' policies on the Kurdish issue.

Turkey's recent military pacts with Israel have further complicated the equation.[8] Reacting to this new alliance, Syria has edged towards a *rapprochement* with Iraq, while finally bowing to pressure from Turkey to close PKK bases in the Baqa'a valley and end its long-denied 'hospitality' to PKK leader Abdullah Ocalan. These moves clearly will influence the future of the PKK, as well as the position of the Kurds in northern Iraq.

By 1997/8, Iraq appeared to be pursuing a strategy of eroding the effects of sanctions 'by other means', by promoting regional trade in defiance of the embargo. There was already clandestine trade on some scale, to which the Security Council, including the US, has turned a blind eye. But the longer sanctions continue, and the less the states in the region are convinced that they serve any purpose, the more this could be a means for Iraq to subvert the continued imposition of sanctions by the Security Council.

Syria, for its own strategic reasons, has chosen to re-establish trade with Iraq, and in July 1998 the two countries agreed to recommission the oil pipeline, closed since

1982, running between the Kirkuk oilfields and the Syrian port of Banias. Meanwhile, in 1998 Turkey decided to 'legalise' the long-standing smuggling trade with Iraq, allowing the Government to profit from it. This is in addition to revenue from renewed pipeline dues paid to Turkey under the oil-for-food arrangements. The gradual improvement in Iraqi relations with Iran may also expand trade links.

Arms control

Continuing regional insecurity has made a mockery of the avowed post-war international policy, enshrined in UNSC Resolution 687, of controlling weapons of mass destruction throughout the Middle East. Paragraph 14 'Notes that the actions to be taken by Iraq [in eliminating nuclear, chemical and biological weapons of mass destruction] represent steps towards the goal of establishing in the Middle East a zone free from weapons of mass destruction and all missiles for their delivery and the objective of a global ban on chemical weapons'.

Soon after the end of the war, President Bush also proposed a US initiative for 'comprehensive' arms control in the Middle East, covering weapons of mass destruction and conventional weapons. It called for a code of 'responsible' arms transfers among major suppliers and the prevention of 'destabilising' arms sales.[9] As things stand, only Iraq is subject to arms control, and no other state has been held accountable for its possession or acquisition of such weapons.

The preoccupation with UNSCOM's efforts to root out all weapons of mass destruction in Iraq has not prevented, and in some respects has encouraged, the continued build-up of conventional arms in surrounding states. Arguably competition between states which are major defence suppliers has increased in the 1990s. There has not been any significant diminution in sales of conventional weapons to the Gulf states, Turkey, Syria, or – despite US efforts – to Iran. Saudi Arabia, Turkey and Egypt were ranked by SIPRI as the leading three recipients of major conventional arms in the world between 1992 and 1996.[10]

In the Gulf, no regional defence organisation has emerged, as was originally envisaged after the Gulf War. The Gulf states have chosen to remain dependent on US military protection. Although their annual military expenditure is now reduced compared with the 1980s, Saudi Arabia and other Gulf states made over $30 billion of weapons orders in the two years following the Gulf War. In those years, the US was the source of some 43 percent of the arms sold to the Gulf.[11] A new factor in the arms market since 1990 has been the crumbling military infrastructure of the former Soviet Union, which has become a source of cheap weaponry and hardware, with no form of accountability for what is sold or bought, or by whom.

It could also be argued that the regional alliance between Israel and Turkey – two major US allies and recipients of US weaponry (one of which also possesses weapons of mass destruction) – does not create a favourable atmosphere for any form of regional arms control. Combined with the competing development of nuclear capability in India and Pakistan, this cannot be said to be enhancing the prospects for regional security and peace. If, while Iraq's armaments programme is blocked, or at least limited by international sanctions, its neighbours build up formidable arsenals, the temptation for any future Iraqi regime to try to 'catch up' by evading residual import control mechanisms will be very great.

NOTES ON PART I OVERVIEW

1   Landgren (1995), p 442.

2   For example, the World Council of Churches and the Middle East Council of Churches, national councils of churches in Europe and the US, Pax Christi, the Catholic Bishops Conference in the US and Quaker organisations in a number of countries have all issued statements and campaigned on the impact of sanctions. There have also been initiatives in congregations at a local level, especially in evangelical communities in the US.

3   Brzezinski and Scowcroft (1997), p 5.

4   'The Gulf, US Policy and Peace', Remarks to the Middle East Insight Conference, College of William and Mary, Williamsburg VA, November 12, 1997.

5   Robert H. Pelletreau, Assistant Secretary of State for Near Eastern Affairs, 'Remarks before the CENTCOM Annual Southwest Asia Symposium', Tampa, Florida, May 14, 1996 (Department of State website, http://www.state.gov).

6   For example, Israel resisted with impunity Security Council Resolution 799 (18 December 1992) calling for the return of Palestinians exiled to Lebanon, until late 1993. Only in April 1998 did Israel adopt Resolution 425 (1978) calling for its withdrawal from Lebanon, and that withdrawal has yet to take place (*Guardian*, 28 November 1998, 'Netanyahu shaken by Lebanon Crisis').

7   Henri J. Barkey (1996), pp 41–42.

8   In an interview with a Turkish newspaper, the then Israeli Defence Minister Yitzhaq Mordechai, commenting on the character of the military alliance between the two countries, was quoted as saying, 'The alliance is not against a third country... However, if a country like Iran, Iraq or Syria wants to use force against Turkey, it will realise that it is facing a united force.' If 'something undesirable' happened in the region, 'coordination and harmonisation' could take place. BBC Summary of World Broadcasts, 2 May 1997, 'Israeli defence minister says pact with Turkey source of regional stability', quoting *Yeni Yuzyil*, Istanbul, 26 April 1997. An Israeli foreign policy expert noted that Israel was also a source of military technology, cheaper than the US, and less hedged around with export restrictions (*Guardian*, 9 December 1997, 'Israel and Turkey forge stronger links').

9   US Congress, Senate, Committee on Foreign Relations, Middle East Arms Transfer Policy: Hearing before the Committee on Foreign Relations, June 6, 1991, pp 6–8. The attempt by the Permanent Five Security Council members to curb arms supplies to the Middle East remains deadlocked.

10   Stockholm International Peace Research Institute (1997), p 272, Table 9.3.

11   E. Gregory Gause III (1997), p 13. The US since the Gulf War was reported to have greatly increased its share of all weapons delivered to developing nations – from less than 20 percent of the total in 1990 to 46.5 percent in 1994 – presumably benefitting both from the dramatic decline in the Russian share of the market and the 'showcase' for its weapons offered by the Gulf War, as well as the security needs of the Gulf states which constituted a major market for US weaponry. *Boston Globe*, 'Armed for Profit: the Selling of US Weapons', Special Report, p 2, quoting the Congressional Research Service, Library of Congress.

PART II

State Power, Survival and Conflict in Iraq since 1991

CHAPTER 4

The Impact of Post-war International Intervention on the Iraqi State

This chapter and Chapter 5 deal with the regions of Iraq which have remained under government control since 1991. Conditions in the three northern governorates, which came under Kurdish control after the withdrawal of Iraqi forces in October 1991 will be discussed in Chapter 6.

In March 1991, the Iraqi army had been routed in Kuwait and the country subjected to intensive bombing. The Government seemed close to collapse. By the late 1990s, however, the same regime was still in power. Arguably a long history of authoritarian rule and a long period of confrontation with external enemies fitted the regime to survive. It has certainly not proved to be as politically vulnerable to effects of sanctions as most observers in the West had expected.[1] The Government succeeded in re-asserting repressive controls over most of the population which, as a consequence, was subjected to economic hardships and continuing human rights abuses.

THE UPRISINGS

In the weeks immediately following the end of the war, many units of the defeated Iraqi army managed to make their way back into Iraq despite coalition efforts to stop them. One soldier who served in Kuwait described how, as the Coalition forces advanced on Kuwait city, he and his fellow soldiers started walking back towards Iraq, their officers having already fled.

Angry and disillusioned elements of this retreating army triggered the uprising in southern Iraq. Speaking in 1994, Saddam Hussein gave the impression he had envisaged 'lur[ing] the enemy troops into urban Iraqi areas and cities so that we could put them through the worst'. He blamed the uprisings for preventing the implementation of this strategy.[2] However, General Wafiq Samara'i, then head of military intelligence, offered a different interpretation. He said that Saddam came close to psychological collapse when Iraqi troops fled Kuwait, and feared the allies would come as far as Baghdad. Only when the Coalition called a unilateral ceasefire did his mood change: 'he felt himself to be a great hero'.[3]

The first signs of rebellion appeared on the last day of February in the predominantly Sunni towns of Abu'l-Khasib and Zubair, south of Basra, near the Kuwaiti border. The uprising spread rapidly to Basra, where the destruction of bridges further north created a bottleneck, concentrating large numbers of retreating troops. Press reports on 1 March said people were in the streets of Basra shouting slogans against Saddam Hussein, while a tank fired shells through one of his large and ubiquitous public portraits.[4] Huge traffic jams were created by military vehicles while government loyalists engaged in shoot-outs with rebels.[5] By 7 March most of the main towns in the south, including the Shi'i holy cities of Najaf and Karbala, were in revolt.

The scale of the rebellions disconcerted both the Iraqi Government and coalition leadership. There had been indications of discontent in the south before the end of the war, but they did not hint at the scale of events which followed. On 10 February, before the ground war began, a crowd of people in the southern town of Diwaniya publicly protested against Saddam Hussein's refusal to end the occupation of Kuwait, and were said to have killed ten Ba'th Party officials.[6] Some sources have suggested that the collapse of public services and infrastructure as a result of coalition bombing played a part in triggering the revolt. At the start of the ground offensive, the Government rationing system reportedly broke down, causing serious food shortages which may have been a further source of popular discontent.[7]

The 'rebels' included army officers and soldiers, ordinary citizens and members of resistance groups from Iran who were able to cross the border without impediment.[8] Iraqi opposition groups based in Iran – including the Supreme Council for the Islamic Revolution in Iraq (SCIRI), al-Da'wa al-Islamiyya and the Badr Brigades – had not initiated the uprisings and did not control their course, but they did play a prominent role in the latter stages, especially in Najaf and Karbala.[9] Not everyone participated in the uprisings, however. Some soldiers and civilians in the cities, and tribal leaders in rural areas supported the Government. There were also instances when the rebellion collapsed after defections to the government side.[10] Many more people stayed at home and tried to keep out of the way.

In the north, the uprising began with popular demonstrations in collective settlements (*mujamma'at*) near Raniya on 4 March.[11] The forces of the Kurdistan Front (KF) rapidly seized control of most of the region, including Sulaymaniya, Arbil, Dohuk and the oil region of Kirkuk. A key element in the KF's initial success was the defection of most of the *jash* (donkeys), the derogatory name given to the National Defence Battalions recruited from the Kurdish areas and used by the Government mainly for internal security and policing work there.

The timing of the uprisings seems to have taken most of the opposition groups by surprise. In the north a KF representative spoke of the Front following the civilians into the streets,[12] though in January the KF leadership, while taking care not to lend any open support to the US-led Coalition's attack on Iraq, had apparently prepared the ground for an uprising by announcing an amnesty for the *jash*. As the uprising began, *jash* members began to defect, 'some out of a change of heart, others out of sheer opportunism'.[13] In Dohuk, for example, *jash* leaders played a key role in creating the uprising and swelling its forces.[14]

However, the regime was able to regroup its forces, particularly because a significant number of the Republican Guard divisions and other elite units had managed to retreat from Kuwait along with some of their armour and weapons.[15] The appointment on 6 March of Saddam Hussein's cousin Ali Hasan al-Majid as Interior Minister had sent a signal – particularly to the Kurds – of the Government's determination to avoid defeat. Ali Hasan was notorious for his role as head of the Northern Bureau of the Ba'th Party, in charge of the Anfal operations in 1988 (see Chapter 6). He was expected to act more forcibly to crush the uprisings than his predecessor, Samir Muhammad Abd al-Wahhab al-Shaikhly.

The decision to concentrate first on crushing the rebellion in the south was both a military tactic – the relatively limited force of 'reliable' Republican Guards could not have attacked on two fronts at once – and a reflection of the regime's priorities. The south – including Iraq's second largest city, Basra, and its surrounding petrochemical industries – was of critical importance to any attempt to retain control of the country. The agricultural hinterland of the north was of less immediate concern, with the exception of the oilfields of the Kirkuk region, undamaged during the Iran-Iraq War, which fell into Kurdish hands during the uprising.[16] Having crushed the southern uprising, the Republican Guard units swept through the north. The last city held by the KF, Sulaymaniya, had fallen to government forces by 2 April, by which time the mass exodus of refugees was well underway.

A further key to the regime's rapid reassertion of control was the fact that in Baghdad, there was no rebellion. News of the military defeat and the uprising in the south was slow to arrive in the capital, since the public media did not reveal the turn events had taken. Aside from external radio broadcasts, people reportedly found out what was happening by waiting at bus stations for news from returning soldiers.[17] Witnesses also spoke of tanks and artillery encircling the poor, predominantly Shi'i areas such as Saddam City (formerly Madinat al-Thawra), preempting contacts with rebels to the south. People were said to be waiting for something to happen, but no arms arrived from the south, nor were effective communications established with the rebels. One witness, a resident of Saddam City at that time, also reported intensive house-to-house searches immediately after the uprisings.

Visitors to Baghdad hospitals in early April, when the Government had already regained control of most areas in the south, heard from staff that gun-shot victims, including women and old people, were being admitted. This may indicate that skirmishes or gun battles did take place in the capital. But there was no serious challenge either there or in the central governorates, the heartland of the leadership's support.

Coalition inaction during the uprisings also suggested to the Government in Baghdad that it would be allowed to deal with internal dissent as it wished. 'Saddam's calculations were eased immeasurably once he could be confident that the Coalition would take a passive stance.'[18] The regime's ability not only to contain but to quell the uprisings was also enhanced by the absence of any ban on the use of helicopters and helicopter gunships in the 3 March ceasefire arrangements. Hence rebel positions were attacked from the air as well as shelled. Karbala and Najaf both fell victim to these onslaughts.[19]

Karbala was said to have held out for twelve days against the Republican Guard, but at very high cost. A number of visitors to the town after the uprising commented on the burned and blackened remnants of the palm groves that surrounded it, destroyed, it seems, by government forces to prevent rebels from hiding there. The main al-Hussein hospital was a key battle site, held for a time by the rebels and retaken by government forces with the patients still inside. Many of the patients were apparently killed in the fighting or deliberately executed afterwards. There was very extensive damage caused by artillery shelling and bombing to the centre of the town, including to the shrines. According to eyewitnesses in both Karbala and Basra, soldiers conducted house-to-house searches after they had entered the city, smashing homes and threatening whole families with death if they did not give up their menfolk.

Iraqi troops and security services acted with great brutality in quelling the uprisings. Both fighters and civilian refugees fled to US military lines in southern Iraq telling of atrocities.[20] Widespread arbitrary executions, disappearances and the use of prisoners as human shields have been documented by human rights organisations.[21] Press reports quoted witnesses fleeing the cities of Basra and Zubair to the border town of Safwan as saying that Republican Guards had been hanging rebels from the gun barrels of tanks.[22]

Characteristically, the brutality of the post-uprising repression was matched by token political concessions. On 23 March, after the rebellion in the south had largely been crushed but before that in the north had ended, Saddam Hussein reshuffled his cabinet, appointing RCC member and former Foreign Minister Sa'dun Hammadi, a US-educated Shi'i Muslim from Karbala, as Prime Minister. Hammadi had been a member of the Ba'th Party since the 1950s and had held a succession of senior ministerial posts. He was one of the few Shi'i political figures who had risen to this level in the Ba'thist hierarchy. Hammadi's appointment was a symbolic gesture apparently intended to suggest a willingness to give Shi'i Muslims a greater role in government, but he only remained Prime Minister until September 1991, when he was replaced by Muhammad Zubaydi, a less weighty Shi'i figure.

A new law allowing the formation of political parties outside the Ba'th Party nonetheless ruled out parties established on the basis of 'race, regionalism, or atheism'. Religious parties were permitted, but not if they were 'sectarian'. The law never took practical effect in any case.

Despite its success in quelling the uprisings, Iraq's political leadership remained in a precarious position. Coalition troops were still on Iraqi soil, the economic embargo was causing serious hardship, and the economy had suffered severe damage during the war.

Visitors to Iraq in the first few months after the Gulf War were surprised both at their freedom of movement and the willingness of people to speak freely, particularly in provincial centres, where central control had broken down or at least was greatly diminished. However, by the end of 1991, the Government's control was reasserted at local level in much of the country, and the security apparatus was back in place.

Besides the internal political threat, the other major area of concern for the Government was the state of the infrastructure and economy. Sanctions, reimposed after the end of the war, made the prospect for post-war recovery bleak. International surveys conducted in the first half of 1991 gave some sense of the magnitude of the problems which were foreseen. In the first post-war report from the UN in March 1991, Martti Ahtisaari spoke of Iraq being bombed into 'a pre-industrial age'. This exaggerated the scale of the problem, but it emphasised that a country which had depended on high levels of imported technology had lost the ability to restore its infrastructure to full working order.

RECONSTRUCTION

As aid agencies discovered when trying to assess needs in the chaotic months after the war, it was often difficult to disentangle problems caused by the 1991 war, the uprisings and economic sanctions from those caused by the Iran-Iraq War. Countrywide, the destruction of infrastructure between 1980 and 1988 was estimated by one source at $126 billion.[23] Iraq's second city of Basra was a major casualty of both wars.[24] Amara, the provincial town of Maysan governorate situated close to the Iranian border, also suffered severe damage during the Iran-Iraq War.

The coalition bombing campaign, it later emerged, did less damage to Iraq's military arsenal than was reported at the time, but rather more damage to the civilian infrastructure than was initially supposed. The key problem was the loss of electric power. A Pentagon draft report leaked to the *New York Times* in February 1992 revealed that more damage was done to Iraqi generating capacity than was originally intended because generators rather than transformers were targeted. The former take longer to repair.[25] The loss of generating capacity caused the collapse of water and sanitation systems, and of irrigated agriculture, all of which relied mainly on electric pumps. Electricity shortages affected health care – especially the refrigeration needed for drugs and vaccines – while lack of clean drinking water resulted in widespread illness.

The uprisings caused further physical damage. Government representatives were quick to blame the rebels for all such damage. Opposition spokesmen, in their turn, have blamed government forces. In the south looting was widespread. It appears that the rebels, the general populace and soldiers all joined in.[26] Government offices were stripped, from air conditioning units down to door handles. One Karbala resident said that a particular target for popular anger was schools, where loot taken from Kuwait was stored: 'Some people burned the goods out of bitterness at the regime, and some took them away'.[27] Aid officials reported food stores were emptied, hospital and water department stores stripped of equipment, spare parts and supplies. The restrictions imposed by sanctions made it difficult to replace them.

Under Saddam Hussein's rule, the Iraqi Government had not been much disposed to long-term planning,[28] and in 1991 its immediate priorities appeared to be political. While it is impossible to know how the leadership assessed the prospects for surviving sanctions in 1991, it seems likely that it shared with most Security Council members the view that sanctions would not last more than a year or two. The Government was certainly prepared to present hardship and belt-tightening as part of the citizen's duty. Its authoritarian grip, once restored, allowed it to maintain this line without unmanageable popular pressure.

Once military control was largely restored, the Government launched a three-month emergency campaign, from April 1991, to restore basic services and infrastructure. Initial repairs – to roads, bridges, telecommunications, electricity and water services – were completed more rapidly than most external observers had anticipated.[29] The rapid restoration of 'normality', particularly in Baghdad, also demonstrated its ability to control events.

Outside Baghdad, however, the restoration of the infrastructure 'soon reached a plateau'.[30] Unexpected success was achieved in the short run using cannibalised parts, but cumulatively these 'solutions', however ingenious, caused a further deterioration in services after a couple of years. As an aid agency official put it: 'If two facilities are damaged, one has been rebuilt using parts from each. This means that repaired installations are forced to run well over capacity, with no fallback facilities at all.'[31]

By 1994, electricity supplies were said to be increasingly erratic, with frequent power failures even in Baghdad. At the beginning of 1998, UN Secretary General Kofi Annan, urging an increase in the funding and scope of the oil-for-food resolutions (see Chapter 7), drew the Security Council's attention to the 'severity of the problems afflicting the sector as a whole. At present, the maximum power generation capacity is about 40 percent of the original installed capacity.'[32]

The International Study Team in September 1991 found water treatment plants were operating on average at about 50 percent capacity. In 1996, the level appeared about the same.[33] As of 1996, Basra's water was contaminated and highly saline, 'unsuitable for human consumption', but the drinking water on sale from tankers was expensive – more so than oil. The governorate's water treatment system had reportedly been reduced to a third of its previous capacity.[34] A UN report noted that by 1995 the Iraqi Government's annual expenditure on water and sanitation was about $8.5 million, compared with annual maintenance expenditure of $100 million before 1991.[35]

Water and sanitation systems remained seriously deficient in most of the southern governorates.[36] Local water officials in the southern towns of Amara and Nasariya, describing their difficulties as of early 1992, said that initially the greatest problem had been loss of dependable electric power to run pumps and generators followed by a shortage of chlorine for water treatment. By 1992, these problems had been alleviated, but difficulties remained with obtaining spare parts, especially for pumping equip-ment, chlorinators and pipes, in addition to vehicle tyres and car batteries. Some items were available on the local market, but at great expense: a submersible pump which would have cost ID250 before the war was going for ID7000. Aid agencies helped with imports, but not on the scale required.[37]

In Amara, a programme in the early 1980s to upgrade the sewage system was halted because of the Iran-Iraq War, leaving only 25 percent of the sewage system piped. The other 75 percent runs in open ditches which get silted up. The regular dredging required was no longer possible because not all the dredgers were working. This seems to have been a problem common to a number of major towns in the south.

Sewage systems appear to have deteriorated further because of lack of spare parts and the priority given to treating drinking water, which meant all available chlorine supplies were generally used for this purpose and not to treat bacteria in waste.[38] In most cities, a substantial proportion of sewage is pumped untreated into rivers. By the end of 1998, the import of spare parts and equipment under Resolution 986 and its successors had barely begun to make a dent in the problem. Outside Baghdad, 'because delays in ordering and installation, pumping stations and treatment facilities are deteriorating rapidly'.[39]

The political implications of reconstruction were not neglected. First, it was evidently necessary to demonstrate a commitment to restoring at least some public services. Second, Iraq's reconstruction by its own efforts would demonstrate the country's (and the leadership's) strength and ability to survive in the face of international pressure.

The 'heroic' model had also formed a theme of reconstruction drives after the Iran-Iraq War.[40]

The Government publicised a variety of prestige projects, including the rebuilding of the Ministry of Defence headquarters, opened in January 1994,[41] and the inauguration in March 1995 of the Saddam Tower – a 'monumental' telecommunications tower in central Baghdad – invoking the glories of the tower of Babel.[42]

A grand state mosque in Baghdad was planned (though by 1998 it had not been built), and new palaces were built for Saddam Hussein. Other reconstruction projects were political in a different sense: the shrines in Najaf and Karbala, severely damaged by shelling during the uprising, were repaired.

In a 1995 message on the fourth anniversary of the war, Saddam Hussein spoke of how Iraq had 'rebuilt what the aggressors had destroyed. Moreover it added all that is new, lofty and grand.'[43] Some Baghdad residents were quoted as justifying the building of these palace complexes on the grounds that they created jobs. Others regarded them as offensive ostentation on the part of the elite while others went hungry.[44]

There developed a strangely symbiotic relationship between this rhetoric, designed to make political capital out of the image of a phoenix rising from the ashes, and that of US officials, for whom such extravagant projects justified their Government's view that sanctions should remain at all costs because Saddam Hussein was redirecting the funds he had available to non-humanitarian ends.

On the industrial front, the oil and petrochemical sectors were operating at a very low level until agreement to UNSC Resolution 986 came into force at the end of 1996. Civilian industrial production suffered shortages of inputs and spare parts as a result of Sanctions Committee policy on inputs to industry.[45]

The Government has never published any figures on military industries. Although imports of military equipment are banned under international sanctions, production of conventional weapons is not. Western analysts consider that Iraq is probably continuing low-level conventional military production.[46] It is therefore unclear whether since the Gulf War part of the civil engineering sector may have been subsumed and concealed under military industrial activities.[47] For example, it is thought that machine tools industries with both civilian and military applications have been revived. Iraq has succeeded in maintaining front companies abroad, and has been able to smuggle in some materials for weapons manufacture.[48]

Certainly the Government has portrayed the rebuilding of its military strength as part of its resistance to international pressure. Addressing the staff of the Military Industrialisation Organisation (MIO) in early 1997, Saddam Hussein spoke of combating the 'aggression' in the following terms:

> Where should the emphasis be placed, then? Emphasis should be placed on the armed forces, in addition to food. Who is the direct supplier of the armed forces in terms of armament and modernisation of what they possess? The direct and basic supplier is you. This shows how important you are to the armed forces, national security and consequently to the steadfastness of those whose duty it is to hold fast.[49]

The MIO became a key focus of both reconstruction activity and industrial production, including military industries. It was supervised between 1992 and 1995 by Hussein Kamil al-Majid, who was responsible for much of Iraq's weapons programme in the 1980s. In 1996, after his death, the organisation was scaled down. Its construction arm, the Fao Company, was transferred to the Ministry of Housing, and the Industrial Engineering Company, to the Ministry of Oil.[50]

Major projects undertaken since the Gulf War in which the MIO played an important part included the drainage and channelling of water in the southern marshes. To carry out the major works of building dykes and channels, the MIO was able to utilise large amounts of earth-moving equipment which had been abandoned by foreign companies when they evacuated in 1990.[51]

The work had several aspects. One, the 'Third River' project, or Main Outfall Drain Scheme, was first mooted in the 1950s and still incomplete in 1990. Its main purpose was to remove saline and polluted irrigation water from surrounding agricultural land, rather than allowing it to flow into the Euphrates and Tigris.

A second scheme was designed to dam the flow of water from tributaries of the Tigris into the Amara marshes, by digging a large drain across the northern end of the marshes, turning southward below the city of Amara and running parallel to the Tigris (see map). This canal is clearly visible on aerial photographs. It is primarily intended to drain large sections of marshland. By 1994, satellite and aerial surveillance suggested that large areas of the Amara marsh had been dried and the Hawr al-Hammar lake was much reduced. Further work was reportedly carried out to build dykes across the Howeizeh marshes close to the Iranian border.

Parts of the marshes had previously been drained, or flooded, for military purposes during the Iran-Iraq War[52] but the scale of the drainage works in 1992–1994 was much larger. However, judging the exact extent of permanently dried areas is difficult since some parts of the marsh are seasonal.[53] The Government has stated its intention to use the drained marsh areas to expand agricultural production (see below), but other priorities have clearly taken precedence.

In the late 1980s the marshes hid many deserters, and their inaccessibility lessened military control over the Iranian border region. After the 1991 uprisings, when many of those involved in the uprisings fled to the marshes, it was evidently decided that draining them would clear out the rebels, whether refugees from the cities or local people, and would facilitate military control of the border region.

A second probable reason for the drainage relates to the negotiations since 1991 with several international oil companies for the prospective development of southern oilfields in close proximity to the marshes. These include the Nahr 'Umar, Majnun, Gharraf, Nasariya and West Qurna fields. Surface facilities at West Qurna were 'badly damaged and pillaged in early 1991 following Desert Storm' during the uprisings.[54] Clearly the Government wants to ensure that the oilfields themselves, and access to them, is secure.

A further development during 1992–4 was the building of sweet water canals, taking water from al-Gharraf river, a tributary of the Tigris north-east of Nasariya, to Basra and to Suq al-Shuyukh, Fuhud and Chabaish because the increasing salinity of the Euphrates made its water unsuitable for drinking.[55] However, the combination of government policies on drainage and water management and the difficulties in obtaining equipment and spare parts caused by the embargo meant that there was little improvement in water availability.

As of 1998, these new water supplies for the region around Nasariya were reportedly still being held up by problems with equipment and pipes for water treatment plants.[56] It also seems doubtful whether the central authorities gave this problem high priority. The population of this area, and particularly the large numbers of people displaced from the marshes to areas around Nasariya, have consequently suffered severe water shortages (see Chapter 5).

TABLE 1 – THE STATE OF IRAQ

Population at official census:

1987	16,278,316
1997	22,017,983[57]

GDP at 1980 prices ($ billion):[58]

1960	8.7
1979	54.0
1993	10.0

Annual value of imports ($ billion)[59]

1980	11.534
1996	0.492

Annual value of exports ($ billion)

1980	28.321
1996	0.502

MANAGING THE ECONOMY

The drastic decline in the Iraqi economy is starkly evident from any set of statistics comparing the 1980s and the 1990s (see Table 1). The Iraqi leadership has sought to blame the entirety of its economic problems on sanctions, but its own economic policies, both before and after 1990, have played a major role in 'these dismal statistics', as one Iraqi economist described them. He points out that by 1993 per capita GDP had fallen almost to 1960 levels. 'Such a drastic collapse in per capita GDP translates into the nullification of nearly half a century of growth and improvement in the living standards of the population.'[60]

Iraq's economy was particularly vulnerable to interruption of its international trade, with oil revenues making up 60 percent of GDP in 1989.[61] It had previously imported a large proportion of its food, medical supplies and spare parts. Although food and medicine are not subject to the trade embargo, imports of these products have declined sharply since 1990. Other imports have been limited by the availability of foreign exchange, as well as by the controls imposed by the UN Sanctions Committee.

At the end of 1994, Western diplomatic sources estimated that Iraq had available from all sources, including smuggling, between $800 million and $1 billion for all its imports.[62] This compared with $11.1 billion spent on non-military imports in 1989, and $4.9 billion on military items.[63] Since 1991 it has been impossible to tell what proportion of available funds has been used for civilian and for military purposes.

From 1992 onwards, there were two areas in which state spending would have decreased. One was a saving on the salary bill for the army. In the year after the war, demobilisation reduced the armed forces from over 900,000 to between 300,000 and

400,000. Though those demobilised from the regular army received a pension, this would cost less than regular pay.[64]

A second decision which may have saved resources was the withdrawal of government forces from Iraqi Kurdistan. This was accompanied by the termination of central funding for the three northern governorates – including wages and, for a time, pensions – and the gradual reduction in the volume of rations being delivered, to around 10 percent of their pre-war level by 1993. The three northern governorates account for roughly 17.5 percent of the total population and, according to FAO estimates, Iraq's bill for rations would have been reduced by 15–20 percent.[65]

Legacies of the Oil Boom

The massive infusion of oil revenues into the Iraqi economy since the 1973 price rises skewed its development, emphasising consumption and trade rather than production. Iraq became increasingly dependent on selling oil in volume and at sustained prices. Rising oil revenues allowed Iraq to import everything from wheat and cosmetics, to hi-tech hospital systems, components for chemical weapons and command and control systems.

Successive Governments neglected investment in agriculture, which generally performed poorly relative to other sectors. For example, in the 1960s Iraq was more or less self-sufficient in wheat production. By the mid-1980s, imports were in excess of 2 million tonnes a year, which averaged four times indigenous production.[66] Prior to 1990, Iraq was spending $2–3 billion a year on food imports. Another consequence was the massive drift of population to the main cities. By 1990, more than 70 percent of the Iraq population lived in urban areas.

The oil boom allowed the Iraqi state to increase its political and social control and to became 'the largest spender in the economy, the largest employer... and the arbiter of the distribution of income among groups, classes, and regions of the country'.[67]

Living standards rose rapidly between the mid-1970s and the early 1980s when oil revenues allowed the Government to continue with high levels of spending to secure popular acquiescence in a war in which Iraq's fortunes deteriorated rapidly.[68] When expenditure on the war, and the destruction of Iraq's southern oil facilities, diminished the Government's income, social investment, not military expenditure, was cut back. After the war, the leadership was said to have allocated $5 billion per year to rearmament and $2.5 billion for reconstruction, including 'victory' monuments and a new presidential palace.[69]

During and after the Iran-Iraq War, the Government embarked on a programme of partial privatisation. Some sectors, such as building and transport, already relied heavily on the private sector, but by 1989 the process had spread much further, creating a substantial group of private entrepreneurs, contractors and landowners. However, strategic oil and military industries remained in state hands.[70]

The economic and physical damage caused by the Iran-Iraq War set back economic and infrastructural development, and generated a range of social problems which had scarcely been addressed by 1990. These were concentrated in the south and in the northern governorates affected by the Anfal operations against the Kurds. The wage-earning classes experienced growing shortages and rising prices, as price controls were removed from all but a handful of basic goods. Inflation was estimated at 45 percent in 1990.[71]

The high levels of expenditure on military hardware and military industry, warfare and reconstruction meant that by 1990 Iraq had a large and growing external debt. The need to reduce this debt was apparently a major factor in the leadership's decision to invade Kuwait – to gain access to Kuwaiti oilfields.

Several external sources of Iraqi funds have been mooted. First, those Iraqi overseas assets which were identified were frozen in 1990. A small proportion were released to pay for humanitarian goods permitted under sanctions until Resolution 778 refroze all assets in October 1992. According to one investigation, a second category was Iraqi government assets, 'monies, stocks in companies, gold' moved out either shortly before the invasion or shortly after it. The third was a mixture of 'sleeping assets' held abroad in companies belonging to Saddam Hussein and his family, to the Government and other regime members. These last two categories, each said to amount to billions of dollars, remained outside the control of the UN sanctions regime.[72] The US Treasury Department, as well as intelligence services, made strenuous efforts to discover these hidden assets which in 1992 were variously estimated at between $10 billion and $30 billion. However, they have not made public any more detailed findings.[73]

Iraq held substantial official gold reserves before the war, though the exact amount was not known. In addition, many Iraqis had gold jewellery, a particularly important asset for women as a part of their dowry payments. At least 100 tonnes of gold were reportedly raised from donations solicited after the Gulf War. It is thought that some merchants were also obliged to surrender gold to the central reserve.[74] A substantial amount of this gold was said to have been sold off in neighbouring countries. Finally, although Kuwait's official gold reserves were returned, some looted gold may have remained in Iraq. By the end of 1992, Iraq was thought to have used 25–30 tonnes of gold reserves to pay for food and medical imports since 1991.[75] The London-based daily *Al-Hayat* estimated that at the end of the same year, Iraq's gold reserves totalled 250–300 tonnes.[76]

For the first year after the war the loot gathered in Kuwait filled warehouses with goods which were released onto the Iraqi market, where consumer goods from Kuwait could often be readily identified. The larger and more valuable items were often re-exported to neighbouring countries.[77]

Since self-sufficiency in food and most other consumer goods, as well as spare parts, was not feasible, Iraq has needed to import goods, whether through Security Council-approved or other channels, and to obtain foreign currency for these purchases. Smuggling has inevitably been rife on all Iraq's land borders. Which routes have been most active has varied over time, depending to some extent on political conditions.

Oil sales continued illicitly, but they were on a relatively small scale. According to one estimate in 1995, Iraq was exporting roughly 110,000 barrels a day (b/d), of which 70,000b/d of crude was to Jordan under the arrangement already described. Exports of 'product' (refined oil – diesel and kerosene) to Jordan, Turkey and Iran amounted to 20–30,000b/d and crude transhipped through the Gulf and Iran to 10,000b/d.[78]

Most of the trade was in the form of barter. Petroleum products, fertilisers and cement are trucked to Iran and Turkey in return for food supplies, medicines and spare parts. The town of Fayda, north of Mosul, became the transit point for the trade with Turkey and was declared a 'free trade zone' in mid-1992. In that year the Iraqi side of the trade in gas oil was said to be under the direct control of the Ministry of Military Industrialisation. In return, it received from Turkey 'goods which it allocated to its own network of distribution centres as well as to cooperatives throughout the country'. The towns of Khisrawi in the central part of the country and Basra in the south are used for trade transactions with Iran.[79] A journalist noted in 1995 that 'everything from Iranian-made toothbrushes to nuts and detergents are crossing the border into Iraq'.[80]

However, the proceeds of smuggling made up only a fraction of Iraq's previous revenues, and there were limits on the quantities of larger items which could be supplied in this way. For example, it would be difficult to smuggle car tyres, which have constantly been in short supply, on a scale which could meet the country's needs.[81]

Shortage of foreign exchange has remained a major problem in economic management. Before the Gulf War, the exchange rate mattered little to the Government because it obtained its dollars through oil sales.[82] Since 1991, the massive loss of dollar payments weakened the dinar and affected Iraq's purchasing power abroad.

Photocopy money

The Government charted a wavering course in this dangerous situation, attempting to juggle import levels and prices. In the short run, the state could print money to buy dollars in order to finance imports and to pay the wages and other costs in the state sector. However, the expanding but increasingly valueless volume of 'photocopy' money, and the traders' anticipation of further falls in the value of the currency, fuelled near hyper-inflation. This in turn further undermined living standards.[83] The dinar's effective market rate began a catastrophic slide, from eight to the US dollar in late 1991 to 2950 by December 1995. Until 1994, the official rate remained ID0.3 to the dollar.

After the war, the Government lifted controls and taxes on imports in order to increase the flow of goods, while making sporadic efforts to control prices. From mid-1992, however, it began to pursue a more interventionist policy and to take various punitive measures to control exchange dealing, imports and price levels in the private sector, with largely negative effects.

Twenty prominent members of the Baghdad Chamber of Commerce were executed in July 1992 and their assets seized for 'profiteering' (see below). Many others were reportedly imprisoned. Consequently, Iraqi merchants working in Jordan, fearing reprisals, suspended consignments to Iraq, including approved shipments of food and medicine. At the end of July, the Iraqi Trade Ministry said the volume of trade with Jordan had dropped by 50 percent. World Food Programme monitors reported price rises on basic goods of 30 percent in late July.

The Government further restricted imports, setting a deadline at the end of 1992 for disposal of stocks of 146 'luxury items', including some foodstuffs and electronic goods, though it seems this ban was never fully implemented.[84] Smuggling in inputs for small-scale consumer industries remained possible, though expensive. Consumer durables were also available, at a price. In 1994 it was reported that sophisticated computer materials were available in Baghdad. One store owner told a journalist that he had no problem in selling them – mainly to Iraqis, but also to foreigners for whom, because of the exchange rate, these goods were very cheap.[85]

In May 1993, the Central Bank withdrew all 'Swiss issue' 25-dinar notes, closing the borders for a week. This appears to have been mainly a political move aimed at Iraqis outside government-controlled areas, particularly in Iraqi Kurdistan (see Chapter 6), but it had a negative effect on trade with Jordan. Many of the notes were held by traders and speculators in Jordan (and also in the Gulf) who had previously accepted local currency from their Iraqi counterparts to pay for imports.[86]

By 1994, after the dinar had sunk to 265 to the dollar, the Government bowed to the inevitable by allowing banks to abandon the official exchange rate. The Central Bank issued licences to 28 foreign exchange houses to buy and sell foreign currency. From that time Iraqis were permitted to deal legally in foreign exchange and to open foreign cash accounts in domestic banks.[87]

These measures did not, however, check the dinar's slide and the continuing rise in inflation. Minister of Planning Samal Majid was fired in August 1994 after his office published a report saying that inflation had reached 24,000 percent.[88] The Government, meanwhile, continued to print money. In January 1995, Saddam Hussein ordered the printing of an ID250 note which would have been worth $800 before the crisis in 1990. In 1995 it was worth barely 50 cents.[89]

In an address to the cabinet on the economy on 2 December 1995, Saddam Hussein spoke of seeking alternative sources of finance for the budget to printing banknotes. He also proposed halting the printing of currency abroad. There were also plans to sell off some state properties below market prices and allow the private sector to participate in operating and financing some state institutions. Taxes were to be imposed on higher incomes.[90] Within months, the economic scenario was changed by Iraq's acceptance of UNSC Resolution 986 and it is therefore difficult to assess whether these adjustment and stabilisation measures had any effect.

Price inflation under sanctions

For ordinary Iraqis, prices, rather than shortages, have been the main problem since 1991. Most products – food, luxury goods, medications, even pumps and spare parts – have been available on the open market, but few can afford them. Shortages of particular mass market products – for example baby milk powder – occurred periodically, driving prices up further.

The level of inflation since 1991 has tracked very closely the declining value of the dinar.[91] The purchasing power of meagre wages has fallen dramatically, but prices would often fluctuate rapidly, making household management a painfully unpredictable experience. In the course of a few weeks the same wages could purchase variable amounts of goods. As one researcher noted, 'Foodstuffs, cigarettes and hard-to-find spare parts are particularly sensitive to currency swings, whereas prices of clothes, cosmetics and other discretionary goods are less volatile'.[92]

The problems were exacerbated by the extreme vulnerability of both dinar value and prices to political events. Government decisions frequently contributed to the crises which caused these fluctuations. President Bush's threat to bomb Iraq in mid-July 1991 was one of the earliest scares to trigger price hikes. At the time of the cruise missile attack on 27 June 1993, the dinar fell by 30 percent, but rose again a few days later to ID45 to the dollar with the news that an Iraqi delegation was going to the UN to discuss oil sales.

After Resolution 986 was passed in April 1995, the value of the dinar against the dollar rose briefly to about ID600 before sliding down again once it was clear that the Iraqi Government would not accept the resolution.[93] After Iraq decided to negotiate in January 1996, its value rose to ID400 to the dollar when talks opened in early

February from an all-time low of ID3000.[94] Prices also dropped dramatically in late January, a kilo of sugar from ID1200 to ID250 and a loaf of bread from ID60 to ID15.

In this case the Government helped to bring down prices and increase the 'feel-good' factor by dumping food and other goods on the market. In February the Trade Ministry was offering a variety of goods – food, household appliances, toys, construction materials and spare auto parts – at central markets in Baghdad and the governorates at prices lower than those on the local market.[95]

The increased flow of imports under the oil-for-food mechanism has alleviated the scale of inflation, but the value of the dinar has remained low, so that inflationary pressures remain. Immediately after oil sales began in December 1996, the dinar strengthened to ID750 to the dollar, but in mid-1998 it had weakened to the range of ID1300–1500.[96] Food prices on the open market declined during 1997, but despite the inflow of foodstuffs under the oil-for-food programme, they began to rise again in 1998.[97]

As an Iraqi economist has noted, the Government in its response to the loss of export earnings failed to match the money supply with the economy's ability to produce and supply goods. While the ration system (see below) made some basic goods affordable, monetary expansion generated high levels of inflation and made non-rationed goods prohibitively expensive. This policy, he concludes, 'shifted the burden of sanctions to the Iraqi population. Only those few Iraqis who possessed dollars benefitted from the policy, since they were shielded from the effects of hyper-inflation.'[98]

Securing food supplies

According to some sources, Iraq held larger food reserves prior to the war than was estimated at that time, allowing it to survive longer without purchasing foods. Indeed, during the period from October 1990 until the end of the war, few shipments of food got through the allied blockade. This meant that Iraq used little of its foreign exchange reserves on food imports during that period.

During the 1990 winter cereal-growing season, after sanctions were imposed, the Ministry of Agriculture launched a campaign to raise cereal production.[99] The Government organised the planting of wheat in the lowlands and valleys of the Kurdish north, including in the rural 'no-go areas' created by the Anfal operations, where agricultural production had effectively ceased. In summer 1991, this crop was harvested with assistance from the coalition forces, with part of it being allocated to the Government, part to the Kurdish farmers.[100]

After government forces and funding were withdrawn from the northern governorates, the trade embargo imposed from October 1991 diminished the region's role as an agricultural reserve. According to the FAO, the three northern governorates accounted for 21.3 percent of 1994/5 cereal yield.[101] However, in the following years some Kurdish landowners sold their cereal crops to the Government, when they were offered prices higher than those obtainable on the local market.

Clearly, in the straitened circumstances of post-war Iraq, boosting agriculture was a key to sustaining living standards. During 1991, the Government had already set a priority on expansion of dryland farming to raise wheat production. With the constraints imposed by sanctions – shortages of fertilisers, pesticides and spare parts for agricultural and spraying equipment – government efforts to increase basic food production have met with fairly limited success. The animal husbandry sector, badly hit by the 1991 war, has remained in poor shape.[102]

Locally-produced food may have increased as a proportion of total stocks, but the overall improvements in agricultural production appear to have been relatively small. Over the period from 1991–5, per-hectare yields of the staple crops, wheat and barley, had fallen but the acreage planted had increased, leading to an overall increase in production.[103] The quality of the grain was said to be low, containing many impurities, leading to complaints about the poor quality of flour available in the government ration. Prior to the war, Iraq had imported much of its wheat seed from Canada and Australia. The diminishing quantities of these higher-yielding and disease-resistant varieties may also have diminished yields.

At the end of 1997, the FAO reported that yields remained low due to 'poor land preparation resulting from a lack of machinery, low use of inputs such as fertilisers and pesticides, deteriorating soil quality and irrigation facilities and increased crop infestation'.[104]

The cultivation of vegetables and fruit saw some revival after the war, both for the market and for home use. In the 1980s, urban-based entrepreneurs with good connections had opportunities to rent or buy agricultural land being sold off by the state. While some of this land was in the grain-growing areas of the north, the choicest leases seem to have been in the central areas around Baghdad where the most lucrative enterprises produced vegetables and poultry by intensive methods rather than extensive grain production.[105] These producers were severely affected by the 1991 war, with the loss of electricity and irrigation leading to the death of large amounts of livestock. However, vegetable production has revived to some degree. The FAO noted in 1995 that 'demand for and prices of vegetables have increased, generating more attractive profit margins'.[106]

The problems of poor drainage and high levels of salinity have afflicted irrigated agriculture in southern Iraq for many years.[107] These problems were exacerbated during the war and its aftermath, when power failure prevented the predominantly electric drainage pumps from flushing out the salt from the soil. Since that time there has been a shortage of spare parts to mend pumps. In 1995, the FAO reported 'vast expanses of waterlogged land and sheets of salt stretching across fields' in the south.[108]

Since 1994, some drained marsh land and marginal desert areas have been distributed for farming, though the scale of this operation is not clear.[109] It is unclear how suitable the drained marshland will be for farming in the long term, given potential problems of salinity. It is also unclear how committed this or any other government would be to continue the expansion of indigenous agriculture once sanctions are lifted and the option of importing food on a large scale is restored.

Since 1991, the Government has bought up cereal crops each year at fixed prices. Reports suggest that it has been able to meet the wheat flour component of the government ration largely from local production, compulsorily purchased from farmers.[110] By 1992 the Government was offering farmers three times the purchase prices offered in 1991 for wheat and barley in an attempt to stop them selling on the private market and thus depleting amounts available to the state for ration distributions. But although the nominal prices set by the Government rose each year, the real prices were much the same as in 1991, because of the declining value of the dinar.

The costs of production were also increasing. Inputs are expensive and scarce – including farm machinery, spraying equipment, irrigation equipment, fertilisers,

pesticides and milling capacity. Furthermore, subsidies and support from the state –
for example veterinary and extension services, and maintenance of the irrigation
system – had been severely reduced.[111] The delivery of agricultural machinery, spare
parts, pesticides, fertilisers and veterinary supplies began to increase in 1998 under
Resolution 986, but the impact on productivity and farm income is not yet clear.

Some reports suggest that farmers have sometimes hoarded crops and resisted
selling them at government-controlled prices, despite the fact that government
inspectors were empowered in 1993 to fine or jail farmers who withheld their crops.
Another way of dealing with recalcitrant farmers was to make them pay the market
price for the shortfall of the crop they withheld.[112]

Food processing industries were returned to the private sector in 1990. Food processing in Iraq was estimated to have dropped to less than 10 percent of pre-1990
levels, so that it is not a major market for local agricultural products. It has generally
been more profitable to import products, legally or illegally, from the cheapest
sources, and often past their expiry dates.[113]

Food rationing and control

Before the sanctions, the import and marketing of wheat flour and some other staples
was largely a state monopoly. These imports were valued not at the market exchange
rate but at the overvalued official rate, which was equivalent to a subsidy to consumers. Soon after the imposition of sanctions the Government withdrew these
general subsidies and replaced them with a subsidised ration system. The private sector
began to play an active role in the import and marketing of all food items, including
wheat flour.[114]

The state's ability to provide services and an acceptable standard of living has
been dramatically diminished by its lack of oil revenues. It has not been able to exercise monopolistic control of food supplies because of the need to import, and to use,
private external capital sources to do this. Nevertheless, the state has remained the
main source of food supplies through the rationing system. Mass starvation has periodically been predicted in Iraq since 1991, and the rationing system has arguably
played an important role in preventing this kind of cataclysm.

The ration system, introduced in September 1990 after the occupation of Kuwait
and the imposition of UN economic sanctions is administered by the Ministry of
Trade, but the rations are distributed from government warehouses to some 50,000
private-sector retail stores, or 'food agents'. The monthly allocation per person for
most of the period from 1991–7 included flour, rice, sugar, oil, tea, soap and deter-
gent. Lentils were removed from the list soon after the war. Baby milk was available
only for children under a year old. The food products included in the list are low in
protein. Experience showed that, for most families, the ration only lasted between
half and two-thirds of the month. They therefore still had to obtain the rest of their
food and basic goods at market prices. Calculations suggest that the value of ration
goods as a subsidy to living costs has declined over the period.[115]

After a series of modest increases in the size of monthly ration allocations during
1993 and early 1994, this basket of goods was reduced by more than 40 percent from
October 1994. Since 1995, the quantity of flour in the ration has risen again, reaching
nine kilograms per month in early 1997, though this amount seldom seems to have

been delivered. In addition, the price charged for the monthly ration – which had remained at ID2.1 until June 1995 – was increased to ID100 per person in mid-1996.

Even the modest increase in rations proposed under Resolution 986 has not been consistently implemented. Iraqi officials complained of delays in the arrival of food-stuffs and related items which made planning for ration distributions difficult.[116] It was not until mid-1998 that the ration was delivered in full for three consecutive months. Nearly two-thirds of households questioned by World Food Programme (WFP) observers in 1998 said the ration still only lasted 20 days. The energy content of the ration has risen from an average of 1295 kilocalories per person per day in 1993–5 to 2030 kilocalories in 1997–8.[117]

UN humanitarian agencies do not regard this improvement as sufficient to counter the prevailing levels of malnutrition, especially among young children. These levels are thought to have stabilised in government-controlled areas since the implementation of Resolution 986 in 1997–8, but have not declined.[118]

Some families reportedly sell parts of the ration – for example oil – in order to buy larger amounts of most basic items such as flour, or to buy medicines or other goods. Others were said to be selling infant formula and feeding their babies ordinary food, occasionally with fatal consequences. It seems that the system of checks against abuse of the ration system focuses mainly on preventing false claims rather than the resale of goods.[119]

There has been considerable debate about how equitable the distribution of the ration has been, especially in regard to food. UN agencies and others researching socio-economic conditions have generally reported the rationing system to be equitable, while human rights and opposition organisations have alleged inequities and exclusions. The UN Special Rapporteur concluded in 1996 that although the rationing system 'has so far functioned in general terms quite efficiently, the procedure to obtain a "rationing card" is onerous and often arbitrary and, moreover, it is evident that the system is easily susceptible to manipulation for political purposes'. According to his informants, when applying for a ration card each person or family is required to produce a civil status identity card, and confirmation of domicile, endorsed by 'the neighbourhood Mukhtar', plus a card containing security information.[120]

Opposition sources have claimed that there are restrictions on who can receive rations. Applicants have to prove that they do not have any deserters or refugees in the family, have to be approved by the local Ba'th Party, and have no criminal record. A food blockade seems to have existed in the marshland areas, though it is not clear how systematic this has been (see Chapter 5). In these areas female-headed households are reportedly regarded as suspect because they may have relatives who have fled to Iran; others have had their ration cards stamped for smuggling food into the marshes in defiance of restrictions.[121] Refugees have frequently alleged that Ba'th Party members get larger amounts of better-quality food, and get rations delivered rather than having to go and queue.[122]

The UN may be able to see that the system of distribution to the retail outlets works smoothly, but has not been in a position to check who receives ration cards or the scale of possible exclusions. Human rights and opposition groups rely mainly on information from those who have fled the country and who are more likely to have been subject to exclusions.

It has been very much in the state's political interest to maintain the system for the majority of the population under its control as a demonstration of its continuing ability to provide for the population. The welfarist strand in state ideology has been strong over many years, and the absence of such provision would suggest that the system was collapsing. The Government's commitment to its maintenance 'is not inconsistent with the generally repressive nature of the regime, but rather, can be seen as an important instrument for the maintenance of political control and support'.[123] The main forms of discrimination are probably not so much in the receipt of rations as in the availability of other forms of perks and additional subsidies.

Besides the part it has played in maintaining the legitimacy of the regime, the relatively inclusive ration system has other political functions. It is an effective way of keeping track on the population and its movements – there is now a computerised list of all beneficiaries[124] – and binds people to the state to maintain a minimum level of life, giving them an incentive to conform and to do what they are told. As one refugee with family still in Iraq observed: 'The need to have a ration card is a form of pressure on families to do what the government wants – for example, to go on a demonstration, or to vote'. The need to produce a ration card, along with other documents, to gain access to services is an additional form of pressure.

The state, the private sector, and the 'black' economy

The increasingly fractious family group around Saddam Hussein has continued to stand at the centre of economic as well as political life, along with a probably diminishing number of clan and tribal groups which have been loyal to the regime. Family and party networks around the ruling group have played a key role both in 'official' economic activity and the 'parallel' economy which has developed in response to sanctions-induced shortages, based on currency dealing, trade and smuggling on a regional scale. These two types of activity seem to overlap to a great extent.

The state has needed a measure of cooperation from certain economic groups for its survival. One aid worker in Baghdad in mid-1991 noted the 'rapidly shifting relationships between the state on the one hand, and farmers, merchants and contractors on the other'.[125]

The two groups which have profited most obviously from the 'sanctions economy' are contractors and import/export merchants. Contracting, trade and transport, the areas where it has been possible to make profits since 1991, had fallen largely into private hands in the 1980s. As the Iran-Iraq War ended, the importance of building and construction works increased, as did the number of contracting companies, both state and privately owned. Many of those who received leases and bought privatised enterprises were close to the leadership, through family, tribal or other connections.[126]

In mid-1992, the Industry and Minerals Minister Amer Hammadi al-Saadi acknowledged that the Government had not been rigorous in taxing local contractors who have earned large sums in reconstruction since the war. 'They are not taxed really. The Government was never very strict about that,' he was quoted as saying.[127]

The rationing system itself has generated considerable commercial activity. Certain merchants were directly licensed by the Ministry of Trade to import goods for distribution as rations. Transportation of rations monthly from warehouses to 50,000 retail outlets round the country is paid for by the Government but provided by private companies, allegedly in the hands of the President's son, Uday.[128]

A number of companies involved in import/export trade operated out of Amman after 1991. Iraqi businessmen, bank accounts and property abroad, mainly in Jordan, provided a channel through which to import goods, food, luxury goods, both legally and by smuggling. Several of the three or four dozen Iraqi companies operating in Amman have been linked to key figures in the regime such as Hussein Kamil (Arabco) and Ibrahim Takriti (Al-Badawi & Co).[129]

For those merchants without direct relations with the leadership, profit does not come without risk. The regime has clearly signalled that this group should not acquire too much power, and their profitable enterprises have been vulnerable to appropriation by members of Saddam's family and members of his inner circle. The result was an increasingly unpredictable and unstable relationship between the various segments of the trading community.

In 1992, as mentioned above, some 40 merchants were executed for profiteering and their assets seized. A number of those executed were senior members of the Baghdad Chamber of Commerce, and belonged to prominent merchant families, Sunni and Shi'a. They included Salim Hamra Abd al-Hadi Hamra, 65, former head of the Baghdad Chamber of Commerce, two other members of the al-Hamra family, and Mustafa Buniya, who was part of a family food wholesale business.[130]

These economic 'opportunities' have also created rivalries within the leadership. Some of the conflicts and killings since 1991 seem to relate not only to political and clan loyalties and internecine conflicts, but to 'turf' wars over control of this parallel economy. Businessmen living both in Iraq and abroad have apparently fallen victim to such feuds. The main contenders for control of trade and currency dealing internationally are reportedly Uday Hussein, Saddam's son, and his half-brother Barzan al-Takriti, who between 1990 and 1998 was based in Geneva. In 1998, a multiple killing in Amman, including two wealthy Iraqi businessmen with links to Barzan, was attributed to this rivalry.[131]

The decision to allow foreign currency dealing in 1994 was followed by a wave of arrests and executions of currency dealers which was apparently part of a bid by Uday to gain control of this sphere of activity.[132] At the end of April 1994 a leading money-changer, Abbas Aun, and four of his collaborators were executed, allegedly because regime members wanted to take over his business interests.[133] Opposition sources also claimed that a major food wholesaler, Abd al-Latif al-Buniya, was killed in a road accident 'engineered' to allow Uday to seize his commercial concerns.[134] In the 1980s, the Buniya family had close business relations with Saddam's half-brother Barzan al-Takriti.

Various other forms of pressure have been exerted on the merchant and business community. The UN Special Rapporteur noted: 'Property rights are also violated on spurious charges in order to enrich government officials or provide revenues for the state. Moreover, violations of property rights are used to alter the ethnic composition of communities or to penalise family members for alleged crimes attributed to their relatives.'[135] This includes confiscation of properties or the use of political pressure to force the sale of businesses cheaply. Reports suggest that a number of businessmen, particularly in the Shi'i community, have fallen victim to these practices. In July 1994, Iraqi press reports said that '39 patriotic Iraqi merchants and industrialists' had 'contributed' $2.75 million to import food. How 'voluntary' these contributions were is not known.[136]

Smuggling and various kinds of illicit business dealing may remain under the control of elements within the political leadership, but since the Gulf War they have

expanded to involve substantial numbers of people for many of whom the army contacts and 'business relationships', often dating back to the Iran-Iraq War, play an
important role.

A substantial number of people seem to have found a viable way to make a living
through black market dealing and smuggling. As one observer described it:

> The people who run the black market in both petrol and basic foodstuffs, and luxury items
> like whisky and Western cigarettes, are actually members of the lower middle strata of
> Iraqi society; hardened war profiteers who managed to survive as soldiers and smugglers
> during the Iran-Iraq war as well as the Gulf war which followed.
>
> Many of these 'new elements' in society have links with Iraq's large and once-powerful
> rural clans. Coming mostly from the lower echelons of these clans, the new merchants are
> both Shi'ites and Sunnis... The goods they handle are mostly smuggled from Syria,
> Turkey and Iran...[137]

NOTES ON CHAPTER 4

1   Patrick Clawson argued that the Iraqi regime soon adapted to the pressures created by
     sanctions. They therefore exercised limited leverage over its actions and were equally
     unlikely to lead to Saddam Hussein's fall (Clawson [1993ii], pp 71–8).

2   Foreign Broadcast Information Service, 'Saddam Addresses Army Commanders 6 Jan',
     quoting Iraqi News Agency, 6 January 1994.

3   *Financial Times*, 5 January 1995, 'Saddam "came close to nervous collapse"'.

4   A variety of images of Saddam Hussein are depicted in the ubiquitous wall paintings in
     public places in every town. The leader is portrayed as a man of all the people: as a Kurd,
     as a southern farmer, as a businessman, as a father and protector, as well as in military
     uniform or a civilian suit. In the south, many of these portraits were destroyed or defaced
     during the uprisings, only to be painstakingly repainted when government forces
     regained control.

5   *Daily Telegraph*, 2 March 1991, '"Saddam is Finished" Cries as Basra Explodes in
     Anarchy'; *Sunday Telegraph*, 3 March 1991, 'Loyalists in Basra Clash With Troops';
     Independent on Sunday, 3 March 1991, 'Iraq Slides Towards Civil War'.

6   Nakash (1994), p 274.

7   Middle East Watch (1992), p 38; Baram (1994), p 553.

8   Al-Jabbar (1994), p 108.

9   The *Independent* reported on 4 March ('Shia Muslims rise up against Saddam in Basra')
     that SCIRI had issued a statement from Lebanon claiming that rebels controlled
     Nasariya, Suq al-Shuyukh, Fuhud, al-Tar and parts of Amara. Its leader, Ayatollah
     Muhammad Baqr al-Hakim, speaking from Teheran, reportedly claimed that 'volunteers
     for martyrdom' had seized control of Basra. It was, however, not clear that any group
     was in full control of Basra at that time (*Daily Telegraph*, 5 March 1991, 'Iran Reveals
     its Hand as Ayatollah's Army Moves on Iraqi Towns'). This headline appears further to
     exaggerate the role of SCIRI. The text of the article in fact pointed out that other forces
     were also in play: 'Various middle class groups have already issued a charter for "pluralist
     democracy" and Leftist groups, including the Iraqi Communist party have always been
     strong among the Shi'ites'.

10   Some leaders may have changed sides once it became clear that Saddam's troops were
     regaining control. A US army intelligence officer was quoted as saying that in the town

of Samawa the rebels were poorly armed and had no training in using the weapons they did have. Once nearby towns had fallen to the Iraqi army, according to refugees, some tribal leaders began hanging up portraits of Saddam Hussein outside their houses. (*Independent*, 2 April 1991, 'Betrayal ends Iraqi Rebellion in the south').

11 McDowall (1997), p 371; Kutschera (1997), p 93.
12 McDowall *ibid.*; Middle East Watch (1992), p 30.
13 Al-Khafaji (1994), p 28.
14 McDowall (1997), p 371.
15 Gordon and Trainor (1995), p 429.
16 Freedman and Boren (1992), p 65.
17 *International Herald Tribune*, 8 March 1991, 'Defeated Baghdad's Market of Rumours'.
18 Freedman and Karsh (1993), p 426.
19 Gordon and Trainor (1995), p 449.
20 *Ibid.*
21 For example Amnesty International (1991); Middle East Watch (1992).
22 *Washington Post*, 13 March 1991, 'Iraqi Troops Reportedly Hang Rebels from Tanks'.
23 Kamran Mofid (1990), *The Economic Consequences of the Gulf War*, quoted in Barakat (1993), p 13.
24 In 1989 a reconstruction drive had begun in Basra, but it had done little more than clear rubble and mines, restore some roads and bridges and give some grants to householders to restore their homes (Barakat [1993], pp 16, 20–22). Little progress was made on infrastructural work, especially water and sanitation. A project to renew the sewerage system in Basra, being carried out by an Indian construction company, was halted by sanctions and the war (*Middle East Economic Digest*, 4 June 1993).
25 *Gulf Newsletter*, February 1992, no. 2, 'The Gulf Environment: Hidden Costs of War', p 4.
26 Middle East Watch (1992), pp 37–8.
27 Interview conducted by Maysoon Pachachi, film-maker, with a former Karbala resident.
28 Alnasrawi (1994) notes that, during the 1980s, economic decisions were increasingly made by political leaders who ignored or over-rode the institutional mechanisms of economic planning (pp 89–91, 107–8).
29 The International Study Team which visited Iraq between 25 August and 4 September 1991 found that electrical generation had been restored to about 68 percent of 1990 peak load and about 37 percent of installed capacity, with 75 percent of transmission lines operable (*Electrical Facilities Survey*, October 1991, p 1). On water treatment plants, the team found them to be operating at between 30 and 70 percent of capacity, with chlorine supplies being rationed. Waste water systems in Baghdad and the south were operating at between 0–70 percent capacity, ie some plants were not operating at all, mainly due to lack of spare parts and electricity supply (*Water and Wastewater Systems Survey*, October 1991, p 1).
30 Kuttab (1992), p 38.
31 An Oxfam official quoted in Hunter (1993), p 25.
32 United Nations Security Council (1998), para. 27.
33 Center for Economic and Social Rights (1996), p 26.
34 United Nations Consolidated Inter-Agency Humanitarian Programme in Iraq Extension of the Cooperation Programme for the period 1 April 1996–31 March 1997, 3 April 1996, p 68.
35 *Ibid.*, p 7.
36 Zaidy (1994), p 150.
37 Information gathered by the author in Amara and Nasariya, February 1992.
38 Center for Economic and Social Rights (1996), p 27.
39 United Nations Security Council (1998ii), para. 34.
40 Barakat (1993), pp 18–19.

41 BBC Summary of World Broadcasts, 20 January 1994, 'Defence minister opens reconstructed ministry headquarters', quoting INA news agency, Baghdad, 18 January 1994.

42 *Monde arabe Maghreb Machrek*, April–June 1995, No 148, p 66.

43 BBC Summary of World Broadcasts, 19 January 1995, 'Saddam Hussein's speech to mark fourth anniversary of start of Gulf war', quoting Republic of Iraq Radio, Baghdad, 17 January 1995.

44 *Middle East International*, 22 September 1995, 'Going Hungry'.

45 Al-Khudayri (1997), quoted an Iraqi government report which stated that some 80 percent of manufacturing facilities were idle (p 12).

46 A US Congressional report in 1993 suggested that much of Iraq's conventional weapons manufacturing capacity – not subject to UNSCOM inspections – had survived the 1991 war and was in operation (Congress, House of Representatives, Committee on Foreign Affairs, Iraq Rebuilds Its Military Industries: A Staff Report to the Subcommittee on International Security, International Organisations and Human Rights, Committee on Foreign Affairs, June 29, 1993). Antony Cordesman, however, commented in 1994: 'Although Iraq has rebuilt much of its capacity, it has not found through its military industries the ability to make up for a structure which was so dependent on military imports that Iraq during the Iran-Iraq War never developed many of the major depot repair-service facilities and other capabilities to keep its high technology weapons going' (Symposium on Dual Containment [1994], p 13).

47 Al-Khudayri (1997), p 13.

48 The best documented case was the Iraqi attempt to import guidance systems and other missile components from Russia. The gyroscopes were intercepted by the Jordanian authorities in November 1995, based on information from UNSCOM (*Bulletin of the Atomic Scientists*, October 1998, quoted in *Washington Post*, 18 October 1998, 'Iraq Sought Russian Arms Technology').

49 BBC Summary of World Broadcasts, 28 February 1997, 'Saddam Hussein's speech while visiting Military Industrialisation Organisation', quoting Republic of Iraq Radio, 26 February 1997.

50 *Middle East Economic Survey*, 5 February 1996, 'New Chairman Appointed For Military Industrialisation Authority'.

51 *Middle East Economic Digest*, 10 July 1992, 'Plant seized for canal project'.

52 Maltby (1994), p 12.

53 According to one estimate made in the 1950s, the marsh areas covered up to 30,000 square kilometres, mostly located between the converging arms of the Tigris and Euphrates rivers (Ali [1955]).

54 *Middle East Economic Survey*, 20 January 1997, 'Iraq Negotiates E&P Agreements with Indian, Russian and Malaysian Firms'.

55 BBC Summary of World Broadcasts, 23 September 1992, 'Saddam Hussein orders fresh water to be supplied to marshlands', quoting Republic of Iraq Radio, 21 September 1992. The raised salinity is thought to be the combined effect of saline run-off from surrounding land and the reduced flow of the Euphrates caused by the series of dams built up-stream by Turkey and Syria. After the Gulf War, the area around Chabaish suffered from high levels of salinity in the Euphrates water, which had become unfit for drinking. Water was tankered from other sources, mainly from the Tigris, though this was laborious and expensive. In 1998, the local authorities were still requesting that aid agencies bring in supplies by tanker, suggesting that the situation had not improved.

56 In 1993, the level of the Euphrates in the Nasariya region was said to have dropped between 2 and 3 metres, leaving the intake pipes of the Suq al-Shuyukh water treatment plant above the river level. According to Baudouin Koenig, a French film-maker who visited the area in 1996, the canal to Basra was not operating when he was there (interview with the author, September 1997).

57 Figures cited respectively in BBC Summary of World Broadcasts, 23 September 1997

and 20 October 1997, 'Population Census to be held on 16 October', quoting INA news agency, Baghdad, 21 September 1997; 'Population Census Results Announced' , quoting INA news agency, Baghdad, 17 October 1997. In the 1997 census it is unclear how the population was counted in areas outside government control.

58   Alnasrawi (1994), p xv.

59   Import and export figures are from *World Bank Development Indicators* 1998. However, since 1991, smuggling has to be added as a component of economic activity, both for government and Kurdish-controlled Iraq. Hence the overall scale of trade may be greater than these figures suggest.

60   Alnasrawi (1994), p xv.

61   Center for Economic and Social Rights (1996), p 7, quoting the Economist Intelligence Unit, *Country Profile: Iraq* 1995/6, p 13.

62   Eric Rouleau (1994). Paul Conlon (1997) notes that 'Iraq's imports in the years 1993–4 are assumed to have been in the area of $800 million to US$ 1.2 billion' (p 262, note 33).

63   Alnasrawi (1994), p 96, Table 5.4.

64   Clawson (1993ii), pp 19–23, *passim*.

65   FAO (1995), Section III, 'Public Rationing System'.

66   Beaumont (1993), pp 126–7.

67   Alnasrawi (1994), p 87.

68   There was a burst of expenditure in the early 1980s on social services, including for example district hospitals in the main towns of the south. In some of the larger cities, water systems were also improved during the 1980s, though little attention was paid to sanitation systems. These improvements depended heavily on the use of imported technologies.

69   Sluglett and Farouk-Sluglett (1990ii), p 23.

70   Sluglett and Farouk-Sluglett (1990ii), p 22. According to al-Shabibi (1997) the private enterprises were sold mainly to contractors who had flourished during the 1980s. These sales were a means by which the Government obtained additional funds from the private sector (p 58).

71   Sluglett and Farouk-Sluglett (1990ii), p 23.

72   Statement of Julius Kroll of Kroll Associates, Congress, House of Representatives. Committee on Foreign Affairs, Iraq's Nuclear Weapons Capability and IAEA Inspections in Iraq: Joint Hearing of the Subcommittees on Europe and the Middle East and International Security, International Organisations and Human Rights of the Committee on Foreign Affairs, June 29, 1993. Kroll Associates' work on Iraqi arms procurement networks was described as an outgrowth of an investigation commissioned by the Kuwaiti Government in 1990 to find Iraq's hidden assets.

73   *Middle East Economic Survey*, 9 March 1992, 'UN Security Council Debates Use of Confiscated Iraqi Financial Assets Abroad'. Some money-laundering operations have been traced, though no attempt seems to have been made to prevent the activities of Barzan Takriti who, in his role as permanent representative of Iraq at the UN, has been based in Geneva since 1990. He is thought to be a key figure in Iraq's financial operations abroad. The Iraqi Government's clandestine dealings abroad in arms and other military equipment in the 1980s means that it has long experience of operating front companies and covering its tracks abroad.

74   *Middle East Economic Digest*, 6 November 1992.

75   The Australian Reserve Bank reported in mid-1992 receiving 10 tons of gold, worth $108 million, in payment for 900,000 tons of wheat purchased by Iraq since February 1991 (*Washington Post*, 22 August 1992, 'Iraq Buying Wheat With Gold').

76   *Gulf Newsletter*, January 1993, no. 5, 'Iraq: Economic News', p 3.

77   Clawson (1993ii), p 52.

78   US Congress, Senate, Foreign Relations Committee, US Policy Toward Iran and Iraq: Hearing before the Subcommittee on Near Eastern and South Asian Affairs, March 2,

1995, Prepared Statement of James Placke, p 64. An article in the London-based daily *al-Sharq al-Awsat* on 8 June 1994 alleged that Iraq was setting up front companies in Jordan and Cyprus to sell oil, while concealing its source. The oil was to be exported by land via Iran, or from Umm Qasr via the Iranian port of Bandar-e Khomeyni from where it was to be re-exported (quoted in Foreign Broadcast Information Service, 9 June 1994, 'Oil Reportedly Being Marketed Via "Front Companies"').

79   *Middle East Economic Survey*, 26 October 1992, 'Iraq Barters Gas Oil for Turkish Products'; *Middle East Economic Survey*, 29 March 1993, 'No Relaxation of Economic Sanctions Against Iraq in Prospect at UN'.
80   *Middle East International*, 22 September 1995, 'Going Hungry'.
81   Dr Paul Conlon, interview, *op. cit.*
82   Chaudry (1991), p 23, note 8.
83   Center for Economic and Social Rights (1996), p 17; Kopp (1996), pp 449–451.
84   *Middle East International*, 22 October 1993, 'Iraq: Life under Sanctions' alludes to a ban on 140 imported luxury items implemented only 'in last few months'.
85   Boone *et al* (1997), p 28; *The Middle East*, April 1994, 'Not Everyone's Gloomy'.
86   *Jordan Economic Monitor*, June 1993, p 4.
87   *Middle East Economic Digest*, 18 February 1994.
88   Graham-Brown (1995), p 10.
89   *Financial Times*, 24 January 1995, 'Iraq issues new banknote'.
90   Reported in BBC Summary of World Broadcasts, 3 January 1996, 'President Saddam Hussein says "economic deterioration" must be halted', quoting INA news agency, Baghdad, 31 December 1995.
91   Boone *et al* (1997), p 14. The authors point out that during the first year of sanctions, 1990–91, prices rose much faster than the value of the dinar fell, but after that time the fall in the dinar was matched by the rise in price inflation.
92   *Middle East International*, 22 October 1993, 'Iraq: life under sanctions'.
93   United Nations General Assembly (1995), para. 42.
94   *Jordan Times*, 26 February 1996, 'Iraqi dinar weakens'.
95   BBC Summary of World Broadcasts, respectively 13 and 24 February 1996, 'Trade Ministry's intervention results in decline in prices', quoting Iraqi TV, Baghdad, 11 February 1996; 'Trade Ministry offers goods at reduced prices', quoting Iraqi TV, Baghdad, 22 February 1996.
96   *Middle East Economic Digest*, 15 May 1998.
97   United Nations Security Council (1998ii), para. 23.
98   Al-Shabibi (1997), p 59.
99   These efforts began soon after the imposition of economic sanctions in August 1990. The Government launched campaigns to increase production, reduced the price of seeds and fertilisers, and raised the producer prices for wheat, rice and barley. Until war was imminent, peasants were exempted from service in the regular army and *al-jaysh al-sha'bi* (the popular army) (Karsh and Rautsi [1991], pp 223, 240).
100 In a curious sidelight on Operation Safe Haven, the Iraqi Government, the Kurdistan Front, DART and the British Overseas Development Adminstration cooperated, albeit with some reluctance, to bring in the harvest in the security zone in the summer of 1991. This was mainly the result of concerns on the part of OFDA/DART officials about future food security in the security zone after the coalition forces left in July 1991 (Brilliant *et al* [1995], p 61).
101 FAO (1995), Section III, 'Food Production in 1994/5'.
102 FAO (1995), Section III, 'Food Availability'. The UN Secretary General's report of 1 February 1998 on the implementation of the oil-for-food resolutions stressed the importance of boosting production of eggs and chickens to improve the nutritional value of foods available to the population (United Nations [1998i]).
103 Boone *et al* (1997), Table 6, quoting FAO figures: average production of wheat 1984–8

was 913,000 tons and for 1990–6 1,241,000 tons. The respective figures for barley were 1,008,000 and 1,259,000 tons. The area planted had also increased but yields had fallen by 20 percent or more.

104 FAO, 'Iraq', 5 December 1997 (http://www.fao.org).

105 Springborg (1987), p 19.

106 FAO (1995), Section III, 'Vegetables and Fruit'.

107 Putting increasing amounts of land under irrigation without sufficient drainage led to heavy salt deposits. This problem began to appear as early as the 1950s and 1960s. See Fernea (1970), p 149.

108 FAO (1995), Section III, 'Food Production in 1994/5'.

109 For example, Foreign Broadcast Information Service, 14 July 1994, 'Allocations of Land Along River Reported', quoting Al-Thawrah, Baghdad, 3 July 1994, reported that it had been decided to distribute 228,000 dunums of agricultural land on the banks of the Umm al-Maarik river (Third River) 'for the cultivation of strategic crops'. A report to the Iraqi Cabinet in late 1996 claimed that 553,000 dunums of land had been reclaimed in the southern region (BBC Summary of World Broadcasts, 9 December 1996, 'Cabinet session discusses land reclamation in the south', quoting INA news agency, Baghdad, 7 December 1996). Baudouin Koenig noted in 1996 that land was being cleared for agriculture and distributed outside the marshlands, nearer to Basra, in areas which had to be cleared of mines and other battle detritus (interview, op. cit.).

110 Boone et al (1997), pp 34-36.

111 The Economist, 2 May 1998, 'Digging for defeat'. A report in 1996 indicated that the Government had imposed a tax on farmers' use of irrigation (previously free of charge), according to the area owned, in order to maintain the system (Jordan Times, 17 January 1996, 'Iraq imposes tax on irrigation').

112 Boone et al (1997), p 35. By 1997, a senior official was threatening to confiscate the land of any farmer or peasant who was 'negligent' in delivering his crop (BBC Summary of World Broadcasts, 29 May 1997, 'Official says land of "negligent" farmers will be confiscated', quoting Iraqi TV, Baghdad, 27 May 1997).

113 FAO (1995) Section III, 'Food Industries in Iraq'.

114 Boone et al (1997), pp 11–12.

115 Boone et al (1997). Table 4 shows the nominal price of the monthly ration for a family of six as ID11.1 in August 1991 and ID600 in May 1996. However, the cost of these ration goods at market prices would have risen from ID212 in 1991 to ID19,048 in 1996. However, most of this apparent increase is accounted for by inflation. The authors calculate that the value of the implied subsidy embodied in the ration in kilograms of wheat flour equivalent actually declined, from 83 in 1991 to 77 in 1996.

116 United Nations Security Council (1997), para. 13–15. As of 31 October 1998, the UN reported $2.128 billion of foodstuffs had been distributed in government-controlled areas since deliveries began in March/April 1997 (United Nations Security Council [1998ii], para. 20).

117 United Nations Economic and Social Council, Commission on Human Rights (1998) Section III A (electronic copy: http://www.unhchr.ch). The proposed increase in the calorific value of the ration to 2,300 Kcal capita per day had not been implemented by the end of 1998 because of lower than expected oil revenues (see Chapter 7) (United Nations Security Council [1998ii], para. 21–22).

118 United Nations Security Council (1998ii), para. 29.

119 Boone et al (1997), p 32.

120 United Nations General Assembly (1996), para. 71–73.

121 Rend Rahim Franke, interview with the author, Washington, 16 October 1996; Dialogue (London) May 1996, 'Iraq and the Question of Resolution 986'.

122 For example, Boone et al (1997) assert that distribution is generally fair and equitable.

The only inequities they heard of were additional goods added to the ration in some areas – mainly Baghdad – and not in others.

123   Center for Economic and Social Rights (1996), p 18.
124   *Ibid.*
125   Jim Fine, interview with the author, 23 May 1997.
126   Al-Khafaji (1986) outlines the connections of some leading Iraqi families with the regime in the 1980s (p 7).
127   *Middle East Economic Digest*, 31 July 1992.
128   United Nations Economic and Social Council, Commission on Human Rights (1996), para. 34.
129   Graham-Brown (1995), p 11.
130   Amnesty International, *Urgent Action*, 'Iraq – Death Penalty', 3 August 1992.
131   *Guardian*, 20 January 1998, 'Jordan Stops Iraqi Diplomats Leaving after Killings'.
132   See, for example, Foreign Broadcast Information Service, 8 February 1994, 'Clashes with Money Changers Reported', quoting (Clandestine) Voice of Iraqi Islamic Revolution, 7 February 1994; *ibid.*, 14 February 1994, 'Police Kill 30 Currency Dealers in Raid', quoting Agence France Presse, Paris 13 February 1994. Before currency dealing was legalised, currency dealers were often rounded up. For instance, in October 1992 hundreds of currency traders were said to have been arrested in a crackdown on illegal exchange dealing (*Middle East Economic Digest*, 9 October 1992).
133   Another source said he worked for an operation run by Saddam's two sons, Uday and Qusay, which traded in hard currency in Baghdad and elsewhere in Iraq, including in the Kurdish-controlled north (Foreign Broadcast Information Service, 7 April 1994, 'Executed Money Change Reportedly Related to Saddam', quoting *Al-Hayat*, London 3 April 1994).
134   *Middle East International*, 10 June 1994, 'Sanctions and Crime'.
135   United Nations Economic and Social Council, Commission on Human Rights (1994), para. 151.
136   *Washington Post*, 30 July 1994, 'Iraqi's Agile Saddam Persists in Power 3 Years After US Pencilled Him Out'.
137   *Middle East International*, 25 June 1993, 'Surviving Sanctions'.

CHAPTER 5

Iraqi Society Since 1991

The economic and political shocks experienced by Iraqi society since 1991 – collapsing social services, sharp declines in living standards, high levels of crime and human rights abuses – have affected both the structure of society and the well-being of the population. Despite reduced resources, the Government has been able to perpetuate the population's dependence on state services, established over two decades, though this has not prevented the embargo from taking the greatest toll on those who are most vulnerable: children, old people and female-headed households.

The effects of the embargo, combined with government policies, has greatly increased the divide between the wealthy and powerful, those whom Eric Rouleau has described as the 'nomenklatura',[1] who have profited from the crisis, and the majority of the population who struggle to maintain themselves at or above subsistence. The regime has reinforced the effects of scarcity by singling out particular groups for privilege or for persecution and has, in the process, increased divisions between different ethnic and religious groups.

Nonetheless, individuals and families have not been entirely passive. They have used whatever means are at their disposal – savings, help from relatives abroad, connections with influential people, the black market or support from their ethnic and religious community – to make a living. In turn, the Government, in order to remain in control, has attempted to manipulate communal loyalties and client relations to its own advantage.

HEALTH AND EDUCATION UNDERMINED

The decline in the provision of health, water purification, and sanitation services has hit hardest those who depend on them most: children, women of childbearing age, the elderly and the chronically ill. The restoration of water and sanitation facilities and electricity is the precondition for a sustainable improvement in health conditions which, despite the oil-for-food deal had not materialised by early 1998. While hospitals and clinics can be restocked with medicines and equipment, basic sanitary conditions will continue to influence overall levels of health. Since 1991, lack of clean drinking water and environmental pollution with sewage lying in pools in city streets, especially in the south, have exposed large numbers of people to illness.[2]

Health care has remained far below pre-war levels, due to chronic shortages of spare parts, vehicles and equipment, basic healthcare inputs, medicines and paper. Before 1990, Iraq imported annually an estimated $500 million in drugs and medical supplies. In addition, about a quarter of annual requirements had been manufactured locally, but the pharmaceutical industry lost most of its capacity as a result of war damage and the restriction on imports of raw materials for manufacturing.[3]

Marked declines in the physical condition of hospital services, including standards of hygiene, led to serious risks of cross-infection among patients. A British charity, Medical Aid for Iraq, which delivered paediatric medical supplies regularly to a number of hospitals noted in late 1994:

> A severe deterioration [compared with the previous year] is detectable in all the hospitals visited… The team had not expected to see such an extreme reduction of resources, given the desperate situation of the hospitals in April [1994]… Basic medicines are absent, routine surgery impossible, and more and more equipment is breaking down and put out of use because of the unavailability of spare parts.
>
> The Baghdad hospitals appear to be suffering particularly acutely. This may be because of the number of referrals of sick children from the provinces in addition to the demand from the local population of around 4 million. Children are referred to Baghdad because treatment is unavailable at their local hospital due to the shortage of drugs. But the Baghdad hospitals cannot provide the treatment either.[4]

Patterns of illness changed, with increases in the incidence of diseases previously not common in Iraq, such as kwashiorkor and tuberculosis, and of illnesses associated with poverty and poor sanitary conditions, especially diarrhoeal diseases and acute respiratory infections. In 1994 hospitals in southern Iraq were reporting a marked increase in children being admitted with tuberculosis, also a sign of growing impoverishment.[5]

Public use of clinics and local hospital services was reduced because they frequently did not have stocks of medications or the equipment to provide treatment. Some rural clinics were reported to be closed or not receiving patients because they had nothing to treat people with.[6] The number of patients attending hospital declined, especially in surgical wards. According to government sources quoted in 1996, 'In spite of an estimated 50% decline in hospital attendance, there have been significant increases in reported rates of mortality in hospitals'.[7]

Internal conflict has at times limited the use of health facilities. In Maysan governorate in the south in early 1992, a number of clinics and sub-clinics were still closed in rural areas for 'security reasons', and in the Suq al-Shuyukh area of Dhi Qar governorate. Officials said it was 'dangerous' to reopen them. Some people from communities in this area, on the other hand, considered that attending a clinic or hospital was in itself a dangerous act, since they feared identifying themselves to any official.

Although there is no doubt that there have been severe shortages of medications and medical equipment since 1991, external observers have at times questioned how equitable distribution of medical supplies has been. This may be the result of government policy decisions, in part because of inefficiencies, but also because drugs (particularly for chronic complaints such as hypertension and diabetes) are expensive and are frequently traded on the black market, a temptation for all health and administrative staff who have access to them. A doctor interviewed by the UN Special Rapporteur's team spoke of 'the unavailability of many medicines and the emergence of a flourishing, but very expensive black market in drugs'.[8] This has created serious problems for sufferers from chronic ailments such as heart disease or diabetes – to cite common examples – which require long-term medication. Not only is it difficult to maintain a regular supply, but the cost is crippling. Many people try to get relatives living abroad to send in medications.

Private hospitals, which do exist in Iraq, can purchase their medical needs outside the state system, but charge high prices and are therefore only open to those with money.[9] Those with wealth and influence can still go abroad for treatment.

The Iraqi health system is particularly vulnerable to the kinds of problems which economic sanctions have created. It is centralised in organisation, highly medicalised, with a heavy dependence on prescribing drugs, so that neither the system nor individual medical staff are accustomed to flexible responses to problems. Staff were initially reluctant to improvise, both because of their medical training and because of the hierarchical and authoritarian system.[10]

According to some observers, the health system had traditionally emphasised curative medicine while neglecting preventive care. This inherited weakness contributed to the disastrous public health situation after 1991. Many senior staff had been trained in the West or the Soviet Union, were used to advanced hospital technology, and depended on nursing staff from overseas. In 1996, medical staff told researchers that 'they were not trained to practice medicine in such primitive conditions'.[11] In common with other states in the region, social attitudes to nursing are generally negative, so that it is difficult to train a new and committed cadre of nurses. Many trained staff have left the health services because of the declining value of earnings.[12] However, good management at hospital level can make a difference, and observers reported that those hospitals where managers deployed scarce resources effectively fared better, even in cities such as Basra and Amara where the overall situation of health and sanitation is poor.

In the first couple of years after the war, the Health Ministry itself appeared to resist attempts by individual doctors and managers to adapt to the new conditions. The Government regarded it as important to demand a return to pre-war conditions, rather than adapt to new ones. Thus it tried to obtain full supplies of chlorine for water treatment but did not conduct a strong public health campaign to persuade people to boil unsafe water.[13] According to one aid consultant, this attitude extended to the heads of all service departments – health, water and sanitation and electricity departments – who did not incorporate into their planning the fact that if the embargo remained in place, they could not restore pre-war levels of service.[14]

Social attitudes to medicine have also influenced responses to the embargo. For example, prolonged breast-feeding was not the norm in Iraq before 1990, especially in urban and middle-class communities. Many women breast-fed only for the first few months, after which bottle-feeding prevailed.[15] Babies and young children were therefore more vulnerable to infection, particularly when there was no clean water with which to mix baby milk or formula. It also led to nutritional problems when mothers fed the powdered baby milk in too weak a solution because of its cost. Powdered baby milk on the government ration is given to families with a child under one year, but shortages pushed up its price on the open market.[16]

The increase in diseases associated with insanitary living conditions and poverty, the declining capacities of the health system, along with a lowering of general nutritional levels, has caused a rise in rates of infant and under-five malnutrition, morbidity and mortality (see Chapter 8). This has to be compared with a situation in the 1980s when, at least for the urban middle classes, health concerns were beginning to focus on excessive and unbalanced eating habits in children similar to those in other wealthy Gulf states.[17]

A less commonly discussed effect of the embargo is the crisis in education. Dwindling resources threaten the system. In rural areas particularly, many schools are said to be in very poor condition. There are chronic shortages of paper, books and other school materials. Teachers have reportedly been leaving the profession or taking on multiple jobs as their salaries, which prior to the war provided a modest living, now do not even cover the necessities of life. In 1994, it was reported that some 12,000 teachers (mainly women) had left their jobs since 1990.[18]

Family income has been progressively undermined by unemployment and low wages in relation to dramatic levels of inflation. The costs of sending children to school – clothes, transport, school materials, even pencils and paper (which previously were provided free of charge and now have to be paid for) – began to influence family decisions about keeping children in school, in a country where primary school attendance levels at least were previously quite high, even in rural areas. Researchers and aid workers, as well as government officials, attest to the rising level of school drop-outs, even at primary level. In 1996, 53 percent of six-year-old rural children were estimated to have entered school, compared with 75 percent of urban children.[19]

Pressure has grown for children to work and contribute to family income. Many more children, it seems, work in addition to attending school. A team conducting an economic survey in 1996 explained what they saw:

> A visible phenomenon is the rise in the number of children working as petty vendors. It is not clear if these children who work as petty traders take up these activities outside of school hours, or whether they have dropped out of school altogether. In our interviews with families whose children are involved in petty vending, the parents generally claimed that their child did attend school, and did the petty trading in his spare time.[20]

The social impact of schooling under an authoritarian regime may be problematic, but the Iraqi system had succeeded in creating skilled and technically proficient cadres. The latest generation of schoolchildren have had at best a depleted education and, given the impoverishment of the professional classes, may have begun to question its value. The situation since 1990 may also be deterring girls from remaining at school, where their enrolment and retention rates are already lower than those for boys, especially at secondary school level.

It is apparently easier to make a living today from trade or manual employment – or by theft, illegal trading and bribery – than it is by being a professor, doctor, teacher or even engineer. In 1993, a thirty-year-old civil engineer working as a taxi driver was quoted as saying: 'Now education is no use. As an engineer I would earn 30 dinars a month; now as a taxi driver I can earn 4000 dinars. And I absolutely need 4000.' The article further commented, 'Mechanics and vegetable and grain sellers are making new fortunes. In contrast, engineers, writers, pharmacists, travel operators, technical consultants, scientists and surgeons find themselves without work.'[21]

According to evidence given to the UN Special Rapporteur, higher education has become very corrupt, driven by the impoverishment of the academic teaching staff. Children of party members gain automatic admission and easy passes; bribes can induce professors to change grades or leak questions in advance of exams.[22]

Many graduates of universities, technical schools and institutions, who used to be allocated positions in ministries or departments in the governorates, are now jobless. By 1996, many firms had fired employees and were operating with skeleton staffs. The lack of work has inevitably encouraged the emigration of people with training and initiative.

THE HAVES AND THE HAVE-NOTS: CHANGING PATTERNS OF POVERTY

Post-war sanctions have undermined the livelihood of Iraq's substantial middle-income group and reduced living standards to subsistence level or below for the already poor. The impact has evidently not been as catastrophic as for example in Haiti, which was chronically poor before sanctions were imposed. Nevertheless, the rapid downward spiral of the economy since 1991 has had a profound impact on Iraqi society.

In all, Iraq has acquired the profile of a poor country in terms of measurable indicators, such as the infant mortality rate. Measurement of the social and economic effect of sanctions is far from being an exact science, and has for the most part been confined to estimates of the fall in per capita GDP, measures of mortality and morbidity, nutritional indices and descriptions of the decline in basic services. These are, however, only part of the picture, recording the most acute forms of suffering. Other indicators of social dislocation and change are less easy to discern and more difficult to measure, but may prove to have longer-term consequences, though conditions in Iraq have made it very difficult to track these trends in any systematic way.

People's ability to cope with the economic crisis was influenced by where they lived, what kind of jobs they had, their ethnic, religious and family background, and their individual and communal relations with the state before the Gulf crisis. Since 1991, the effects of the embargo and the policies of the Government have brought often bewildering changes in the status of social groups as new forms of economic difference emerged.

Visitors to Baghdad since mid-1991 have been surprised at signs of comfort and even affluence in middle-class suburbs and the areas where international hotels and restaurants are located. The weekend ritual of large and noisy wedding processions in the streets soon resumed after the war, and wedding parties in smart clothes took suites in the major hotels where, until 1994, when the sale of alcohol in public places was banned, pyramids of Black Label whisky were usually on display. Even allowing that weddings are accepted at all levels of Iraqi society as a time for expenditure which often taxes family budgets, these scenes do not fit the picture being painted by the Government, and indeed UN organisations and aid agencies, of 'pre-famine conditions'.

But only a few miles away, in the poor satellite city of Saddam City (formerly Madinat al-Thawra) a very different picture emerges. This has always been a poor area, consisting mainly of Shi'i migrants from the south who first began arriving in the 1950s. In this and other poor quarters of Baghdad, life was never easy, but has become increasingly harsh since 1991. In Basra, Iraq's second city, the decline in living standards has been far more dramatic. The basic infrastructure was severely damaged, and the collapse of industry, especially of petrochemicals, put many people out of work.

In late 1995, an FAO team reflected this mixed picture of Iraqi society:

> The urban population accounts for about 71 percent of the total population. Of the remaining 29 percent in rural areas, farmers constitute about three quarters. The other 8 percent of the population in the rural areas are in bad shape in the absence of earning opportunities. Of the urban population 10–12 percent (7–9 percent of the total population) may be doing very well through trade and access to other attractive means of making money. Most of the rest of the population is in a precarious condition (perhaps 70 percent of the total).[23]

For the rural population, living standards have always been lower, so that the decline since 1990 has been less drastic than for the urban middle class. The state of the infrastructure in rural areas is far worse than in the cities, though this discrepancy existed before 1990. For example, only 50 percent of the rural population is said to have access to a water supply from a network, compared with 96 percent in the cities.[24]

However, people with access even to small amounts of land can grow some food for themselves, and are therefore less affected by inflation than are townspeople. Even in urban areas, or on the outskirts of towns, those able to keep poultry or grow vegetables are said to be in a better position. The decline in the earning-power and status of salaried employment and the difficult conditions in urban areas also seems to have stimulated a return to rural employment. The Ministry of Labour and Social Affairs estimated in 1996 that nearly 40 percent of the workforce were now engaged in some form of agriculture.[25]

The worst hardship has probably fallen on the urban poor, measured in terms of the ability to feed their families, childhood illness and mortality, and loss of education. They are also the group least able to bribe their way out of difficulties or leave the country. However, the middle classes, built largely on state employment and benefits, have seen the greatest fall in living standards. 'Those classes and communities that had acquiesced with the 1980s status quo... were no longer able to do so. The pie had simply shrunk to a degree that the regime monopolised it and distributed the bulk of it to [Saddam's] closest allies in order to keep their loyalty.'[26]

A further source of differentiation between various parts of the country is based on the importance of a particular region or city for the survival of the Government.

> The central cities of Iraq, especially Tikrit, Samara and parts of Baghdad, continue to enjoy privileges in the distribution of limited resources... Among social groups of Iraqi society, certain groups remain privileged by comparison with others, eg the military and Baath Party elite, although the number of privileged groups appears to be declining along with the number of persons enjoying special privileges within the protected groups.[27]

The meagre state ration has prevented mass starvation, but urban living standards still depend mainly on people's ability to purchase goods on the free market. For those on the still sizeable state payroll, salary increases and additional subsidies have been immediately eroded by massive price inflation. On 6 December 1991 the Government announced the first wage rise in 13 months for civil servants, of between 30 and 55 percent. The highest increases went to judges, professors, senior civil servants, families of those killed on active service, and disabled veterans of the 1980–88 and 1991 wars. Security and intelligence service personnel and other civil servants received a 30 percent rise, and the army, which had already received two pay rises in the year, received 40 percent. But prices had already risen 1500–2000 times between August 1990 and August 1991.[28]

By 1994 token attempts were still being made to cushion state employees, especially more privileged groups. In July, a flat rate rise of ID200 per month was announced for all state employees, members of the armed forces, internal security services and 'special agencies'. Their wives and up to five children were to receive ID50 each. Transport allowances, highest for those working outside the main cities, were instituted. Pensioners with 25 years' government service also received increased payments.[29] When rations levels were reduced in September 1994, civil servants, armed forces personnel, families of war dead and certain categories of pensioners – some 3.5 million people – received a monthly allowance of ID2000. However, the value of such compensatory payments was almost immediately swallowed up by inflation.[30]

Civil servants and army personnel have the additional perk of access to state stores which sell non-ration goods at subsidised prices. Before 1989 these shops had been open to all citizens but subsequently access was restricted.[31] Military officers have much higher salaries than civil servants, and it has been alleged that the Republican Guard is paid in US dollars.[32] Government employees who have been in the Ba'th Party for ten years or more are said to receive much higher salaries than their non-party counterparts. The government practice of printing large amounts of money has also reportedly been used to provide favoured individuals with funds which can be changed for dollars.

The collapse of the purchasing power of the salaried middle class has begun to undermine the social ranking of different forms of employment. According to a 1995 FAO report, the average monthly emoluments (salary and allowances) of a lower-level government employee were ID500–600. Average monthly wages for all civil servants were about ID5000.[33] The same report gave the cost of a kilo of chicken as ID2500 on the open market. In 1991, when average public sector wages were about ID100–200, the same amount of chicken would have cost ID3.

In the public sector, people are either leaving their professions or taking additional jobs because the pay no longer sustains them. A refugee from Saddam City remarked that in the past it had been rare for men to have two jobs, but by 1992 it had become common. He knew a specialist working in a government hospital who was driving a taxi in the afternoons and a secondary school teacher who sold oranges on a street stall.

According to the International Committee of the Red Cross (ICRC), which works with government water departments, many Iraqi engineers have left their jobs or gone abroad because of the impossibility of earning a living wage in what used to be a prestigious profession. In 1996 a research team found that almost all engineers who have remained in water treatment plants had taken additional jobs in the private sector to sustain their families. Staff interviewed by the team reported very low morale.[34]

For many people, the war was followed swiftly by unemployment. Many small businesses, and much of the industrial sector, collapsed for lack of electricity, inputs and spare parts. The reduction in the size of the army to 300,000–400,000 in 1991–2 caused a further sharp increase in the numbers of unemployed. Those who had been drafted into *al-jaysh al-sha'bi*, the Ba'th Party militia, rather than into the regular forces, received no pension after they were stood down. Reconstruction projects which involved large amounts of manual labour created some employment, but not sufficient to absorb the large numbers of newly unemployed.

Loss of employment could also result from belonging to the 'wrong' religious or ethnic group. It is alleged that in August 1993, 900 teachers, most of whom were said to be Assyrian Christians, were 'pensioned off' in Nineveh governorate, while 100 other Assyrian teachers were said to have been dismissed in Kirkuk governorate.[35]

It is difficult to say what impact the situation since 1991 has had on women's employment, since it is not clear exactly what participation rates were prior to 1990. There was a considerable expansion in women's presence in certain professions by the early 1980s – teaching and pharmacy, for example, became largely women's preserves. During the Iran-Iraq War, women and migrant workers were increasingly substituted in the public sector for men drafted into the army.[36]

However, since 1990 the types of white-collar jobs which women held have suffered a dramatic loss in earning power. It is likely that the numbers of women in the professions has declined while more women may now be entering informal employment – selling goods, cleaning and working from home. This may include women who would not have worked for wages before 1990 and are now forced to do so by poverty or the loss of male breadwinners. In areas such as Saddam City it has reportedly become more common to find women doing paid work.

Although there had been some erosion of living standards in the late 1980s, the abrupt crash in 1990–1 left many people in shock. Salaried employees parti-cularly found it hard to adapt to the new situation of impoverishment and insecurity, and to accept that the pre-1991 situation would not be quickly restored. It there-fore took time for people to find other ways of surviving. Researchers have been struck by the sharp differences within the middle class, within neighbourhoods, and even in one street. Some households are stripped down to basics, clearly only just surviving. In others, inessentials like freezers are still in evidence. Much of this has depended on the skills within the family and the opportunities which come their way.

Those with a practical bent or good connections have found work outside the salaried state sector – driving taxis, doing repair or construction work, smuggling, trading or working in the few surviving industries. Even in 1991 it was evident that those who were engaged in trade, especially bringing goods in (legally or illegally) from abroad, or trading in items which could be bought cheap and sold at high prices, were doing relatively well. A survey conducted in 1996 calculated that the average percentage decline in monthly salaries in Iraq between 1991 and 1996 was 56 percent, but for a middle-ranking civil servant it was 80 percent, and for an unskilled worker in a public enterprise 62 percent. In contrast, skilled textile workers in the private sector suffered only a 17 percent drop in salary and unskilled workers in the private sector 43 percent.[37]

Some more lucrative areas of work are not necessarily the same as those which paid well before 1991. Those working on 'special reconstruction projects', including engineers, unskilled and semi-skilled workers, receive better pay. In 1993, an unskilled worker on the Saddam Tower was said to be earning more in a day than most government employees did in a week.[38] In 1995, unskilled workers could earn about ID500 a day, provided they found work. However, unskilled workers waiting on street corners in Baghdad and other towns in the hope of being picked up by prospective employers claimed that it was rare for them to find work for more than one day a week.[39]

As is common in such harsh situations, people find a variety of niches in which a small profit can be made. For example, in the vicinity of the special government stores a further layer of informal trade developed. Customers sold their purchases for a higher price to people waiting outside, who are not entitled to use these stores. Some merchants apparently resorted to buying large quantities of goods in state cooperatives, and then selling them at higher prices on the free market.[40]

Taxi drivers and lorry drivers plying the road between Baghdad and Amman frequently carry 'gifts' or portable goods, such as medicines, for sale. This may be done to help friends, to use as bribes, or to sell for profit. The exchange rate with the Iraqi dinar meant that goods brought from Iraq, though expensive for Iraqis, were very cheap in Amman's highly-priced consumer market. So another way to make money was to take goods to sell in Jordan. This could be done by business people who have permission to travel or by ordinary travellers taking personal possessions to sell. For a time, it was also a way for the poor to make some money. Some people, particularly from the poor areas of Baghdad, took goods to sell on the streets of Amman, sleeping rough in parks and on pavements. In 1993 the Jordanian authorities took action to clear out these illegal traders.[41]

Anecdotal evidence and official decrees suggest prostitution is on the increase, frequently a sign of increasing impoverishment. A decree in 1993 making procurement of prostitutes punishable by the death penalty was followed by Decree 118 of 27 August 1994 establishing the death penalty for organising prostitution (paragraph 1): 'The death penalty shall be imposed on anyone who organises a gang for the purposes of pandering, as defined in article 1 of the Anti-Prostitution Act No. 8 of 1988'.[42]

Role of family in survival

Family ties have undoubtedly been important in sustaining people under the economic pressures of the embargo, but families themselves are subjected to considerable strain. The burdens on women as household managers have intensified. Simply keeping the family fed and dealing with illness, without the access to reasonable health and sanitation services, has become extremely time-consuming, even for women who do not go out to work.

The most publicised aspect of impoverishment has been the progressive selling off of property and family possessions including furniture, electrical goods, personal belongings, clothes, and even parts of houses: doors, windows, cement blocks. In the south, people were reported to be reduced to selling single garments and household items in the streets in order to buy food or other necessities. Another practice was to trade expensive items such as a large fridge for a smaller model.[43] All except the poorest women have some gold as part of their dowry. Much of this gold has now reportedly been sold. Barter and borrowing money, as well as selling jewellery and household goods have become common ways of surviving. Small-scale surveys suggest that many women have incurred debts negotiated for themselves and their families.[44]

This process, what economists call 'dissaving', transfers resources from the majority, who have to sell assets in order to meet family needs, to the few who still have purchasing power, so further altering the distribution of income in society.[45]

Those who still have assets often support a network of relatives and other dependents. There are apparently instances of people passing on rations which they do not need to poorer families. However, in poor communities, few have much to spare. One refugee in Iran from a poor community in southern Iraq commented that people would try to help the destitute, particularly women on their own, but most did not have anything to spare.

There is considerable evidence that many families, and whole communities, in both government and Kurdish-controlled areas, have been kept afloat by funds from family members or friends abroad. Some communities have charitable institutions attached to the mosque or the church through which funds from expatriates can be collected. Although there is no way of measuring this flow of funds, it is thought to be very substantial, coming mainly from relatively affluent exiles and expatriates in Europe, the US, Australasia and parts of the Middle East.[46] Not only is support provided in cash, but also in kind, particularly in an effort to maintain supplies of medication for chronic conditions such as hypertension and diabetes. These transfers create a further form of differentiation – between those people with family members abroad who are able to help, and those who have no-one, or whose relatives abroad are also poor.

The high level of male unemployment in urban areas – the result both of factory and business closures, and large-scale demobilisations from the army during 1991 and 1992 – has undermined the role of men as breadwinners. In some cases, the burden of earning is spread over the whole family as increasing numbers of children work in order to contribute to family income.

In families where there is a male head of household, women remain heavily dependent on the men's earning power, as many men still do not like their female relatives working outside the home. Among poor families, households as large as 20 people may all depend on one or two breadwinners. If the earner loses his employment or becomes ill, the situation can become desperate.[47]

Some of the problems families face today are a legacy of the Iran-Iraq War, when conscription disrupted employment, educational and social patterns for many young men. In 1970, 2.9 percent of the labour force was in the armed forces; in 1988, this figure had risen to more than 21 percent.[48] Many were kept in the army well beyond the normal conscription period of four years, or were recruited into *al-jaysh al-sha'bi*, for which people were expected to 'volunteer'.[49]

Thus at the end of the Gulf War, the army demobilised many men whose main experience in the previous decade was of fighting, who had not married, or had barely seen their wives and families. They had difficulty in finding jobs, and many were physically disabled or psychologically disturbed as a result of the brutalities of trench warfare. One researcher noted the high number of disabled people identified in household surveys. With the poor state of the health service, families were left to care for the disabled, creating further demands on women. Although both international and Iraqi researchers have discussed the effects of bombing on children and other civilians in 1991, men affected by years of trench warfare or the traumatic effects of intensive bombing during the 1991 war seem to have received little attention.

The tensions caused by disability, loss of status and fear of the future, sometimes leading to drinking and other substance abuse, have in all probability heightened domestic violence. Violence in the family is something which the state has not openly acknowledged, but by 1996 even a Ministry of Information and Culture report on the situation of school children referred to 'tense social relations inside the family'.[50]

An increasing number of women have been left to fend entirely for themselves. Some families lived for a number of years without a male head of household during the Iran-Iraq War. In the intervening years, women had got used to managing without them, which made their return, especially if unemployed, very difficult. Since 1990, a substantial number of men have been imprisoned, have disappeared or fled the country. Others have gone abroad in search of work.

Women who are widowed, divorced or deserted and do not have the support of other family members are most vulnerable. From 1980 onwards, the Ministry of Labour and Social Affairs had given assistance to those it defined as 'destitutes': those on very low incomes, female heads of household, invalids or elderly people without support. Until 1990, applicants had to go through a rigorous checking process to get on these lists, which often took months. After 1991 the Ministry was said to have discontinued new registrations.[51] Consequently the lists ceased to represent, even approximately, the numbers of those in acute need. In the latter part of 1994 UNICEF and the Iraqi Red Crescent were reported to be carrying out surveys to redefine the numbers of people classified as destitute. In 1996, the World Food Programme (WFP) reported the number of registered destitutes as 450,000. However, it had identified an additional 765,000 people from poor urban families (mainly female-headed households with children under five, of whom 153,000 were said to be seriously malnourished) who were in need of food aid.[52]

Other sources of assistance are provided by state-supervised organisations: for example, the General Federation of Iraqi Women, or the Iraqi Red Crescent. Charitable assistance also exists within communities, particularly centring on mosques and churches, as well as on wealthy individuals (see also Chapter 8). Such activities are permitted by the state on a discretionary basis, dependant largely on whether those involved are suspected (with or without good reason) of using charitable work to build any kind of base for opposition. Among the Shi'i community and in the minority communities this work is therefore done discreetly to avoid problems with the authorities.

In the 1980s, there were debates among academics and researchers about how far the extended family structure in Iraq had been weakened by the increase in nuclear family units among urban people and by the growing number of women, particularly among the middle classes, who took up paid employment.[53] Since 1990, extended family networks seem to be playing an enhanced role in survival, whatever the preferences of individuals, as dependence on relatives for money, connections and other services has increased.

The trend towards nuclear family households may have been arrested and even reversed because young families cannot afford to live on their own, but are forced to live with their parents or in-laws. Poorer families are still more likely to live in extended groups. This obviously helps to support those unable to earn but places a considerable burden on the women of the household, in conditions where everything from food to medicines is an economic and sometimes a practical problem.

The Ba'th Party has often manipulated family relations for its own ends, for example by pro-natalist policies during the Iran-Iraq War. At that time Saddam Hussein, urging women to have five children or more, proclaimed, 'We hope that a woman's inclination to go out to work will not take her away from her family or from giving birth along the lines of our slogan'. Such messages were no longer so prominent in the 1990s.[54]

In other respects, women's freedom of action in relation to family and male relatives may have been curtailed, especially among middle-class women who previously had some choices, albeit limited, in regard to education and work. Fear of crime may also have led to greater restrictions on women's freedom of movement.

In Iraq today, family ties can be dangerous as well as beneficial. Families are often made to suffer for any member who is politically suspect. For example, if a family fails to report that one of its members is a deserter, this may lead to eviction from their home and loss of their ration card. Families with relatives in jail for political reasons can also face harassment by the authorities.[55] Women who remained in Iraq after their husbands, fathers or sons had fled to Iran after the uprisings reported that they received frequent visits from security officials.

In November 1993 the official newspaper *Babil* announced a Revolutionary Command Council (RCC) decree which used marital relations as a weapon against political opponents. A woman could divorce her husband if he 'switched to serve the enemy'. She kept her rights as a wife and the divorce could be annulled if the husband returned to her and 'to the patriotic line' within the period of '*idda* (ie within three months of the divorce).[56]

Recent amnesty decrees contained clauses whereby relatives are held responsible for the return of miscreants to the fold. RCC decree No. 61 dated July 22, 1995, 'remits the remainder of the sentences of Iraqi prisoners and detainees, commutes death sentences to life imprisonment and pardons persons liable to the penalty of amputation of the hand or the auricle of the ear'. However, remission of sentence is conditional: 'if [the detainee's] relatives undertake to ensure their good conduct, provided that the said undertaking is endorsed by a member of the Arab Ba'ath Socialist Party'.

CRIME AND PUNISHMENT

'If help does not come soon, the survivors will be the sanctions-breakers, the black marketeers and the thieves.'[57] This rather melodramatic statement by a WFP official reflects the gulf which has emerged since 1990 between the privileged and the rest of the population. It also indicates the role extra-legal activities have played in survival and profit since 1991.

Undoubtedly the main reason for the dramatic rise in crime at all levels of society is that it has become a means of survival. A refugee from central Iraq commented in 1993 that people resorted to theft if they were poor or to bribery if they had money. 'Those who keep to their own values are very hungry.'[58]

Theft – particularly of cars – is increasingly common, sometimes accompanied by violence, in a society where this type of crime was previously rare.

Typically, the criminals come from the ranks of young men who were drafted into the army [in the 1980s and early 1990s]... They have lost their youth; demobilised without compensation, often without education or training, without jobs or the prospect of them, inured to the cruelty and harsh, survivalist lessons of war, they turn to violence of another kind. The law encourages them: in a bid to stem the contagion, Saddam has decreed that theft is a capital offence, so thieves kill, the better to ensure they are not caught.[59]

Collaboration between police and criminals is apparently not uncommon. Bribery appears to have become endemic in daily transactions. According to one journalist, shopkeepers say they have visits from policemen or Ba'th Party officials seeking protection money.[60]

Refugees from southern Iraq have spoken of arrests by the army whose main purpose was to elicit payment from the family to get their relative out of prison. Witnesses to the UN Special Rapporteur have alleged that it was possible even to bribe a judge or executioner to avoid the death penalty – but someone else had to die instead so that the executioner could deliver a body.[61]

Since civil servants do not earn a living wage, bribery has become widespread even for mundane transactions. One man was reportedly taken aback when he went to renew his driving licence to be asked by the officials concerned to go to a restaurant and buy them a round of kebabs – more valuable than money in times of inflation.

Many ordinary people, while accustomed to arbitrary actions by state and party agents, were shocked by the rising levels of lawlessness. The decline in standards of public behaviour has also been fuelled by the ostentatious way in which the nomenklatura has escaped the rigours of sanctions.[62]

The scale of the post-war crime wave seems to have worried the authorities, who initiated measures to check it, beginning in January 1992 with the imposition of the death sentence for theft, burglary and looting, as well as car theft. However, these measures appear to have had little effect. At the beginning of 1993, the RCC exempted Ba'th Party members and others on 'security missions' from any legal proceedings for 'confronting thieves and those who infringe law and order, even if this leads to their [the thieves'] injury and death'.[63]

Efforts to dress up new controls on crime as 'Islamic' forms of punishment resulted in a whole array of laws and regulations prescribing brutal punishments, including in 1994, the penalty of amputation of a hand or foot for the theft of goods valued at more than ID5000. In January 1995, the opposition Iraqi National Congress released a videotape recorded from Iraqi television 'showing the mutilations inflicted on an Iraqi army deserter and a petty thief as punishment for their crimes'. The Government's aim in showing the mutilations was said to be to deter potential deserters and thieves.[64]

The detail of the decrees gives some indication of the type and scale of the crimes anticipated, and the harshness of the response. For example, Decree 95 of 27 July 1994 stipulates (paragraph I): 'The death penalty shall be imposed on anyone who smuggles an automobile, a truck or any machinery or apparatus used for drilling, earth moving or any similar purpose outside Iraq or to a hostile body'.[65]

Decree 114 of 25 August 1994 amended Decree 59 paragraph 2, which had called for execution if a robbery is committed by a person carrying a visible or hidden weapon or if the crime results in the death of a person. Decree 114 extended the provision for execution to include any theft perpetrated by an individual 'affiliated with the Armed Forces, the Security Services, or a state employee'. The death penalty can be commuted to life imprisonment if the court finds the circumstances warrant mercy.[66] Decree 74 of 4 July 1994 called for the detention, 'for a period of one to three years, [of] anyone who sells or purchases foreign currency outside the licensed offices or, to that end, conspires with employees of licensed offices or banks'.[67]

Iraq is a highly bureaucratised society regulated by a large number of laws and RCC decrees decided by a small inner group around the president or by Saddam Hussein himself. Yet enforcement of these rules is often arbitrary. Hence even this attempted crack-down on crime did not affect all parts of society equally, so that some favoured individuals carrying on these illicit activities continued with impunity.

The laws may be used by officials for self-aggrandisement, to reward those in favour or protect them from punishment, and to dispossess those they want to exclude. Furthermore, enforcement of all laws seems to be selective and may be used against those who are thought to have dissident views, or who are potential economic or political rivals of individuals favoured by the inner circle. Since 1990, this has become part of the structure which allows the 'winners' to retain their privileges despite sanctions.

THE STRUCTURES OF COERCION

Since the 1991 Gulf War, US officials have frequently spoken of 'thinning support' for Saddam Hussein and the 'narrowing base' of his leadership. Analysts who have followed the fortunes of the Ba'thist regime since the 1970s emphasise that even before 1991 its base was narrow. In the late 1980s perhaps 700 people were said to be considered 'reliable supporters' of the regime although many others – senior civil servants, members of state security services, party officials and senior army officers – were dependent on the status quo for their livelihoods and status.[68]

During the 1980s, inner councils were established within the Government, staffed by loyal adherents and relatives of the ruling family. These bodies appear to make most key decisions and can override the more formal decision-making structures, including the RCC and the Ba'th Party Regional Command. In addition to the circle of close relatives, a small group of 'loyal outsiders' hold senior posts: for example Tariq Aziz, an Assyrian from Mosul, and Taysir Taha Ramadan, also from Mosul.

Some members of this inner circle have lost their lives because of some perceived disloyalty, and many others have gone through cycles of disgrace and rehabilitation. This tactic appears to be part of Saddam's method of retaining control. Hussein Kamil was an example of this process. A man of strong ambition, he was promoted rapidly until he was abruptly demoted from the post of Defence Minister in 1991, only to be reinstated later in an influential position as Minister of Industry and Minerals and Director of the Military Industries Organisation, where he remained until his defection in August 1995 and subsequent return to his death in January 1996.

Since the 1991 war, elements within Saddam's immediate family circle and among the tribes and clans on which he relied for recruitment to senior army and security service positions have showed signs of dissent. His son Uday's temperament, described as that of a psychotic playboy, appears to have caused many of the problems among close family members. There have also been struggles between different factions of the al-Majid clan.

After the experience of the uprisings, in which discontented and defeated soldiers played a significant role, a major priority has been to retain the allegiance of the armed services and to reinforce the army and security services' role in internal security. Republican Guard regiments have been deployed for internal security duties and along the *de facto* border with the Kurdish-controlled north between 1992 and 1996. Large forces were periodically despatched to the southern marsh areas for large-scale offensives. The security services have been highly active in conducting security sweeps, arresting the politically suspect and those they wish to intimidate.

Since the 1970s, the armed forces have been increasingly removed from the inner circle of political power, with the exception of certain elite troops. Until 1991, the Republican Guard filled this role. However, it seems that in the constant search for 'reliable' elements, only certain sections of the Guard now have this privileged position.

The weakening of ties between the military and particular Sunni clans previously loyal to the regime led to a proliferation of new units (see below). After the 1991 war, a new security unit known as the Special Republican Guard was apparently established as a counter-balance to the main Republican Guard force.[69] A unit called 'Saddam's *fiday'in*' was said to have been formed in 1995, apparently because of Saddam's increasing distrust of Republican Guard officers belonging to clans or tribes from Ramadi and Mosul.[70]

Following the assassination attempt on Uday in December 1996, another new army unit, *jaysh umm al-ma'arik*, was set up under the control of his brother Qusay, while the activities of a group within Special Security (*amn al-khass*) known as the 'Emergency Organ', were reportedly extended from Baghdad to the provinces.[71] The problems in finding those responsible for the attack on Uday suggest that the proliferation of competing security services may have become inefficient and counterproductive.

After the Gulf crisis, the level of Iraq's military forces has been dramatically reduced – to between 300,000 and 400,000 from close to a million men under arms (including the poorly-trained party militia, *al-jaysh al-sha'bi*). Army officers and elite forces continue to receive a variety of additional benefits and bonuses, including grants of state land and cheap home loans. However, the impact of sanctions meant that by 1993 living conditions for non-elite regiments had reportedly deteriorated. Life for ordinary soldiers was said to have become very harsh. An ordinary soldier's pay in mid-1991 was about ID53 a month, compared with ID100–200 for a low-ranking civil servant. By 1994 it was reported that even Republican Guard units were less pampered than in the past. The decline in the status and income of the officer class, except in the 'inner circle' of units, has been compared by one author to that of Russian military officers today.[72]

Significant numbers of army deserters fled to Iraqi Kurdistan between 1993 and 1996 when the Iraqi National Congress was based there. By that time the southern marshes, previously the main refuge for deserters, had been largely ruled out as a hiding place.[73] That the problem of desertion had become widespread was indicated by the brutal punishments of ear-cutting and branding meted out to deserters and draft evaders from 1994 onwards. Reports indicated, however, that by 1996 these penalties were being used less frequently.[74] It was suggested that they were proving unpopular even among the regime's supporters.

The possibilities for opposition

Since the Gulf War there have been a number of attempts to change the Government by force. During each year since 1992, several abortive coup attempts have been reported, though the reliability of the reports is always uncertain. However, to put this in perspective, there had been numerous attempted coups and assassinations directed at Saddam Hussein prior to the Gulf crisis.[75]

Most of the reported 'coups', whatever their reality, have been followed by widespread arrests and executions. After reported coup attempts in July 1992 and in July or August 1993, members of clans usually considered loyal to Saddam Hussein were executed. In May 1995, according to the UN Special Rapporteur, an uprising took place in the city of al-Ramadi after the body of Brigadier General Muhammad Madhlum Dulaymi was returned to his family in Ramadi, reportedly bearing the marks of torture. The riots which followed this event led to an 'allegedly disproportionate and indiscriminate use of force' by the authorities, including arbitrary killings and numerous arrests.[76]

By the end of 1998, none of these attempts to change the Government, either by a coup or assassination had succeeded. There is some evidence to suggest that the Government's control in the south, outside the cities, continued to be patchy. There have been many stories of armed groups attacking army or government or Ba'th Party property and officials in the south. Government sources usually attributed incidents to 'bandits and robbers', while opposition sources speak of planned attacks on government targets.[77] In the Amara marshes in 1992, soldiers on checkpoints on marsh roads were said to be withdrawn to garrisons or strongpoints at night. Drainage of the marsh areas has undoubtedly increased the degree of military control since that time, but up to the end of 1998 there were persistent reports of both government military attacks in the marshes and rebel activity.

The state's grip proved sufficient to prevent the widespread emergence of alternative forms of organisation. By the time Saddam Hussein took formal power in 1980 most organised political opposition had already been suppressed and destroyed, or bought off. Such opposition as may exist inside government-controlled areas today is clandestine and probably fragmentary. Adherents of various political groups banned by the Government – including the INC, SCIRI and the Da'wa Party – have reportedly been arrested, usually tortured and executed.[78] Periodically mass arrests sweep hundreds into jail, while mass executions of prisoners are not uncommon.[79]

In such a repressive climate, concern at the degree of social disintegration which has occurred since 1991, and anger directed against the leadership, cannot easily be translated into popular, organised action against the state. The regime has been able to channel some of the popular resentment caused by the war, the uprisings and the economic embargo towards external enemies, particularly those states which have implemented sanctions most energetically. Even those who might have welcomed a change in government, especially among the urban middle classes, felt let down when the embargo dragged on for so long. They felt they had already suffered during the war, and did not see why they should be further victimised.

The failure of the uprisings left a legacy of anger and bitterness at the absence of international support. One of the longer-term effects of the experience in the south was to make people fear any further open defiance of the regime in view of the retribution meted out afterwards. The regime has also played on fears of the possible anarchy and vengeance which might follow its collapse. During the 1991 uprisings in the south, and to a lesser extent in the Kurdish areas, rebels took brutal revenge on party officials and those identified as informers.[80]

Anecdotal evidence nonetheless suggests that since 1991 there have been periodic outbursts of public indignation and violence, quickly suppressed. Some have been triggered by food shortages and government price controls, but the most obvious backlash came as a result of the imposition of so-called Islamic punishments for desertion, theft and other economic crimes. Branding and cutting the ears of army deserters led to incidents in several southern cities. For example, according to one report, in Amara several Ba'thist officials reportedly had their ears cut off by an irate crowd. In Nasariya, a doctor who cut the ears of several deserters was killed with his family in his own house.[81]

A protest strike by several hundred doctors following the announcement of the amputation and branding decrees was called off when they themselves were threatened with imprisonment and execution. Sixty medical students were reportedly arrested in Basra in December 1994 for refusing to carry out the punishments or for performing cosmetic surgery on the victims.[82] Doctors were reportedly warned that if they performed any operation to reattach the ear immediately after the amputation, their own ears would be removed.

MANIPULATING SOCIAL GROUPS

Since the 1970s, Ba'thist governments have engaged in active social and political manipulation, both by inducement and coercion. Its strategies of control under the restrictive conditions imposed by sanctions have contributed to changes in Iraq's social order.

Within the ranks of the leadership and in society at large, the hunt for enemies is accompanied by a constant search for allies. Since 1991 these divide-and-rule tactics have become far more explicit. The regime, without a broad base of support, has relied on buying support or acquiescence, with money or other favours. The economic problems which the regime has experienced since the Gulf War have limited the inducements it can offer. Its largesse is now distributed more selectively to those who can be induced to remain loyal and can control their own followers or clients. The Government, while continuing to stress the theme of an Iraqi people united against the world, has increasingly singled out particular ethnic, religious or tribal groups for favours or for repression.

The Special Rapporteur has argued that 'In the process of subjugating the population, power is abused not only vertically, ie through immediate and direct oppression upon the population, but by means of horizontal effects, whereby social ties are also exploited'. This includes collective family responsibility for alleged crimes by an individual and manipulation of tribal and religious leaders, who are forced to swear allegiance to Saddam Hussein on behalf of their communities – either to avoid punishments or to gain privileges.[83]

The economic collapse created by the embargo may well have reinforced communal solidarities. Individuals and families may be more inclined to turn to kin, or to members of their own ethnic or confessional group, to help and protect them in a time of economic difficulty. At the same time, economic hardship may reinforce prejudices and even hostility against other groups. In any society where, as in present-day Iraq, many people are compromised by informing and cooperating with the authorities in order to safeguard their own position and that of their families, mutual suspicion, at the individual and community level, is never far from the surface.

Nonetheless, the simplistic shorthand for religious and ethnic divisions commonly used in the West since 1991 – 'Sunni centre, Shi'ite south and Kurdish north' – is misleading, and masks more complex patterns of social identity. Since the 1960s, migration, both voluntary and forced, has altered the demographic balance between different communities. After the Gulf War, further changes have occurred as a result of displacement, economic pressures and emigration.

In urban areas, many people live in mixed communities in which class and social status may have as much significance as ethnic origin or religious affiliation, except where these divisions coincide. In Baghdad, for example, there is a very sizeable Shi'i population. The majority are poor migrants from the south who are the predominant group in several of the poorest neighbourhoods, but there is also a sizeable group of Shi'i professionals and merchants who would associate more readily with people of their own class than with their poorer co-religionists.[84]

Many Kurds live in Baghdad and the south as a result of migration or forced displacement (see Chapter 6). There are also Christian minorities – predominantly Chaldean – in the Baghdad region. On the other hand, the number of Christians in northern cities such as Mosul has diminished significantly since the 1960s. Christians, like Kurds and Turcomans, formed part of rural as well as urban communities in the northern part of the country. The Christian community as a whole has shrunk markedly as a result of emigration, particularly since 1991.

Tribal Allegiances

In Saddam Hussein's view, the Ba'th Party failed him during the uprisings, and its position in the overall structure of power seems to have weakened significantly since the 1980s.[85] In its place, the leadership has chosen to promote, more strongly than in the past, 'primordial' loyalties of tribe and clan. These may be real – in the form of membership of an extended family network – or imagined common tribal ancestry.[86]

In Arab Iraq, some of the mores of bedouin tribal life survived the settling of tribal peoples from the Arabian peninsula in the Iraqi countryside in the eighteenth and nineteenth centuries. Some of the concepts of honour and deference to tribal leaders remained, although roles within the tribal group were altered by settled life, and by the conversion of large numbers of those who settled in the south from Sunni to Shi'i Islam. Many of the historical forms of communalism – and the pre-eminence of landlords, tribal and religious leaders – were eroded by economic and social changes: the diminishing importance of agriculture, the growth of opportunities in cities and the oil boom from the 1970s. However, elements of communal organisation remained, reconstructed 'not necessarily in terms of historical continuities with traditional formations, but on bases favoured by the current situation'.[87]

In its early years, the Ba'th Party sought to subordinate communal ties to party and state power, but under Saddam Hussein, the leadership has relied heavily on ties of tribe, clan and family to build loyalty. The regime's support has come mainly from the small town of Takrit in Central Iraq, where bonds of family, clan and tribe still have importance. This inner circle appears to consist mostly of members of Saddam Hussein's own immediate family and clan (the Be'jat section of the Al bu Nasir tribe)[88] and of several major tribal groups including al-Dulaym, al-Duri, al-Jubur, al-Shammar. From these groups come most of the key figures in the leadership, especially in the intelligence and internal security establishment.

The 1991 uprisings did not touch this core of support but, after he had reasserted his control, Saddam appeared to become increasingly suspicious of their loyalty. From 1992 onwards, reports of attempted coups increasingly involved members of these tribes. Whether this was because, in their discontent with the regime, they did indeed rebel, or because they were 'framed' by the leadership is not clear.[89]

By 1995–6, the leadership was actively seeking to gain the allegiance of a wider group of tribes, and was promoting the role of tribal *shaykhs* in tax collecting, army recruitment and administration. Sunni tribes were a particular focus of attention, including several in the western governorate of Ramadi, where Saddam was also trying to mend relations with the al-Dulaym clan after the violent clashes of 1995.[90] Efforts were also made to recruit tribal leaders in the south, and Saddam Hussein 'presented the tribal principle as a bridge which transcends the Sunni-Shi'i divide' which the regime has done so much to exacerbate (see below).[91]

This trend was accompanied by a greater public emphasis on the values of rural life and agriculture, as urban society, previously sustained by bureaucratic and professional classes, began to crumble. In June 1994, the Council of Ministers announced that the issuance of building licences in Baghdad and other provincial centres had been stopped in order to promote building in the countryside. Saddam Hussein spoke of the short-term and long-term social and economic benefits 'of the continued promotion of the countryside, districts and subdistricts, which will settle people in these areas and upgrade their standard of living'.[92]

Many Iraqis whose urban, middle-class existence has collapsed (at the most optimistic reading, temporarily) may be tempted to return to the village or small town from which they came. Those who still have family connections may acquire a new status as a local notable, performing services for the state for a share of the takings.

However, the promotion of tribal power clearly had some drawbacks. It appears to have revived old feuds and disputes and has created urban/rural tensions, presumably as rural-based clans wield greater influence through the increased power of tribal *shaykhs* and through further recruitment of rural elements into the security services. A decree published in March 1997 indicated problems with the promotion of tribal authority outside the core group of tribes which have formed the basis of the regime's support.

It states that 'anyone making a claim in accordance with tribal traditions against anyone carrying out an action in implementation of a law or an order issued to him from a higher authority shall face a penalty of at least three years in prison'. The commentary added that there were 'two issues which should not be confused, namely, the issue of respecting tribes which are a genuine part of the social and national fabric, and the issue of acting against general state law and tribalism in a lawless community. Tribalism should not be viewed as something above the law.' It also stressed that if the law was not observed by the whole civil community 'anarchy would prevail among the groups that make up the urban community'.[93]

Class, religion and tribe in the south

In the south, religious, tribal and class identities have played their part in shaping society. Shi'i Muslims today make up at least 60 percent of the population of Iraq. They comprise the vast majority of those living in the region to the south of Baghdad. This area suffered most as a result of the wars of 1980–88 and 1991 and, with the exception of the petrochemical and related industries located around Basra and the Shatt al-Arab, was generally discriminated against in the allocation of resources.

Since 1991, the Ba'thist regime has both openly persecuted the Shi'i Muslim community and sought to co-opt elements of rural society in the south. By the time of the uprisings in the south in 1991, the regime's relationship with the Shi'i community was already one of mistrust. The hatred and violence directed against the Ba'th Party during the uprisings and the regime's retribution caused further antagonism. Since that time, the regime has taken particularly harsh measures against any signs

---

A History of Repression

Returning refugees to rural areas in the south in late 1991 reportedly remarked that 'our troubles did not begin with this last war'.[94] The Shi'i community, though it forms the majority of the population, has long been treated as an underprivileged minority.

The Shi'a became a majority of the population of Iraq due mainly to the conversion of bedouin from formerly nomadic Sunni tribal confederations which settled in Iraq, for example al-Muntafiq, al-Zubayd, al-Dulaym, Al bu Muhammad and Bani Lam. The Ottoman Government encouraged their settlement in the late nineteenth century, mostly in the southern and western parts of what became the state of Iraq.

Grants of land to tribal *shaykhs* following changes in Ottoman land law in 1858 turned some of them into major landowners.[95] *Sayyids* from the Shi'i holy cities of Najaf and Karbala, until that time the centres of Shi'i habitation, with substantial populations of Persian origin, proselytised among the settled tribesmen.[96] In some cases only sections of a tribe or confederation would be converted, and to this day there are tribes in which some sections are Sunni, others Shi'i. For example, the Dulaym clans which settled north of Baghdad remained Sunni, whereas the branch which settled in the Hindiya district in the south converted to Shi'ism.[97]

The Shi'i community remained divided along class and status lines: between urban and rural dwellers, those who follow a secular or religious mode of life, merchants, businessmen, professions, landowners and peasants. Batatu noted that in 1958 'if the richest of the rich were often Shi'is, so were also predominantly the poorest of the poor'.[98] Nonetheless, a common political issue since the time of the monarchy has been the demand for access to political power and representation commensurate with the community's majority status. In contrast to the Kurds in Iraq, the debate has not been over whether or not to be part of the Iraqi nation, but how to be part of it.

For some, the issue is essentially secular, relating to political rather than strictly religious representation. For others, it is a class issue, since the Shi'a have historically made up the majority of the poorest in Iraqi society and the divisions between rich and poor – landowners and peasants – were very sharp.[99] The power of the landowning class was seriously weakened by the land reforms of the 1960s, but the Shi'i merchant community in Baghdad had grown in importance when much of the wealthy Jewish commercial community left for Israel after 1948. However, politically speaking, the Shi'i merchants tended to seek individual mobility rather than political solidarity with the wider Shi'i

---

of popular dissent – real or imagined – and has further curbed religious worship and organisation.

The uprising had raised the spectre of an open Sunni-Shi'i split, and Saddam Hussein has sought to build some alliances within the Shi'i community. In the south, both in the marshes and outside them, and in the small towns, the Government is said to have made systematic efforts since 1991 to co-opt tribal leaders. As early as August 1991 in the weeks before the Ba'th Party's tenth Congress, Iraqi television featured tribal personalities from the south pledging fealty to Saddam Hussein and begging pardon for the seditious behaviour of 'a few paid saboteurs'. Representing a regime that once banned the use of tribal and clan names (except in Kurdistan where it was encouraged) the President himself admitted to a delegation from Kut that his regime had been mistaken in 'inciting the people against feudalism'.[100]

In 1992, when signing a 'treaty' with some tribes in the Suq al-Shuyukh district, Saddam Hussein spoke of the 'Ba'th party as the tribe encompassing all tribes'. They

community. In contrast with Iran, the merchant community has not generally had a very close relationship with the 'ulama (scholars of Muslim theology and law). The Ba'thist Government had some success in detaching them from the 'ulama's interests.[101]

The Iraqi Communist Party had considerable success in recruiting in the 1950s among poor Shi'i urban migrants, as indeed did the Ba'th Party in that first decade of its existence. After the earliest decade of Iraqi Ba'thism, during which Shi'a in the south played a considerable part in the small beginnings of the party, they have always held some offices in government, the party and the army. However, overall, their representation in the RCC and in the regional Ba'th Party command appears to have been reduced since the 1980s, along with that of other minority groups. Their influence in key circles of power has certainly never been commensurate with the size of the Shi'i population.[102]

The Shi'i religious establishment in Najaf and Karbala was not able to gain a coherent role in political life, even as far back as the British mandate period in the 1920s. However, in the 1960s and 1970s, reacting to the growing secularism within the Shi'i community, some of the 'ulama sought to rebuild faith and adherence to traditional rites. Others began to develop an explicit Shi'i religious political message. Several political groups emerged, the oldest of which is the clandestine al-Da'wa al-Islamiyya party, formed in the 1960s, which established itself during the 1970s as a significant force.

After the Iranian revolution in 1979, Saddam Hussein's suspicion of the Shi'i community's links with Iran increased, as did Iraqi Shi'a political activism against the regime. This was answered with fierce repression, including the execution in 1980 of Ayatollah Muhammad Baqr al-Sadr (whose thinking and writings on the political role of Shi'ism were the main inspiration of al-Da'wa) and his sister, Bint al-Huda. In the late 1970s and early 1980s the Government also deported hundreds of thousands of Iraqi Shi'a to Iran on the grounds that they were 'of Iranian origin'. Despite this repression, significant material improvements in the late 1970s and early 1980s may have placated part of the Shi'i population. The war with Iran did not lead to significant levels of defection or any open rebellion, as some commentators had anticipated.[103]

This wave of repression marked the end of open Shi'i political opposition inside Iraq for over a decade. From 1980 onwards Iraqi Shi'a opposition groups had to operate from Iran. This also brought new levels of interference in Shi'i religious affairs by the Ba'thist regime, including government control over Shi'i religious revenues through the Ministry of Awqaf, official salaries for Shi'i 'ulama, and supervision of school curricula.[104]

pledged to 'defend Iraq's national soil and confront the scheme of infiltration, sabotage and partition, and sanctions the shedding of the blood of any of their sons whose betrayal of the homeland is proven'. In return Saddam agreed to give them arms and pledged to implement 'additional service projects to serve the citizens'.[105] This gives some indication of the opportunities offered to local leaders to boost their prestige and power at the expense of those unwilling to cooperate with the Government.

Along with the widespread arrests and 'demotion' of local tribal chiefs who were involved in, or supportive of, the uprisings, the selection, promotion and payment of new chiefs loyal to the Government has been a means of exerting control in a strategic region where the Government knows much of the population is discontented, if not hostile. These local forces may be used to supplement the military and internal security services saving the regime 'from having to spread its armed forces too thinly'.[106]

Since the time of the uprisings, hostility to Shi'ism as a religion has been quite explicit. Perhaps most symbolic was the slogan said to have been painted on Iraqi tanks entering Najaf: 'No more Shi'as after today'. This has subsequently been reinforced by the treatment of the Shi'i religious establishment, and continued public slurs on Shi'i religion. In the towns of the south, the once-influential religious forces have been rendered largely powerless; political parties with an Islamist agenda were long ago banned, and even Shi'i social organisations are restricted in their work.

In the shrine cities and other provincial centres, it has been suggested that impoverishment has increased people's dependence on assistance from communal sources, and that wealthier people have used traditional religious forms of charity to assist the poor. It seems the Government permits this as long as it is discrete and the persons involved are not seen to be gathering any kind of a following or political power as a result.

For the two million or more Shi'a living in the Baghdad metropolitan area, the communal ties which may operate in the shrine cities and other towns in the south do not necessarily have the same strength. There are fewer Shi'i mosques around which communities can gather for help or solidarity, and communities are more fragmented and subject to forces created by class and income differences. The poorest communities in Baghdad are largely, though not exclusively, Shi'i, and it is probably poverty as much as religious affiliation which determines their allegiances. For most, the acute problems of crime and unemployment are shared with all the other poor.

The effect on the religious establishment of Najaf and Karbala, already weakened by the events of the 1970s and 1980s, has been further to restrict religious activity. The regime has interfered with Shi'i devotional practices, particularly in public places. Religious institutions have been closed. There was large-scale destruction and desecration of Shi'i shrines during and after the uprising, particularly in the holy cities of Najaf and Karbala. While restoration work has been done on the main shrines of Imam Hussein and Imam Ali respectively, many other mosques, *husayniyas* and libraries remained ruined despite offers from the community to pay for their restoration. Some *husayniyas* which were restored could only be rebuilt on condition that they were no longer identified as Shi'i centres of learning and worship.[107]

Many clergy were arrested. The Grand Ayatollah Abu al-Qassim al-Kho'i, who was Shi'i Islam's most senior cleric, known as the *marja'*, was held under virtual house arrest from the time of the uprising until his death in August 1992. Ayatollah al-Kho'i was not a political figure but had wielded very great influence throughout the Shi'i world. During the uprising in Najaf, he called for the establishment of a 'Supreme

Committee' under whose leadership the Shi'a would preserve Iraq's security and stabilise public, religious and social affairs. He was later forced to appear on Iraqi television and call for an end to the insurrection.[108] According to Amnesty International, 106 of his relatives, members of his staff and theology students arrested during the uprising 'disappeared' while in custody.[109] In July 1994 one of his sons, Hojjat al-Islam Sayyid Muhammad Taqi al-Kho'i, was killed in a car crash which the al-Kho'i family alleged was 'arranged' by the regime. He had reportedly been warned by the authorities in Baghdad not to continue speaking out about persecution of the Shi'a.

The emergence of the *marja'*, the religious figure of greatest eminence within Shi'i Islam, has always been a process which has taken place within the Shi'i community worldwide. After Ayatollah al-Kho'i's death, the Iraqi regime attempted to interfere in the appointment of the next *marja'*, nominating its own candidate who, though not widely accepted, has assumed a role as a kind of religious functionary. Meanwhile, two senior figures, Grand Ayatollah Sayyid Ali Sistani and Grand Ayatollah Shaykh Mirza Ali al-Gharawi, both of whom would have been popular candidates for *marja'*, have been harassed, and al-Gharawi was reportedly assassinated along with three companions on 18 June 1998.[110]

While suppressing or coopting the religious establishment, Saddam Hussein sought to legitimise his rule over both Sunni and Shi'i Muslims by claiming that his family is descended from the family of the Prophet, and therefore that of Ali and Hussein.[111] In March 1996, the Iraqi media reported him as visiting 'the tomb of his great-grandfather, Imam Ali al-Hadi [the 10th Shi'i imam]... in Samarra district' and, soon afterwards, 'the tombs of the righteous imams, his grandfathers and heroes of Arabism, Islam and the sublime principles: Ali Bin Abi Talib in holy Najaf Governorate and his sons Hussein and Abbas in Karbala Governorate...'[112]

INTERNAL DISPLACEMENT AND EMIGRATION

The regime's forcible relocation of populations – to destroy political opposition, for 'border security' and to prevent any concentration of groups which might present any kind of threat to its rule – was seen in its most extensive and brutal form during the Anfal operations in Iraqi Kurdistan in 1988. But since the Gulf War, both the Kurds and other communities have been victims of forced displacement.

Human rights organisations and the UN Special Rapporteur have documented the increasing pressure on Kurds and Turcomans to move from both Kirkuk and Mosul and their environs. The 'Arabisation' of these cities and the surrounding region, begun well before the 1991 war, continues to be a goal of the Government. In 1993, it was reported that the Iraqi authorities were encouraging Arab families from Central Iraq to resettle in these cities by offering them money and other incentives. Meanwhile, Kurdish residents were given the choice of moving to southern Iraq with their possessions or going to the Kurdish-controlled north leaving their possessions behind, forfeiting their property and their ration cards.

Reports in subsequent years suggested the pressure on these communities has continued. In 1997 and 1998, human rights sources reported that the 'Arabisation' campaign had intensified in the Kirkuk and Khanaqin region, where there was evidence of that deportation orders had been issued to several thousand Kurdish and Turcoman residents. Many of these families have moved into Kurdish-controlled areas, adding to the internally displaced population there.[113] UN sources were quoted as saying that at least 500 families displaced from the Kirkuk/Khanaqin area had registered with the UN in Iraqi Kurdistan in the first half of 1997.[114]

Turcomans have been forced to leave Kirkuk and villages in this region, and to choose between going to the Kurdish-controlled region without their possessions, or with their possessions to southern Iraq. The minority of Turcomans in Iraq who are Shi'i, rather than Sunni, Muslims have reportedly received the harsher treatment. The Government has banned both groups from selling property to any non-Arab buyer.[115]

After the 1991 war, many people moved to Baghdad from the south, especially from the Basra region, where conditions were bad and work opportunities few, especially because of the destruction of the petrochemical industry. In August 1994, the Government reportedly issued a decree forbidding those who had moved into Baghdad after 1991 to remain there, and prohibiting further in-migration. Exceptions were made for the predominantly Sunni governorates of Mosul, Salahadin, Diyala and al-Anbar. All others were apparently ordered to leave Baghdad. The Government justified this move by saying that it was overwhelmed by the demand for housing, health and education services which this additional population caused. According to an informed source, the Baghdad police took strong measures to execute this decree. Families were forced to leave their houses, and their effects were dumped in the street. They were said to have been given a sum of ID6000 (about $8 at that time) as moving expenses.

The southern marshes

The regime's efforts to remove by force the inhabitants of the marshes between the Tigris and Euphrates constitutes the most extensive forced displacement of population since 1991. The drainage project already described was accompanied by a systematic military campaign to clear the area.

The marsh-dwellers had mixed origins. Some bedouin tribes settled in the marsh areas in the nineteenth century, but they despised and did not intermarry with the pre-existing marsh inhabitants, whom they regarded as 'yokels' or *Ma'dan*, a term of contempt for marsh dwellers to this day.[116] The marsh inhabitants had historically lived either by buffalo herding and by making and selling reed matting, or by cereal cultivation. They also fished for their own subsistence. In the early 1960s the population was estimated by an Iraqi anthropologist to be about 400,000.[117] Over the past 50 years, the economic isolation of the marshes has progressively diminished, with the advent of some government education and health services, recruitment of people from the marshes into the army and government service, and the increasing development of commercial links with the towns. Since the 1950s, many inhabitants have migrated from the marshes in search of work.

These changes altered somewhat the lives of the marsh-dwellers, but their communities still remained largely intact. It was during the Iran-Iraq War that the ecology and geographical position of the marshes brought more violent intrusion by the state. Forgotten casualties of the Iran-Iraq War were the peasants and marsh-dwellers in areas drained or cleared as battle zones both in the Fao area and in the region of the Amara marshes adjacent to the Tigris. Many of those displaced apparently ended up living in half-finished buildings on the outskirts of Basra and other cities, where some of them remain today.[118]

The marshes also became a haven for large numbers of deserters and were periodically bombed and shelled by the Iraqi army. Documents later captured in the Kurdish city of Sulaymaniya suggest that even by the late 1980s the Government was determined to regain control of this area and had a strategy to do so. One of the documents recommended that an economic blockade be applied to villages in the marshes 'through the withdrawal of all food supply agencies; a ban on the sale of fish... by prohibiting goods traffic from entering those villages and areas'. These sanctions were to be lifted only if local tribal chiefs cooperated in the campaign against deserters. 'Consideration must be given to the possibility of regrouping the marsh villages on dry land (which is easy to control) and opening roads and points of access deep inside the marshes.'[119]

In 1991, the marshes were the obvious refuge for those fleeing after the uprisings collapsed, and a way to reach Iran. For townspeople, it was certainly an uncomfortable refuge. One refugee from Saddam City described his experience of hiding in the marshes to escape conscription. The winter was very cold and damp, the summer very hot and mosquito-infested. When he began working, 'cutting reeds ripped up your hands. You could go a few hundred metres from the village and easily get completely lost in the reed beds.'

The political allegiances of the marsh inhabitants are apparently mixed. Some of the tribes fought in the Iraqi army during the Iran-Iraq War. Many took part in the uprisings, though others have since taken the government side and been rewarded. Some recalcitrant *shaykhs* were apparently replaced after the uprising while others were jailed or killed.

In April 1992, the army and security forces began a campaign of bombardment (with artillery and, until the no-fly zone was imposed in August 1992, with helicopter gunships and fixed-wing aircraft) and burning reeds, particularly in the central area of the Amara marshes. After the imposition of the no-fly zone, the ground-based attacks continued unabated, indiscriminately targeting young and old, men and women.[120] There were also reports of many people being arrested or at least removed from the area.[121]

At the same time, the Government announced a programme to move marsh inhabitants to the fringes of the marshes to be rehoused and provided with amenities. National Assembly speaker Saadi Mehdi Saleh said, however, that 'they would not be allowed to settle back in the places they were taken from'.[122] In practice, the drive to remove people from the marshes, destroying the economic basis of their livelihoods, left most of them with little choice. It was a violent and forcible displacement of population on a large scale. The army was also said to have imposed restrictions on food being taken into the marsh areas. Soldiers at road-blocks near the marshes checked vehicles. Many families did not have ration cards, or at least not up-to-date ones. It is unclear how effective or systematic this embargo was. Women were reportedly sent to town to sell fish and other produce, and to buy supplies for several families. Family connections in the towns apparently facilitated quite extensive smuggling.

Fighting nonetheless continued, with Iranian-based opposition groups using the marshes as a base from which to carry out sporadic attacks and hit-and-run raids on government and Ba'th Party buildings and military units. They also claimed to have tried to sabotage the dykes associated with the drainage project. The level of rebel activity seemed to depend to some extent on how cooperative the Iranian authorities at the border were being at any particular moment. How far these forces were actively assisted by the marsh inhabitants is not clear. Villagers seem on occasion to help and shelter fighters at some risk to themselves, though other reports spoke of villagers who were Ba'th Party members informing on rebels in their area.[123] Government forces continued their artillery attacks and raids in the marshes, with access made easier by the extensive drainage.

As early as 1992, some families living on the fringes of Chabaish (a larger settlement drained at an earlier date) had moved to Nasariya for greater security, while others from inside the marshes had taken over their vacated houses. Other families were already living in dwellings constructed from reed mats, plastic and canvas on the sides of the road from Chabaish to Nasariya, probably displaced from marsh villages, after attacks early in the year.

By summer 1993, the situation, particularly in the Amara marshes, evidently became much worse. The water levels dropped, leaving sticky mud in which fish died. There were allegations that the water was poisoned, but it may have simply been too brackish. Water buffalo, an important economic asset, died through lack of water. Transport by boat – the usual mode of travel – became more difficult. People whose homes had been destroyed by government attacks, or in areas where water levels had dropped too low, moved to deeper areas of marshland or settled on the margins of the large new canal taking the water from the Amara marshes, where they could live by fishing.[124]

Larger numbers of people began to leave the area altogether. Ten thousand or more headed for Iran between summer 1993 and the end of 1994. Some of the refugees said they had survived the bombardments and food shortages, but lack of water in the summer heat made it impossible to continue living in the dried areas.[125] The exact scale of internal displacement as a result of the destruction of marsh areas is not known, but there are now reported to be communities of displaced marsh people around several of the main towns such as Amara and Nasariya. One source said that some of the displaced had tried to move to Baghdad but had been forced out and had to return to the south, where the local authorities complained they did not have the resources to cope with them.

In 1998, there were reports from the Nasariya area of numerous internally displaced people from the southern marsh areas living in very primitive housing with an extremely low standard of living, and without any support from the authorities. People living on the periphery of the marsh areas have also experienced difficulty with supplies of drinking water. Many of the displaced were thought to have no ration cards or even proper ID cards. Concerns have been voiced as to whether this group has been receiving rations under the auspices of the oil-for-food resolutions.[126] There are reported to be large numbers of female-headed households among the internally displaced or those whose male relatives are deserters or in prison. In the marshes, even in villages which are still intact, it seems that few men of working age are to be found: either they are working outside the area, or in hiding, in prison, or in Iran.

By 1995–6, some new agricultural land appeared to have been opened up in the drained marsh areas, although few outside observers have had access to the area to confirm its extent. Land seems to have been distributed through local tribal *shaykhs*, with the Government providing seeds and irrigation pumps (reportedly using adapted old military tank engines). Apparently priority was given to marsh-dwellers, but the opportunity to acquire land also attracted people from outside the region.[127] Several settlements were reported to have had new houses built for the farmers.[128]

The dispossession of the community as a whole means a loss of a range of skills and occupations. According to one interviewee, there were some 400 boat-builders and carpenters in the marshes before the Gulf War, now there are only said to be between six and ten workshops left.[129] Meanwhile, the poorest members of the marsh communities have joined the ranks of the unemployed and day labourers. Many of the displaced had to sell off their water buffaloes after they moved from the dried marshes and had nothing to live on.

Although it is likely that many young people would have left these communities in the next generations, the drainage and displacements since 1991 have put a definitive and brutal end to a distinctive culture and the ecosystem which sustained it.

Leaving the country

The traffic of people over the Jordanian border began as soon as the Iraqi authorities opened the border on 15 May 1991.[130] Since there has been a steady stream of people leaving Iraq – mainly those with more money and education – to join several million Iraqis already living outside their country. 'The trend of emigration from the country, especially among the youth,' one observer noted in 1996, 'continues in spite [of] restrictions imposed by the authorities'.

Most of the stream of hopeful emigrants failed in their efforts to find countries of asylum or emigration and, having spent frustrating months in expensive apartments or hotels in Amman which consumed their savings, went home disappointed. A smaller group managed to stay in Jordan, some awaiting resettlement by UNHCR, some in penurious conditions, with no rights to Jordanian public services. Furthermore, until 1994 at least the presence of Iraqi security agents was said to be ubiquitous – including some for a time stationed in Amman in a building adjacent to that of UNHCR where asylum applicants congregated. Killings of dissidents in Amman added to the uneasy feelings of those remaining there.

In 1991, the exodus through Amman was mainly of people from the Christian community, along with a few Kurds. By 1992–3, UNHCR figures showed that the majority of asylum applicants were Shi'a from Baghdad and the south. Few were accepted for resettlement.[131] Many people nonetheless remained in Amman, living in a kind of limbo.[132] A source of fear and insecurity for Iraqis living in Jordan was the presence of Iraqi security agencies which, with the exception of a brief period in 1995 when cooler political relations temporarily limited their influence, appear to have operated freely in Amman.

Although the Iraqi Government has continued to allow people across the Jordanian border, it has progressively tightened the exit conditions. An exit tax of ID15,000 was first imposed in May 1993, and by the end of 1995 it had risen to ID400,000. In 1995 restrictions were imposed on the categories of people allowed to travel outside the country. Skilled persons such as engineers, architects and doctors are required to post a guarantee of return of ID1 million in cash in a bank account or fixed property. All applicants for exit permits have to present security clearances, ration cards and certification from the Ministry of Defence that they have fulfilled their military service obligations.[133] Many of the potential problems involved in getting the correct documents can be circumvented by bribery or by buying the relevant documents. Again, those with access to money therefore have the opportunity to leave which is not available to the poor.

These controls affect people travelling via Amman, the 'legal' exit from Iraq. Since the end of 1991, another way to leave the country has been through the north. This direction has mostly been taken by those under pressure from the authorities in one way or another. Some of these people, especially Kurds, have stayed in the north, others have gone on to Iran or tried to get to Europe via Turkey. People who have travelled this way speak of needing money or influence to bribe their way through internal check points, and to get across the *de facto* line to Iraqi Kurdistan. From 1992 until September 1996, army deserters and political refugees were supported by the Iraqi National Congress or other opposition groups in the north. The occupation of Arbil by the Iraqis had tragic consequences for some of these people. Some families who were refugees from the south found themselves fleeing to the Iranian border with the PUK.

NOTES ON CHAPTER 5

1   Rouleau (1994).
2   Injuries and illness due to war-induced pollution have not been measured. Some doctors have mentioned health problems and birth defects that they attributed to these causes. No comprehensive studies are available, but given the problems among US and UK servicemen since the Gulf War this cannot be discounted. A UN report in June 1998 quoted Iraqi government figures as showing that cancer cases in Basra almost doubled between 1989 and 1994, while there was a six-fold increase in Maysan governorate, also in the south. In the rest of the country under government control, no change in rates was reported. It is currently impossible to get independent confirmation of the figures or to be sure of the causes (*Guardian*, 22 June 1998, 'Gulf war linked to sixfold rise in Iraqi cancer rates'). Ordnance and war debris also pose dangers. Most are out in the desert, therefore less likely to become children's playthings, but after the war, the Government was said to be offering cash for weapons, and people were going out in to the desert and digging up war materials, including mines, near the Saudi border (interview with an IOM official, 8 April 1997).
3   Hoskins (1997), p 106.
4   Medical Aid for Iraq, 'Report on delivery of medical supplies to paediatric hospitals in Iraq, October 1994'.
5   *Ibid*.
6   United Nations Economic and Social Council, Commission on Human Rights (1998), Section III A (electronic copy: http://www.unhchr.ch).
7   Center for Economic and Social Rights (1996), p 20, quoting government figures cited by the World Health Organisation of 90,000 excess deaths in public hospitals annually since sanctions were imposed.
8   United Nations General Assembly (1995), para. 33.
9   UN General Assembly (1996), para. 85. An Iraqi newspaper reported in January 1998 that the Government intended, on a one-year trial basis, to transform an unspecified number of state-owned hospitals into 'self-financed hospitals, which rely on revenues generated from rendering high-quality medical services at appropriate price rates to

cover their expenses'. BBC Summary of World Broadcasts, 17 February 1998, 'Health Minister says state hospitals to be privatised in one-year trial', quoting *Al-Zawra*, Baghdad, 29 January 1998.

10 Author's discussion with a doctor working with ICRC, September 1991.
11 Center for Economic and Social Rights (1996), p 23.
12 *Ibid.*, pp 10, 27.
13 Jim Fine, interview with the author, 23 May 1997.
14 Kuttab (1992), p 37.
15 Fawzi *et al* (1997), p 781.
16 FAO (1995), Section III, Public Rationing System.
17 Center for Economic and Social Rights (1996), p 10.
18 *Guardian*, 29 October 1994, 'Desperate unity of a pariah state', quoting Mohammed Zijjari, the UN Coordinator in Baghdad.
19 United Nations Economic and Social Council, Commission on Human Rights (1998), Section III B. According to figures given by the UN, net primary enrolment rates fell from 94 percent for children of school age in 1991 to 84 percent in 1996 (United Nations Security Council [1998ii], para. 47). According to the 1988 *World Development Report*, primary school enrolment as percentage of the primary school age group was 96 percent for all children and 87 percent for girls; at secondary levels the figures were 47 and 37 percent respectively.
20 Boone *et al* (1997), p 24.
21 *Guardian Education*, 26 January 1993, 'Iraq: Where Students Struggle to Survive'.
22 United Nations General Assembly (1995), para. 38.
23 FAO (1995), Section III, Access to Food: Prices and Incomes.
24 United Nations Economic and Social Council, Commission on Human Rights (1998), Section III A.
25 Boone *et al* (1997), p 20.
26 Al-Khafaji (1995), pp 31–32.
27 United Nations General Assembly (1994), para. 92.
28 Dreze and Gazdar (1991), p 16.
29 *Gulf Newsletter*, June/July 1994, no. 10, 'Saddam Hussain tightens his grip on the economy', p 5.
30 *Gulf Newsletter*, November/December 1994, no. 11, 'New punishments, new hardships', p 5.
31 Chaudry (1991), p 17.
32 United Nations Economic and Social Council, Commission on Human Rights (1996), para. 34.
33 FAO (1995), Section III, Access to Food: Prices and Incomes.
34 ICRC, *Water in Iraq*, Special Brochure, Geneva, July 1996; Center for Economic and Social Rights (1996), p 27.
35 United Economic and Social Council, Commission on Human Rights (1994), para. 97.
36 According to official figures, in 1977 women made up 17.6 percent of the workforce excluding farm workers (Omar [1994], p 62). The decline of the small family farm sector and rural-urban migration in the 1970s and 1980s appeared to have led to a decline in the numbers of women in agricultural employment (Mahdi [1995], p 205). According to a representative of the General Federation of Iraqi Women, 27 percent of the workforce before the 1991 war were women, a very high percentage for the region. She asserted that the level of women's participation had increased since 1991 because women were taking jobs in the public sector previously held by men, who were now working in construction (Comité de Solidaridad con la Causa Arabe, 'Informe de la segunda delegación espanola a Irak', March 1994, p 41).
37 Boone *et al* (1997), Table 3.
38 *Middle East International*, 22 October 1993, 'Iraq: Life under Sanctions'.

39 FAO (1995), Section III, Access to Food: Prices and Incomes.

40 *Jordan Times*, 26 February 1996.

41 *Gulf Newsletter*, July 1993, no. 7, 'Refugees and displaced people', p 6.

42 BBC Summary of World Broadcasts, 23 October 1993, 'RCC decree says procurement of prostitutes carries death penalty', quoting Republic of Iraq Radio, Baghdad, 21 October 1993; UN Commission on Human Rights (1995), para. 41.

43 Boone *et al* (1997), p 25.

44 Bhatia *et al* (1992), pp 39, Appendix 2b.

45 Al-Shabibi (1997), p 59.

46 See, for example, *Washington Post*, 6 October 1996, 'The Iraqi Example: Saddam Has Thrived Under Sanctions While Innocent Civilians Suffer'.

47 Boone *et al* (1997), p 26; Bhatia *et al* (1992), *passim*.

48 Alnasrawi (1994), p 92.

49 One refugee from Basra recalled that in the late 1980s a person working in the private sector might be able to avoid service, but anyone with a government job had to serve if asked, or lose their position. Young and old alike were called up, frequently to do guard duty or dig ditches, though during wars members of the popular army also had to fight.

50 *Baghdad Observer*, 10 April 1996, 'Lost dreams of Iraqi school children'.

51 Von Braunmuhl and Kulessa (1995), p 102. The figure given for registered destitutes by WFP in September 1991 was 394,005. WFP was assisting a further 224,500 people it regarded as vulnerable.

52 United Nations Consolidated Inter-Agency Humanitarian Programme in Iraq Extension of the Cooperation Programme for the period from 1 April 1996–31 March 1997, 3 April 1996, p 20.

53 See, for example, Joseph (1982), Omar (1994), pp 62–3.

54 Omar (1994), pp 64–5. After the 1991 war, it seems that contraceptives were available in some places. The main problem was to afford them. In late 1991, a hospital doctor told the author that the pill had gone up from 250 fils to ID5 (presumably for a month's supply) while the cost of an IUD had risen from ID3 to ID30. This might have discouraged some women from using them.

55 United Nations General Assembly (1996), para. 20–21. As early as 1982, the Ministry of Defence had ordered the arrest and detention of wives and children of deserters (Omar [1994], p 63).

56 Omar (1994), p 64.

57 WFP/FAO, 'Time running out for Iraqi children', 26 September 1995, Press Statement by Dieter Hannusch, WFP's Chief Emergency Support Officer.

58 The breakdown of social norms under these economic pressures even seemed to be invading the school yard. A study by the Ministry of Information and Culture reported that theft – of money, school stationary and food (sandwiches, sweets, eggs, all of which can be sold) – 'has become a common problem in schools' (*Baghdad Observer*, 10 April 1996, 'Lost dreams of Iraqi school children'). A refugee from Baghdad said he knew of a school where the pupils were stealing the desks to sell them or use them for fuel.

59 *Guardian*, 5 April 1994, 'The Father of Battles'.

60 *Wall Street Journal*, 25 August 1994, 'Saddam Hussein's Draconian Decrees Fail to Slow Iraqi Economy Descent'.

61 United Nations General Assembly (1995), para. 38.

62 Rouleau (1994).

63 *Gulf Newsletter*, January 1993, no. 5, 'Iraq: economic news', p 3.

64 *Middle East International*, 20 January 1995, 'The Tragic Toll of Sanctions'.

65 United Nations Economic and Social Council, Commission on Human Rights (1995), para. 41.

66 Human Rights Watch/Middle East (1995), p 14.

67   United Nations Economic and Social Council, Commission on Human Rights (1995), para. 37.
68   *Middle East International*, 14 September 1990, 'Saddam Hussein and the government of Iraq'.
69   Baram (1993), p 35.
70   BBC Summary of World Broadcasts, 6 May 1995, 'Opposition radio says "Saddam's Fida'iyin" to replace Republican Guard officers', quoting Voice of Rebellious Iraq, 4 May 1995.
71   Jabbar (1998); BBC Summary of World Broadcasts, 10 March 1997, 'Saddam reportedly tightens security after assassination attempts', quoting *Al-Quds al-Arabi*, London, 7 March 1997.
72   Jabbar (1998).
73   At the beginning of 1996, the Baghdad press reported that the price for buying out of army service was between $600 and $800 (ID1,200,000–1,600.000 at the exchange rate of ID2000 to the dollar which prevailed the time) (*Le Monde*, 2 January 1996, 'Iraq: le forfait...').
74   Amnesty International (1996), p 1.
75   There were reportedly four such attempts between late 1988 and January 1990 (Karsh and Rautsi [1991], p 207).
76   United Nations Economic and Social Council, Commission on Human Rights (1996), para. 21.
77   Most of the reports come from opposition radio stations, but evidence has also come from visitors and aid workers. In 1992/3, officials were said to be reluctant to travel off the main roads in the afternoons or evenings, and some attacks were even acknowledged by the official media. In 1994, a group of foreign journalists was attacked near Basra, and there were reports of gun battles in the Nasariya area.
78   See, for example, United Nations General Assembly (1997), para. 15.
79   See, for example, Amnesty International (1998), section on the Republic of Iraq.
80   Baram (1993), p 36; Maysoun Pachachi, interview with former Karbala resident, *op cit*. In the north, Kutschera (1997), p 93; Randal (1997), p 40.
81   *The Times*, 13 September 1994, 'Iraq mob cuts officials' ears off'.
82   Amnesty International (1996), p 9. The UN Special Rapporteur wrote that in a situation of acute shortages in the health sector, 'a particularly sad aspect of the effects of the decrees is the prescribed diversion of medical services, including personnel and material resources such as drugs and surgical instruments, away from health-related activities and for the purposes of legalised mutilations' (United Nations General Assembly [1994], para. 70).
83   United Nations Economic and Social Council, Commission on Human Rights (1994), para. 180.
84   For a description of the communal geography of Baghdad, see Luizard (1994).
85   *Middle East International*, 14 September 1990, 'Saddam Hussein and the government of Iraq'; Baram (1997), p 7.
86   Tripp (1995), p 135.
87   Zubaida (1991), p 209.
88   Batatu (1978), p 1084.
89   See, for example, reports of a purge in 1994 against a number of senior security and party officials belonging to the al-Duri clan (from the village of al-Duri in the Takrit area). This clan has been closely allied with Saddam Hussein, and his Vice President, Izzat al-Duri, comes from this area. Foreign Broadcast Information Service 'Saddam Launches "Purge" Against al-Duri Officials', 25 May 1994, quoting *al-Hayat*, London 21 May 1994.
90   *Middle East International*, 25 June 1993, 'Surviving Sanctions'. In the National Assembly elections of 24 March 1996, representatives of tribes constituted the largest number of

persons elected, and they were still predominantly from the 'core' tribes of al-Takriti, al-Jabbur, al-Dulaymi and al-Shamri. United Nations General Assembly (1996), para. 50.

91   Baram (1997), p 18.
92   *Independent on Sunday*, 8 January 1995, 'Famine after Desert Storm'; BBC Summary of World Broadcasts, 30 June 1994, 'Ban on urban construction intended to promote rural development', quoting Republic of Iraq Radio, Baghdad, 28 June 1994.
93   BBC Summary of World Broadcasts, 27 March 1997, 'TV broadcasts decree on tribal traditions, explanation of rationale', quoting Iraqi TV, Baghdad, 25 March 1997.
94   As recalled by an official of the International Organisation for Migration while he was accompanying refugees returning from Iran.
95   Farouk-Sluglett and Sluglett (1983), pp 493–495.
96   Nakash (1994), p 25ff.
97   *Ibid.*, p 43.
98   Batatu (1978), p 49.
99   For example, in 1951 eight shaikhly families in the province of Amara held 53 percent of agricultural land, and eighteen other individuals 19 percent of all land-holdings in the province. The high levels of landlessness, unemployment and impoverishment in rural communities in the south led to a trend of rural urban migration which began in the 1920s, and intensified in the 1950s and 1960s as the oil boom began (Farouk-Sluglett and Sluglett [1983], pp 498, 500–501).
100 *Le Monde*, 4-5 August 1991, 'Le pouvoir ébranlé de M. Saddam Hussein'.
101 Nakash (1994), pp 271–2.
102 Al-Khafaji (1994), p 29.
103 Chubin and Tripp (1988), p 104. A number of commentators have noted that despite being co-religionists, Iraqi and Iranian Shi'ism have evolved in different ways, and there is less common ground politically than might be expected even among those with a Shi'i political agenda.
104 Stapleton (1993), pp 18–24.
105 Foreign Broadcast Information Service, 3 December 1992, 'Saddam Receives Dhi Qar Group, Promises Firearms', quoting Iraqi news agency, Baghdad, 2 December 1992; BBC Summary of World Broadcasts, 2 December 1992, 'Delegation from Suq al-Shuyukh renews allegiance to Saddam Hussein', quoting Republic of Iraq Radio, Baghdad, 30 November 1992.
106 Baram (1997), p 19.
107 United Nations Economic and Social Council (1994), para. 131.
108 Nakash (1994), pp 276, 278.
109 Amnesty International (1993).
110 *Dialogue*, July 1998, 'The Murder of Shi'a Clerics: The UN Speaks Out'.
111 According to Baram (1991), p 138, a book published in 1989 claimed descent from the Prophet's family through Saddam's mother, who was from the Al bu Nasr tribe. The use of Islamic images and rhetoric to legitimise the regime was already emerging in the 1980s. After the Iranian Revolution when rivalry with Iran became paramount, the state promulgated the idea that Iraq is the bearer of Islamic values in the region. This was superimposed on the older official view of Iraq as the leader and protector of the Arabs and a great society with roots in ancient civilisations. Since the 1991 war, religious symbolism generally has taken an increasingly heroic tone, to the point where in 1996 and 1997 Saddam Hussein was being described in the state-run media as 'the mujahid' or 'the God-supported leader'. For example, BBC Summary of World Broadcasts, 10 June 1997, 'Saddam chairs meeting which denounces UN Resolution', quoting Iraqi TV, Baghdad, 8 June 1997, in which he is referred to as the 'leader mujahid'.
112 BBC Summary of World Broadcasts, respectively 22 March 1996 and 25 March 1996, 'Iraqi president visits Shi'i tomb, quoting Iraqi TV, Baghdad; 'Saddam Hussein visits tombs of Shi'i imams', 3 April 1996, quoting Iraqi TV, 1 April 1996.

113 According to the UN Special Rapporteur, deportation orders were issued on 13 May 1997 to 1300 Kurdish and Turcoman families from Kirkuk; in August to 440 Kurdish families in Jalula and Qara-Tepa (west of Khanaqin) (United Nations General Assembly [1997], para. 27; United Nations Economic and Social Council, Commission on Human Rights (1998), Section II B). The US State Department gave somewhat larger numbers for deportations in 1997 from Kirkuk and Khanaqin: 1500 persons in April; 1000 families in September and 1750 families in December 1997 (US Department of State [1998], Section 2D, electronic copy, http://www.state.gov). In a press release on 30 April 1998, Amnesty International reported that several hundred more Kurdish families had been forced to move from the Kirkuk area since November 1997, and more were targeted for expulsion.

114 Human Rights Watch, *World Report* 1998, p 334.

115 United Nations Economic and Social Council, Commission on Human Rights (1994), para. 139–40.

116 Nakash (1994), p 47.

117 Salim (1962), p 21.

118 Minority Rights Group (1993), p 14ff.

119 'Plan of action for the Marshes' from the Directorate of Security, Arbil Governorate, 30 January 1989, quoted in United Nations Economic and Social Council Commission on Human Rights (1993), Document no. 18.

120 *Gulf Newsletter*, January 1993, no. 5, 'Human rights in southern Iraq', p 5, quoting information from Amnesty International.

121 There have been persistent reports of people from this region being sent to Abu Ghraib and other prisons in the central region. Some of them were probably killed, but no reliable figures are available. It is unclear whether these were punitive sweeps picking up people uninvolved in any opposition activity or whether they targeted individuals thought to support the insurgents.

122 *Middle East Economic Digest*, 22 May 1992.

123 BBC Summary of World Broadcasts, 1 February 1996, 'Returning travellers report "massacre" of Shi'i rebels, villagers in Adl area', quoting *Al-Hayat*, London, 31 January 1996.

124 Hilterman (1993), p 36.

125 *Gulf Newsletter*, October/November 1993, no. 8, 'Marsh dwellers forced from their homes', p 4.

126 In September 1998, UN observers' attempts to verify that the displaced population in the Nasariya area had equitable access to the government ration were 'inconclusive' and were to be 'kept under review' (United Nations Security Council [1998ii], para. 17).

127 Baudouin Koenig, film-maker, interviews in the village of al-Imarat, 1996.

128 However, in 1996 Saddam Hussein conceded that the state had not given proper attention to those living in 'reclaimed' areas of Maysan, Basra and Dhi Qar governorates (BBC Summary of World Broadcasts, 9 December 1996, 'Cabinet session discusses land reclamation in the south', quoting INA news agency, Baghdad, 7 December 1996).

129 Baudouin Koenig, interviews in the village of al-Ouain 1996.

130 After the Gulf War 'more than 100,000 Iraqis' moved to Jordan, at least temporarily. While many were believed to have repatriated or moved elsewhere, some 30,000 remained in Jordan (US Committee for Refugees [1994], p 110).

131 In June 1993, out of 2800 applications for asylum to UNHCR (both individuals and family groups) since mid-1991, only 171 cases (about 560 people) were reportedly resettled from Jordan, with a further 36 cases awaiting resettlement (*Gulf Newsletter*, July 1993, no. 7, 'Iraqi Refugees in Jordan', p 6). During 1994 and 1995, the US Committee for Refugees reported that a 'relatively small number of Iraqi nationals have approached UNHCR in Amman to be recognised as refugees. UNHCR estimated that about 150 Iraqi refugees in Jordan would require settlement to third countries' (US Committee for Refugees [1995], p 118).

132 In mid-1995, there were still said to be some 30,000 Iraqis living in Jordan: 'street traders, long term residents or asylum seekers hoping for visas to a third country' (*Guardian*, 'Fear and Loathing and a Little Hope', 19 August 1995).

133 *Middle East International*, 22 October 1993, 'Iraq: Life under Sanctions'; United Nations General Assembly (1995), para. 49; United Nations General Assembly (1996), para. 40.

CHAPTER 6

Iraqi Kurdistan Since 1991

S ince the Gulf crisis of 1991, the three predominantly Kurdish northern governorates of Iraq have existed in a state of limbo, still part of Iraq yet under the
political control of Kurdish parties and largely cut off from the rest of the
country by an economic embargo imposed by the Iraqi Government.

The Government's decision to withdraw its troops and administration from the
region at the end of 1991 created a new and unusual situation which, for the Kurds,
opened the way for some form of self-rule, more extensive than anything they
had experienced in Iraq before. At the very least, it meant an end to direct Ba'thist
repression. For a time, some Western supporters of the Kurds saw the Iraqi withdrawal as a real opportunity to give democracy a chance to work. The decision of the
Iraqi opposition to establish a presence in the north in late 1992 made Iraqi
Kurdistan a potential base from which to overthrow the regime.

By 1996, the two major Kurdish parties, the Kurdistan Democratic Party (KDP)
and Patriotic Union of Kurdistan (PUK), were locked in a war for geographical and
economic hegemony, splitting the region between them and leaving many ordinary
citizens impoverished, fearful and despairing of the future. Many had left the country
or were trying to leave. The Western coalition states appeared to have no solution to
the conflict and indeed no policy for the future of the region. Meanwhile, the influence of Turkey and Iran in Iraqi Kurdistan had significantly increased.

The outcome of these events cannot be explained by any single factor.
International intervention in 1991 created new political dynamics which, in the
volatile local and regional context, had unpredicted results. Kurdish political and
social history explains other aspects of the story. The violent struggles with the Iraqi

state over the last half century shaped not only its people's material circumstances, but their attitudes, sense of identity and expectations.

The Kurds under Ba'thist Rule

Under the March 1970 Manifesto, the Iraqi Government proposed regional autonomy for the Kurds and proportional representation in the affairs of the state. However, mutual suspicion and the Government's reluctance to cede the key asset which the Kurds demanded – the city of Kirkuk and its oil resources – led to stalemate. In 1974 the Government unilaterally issued a less favourable Autonomy Law which was rejected by the Kurdish leaders.[1] Encouraged by the Shah of Iran, the Iraqi Kurds launched a military campaign against the state. Under the terms of the 1975 Algiers agreement between Iran and Iraq, Iran agreed to end its support for the Iraqi Kurds and the revolt in northern Iraq collapsed.[2]

In 1976 Iraq declared a security zone of between five and 30 kilometres along the mountainous Turkish and Iranian borders. Between 1976 and 1978 an estimated 600,000 people were resettled either in the first generation of *mujamma'at* (collective settlements) or were removed to the south of the country.[3] Most of these new settlements were located well away from the Iranian and Turkish borders, in the lowlands of the Kurdish region.

Military campaigns against the *peshmergas* during the Iran-Iraq War (1980–88) were accompanied by an economic blockade, aerial and artillery bombardments, forced displacements of population – including the abduction by Iraqi troops of 5000–8000 male members of the Barzani clan in 1983 – and destruction of villages. However, the *peshmergas* did succeed in establishing a degree of control over the mountainous regions near the Iranian and Turkish borders.

In 1987 the Iraqi Government had already begun to define larger 'prohibited rural areas' in the Kurdish mountains in which 'all resident Kurds were co-terminous with the *peshmerga* insurgents, and they would be dealt with accordingly'. Foodstuffs, persons and machines were prohibited from the villages in the prohibited 'security zones'; agriculture and animal husbandry were banned; and the military were ordered to kill 'any person or animal found in these areas'.[4]

This prefigured the four military campaigns under the code name Anfal (the spoils) in 1988. Since 1991 a large amount of evidence of what happened during the Anfal operations of 1988 has come to light. The intention of the campaigns was primarily to regain control over the mountainous regions held by the *peshmerga* but the scale of the operation went far beyond any previous campaign. 'Baghdad's objectives seem to have included the destruction of Kurdish nationalist forces and the removal of all inhabitants and livestock from the captured areas.'[5]

It is estimated that some 4000 settlements – from small villages to medium-sized towns such as Qala Diza, Raniya, and Halabja – in the three predominantly Kurdish northern governorates were systematically bulldozed and dynamited.[6] Some settlements were subjected to aerial bombing, in which chemical weapons were used. The largest death toll resulted from the chemical attack on the town of Halabja in March 1988, in which between 3200 and 5000 people died. Following the bombing, an estimated 60,000 civilians fled to Turkey and about 70,000 to Iran.[7] Many thousands of men were arrested and subsequently disappeared, or were forcibly moved to other parts of the country. Much of the remaining rural population was forced into new *mujamma'at* away from the border areas.[8]

The 1988 chemical attack on the town of Halabja was only the culmination of years of systematic and forcible resettlement of the Kurdish rural population. As this violent process left scars on the landscape, it also left scars on individuals and communities.

From 1970 to 1990, relations with the Government of Iraq and with the governments of neighbouring states, particularly Iran and Turkey, have dominated Iraqi Kurdish politics. The Kurds have been sporadically at war with the Iraqi Government since the collapse of the 1970 autonomy talks, initiated by the Ba'thist Government which had come to power in 1968.[9] The experience of alternately negotiating and fighting with this Government certainly influenced the strategies and expectations of the current Kurdish leaders, while the Ba'thists' ruthless repression of Kurdish opposition – to the point of genocide in the late 1980s[10] – has marked the entire population.

KURDISH IDENTITY

Most Kurds in Iraq regard themselves as both Iraqis and Kurds. Unlike the Kurds in neighbouring Turkey, they have not had to struggle for recognition of their existence as an ethnic, linguistic and cultural group. Hence outright separatism has not, for the majority, been part of the political agenda. The most common position articulated, at least in the early 1990s, favoured some form of autonomy or federal structure which would allow a degree of distance from Arab Iraq.

However, divisions within the Kurdish community remained a major factor in the convoluted politics of the region. In Iraqi Kurdistan, divisions are not primarily on religious lines, since the majority of Kurds in this region are Sunni Muslims. The only exceptions are the Shi'i Fayli Kurds, most of whom were deported to Iran in the 1970s and 1980s, and who had previously lived mainly in Baghdad or in the main cities of central Iraq as far north as Khanaqin.[11] Some Fayli refugees who have recently returned from Iran have gone to northern Iraq because they cannot return to their homes.

The major fault-lines in Iraqi Kurdish society follow linguistic, regional and tribal divisions. The division between speakers of the two Kurdish dialects, Surani and Kurmanji, cuts through northern Iraq. Those in the north and west, the region known as Badinan, speak Kurmanji, while those in the south and east use Surani, the dialect which the Iraqi Government treated as the 'official' Kurdish language used in the education system. In contrast to Turkey, suppression of the Kurdish language has not been a feature of government policy.[12]

Linguistic and cultural differences between the two regions have been overlaid by political differences. The division between adherents of the Kurdish national movement in Iraq and supporters of the Government has not been along either religious or linguistic and regional lines. However, rifts within the Kurdish national movement do reflect regional divisions. Today the zones of influence of the two main parties coincide roughly with the language boundaries. While this has probably helped to reinforce the animosities fostered by party conflict, the picture is not entirely clear-cut, since each of the two main parties has supporters in the territory of its rival.

In some parts of Iraqi Kurdistan the notion of tribal or clan loyalty is still strong. In the north-western Badinan region, strong clan structures still control particular valleys and mountains and retain an allegiance to a particular *agha* (tribal leader). In some clans, including the Barzanis, these ties are intensified by the religious roles played by members of the leading families, particularly in Sufi orders.[13]

However, even in the past, not everyone was part of this tribal structure. Many Kurdish peasants lived outside the tribal structures and often perceived their relationship with the *aghas* as one of exploitation rather than loyalty.[14] The growth of a professional and intellectual class from the 1950s onwards, particularly in Sulaymaniya, created a social order with very different kinds of allegiance. Some authorities estimate that in 1960, 60 percent of Iraqi Kurds claimed a tribal affiliation, but by the late 1980s this figure had fallen to 20 percent.[15]

From the 1970s, the oil boom had drawn more and more people to the towns: to Dohuk, a small town which had grown rapidly in the 1960s; to Arbil, an ancient centre which expanded as people from its lowland hinterland moved in; and to Sulaymaniya, which became the largest city in the region with over a million inhabitants.[16] Many people from the northern governorates were also attracted further afield in search of employment, to Baghdad and to the oil industries of Kirkuk. Therefore, in addition to those whom the Government forcibly displaced, many other Kurds voluntarily made their homes outside this region.

Political parties in Iraqi Kurdistan are neither substitutes for tribal groups nor necessarily identified with them, though the two have often been closely linked. Parties have run the gamut from ideological groupings, including a variety of leftist parties, to clan-based organisations. An example of the latter is the Conservative Party, formed after the 1991 war as a base for the Surchi, Herki and Bradost chiefs and their allies, constant rivals of the Barzanis in the Badinan area.

The KDP (Kurdistan Democratic Party), by far the oldest Iraqi Kurdish nationalist party, dating back to 1946, developed as an alliance of political forces, but the Barzani clan has always formed its core. In the 1960s, urban intellectuals joined it in an uneasy alliance. In the early 1970s, Mullah Mustafa Barzani managed for a brief period to dominate the entire Iraqi Kurdish movement. However the KDP collapsed after the Shah withdrew support from the Iraqi Kurds in 1975. After the party's revival in the 1980s under the leadership of Masud Barzani, one of Mullah Mustafa's sons, the central role of the Barzani clan remained.

In 1976, after the exile of Mullah Mustafa Barzani and the collapse of the 'old' KDP, Jalal Talabani broke away to form the PUK (Patriotic Union of Kurdistan). At the time it was viewed as a radical alternative to the KDP and had a stronger urban base. While Talabani appears to have a loyalty to his home region of Sulaymaniya, allegiance to him or to the party was not built on tribal or family loyalties. In contrast to the Barzanis, for example, Talabani did not initially organise PUK *peshmergas* along tribal lines. However, the original left-oriented ideological base of the PUK has been much diluted, and it is now a coalition of forces whose main *raison d'etre* appears to be to contest KDP control of the region.

In their struggles with each other and with the Iraqi Government, all the Kurdish parties have depended on external support. As a consequence lines of communication have always been kept open to Baghdad, Teheran, Ankara and Damascus, whatever the political rhetoric of the party or leader concerned. During the Iran-Iraq War, for example, the KDP was allied with Iran. The PUK, suspicious of Iran's intentions, in December 1983 entered into negotiations with the Iraqi Government on revised autonomy demands. Discussions continued until the end of 1984 without agreement. The PUK then resumed hostilities against the Iraqi Government and subsequently forged closer links with Iran. Close ties were maintained with Iran's ally Syria.[17]

After the catastrophe of the Anfal, political activity was disrupted by the large numbers of activists who had been killed, deported to other parts of the country, or fled abroad. The formation in 1988 of the Kurdistan Front (KF), which included the majority of Kurdish political groups, papered over the simmering rivalry and distrust between the PUK and KDP until the elections of 1992.[18]

Most political groups recruited their own *peshmerga* forces. This has highlighted the military rather than political character of the parties and the increasing role of rural and tribal recruits at the expense of urban intellectuals.

The Iraqi Government further manipulated local allegiances by recruiting the so-called National Defence Battalions (known to most Kurds as the *jash* or 'donkeys'). These were militia units with low-level military and security duties mainly in the Kurdish region. They were recruited by tribal leaders or other persons appointed by the Government. These *mustashars* (literally 'advisors') received a payment for every 'paper' recruit. Some accepted the role out of hostility to the 'nationalist' Kurdish leaders, some because of local tribal rivalries, others simply to make money.

The *mustashar* system strengthened the political and economic position of certain tribal leaders as well as contributing to rivalries between tribal groups, though some *mustashars* managed to raise troops without a tribal base, profiting economically in the process. Some of the *mustashars* became very rich and have been able to use their wealth to advantage in recent years.[19] Many of the recruits never bore arms, but were excused from service in the regular army – a considerable advantage during the long years of the Iran-Iraq War.

In the 1980s this force could apparently mobilise at least as many men as could the Kurdish *peshmergas*. *Jash* forces played a considerable role in the Anfal campaigns, sending many fellow Kurds to their deaths and destroying their property, although there were instances in which *jash* soldiers saved Kurdish lives, even if they sometimes took bribes to do so.[20]

The system of *mujamma'at*, or collective settlements, seems to have reinforced the power of those tribal leaders who were involved in the distribution of government supplies to the settlements, which create new opportunities for clientelism. The resettlement process in some cases refocussed tribal ties. 'Tribal groups were resettled together in the townships, where the absence of alterative employment reinforced their dependency on their chief and his dependency on government, and this began to replace territoriality as a defining basis for tribal solidarity.'[21]

During the uprising, many *mustashars* and their *jash* forces went over to the Kurdish side, since Baghdad appeared to be in full retreat, though some retained ties with Baghdad. Some of the *jash* leaders were made *peshmerga* commanders by the main parties, while many of their followers became part of the parties' *peshmerga* forces, though their integration was not always successful. Some of the *mustashars* who remained independent, still commanding large forces of their own, were prone to switch allegiance between parties or play one party off against another.[22]

The history of one *mustashar* leader illustrates the profit and power – but also the danger – involved in these manoeuvres. Hussein Agha al-Surchi, a leading member of the Surchi clan, had worked 'as a little soldier under Saddam' as a *mustashar*, until 1991, becoming a very wealthy man in the process. After the uprisings, he challenged Masud Barzani for calling him a traitor, saying 'My villages are still standing and still wealthy, my people still dress as Kurds, speak Kurdish and have a good life. Look what your nationalism has done for you...'[23] Hussein Agha was subsequently involved in forming the Conservative Party.

Once fighting began between the KDP and PUK in 1994, the two main parties became increasingly determined to gain the allegiance of hitherto unaffiliated tribal groups and to prevent other parties or clan leaders from shifting their allegiances. In 1996 there were allegations that some members of the Surchi clan intended to join forces with the PUK. The KDP wanted to prevent the area controlled by the Surchis, which lies on the strategic 'Hamilton road' from Arbil to Hajj 'Umran, from falling under PUK influence. The KDP therefore attacked the Surchi's base in the village of Kalkin, killing Hussein Agha.[24] After this incident, some of the clan's members worked with the KDP, others with the PUK, and others based in Mosul continued to cooperate with the Iraqi Government.

A further grey area, both politically and socially, is the precise definition of who is a Kurd. Within the *de facto* Kurdish-controlled area, the population is predominantly Kurdish, but includes substantial communities (urban and rural) of Assyrian Christians, a smaller number of Chaldean Christians, a community belonging to the heterodox Yezidi religion (Kurmanji speakers mostly living in the Sheykhan area between Mosul and Dohuk) and a substantial Turcoman community.

Alliances in the region are generally based on family and tribe, rather than religion, but religious cleavages certainly exist, not least between the various Christian groups. Within some of these groups, particularly the Assyrians, are people who have identified closely with the Kurds, even fighting with the Kurdish *peshmergas*. Other Christians have preferred to retain their separate religious and political identity.

The Kurds themselves seem to have ambiguous attitudes to minority groups. Some give an inclusive definition of 'Kurdishness' which includes Christians and sometimes Turcomans as well and does not accept their existence as separate communities. Others see much sharper divisions between the communities.

The Iraqi Government has also intervened in 'defining' ethnicity and religious identity. In the 1987 Iraqi census, Yezidis, Assyrians and Chaldeans who chose to be designated as 'Kurds' rather than 'Arabs' (no other option was offered) and who remained in Kurdish-majority areas, were victimised during the Anfal campaign. As many as 200 Assyrian villages, mainly in the Dohuk region, were destroyed.[25] All minorities – Christians, Yezidis and Turcomans – suffered during the Iraqi suppression of the 1991 uprising, and many fled to the borders along with the Kurds.

Although the post-Gulf War Kurdish administration recognised formal rights for minority groups, there have been tensions with the Assyrian and Turcoman communities. Assyrian Church leaders in Zakho and Dohuk allege that in some cases Christians have been discriminated against, especially in relation to land disputes. The open conflict between the PUK and KDP made life difficult for all the smaller political groupings, and it seems the Assyrian parties were no exception. While some Christians have returned to the north from Baghdad and other cities, large numbers have been leaving Iraq altogether.

The position of the Turcomans has become politically more prominent in recent years. Turkey has taken a hand in trying to boost Turcoman status and influence in the region. In late 1996, Turcomans became active participants in peace efforts (see below) and the Turkish authorities have encouraged local Turcoman organisations to register people as Turcomans in order to benefit from aid from Turkish organisations. It is unclear whether Turkish patronage will work to the advantage of this community in the longer run or create more local resentment against them.

THE FORMATION OF THE KURDISH REGIONAL ADMINISTRATION

When Iraqi troops withdrew from the region in late October 1991, all this historical and political baggage – convoluted relations with the Iraqi state and with neighbouring states, internal rivalries, and conflicting ideas of Kurdish identity – remained in place.

The *de facto* line drawn between the three northern governorates and government-controlled Iraq, which from November 1991 to September 1996 formed a *de facto* border, created a predominantly Kurdish enclave with a total population of 3–3.5 million.[26] The total Kurdish population of Iraq is probably about 4 million but substantial numbers of Kurds still remain in areas under Baghdad's control.

Administratively, the region which fell under Kurdish rule consisted of three governorates, Dohuk, Arbil and Sulaymaniya, with the city of Arbil as the regional capital. Small sections of Nineveh and Kirkuk governorates also fell inside the Kurdish-controlled region. The Iraqi Government retained control of strategically important areas of Kirkuk, Khanaqin and Sinjar.[27]

The Iraqi withdrawal left the KF as the main organised force in the region, politically and militarily. There was an urgent need to fill the administrative and legal vacuum left by Iraq's withdrawal. The KF, as an umbrella organisation, was not an appropriate instrument through which to raise taxes and administer services. Its constituent parties controlled what customs revenues were available, and local *peshmerga* commanders were running their areas as personal fiefdoms.[28] Decision-making also proved to be a problem. Any of the eight parties could veto proposals for action by the front. The parties all had separate political structures, including politbureaus, and armed *peshmerga* under more or less effective control.[29]

By December 1991, it was clear that the autonomy talks were unlikely to make progress, while Iraq's economic embargo seemed set to continue. The KF therefore declared its intention to elect a regional parliament to replace the regional assembly which had existed under Ba'thist rule. In January 1992 the KF formally withdrew from autonomy negotiations with Baghdad.[30]

The failure of the autonomy negotiations had created severe strains between the KDP and PUK, and particularly between Masud Barzani and Jalal Talabani. Aside from administrative needs, the Kurdish leadership saw the opportunity created by Iraqi withdrawal and a measure of continued Western protection to clarify who was to be overall leader. According to some commentators, this 'display of democracy' was also intended to make it more difficult for the coalition allies to abandon the Kurds or to allow the reimposition, without negotiation, of Iraqi government control.[31] However, the KF leadership was also well aware of the 'anti-separatist' sentiments among the Western powers as well as Turkey, Iran and Syria.[32] This consciousness was intensified after Iraq's withdrawal. Thus the KF was careful to model the elections on the 1970 Autonomy Agreement originally framed by the Iraqi Government.

The KF held elections on 19 May 1992 throughout the areas it controlled. The election process was hastily prepared with some external assistance. No census of electors was taken in advance of the poll. Most of the main political groups took part, with the exception of the Conservative Party and the Iraqi National Turcoman Party.[33] There were five reserved seats for Assyrian candidates.

The result was announced as a tie between the PUK and the KDP. In fact, the KDP received 45.3 percent of the vote, and the PUK 43.8 percent. It took three days of tense negotiations to decide on the reallocation of votes from the smaller parties –

all of which received less than the 7 percent of the vote required to gain a seat – to the two main parties.[34] As one group of observers noted, 'the problem was not merely achieving a compromise with which neither party would lose face, but also getting both leaders to accept the results in the first place'.[35] The figures finally published showed KDP with 50.8 percent and PUK 49.2 percent.[36]

Despite some irregularities, the poll probably reflected the broad pattern of support for the two main parties. The vote for the KDP and PUK was predictably divided on a regional basis, but there were variations in the levels of support. In Sulaymaniya governorate the PUK took 60 percent of the vote and the KDP 27 percent. A similar pattern emerged in the much smaller section of Kirkuk governorate which lay within the Kurdish-controlled area. The KDP took 85 percent of the vote in Dohuk governorate, but in Arbil governorate the two parties received almost equal shares of the vote.[37]

The contest for sole leadership of the Iraqi Kurdish movement between Jalal Talabani and Masud Barzani was not resolved. Barzani took 47.5 percent of the vote and Talabani 44.9 percent. A proposed run-off between the two candidates was never held.

The very fact that the elections were held created a climate of optimism, leading both local and international analysts to believe that a democratic experiment could take place in this region outside Iraqi government control. For many people living in Iraqi Kurdistan, the opportunity to vote was a positive experience and symbolised their new-found freedom from Ba'thist control. On the other hand, most of the political parties were discontented with the outcome.

The consequence of the marginal loser's refusal to accept defeat was a 50-50 power sharing arrangement which never had much chance of working, despite the undoubted goodwill of some of the participants. There were soon warning signs of the internal difficulties to come. On 8 June 1992, shortly after the results were announced, about 10 people were killed in armed clashes in Chamchamal between the PUK and KDP. Iraqi forces, located on the *de facto* line close by, were reported to have joined in the fighting, siding with the KDP. This conflict was apparently triggered by the KDP's unexpectedly good electoral showing in the Chamchamal area.

The smaller KF parties did not gain any parliamentary seats because of the 7 percent threshold rule in the elections, though some representatives of these parties were included in the first administration. As a result, within a year, most of these parties had dissolved themselves or merged with the PUK or KDP. Only the Islamic Movement of Iraqi Kurdistan (IMIK), which gained 5 percent of the vote, strengthened its position as a 'third force' after the elections, though it was not represented in the Kurdish administration.

The PUK and KDP saw the diminution of the small parties' influence as a positive outcome of the election.[38] Even prior to 1991, the small parties were not really independent actors. They had usually operated in alliance with either the KDP or PUK, sometimes changing allegiances. However, they had allowed expression of a greater diversity of views than prevailed after the elections.

The two main parties' policies were heavily influenced by the mutual suspicion of their leaders, and the administration remained, in many respects, 'merely an extension of the power base of... the PUK and KDP'.[39] The 50-50 power sharing system induced administrative paralysis and exacerbated the long-standing competition between the main parties for influence, power and funding. As a consequence, one of the original goals of the election – to give the new assembly the main voice in decisions about future negotiations with the Iraqi Government – was never fulfilled.

The Kurdish leadership continued to hope that Western governments would make some kind of political commitment to the Kurds. In fact, the coalition allies had regarded the elections with very mixed feelings, emphasising that they should not lead towards independence.[40] Despite repeated invitations from the KF, the US State Department did not give permission for US nationals to travel to Iraqi Kurdistan as election observers. The Turkish reaction, especially from military circles, was predictably hostile.[41]

The new order in Iraqi Kurdistan never received formal international recognition. For a time, the Kurdish administration had representatives in London, Washington, Paris, Bonn and Ankara, and Kurdish ministers paid visits to Europe and the US. However, substantive discussions with these governments, insofar as they occurred, were conducted mainly with the Kurdish political parties and their leaders.[42] The US and Turkish Governments, in particular, only dealt with the party leaders, arguably contributing to their endemic rivalries and further marginalising the administration.[43]

ROLE AND EFFECTIVENESS OF THE ADMINISTRATION

The new administration retained many features of the previous Ba'thist system, including the provincial governors and their offices, whose appointments became increasingly determined by party considerations. The police force, apart from its senior Iraqi officers, remained in place, and in fact had policed the elections. Temporary courts had been established after the Iraqis withdrew. Although Iraqi government rations were progressively withdrawn, the system of food agents which the Government had set up throughout the region was still in place, and was used by WFP and other aid agencies to distribute food and other relief goods.

The 50-50 power-sharing system undoubtedly reinforced the networks of patronage operated by each of the two main parties. The system of dual patronage filtered all the way down to the appointment of teachers in local primary schools and the number of policemen on patrol. If one administrator, policeman or school principal was a PUK supporter, then he or she had to be 'balanced' by a KDP member of equivalent rank. At senior levels, the appointment of governor and ministerial staff often depended as much on their status in their parties or their previous roles as *peshmerga* heroes as on their administrative abilities.[44] Patronage extended not only to individuals and families, but also to party or tribal groups which had no direct say in political affairs under this system.

There was no effective integration of the parties' military forces into unified police and army structures, as had initially been proposed. *Peshmerga* groups never surrendered their separate roles, nor was the regional pattern of control between the two major parties significantly altered. Meanwhile for young men, joining the *peshmerga* offered an income and some security, which was more than could be said for most civilian jobs.[45]

The police and the judicial system had to contend a large number of land disputes, as a result of people returning to their homes in destroyed villages and towns, and crimes of violence. The courts often faced political interference in their decisions. For example, judges and lawyers found that people who had protection from a particular party, when sentenced to jail terms, were sometimes released without any authority from the courts. Although in 1992 the parties had largely given up their separate systems of detention, the 'unified' system was very fragile and once internecine conflict began in 1994 there was a rapid return to separate and arbitrary systems of justice.[46]

The near paralysis of the administration was compounded by the fact that the two main party leaders remained outside the parliamentary and administrative structures.[47] The rivalry between Masud Barzani and Jalal Talabani was of long standing, and despite their periodic protestations of cooperation each seemed obsessed with outmanoeuvring the other. The party structures of the KDP and PUK continued to dominate proceedings, creating power without responsibility. This left both the assembly and the administration – despite the good intentions and independence of view among some of their members – powerless to act in important matters except with the consent of main parties.

From the end of 1992 until early 1994, the KDP and PUK did surrender to the administration at least a portion of the customs revenues they collected but the finance ministry was not able to achieve effective fiscal control. The difficulties in developing any credible programmes to assist the population further undermined the administration's political position. It was also subject to two sets of externally-imposed constraints.

Iraqi Kurdistan was not exempt from the terms of UN sanctions against Iraq despite repeated requests from the Kurdish parliament and administration.[48] The embargo limited the possibility of improving or even refurbishing the infrastructure, exploiting small-scale oil reserves or rebuilding the few existing local industries.[49] The US in particular made it clear that economic aid, over and above strictly humanitarian needs, was not on offer. A further inhibiting factor was the suspicion voiced by the Turkish authorities at the prospect of any project which might contribute to the self-sufficiency of the Kurds, for example by restructuring the electricity grid to lessen dependence on the Iraqi system of which it is part.

The Iraqi 'internal' embargo withdrew the wages and emoluments of all public employees who remained in the three governorates, as well as cutting off funds for investment and running costs of public institutions. The KF and later the Kurdish administration were left to find the salaries of the 165,000 people on the payroll, including teachers and medical staff.[50] For political reasons, it proved very difficult to lay off employees, even in overstaffed departments.

All goods coming from government areas were (at least theoretically) stopped at the checkpoints along the *de facto* Iraqi lines. The only exception was for UN humanitarian convoys. In addition, the Iraqi Government progressively cut ration allocations to the three governorates. By 1993, government ration deliveries had diminished to less than 10 percent of full supply for the whole area. The token deliveries allowed the Government to say that rations were being supplied, if only at reduced rates. The decline in supplies hit Dohuk governorate least severely at first. It seems that the Government deliberately fostered these discrepancies, which predictably created tensions between governorates. For example, preferential fuel supplies to Dohuk encouraged this governorate to restrict fuel supplies to Arbil and Sulaymaniya governorate in order to maintain its advantage.[51]

The Kurdish administration did not substitute its own general ration distribution. The WFP has been the main source of food aid since 1991, with a limited target group of some 750,000 out of a population of 3–3.5 million (see Chapter 7).

Similarly, supplies of oil products from government-controlled areas were drastically reduced in 1992, so that the UN had to import most of the region's winter needs from Turkey. As of 1993, this particular aspect of the embargo was relaxed in an arrangement whereby kerosene, gas-oil and gasoline were delivered to private Kurdish companies from private Iraqi companies, though the latter were supplied by the state-controlled Military Industrialisation Organisation. However, the flow of kerosene, used for home heating, remained unreliable in the following years.

In August 1993, the Iraqi Government cut electricity supplies to the Dohuk region. Dohuk governorate had no other source of power and the UN was obliged to import and install temporary generators to maintain water and health services.[52] Supplies from Turkey were only sporadically available. In August 1994, electricity supplies to the Aqra area, near the *de facto* line, were also cut. Power was not restored to Dohuk and Aqra until August 1995. In Arbil and Sulaymaniya governorates supplies from the national grid were also cut, some power was available from local hydro-electric sources.

In May 1993, the Iraqi Government withdrew the 25-dinar note from circulation, closing its borders for six days. Those in government-controlled areas could exchange the notes for other denominations, but those in the Kurdish region were left with technically valueless notes.[53] The Kurdish-controlled region has therefore continued to trade in dollars and the so-called Swiss-issue dinars which the Government had withdrawn, as well as in Turkish lira and Iranian rials.

Ironically, the value of the 'Swiss' dinar against the dollar – the all-important measure – held up much better than the currency in government-controlled Iraq. Between 1993 and 1995, the dinar's value against the dollar in the north fluctuated between about ID20 and ID80, at the end of 1995 there being 50 to the dollar, as against 2000–3000 in government-controlled areas. In contrast to the rest of Iraq, where the government policy of printing money fuelled high levels of inflation, the use of the 'Swiss' notes had the effect of limiting the supply of currency. The constant inflow of foreign currency, especially of US dollars through aid agency activity, trade with neighbouring countries, and remittances from Kurds abroad, all helped to steady the exchange rate.[54] The greater purchasing power of the dinar, and continued flows of humanitarian aid meant that between 1993 and 1995 the economic situation in the north, though difficult, was probably not quite as bad as it was in the worst-hit sectors of Iraqi society under government control.

Nonetheless, the economy was precarious even before civil strife set in. There was no proper banking system since Iraq had closed all the banks when it imposed the embargo in 1991 and halted replenishment funds to the Agricultural, Estate and Industrial Banks.[55] The vagaries of trade with neighbouring countries and changes in both the internal and international political situation caused currency values and therefore prices to fluctuate, and to differ from one area to another. The ongoing problems with supplies of food, fuel and power increased the structural dependence of the region on external assistance.

These external and internal obstacles and the lack of political stability have limited the opportunities to rebuild the region economically. The three governorates had previously served as an agricultural hinterland for the rest of Iraq, producing cereal crops in the plains and fruit, vegetables and livestock in the mountains.

Agriculture did undergo a revival after 1991, first and foremost in the large-scale lowland farms, where the main commercial crops are rain-fed cereals. This was despite difficulties with obtaining inputs such as fertilisers and pesticides since 1990. From 1992 onwards, a number of major Kurdish landowners reportedly sold their cereal harvest to the Iraqi Government, which offered higher prices than those prevailing on the local market in the north.

In the mountains, commercial production has been slower to revive, since the small-scale farms in the rebuilt villages first produced crops for their own subsistence and then vegetables, pulses and other crops for the market. Farmers producing for the market also encountered a number of problems, including the poor state of the roads, competition from imported produce – especially from Turkey – and a shortage of local processing facilities for canning and milling. In the past, much of this was done in other parts of Iraq.

Fruit orchards, for which the region was famous, and which were razed during the Anfal operations, will take many years to restore. Other types of trees were similarly destroyed, and subsequent felling for domestic fuel because of shortages during and after 1991 further depleted tree cover on the mountains. Livestock – sheep, goats and chickens – was lost in the 1980s, and stock has slowly been rebuilt, hampered by lack of veterinary services and high levels of disease from animals being brought in without controls from Iran and Turkey.

The few industrial plants – cement, cigarettes, marble quarrying and textile production – supplied both the local market and other parts of Iraq.[56] The Iraqi embargo interrupted this trade, at least until the end of 1996, since when trade relations with government-controlled areas have been partially restored.

Neither economic nor social contacts with government-controlled areas were completely cut. Many residents of Iraqi Kurdistan have relatives in other parts of the country. Kurds in Mosul and Kirkuk, for example, frequently remained in contact with their relatives in the north. While the internal embargo was at times stringent, there was always a good deal of smuggling. Some bizarre examples of 'legal' trade also continued. According to the Minister of Finance in the first Kurdish administration, marble from quarries in Iraqi Kurdistan was still being shipped to Baghdad in 1993, and the Kurds were levying taxes on it.[57]

The Iraqi embargo, however, shifted the focus of trade to neighbouring countries. The Kurdish administration was dependent for its income on customs revenues, most of which came from trade with Turkey. The routes to Iran are more difficult, and in winter heavy traffic on the mountain passes is limited. Nonetheless trade continues in all seasons using pack animals or porters.

The chaotic situation after the 1991 Gulf War greatly increased the scale of smuggling and asset-stripping. In 1991 and 1992, there were persistent reports that large quantities of vehicles, building materials and machinery, agricultural equipment and even industrial plant were being sold off cheaply to Iran by local Kurdish 'entrepreneurs'. According to one report, of 700 municipal vehicles in Arbil (including garbage trucks and bulldozers) before the uprising, only 90 remained in mid-1992. The police force only retained 18 out of 345 patrol cars.[58] It seems that the political parties did nothing effective to stop this traffic.[59]

The northern part of Iraq lies on a network of trade routes used for smuggling from Iran, and to a lesser extent from Afghanistan and Central Asia to Turkey. The embargo did not stop this trade. Cigarettes and alcohol, for example, are traded from Turkey to Iran, with the middlemen in Iraqi Kurdistan profiting from these transactions. The goods come into the region through the KDP-controlled Habur crossing from Turkey and entered Iran through the Hajj 'Umran frontier post, over which the PUK, KDP and IMIK have vied for control.[60] It is rumoured that drugs are smuggled via Iraqi Kurdistan, though this is not a major route. Shorter distance cross-border smuggling of food, clothing, livestock, oil products, tyres, spare parts and car batteries also continues to and from Turkey, Iran and government-controlled Iraq, alongside trade cleared by the UN Sanctions Committee. Merchants and traders on all sides have profited considerably over the past six years from these transactions, as have those involved in transport and other services.

The progressive fragmentation of Iraqi Kurdistan since 1994 has led to the imposition of further tariffs on the movement of goods. 'Taxes' are often levied at road blocks between the territories controlled by rival Kurdish forces. Since the main flow of goods is from the Turkish border, the additional costs are mainly felt by those furthest away in the south-east, especially in Sulaymaniya governorate.

Trade, humanitarian aid, and what one analyst has described as 'predation' – the gathering of taxes by armed groups without an agreed basis regulated by a state authority[61] – has undoubtedly generated new wealth, but this has neither been translated into productive economic activity, nor has it provided services for the public. Even during the short period when the Kurdish administration received a share of revenues from these taxes, they were still gathered through party mechanisms. The first Minister of Finance suggested that responsibility for customs and excise be assigned to a specialised department and a commission should be appointed to collect taxes throughout the region.[62] This, however, was never achieved, and after mid-1994 predation again prevailed.

Although exact measurement is impossible, it seems that by 1996, unregulated 'entrepreneurial' business had become more important than formal economic activity, except in the agricultural sector. Though many people have made some kind of living in this informal sector, the large profits appear to be monopolised by a small group of party officials, *mustashars*, merchants and entrepreneurs.

The KDP and PUK became deeply involved in a struggle to control regional trade. Not only have some individuals within these parties made fortunes, but the struggle for control of borders and routes on which customs revenues could be levied became a key issue in the conflict between the parties. As the fighting escalated, more and more of the revenue gathered was devoted to paying *peshmergas*, purchasing arms and buying the loyalty of individuals and groups, thereby fuelling conflict rather than improving the economic circumstances of the population. The profits from these activities were not confined within the borders of Iraqi Kurdistan. In Turkey and Iran, as well as in government-controlled areas of Iraq, individual merchants, private companies and military or government organisations participated in this lucrative activity. In Turkey, both the PKK and elements of the Turkish army stationed in the south-east have reportedly been deeply involved in contraband trade. These economic interests add a further dimension to the political struggles between the Iraqi Kurdish parties and to the regional interests which have had an increasing influence in events in Iraqi Kurdistan.

THE DYNAMICS OF CONFLICT

In March 1993, Fuad Ma'sum, the first Prime Minister of the Kurdish administration, submitted his resignation. He had succeeded in creating a measure of cross-party cooperation, but the pressures endemic in the power-sharing system frustrated his efforts. Further danger signs were the number of apparently politically-motivated assassinations during 1992 and 1993. Eleven victims documented by Amnesty International included a judge, a Sunni Muslim cleric, two prominent businessmen and several members of small political parties, mainly those of the left. In most cases, no-one was ever apprehended for the killings.[63] At the end of the year, tensions between the PUK and KDP rose sharply after fighting broke out, first between the KDP and a breakaway faction of the Kurdistan Socialist Party (KSP), and then between the IMIK and PUK, rivals for influence in the Sulaymaniya region.

The credibility of the assembly and the administration was also undermined by the failed attempt to bring the KDP and PUK leaders more directly into the decision-making process and create a more collective style of leadership by the formation of a Presidential Council. This proposal was ratified by the Assembly on 20 December 1993 but was almost immediately undermined by the PUK-IMIK fighting. Barzani's efforts to prevent the fighting spreading to urban centres were ignored by the PUK leadership.[64] For the first time, citizens of Arbil and Sulaymaniya witnessed Kurds fighting Kurds on their streets, causing up to 300 casualties.

In early 1994, proposals for new elections created further tensions. While the main parties publicly supported the idea, neither was prepared to find itself in opposition.[65] In May 1994, a minor dispute over ownership of a piece of land in Qala Diza sparked widespread fighting between the KDP and PUK, during which the PUK stormed the parliament building in Arbil.[66]

The opposition Iraqi National Congress based in Salahadin (of which both the KDP and PUK were members) and the smaller Kurdish parties negotiated a series of ceasefires between the KDP and PUK but fighting did not cease entirely until September 1994. The situation was complicated by renewed clashes between the PUK and the IMIK—the latter in loose alliance with the KDP and backed by Iran.[67]

A peace accord reached in Paris between the PUK and KDP in July 1994 proposed new elections and the unification of *peshmerga* forces. It was ratified in November by an 'agreement of alliance' between the parties' political bureaus.[68] Nonetheless, serious fighting between the KDP and IMIK on one side and the PUK on the other resumed in late December 1994, and continued sporadically until March 1995. On 28 March, KDP sources announced that PUK forces were besieging the parliament building in Arbil where a number of deputies had staged a sit-in to demand an end to the fighting.[69]

The failure in March 1995 of the strategy devised by General Samara'i and the INC to trigger a military coup against Saddam Hussein and to mount a challenge to Iraqi forces across the *de facto* line further exacerbated tensions between the PUK and KDP. Renewed clashes occurred in July 1995.

The human rights situation deteriorated sharply after the outbreak of fighting in May 1994. Amnesty International's report of February 1995 documented 'unlawful and deliberate killings', assassinations and an increasing tendency for all party militias to act outside the rule of law.[70]

From early in 1995, Iraqi Kurdistan was effectively partitioned, with the KDP dominating the north-western area along the Turkish border and the PUK controlling the south-east, centred on Sulaymaniya. Arbil governorate was divided between the parties, with the PUK controlling Arbil city. A further *de facto* border was therefore established between the areas controlled by the PUK and KDP, with road-blocks which made it difficult for people to move around freely and created another opportunity for the two sides to tax trade and goods moving from one area of control to the other. The Hamilton road, linking Hajj 'Umran to Arbil, became a major strategic asset which each party sought to control.

This rift led to the administrative fragmentation of Iraqi Kurdistan. Arbil was the regional capital, but when the city was taken by the PUK, KDP staff from the ministries had fled. Most went to Salahadin, but some moved to other towns where the minister or deputy minister happened to live. From 1995, therefore, most sectors – for example education – had two ministries, one in the KDP-controlled area, the other in PUK territory. By early 1997, the two parties had effectively created separate political administrations.[71]

During the period from the end of 1992 until 1994, employees of the administration – teachers, doctors, nurses, clerical and manual staff – generally received their pay, albeit meagre, at fairly regular intervals. Funds for public institutions were

---

The Turkish Army and the PKK

In April 1991, while Iraqi Kurdish refugees were still on the Turkish border, skirmishes occurred between the PKK and the Turkish army, culminating in the first major Turkish attack in northern Iraq on 8 August 1991, soon after the last coalition troops had left.[72] When the Iraqi Government protested, Turkey invoked the pre-war bilateral agreement, which had lapsed with the end of the Iran-Iraq War in 1988, and had allowed Turkish forces to conduct cross-border incursions in pursuit of PKK members.[73]

Since 1991, the Turkish army has continued to shell and bomb border areas, periodically resorting to large-scale ground offensives into northern Iraq, backed by air strikes, to attack PKK bases. These attacks all took place within the northern no-fly zone, which only applies to Iraq. Most of the Turkish operations have been conducted within the so-called 'security zone' along the Iraqi-Turkish border, though as the PKK moved further away from the border areas, Turkish incursions also moved progressively deeper inside Iraq. Civilian deaths and injuries and disruption of village resettlement, especially in northern Dohuk governorate, have often been reported.[74]

- The first major ground incursion, involving 20,000 troops, took place in October 1992.
- In late 1993, Turkish forces launched air and ground attacks on alleged PKK bases in northern Iraq.
- In March 1995, some 35,000 Turkish troops backed by tanks, helicopters and F-16 fighter aircraft remained in the north for almost two months.
- In May 1997, 50,000 Turkish troops, joining KDP forces, launched their largest and most extensive campaign yet against the PKK in northern Iraq, occupying a large swathe of territory along the Turkish border, and remaining there until the end of June. Further incursions took place in September, November and December 1997.
- In November 1998, Turkish troops, with KDP forces, again attacked the PKK in northern Iraq. On this occasion PKK fighters, under added pressure after losing their bases in Syria, fled to the Iranian border.

scarce but did exist. After fighting broke out in 1994, control of revenues reverted entirely to the two major parties, amid mutual accusations of embezzlement.

Increasing amounts of money on both sides were poured into supporting military expenses, the maintenance of party structures and *peshmerga* forces (an estimated 160,000 are thought to be on the payrolls of the parties)[75] and into the pockets of profiteers rather than into paying teachers or hospital staff. Consequently the living conditions of all those dependent on public sector pay became even more precarious. From 1995 to 1997, salary payments became irregular and at times non-existent.

Ministers essentially became party officials. Although the split had ended the paralysis associated with the 50-50 arrangement, they had little money at their disposal for public services until the oil-for-food arrangements came into operation in 1997. As one aid worker observed in 1996: 'Only for "firefighting" is money available. If there is a crisis, for example, if people go on strike, the relevant party will find them a month's wages; if there is a cholera outbreak, some money will be found to deal with it.'

Trade revenues both from Turkey and Iran increased between 1994 and 1996, particularly through the Habur crossing from Turkey, after that country resumed trade with government-controlled Iraq. The KDP, which controlled the Kurdish side of the border, benefited by levying 'taxes' on goods imported, with the main revenue coming from the revived oil trade between Iraq and Turkey. The PUK had more difficulties in raising revenues, and the extension of its control to include the city of Arbil put additional strain on its resources, since between early 1995 and August 1996, some 75 percent of the Kurdish region's population lived under its rule.

THE IRAQI KURDS AND THEIR NEIGHBOURS 1991–4

Historically the conflict between Kurdish nationalist movements and governments has always had a regional dimension. The relative weakness of the Iraqi Kurdish political forces in relation to their own Government led to alliances and 'understandings', most often with Iran, but also with Syria in the case of the PUK, and recently Turkey. But the emergence of a Kurdish-controlled enclave in northern Iraq in 1991 created a new political situation for neighbouring states.

Turkey and Iran, the two main protagonists, have intervened militarily with impunity. Both countries have had a growing intelligence presence in Iraqi Kurdistan since 1992 and have used the PUK and KDP as surrogates in battles with their own Kurdish opponents. Meanwhile the Iraqi Kurdish parties have tried to use these two states as allies in their own power struggles, or in order to gain leverage with Western governments.

Successive Turkish governments have opposed any 'democratic experiment' or any sign of permanence in the separate Kurdish administration of northern Iraq. On 4 October 1992, the new administration in Iraqi Kurdistan took steps to define its legal relationship to the rest of Iraq 'on the basis of the federation [*al-ittihad al-fidiraliy*] within a democratic parliamentary Iraq...'[76] Turkish Prime Minister Demirel described a federated state as 'a stage... on the way to an independent state'.[77]

The Iraqi Kurdish leaders were certainly conscious of Turkish sensitivities. Barzani stressed to the Turks that the parties' political objectives were limited to Iraqi Kurdistan, and that they did not seek independence. Talabani was assiduous in courting the

Turkish leadership during 1991 and 1992. However, the Turkish political and military establishment viewed as highly dangerous the potential impact on the Turkish Kurds of an 'example' of autonomy in any form, and the federalist formula seemed no less threatening.

Turkish political and military chiefs have, however, differed on how to deal with Iraqi Kurds. President Ozal favoured efforts to establish Turkish control over what went on in northern Iraq and to coopt the Iraqi Kurdish parties: 'we should try to keep them under our spell as much as possible and even try to assume the role of their guarantors'.[78] The Iraqi Kurdish parties were therefore put under pressure to cooperate in securing the border areas against the PKK.[79]

Mainly for reasons of geography, the PUK had more cordial relations with the PKK than the KDP. The PKK has operated mainly in the Badinan region, encroaching on the KDP's territory. A further reason for rivalry is the Barzani clan's strong ties in the Hakkari region, across the border in Turkey, which the PKK has claimed to control.[80] Further cementing the PUK-PKK relationship is their common and long-standing relationship with the Syrian Government. However, the pressures of events since 1991 have not allowed the PUK to ignore Turkish influence. On a number of occasions, Talabani has been obliged to accept arrangements which, at least in the short term, involved distancing the PUK from the PKK.

During the Turkish incursion into northern Iraq in October 1992, the Iraqi Kurdish leadership announced that it would expel the PKK from northern Iraq, arguing that the latter's actions, and Turkish retaliation, were hampering resettlement of the areas bordering on Turkey. The KDP and PUK were, however, not wholly at one on the issue. Only a few months before, Barzani had reportedly criticised Talabani for 'playing games' with the Turks '[by] facilitating the PKK in order to embarrass the KDP'.[81] After Turkish troops withdrew in early November, the KDP and PUK undertook to limit the PKK's presence to a camp at Zaleh near the Iraqi-Iranian border, and to patrol a security zone along the Iraqi-Turkish border.[82] However, KDP fears that PUK links with the PKK were growing stronger during 1993 drove Barzani closer to the Turkish Government and heightened the tension and distrust between the PUK and KDP.

In March 1993, the PKK leader, Abdullah Ocalan, declared a unilateral ceasefire which lasted several months. However, the death of President Ozal deprived the Turkish Government of an influential voice in favour of a political settlement with the Turkish Kurds. It seems he had never convinced either the general staff or most leading Turkish politicians that military means alone, inside Turkey or in Iraqi Kurdistan, would not solve the Kurdish question. When fighting resumed in June 1993, the PKK continued to operate in Iraqi Kurdistan.

After Ozal's death, prevailing opinion in Turkish government circles shifted in favour of closer relations with Iraq, which suggested a different strategy for Iraqi Kurdistan. Some Turkish opinion saw an advantage in the restoration of Iraqi rule, with two provisos: that 'hot pursuit' arrangements, comparable to those which existed in the 1980s, could be reinstated; and that there would be no further mass exodus of Iraqi Kurds.

Neither the Iranian Government nor the Supreme Council for the Islamic Revolution in Iraq (SCIRI), the main Iraqi opposition group operating under the aegis of Teheran, liked the federalist stance taken by the Kurdish parties. Both apparently felt that the Shi'i majority in Iraq would benefit more by maintaining a unitary system of government. Furthermore, proposals for any kind of separate or autonomous entity on ethnic lines were not welcomed since this option is not on offer to Iran's substantial Kurdish minority.

Between 1992 and 1994, Iranian military action was confined to air raids and bombardment of Iranian Kurdish groups – the Kurdistan Democratic Party of Iran (KDPI) and Komala – which had been based in PUK-controlled areas near the Iranian border since the 1980s.[83] The most intense attacks occurred during 1993, and forced the KDPI to move its base away from the border to the vicinity of Koisanjaq.[84]

At various times both the KDP and PUK leadership had been based in Iran, or were allied with the Iranian Government. Iranian officials therefore had long-standing, though frequently uneasy, relations with most of the Iraqi Kurdish parties and a close knowledge of their leaders. The Iranians gave some support to IMIK and, after the IMIK/PUK fighting in December 1993, allowed Iraqi opposition parties based in Teheran (representatives of the Da'wa party and SCIRI) to mediate between the warring parties. Iranian forces or their surrogates are also thought to have intervened during the fighting in mid-1994 in the Penjwin area.[85]

Making peace or sustaining conflict: external powers and peace initiatives 1994–6

During 1994 and 1995, the conflict between the KDP and PUK deepened international involvement in the affairs of Iraqi Kurdistan. There was no shortage of mediation attempts, but their seriousness was questionable. This applied not only to the efforts of Turkey and Iran, but also those of the Western coalition partners, particularly the US.

The Turkish response to the inter-Kurdish conflict was ambivalent. The Government, and especially the military, had not wanted to see the experiment in *de facto* autonomy succeed, so that the party rifts were in one sense welcome. On the other hand, there were fears that the fighting would create a power vacuum, which would be to the advantage of the PKK and give undue influence to other neighbouring states such as Iran.

The Turkish Government had been involved in discussions to end the May 1994 fighting.[86] However, angered that its representatives were not invited to the talks which led to the Paris accords in July 1994, it reportedly refused to grant visas to the Kurdish leaders to attend the projected signing ceremony in Paris in September.[87] Some observers consider that the 'Paris Accords' would have had some chance of success if Turkish acceptance could have been secured.[88]

In early 1995, Turkey's relations with the Iraqi Government were improving and it was apparently urging the Kurdish parties to resume negotiations with Baghdad.[89] By mid-year, however, this demand was dropped as it moved closer to the US, which opposed any Kurdish contacts with the Iraqi Government.[90] With US encouragement, Turkey became a participant in peace negotiations in August and September 1995.

One commentator described successive US administrations' policies towards the Kurds after 1991 as 'a policy of avoidance'.[91] However, the apparent growth of Iran's influence in Iraqi Kurdistan was one reason for the US-initiated peace talks between the KDP and PUK in August 1995. UK and Turkish representatives attended, as did members of the Iraqi National Congress (INC). The first meeting in Drogheda in the Republic of Ireland on 10–11 August, resulted in an agreement which in principle included the prospect of future elections. It envisaged the formation of a neutral commission under INC auspices to oversee the demilitarisation of Arbil (still in PUK hands) and to supervise the transfer of customs revenues to the Kurdish administration. The Turkish presence ensured that emphasis was also placed on the importance of border security.

A second meeting in Dublin between 12 and 15 September failed to agree on how to implement this plan.[92] The PKK, Iran and Syria were clearly hostile to US intervention in the conflict, and the PKK launched a major attack on the KDP at the end of August, soon after the first round of talks ended. This was seen as a direct attempt to sabotage US-sponsored peace efforts. Fighting continued until late in the year, with the KDP unable to gain the upper hand. Eventually, in December, the KDP signed a ceasefire agreement with the PKK.[93]

After the failure of talks in Ireland in September, Iran convened discussions between the KDP and PUK in Teheran on a range of issues similar to those discussed at the talks in Ireland, but with no substantive outcomes.[94] In a further mediation effort in late December 1995 a delegation headed by Ali Aqa-Mohammadi, representative of President of Islamic Republic, held separate talks with PUK and KDP leaders, as well as Islamic figures in Iraqi Kurdistan. There were signs that the PUK's relations with Iran were becoming closer. This was thought to reflect the PUK's limited options for making alliances, rather than any commitment to Iranian interests.[95]

Despite Iran's efforts, both parties appealed to the US to continue its involvement in mediation.[96] Some observers insist that the failure of the US State Department to follow up effectively on its 1995 mediation efforts constituted a further opportunity thrown away. State Department officials acknowledge that funds were not made available for the establishment of a neutral monitoring force in Arbil, as part of the agreements made in Ireland.[97] Only in April 1996 was there any further indication of interest in the issue, when the State Department's Director of Northern Gulf Affairs, Robert Deutch, accompanied by Turkish foreign ministry officials, visited Iraqi Kurdistan and had separate but inconclusive talks with the PUK and KDP leaders.

Senior State Department officials argue that intervention at a higher level would have made no difference since the Kurdish leaders had no will to agree. On the crucial issue of dividing customs revenues, there was an *impasse*. Talabani refused to give up control of Arbil because it constituted a bargaining counter against KDP control of Habur revenues, which the latter refused to share without an agreement on Arbil. With the various mediators unable or unwilling to break this *impasse*, the Iraqi Government was able to return to the stage.

The crisis of 1996

While the power struggles continued, the vexed question of Iraqi Kurdistan's future relations with the Iraqi state remained unsolved. In January 1995, the British Government warned that the inter-party conflict would provide an excuse to Saddam Hussein to restore his control over the north. Offers from the Government of Iraq to mediate in the conflict were refused by the Kurds, but both the PUK and KDP had maintained informal contacts with Baghdad since 1991.[98]

As early as 1994, Masud Barzani had suggested that if he did not find more support from the West he would, as a last resort, return to negotiations with Baghdad.[99] This may have been more of a bargaining position than an expression of intent at that moment, but government contacts with the KDP reportedly intensified early in 1995 after the PUK/INC attack across the *de facto* border. These contacts, and the supply of arms to the KDP were said to be 'common knowledge by spring 1995'.[100]

Events in the second half of 1996 brought to a head the contradictions which had built up since coalition troops left the area in 1991. They emphasised the limited credibility of Western claims to provide protection to the Kurds, and highlighted the almost suicidal determination of the two main Kurdish parties not to lose ground. Their search for external allies further increased interference by regional and international powers, all with their own political agendas.

By June 1996, the situation in Iraqi Kurdistan had become very tense. Turkish ground and air attacks intensified, and there were reports of renewed confrontations between PUK and KDP. Talabani openly accused the KDP of having re-opened relations with Baghdad. Alleging a KDP attack on PUK forces in the Hiran area on 5 July, he stated: '[The PUK] will not remain silent about these assaults, the motive for which we believe is the KDP's relationship with Saddam, the executioner. Saddam wants to prevent Kurdistan from becoming an Iraqi opposition base from which an attack can be launched against his tottering dictatorship. They must stop playing with fire, because it might burn not only their fingers but also their very homes.'[101]

During the night of 27–28 July, a force of Iranian Revolutionary Guards advanced into Iraqi Kurdistan to attack the KDPI's base at Koisanjaq. The incursion lasted about 72 hours. There were conflicting reports on whether the PUK actively facilitated this attack given that in the past the party had close links with the KDPI. The KDP accused the Iranian forces of leaving behind weapons for the PUK.[102]

During August, PUK-KDP clashes were said by UN officials to be the most intense in two years. The PUK offensive aimed to seize control of the border post of Hajj 'Umran and the Hamilton road in order to secure customs revenues which at that time were accruing to the KDP. It was facilitated by the neutrality, at the behest of Iran, of the IMIK and Kurdish Hizbollah, formerly allies of the KDP.[103] On 23 August, a first attempt by the US to establish a ceasefire lasted less than 24 hours. Iran's interest in continuing its mediating role was rejected, with the State Department saying it had 'no useful role' in northern Iraq. Finally, the KDP and PUK both agreed to a meeting in London on 30 August.

The discussions were abandoned on 31 August as news broke of the Iraqi advance on Arbil, at the invitation of the KDP, with a force of 30,000 men and 400 tanks. Some prior warning of Iraqi troop movements had come from the INC and PUK, while the CIA had reportedly concluded by 26 August 'with reasonable confidence' that Iraqi troops were planning an advance on Arbil. On 28 August, President Clinton had approved a diplomatic *démarche* warning Iraq not to take aggressive action around Arbil. Nonetheless, administration officials claimed to be unaware of the KDP's involvement.[104]

On 31 August, Iraqi Deputy Prime Minister Tariq Aziz published a letter allegedly written by Barzani to Saddam Hussein on 22 August in which he asked for assistance. A day earlier, Barzani had addressed a letter to the Clinton administration appealing for help. In both instances, Barzani justified his appeals by alleging Iranian intervention on the side of the PUK.[105]

PUK forces withdrew rapidly from Arbil, as the advancing Iraqi and KDP forces sealed off the exits to the city to prevent any repetition of the refugee flight of 1991. The Iraqis did not remain long in the city, beginning their withdrawal on 2 September. By 4 September their forces were reportedly dug in near Qushtepe, some 10 miles south-east of Arbil. Baghdad signalled early on that it did not intend an immediate reoccupation of the north. However, the short incursion allowed the KDP to seize control of the regional capital, held by the PUK since early 1995.[106]

The Iraqi forces, with KDP cooperation, used the incursion to target all the opposition parties with bases in Arbil – including the INC, SCIRI, the Iraqi National Turcoman Party, the Islamic Action Organisation and, of course, the PUK – arresting and taking away personnel who were still in the Arbil area. Their particular target was INC forces working with the CIA unit. On 31 August, as the Iraqis advanced, they executed 96 members of Brigade No 3 of the INC's forces near their camp at Qushtepe, south-east of Arbil.[107] In addition, the Iraqis established their own security and intelligence personnel in KDP-controlled areas. The head of KDP intelligence, Karim Sinjari, later conceded, 'It is likely there are intelligence agents and Iraqi secret police here, but publicly, there is nobody here'.[108]

By 5 September, the KDP began a new military push to the south-east, taking Sulaymaniya, as one journalist observed, in a 'chaotic' fashion, with little opposition.[109] The PUK leadership and military cadres, along with many civilians, had already fled towards the Iranian border. The KDP may have received Iraqi assistance in this push, at least in terms of equipment, but it does not seem that Iraqi troops were involved. The US administration continued to stress that this was a 'civil war' situation in which it would not intervene.[110]

By 11 September, the KDP appeared to be in control of most of Iraqi Kurdistan. However, a month later, in a swift reversal which few had anticipated, the PUK retook Sulaymaniya. By 21 October, the PUK had regained most of the lost territory, with the exception of Arbil. Talabani was said to have received a direct warning from Saddam Hussein, and requests from the US and Iran, not to attempt to retake Arbil.[111]

The US and UK secured a ceasefire on 23 October, and US Assistant Secretary of State Robert Pelletreau convened talks between the Kurdish parties in Ankara in an attempt to revive the agreements made in Ireland the previous year. According to Pelletreau, a peace settlement under Washington's auspices was to prevent the return of Iraqi authority to the region and to support the US policy of containment.[112]

In talks involving the US and UK Governments, as well as Turkish officials and the Turkish army's General Staff, the KDP and PUK agreed to make the ceasefire permanent. They agreed to end media attacks, to exchange prisoners, restore civilian services and give equal access to aid for all displaced persons. It was agreed that the parties should not seek intervention by external forces. In regard to political conciliation, further discussion was to take place on a 'Temporary Local Administration', the sharing of customs revenues and new elections.[113] Turkey and the US wanted the Kurdish parties, in particular the KDP, to cooperate in combatting the PKK. They also wanted to close Atrush camp in Dohuk governorate, which held some 14,000 Turkish Kurdish refugees.[114] At a second round of talks on 15 November, Pelletreau announced a further inducement – $11 million in US humanitarian aid for northern Iraq channelled through WFP and UNICEF.[115]

A peace supervision committee, including representatives of the American, British and Turkish Governments, the PUK, KDP, Assyrian Democratic Party and the Turcoman Front, was to meet regularly in Ankara. This so-called 'Ankara process' was the most concerted effort made by the US, Britain and Turkey to achieve a reconciliation between the PUK and KDP leaders. This time, some $3 million was found by the US administration to finance a 2000-strong peace monitoring force, composed mainly of Turcomans and Assyrians along with neutral Kurds, to patrol the ceasefire line they had established. Training and logistics for this force came from the Turkish army.[116]

Despite these measures, US negotiators found that both parties remained completely intransigent on the key points of conflict: control of revenues and territorial control of contested areas, especially of the regional capital, Arbil. In March 1997, the KDP withdrew from the 'Ankara process', accusing the PUK of carrying out assassinations of three of its officials.[117] A visit by US Acting Assistant Secretary of State David Welch to Iraqi Kurdistan in April 1997 produced little progress.[118] Turkey's continued engagement with the PKK in northern Iraq meant that its position fell far short of neutrality.

Shifting alliances

The KDP's discussions with Baghdad did not result in any substantive agreement and by 1997 the KDP had repaired relations with the US, leaving it little option but to become more explicitly aligned with the Turkish Government in trying to crush the PKK. Early in 1997, there was reportedly a marked deterioration in relations between the KDP and the PKK, culminating in an armed clash between KDP *peshmerga* and PKK militia after KDP forces surrounded the PKK office in Arbil.[119]

On 14 May, the Turkish army launched a major cross-border operation known as Operation Sledgehammer, acting in support of a KDP operation against the PKK. It involved a force of up to 50,000 Turkish troops which remained in the region until the end of June.[120] In October, the PUK, reportedly with support from the PKK, launched a major offensive against the KDP, taking territory along the Iranian border and pushing towards the strategic Hamilton road leading towards Arbil.[121] The previously separate PUK-KDP and PKK-Turkish Army conflicts converged for the first time in November when Turkish air and ground forces joined the KDP in forcing the PUK and the PKK to retreat to the previous ceasefire line. The fighting was reported to have left 1000 dead by the time the US and UK arranged yet another ceasefire on 24 November.[122]

The intersection of the two conflicts undermined the 'Ankara process' and left the way open for other mediators. Unconfirmed reports further suggested that the Iraqi Government may have mediated between the two sides during the October and November fighting.[123] The KDP's *rapprochement* with Baghdad had proved to be only partial, and reports from the region indicated that the PUK had intensified contacts with Baghdad since mid-1997.[124] In January 1998, Jalal Talabani met with the Director of Iraqi General Intelligence, Rafi Dahham al-Tikriti in Sulaymaniya.[125]

Economically speaking, Iraq has restored ties with its northern governorates. The economic embargo and restrictions on movement imposed at the end of 1991 appeared to have been gradually lifted since late 1996 and the implementation of the oil-for-food resolution (see Chapter 7). However, some sources allege that during 1997 the Iraqis were still restricting trade in goods which were not part of the oil-for-food programme to areas under PUK control.[126]

By early 1998 both parties appeared more inclined to compromise and put forward peace proposals.[127] The escalating conflict with the PKK during 1997 had taken a toll on KDP forces and funds, while the PUK lost badly in the October and November 1997 fighting. The UNSCOM crisis of February 1998 also appears to have given impetus to the discussions. The flow of goods under the oil-for-food programme lessened to some extent the intensity of competition over customs revenues.

Signs of greater cooperation appeared first over humanitarian issues. A joint Higher Coordination Committee was set up in 1997 to improve coordination between the separate PUK and KDP administrations on civilian services. Its work was interrupted by the October and November fighting, but in March 1998 the two parties sent a joint delegation to Washington to discuss the implementation of the UN humanitarian programme in the north.[128]

The Iraqi Government's growing involvement disturbed the US and UK and led to a series of moves to recapture the initiative. The aim was first to reassure the leaders of both parties who feared the possibility that sanctions might be lifted, which would bring the issue of their relations with the rest of Iraq into sharper perspective. Second, a more energetic effort was made to reconcile the two leaders. When Assistant Secretary of State Welch visited Iraqi Kurdistan in July 1998, he invited Barzani and Talabani to Washington. The meeting, the first between the two leaders for several years, resulted in an agreement which was intended to lead to revenue-sharing, a re-united administration and elections.

The situation on the ground has been much improved as a consequence of the agreement and the changes in the economic situation. It remains to be seen whether signatures on paper can can result in longer-term cooperation, given the deep distrust between the two leaders and the potential for interference by regional powers. Turkish officials, as before, expressed reservations about the terms of the agreement and in January 1999, the Iraqi Government was making new overtures on autonomy talks.

Plans to hold elections in July for a new Kurdish administration, if they go ahead, will test the willingness of the main parties to abide by the results. If the PUK and KDP share of the vote is as close as it was in the 1992 election, the challenge will be to form an administration which gives each party adequate representation without returning to the paralysis of the previous 50:50 power-sharing arrangement.

Meanwhile, Iraqi Kurdistan's position remains an anomaly which the international community has found no way to resolve while Saddam Hussein remains in power. The lack of any formal status and the economic problems which have accompanied it arguably contributed to the growth of internal conflict. Meanwhile the interference of Iraq's neighbours in Iraqi Kurdish affairs seems unlikely to abate. How Iraqi Kurdistan could be reintegrated into Iraq without losing whatever gains have been made since 1991, and with assurances that its population could live in safety, is a question which remains to be answered.

THE SOCIAL IMPACT OF EMBARGO AND CONFLICT

Internecine strife and the economic impoverishment of many citizens soon dimmed the hopes for a better life which the 1992 elections had raised. The sense of freedom created by the Iraqi Government's withdrawal was overshadowed by the impact of inter-party conflict and the accompanying abuses of power. There have been significant achievements, not least the rebuilding of several towns and many of the villages which had been destroyed since 1975. According to the Kurdish Ministry of Reconstruction, by 1996, 2850 villages had been rebuilt, constituting an unusual example of a return to rural life, after many years when forced or voluntary movement to urban areas had been the norm.[129]

In 1991, a significant number of those who originated from destroyed villages chose to return to the sites of their villages, rather than going back to *mujamma'at* or to the cities where they had been forced to resettle. Until late 1991, Iraqi troops were still present in many towns and *mujamma'at*. People therefore felt safer in the mountainous areas along the Iranian and Turkish borders where many of the destroyed settlements were located, and which were controlled by coalition troops or Kurdish *peshmergas*.

This more or less spontaneous movement on the part of returning refugees marked the beginning of efforts, supported by the UN and aid agencies, to re-establish rural communities. But restoring a semblance of rural life occurred in a patchwork fashion, with no overall plan. Resettlement was slower to start in regions which remained under Iraqi control until October 1991 and slower still in areas which lay close to the Iraqi lines, where the line of tanks on the horizon was a constant reminder of the fragility of the new order. For example, in the Germian region, which had suffered very severely during the Anfal campaign and lies close to the Iraqi lines around Kifri and Kalar, resettlement only gained momentum in 1993.

On the *de facto* line with Iraq, in the region around Kifri, Kalar and Chamchamal, the inhabitants have not only suffered shelling but have also been forced to flee their homes. On the whole, people usually return to their homes after each incident, but it can cause economic disruption and interruption of agricultural work. Occasionally there have been incursions by Iraqi troops, or, as in one bizarre incident, 'tribesmen' who were thought to be soldiers in disguise.[130]

Which groups of people moved back to their villages depended on a variety of factors. In the valleys and plains, Kurdish landowners who had been dispossessed or had joined the *peshmergas* returned to claim their land, bringing with them relatives, members of their tribe or clan and clients who would rent land and farm it for a share of the crop. In the mountain valleys, families returned individually or in groups to the piles of rubble which were all that remained of their mountain villages. Fruit orchards had been uprooted, livestock killed or dispersed, and wells poisoned or concreted over.[131]

During the first wave of returns in 1991, initial aid agency research in Sulaymaniya governorate detected little conflict over land ownership among returning villagers, but such disputes were later found to have had a significant inhibiting effect on village reconstruction.[132] After the Anfal operations, the Iraqi Government had expropriated agricultural land in areas which had been largely cleared of their Kurdish population. This land was then leased to either Arabs or Kurds to farm. Most of the Arab tenant farmers fled once the Iraqis withdrew. However, in some places those who had been displaced found their land had been taken over by tribes and clients of powerful *mustashars*, big landowners, or was claimed by adjacent villages. In the Dohuk region, Assyrian families moving back reportedly found that Kurdish farmers had taken over some of their land.

The Kurdish administration and political parties appeared reluctant to tackle the touchy question of disputed land or challenge powerful owners. They reportedly cited the need for Kurdish unity, and argued that larger landowners would be better able to bring lands under cultivation than the more impoverished smaller farmers. However, as one commentator noted, 'the fact that many Kurds have benefited from the Anfal is clearly an emotional and divisive issue; the continuing political influence of these beneficiaries is also a cause for concern'.[133]

In some instances, people moved from Baghdad and the south to live in rebuilt villages. In others, there were not enough surviving members who could return to create a viable community. Rebuilding villages in very remote areas sometimes proved too difficult because there were virtually no roads and no water supply within a reasonable distance. The pattern of resettlement was also influenced by the activities of UNHCR in 1991–2 and in the longer term, the support available from international and local NGOs (see Chapter 8).

Poverty was an inhibiting factor. Some families could not afford the cost of transporting their belongings and building materials to the village site. Once in place, they also needed money to purchase livestock, including draught animals. The alternative was the costly hire of tractors – and the purchase of fuel to run them – in addition to other farm equipment, fertilisers and seeds.[134] Those who owned all or part of the land to which they returned were likely to re-establish themselves more easily than those who had to rent land (usually for a share of the crop), whether from the local *agha*, another villager or someone who had remained in the town or *mujamma'at*.[135]

The disappearance of so many men in the 1980s had created a sizeable population of female-headed households, many of them displaced. In the Barzan valley alone, relief workers found in 1991 a population of between 3000 and 3500 female-headed households. Some ruined villages were populated only by women and children. In the early days of 1991, some of these women were said to be living from gathering and processing for sale herbs such as *sumak* (used to flavour kebabs), nuts and plants used as animal fodder.

Re-establishing life in a village was particularly hard for this group of 'Anfal widows', unless they had other family members of their family to help them. Their opportunities for income generation were very limited, and many depended on relief supplies or help from their neighbours, local clan leaders or political parties. There were also problems in gaining access to land, particularly because women have difficulty in claiming their dead husbands' property, which usually passes to male relatives. The only counterbalancing factor was the aid agencies' focus on assistance to female-headed households, both in the *mujamma'at* and in resettled villages.[136]

By no means all of those who had been forcibly displaced moved back to the rural areas. Although some of the *mujamma'at* have been virtually emptied since 1991, the figures show that they still house some 20 percent of the population. Families which moved back to villages sometimes left members in the *mujamma'at* or in town, in order to collect food rations, or to keep their children in school. The lack of facilities in the rebuilt villages and their uncertain future encouraged people to keep their options open. In some cases, people leaving collective towns virtually dismantled their houses, taking with them or selling windows, doors, everything that could be removed. In other places the housing remained more-or-less intact. Recent research suggests that up to half of those living in rural areas still have an urban winter base.[137]

Those who had grown up in the *mujamma'at* had no experience of agriculture or village life. Some of those returning to their villages after 1991 had only lived in the settlements since 1987 or 1998, but others moved as much as a decade earlier. The *mujamma'at* resembled refugee camps in the sense that they made people dependent on the Government for their food supplies, and were designed to thwart any kind of initiative. Few had the opportunity to earn a proper living, either by farming or work in urban areas.

Despite the effects of this culture of dependence, aid workers found most of those who returned to rebuild their villages were determined to succeed. Conditions were very harsh, especially for the first two or three years of rebuilding. Even with assistance from aid agencies, facilities were minimal and women in particular had to work very hard. Nonetheless, many of these villages managed to produce enough to feed their families and in some seasons a small surplus to sell.

Anti-personnel mines constitute a serious obstacle to rural resettlement, limiting access to arable land and pastures. Most of them look like large brown pebbles, the size of a fist or smaller. In the stony mountain landscape, they are frighteningly hard to spot. For anyone tilling land, and especially for shepherds, they are a lethal hazard. Women, often accompanied by children when fetching water or collecting firewood, are also likely victims. Mines can be washed into rivers by heavy rain or mud flows and end up many miles from where they were laid, so that even washing clothes in a stream can be dangerous.

Since 1991, anti-personnel mines and unexploded shells, left behind by the Iraqi army, have caused thousands of casualties. Hospital records up to 1996 showed that 2126 people died and 3651 were injured. This does not include numerous casualties in very remote areas who never reach hospital.

The total number of mines in Iraq is now calculated at ten million, of which eight million are thought to be anti-personnel mines from a variety of sources: Italy primarily, but also the US and Soviet Union. The majority of these were laid in the north by Iraq, and in the eastern border areas by Iran, during the 1980–88 war, or by the Iraqi army as part of their operations to clear the civilian population from the Kurdish rural areas. After Iraq's occupation of Kuwait, new minefields were laid near the Turkish border to hinder a possible coalition attack from Turkey, and more were apparently laid during the uprising in 1991. Finally, the Turkish army reportedly laid some mines during its 1995 cross-border operation against the PKK.[138]

Those who go on foot or with donkeys on mountain tracks to smuggle goods across the Iranian or Turkey borders are also at risk. Children, especially young boys, develop what Rae McGrath of Mines Advisory Group called 'a land mine culture' – collecting different types of mines and swapping them. When Iraqi troops withdrew they also left extensive dumps of live ammunition and shells. Youngsters have been killed trying to extract valuable metals from unexploded shells by setting fires under them, or shooting at them.[139]

Other extraneous factors have disturbed efforts to re-establish the rhythms of rural life. For those settling in areas close to the borders of the region, military attacks have been commonplace. On the Iranian border they were relatively small scale and sporadic, involving some internal displacement away from border areas, both of Iraqi Kurds and refugee Iranian Kurds.[140]

On the Turkish border, disruption has been more severe and frequent, beginning in 1991. Frequent Turkish bombing raids on PKK bases and periodic ground campaigns have disrupted settlement, mainly in the north of Dohuk governorate.[141] The presence of the PKK and its military actions have also caused difficulties for villagers.[142] In 1996–7, reports suggest that in areas close to the Turkish border resettled villagers have left their homes, finding the security situation too difficult. Some of these displaced people appear to have returned to the *mujamma'at* where they were previously housed.

The long-term future of this restored small farm sector, economically and socially, is still in question. Socially speaking, it is hard to know how cohesive these new communities will prove to be. Only a fragment of the previous population has returned, and therefore the social hierarchies of the past cannot be restored. It is unclear whether the young people now growing up in these villages will see a future for themselves there.

Economically, much depends on the policy of whatever government the region has in the future. In addition to the political and security policies of previous governments, little was done economically to encourage small farmers in mountain areas, and since 1991 the Kurdish adminstration has provided little support. The reestablishment of food rations provided under Resolution 986 and the consequent depression of agricultural prices caused by large imports of food may also deter some villagers from persevering with farming (see Chapter 7).

Urban life

For many people in the West, the dominant images of the Kurds are either of hardy mountain people or pitiful refugees freezing on mountain tops. In fact, data collected in different surveys in 1994 and 1995 variously suggested that 58 or 64 percent of the population lived in cities and towns, 19 or 22 percent in collective settlements, and 23 or 13 percent in villages.[143] These figures are a useful corrective to the idea of Kurdistan as a largely rural society, but many more people have rural links than the figures suggest. *Mujamma'at* dwellers in particular often work in agriculture during the growing and harvesting season, while they and urban dwellers are involved in trade in agricultural goods or are dependent on agricultural production by family members.[144]

By 1994, both local officials and aid agencies conceded that urban dwellers and those in collective settlements were under increasing economic pressure. A 1994 survey found that those in collective settlements and among those registered as displaced had the highest percentage of poor households.[145] Just over half of the total number categorised as poor lived in towns and cities. The proportion of poor families in resettled villages was little better, but there seemed some prospect that this group could secure a livelihood through agriculture if political circumstances permitted.[146]

In some respects, the pattern of urban economic decline replicated the situation in government-controlled areas, though the dynamics were somewhat different. Prices rose, but not as dramatically as in government areas. Food and other basic goods were usually available, but low wages and salaries meant that prices were often beyond what most people could afford. After the harvest, food prices usual · fell, but for the rest of the year the internal embargo caused dependence on more expensive imported goods.

The most vulnerable were those without rural links, who had fixed and low salaries and who purchased all their goods in urban markets. After 1992, the minimal security provided by government rations was withdrawn, removing a safety-net for the poorest. However, it seems that even during 1991, when the Iraqi Government remained in control over a large part of the region, many people were not receiving government rations because they did not have ration cards or had not registered for them.[147]

By 1992, salaries of public servants were being paid regularly but, unlike in government areas, there were no pay rises. Public servants, who constituted an estimated 45 percent of the workforce in northern Iraq (approximately 200,000 employees), found that their pay fell below subsistence levels. Pension payments to retired civil servants also ceased for a time under the internal embargo.[148] In 1994 salaries averaged 250–300 Iraqi dinars per month, when an average family needed 2000–3000 for basic amenities. One NGO official said that ID300 would barely cover the cost of a bag of rice.

Since 1995 and the virtual collapse of the administration, salaries have been paid irregularly. Teachers recalled going five months without pay. What is more surprising is that they have the commitment to go to work at all. Most teachers, health workers and other salaried groups have other jobs, mainly in the informal sector and services, including involvement in smuggling. People also take advantage of any form of aid or subsidy on offer. For example, for a time workers in certain ministries – mainly education and health – received a food ration paid for by external aid. Given the meagre pay of teachers and medical staff this seems justified, but it also led to the proliferation of ancillary staff such as cleaners and office staff. Although such jobs pay a pittance, they were worth having because of the food ration.

Rather better off were families, both urban and rural with menfolk recruited into the *peshmerga*, who receive regular pay at a higher level than public employees. In addition skilled labourers and entrepreneurs have profited from smuggling and from the construction work generated by aid agencies and latterly by funds under the oil-for-food programme.

As elsewhere, many people have sold personal possessions – jewellery, furniture and electrical goods – while help from relatives overseas has become more and more important. A 1994 survey found that over 20 percent of households sampled gave as their primary source of income 'assistance or borrowing from non-relatives; sale of household goods; drawing on savings; assistance from relatives'.[149] In both rural and urban areas, it seems many poor families periodically receive *zakat* (religious tax) payments either in cash or kind.[150]

According to a primary school head teacher with seven or eight dependents, interviewed in 1995:

> My salary is around ID500… and I have not had my salary paid for three months now… We get some help from NGOs who provide teachers with food items now and then. Also, I am lucky because I have a brother-in-law who lives in Europe and sends us dollars now and then. If it were not for him, I cannot imagine how we would survive. However, others are not so lucky and I know many of my staff and pupils cannot afford even to buy enough bread and yoghurt to eat.
>
> Many of the teachers come to work just for one or two hours. Then they leave and go to the market where they have another job, or maybe more than one job to support their

families. It has now become the norm for people not to depend on their salaries and turn to other jobs to survive. Even our pupils sometimes work to support their families.[151]

Health services suffered erratic power and fuel supplies, and the perennial lack of spare parts and medical supplies which are common throughout Iraq. There has been a greater input from aid agencies in Iraqi Kurdistan, but mainly in response to breakdowns and shortages rather than the redevelopment of services. In 1993–4, the situation in health was probably better than in some government-controlled areas, but the collapse of the administration since that time and the ensuing funding problems may have altered that balance.

In the early period after the refugee returns of 1991, imbalances developed in educational provision in the Kurdish region. In some areas where rural resettlement was taking place, there were still no schools. In others, schools were built, but they did not function because no teachers were available. In Sulaymaniya governorate in early 1993, according to UNICEF's education officer, there has been a 50 percent increase in the number of primary schools (as schools in destroyed areas were rebuilt), but an acute shortage of teachers to go and work in the villages. Teacher-pupil ratios varied widely, from 1:20 to 1:80. In larger settlements and towns such as Qala Diza and Halabja, which were being rebuilt on the ruins of previous structures and to which substantial numbers of people had returned, there was a great shortage of teachers and classrooms at all levels. In Qala Diza, for example, some secondary school teachers said they were teaching two shifts with classes of more than 60 students in each shift.

In urban areas aid agencies noticed increasing problems with school attendance. By 1994, the pattern whereby children dropped out of school to work or worked as well as going to school was recognised as increasingly common, to the point were a Kurdish organisation established a 'catch-up' centre for out-of-school children. Even before this period, children could be seen selling goods or kerosene and petrol by the roadsides.

Displacement

As the parties struggled for control of the region, population displacement further contributed to impoverishment. The massive population movements of 1991 have not been repeated – though governments (especially that of Turkey), aid organisations and the UN periodically anticipated this – but there have been numerous smaller displacements.

In 1994, the UN estimated that some 25,000 fled their homes, at least temporarily, because of the fighting.[152] The sense of insecurity has grown since early 1995 when the PUK's capture of Arbil led to the *de facto* partition of Iraqi Kurdistan. It became common for the incoming party members and *peshmergas* to seize the property and goods of those who fled, without discussion or redress.[153] Although the main targets were those with overt party affiliations, others have also suffered. A visitor in August 1996 reported, 'In all major Kurdish cities, hotels, public buildings and camps are cramped with awara (aliens) – Kurds seeking refuge from, or deported by, the rival party, living on meagre aid from their respective parties or recruited and sent to the front lines to face their "fraternal enemy", leaving their families behind as awara'.[154]

The crisis of September 1996 created the largest movement of people since 1991. Fear of the Iraqi army and its security services was added to the fear of rival Kurdish factions. In the south-east, the PUK's announcement of an imminent Iraqi attack on Sulaymaniya undoubtedly contributed to the scale of the exodus towards the Iranian border. Further confusion was caused in areas over which the conflict ebbed and flowed – for example Koisanjaq was reported to have been overrun by competing parties five times during this phase of the conflict.

According to the International Committee of the Red Cross (ICRC), some 80,000 people in all were displaced, mostly in Sulaymaniya governorate, when the KDP took Sulaymaniya city in September 1996. Of these, about half fled to Iran. The majority returned to their homes when the PUK retook Sulaymaniya.[155] After the ceasefire agreement brokered by the US in October, thousands more people identified with the 'wrong' faction were reportedly displaced as the PUK reasserted its control in Sulaymaniya and the KDP strengthened its grip in Arbil.

While accurate figures are not obtainable, the KDP alleged that 58,000 KDP supporters were expelled from Sulaymaniya and other PUK-controlled areas between October 1996 and October 1997, while the PUK alleged that more than 49,000 of its supporters were expelled from Arbil and other KDP-controlled areas between August 1996 and October 1997.[156] UN sources estimated that 3000 people were displaced from January to August 1997, mainly as a result of the Turkish incursion, and a further 10,000 by the fighting in October and November 1997.[157]

RESPONSES TO CONFLICT

After the hope and traumas of the uprising, many Kurds clearly felt that once the Iraqis left there might be a better future. Hence the shock at the first urban clash – between the PUK and IMIK in December 1993 – with Kurd shooting at Kurd, not on an isolated mountainside but in the streets of a city. During the much more intense and widespread fighting in May 1994, popular discontent with the behaviour of both parties was evident when a group of 200 women marched from Sulaymaniya to Arbil to demand that the two parties desist from fighting. More independent-minded members of parliament staged a sit-in at the assembly building in Arbil in January 1995.

However, once hostilities took hold, for most people survival was the main aim. People who fled could not easily return to their homes once the region was divided. At least until 1998, both the KDP and PUK were vocal in mutual blame for outrages, thereby stirring up prejudices and reinforcing stereotypes between the language-based regions.[158]

Economic conditions and political difficulties combined to induce many people to leave the country, despite the considerable cost of purchasing an Iraqi or other passport and visa, and paying the necessary 'sweeteners' to jump the enormous queues to get into Turkey. In the past few years as conditions worsened, a lucrative trade developed for those controlling the border (on both sides) in selling passports and visas.

The flow of people leaving the country continued unabated in 1997 and early 1998, to the point where it was causing alarm among European governments. In the view of one Kurdish observer, 'These parties [the KDP and the PUK] have created an unstable environment where people are constantly worried and frightened. They have used the region's limited revenues to purchase weapons and enhance their wealth, power and control'.[159]

It is evident that some people in Iraqi Kurdistan have done very well out of the uncertainties of the 1990s. Visitors soon after the initial refugee crisis witnessed smart receptions at which the entrepreneurs of the crisis ostentatiously displayed their wealth. Since then, the scale of smuggling and every kind of import-export and transport business has grown apace. Particular beneficiaries are those with good party connections or links with entrepreneurs in Turkey or government-controlled Iraq. An often-cited example is the growing wealth and influence of Nechirvan Barzani, Masud's nephew, who has established companies in Dohuk through which all goods coming from Turkey and those transhipped to Iraq have to pass.[160]

There were also differences in patterns of need and poverty between different areas. The importance of trade with Turkey meant that the relative economic position of Dohuk governorate was substantially improved. Before 1990, this northern Badinan region had been the least economically developed of the three governorates. The situation after 1991 put Sulaymaniya and Arbil, previously more prosperous and urbanised governorates, at a disadvantage. A 1994 survey suggested that Sulaymaniya governorate had become the poorest of the three.[161] However, there have been pockets of impoverishment in all governorates: for example, the disruptions caused by the Turkish-PKK war have impoverished rural life and caused displacement in the mountainous border regions of both Dohuk and Arbil governorates.

Another area with particular problems – in the south-east around the town of Halabja – remained under the control of the IMIK, and was not integrated into the PUK administrative region.[162] This is a region with an especially vulnerable population, since it suffered the worst of the chemical attacks carried out in 1988. The impact on the health of the population, and on agricultural production, has yet to be properly surveyed. However, initial research in 1997 suggested that the population which survived the attack is characterised by severe health problems, impoverishment and depression.[163]

The scarcity of work and resources appears to have strengthened ties of clientelism both to the main parties and to powerful clan or tribal leaders. Those with strong party, family and tribal ties are more likely to be 'looked after' than those without such connections. Those in positions of power therefore tend to regard all resources – including international aid and funds from the oil-for-food programme – as a vehicle for further patronage, whether at a personal or party level.

From early 1997, however, these funds did make a difference, even before the fighting stopped. Some argue that once more money was available the two separate administrations proved more efficient than the paralysed 50-50 adminstration of 1992–4. Significant amounts of '986' money has undoubtedly gone into the pockets of contractors and party-related interests, but up to late 1998, the overall standard of living had improved more rapidly than in government-controlled areas. Nonetheless, the question of the region's long-term future and the sustainability of the current political and economic situation still remain.

NOTES ON CHAPTER 6

1   Entessar (1992), p 76.
2   Sluglett and Farouk-Sluglett (1990i), pp 164–70.
3   McDowall (1997), p 339.
4   Human Rights Watch/Middle East (1995), pp 4–5; Order no 28/3650 of 3 June 1987, signed by Ali Hassan al-Majid, Secretary-General of the Office for the Organisation of the North (United Nations Economic and Social Council Commission on Human Rights [1992], Annex II).
5   McDowall (1992), p 110.
6   Van Bruinessen (1992) states that by 1990 4000 villages had been destroyed out of a total of 7000 in the Kurdish region (p 44). Human Rights Watch/Middle East (1995) describes in detail the eight campaigns, covering, in sequence: first, the siege of Sergalou and Bergalou (near the Dokan dam); second, the Qara Dagh region (south of Sulaymaniya); third, the Germian region (between Kirkuk and Qalar); fourth, the valley of the lesser Zab river (between Kirkuk and Taqtaq; the fifth, sixth and seventh, the mountain valleys of Rawanduz and Shaqlawa, and the eighth, in Badinan (see map).
7   UNHCR gave figures for three waves of Kurdish refugees in this period: in May 1987, some 10,000 people fled; in spring 1988 after the bombing of Halabja, 70,000; and a further 22,000 in October 1988.
8   Human Rights Watch/Middle East (1995), p 8; McDowall (1992), p 110.
9   The 1970 autonomy proposals emphasised linguistic and cultural autonomy, educational reforms and the implementation of land reforms (already implemented in the rest of the country in the 1960s). Kurds were to be represented in central government, and organs representing the region were to be established. In a 1972 document, the Kurdistan Democratic Party was still pressing for inclusion of Kirkuk in the autonomous region. Ite challenged the veracity of the 1965 census as a basis for determining areas with a Kurdish majority. Mustafa Barzani said that if a new census did not show a Kurdish majority in Kirkuk, he would not accept it. (KDP, Settlement of the Kurdish Problem in Iraq, 30 October 1972 in Weller [1993], pp 580–81).
10 For arguments that the Anfal campaign and associated Iraqi actions constituted genocidal action, see Human Rights Watch/Middle East (1995), Introduction, pp 1–15.
11 According to van Bruinessen (1994), the majority of the Faylis, who originated from western Iran but had lived for generations in Central Iraq, did not have Iraqi citizenship (p 28). They have their own dialect of Kurdish, though the majority who lived in Iraq also spoke Arabic. Although they lived somewhat separated from the majority of the Kurdish population in Iraq, they occupied important positions in the Iraqi Kurdish nationalist movement in the 1970s, and wealthy Faylis contributed significant financial resources to the movement.
12 Van Bruinessen (1994), p 29.
13 The Barzani clan developed around a succession of charismatic *shaykhs* associated with the Naqashbandi order in the late nineteenth century. Their following, centring on the village of Barzan, grew as they attracted peasants and others who felt oppressed by neighbouring tribal chiefs. See van Bruinessen (1992), pp 329–335.
14 Van Bruinessen (1992), p 309.
15 McDowall (1997), p 354.
16 This urban population generally speaking did not adhere closely to tribal identities, although in Dohuk – which grew into a large town only in the 1960s – tribal divisions were imported into the urban structure, with particular tribes controlling quarters of the town.
17 McDowall (1992), pp 104–106.
18 The Iraqi Kurdistan Front was first established in May 1988 as an umbrella organisation for Kurdish political groups (Francke [1994], p 165). Initially it was said to have

been composed of five political parties: The Kurdistan Democratic Party (KDP), the Patriotic Union of Kurdistan (PUK), the Kurdistan People's Democratic Party (KPDP), the Kurdistan Socialist Party – Iraq (KPS–I) and the Kurdish Socialist Party (PASOK). Three more parties subsequently joined: The Assyrian Democratic Party (ADM), the Iraqi Communist Party – Kurdistan Region and the Kurdistan Toilers' Party (KTP) (Amnesty International [1995], p 9).

19   Leezenberg (1997), pp 49–50.
20   Van Bruinessen (1994), pp 28–29. For details of *jash* activities during the Anfal see Human Rights Watch/Middle East (1995), *passim*.
21   McDowall (1997), p 357.
22   Muller (1992), p 20. Examples of the relative independence of some local strong-men who were not tribal leaders and gained their status as *mustashars* in the 1980s are Tahsin Shawais in Chamchamal, who had a reputation as a brave *peshmerga*, but had also sided with Baghdad in the 1980s, and Mamand Qashqai, a former petty criminal who became a *mustashar*, and after 1991 became a warlord with his own forces, dominating one city quarter in Arbil (Leezenberg [1997], p 61).
23   Quoted in McDowall (1997), p 377.
24   BBC Summary of World Broadcasts, 21 June 1996, 'Seven People Reported Killed in Kurdish Clashes in North', quoting *Huriyet*, Istanbul, 18 June 1996; al-Khafaji (1996), p 36.
25   Hoff *et al* (1992), p 5.
26   See Hoff *et al* (1992), p 4; Ward and Rimmer (1995) in the Overseas Development Institute's poverty study gave a total population for the Kurdish-controlled area of 3,052,000, while an estimate (January 1995) from the UNDHA's Inter-Agency Relief Coordination Unit (IRCU) put the total population at 3,280,270.
27   Kirkuk city and Khanaqin are the sites of oil refineries, and there are substantial oilfields in this region (Muller [1992], p 30).
28   *New York Times*, 6 February 1992, 'Kurds' Dream of Freedom Slipping Away'. According to Kutschera (1997), p 122, the division of revenues was 30 percent each to KDP and PUK, and 10–15 percent each for the smaller parties.
29   McDowall (1997), pp 379–80.
30   *Daily Telegraph*, 16 December 1991, 'Kurds to Vote for Assembly in Iraq'; McDowall (1997), pp 379–80. This did not mean that contacts ceased. In early March 1992, a KDP delegation was in Baghdad to discuss clashes which had occured with the Iraqi army in the previous week, and the issue of the Iraqi embargo (BBC Summary of World Broadcasts, 11 March 1992, 'KDP delegation reported to have held talks in Baghdad', quoting Agence France Presse in English, 9 March 1992).
31   *Middle East International*, 15 May 1992, 'Election Fever'.
32   Lawyers Committee for Human Rights (1992), pp 9–10.
33   The Turcoman Party argued that participation in the election would jeopardise the position of the large number of Turcomans still under Ba'th Party rule. The decision may also have reflected Turkish government hostility to the elections.
34   According to some Kurdish sources (for example Dr Mahmud Uthman; Dr Fuad Hussein, interview, *op. cit.*) the PUK threatened that there would be armed conflict if the KDP capitalised on this marginal victory.
35   Hoff *et al* (1992), p 31.
36   Four of the five reserved seats went to the Assyrian Democratic Movement and the fifth to Kurdistan Christian Unity.
37   Meadowcroft and Lunn (1992), pp 15–17.
38   Some of the parties had combined forces or joined one of the larger parties in advance of the elections (McDowall [1997], p 380). After the 1992 elections, the KPDP and the KSP/PASOK joined to form the Unity Party of Kurdistan. In August 1993 the Kurdish Unity Party united with the KDP.

39   Amnesty International (1995), pp 6, 20.
40   The European Parliament was more positive but encouraged the Kurdish leadership to pursue the path of autonomy (Cook [1995], p 79).
41   Hoff *et al* (1992), pp 18–19.
42   Until 1994, the members of the MCC based in Zakho – the US, UK, France and Turkey (from 1993) – maintained regular contact with the Kurdish leadership in Salahadin.
43   Gunter (1993), p 304.
44   *Middle East International*, 27 May 1994, 'Dicing with Death: The KDP and the PUK in Conflict'; Leezenberg (1997), p 58–9.
45   *Gulf Newsletter*, June/July 1994, no. 10, 'Conflict in Iraqi Kurdistan', p 2.
46   Amnesty International (1995), *passim*.
47   *Ibid.*, p 18.
48   The first of a number of such appeals was made by Dr Fuad Ma'sum, Chairman of the Council of Ministers, to the UN Security Council on 4 August 1992 (BBC Summary of World Broadcasts, 10 August 1992, 'Iraqi Kurdistan Premier Appeals for UN Assistance', quoting Voice of the People of Kurdistan, 8 August 1992).
49   Keen (1993), p 37.
50   Public employees made up some 45 percent of employed persons in the three gover-norates. Until October 1991, the Iraqi Government had apparently continued to pay salaries to at least some of the officials who had stayed in areas under *peshmerga* control as well as those working in the parts of the region still held by the Government (Dammers [1994], p 405).
51   Keen (1993), p 60.
52   Human Rights Watch/Middle East (1994), p 46.
53   Cook (1995), p 51; BBC Summary of World Broadcasts, 12 May 1993, 'Iraq Reopens Its Borders Following Withdrawal of the 25-dinar Note'.
54   Bozarslan (1996), p 111.
55   UNHCR (1992i), p 14.
56   Graham-Brown (1995), p 8.
57   *Gulf Newsletter*, September 1992, no. 4, 'Kurds Struggle Against the Odds', p 4; Dr Salahaddin M. Al-Haffid, interview with the author, March 1993.
58   Keen (1993), p 40.
59   McDowall (1997), p 383; Kutschera (1997), pp 115–6.
60   Bozarslan (1996), pp 114–5.
61   *Ibid.*, pp 112–114.
62   Al-Haffid (1992), p 51.
63   Amnesty International (1995), pp 89–93.
64   *Gulf Newsletter*, March 1994, no. 9, 'Tension in the Kurdish Region', p 5; Leezenberg (1997), p 60.
65   *Gulf Newsletter*, ibid.
66   Kutschera (1997), p 132; Amnesty International (1995), pp 111–112.
67   *Gulf Newsletter*, November/December 1994, no. 11, 'Turkish Policy and the Iraqi Kurds', p 4.
68   BBC Summary of World Broadcasts, 24 November 1994, 'PUK and KDP Sign Agreement on Alliance', quoting Voice of Iraqi Kurdistan, Salahadin, 22 November 1994.
69   BBC Summary of World Broadcasts, 30 March 1995, 'KDP Claims PUK Force has "Stormed" Kurdistan Parliament in Arbil', quoting Voice of Iraqi Kurdistan, Salahadin, 28 March 1995.
70   Amnesty International (1995), pp 5–6.
71   See, for example, BBC Summary of World Broadcasts, 29 January 1997, 'KDP says PUK appointment of new ministers has "no legal grounds"', quoting the Voice of Iraqi Kurdistan, Salahadin, 27 January 1997.

72   Lawyers Committee for Human Rights (1992), p 16.
73   *Turkey Briefing*, August 1991, vol. 5, no. 4; Phebe Marr (1996), p 61.
74   For example, US Department of State (1995), p 1090.
75   Majid (forthcoming).
76   BBC Summary of World Broadcasts, 8 October 1992, 'National Council of Iraqi Kurdistan Issues Statement on Federation', quoting Voice of the People of Kurdistan, 5 October 1992.
77   Foreign Broadcast Information Service, 12 November 1992, p 52, 'Interview with Prime Minister Demirel', quoting *Turkiye*, 10 October 1992, p 14.
78   From a letter from Ozal to Suleiman Demirel at the end of February 1993, soon before his death. Published as 'Ozal's Will' in *Huriyet*, 12 November 1993. The whole passage reveals Ozal's thinking: 'it would be a lot more useful for us to have influence over these groups (KDP and PUK) in northern Iraq rather than letting them be influenced by external forces that have dubious intentions. We should try to keep them under our spell as much as possible and even try to assume the role of their guarantors. We know that the Saddam regime supports the PKK and helps it any way it can. If Saddam succeeds along with the PKK, in weakening the Kurds and the Turcomans of northern Iraq, then the terrorist organisation will be better situated to manoeuvre in those territories. It also goes without saying that it does not serve our interests to make enemies of Talabani and Barzani in addition to the PKK' (quoted in Ozel [1995], p 180).
79   Robins (1993), pp 674–675.
80   Bozarslan (1997), p 251.
81   Victor Tanner, interview with the author, May 1997, citing an interview between Masud Barzani, Tanner and Fred Cuny, 19 June 1992.
82   *Gulf Newsletter*, January 1993, no. 5, 'Turkey and the Iraqi Kurds', p 4.
83   *Gulf Newsletter*, July 1993, no. 7, 'Iranian Attacks', p 4.
84   US Department of State (1995), p 1090.
85   According to a British official, Iranian forces were seen in Pengwin during the May 1994 fighting.
86   Cuny (1995) says some *peshmerga* leaders credited Turkey with providing the framework which ended the fighting in summer 1994 (p 11). A British official source also mentioned that Barzani and Talabani had talks with Turkish officials in Silopi in early June 1994.
87   *Turkish Daily News*, 16 August 1994, 'Ankara feels Iraqi Kurds creating confidence crisis'; Dr Fuad Hussein, interview with the author, July 1997. In fact, these talks were not officially sanctioned by the French Government, and France and the UK only sent diplomatic observers (Kendal Nezan, interview with the author, 21 October 1997).
88   Kendal Nezan, interview, *op. cit.*
89   *Turkey Briefing*, Spring 1994, vol. 8, no. 1, p 7; BBC Summary of World Broadcasts, 13 February 1995, 'Turkey Seeks New Relationship with Iraq', quoting TRT TV, Ankara, 11 February 1995.
90   For a discussion of the complex issues involved see Leezenberg (1997), p 71–2.
91   Randal (1997), p 296.
92   *Middle East International*, 22 September 1995, 'Peace Talks Fail'.
93   *International Herald Tribune*, 'The Bad News From Kurdistan Is Bad for Washington, Too', 1 April 1996.
94   BBC Summary of World Broadcasts, 14 October 1995, 'PUK, KDP Issue Communique on Tehran Talks', quoting Voice of the People of Kurdistan, Sulaymaniya, 12 October 1995.
95   *Middle East International*, 8 November 1996, 'Iraq and Turkey: Dealing With the Kurds'.
96   See, for example, BBC Summary of World Broadcasts, 21 March 1996, 'Kurdistan Democratic Party Leader Comments on Situation in Kurdistan', quoting Voice of Iraqi

Kurdistan, Salahadin, 18 March 1996; *ibid.*, 'PUK Welcomes Kurdistan Democratic Party Response to Peace Proposals', 29 March 1996, quoting Voice of the People of Kurdistan, Sulaymaniya, 27 March 1996.

97 State Department official interviewed by the author, May 1997. See also Randal (1997): 'The missing money, some said, had fallen victim to the penny-wise, pound foolish budget war between President Clinton and the Republican-controlled Congress, which briefly shut down the federal government in early 1996" (p 295).

98 BBC Summary of World Broadcasts, 15 February 1995, '"Babil" Newspaper Says Dialogue Between Kurds and Government "the Only Way Out"', quoting Iraqi News Agency, Baghdad, 14 February 1995.

99 In an interview with the Austrian publication *Profil* (Vienna, 31 January 1994) when asked whether he could envisage a resumption of negotiations with Saddam Hussein, Barzani replied: 'Actually, we only want to negotiate with a democratic government. But if the Kurdish people are threatened with destruction... then negotiations with Baghdad will perhaps be necessary' (p 56). Quoted in Foreign Broadcast Information Service, 31 January 1994, 'Kurdish Leader Warns Against Mass Exodus of Kurds'.

100 *Middle East International*, 8 November 1996, 'Iraq and Turkey: Dealing With the Kurds'. Randal (1997) wrote that in February 1996 he had heard rumours that Barzani had been negotiating with Baghdad for months and had purchased tanks and other equipment from the Iraqi Government (p 293).

101 BBC Summary of World Broadcasts, 8 July 1996, 'PUK Leader Threatens Retaliation For Attacks by KDP Forces', quoting Voice of the People of Kurdistan, Sulaymaniya, 6 July 1996.

102 BBC Summary of World Broadcasts, 31 July 1996, 'Iranian Forces Kill 20 Kurds Based in Iraq', quoting Vision of the Islamic Republic of Iran Network I, Teheran, 29 July 1996; al-Khafaji (1996), p 37. However, the KDP asserted that the Iranian forces left behind arms for the PUK. *Washington Post*, 1 September 1996, 'Kurdish Feuds Put US in Quandary'.

103 Kutschera (1997), p 138.

104 *Washington Post*, 4 September 1996, 'Why Clinton's Response Fell Far From Site of Saddam's Aggression'; *Frankfurter Allegemeine Zeitung*, 19 August 1996, 'Bagdad zieht Truppen im Norden zusammen'.

105 *Le Monde*, 3 September 1996, 'L'armée de Bagdad commence à quitter le nord du Kurdistan irakien'; *Independent*, 6 September 1996, 'US Blamed For Causing Iraq Crisis'.

106 BBC Summary of World Broadcasts, 2 September 1996, 'Iraqi Forces Will Not Remain in Arbil, No Iraqi Government to be Established there "Yet"', quoting Iraqi TV, Baghdad, 31 August 1996; *Independent*, 5 September 1996, 'Kurdish Capital Left to Lick its Wounds as Iraqis Withdraw'.

107 United Nations General Assembly (1996), para. 93.

108 *Guardian*, 28 April 1997, 'Rival Kurds Threaten Iraqi Oil Deal as Relief Arrives for Desperate People'.

109 Randal (1997), p 309.

110 *Le Monde*, 11 September 1996, 'Les Kurdes soutenus par Bagdad prennent le contrôle du nord de l'Iraq'.

111 BBC Summary of World Broadcasts, 25 October 1996, 'PUK Not Advancing on Arbil "For the Time Being"', quoting MBC TV, London, 23 October 1996.

112 *Al-Hayat*, 2 August 1998, 'Robert Pelletreau, the Kurdish Negotiations'.

113 United States Information Agency, 31 October 1996, 'Statement on Enforcing Iraq Kurd Ceasefire'.

114 Pelletreau, interview, *op. cit.*

115 BBC Summary of World Broadcasts, 18 November 1996, 'KDP, PUK Sides Back "Lasting" Ceasefire', quoting TRT TV, Ankara, 15 November 1996; Robert Pelletreau, interview, *op. cit.*

116 BBC Summary of World Broadcasts, 11 December 1996, 'Kurdish Groups Reportedly Make Good Progress on Northern Iraq Ceasefire', quoting Anatolia news agency, Ankara, 9 December 1996.

117 BBC Summary of World Broadcasts, 22 March 1997, 'KDP Sets Out Conditions for Resuming Ankara Peace Talks', quoting Voice of Iraqi Kurdistan, Salahadin, 20 March 1997. The three officials assassinated were Sirwan Nawroli in January 1997, the KDP governor of Arbil, François Hariri, in February, and Mouhiddin Rahim in March (Human Rights Watch, *World Report* 1998, p 336).

118 US Department of State, Office of the Spokesman, Press Statement 'Acting Assistant Secretary Welch's Arrival in Northern Iraq', 3 April 1997. Welch was the highest-ranking State Department official to visit Iraqi Kurdistan – as opposed to attending meetings in Ankara – since Secretary of State James Baker's visit to the border region during the refugee crisis of 1991.

119 BBC Summary of World Broadcasts, 10 March 1997, 'Clashes Reported Between KDP forces and PKK in Arbil', quoting Voice of the People of Kurdistan, 7 March 1997. The KDP in its own propaganda identified the PKK as a local political threat. Some Western officials asserted that the PKK had indeed increased its local support in Iraqi Kurdistan, perhaps as a result of popular disillusionment with Iraqi Kurdish parties. Martin van Bruinessen, on the other hand, argues that the PKK had considerable support, especially in Badinan before August 1995, when it alienated some of these supporters by attacking the KDP during the peace negotiations (Interview with the author, 25 September 1997).

120 BBC Summary of World Broadcasts, 15 May 1997, 'Turkish Army Enters Northern Iraq to Support KDP Operations against the PKK', quoting TRT TV, Ankara, 14 May 1997; *Financial Times*, 30 May 1997, 'Turkey Finds Ally in Advance on PKK'.

121 BBC Summary of World Broadcasts, 17 October 1997, PUK Spokesman Confirms It Started Fighting in North', quoting *Al-Sharq al-Awsat*, London, 15 October 1997; *Independent*, 'As Kurds Fight Over a Road, Saddam Tightens His Grip', 13 November 1997.

122 US Department of State (1998ii) (electronic copy, http://www.state.gov).

123 BBC Summary of World Broadcasts, 8 November 1997, 'Iraq Reportedly Brokering Contacts Between Kurdish Sides', quoting *al-Hayat*, London, 6 November 1997.

124 For example, BBC Summary of World Broadcasts, 18 June 1997, 'Arabic Paper Reports Baghdad-PUK Contacts via Intermediaries', quoting *Al-Hayat*, London, 14 June 1997; 'Saddam Said to Have Received Envoy of PUK Leader Talabani', 17 July 1997, quoting *Al-Majd*, Jordan, 14 July 1997.

125 BBC Summary of World Broadcasts, 22 January 1998, 'Intelligence Director Reportedly Holds Talks With PUK's Talabani', quoting *Al-Hayat*, London, 20 January 1998.

126 US Department of State (1998ii), Introduction.

127 BBC Summary of World Broadcasts, 20 January 1998, 'KDP Leader Barzani Responds to PUK Proposal With His Own Peace Plan', quoting Voice of Iraqi Kurdistan, Salah al-Din, 17 January 1998.

128 BBC Summary of World Broadcasts, 31 March 1998, 'Joint PUK-KDP Delegation Holds Talks at UN in New York', quoting Voice of the People of Kurdistan, 29 March 1998.

129 United Nations Consolidated Inter-Agency Humanitarian Cooperation Programme for Iraq, *Mid-Term Review*, September 1995. According to UNDHA/IRCU figures, 69 percent of villages in Dohuk governorate had been rebuilt by early 1995, 85 percent of those in Arbil governorate, and 50 percent of those in Sulaymaniya governorate.

130 On 12 March 1992, after an incident in the village of Awayna (about 37 kilometres from Arbil, near the Iraqi lines) in which four armed intruders tried to steal a tractor, some 400 armed men reportedly entered the village and shot dead at least 15 people, injuring ten others. The dead apparently included women and children. Some sources said the

attackers were Iraqi soldiers dressed as civilians; others that they were Arab tribesman working for the Iraqi Government (*Gulf Newsletter*, April 1993, no. 6, 'Lack of funds slows Kurdish reconstruction', p 7).

131 In the three governorates, about half the cultivable land is privately owned, the other half was distributed by the state under the 1975 land reform for the Kurdish region. Only a small proportion of this was on a rental basis from the state. However, in the latter part of the 1980s, government policy of privatisation in the agricultural sector created a much larger number of lessees, many of whom were large landowners, or absentee landowners. Large estates are concentrated in the southern plains of Kurdistan, where the main crop is wheat, similar to adjacent areas of Mosul and Kirkuk governorates. This area constitutes the 'breadbasket' of Iraq. In Dohuk governorate in 1997 it was estimated that 85 percent of land was farmed on a large-scale commercial basis.

132 Leezenberg (1997), p 63–4.
133 Keen (1993), p 60.
134 *Ibid.*, p 38.
135 Silva-Barbeau *et al* (1994), p 74.
136 Netherlands Kurdistan Society (1996), p 27.
137 Majid (forthcoming).
138 UN Department of Humanitarian Affairs, Mine Clearance and Policy Unit, 'Demining Country Report: Iraq. Update', 30 April 1996.
139 *Ibid.*; Middle East Watch (1992).
140 *Gulf Newsletter*, October/November 1993, no. 8, 'Refugees and Displaced People', p 6.
141 US Department of State (1995), p 1090.
142 For example, the PKK allegedly kidnapped four people from the village of Gunda Jour in August 1997, and in October Iraqi Kurds reported 14 civilians killed and nine others wounded in PKK attacks on the villages of Korka, Chema, Dizo and Selki. Seven Assyrian civilians reportedly were ambushed and killed near the village of Mangeesh on 13 December (US State Department [1998ii] Section IG).
143 The first figure is from Ward and Rimmer (1995), p 23, Table 4; the second from UN DHA/IRCU Statistics, January 1995.
144 Majid (forthcoming).
145 Ward and Rimmer (*op. cit.*) used a measure of absolute poverty and a relative poverty line set at two-thirds of mean household expenditure.
146 Ward and Rimmer (1995), pp 23–4, 30.
147 The large movements of population during early 1991, and the shifting pattern of control between the Iraqi authorities and the KF between April and September 1991, had prevented the full restoration of the ration system. Some people may also have feared to register with the Iraqi authorities. A sample survey in the eastern part of Dohuk governorate in August 1991 suggested that only 62 percent of the sample were in receipt of government rations. The majority of non-recipients said they could not get rations because they were not registered.
148 Ward and Rimmer (1995), p 4.
149 *Ibid.*, p 17.
150 Silva-Barbeau *et al* (1994), p 25.
151 Amin and Yildiz (1996), p 91.
152 *Gulf Newsletter*, June/July 1994, no. 10, 'Conflict in Iraqi Kurdistan', p 2.
153 *The Economist*, 10 August 1996, 'Kurdistan? Which One Do You Mean?'.
154 Al-Khafaji (1996), p 36.
155 ICRC, 25 September 1996, 'Update No. 3 on ICRC activities in Iraq'; 7 November 1996, 'ICRC aid to internally displaced people'. Both reports on ReliefWeb. The UN Secretary General reported a total of 100,000 people displaced in the north during 1996. United Nations Security Council (1997), p 11, para. 34.
156 US Department of State (1998ii), Section 2 D.

157 United Nations Security Council (1997), p 11, para. 34; Office of the UN Humanitarian Coordinator for Iraq, 'Implementation of Security Council Resolution 986 (1995) and the Memorandum of Understanding: Chronology', 3 November 1997.

158 Van Bruinessen (1994), p 30.

159 *Kurdistan Observer* (Washington Kurdish Institute website, http://www.clark.net/kurd/), 22 January 1998, Kamran Karadaghi, 'Refugees: The Kurds Are Also to Blame', translated from Arabic.

160 Uday Hussein was said to be one of his major partners.

161 Van Bruinessen (1994), p 29; Ward and Rimmer (1995), p 20.

162 Fighting in April 1997 between the PUK and IMIK was alleged to have been caused by IMIK's refusal to link Halabja to the Sulaymaniya Governorate's PUK administration. BBC Summary of World Broadcasts, 1 May 1997, 'Iran Said to be "Apprehensive" About Egyptian Role in Kurdish Mediation Efforts', quoting *Al-Hayat*, London, 29 April 1997.

163 Channel 4 Television, 'Despatches Special: Saddam's Secret Timebomb', 23 February 1998 (Roberts and Wykeham Films).

PART II
OVERVIEW

SANCTIONS, POLITICAL POWER AND SOCIAL CHANGE

The period of isolation since 1991 may have 'contained' Iraq's territorial ambitions, but has not prevented economic and social changes occurring within its boundaries. The state has not collapsed, though it retrenched in terms of geographical and economic control. In the north, its place was taken by non-state forces – the contending Kurdish political parties. Nonetheless, the regime continued, along with Turkey and Iran, to influence events there. Since 1996 this influence has increased in both economic and political terms.

Holding on to power

Iraq as a nation has historically had difficulty in establishing a form of identity acceptable to its disparate cultural, religious and ethnic groups. Under Ba'thism, and particularly since Saddam Hussein became president, various sorts of 'glue' have been applied. The state has enforced a measure of cohesion by coercion, but this has always gone along with clientelism, using favours to bind those with real or imagined primordial ties[1] to the leadership group. Large oil revenues helped to effect a redistribution of resources, creating groups which became allies of the state.[2] Finally, finding, or creating, external enemies has promoted the sense of an embattled nation which needs the loyalty of its citizens to survive.

The impact of sanctions in the post-Gulf War period on these structures has been complex. The embargo has intensified competition for scarce resources and thereby probably sharpened pre-existing social tensions. The leadership has been able to play on these rivalries and yet convey the sense that Iraq is standing 'against the world'. Pan-Arabist sentiments have been replaced by a token Islamic rhetoric, but the appeal to national honour and endurance – while laying the blame for the misery of the post-Gulf-War era on the international community – still has resonance in a society where open debate on the issues is not possible. In consequence, the political perspectives which made many South Africans support the imposition of an international embargo, even if it resulted in hardship, do not seem to have taken root in Iraq. The harsh and punitive tone of many US pronouncements may in this respect have played into the Iraqi leadership's hands.[3]

Many of the regime's opponents thought it possible that the war and the economic collapse caused by sanctions would undermine the apparently precarious foundations of Saddam Hussein's power. But the tenacity of the regime, and hardship experienced by much of the population since 1991, blunted that hope.

The economic embargo undermined the earnings and status of the stratum of salaried state employees and professionals which had been the main beneficiary of the oil boom. Despite the development of the private sector in the late 1980s, prosperity was largely in the gift of the state. Economic sanctions have undoubtedly weakened the state's ability to use largesse, well-paid employment and social services to achieve popular acquiescence. Since 1990, however, the rationing system has given the Government a new form of leverage, perpetuating, at a lower economic level, people's dependence on the state for their basic livelihood.

Analysts have noted the heavy dependence of the Iraqi economy on trade and consumption.[4] Before 1990, oil exports financed both investment and high levels of consumption in the domestic sector. With oil exports drastically reduced and domestic investment curbed, wealth and savings have been used almost exclusively to finance consumption, whether the continued conspicuous consumption of the *nomenklatura* or the use of savings to meet basic needs.

Although the state controls distribution of basic necessities for the population, the 1990s have seen the development of new forms of economic activity under the conditions of embargo.[5] In government-controlled areas a number of 'private' enterprises have been set up by members of the leadership circle, taking advantage of state power to control lucrative sectors such as transportation of goods and monetary exchange. Acting sometimes in collaboration and sometimes in rivalry with these companies are established merchants, entrepreneurs and contractors upon whom the regime has had to depend for external trade (legal and illegal) and reconstruction activities.

The leadership has clearly feared at times that the 'profiteering' in which its own members are so deeply involved might get out of hand and slip from its grasp. Rivalries also develop between different entrepreneurs within, or protected by, the ruling family:

> Il apparaît clairement, que même lorsque les plus hautes sphères de l'État sont impliquées dans la création de structures parallèles, la loyauté de ses serviteurs laisse souvent à désirer. De manière désorganisée et souvent antagonique, chaque clan essaie de tirer son épingle du jeu et d'amasser de l'argent le plus rapidement possible. La défection, l'opportunisme et les trahisons sont le lot commun de telles structures.[6]

In the three northern governorates, where the structure of state control has been drastically weakened, the scale of 'parallel' economy relative to any other form of economic activity, became much more extensive. It was based on regional trade and controlled by a small number of individuals either with party patronage or a strong tribal or military base.

Retribalising society?

Since 1991, some external observers have spoken of the 'retribalising' of politics in Iraq. This description could be misleading in two respects: first, it implies that primordial ties as part of the mechanism of politics had previously played no part in political life, which was far from the case. Second, it suggests a return to relationships which had existed many years ago, before the formation of the state. Some commentators describing trends in Iraq since 1990 have used the term 'neo-tribalism'.[7] This indicates rather that tribal and family ties have re-emerged in new political forms. By definition, such ties need to be sufficiently fluid if they are to be effective – in the past too they were constantly shifting for new purposes.

The creation of bureaucracies, armies and militias since Iraq became a state has changed the way these allegiances operate. In Kurdish-controlled areas, the trappings of the Ba'thist state have been withdrawn, but the structure of society had been significantly changed by the impact of its rule. Thus the allegiances described as 'tribal' or primordial may today serve quite different purposes and bring together groups of people who in the past would not have worked together.

The absence of effective state power since 1991, combined with internal conflict, has probably increased the overlap between ties of family and tribe with those of party or militia. Economic dependence on the state has been transferred to other economic actors: essentially political parties and, to a lesser extent, aid organisations. The majority of people in the region had become used to dependence on the state before the Gulf War. In the absence of a viable economy, people have turned to whatever sources of patronage are available.

The promotion in recent years of certain 'tribal' leaders by the Iraqi Government is another example of the constantly changing use of such allegiances. Local shaikhs pledge loyalty and 'deliver' their people in exchange for weapons, services or land all the more important in the straitened circumstances of the 1990s. However, those who hold this power are not necessarily the 'traditional' leaders of their communities. Many of the previous occupants of these positions are either dead or in exile. They are appointees of central government – like many of the shaikhs under the British mandate – but their local power is still exercised in the 'old ways' of patronage and distribution of largesse.

The perceptions of ethnic and religious difference may also have been altered by the experience of the past decade. Under Ba'thist rule, the Iraqi Shi'a have often been equated by the state with their Iranian co-religionists, from the time of the 'Persian' deportations of the 1970s onwards. Since the Iran-Iraq War began they have been perceived not simply as a dissident religious group, but as allies of a rival state. This barrier of distrust has ironically been echoed in the West since the Gulf War.

In fact most observers consider that the majority of Iraqi Shi'a do not identify closely with Iran. A part of the Shi'i elite has always had connections with Iran and Lebanon, both by their origins and family ties among ulamas' families. But for most people, the reaction to pro-Iranian slogans during the uprisings suggests considerable unease with this political orientation. However, years of economic deprivation – which had blocked the individual mobility which was possible in the past – and the overt hostility shown by regime to Shi'i religious belief, may have altered thinking within this community, especially among young people growing up today.

Historically speaking, the Kurdish movement was based on ties which are both narrower and wider than the boundaries of Iraq. The last few years have accentuated the narrow and divisive allegiances within Iraq, reinforced by the perennial search for external allies. Van Bruinessen argues that these intra-Kurdish divisions are not simply remnants (*témoins*) of a past which is destined to disappear if the nationalist movement continues its development. The narrower identities of regional, linguistic, religious communities have to some extent been reinforced by the same factors – war, insecurity and persecution – which have stimulated the sense of national identity.[8] Certainly recent developments in Iraqi Kurdistan fit this pattern. The events of 1991 raised the international profile of Kurds in Iraq, and created a consciousness of Kurdish identity which reflected back to broad sections of the population. Yet the political and economic dynamics of the post-war 'enclave' exposed starkly the fissures in the society and its political organisations.

The removal of Iraqi government control has also removed a major actor in the struggle for the allegiance of 'tribal' and other rural groups and leaders. Arguably this has been an element in sharpening the competition between the two main Kurdish parties. Since 1991, the historical differences in the composition and political dynamics of the KDP and PUK have faded. In both parties, the importance of gaining the allegiance of tribal groups to swell the ranks of fighters, and the integration of *jash* forces has weakened their civilian structures. In so doing, the parties manipulated a variety of loyalties – of kin, tribe and region. Ideological considerations are of little importance.

As Kutschera notes, once the internal conflict took hold, Masud Barzani and Jalal Talabani 'ne se comportent plus en chefs de parti mais en chefs de guerre'.[9] It is hard to see how, in the near future, this rivalry will be diminished because the present structures of power and influence encourage conflict, not peace. Whether in direct control or *in absentia*, the current Iraqi leadership has every interest in exploiting these rifts, and the same can be said for the Governments of Turkey and Iran.

Looking to the future

It is unclear how far trends towards new sources of power and influence will outlast this particular phase of Iraq's history. However, anyone returning to Iraq after an absence of 10 years or more would sense considerable change, very little if any of it for the better. Although some of the trends towards impoverishment and malnutrition evident under the economic embargo will probably be reversed once it is lifted – at what speed depends on inflows of funds and what priorities the Government chooses – it seems likely that the era of isolation since 1990 will result in longer-term changes in Iraqi society.

Some of the social and economic effects of the Iran-Iraq War and of the years of embargo can be expected to persist. Fundamentally, the fault-lines in Iraqi society remain, and the encouragement of primordial loyalties – to family, clan, religion and ethnic group – during the 1990s will probably leave their mark on social and political relations.

A further change with possible political ramifications is the shrinkage of the salaried middle class dependent on state employment. The end of the embargo, and perhaps a new political climate, might attract some of the professional class to return, but this would depend on how secure their future appeared to be. Even if the current regime remains in power, it is not clear whether the economic structures which maintained state employment at such a high level in the 1980s would be reinstated. In the meantime, the accumulated educational deficit and changes in attitudes to education may have long-term effects on the level of skills and ambition among the younger generation. On the positive side, the initiative and inventiveness shown by many individuals in surviving the years of economic crisis could, given a less authoritarian regime, make a contribution to a less dependent society.

A major problem which will face Iraq, whatever government is in power when sanctions are lifted, is the burden of external debts created by economic mismanagement and the priority given to military expenditure during the 1980s. Estimates of Iraq's external debt by 1998 run at $60–80 billion.[10] To this will probably be added the burden of war compensation payments, currently set at 30 percent of all Iraq's oil revenues, with the bill for reparations running to more than $2 billion. If the decline in oil prices which occurred in 1997/8 persists, these payments will prove all the more onerous.

Unless a new government can persuade the international community to modify reparations or restructure Iraq's external debt, it will face very great pressures from the population's understandable impatience to see a reasonable standard of living restored. A German business association spokesman remarked in 1995 that Iraq 'runs the risk of having a terrible awakening when the embargo is lifted and there are expectations in the population that can't immediately be fulfilled'.[11]

Questions arise as to how the remaining oil revenues would be used. Clearly large sums would need to be spent on rehabilitating the infrastructure and services. Even if there was no return to military spending on the scale of the 1980s, it might seem easier, or politically expedient – if the government was not very stable – to respond by raising the levels of imports and the availability of a wide variety of consumer goods while neglecting, as in the past, the creation of a more solid and diversified economic base. A number of Iraqi economists have noted the dangers which continued reliance on oil revenues could therefore pose in the long term.

There are considerable dangers that the culture of the black economy and the scale of corruption generated by scarcity could survive sanctions, and even a change of regime. Its persistence would challenge any government which attempted to create a more open or pluralistic model of politics or a more diversified economy.

NOTES ON PART II OVERVIEW

1   What Clifford Geertz (1973) called 'assumed blood ties' (p 261).
2   Bozarslan (1997), p 17.
3   For a discussion of the political factors influencing the effectiveness of sanctions, see Dowty (1994), pp 193, 195.
4   During the 1970s and 1980s the oil boom led to the rapid growth of a stratum of professionals and public servants whose economic role was mainly as consumers, not producers. Hamit Bozarslan has described social developments in Iraq during the 1970s and 1980s as a process of 'embourgeoisement' – not to be confused with the creation of a bourgeoisie – emphasising their role as consumers, not producers (*op. cit.*, pp 153–4).
5   Kopp (1996), pp 435–7.
6   *Ibid.*, p 439.

7   McDowall (1997), p 385–6; Baram (1997).
8   Van Bruinessen (1994), p 12.
9   Kutschera (1997), p 132.
10   Shabibi (1997) estimated a figure of $80 billion owed to non-Arab creditors. Iraq gave its official estimate in 1991 as $42.1 billion, but Shabibi's figure takes into account interest payments due since that date, in addition to Iraq's current trade deficit (footnote 11, p 78).
11   Peter Jungen, Near and Middle East Association, quoted in *Jordan Times*, 9 August 1995.

PART III

Picking Up the Pieces? Humanitarian Aid Programmes in Iraq 1991–8

CHAPTER 7

The Aid Programme and its Constraints

The humanitarian crisis in northern Iraq in April and May 1991 had drama, pathos and media appeal. Its messy and protracted aftermath attracted less public attention and sympathy. The scale of humanitarian action masked for a time the political dilemmas which Iraq continued to pose for the international community. But those dilemmas returned to haunt the providers of humanitarian aid.

Terms such as 'complex emergency' have been coined to describe crises which combine internal conflict, population displacement, famine and/or failing economic and political structures. When it is impossible – and undesirable – to restore the situation to what it was before, these crises may also be prolonged. Continuing conflict prevents a new political or social order from emerging. Meanwhile, since life has to go on, people seize opportunities for survival, or for aggrandisement. Aid agencies may become embroiled in these struggles for power and survival. Such a crisis has unfolded in Iraq since 1991, with its particular combination of internecine conflict and repression by an authoritarian government which itself is under pressure from international sanctions and an ongoing confrontation with leading powers in the international community.

The aid effort had several phases. During the 1991 Gulf War, a number of aid agencies assisted third-country nationals fleeing to Jordan and Turkey. From April 1991, a large number of NGOs of all kinds arrived on the Turkish border to assist the refugees, and some moved into Iraq with the coalition forces of Operation Provide Comfort to provide assistance to those who returned. Some of these agencies worked directly with the US DART teams in Zakho,[1] while others worked with the various military contingents of Operation Provide Comfort or operated independently outside the safe haven area.

Most observers report that despite mutual suspicions, cooperation between the NGOs and the military was in practice quite good. The aid agencies more or less grudgingly accepted that for efficient logistics, there was much to be said for military involvement in a major crisis, although, as already noted, some of the agencies working in Turkey were critical of the military's management of the camps on the border. There were more general concerns that working closely with armed forces, particularly those of the US, would make NGOs appear tools of US policy, about which many agencies had reservations. Organisations which wanted to work throughout Iraq also feared that evidence of close association with coalition forces – for example, by working in the Zakho camps – would result in their exclusion from areas under government control.[2]

On 7 June 1991, overall responsibility for humanitarian relief operations in the allied security zone in northern Iraq was formally transferred from the Combined Task Force Provide Comfort to UNHCR. Security remained the responsibility of the allied forces until July. A residual military staff, the Military Coordination Commission (MCC), remained in Zakho after ground troops were withdrawn from the safe haven. The MCC was involved in the humanitarian effort to the extent that it cooperated with some NGOs working in Dohuk governorate within the security zone, particularly during the winter of 1991. Between 1992 and 1996 it was also the base for USAID's Office of Foreign Disaster Assistance (OFDA) (see Chapter 8).

The UN's Office of the Executive Delegate (OED), headed by Sadruddin Aga Khan and based in Geneva, had taken over coordination of humanitarian assistance to Iraq from the UN Disaster Relief Organisation (UNDRO). The OED's first tasks were to establish the UN Guards, to set up the consolidated appeal for all UN aid activities in Iraq and on its borders, and to establish a political coordination unit in Baghdad.[3] Money was a constant problem. Sadruddin pointed out that, in contrast to the billions poured in the Gulf War, little money had been donated to the UN's humanitarian appeals by late May and June, hindering its operations in Iraq.[4] 'People were being hired on the basis of pledges of funds because money had not yet come in from the appeal', one former OED official recalled.

The other key UN agencies operating in Iraq at that time were UNICEF and the World Food Programme (WFP). UNICEF focused on the refurbishment of water and sanitation systems throughout the country, provision of chemicals and spare parts for these systems, and basic health-care needs focused on children. WFP provided food for around 700,000 beneficiaries in the north, and in government-controlled areas to social institutions such as orphanages, hospital in-patients and to officially registered 'destitutes'. Other UN agencies – such as WHO, FAO and UNDP which, like UNICEF, had a presence in Iraq before the war – played a smaller role. They normally work on more development-oriented projects which have been largely untenable under sanctions, ruled out by the 'emergency' focus of the UN programme, or by lack of money.

Until December 1992 the International Organisation for Migration (IOM) played an important part in assisting with the movement of refugees and the repatriation of third-country nationals stranded in Iraq and surrounding countries by the war. Between 1994 and 1998, IOM provided transport for Iraqi refugees returning from Iran to Iraqi Kurdistan. The International Committee of the Red Cross (ICRC) ran medical, water and sanitation programmes until the end of 1991. From the end of 1993, it re-started its water and sanitation programme in government areas, began providing medical supplies to Iraqi hospitals in cooperation with the British Red Cross, and initiated programmes for the war disabled, both in government and Kurdish areas. Its protection and tracing work has continued throughout the period since the war, and recently it has been monitoring and assisting displaced people in the Kurdish-controlled region.[5] The International Federation of Red Cross and Red Crescent Societies (formerly the League of Red Cross and Red Crescent Societies) also worked in Iraq throughout the post-war period, intensifying its operations from 1994 onwards to provide medical supplies and distribute food to vulnerable groups.

Non-governmental international aid organisations working in Iraq have been of two basic types. First, the large 'professional' agencies which themselves are diverse in structure and goals, of which some are secular (for example Save the Children Fund and Oxfam) and have organisations in a number of countries; others are affiliated to church organisations (for example Christian Aid, Danchurchaid, the Catholic Fund for Overseas Development [CAFOD] and Catholic Relief Services). These agencies may also work under umbrella organisations such as the Middle East Council of Churches and the World Council of Churches, or in association with the Catholic organisation Caritas.

NGOs such as Médecins sans Frontières (MSF) and the International Rescue Committee specialise in emergency work. Many of the major development agencies have become increasingly drawn into emergency work, partly because the high-profile emergencies of the late 1980s and 1990s have been difficult to ignore, and partly because of the increasingly fierce competition for the funds which are available from both donors and the public for such emergencies. Some large agencies have consequently developed specialisms in emergency logistics, water and sanitation, or healthcare.

The agencies represented in Iraq in the early 1990s varied greatly in size and organisational sophistication, and differed widely in outlook. One European strand of 'activist' emergency aid, which was willing to disregard the constraints of borders and government control, was exemplified by MSF, Médecins du Monde, France Liberté, and Medico International. Other 'emergency specialists' had a more pragmatic and technical approach.

The second category of organisations were those established in direct response to the Iraq crisis by groups of people in a number of countries who wanted to help the Iraqi population as a whole, or to assist particular groups, mainly but not exclusively the Kurds. Iraqis living abroad – in the US, UK, Europe and in the Middle East region, including Iran – also became involved in the relief effort, as did Islamic and other charities based in the Middle East. When the crisis became prolonged, some of them became involved in rehabilitation in Iraqi Kurdistan, and with Iraqi refugee communities, mainly in Iran.

Relations between the UN and this diverse group of NGOs were far from easy. UNHCR's failure to engage effectively in the early months of the crisis, and poor coordination between the major UN agencies gave the UN a poor reputation among NGOs. However, criticisms have been levelled at NGOs themselves for their unwillingness to cooperate with the UN, while expecting it to provide resources. The very marked lack of coordination between NGOs during the emergency period hampered cooperation with the UN, and sometimes caused problems in NGOs' relations with the Governments of Turkey, Iran and Iraq.[6]

After the initial emergency of April and May 1991, NGOs had to decide whether to continue working only in the north, to extend their programmes to the whole of Iraq, where there was a health, nutrition, water and sanitation crisis, or to withdraw altogether. While aid agencies differ in size, style, philosophy and affiliations, most work within certain parameters. They have to assess the needs of the population and their own capacity to respond. They have to balance the scale and acuteness of need in one region of the world with that in another. They have to gain access to those in need, and in most cases cooperate to some extent with local organisations or the Government. They are all subject to similar constraints: for example, the availability of funding, and conditions of reasonable safety for their international and local staff.

Before the war, Iraq was a relatively wealthy country and its authoritarian regime did not welcome aid organisations, except those UN bodies which worked directly with the Government. Consequently the international NGO community had little or no knowledge of the country. Exceptions were the Iraqi organisations, though many of their members had been outside the country for a number of years.

For the major NGOs, the refugee crisis and the decision of the main Western powers to intervene created strong pressures to join the relief effort in northern Iraq. In the UK, for example, some of the main aid agencies would have preferred to maintain their focus on Africa, where they judged the needs to be much greater. However, they faced strong official pressure to participate in Operation Provide Comfort and the effects of high-profile public fund-raising efforts on behalf of the Kurds.[7]

When the coalition forces withdrew without a political settlement in the region, the role of aid agencies was presented as a crucial element in the 'protection of the Kurds'. In fact, a number of the NGOs which had worked in Turkey and the safe haven chose not to stay on beyond the early summer of 1991, thereby partially frustrating the hope entertained in London and Washington that a large-scale NGO presence would strengthen this protection.[8] Of the NGOs which remained, several began exploring the possibilities of extending their work to areas outside the security zone in Arbil and Sulaymaniya governorates, where large numbers of refugees were still returning and needs were arguably greater than in Dohuk governorate, where most help had been given.

The main problem facing agencies which contemplated working throughout Iraq was to assess the extent of need and the ability of NGOs to fulfil it. It was quickly evident that the scale of infrastructural damage and the needs in health and nutrition in Iraq were far beyond NGO capacities. In the summer of 1991, the situation was also shifting constantly, so that it was difficult to decide which sectors to concentrate on. A further deterrent was that by the end of the summer the UN and NGOs found their work hampered by government delays in issuing visas and internal travel permits which were required in order to move outside Baghdad. Balanced against this was the pressure to use the large amounts of money which had been donated by the public in many countries during the emergency. It was also regarded as important to retain the capacity to respond if a further emergency situation developed.

PREPARING FOR WINTER

During 1991 the UN and NGOs concentrated primarily on the repatriation of refugees in the north. From July onwards, UN humanitarian agencies, the UN Guards contingent and NGOs inherited from Operation Provide Comfort the function of delivering material assistance in northern Iraq. Their presence was also supposed to help in providing a measure of protection to the population.

During July and October, a major difficulty for the UN was the uncertain political situation in the northern governorates. In June and July there was still some optimism that the autonomy talks would result in a political settlement. Meanwhile, despite the patchwork of authority in the region, UNCHR workers described cooperation with local Iraqi officials in areas under government control as generally good. In some places, these officials worked alongside KF representatives and for a time there were even joint KF/government patrols in the main cities.

UNHCR's strategy was based on the assumption that an agreement between the Government and KF would allow it to withdraw within a few months. Its officials therefore stressed the importance of linking NGO activities with those of government agencies, arguing that the only possible long-term structures were those built on the government infrastructure. They also encouraged links between areas controlled by the Government and those regions close to the Iranian and Turkish borders controlled by the KF. They wanted to see government services and the state food rationing system re-established in Kurdish-controlled areas.[9]

The belief within the UN that there would be a political settlement seems to have lasted until the end of August.[10] Consequently, although planning for the winter had been initiated in July, no action was taken until late August. According to one staff member, the organisation 'wasted two months waiting for an agreement' between the Kurdish leadership and the Government.[11]

During the summer, a significant number of returnees had gone to the sites of villages destroyed before the Gulf War (during the Anfal or earlier) rather than returning to the *mujamma'at* or the towns from which they had fled in March and April 1991 where, for the most part, Iraqi troops were still present. With winter approaching, many people in these villages had no proper shelter. The continuing refusal of the Baghdad Government to allow UNHCR to establish a sub-office in Kirkuk meant that Kirkuki refugees remained displaced in the north and were dependent on humanitarian aid organisations for food and shelter. In September, UNHCR estimated a still displaced 'floating population' in the three governorates of about 640,000.[12]

Serious outbreaks of fighting in September and October caused people to flee back towards the safety of the mountains. These new population movements made planning the logistics requirements of the shelter programme and food distribution all the more difficult. UNHCR wanted to use food distribution as part of a strategy to control the movement of people, arguing that timing was crucial so as not to encourage people to stay in the mountains.

A dispute reportedly broke out with some of the NGOs operating in the north over UNHCR's placement of food distribution points in the lowlands, discouraging the refugees from fleeing into the mountains in response to renewed violence. While this may have had the advantage of concentrating people in accessible areas where they could be provided with shelter and food and which had less harsh winter weather, the

NGOs argued that the priority should be placed on rebuilding homes in the destroyed villages (mainly in the mountains) where the Kurds would be better protected from Iraqi attacks.[13] Eventually, the security situation dictated that deliveries of shelter materials had to be made to the mountain regions as a priority.[14]

UNHCR's initial idea had been to give cash grants for shelter – which would have avoided its involvement in the major logistical exercise of importing shelter materials – but this was rejected by NGOs and discarded as impractical.[15] Once it was decided that UNHCR should import shelter materials, these were not cleared through the Sanctions Committee until the third week in September. Movement of stores for the programme only began on 25 September, and distribution of materials on 15 October. During October, movement of materials was disrupted in Sulaymaniya governorate by fighting, while Turkish air strikes halted work in some villages near the Iraq-Turkish border.

By the end of October, UNHCR acknowledged that it would need to maintain the programme throughout the winter. The numbers requiring shelter had risen from an initial estimate of 40,000 to 62,000 families (372,000 people). During November, fighting caused a further 200,000 people to move back towards the mountains. Thousands of people were still living in tents, particularly in the Said Sadiq area (6800 families). These were mainly refugees from Kirkuk and others displaced from the Kifri, Kalar and Chamchamal areas by government shelling in September and October. Kurdish protests led UNHCR to move some of the tent-dwellers into abandoned public buildings, mainly in Sulaymaniya.

UNHCR did the general planning and organisation for the so-called 'winterisation' programme, but most of the practical work was done by NGOs. In late 1991, UNHCR had agreements with over 20 international NGOs working in the north, with an emphasis on health and shelter projects. Essentially UNHCR worked with whatever agencies were in place and appeared to have the capacity to do the work. Because there was a shortage of international NGOs, particularly in Sulaymaniya governorate, where the numbers of displaced were greatest, UNHCR began working through newly-established Kurdish NGOs – such as the Kurdish Reconstruction Organisation (KRO), the Kurdish Shelter and Reconstruction Organisation (KSRO), the Kurdish Relief Association (KRA) and KURDS – which also cooperated with international NGOs involved in the shelter programme.[16]

On 23 October, the Iraqi Government began withdrawing its forces from the parts of the three northern governorates which it still controlled. The ensuing economic blockade caused prices for basic commodities to rise. Shortages increased the need for food and fuel to be imported via Turkey. UNHCR's original plans had assumed that government rations would be available for much of the population. The internal blockade also meant that fuel, which had not been included in UNCHR's distribution plan for the displaced because it had previously been very cheap, 'went up six to eight times', leaving people short of heating fuel during a very cold winter.[17] In January and February 1992 a strike by Turkish lorry drivers further interrupted the flow of supplies.[18]

In mid-January the KF announced its formal withdrawal from the autonomy negotiations, while no progress had been made in ending the Iraqi blockade. By February, UNHCR estimated that only about 25 percent of fuel supplies and 40 percent of government rations were reaching the Kurdish-controlled region. According to WFP, the price of food had doubled. As a result, the situation during the winter became increasingly difficult for people not covered by UNHCR/WFP food distributions – only 700,000–750,000 from a population of 3.2–3.5 million were receiving WFP food.

This winter crisis emphasised the difficulties of operating in such politically uncertain conditions, and the weaknesses of UNHCR in responding to a situation which required high levels of flexibility. A major humanitarian disaster was, in the judgement of some observers, only narrowly avoided. In March 1992, UNHCR estimated there were still 400,000–500,000 persons internally displaced in the north.[19] At this stage, rehabilitation of villages consisted only of rudimentary shelters or houses which were mostly temporary structures.

NGOs working with UNHCR criticised the slow delivery and high cost of the original shelter materials (particularly the prefabricated housing units), slow decision-making at UNHCR's Baghdad headquarters and poor liaison with the field. A report on UNHCR's role in Iraq in 1991/2 criticised the lack of clear chains of authority between UN agencies and those with coordinating roles, and sharp differences of perspective between head offices and field staff. It noted particularly the lack of clarity between the tasks of the UN humanitarian coordinator in Baghdad and of UNHCR as 'lead agency'.[20]

UNHCR was slow to respond for political as well as organisational reasons. The UN humanitarian operation as a whole was hampered by the tendency to look over its shoulder to the Government of Iraq, under whose aegis it was operating. NGOs particularly resented demands from UNHCR that they hand over the names of their local staff for submission to the Iraqi Ministry of Foreign Affairs.

1992: A TEST OF WILLS

The *de facto* separation of Iraqi Kurdistan from the rest of Iraq after October/November 1991, and the imposition of the internal embargo, altered the prospects for the aid programme. The Iraqi Government had turned the whole population of the three northern governments into a potential 'caseload' for the UN. The short-term emergency of 1991 was now turning into a longer-term problem of chronic need.

In December 1991, UN organisations in Iraq had expressed concern to the Government at its embargo on the north, 'noting that United Nations humanitarian agencies are not in a position to replace essential services and assure the provision of goods denied to the Kurdish population at large'.[21] The Government ignored these representations, and in early 1992, UN officials in Baghdad were still referring euphemistically to the embargo by the Government's term – 'internal supply restrictions'.[22]

In February, the UN was reportedly still trying to 'kickstart' the government rationing system in the north, using UNHCR/WFP supplies to supplement the diminishing portion of the ration still being supplied by the Government. This strategy was undermined by the continuing decline in the volume of government rations reaching the north – to less than 10 percent of pre-embargo amount by the beginning of 1993.

To survive the harsh winters, the Kurdish-controlled areas were thereafter heavily dependent on the UN and other donors bringing in food and fuel via Turkey. If UN humanitarian organisations brought materials destined for the north via Baghdad, they came under pressure from the Government to allocate a percentage to government-controlled areas, even when donors had earmarked the goods for the north. This increased the tendency to use the Turkish route, thereby making the aid programme more dependent on Turkish goodwill.

On the other hand, although the three northern governorates were no longer under government control, all UN humanitarian operations in Iraq, including those in Iraqi Kurdistan, continued to be run from Baghdad. All UN staff had to get visas from Baghdad and enter and leave Iraqi Kurdistan via government areas. These contradictory arrangements were a recipe for confusion which was compounded during 1992 by changes to the UN bodies responsible for humanitarian assistance in Iraq.

By the end of January 1992, UNHCR had already publicised its intention to wind up its emergency programme in northern Iraq by April. The aim was to have the more development-oriented UN agencies such as UNDP, UNICEF and FAO begin rehabilitation work in the north after UNHCR phased out its operation. A potential difficulty was that agencies like UNICEF and UNDP generally work closely with governments, and it was not clear what implications this would have for rehabilitation work in northern Iraq, now effectively outside government control.

The UN Executive Delegate, Sadruddin, who had played a key role after his UN Inter-agency Mission in July 1991 in focusing Security Council concern on humanitarian issues and pushing for a limited oil sale, had announced his resignation as Executive Delegate at beginning of December 1991. His last action, in November 1991, was to negotiate a six-month renewal of the Memorandum of Understanding (MoU) first signed in April 1991.[23]

The Office of the Executive Delegate subsequently handed over its responsibilities to the newly-established UN Department of Humanitarian Affairs (DHA) headed by Under Secretary General Jan Eliasson, who began work on 1 April as Emergency Relief Coordinator. The aim of the new body was to coordinate the UN agencies' response to humanitarian emergencies round the world (see below). International NGOs pressed for an early decision on which UN agencies would work in northern Iraq once UNCHR's relief programme was phased out.

However, decision-making was complicated by the transfer of political liaison and coordination from the Office of the Executive Delegate to the DHA's Special Unit for Iraq in Geneva and the Inter-Agency Relief Coordination Unit (IRCU) in Baghdad. UNICEF was reluctant to take over all the sectors previously overseen by UNHCR – especially food distribution and shelter – in addition to water, sanitation and health, the sectors in which UNICEF had worked thus far.[24] By May, UNHCR was winding up its sub-agreements with NGOs and handing over health, water and sanitation projects in the north to UNICEF. Eventually it was decided that procurement, transportation, storage and monitoring of fuel, as well as food distribution on behalf of WFP, were to be undertaken by Care International/Care Australia.

The difficulties over renewing the MoU, which expired in June 1992, added to the confusion. In the interim, the UN asserted that the terms of the previous MoU remained in force, but during the summer of 1992, most of the aid programme ground to a halt. The handover of functions to UNICEF was further delayed by the Iraqi refusal to grant visas and travel permits to new UNICEF and NGO staff recruited for the north. The work of UNICEF and WFP was also restricted by the halving of Iraqi fuel supplies delivered to the UN in the north during the period up to October 1991. Further disruption was created when traffic into the north from

Turkey was halted when the PKK forced the closure of the border in July and August.

The Iraqi Government also appeared set on creating security problems for NGO and UN personnel. In early March 1992 the first bomb explosions occurred in northern Iraq, and a series of attacks culminated in the death of a UN Guard in Dohuk on 22 July. Some harassment of UN personnel and damage to vehicles was reported in Baghdad in the summer of 1992. There were no claims of responsibility, but Iraqi agents were suspected. During this period Iraqi forces frequently shelled areas of Iraqi Kurdistan adjacent to the *de facto* border.[25]

Renewing the Memorandum of Understanding

Articles 3–6 of Resolution 688 had called for humanitarian assistance to the Iraqi population. This was the other 'leg' of the resolution and was the first time that the UN had insisted that a state allow international agencies to deliver humanitarian aid. In 1991, the immediate priority was the repatriation of refugees, but by the end of the year the focus had turned to more general assistance to vulnerable groups in the Iraqi population. In reality, access to these groups had been limited.

A US Congressional Committee was told in November 1991 that Iraq had refused to allow the UN to set up humanitarian centres in Kirkuk and Nasariya, in the former case preventing many refugees returning home. '[Iraq] bases its refusal on a deliberate misinterpretation of the MoU it signed with the UN in April which provides for both the Iraqis and the UN to agree on locations for UN humanitarian centers. The Iraqis now claim the unilateral right to designate the location of these centers...'[26]

As of early 1992 therefore, the UN had been unable to establish sub-offices outside Baghdad or to prevent the Government imposing an internal embargo on northern Iraq. Its lack of access to the southern marshes and the circumscribed role of UN Guards attested to Iraq's evident disregard of Resolution 688 and its determination to impose its own priorities. The renegotiation of the MoU was a striking example of how humanitarian concerns became entangled, to their detriment, with other strands of international policy on Iraq, and how the Iraqi Government played one issue against another.

The Government's evident suspicion of the UN and its aid programme meant that it would try to limit as far as possible the UN's freedom of manoeuvre. In Baghdad's view, 'political considerations and interests were the prime motivation for the aid that was given, articulated and implemented by the international community'. A Foreign Ministry official outlined Iraq's objections. The aid provided under Operation Provide Comfort had entered across the Turkish border without Iraqi government consent; this programme had sought out minority populations in revolt against Baghdad, but had not addressed serious needs elsewhere in the country; it came from the same United Nations that had blessed the war and was seeking concessions from the Iraqi Government on a range of issues.[27]

In the view of some UN officials, UNHCR's withdrawal may have sent a signal to the Iraqi Government that the emergency was over and the situation had 'normalised'. In February 1992 a UNHCR official noted that the initial *quid pro quo* that allowed the humanitarian wing of the UN to provide a convenient substitute for what was really intended to be a 'peace-keeping' or 'human rights' undertaking under Resolution 688 was rapidly fading away.

Attempts by the UN to prepare a new plan of action in advance of the MoU negotiations were squeezed from different directions. The Iraqi Government objected to proposals for reconstruction and medium-term development which it saw as too focused on the Kurdish-controlled north. But to gain approval from the hardline Security Council members who wanted to keep up the pressure on Iraq, plans had to avoid putting too much emphasis on reconstructing Iraq's infrastructure, and were instead confined to a relief focus, with only small-scale rural reconstruction and development (which mostly applied to the north).

The initial discussions of the DHA's coordinator, Jan Eliasson, in New York with the Iraqi Ambassador to the UN, Abdul Amir Al-Anbari, had already indicated likely points of disagreement. Iraq claimed that the country only required normal assistance activities and it saw no need for the extension of the MoU. The UN did not, in the Iraqi view, need any permanent presence outside Baghdad, nor any UN Guards.[28] The UN pointed to the internal embargo on the north as evidence that the situation was far from normal.

Attempts to get these negotiations started coincided with the crisis in July 1992 over the barring of UN weapons inspectors from the Ministry of Agriculture. The issues seem to have become further entangled because the UN Secretary General Boutros Boutros-Ghali had asked the head of UNSCOM, Rolf Ekeus, to raise the question of the MoU with Iraqi Deputy Prime Minister Tariq Aziz while Ekeus was still in the midst of the dispute over the inspectors. In a letter to Tariq Aziz of 4 August, the Secretary General expressed his disappointment at the Iraqi Government's response on the MoU: 'I regret the difficult circumstances under which the meeting took place may have adversely affected the possibility of any consideration of our detailed proposals in this regard'.[29]

By the time Eliasson finally arrived in Baghdad for talks about the MoU on 17 August, leading coalition members were already publicly discussing the imposition of a no-fly zone in southern Iraq, finally implemented on 26 August. In this round of negotiations, Eliasson found that Iraqi officials were initially very negative towards international NGOs operating in Iraq, but by the end of the discussions the main stumbling-blocks were the continued presence of the UN Guards and UN access to the south. Boutros-Ghali, in a letter to the Security Council on 24 August, said that Tariq Aziz 'explicitly linked the implications of these declarations [of the no-fly zone] to the continued presence of the Inter-Agency Humanitarian Programme in the south of the country and the Government's refusal to permit the maintenance of sub-offices under a renewed MoU'.[30] Tariq Aziz then 'strongly recommended' that UN agencies leave the south because of the impending events there. All remaining international staff were 'temporarily' withdrawn from locations outside Baghdad immediately after Eliasson's departure.

Although the UN had retained a presence in Amara, Basra and Mosul until August 1992, DHA officials said that problems of access – including problems with visas and travel permits for UN and NGO staff – had begun well before that date. Increasingly UN staff were required to be accompanied by government officials on trips outside Baghdad, and from July UNICEF and WFP staff in southern Iraq came under severe pressure from government officials to leave their duty stations.[31]

The UN Secretary General was active in pursuing the MoU renewal, but Security Council support was limited to two statements, only one of which directly related to the MoU. On 17 July the Security Council 'deeply deplored' the murder of a UN

Guard in Dohuk, and on 2 September it issued a presidential statement expressing 'deep concern' at Iraq's failure to renew the MoU. It urged Iraq 'in the strongest possible terms' to cooperate with the UN, affirming the need for access to vulnerable groups in all parts of the country and for UN field offices with UN Guards to protect them. It was 'disturbed' at Iraq's failure to provide adequate security for UN and NGO personnel: '… the Council considers unrestricted access throughout the country and the assurance of adequate security measures as essential prerequisites for the effective implementation of the programme'.[32]

By the end of September, the Iraqi Government was trying to use the MoU as a bargaining chip to head off Security Council plans to implement Resolution 778, re-freezing Iraqi assets. Foreign Minister Mohammed al-Sahaf threatened that Iraq would not cooperate over the UN's winter plans for aid to the north if the resolution was passed.[33] At a meeting between Iraqi Foreign Minister Muhammad al-Sahhaf and Eliasson at the end of September, the issues were whittled down to the question of field offices, on which the Government offered simply that it would 'make office space and communications links' available to UN staff and the UN Guards, whom the Government insisted should only operate in the north.

After further negotiations in New York and Baghdad – the last round bringing in UNICEF's Director, James P. Grant – a new MoU was finally signed on 22 October, to last until 31 March 1993. Diplomats described the outcome as satisfying neither the UN nor the Iraqi Government.[34] At the time Boutros-Ghali told Security Council members, 'The agreement does not fully meet our aspirations, however I believe that under the circumstances and given the need to urgently provide humanitarian assistance to the affected population in the north as well as in the south, it is necessary to proceed to sign and implement it without any further delay'.[35]

The new agreement placed stronger emphasis on 'cooperation' with the Iraqi authorities. The UN had demanded 500 UN Guards stationed throughout the country as before, but the Iraqis had wanted only 150, all stationed in the north. The final figure was 300 Guards, stationed only in the Kurdish-controlled north, with the exception of a handful of Guards at UN headquarters in Baghdad. According to one UN source, the Western powers, having decided on the no-fly zone in the south, were willing not to insist on the Guards being retained there.[36]

On the issue of the UN's access to all parts of the country, the UN also had to make concessions. The new agreement did not permit the UN to have sub-offices outside Baghdad. UN staff travelling outside Baghdad were required to be accompanied by government staff from the relevant ministry (though in practice this rule has apparently not been consistently adhered to). UN staff could therefore no longer be based anywhere outside Baghdad (with the exception of the three northern governorates which the Government did not control), further reducing their ability to track conditions in different parts of the country.

NGOs had to sign a tripartite agreement with the Government and the UN in order to work in government-controlled areas. The proposed establishment of a special rate of exchange for UN and NGO operations remained a dead letter. The UN continued to accept the 'official Iraqi dinar rate' for transactions within Iraq.

With the approach of winter in northern Iraq, the UN humanitarian programme was under great pressure, a fact well-known to the Iraqi Government. A DHA official argued that while concessions had to be made, the UN had managed to save a lot, especially by keeping the Guards in the north where their presence was important as a visible symbol.

The US initially opposed acceptance of the new MoU terms as conceding too much to Iraq, but the UK and France were willing to accept them, mainly because of the need to begin winter aid to northern Iraq. After a few days, the US ceased its objections. A *Washington Post* article speculated that the initial rejection had more to do with looking tough for the election campaign than with serious opposition to the terms.[37]

The UN Department of Humanitarian Affairs and the UN humanitarian agencies were not able to recoup the ground they lost in 1992. When the Iraqi Government refused visas to representatives of Western donor nations to accompany a UNICEF-led needs assessment mission in March 1993, the DHA reportedly did not challenge the decision.[38] The inability of the UN in Baghdad to insist on access to vulnerable groups was further illustrated by the failure of its efforts in October and November 1993 to send an inter-agency mission to find out if any assistance was reaching the southern marshes. This followed a summer when thousands of people fled to Iran because of falling water levels following the draining of parts of the marshes. The request was never agreed by the Government. In contrast, in November 1993, after allegations by Iraqi opposition groups in Iran of chemical weapons attacks in the Basra marshes, an UNSCOM inspection team not only travelled to south-western Iran to interview refugees, but also visited parts of the Iraqi marshes.[39]

When the MoU again came up for renewal at the end of March 1993, no further negotiations took place. The UN 'assumed' the *de facto* continuation of the aid programme 'within the framework' of the October 1992 MoU. The Iraqi Government made no formal response at all, though for the most part it continued to renew the visas of UN staff and those of signatory NGOs. IRCU avoided any direct confrontation with the Iraqi Ministry of Foreign Affairs, preferring to maintain this anomalous arrangement which continued until 1996, when Resolution 986 brought changes to the terms of the UN humanitarian presence in Iraq (see below).

Winter crisis 1992

After the failure of the August 1992 talks there were fears that the UN, or at least the UN Guards, would be forced to leave Iraq altogether, with serious consequences, especially for the Kurds. As the winter approached, the DHA faced mounting criticism both from NGOs and from donor states for its apparent lack of preparedness. The DHA and the UN humanitarian agencies appeared paralysed both by the political and practical obstacles. In the absence of an MoU, the DHA would be forced to look at other – in its view unpalatable – ways of operating, including the possibility of a cross-border operation via Turkey. The UN was profoundly reluctant to send its staff over the Turkish border without Iraqi permission, thereby jeopardising future work in government-controlled areas.

The winter plan for the north, presented to donors on 1 October when there was still no certainty about the outcome of the MoU negotiations, depended on government-controlled Iraq in several respects. It required the use of the 'front road' from the Turkish border via Mosul into the Kurdish-controlled areas because, despite repairs, there were fears that the Zakho/Dohuk-to-Arbil road through Kurdish-held territory would not withstand heavy traffic in winter weather. The plan depended on Iraqi fuel supplies, without which all supplies (diesel, petrol and kerosene for heating) would have to come from Turkey. There were already serious concerns over kerosene and diesel supplies in the north because the Iraqis had reduced supplies to the UN earlier in the year. In Iraqi Kurdistan, people were reportedly cutting down trees to secure fuel for the winter. The Turkish attack into northern Iraq with 20,000 troops in early October 1992 against the PKK closed the border, further hampering aid operations.

In the view of some NGOs, the DHA plan required large numbers of highly experienced UN personnel to implement it effectively. Criticisms of UNHCR's operations during 1991 and 1992 faded into relative insignificance compared with worries about the ability of coordinators, DHA and IRCU, and main operational agency, UNICEF, to implement the programme. Visa problems during the summer meant that UNICEF did not have an effective presence on the ground. The division of responsibilities between different UN agencies and the role of NGOs had still not been sorted out.[40]

Meanwhile the US and UK were looking at the option of a cross-border operation. During September, the US was reportedly sounding out the Turkish Government on the possibility of importing all northern Iraq's winter needs through Turkey. A joint needs assessment mission to the north in October by OFDA, the ODA and the CEC Humanitarian Office (ECHO, founded in 1992) judged that the UN's assessment of the numbers in need in the north was too low, and pointed out that needs varied from sector to sector. For example, it estimated that most of the population of over three million would need kerosene, rather than the UN's target group of 750,000 for both food and fuel. In fact, the UN later raised its fuel imports to meet the greater need.

The joint report also strongly hinted that unless the UN moved quickly, the aid effort would be carried on through bilateral channels, threatening to marginalise the UN: '... the coordinating role of the UN, inside or outside of an MoU, does not mean that all funds will of necessity be channeled through it. Many donors will undoubtedly feel the need to transfer funds directly to an operating NGO and even when it is through a UN agency it will be necessary to check on unit prices rather than make block payments.'[41]

NGOs highlighted the reluctance in the UN to act on longer-term rehabilitation needs. Since the summer some had urged that planning and pre-positioning of supplies should begin and that agricultural inputs – seeds, fertilisers and fungicides – should be included in the winter plan in order to prevent a similar emergency arising the next year. They also argued that the plan did not address the needs of all those who were most vulnerable. For example, no shelter component was included among the 'urgent needs', despite the fact that some 200,000 displaced people were still living in overcrowded, dilapidated and unsanitary public buildings.

Once the MoU was signed, visas for UN staff became available and the winter programme finally ground into action, but deliveries only started on a large scale in December. The UN was obliged to buy kerosene from Iraq for the north above the going price – the Government reportedly referred the DHA to a private contractor for its fuel purchases. UN officials argued that this was still cheaper than bringing all the fuel from Turkey. A further supply of kerosene from Turkey was funded by the EU.

Many observers considered that a serious humanitarian crisis was avoided only because 1992/3 was a comparatively mild winter. The whole winter peri d, up to

March/April, was plagued by security problems, including several instances of time-bombs being attached to lorries in UN convoys from Turkey, it seems, by Iraqi agents. After a series of such incidents in December, the UN Secretary General issued a statement that he had decided to assign UN Guards to strengthen the protection of the convoys going through government-controlled areas via Mosul. The Iraqi Government initially objected, and UN convoys were briefly suspended from 19 December. However, from the end of December UN Guards accompanied all such convoys. Tensions in the region were further exacerbated by the clashes at the end of December and beginning of January between coalition air forces and the Iraqis over infringements of the no-fly zones.

The changing role of NGOs

1992 was a turning-point for many NGOs working in Iraq. When UNHCR wound up its operational role in the north, a number of agencies which had sub-agreements with it closed their operations. For those which chose to remain, there were new questions: whether to work in the whole of a now divided Iraq or only in the north, outside Iraqi government control; and how to shift the focus of humanitarian aid from emergency work to rehabilitation.

These decisions had to be taken during the summer of 1992 against the background of continuing political uncertainty, confusion over the UN's programme, and doubts over the future of the MoU.[42] A number of agencies were already questioning the viability of programmes in government-controlled areas, and their ability to 'make a difference' in the context of sanctions. Some agencies, and their donors, argued that the difficulties of working in government areas outweighed the needs they could meet. They pointed to the problems in monitoring the effectiveness of their work, and the Iraqi Government's lack of transparency in accounting for projects. Security problems and freedom of movement for staff also became significant issues.

The deciding factor for many agencies was the refusal of the Iraqi Government to renew their visas during the summer of 1992. For others, the final straw was the new MoU, under which agencies had to sign an agreement with the Government and the UN which they had not been a party to negotiating.

Some withdrew from Iraq entirely. Others decided to work only in Iraqi Kurdistan, where they would be freer to decide on their own programmes. Furthermore, the Iraqi internal embargo had clearly increased the immediate needs of the population in the north.[43] The arguments in favour of continuing to work throughout the country included the assertion that maintaining a presence in the whole of Iraq would enable NGOs to respond if the political situation changed – in particular, if an agreement was reached under which Iraqi Kurdistan returned to government control. In addition, from an advocacy perspective, it would be difficult for NGOs to comment on humanitarian conditions in the government areas if they had no presence there. Finally, some agencies hesitated to support only one section of the population.

The question of where the Iraq programme stood in agencies' broader priorities was also a factor in decision-making. The great public outpouring of funds for Iraq in 1991 had created its own pressures to work there. Many NGOs still had 'Gulf funds' to expend. Others were beginning to use government or multilateral funds for their Iraq programmes. For those which no longer had public funds earmarked for Iraq, there was some pressure from inside their own organisations to withdraw. Other demands for relief aid – particularly in Somalia, and nearer home with the breakup of Yugoslavia – made it hard to justify continuing work in Iraq.

In the event, only Care International/Care Australia and Oxfam (UK) signed the MoU. By the end of 1992, no other NGOs had offices in Baghdad. NGOs which decided to work exclusively in Iraqi Kurdistan joined those organisations which had never applied for Iraqi visas, entering Iraqi Kurdistan via Turkey. In the eyes of the Iraqi Government, all these aid workers were entering the country illegally, without visas from Baghdad, and the NGOs' local employees were thus working for illegal organisations.

The second winter of crisis in Iraqi Kurdistan also strengthened the bilateral role of major donors, as OFDA, ODA and ECHO put increasing emphasis on the direct funding of NGOs in the north. Meanwhile, the UN humanitarian agencies, with the two signatory NGOs, remained the main source of humanitarian assistance in government areas through 1992–6, with the exception of organisations which delivered supplies to Iraq but had no base in the country. During this period, overall donor contributions to the humanitarian programme took a nose-dive.

CHOOSING PRIORITIES: DONOR ATTITUDES TO THE HUMANITARIAN PROGRAMME 1991–1996

In mid-November 1991, Lynda Chalker, Britain's Minister for Overseas Development, visited Geneva for talks on the UN's role in Iraq. Before her visit she spoke of 'the British Government's grave concerns at the seeming inability of the UN to utilise properly the resources raised for Iraqi people...' Although she subsequently pronounced herself more satisfied with the UN's operation, she was said to be noticeably less enthusiastic about the work of the UN than that of the Red Cross.[44]

Scepticism and criticism of UN humanitarian agencies working in Iraq, and the emphasis on working with NGOs, was the frequent theme of British and American officials. The donors complained increasingly of the UN aid programme's ineffectiveness, but in practice did little to improve it. A report on UN coordination during the 1991 crisis noted the contradiction between the bilateral preoccupations of donor-governments and their oft-stated insistence that the UN exercise a coordinating role.[45] This observation was borne out by subsequent developments.

By the end of 1991, growing criticism of UN agencies and the way they operated appeared in the Western press, highlighting their expensive expatriate staff, organisational problems and the fact that they still had to make local currency transactions at the 'official' rate of exchange of the Iraqi dinar (ID0.3 to the dollar) when by that time the unofficial rate was ID8 to the dollar and falling fast. UN officials pointed out that only a small proportion of expenditure was incurred in Iraqi currency, but the impression remained that the Iraqi authorities were running rings around the UN.[46]

From 1992 onwards, political developments diminished donors' willingness to fund the aid programme. The demands of the emergencies in former Yugoslavia and Somalia were also consuming emergency funds, while the refusal of Iraq to sell limited amounts of oil under UN control to fund humanitarian needs (Resolutions 706 and 712) further diminished interest in assisting government-controlled Iraq.

This was compounded by the UN's increasing difficulties in operating freely in government-controlled areas. While NGOs carried out their own monitoring and evaluation, monitoring of UN programmes has been limited. This was another reason given by donors for not funding assistance in government-controlled areas. An increasing proportion of funds therefore went directly to NGOs, mostly in the north. By 1995/6, voluntary contributions to NGOs and other non-UN programmes in Iraq made up $61.4m, while voluntary contributions to UN agencies and programmes amounted only to $58m.[47]

Another controversial question was whether aid should be given for costly rehabilitation of water treatment, sanitation and other infrastructure which had been damaged in the war and its aftermath and which, according to the reports of Martti Ahtisaari and Sadruddin, was seriously affecting the health of the civilian population. This was politically contentious since it clearly went beyond simple relief aid. The US and UK had demonstrated their reluctance to provide aid even for basic relief, with the exception of the north, as early as May 1991[48] and remained reluctant to allow major infrastructural repairs, particularly if they related to the electricity system. Therefore a tension remained between what UN agencies and NGOs saw as necessary work – particularly in water and sanitation – to secure the basic health of the population, and the donors' reluctance to pay for these large-scale works. This became an ongoing difficulty since Iraq did not agree to proposed oil-for-food deals for five years, during which time the infrastructure deteriorated further.

With a growing crisis in funding for the UN humanitarian programme as a whole, UNSC Resolution 778, passed in October 1992, provided some extra funds.

The Record of Donors 1991–1996

Large amounts of money were expended on the humanitarian effort in Iraq. However, it was not distributed equally either over time or between different parts of Iraq. Almost half of total expenditure occurred during the 1991 emergency, and in the following years, the preponderance of assistance continued to go to Iraqi Kurdistan.

Between 1991 and 1996, more than $1.2 billion worth of humanitarian relief assistance was channelled through the UN system, through quasi-bilateral channels and through some 60 NGOs.[49] However, much of this amount was spent during the refugee crisis of 1991. UNHCR alone spent almost $230 million on the Gulf crisis up to January 1992, mainly to assist returning refugees in the north and to provide them with food and shelter.[50]

The preponderance of US funds did not go through the UN. During the 1991 crisis, out of a total of $1.4 billion spent on the Kurdish relief operation, $581 million came from the US for Operation Provide Comfort and associated costs.[51] Total US expenditure 1991–4 was approximately $1.1 billion, making it the largest national source of bilateral assistance in Iraq.[52] However, apart from providing frozen Iraqi assets to match voluntary contributions to the escrow account, much of which was used in government areas, its direct assistance was targeted on the Kurdish-controlled areas. OFDA stated the official position: 'The US does not fund humanitarian programmes in central and southern Iraq because of the inability to monitor humanitarian aid and prevent interference by the GOI'.[53] In Iraqi Kurdistan, US bilateral contributions were important, particularly in supporting winter programmes to import food and fuel, but only a small proportion was channelled through the UN humanitarian programme, mainly to WFP.[54]

Until FY 1995 (October 1994–October 1995), most US funding came in the form of allocations from Congress to the Department of Defence.[55] Only a very small proportion

The US used funds from its frozen Iraqi assets to 'match' voluntary donor contributions to the UN humanitarian programme which were deposited in the UN escrow account.[56] Most major donors took advantage of the 'value-added' created by using the escrow account, and between late 1992 and January 1996, $204.78 million had been disbursed from the escrow account for humanitarian needs, plus another $25.72 million for the UN Guards.[57] Nonetheless, the decline in the total funds available for the UN programme continued.[58]

Many donors earmarked their funding to a particular region – usually to Iraqi Kurdistan – or to a particular UN agency. The DHA was critical of this approach, arguing that it made a nonsense of donor pressures to 'prioritise' aid according to need and suggesting that donor behaviour ran counter to Security Council members' commitment to keep Iraq 'as a whole'. It tried to redress the balance by relying on 'matching US funds' to support work in government-controlled areas. The donors on the other hand argued that Iraq, by maintaining the internal embargo on the north, was itself creating additional humanitarian needs.

The outcome was an imbalance in funding between government and Kurdish-controlled areas. The northern governorates received an estimated two-thirds of total assistance, both in relief supplies and rehabilitation. Thus some 17–18 million people in government areas benefitted far less from humanitarian assistance per capita than some 3.5 million inhabitants of Iraqi Kurdistan.[59]

The overall contribution of humanitarian aid to the Iraqi economy under the embargo was relatively small. Humanitarian deliveries – donations from humanitarian non-governmental organisations and goods and materials from international

of funding came from USAID's budget. Much of the US assistance was in the form of goods in kind, purchased in Turkey and transported to northern Iraq. Between 1993 and 1995 the sums for direct assistance varied between $30 million and $50 million a year.

In 1991 the European Commission granted ECU111 million to Iraq as a whole, only 8 percent of which was expended inside Iraq. The rest was used for refugee repatriation on the Iranian and Turkish borders. Total funding for the humanitarian programme via ECHO between 1992 and 1997 was estimated at ECU103 million.[60] ECHO reported the average distribution of its funding in Iraq between 1992 and 1996 as 65 percent of the total to the north and 35 percent to government areas. In 1997 this was adjusted to 53 percent and 47 percent respectively.[61] In August 1997, European Commissioner Emma Bonino visited Baghdad, the first senior EU official to visit Iraq since the Gulf War, signalling a further shift of funding away from the north.[62]

The British Overseas Development Administration (now Department for International Development), a major bilateral donor, also continued to give the preponderance of its aid to the Kurdish-controlled region. During the years 1992/3–1996/7 only 22 percent of its total assistance went to the 'centre and south'.[63] Of the other permanent Security Council members, France made only modest contributions to the UN Guards and UN humanitarian agencies, though it contributed to the work of French NGOs in the north, mainly via the EU and the French Red Cross. The Russian Federation made periodic bilateral donations in kind to the Iraqi Government.

A number of European states, including the Netherlands,[64] Sweden, and Germany, channelled significant sums directly to the UN aid programme and to the UN Guards, in addition to contributions via the EU. In later years, Japan also became a sizeable donor to the UN Iraq programme. Since 1993, Turkey had made several major in-kind donations for both the north and government areas.

organisations including WFP and UNICEF – were estimated to average some 2–5 percent of total annual requests to the Sanctions Committee for clearance under either notification or no-objection procedures. The remaining 95 percent were strictly commercial transactions. In 1994, for example, only $57 million or 1.3 percent of all clearances were submitted and paid for by UN agencies. On the other hand, the proportion of these orders actually delivered would have been much higher than those for commercial clearances.[65]

In Iraqi Kurdistan, the contribution of humanitarian assistance was much greater, but this had to take into account the fact that the economy of the region had been largely destroyed, cut off from markets in the rest of Iraq, and subject to both an Iraqi and international embargo. UN agencies asserted, from 1993 onwards, that humanitarian aid should focus on rehabilitation, but in fact relief assistance, particularly food aid and fuel for the north in winter, continued to make up almost half of expenditure.[66]

The uncertain political situation and lack of secure funding encouraged the tendency to 'short-termism' among UN agencies, and frustrated any attempts at strategic planning. This short-range thinking did not end with the initial emergency. In the UN humanitarian programme, it was April 1993 before DHA appeals covered a year rather than six months. Annual plans seem to have been based less on any realistic assessment of what could be achieved or of longer-term goals than on their value as a bargaining chip with donors and a way of responding to pressures and demands from the Iraqi Government.

In Iraqi Kurdistan, some NGOs campaigned for the UN to engage in longer-term planning, and for the donors to provide funds for longer projects and to cooperate with the Kurdish administration. They pressed the UN to accept that basic agricultural needs should be considered an integral component of emergency aid. These needs were defined as seed, fertilisers, insecticides and pesticides, as well as fuel for ploughing. It was argued that meeting these needs would restore agricultural production and thereby lessen the need for food aid the following year.[67]

For NGOs, donor attitudes to medium or long-term funding have also hampered their own ability to plan. Once their public donations ran out, NGOs, like the DHA, had to seek funds from donor governments and the EU. Most funding on offer was for a year at a time or less – ECHO for example usually gave six month contracts, which were not automatically renewable. In 1994 the British ODA began to give funds for projects of more than a year in duration, but few other donors took this step.

Much of the substantial volume of US aid to Iraqi Kurdistan came from the Department of Defense, which had its own rules for disbursement, and its contribution was largely confined to the delivery of materials. OFDA funded local organisations and international NGOs – but not the Kurdish administration – to implement rehabilitation as well as relief programmes. However, because OFDA's usual role is to provide emergency relief, there were strict limits on the purpose of rehabilitation projects to those which restored the *status quo ante*.

As one advisor to OFDA commented, '...the policy of limiting aid to narrowly defined relief and humanitarian assistance, has hobbled the economy and produced frustrations that have destabilised the area and fueled the inter-party fighting. By refusing to deal with the Kurdish regional government, the allies have undermined the only authority capable of sorting out the squabbling and preventing or controlling internal Kurdish conflict.'[68] Ironically, in 1993–4, departments in the Kurdish administration were in fact indirectly funded by US and other donor agencies, winning contracts for work which these agencies had put out to tender.

By 1996, OFDA officials admitted that their approach had been too 'commodity driven'. This was ascribed to the military control of the programme dictated by the use of Department of Defense funds. However, '[the programme's] over-emphasis on inputs was drawn out far long than necessary… The result was a situation over several years, in which the wrong response (relief) continued to be applied to a changing situation (rehabilitation).'[69]

Other major donors were less rigid, but some infrastructural projects proposed by the Kurdish authorities, especially those relating to oil exploration, would have infringed UN sanctions restrictions, which the international community had not been willing formally to lighten. Furthermore, the political sensitivities of Turkey to any work seen as promoting a 'separate' entity in northern Iraq – for example, the refurbishment and development of the electrical grid – limited the type of projects which most Western donors would fund.

At times of crisis, donors might suddenly withdraw or become temporarily paralysed by the political uncertainties, leaving NGOs wondering if they would be able to continue their programmes. For example, after the crisis of September 1996, in addition to the abrupt removal of OFDA and all US aid agencies from the scene, all US aid money was halted, while ECHO gave no clear signals until well into 1997 as to whether it would be providing funds for its NGO partners for the next year. Its representatives, in common with other aid agency personnel, were having problems in visiting Iraqi Kurdistan.

The focus on assistance to the north was in part the result of real and justifiable doubts as to the viability of aid projects in government areas. However, the political agendas of the main donor states made their motives problematic. Since little international weight was put behind the DHA and UN humanitarian agencies to induce the Iraqi Government to accept a more vigorous approach to humanitarian aid, there was little chance of proper monitoring or accountability for aid given for projects in government-controlled areas. The reluctance to expand the scope of the humanitarian programme rested in part on the hard-line states' strategy of 'maintaining pressure' on Saddam Hussein and was justified by Saddam's refusal to accept the oil-for-food resolutions until 1996. In Iraqi Kurdistan, humanitarian aid fulfilled an obligation from which the major powers had not been able to escape after the refugee crisis of 1991. It provided a visible but not necessarily appropriate response to a political problem for which these donor governments had no solution.

UN INNOVATIONS

The Gulf crisis led to several innovations in the international community's methods dealing with humanitarian emergencies. One of these, already discussed, was the use of coalition troops to 'bring home' the refugees, rather than insisting that neighbouring states provide asylum. But several other developments took the UN and its humanitarian agencies into new territory. The Gulf crisis acted as a trigger for the establishment of the Department of Humanitarian Affairs to coordinate the UN's humanitarian work. Iraq was one of its early testing grounds. A second departure was the use of civilian UN Guards to provide protection for UN staff and property in

Iraq, and the third was the much delayed implementation of the oil-for-food reso-lution, which has been an uncharted territory both for the UN Secretariat and for UN agencies working in Iraq.

The Department of Humanitarian Affairs 1992–1997

Donor dissatisfaction with the UN's record in handling complex emergencies through UNDRO dated back to the early 1980s, as did NGO lobbying for greater coordination within the UN.[70] The problems of coordination and the confused lines of authority and responsibility within the UN, glaringly exposed during the Gulf crisis, speeded up moves to establish a new coordinating body.[71] The DHA was set up under a UN General Assembly resolution on 19 December 1991, headed by an under secretary general reporting to the Secretary General.[72]

The DHA's main goals, to improve coordination between the political and humanitarian arms of the UN, proved very difficult to realise. The first problem arose from the failure to establish relations on an equal basis with other parts of the UN administration, namely the Department of Peace Keeping Operations and the Department of Political Affairs. Second, the role of coordinator of the main UN humanitarian agencies did not materialise. With the exception of UNICEF, these agencies did not take kindly to the DHA's intervention: '… humanitarian agencies and programmes used to operating independently, resist centralised control and have far more experience in what they are doing than the DHA. In addition the Secretary General has not pressed the humanitarian agencies to accept the [DHA's] coordi-nating authority.'[73]

A 1992 report on the UN's humanitarian role in Iraq during 1991 identified an 'ongoing tension between the Security Council and the UN's humanitarian machin-ery'.[74] The advent of the DHA did little to resolve this problem. Although it was headed by an under secretary general who reported to the Secretary General, it appears to have had little ability to influence decision making at the level of the Security Council. Boutros-Ghali, who became Secretary General in 1992, often had abrasive relations with the Security Council, and in particular with some of the five permanent members, though mostly over Somalia and former Yugoslavia. On Iraq, Security Council resolutions gave him a specific role in pursuing the oil-for-food arrangements, and he made some efforts to intervene on issues relating to the humanitarian programme. However, none of this was effective in boosting the posi-tion of the DHA within Iraq or in resolving the tensions between the views of the Security Council and the humanitarian agencies over Iraq.

Jan Eliasson resigned as Under Secretary General for Humanitarian Affairs in November 1993 and was replaced by Peter Hansen. Press and diplomatic sources said Eliasson was frustrated by the inadequate funding of the DHA, tensions with the Secretary General and the lack of political support. No subsequent head of the DHA seems to have succeeded in significantly improving the organisation's position in the UN power structure as it has affected Iraq. The Special Unit for Iraq (SUI, later the Special Emergency Programme for Iraq) dealt with the Iraq programme within the DHA and related directly to the Inter-Agency Relief Coordination Unit (IRCU) in Baghdad. SUI laboured under constant problems in its key task of raising funds for consolidated UN appeals to donors for the Iraq humanitarian programme. The preparation and implementation of consolidated appeals for donor funds – an important role assigned to the DHA in emergency situations – proved an uphill battle. In late 1994, most of SUI's staff working on Iraq were moved from Geneva to UN headquarters in New York.

The DHA had surprisingly little contact with other parts of the UN machinery relating to Iraq, either in Baghdad or at headquarters level. In some cases this was a deliberate policy. For example, officials say the DHA always tried to keep a distance from the activities of UNSCOM. Nonetheless, the DHA's fluctuating relations with the Iraqi Government were undoubtedly affected to an extent by the periodic stand-offs with UNSCOM. Relations at headquarters level with the UN Compensation Commission became somewhat closer when both agencies were dealing with funds obtained under Resolution 778.

Perhaps more surprisingly, the DHA had no formal relations with the UN Sanctions Committee, despite the fact that the latter was dealing with humanitarian exceptions to sanctions, and that UN agencies were applying for waivers. Until 1995/6, DHA officials never appeared before the Committee or attended its meetings, and it was not routinely notified of Sanctions Committee decisions. This was said to be a choice made by the Committee, with the US and UK reportedly being especially keen to limit the involvement of other agencies in its work.[75] Equally, relations with the UN Special Rapporteur's staff at the Centre for Human Rights in Geneva were not close. Essentially, for DHA officials the Special Rapporteur was making their job more difficult inside Iraq by seeking to publicise sensitive information. For the Special Rapporteur's staff, the DHA appeared defensive and determined to avoid conflict with the Iraqi Government.

The institutional culture of most recruits to both the Office of the Executive Delegate and DHA was one which emphasised close cooperation with governments. Indeed, this is part of the broader institutional culture within the UN, whose humanitarian and economic organisations usually work with governments, rather than replacing or overriding them. Even UNHCR, which is often confronted by inter- and intra-state conflict, is reluctant to challenge governments' sovereignty.

The experiences of 1992 had demonstrated, as one DHA official put it, 'just how difficult the Iraqis could make things'. With no formal MoU in place from 1993 onwards, there was little incentive to challenge the Iraqi Government or put pressure on it. This was a highly politicised situation in which the DHA saw itself as balancing all the pressures – as a broker between the Government and the UN agencies as well as other organisations which were part of the humanitarian programme. Later it also had to negotiate with the Turkish Government over aid-related matters. The DHA had little leverage and there were limits to the support which could be expected from the Security Council, which had other priorities. Furthermore, the DHA wished to distance itself from the Security Council in order to maintain cooperation with the Government.

Many NGOs had welcomed the DHA's establishment, hoping that it would improve coordination, but its limited impact in practice was ascribed to its lack of political clout. There was increasing concern on the part of many NGOs in Iraq that both bureaucratic and political constraints had locked the DHA and the other UN humanitarian agencies into taking the least controversial options, refusing to challenge the Government on anything.

DHA officials acknowledge that relations with NGOs got off to a bad start in 1992 when the DHA was widely viewed as siding with the Baghdad Government.

The fact that UN agencies continued to run programmes in the north from Baghdad caused problems for NGOs working outside the framework of the MoU. UN officials reportedly put pressure on some of these NGOs to sign the MoU but all the 'non-signatory' groups maintained their refusal to sign. They particularly objected to UN pressure to provide the Iraqi Ministry of Foreign Affairs with lists of their staff, including local employees, potentially putting them at risk. Baghdad appears to have been well aware of who was working for 'illegal' international agencies in the north, but NGOs argued, as they had to UNHCR in 1991, that in principle there was no reason to hand this information over.

During the winter of 1992–3, there were also differences of opinion between the Special Unit's New York office, which dealt mainly with policy matters, and its Geneva office, which dealt with operational matters. The Geneva office took a much more flexible view of working with non-signatory NGOs than did New York, which sometimes tried to prevent this happening. By spring 1993 it had become clear to the DHA that the UN would have to find a *modus vivendi* with non-signatory NGOs as they were needed in order to implement aid programmes in Iraqi Kurdistan. This led to a greater acceptance of their diverse strategies and styles of work. DHA officials consider that relations improved after that time. The DHA's coordination role was somewhat strengthened after the first disastrous winter: planning for winter 1993–4 was certainly better than the year before. By 1994–5 the majority of non-signatory NGOs had some form of cooperation with UN agencies, especially with UNICEF in the north.[76]

The DHA's role in coordinating the work of the disparate group of NGOs in the north was limited. Although there were regular meetings in Baghdad and regional centres in the north between IRCU, other UN agencies and NGOs, these for the most part were limited to exchanging information. The overall distrust of the constraints on UN operations remained, and some NGOs in the north chose to keep well away from the UN.

NGOs working in Iraqi Kurdistan also felt that co-ordination based centrally in Baghdad did not take account of the specific needs of Iraqi Kurdistan, particularly in view of the Iraqi embargo. On the other hand, UN and especially DHA officials often resented the focus of both NGOs and major donors on assistance to the north. The views of UN staff working in the north were sometimes influenced by NGO perspectives, while those based in Baghdad might reflect some sympathy for the Iraqi Government or simply a strong perception of the limitations imposed by the regime. When Baghdad-based agencies such as FAO or WHO sent staff to Iraqi Kurdistan, some local opinion branded them 'government spies'. Their credibility was also reduced by the fact that they had very limited funds to carry out planned programmes and were therefore regarded as ineffective.

Between 1993 and 1995, DHA officials began to see NGOs as potential allies in the struggle to fund the Iraq humanitarian programme. They were therefore listened to and their views taken into account to some extent. On 1 and 2 June 1993, the DHA called a conference of donors in an attempt to resolve a funding crisis. For the first time, NGOs were invited to attend the entire meeting. By 1994 there was also more acceptance within the Special Unit for Iraq of the NGOs' emphasis on longer-term planning. The irony was that by that time, these meetings were increasingly regarded as unproductive, as donor interest in Iraq declined.

The downward spiral in the provision of international humanitarian aid was accentuated by Iraq's acceptance of UNSC Resolution 986. The DHA was reportedly under pressure not to make further appeals for donor funds once Resolution 986 was agreed. This reflected the view that all humanitarian aid and payments for the UN Guards should come out of Iraqi oil revenues. The last consolidated appeal covered the period from April 1996–March 1997. Resolution 986 ended the DHA's role in Iraq. Supervision of the resolution's implementation passed to the Office of the Iraqi Programme (OIP) within the UN Secretariat as of 15 October 1997. In Baghdad, the new Office of the UN Humanitarian Coordinator for Iraq (UNOHCI) superseded IRCU.[77]

Role of the UN Guards

The UN Guard unit in Iraq, a civilian police force without any real jurisdiction, suffered from a confusion of rôles. It was a unique experiment which has not been repeated. The Guards were established as a compromise measure intended to send a political signal that international protection was being given to the Kurdish population while still securing the acquiescence of the Iraqi Government.

The UN Guards were obviously a much cheaper and less politically problematic option than maintaining coalition troops in the region, but in contrast to military troops, their role has been highly circumscribed. In practice it was limited to guarding UN personnel and convoys and providing security information and communications. With the exception of a few early incidents when guards were present at clashes between the Iraqi army and Kurdish *peshmergas*, they have played no part in mediating or containing conflicts in the north. In government-controlled areas, until they were excluded in mid-1992, they acted solely as guards of UN property and staff. From that time, their numbers were restricted to 300, based in the north, though entering and leaving Iraqi Kurdistan via Baghdad.

A further criticism was that UN Guards were not even equipped to do the minimal job of guarding UN personnel and property. They were largely civilians, from a variety of backgrounds, 'donated' by their governments, with little training or understanding of the complex situation in which they were supposed to work. Criticisms that they were both unnecessarily expensive and ineffective led in July 1993 to the appointment of a Danish former army officer to head the contingent. Some improvements resulted, including a more professional command structure.

Established without the force of a Security Council resolution, the Guards had to be financed as part of UN appeals for voluntary contributions by member states to fund the aid programme.[78] Throughout the period up to the end of 1996, the UN's expenditure on security in northern Iraq – primarily for the UN Guards contingent – comprised up to 10 percent of the annual budget. Even in the period October 1992–August 1993, when there were serious security problems, the Guards unit was always below its full strength of 300, and in June 1993 the number fell to about 100. Since that time, they have rarely reached full strength. In March 1995, for example, a total of only 85 Guards were deployed.[79]

During 1993 and 1994 shortages of funds led to frequent warnings from the DHA that the UN Guards would have to be withdrawn. Ironically, given their marginal role as a protective force, their symbolic importance in Iraqi Kurdistan was such that withdrawal would have sent a signal of diminished international commitment. Thus it was only by threatening that lack of funds would result in a total withdrawal of the Guards that the DHA could convince donors to contribute, though often funding was secured only for a few months at a time. Fund-raising for the Guards also became a 'lever' to obtain funding for the aid programme, the argument being that there was no point in funding the Guards if the aid programme did not continue.[80]

The UN Guards were not generally felt to have provided effective security for NGOs, which suffered serious security problems in the north, especially in 1993–4. Their role in protecting UN personnel and property supposedly extended to NGOs working with the UN. However, the majority of 'non-signatory' NGOs could only benefit from limited security information, and many felt their own sources of information were more reliable. Not all agencies wanted to be part of the UN's emergency evacuation plan, preferring to keep their options open in addressing any future emergency.

THE OPERATION OF THE OIL-FOR-FOOD RESOLUTIONS: 1997–1998

This arrangement, under which Iraq, a state under an international economic embargo, was to pay for humanitarian needs from its own funds, was unique in Security Council annals. After acrimonious discussions over the MoU which spelled out how the resolution would be implemented the UN Secretariat, the DHA and the UN humanitarian agencies were faced with carrying out a highly complex administrative exercise which was constantly subject to political pressures.

UN Security Council Resolution 986 allowed Iraq to sell $2 billion of oil over six months, with provisions for the agreement to be renewed. Deductions of 30 percent for the UN Compensation Fund, and an additional percentage for the cost of UN operations in Iraq, were made under the formula developed for Resolutions 706 and 712. In addition, approximately 13 percent of the oil revenue allocated to humanitarian aid in each phase was reserved for the three northern governorates.[81] Therefore, from each $2 billion of oil sold, the Iraqi Government disposed of just over $1billion to import goods for humanitarian needs in the areas under its control. For each six-month phase, the Iraqi Government was to prepare a distribution plan which covered the whole country.

In the north, the UN was to act as the main purchaser and distributor of goods. However, the MoU allowed basic foodstuffs for the north to be purchased in bulk by the Iraqi Government and distributed from its warehouses in Kirkuk and Mosul. Wheat flour for the north was also milled in government-controlled areas. Medicines for the whole country were to be purchased in conjunction with WHO, with UNICEF covering vaccines. The value of these purchases for the north was then deducted from the so-called '13 percent' account.[82]

Although the MoU under which Resolution 986 was to operate had been agreed in May 1996, oil only began to flow in December 1996.[83] The first deliveries of food purchased from the proceeds began to arrive in Iraq in late March 1997, while the first medical supplies did not arrive until May.

The resolution was renewed in July 1997 (UNSC Resolution 1111), and again in December 1997 (UNSC Resolution 1143) without substantial changes. The Security Council avoided changing what were admitted to be unsatisfactory aspects of the MoU because this might jeopardise the renewal of the resolution. Even the US and

British Governments, which had numerous complaints about the arrangements, very much wanted to keep the resolution in place.

There were a number of causes for dissatisfaction at the way the first two tranches operated. In December 1997 it was reported that 90 percent of the applications made under the first phase (10 December 1996–7 June 1997) had been approved but not all had arrived in Iraq, and only 15 percent of supplies under the second phase (8 June–4 December 1997) had arrived in the country.[84]

There were hold-ups in processing applications for the sale of humanitarian goods to Iraq in the UN Secretariat and in the Sanctions Committee. Some of the delays were due to the backlog of paperwork both in the Secretariat and the Committee. Sanctions Committees already dealt with 'huge flows of paper',[85] and now the Iraq Committee was charged with scrutiny of applications for the purchase of humanitarian goods using oil funds under Resolution 986. The volume of paper became even greater and UN Secretariat sources admitted to problems in adapting the procedures under Resolution 661 to fit the new demands of Resolution 986.

In addition, there does seem to be some foundation to Iraqi complaints of undue delays to Sanction Committee approvals, particularly in the initial phases of the programme. Most of the objections and queries, said to be both 'technical and political', seem to have come from the US and UK, and often related to potential dual-use items. According to informed observers, objections were often based on information about the record of the supplier making the application. This was available only to the objecting country. Applications for goods which had not been included in the Iraqi Government's distribution plan also met with objections from some committee members. Although the secrecy surrounding the operation of the Committee was not as complete as it had been in earlier years, it was still difficult to substantiate any specific allegations of political obstruction. Some modifications were made in 661 rules after strong criticism that the US and UK were responsible for holding up the flow of supplies.

Meanwhile the Iraqi Government, which was very ambiguous about continuing with limited oil sales, created further delays to the flow of goods by halting the sale of oil in June and again in December 1997, ostensibly while awaiting UN approval of its distribution plan. On the first occasion, this hold-up led the Security Council to pass a special resolution which allowed a rollover of the first 180 days' oil sale to the next period. In the second phase, the Iraqi Government also placed restrictions on which oil companies could buy Iraqi oil, excluding British and Japanese, but not US, oil companies.[86]

By the end of 1997, all parties agreed that the system for purchasing and delivering humanitarian goods was not working effectively. The Iraq's stop-go policy on oil sales further complicated the picture, as did slow delivery by suppliers once clearance had been obtained. Some Security Council members had begun to press for the amount of oil sold in each phase to be raised. In February 1998, UN Secretary General Kofi Annan submitted a report to the Security Council calling for the ceiling on oil sales to be raised to $5.52 billion per months.

Central to his argument for the increased level of oil sales was the need to restore Iraq's crumbling infrastructure. Although this had been dubbed an oil-for-food deal, it did allow the import of other humanitarian goods, although until the end of 1997 the Iraqi Government's distribution plans had allocated the funds mainly to buy food and medicines.[87] UN and other aid agencies argued that food and medicine alone would not fully address the basic problems, and that a major rehabilitation of electricity, water and sanitation facilities was critical to improving health conditions.

In his February 1998 review of the programme, Kofi Annan emphasised that 'the scale of the problems [in the electricity sector], and the resources required to address them, were completely different from those which affect other sectors'. The refurbishment would take two years or more, and was evidently beyond the scope of Resolution 986 and its successors, yet there was a 'clear humanitarian justification' for considering it an area for assistance.[88]

These changes were largely embodied in UNSC Resolution 1153 (20 February 1998), passed at the height of a major crisis over UNSCOM inspectors. It envisaged more than doubling the amount of oil to be sold to $5.52 billion every six months, improving administrative procedures, focusing on the urgent need to restore the infrastructure, including the electricity system in areas under both government and Kurdish control, and targeting humanitarian aid to the most vulnerable groups inside Iraq.

The US had initially emphasised that Resolution 986 was intended to meet minimum humanitarian needs, not to rehabilitate the country's infrastructure.[89] However, Resolution 1153 indicated its acceptance that the scope of the so-called oil-for-food resolutions needed to be widened to cover materials for infrastructural repair, including electricity. Iraq also argued that it needed funds to refurbish its oil industry if sufficient oil was to be pumped to reach the new ceiling. The priority attached to retaining sanctions and therefore keeping the limited oil sale in place was evident in the fact that the US accepted in principle that after UN investigations such investment should be allowed. If the limited oil sales proved wholly inadequate as a form of mitigation, the pressures to lift sanctions would immediately increase.

However, the impact on living conditions in Iraq as a result of the expansion of the programme has been undermined by the sharp and unexpected fall in international oil prices. By October 1998, when the new level of oil sales had been in place for two months, the UN estimated that, instead of the $3.1 billion anticipated for the humanitarian programme, the net amount available for humanitarian supplies and oil spare parts equipment would be $1.98 billion.[90] This would not cover the increased expenditure on infrastructural repair projected in the distribution plan for the second half of 1998. In practice, the pattern of expenditure for this phase has differed little from the previous ones, with the emphasis still on food and medicines.

Blockages have also developed at the Iraqi end of the chain. By late 1998, the Secretary General reported that medical and educational supplies already delivered were sitting in warehouses because there was inadequate transport to distribute them.[91] Furthermore, the programme does not allow for any in-country expenses, since all funds are disbursed from the UN escrow account outside Iraq.[92] As more emphasis is put on restoring the infrastructure, Iraqi government departments increasingly say that they do not have the funds to pay for labourers or building materials which are needed in order to install the imported spare parts and equipment.

The presence of UN 'observers' would be of increased importance if the scale and variety of projects to be monitored were to increase. In the north, the implementation of longer-term projects, in particular where these involve using subcontractors, requires more rigorous monitoring and control than exists at present. In government-controlled areas, the system is in no sense up to the task of ensuring that the regime gives priority to the most vulnerable groups and focuses on improving the civilian infrastructure.

The issue of monitoring has predictably proved a difficult one. While there was little difficulty in installing the observers for oil exports, based in Zakho, Umm Qasr and Trebil, Resolution 986 and its MoU also called for country-wide observation of humanitarian goods coming into Iraq. Of the 150 sectoral and regional observers placed in government-controlled areas in 1997, only about half, according to DHA sources, had previous experience of Iraq. They are based in Baghdad and have to notify the Iraqi Government of their wish to travel outside it. They travel in pairs on tours of five days in the region around Baghdad and 12 days to areas further away, and are accompanied by local officials in their inspections. UN reports admit to occasional objections by minders to visiting certain places, or complaints about the questions asked. They also note hostility from beneficiaries, reporting that a growing number declined to be interviewed. The report ascribed this to 'erratic food distribution, delays in the arrival of medicines and severe power cuts', for which the UN was apparently being blamed.[93]

In September 1998, Benon Sevan, the Executive Director of the UN Iraq Programme told the Security Council, 'Assessing the impact of the programme is far easier in the three northern governorates than in the centre and south where we have been unable to receive detailed information on the imputs provided by the Government. In the centre and south, our observers can assess only the extent of the deliveries and how far [they conform] to the allocation plans of the ministries concerned...'[94]

A basic problem for the monitors is the absence of a body of information and experience such as could have been provided if UN officials had previously been resident in provincial centres. Reliable health and nutritional survey data, against which changes can be assessed, is not always readily available. Hence not too much can be expected in terms of rigorous monitoring or identifying trends in the population's welfare.

The nature of the oil deal, renewed every six months, further encourages the short-term approach to assistance which has dogged aid programmes since 1991. Both the Iraqi Government and the Kurdish authorities tend to focus on 'shopping lists' of goods, while the UN, which administers a large proportion of the funds for the north, has yet to address coherently how they can be used for longer-term rehabilitation or income generation.

The structure of the so-called 'two percent fund' for UN expenses (including staff salaries) makes it difficult to hire staff on contracts longer than six months, even when the programme concerned in designed to continue over a longer period. Consequently, there is very little continuity of programme staff or institutional memory in programme work.

Overall, given the scale of the programme, its impact over two years has not been spectacular.[95] In part this is due to the scale of the problems it is intended to address, in part to the numerous logistical problems in administering the programme, from both the UN and Iraqi sides, and also in part to the political undercurrents which continue to influence its implementation. Indeed some UN aid officials perceive it as a political programme which they have to implement at the behest of the Security Council.

There is still a sense in which the humanitarian needs of the Iraqi people remain a political football, with no party to the conflict willing to give them primacy. The limited oil sales allow the leading protagonists of continued sanctions to say that they are addressing concerns over the impact of sanctions on the people of Iraq. The Iraqi Government, meanwhile, continues to look for ways to end sanctions altogether.

NOTES ON CHAPTER 7

1 Several NGOs were directly contracted by OFDA: for example, International Rescue Committee (IRC) in camp management; Care in food distribution; Northwest Medical Teams, Médecins sans Frontières, the German Red Cross, and the US International Medical Corps in health. There was a legal prohibition in place against US agencies working in Iraq, which had to be formally waived for these contracts to be implemented.

2 Minear et al (1992), pp 36–7; Ross (1991), p 24; Washington Post, 25 April 1991, 'Relief Agencies Balk at US Enclave Plan'.

3 The OED had no presence in the north, where UNHCR was the lead agency. However, UNHCR's operations were controlled from its own headquarters in Baghdad.

4 Guardian, 4 May 1991, 'UN aid "short-changed"'.

5 ICRC has maintained its tracing and protection work in Iraq and surrounding countries since the end of the Gulf War. This includes delivering messages between countries without diplomatic relations, tracing missing persons, protecting POWs and, in northern Iraq since 1996, visiting detainees.

6 Minear et al (1992), pp 34–35.

7 In particular, the Simple Truth appeal organised by Jeffrey Archer (now Lord Archer) soon after the main joint body of NGOs, the Disasters Emergency Committee (DEC), had launched its own public appeal (Minear et al [1996], p 53).

8 Brilliant et al (1995), p 56.

9 See, for example, UNHCR's statement of policy: 'UNHCR has, from the beginning of its programme, been guided by the principle that the aid it gives should be consistent with what the relevant departments of the Government of Iraq would themselves have provided had conditions permitted. Wherever possible the UN/NGO programme of assistance is managed so as to encourage or strengthen government involvement in caring for the entire population in a given region – displaced and indigenous alike.' (UNCHR [1992i], p 6).

10 This was despite fighting in July which caused up to 50,000 newly-arrived refugees to move back towards the Iranian border. On 7 and 8 August there were also the first reports of Turkish bombing across the border to the north of Kani Masi.

11 Lawyers Committee for Human Rights (1992), p 19.

12 This group would have included 'refugee-like' displaced people from areas like Kirkuk and so-called 'floaters', who had not yet returned to their homes within the northern governorates (Lawyers Committee for Human Rights [1992], p 18).

13 Lawyers Committee for Human Rights (1992), pp 18–19. Within the 'security zone' in the north-west, the Military Coordination Centre in Zakho sometimes used its helicopters to ferry basic supplies to villagers during the severe months of the 1991 winter.

14 According to UNHCR, the total number of families in villages assisted under the winterisation programme was 51,544, covering 713 villages in Sulaymaniya governorate, 327 in Arbil, and 216 in Dohuk governorate (UNHCR [1992i], p 19).

15 This strategy had been used for Afghan refugees returning from Pakistan, but in that case the exercise had involved a clearly-defined number of people, all of whom had UNHCR ration cards; there were functioning banks in Pakistan; and at that time there were no security problems. None of these conditions obtained in Iraqi Kurdistan at that time.

16 For example, Caritas (Switzerland) worked with KRO, Save the Children Fund (UK) with KSRO, while Christian Aid and CAFOD financed projects with both these organisations. The main international NGOs working with UNHCR on its shelter programme were the International Rescue Committee, Action Contre la Faim, AIM, Christian Outreach, DanChurchAid, Equilibre, Medico International, Save the Children Fund (UK), Oxfam (UK), Action Nord Sud and Caritas (Switzerland) (UNHCR [1992i], p 19). Care International/Care Australia took over the logistics for the UN winter programme at the end of September 1991.

17   Testimony of Shep Lowman, Migration and Refugee Services, US Catholic Conference, US Congress, Senate, Committee on Foreign Relations, Mass Killings in Iraq: Hearing before the Committee on Foreign Relations, March 19, 1992, p 33.

18   The drivers were protesting because the Turkish authorities had limited trucks to one extra fuel tank when crossing into Iraq. They had previously made money by buying cheaper Iraqi fuel and selling it at a higher price in Turkey.

19   UNHCR [1992i], p 3.

20   Minear *et al* (1992), p 20.

21   Further report of the Secretary General on the status of compliance by Iraq with the obligations placed upon it under certain of the Security Council resolutions relating to the situation between Iraq and Kuwait, S/23687, 7 March 1992, Annex III (in United Nations [1996i], Document 107).

22   UNHCR (1992i), p 4.

23   The terms of the renewed MoU were much the same as those agreed in April 1991, except that the continued presence of the UN Guards was written into the November MoU instead of being a separate agreement. The Iraqi Government still had not accepted the establishment of a special exchange rate for relief operations under the UN and it did not subsequently do so. The renewed MoU also contained the stipulation that 'UN staff will be allowed, in coordination with the GOI, to accompany returnees to their homes as required'.

24   There seemed to be differing messages from within UNICEF as to whether it was willing to play the role of lead agency in the north. Decision-making was probably not helped by a chronic shortage of funds. In late March 1992, according to one UN source, UNICEF was in 'very severe' financial straits, it being impossible to run a programme on pledges alone, without money in the bank.

25   On 9 July the UN Secretary General characterised 'the deplorable attacks on personnel engaged in the provision of essential humanitarian assistance' as 'totally unacceptable' (Letter dated 15 July 1992 from the Secretary-General to the President of the Security Council concerning implementation of Security Council Resolutions [United Nations (1996i), Document 123]).

26   Statement by Jackie Wolcott, Deputy Assistant Secretary of State, International Organisation Affairs, Congress, House of Representatives, Select Committee on Hunger, Humanitarian Crisis in Iraq: Challenge for US Policy: Hearing before the International Task Force of the Select Committee on Hunger, 102nd Congress, 1st session, November 13, 1991, p 11 of the statement. It seems that the UN in Baghdad continued to hope for progress on the establishment of a sub-office in Nasariya. In February 1992, an official still insisted that it was important to establish a sub-office there to demonstrate that the Government was accepting a UN presence.

27   Riyad al-Qaysi, interviewed by Larry Minear and Thomas Weiss in *International Herald Tribune*, 1 July 1992, 'Iraq Puts the "New Humanitarian Order" to the Test' . On 25 June 1992, Saddam Hussein had been quoted as saying that the United Nations and the Security Council 'lost all credibility when the United States started imposing its will on them'. *International Herald Tribune*, 'Saddam and UN Head for Clash on Aid'.

28   United Nations (1996i), Document 123, *op. cit.*

29   Letter dated 4 August 1992 from the Secretary-General to the Deputy Prime Minister of Iraq concerning the work of the Special Commission and humanitarian programmes in Iraq. United Nations (1996i), Document 126.

30   Letter dated 24 August 1992 from the Secretary-General to the President of the Security Council concerning the MoU governing the Inter-Agency Humanitarian Programme in Iraq (United Nations [1996i], Document 127). UN sources in Iraq confirmed that the GOI clearly stated that the threat of imposing an no-fly zone affected the negotiations.

31   According to information from the DHA, UNICEF and WFP staff had already been

told to leave Basra in July, though at the time the Ministry of Foreign Affairs denied having issued the order.

32 Statement by the President of the Security Council concerning the Inter-Agency Humanitarian Programme in Iraq, S/24511, 2 September 1992 (United Nations [1996i], Document 129.

33 *New York Times*, 30 September 1992, 'Iraq says it will not assist UN's efforts to help Kurds', although the Government was reported to have renewed the visas of UN staff in Iraq for a further month; (*New York Times*, 29 September 1992, 'Iraq, assets at risk, asks to reopen oil talks').

34 *New York Times*, 23 October 1992, 'UN Chief in accord with Iraqis on food and medicine for Kurds'.

35 Quoted in *Washington Post*, 22 October 1992, 'US Pulls Back From Opposing UN-Iraq Pact'. Boutros-Ghali, in a later account for a UN volume on Iraq, glosses over the very substantial areas in which the UN lost the argument with the Iraqis (The UN and the Iraq-Kuwait Conflict [1996], p 59).

36 Dr Juergen Dedring, formerly a UN official working in the Department of Humanitarian Affairs, interview with the author, July 1998.

37 *Washington Post*, 22 October 1992, 'US Pulls Back From Opposing UN-Iraq Pact'.

38 Human Rights Watch (1993), p 169.

39 *Gulf Newsletter*, October/November 1993, no. 8, 'Marsh dwellers forced from their homes'.

40 UNICEF was therefore reluctant to extend its work and stated that it would not be coordinating the fuel distribution in the north, as stated in the draft plan. The DHA had to appeal to NGOs to fill this role, which was finally taken on by Care International/ Care Australia.

41 Office of US Foreign Disaster Assistance, US Agency for International Development, 'Joint Emergency Winter Humanitarian Needs Assessment Mission to Northern Iraq October 9–16, 1992', p iv.

42 Even by September 1991 there were hints from Iraqi officials that if NGOs wanted to remain in Iraq they would have to sign individual agreements with the Government.

43 Among those NGOs which withdrew from Iraq in 1992 were: Catholic Relief Services, Quaker Peace and Service/American Friends Service Committee, Save the Children Fund (US). Those which ceased to work in government-controlled areas included: Save the Children (UK), MSF, Equilibre, Christian Aid, and Medair.

44 Overseas Development Administration, press release, 12 November 1991, 'Lynda Chalker in Talks on Iraq'; *Independent*, 15 November 1991, 'Chalker satisfied with aid to Kurds'. In fact part of the background to these concerns was the disbursement of £57 million raised by Jeffrey Archer's 'Simple Truth' appeal for Kurdish refugees in May 1991 under the auspices of the Red Cross. Some of this money had gone to the UN and the remainder to NGOs, but there were accusations that it had not been properly used. The appeal had also brought criticisms of the British Red Cross since this appeal overlapped with another major Gulf appeal by the Disaster Emergencies Committee (comprising a number of major British NGOs). This was one example of the increasingly fierce competition for emergency funds in major crises, both nationally and internationally, and the difficulty of adequate accountability for their use.

45 Minear *et al* (1992), pp 29–30.

46 See, for example, David Hirst's critique in the *Guardian*, 13 November 1992, 'A land out on a limb'. According to UNDHA/IRCU, 'Since 1991 the government of Iraq has provided local currency in the amount of ID2.5 million as a contribution which has covered the majority of local costs of the Programme. Expenditures in local currency are limited to salaries of local staff and local operating costs of vehicles and other minor expenditures' (UN Inter-Agency Humanitarian Programme in Iraq, *Implementation Report* 1 July 1992–31 March 1993, June 1993).

47   United Nations Consolidated Inter-Agency Humanitarian Programme in Iraq, *Extension of the Cooperation Programme for the period from 1 April 1996–31 March 1997*, 3 April 1996, p 8, Table I.

48   See, for example, the *Independent*, 11 May 1991, 'UK adopts tough line on humanitarian aid for Iraq'.

49   UN Department of Humanitarian Affairs United Nations Consolidated Inter-Agency Humanitarian Programme in Iraq, *Extension of the Cooperation Programme for the period 1 April 1996–31 March 1997*, 3 April 1996, p 5.

50   UNHCR, *Information Bulletin*, No. 8 on Operations in the Persian Gulf Region, 27 January 1992.

51   Commission of the European Community, *Humanitarian Aid from the European Community: Emergency Aid, Food Aid, Refugee Aid*, DE 70, Brussels, January 1992.

52   'Humanitarian Assistance in Iraq', US Department of State Despatch, 13 January 1992, vol. 3, no. 2, p 26; *Turkish Daily News*, 9 September 1994, quoting Congressional Research Service, Washington.

53   US Agency for International Development, Office of US Foreign Disaster Assistance (OFDA) *Situation Report: Northern Iraq – Displaced Persons*, no. 1 (FY 1995), December 9, 1994; no. 3 (FY 1995), April 26, 1995, p 2. In 1996, after Congressional allocations of humanitarian aid funds through the Department of Defence had ended, US funding for WFP ($7.3 million) announced in October 1996 came 'with the caveat that the money should be used to assist the Kurds in northern Iraq' (US Department of State, *Daily Press Briefing*, 30 October 1996).

54   For example, in 1995–6 the US provided 18.51 percent of total humanitarian assistance to Iraq, but only 8.26 percent of UN programme funding (UN Consolidated Inter-Agency Humanitarian Programme in Iraq, *Extension of the Cooperation Programme for the Period 1 April 1996–31 March 1997*, p 131).

55   Aid officials said the Department of Defense was always uneasy with this humanitarian aid role, and did not want it to continue. US funding was halted by the withdrawal of OFDA and all US aid workers from northern Iraq in October/November 1996 (see Chapter 8)

56   For details of the working of the UN escrow account (The United Nations Trust Fund for Humanitarian Assistance to Iraq) and contributions to it, see UN Department of Humanitarian Affairs, United Nations Consolidated Inter-Agency Humanitarian Programme in Iraq *Extension of the Cooperation Programme for 1995–1996 (March 1995)*, Annex I, 'United Nations SCR 778 Escrow Account', pp 93–4. Up to 70 percent of the US 'matching funds' from oil-related frozen assets could be assigned to the humanitarian programme. The other 30 percent went to the UN Compensation Fund. Voluntary contributions from donors were not subject to the 30 percent deduction.

57   For example, the ODA used it as a channel for most aid contributions until the end of 1995. The only exceptions were grants to small NGOs where the delay in payment caused them problems. Once the escrow system had been established, it worked reasonably well, though during the summer of 1993 delays were caused by disputes on the management of voluntary contributions between the DHA and ECHO.

58   The following table shows the decline in overall funding for assistance programmes in Iraq, the decline in the UN programme's share of that funding, and the large discrepancies between the amounts projected in the annual or bi-annual appeals, and the amounts actually received.

	Total appeal	Funds to UN	Funds to other organisations
	(US$ million)	(US$ million)	(US$ million)
January–June 1992	143.2	89.1	—
July 1992–March 1993	201.7	134.7	—
April 1993–March 1994	467.1	95.2	77.9
April 1994–March 1995	288.5	61.2	53.4
April 1995–March 1996	138.8	39.4	34.3

Source: United Nations (1996i), p 59

59   The record of the World Food Programme, which received on average almost half the funds provided by donors to the UN humanitarian programme, illustrates the skewing of contributions to the north and the effects of shrinking availability of funds. WFP's beneficiaries in Iraq in 1992/3 totalled 1.26 million people, of whom 750,000 were in the north and 510,000 in government areas. In 1995–6 diminished funding reduced this number to approximately 400,000, of whom 300,000 in the north received reduced rations monthly, and 100,000 in Government areas (refugees, hospital in-patients and persons in social welfare institutions) received a regular full ration. For the first time since 1991, WFP failed to deliver any rations for over four months to those on the Ministry of Labour and Social Affairs 'destitute' list. In 1996/7 the target was raised to 2.15 million beneficiaries. For the first time, the majority were in government areas. However, towards the end of the year the agency was reporting 'alarming' stock shortages and lack of donor response (Department of Humanitarian Affairs, UN Inter-Agency Humanitarian Programme in Iraq, *Implementation Report* [1 July 1992–13 March 1993], Geneva June 1993; United Nations Consolidated Inter-Agency Humanitarian Programme in Iraq, *Extension of the Cooperation Programme for the period from 1 April 1996–31 March 1997*, 3 April 1996, pp 5, 20).

60   Information from the EC Humanitarian Office (ECHO), which began operating in 1992, and became one of the largest donors in the north, working via international and local NGOs. French NGOs have generally had close relations with ECHO, though others, including UK and Dutch agencies, have experienced more difficulties, often complaining of slow decision-making and bureaucratic obstacles.

61   The balance was further tipped to the north from 1994 onwards when the Council of Ministers and the European parliament decided to allocate further assistance, specifically for rehabilitation work in the northern governorates, through Directorate General (DG) 1B. Between 1994 and 1996 this amounted to ECU8 million. From 1997 this was to be administered through DG8.

62   Reuters, 4 August 1997, 'EU's Bonino visits Iraq to study humanitarian needs'. By 1998 a number of European NGOs working in Iraqi Kurdistan had their ECHO funding terminated and therefore closed their programmes.

63   This includes contributions via the EU, totalling £57.5 million from 1992/3–1996/7. Just over £1 million was spent on Iraqi refugees in Iran in this period (calculated from ODA, 'Emergency Aid to Iraq 1991–1996', 28 May 1997).

64   The Netherlands in 1995–6 was the largest donor to the UN programme – 22.42 percent of the total – and provided 14 percent of overall aid to Iraq (extension of the Cooperation Programme for the Period 1 April 1996–31 March 1997, *op. cit.*, p 131). The Government apparently tried to persuade the main Dutch aid agencies grouped in the Dutch Consortium (comprising Memisa, Terre des Hommes, Dutch Interchurch Aid and Caritas Nederlandica) to work in government areas but they refused, in view of the difficulties already outlined.

65   Conlon (1997), pp 261, 262. Only during the emergency of April–July 1991 were most of the applications for humanitarian goods. See discussion in Chapter 2.

66   Sixty percent of UN expenditure between April and December 1993 went on relief and

on the UN Guards. Health, for the whole country, made up 13 percent, and agriculture, mainly in the north, 14 percent. The proportions of projected expenditure for 1996–7 were little changed: food assistance and nutrition plus the cost of the UN Guards still made up some almost 48 percent of the total, with agricultural rehabilitation making up 15.5 percent, water and sanitation 14.7 percent, and health 15.8 percent. Education, a sector where there is an acknowledged crisis in areas under both government and Kurdish control, received 1.7 percent (*Gulf Newsletter*, March 1994, no 9, 'Security Council members differ on sanctions', p 2; United Nations Consolidated Inter-Agency Humanitarian Programme in Iraq, *Extension of the Cooperation Programme for the period from 1 April 1996–31 March 1997*, 3 April 1996, Table II, p 9).

67 For a clear statement of this position on behalf of Save the Children Fund (UK) see Keen (1993).

68 Cuny (1995), p 4.

69 OFDA (1996), pp 11–12.

70 Dammers (1994), p 409.

71 By June 1991, Britain, Germany and the US were pressing for the appointment of a UN emergency relief coordinator to be based in New York and be directly responsible to the UN Secretary General (*Independent*, 10 June 1991, 'UN urged to act over refugees').

72 UN General Assembly Resolution GA 46/182.

73 Durch, *op. cit.*, p 158; Juergen Dedring, interview with the author, July 1998.

74 Minear *et al* (1992), p 21.

75 Dr Paul Conlon, interview with the author, 29 September 1997; Dr Juergen Dedring, interview, *op cit*.

76 Out of about 40 NGOs working in Iraqi Kurdistan in 1994, 30 were said to have some form of cooperation with the UN.

77 At the same time, the DHA as a whole became the UN Office for the Coordination of Humanitarian Affairs (UNOCHA). The Coordinator in Baghdad has changed several times since August 1996, when Gaultiero Fulcheri replaced Mohammed Zijjari (who had been in post since early 1993). Fulcheri was replaced by Stefan di Mistura in February 1997. In September 1997 Dennis J. Halliday became coordinator. He resigned in September 1998.

78 Minear *et al* (1992), p 6–7. The contingent received two forms of international support: first the provision of personnel from donor states to staff the contingent, and second cash contributions for operational costs.

79 UN Inter-Agency Humanitarian Cooperation Programme for Iraq, *Implementation Report 1994–5*, p 108.

80 In May 1993, DHA/IRCU announced that the UN Guards would have to be withdrawn altogether from northern Iraq unless new funds were forthcoming. This threat was repeated in July 1994.

81 For example, in Phase I $1066.9 million was allotted for the purchase of humanitarian goods for government-controlled areas. A further $231.5 million were allotted for Kurdish-controlled areas, of which $55.4 million were used by the GOI for bulk purchases (mainly of food) for delivery to the three northern governorates (UN Security Council (1997), para. 9.

82 UN Security Council, *ibid.* pp 7–12.

83 In September 1996, the UN Secretary General had halted preparations for implementation because of Iraq's incursion into Arbil.

84 *Middle East Economic Survey*, 8 December 1997, 'Security Council Rolls Over Oil-For-Food Program Leaving Door Open for Changes In 1998; Iraq Delays Oil Exports Until Grievances Are Settled'.

85 Conlon (1997), p 272.

86 Shell and BP, along with Mitsubishi of Japan were informed by the Iraqi state oil company SOMO had decided against renewing their contracts (Reuters, 7 August 1997,

'Iraq snubs British requests for oil sale contracts'). US companies listed as having contracts for both tranches were Coastal, Chevron and Mobil.

87   In phases one and two, the Government's distribution plan for the whole country allocated just over $1 billion out of the total available of around $1.3 billion for food and medicines (food in each case made up just over $800 million). The remainder had to cover repairs in the health service, education, water and sanitation, agriculture and electricity (*Middle East Economic Survey*, 11 August 1997, 'Mimimal Allocation Changes To Distribution Plan; EU Commissioner Visits Baghdad').

88   Provisional estimates, he added, put the cost of immediate rehabilitation and maintenance needs for the whole infrastructure (generation, transmission and distribution) at some $870 million and the total value of projects to address the whole system's operating problems at about $7 billion. UN Security Council (1998i), para. 26.

89   *Middle East Economic Survey*, 17 November 1997, 'Iraq Crisis with Security Council Spills Over into Oil'.

90   UN Security Council (1998ii), para. 4.

91   UN Security Council, *ibid.*, paras 25, 45.

92   UN Security Council, *ibid.*, para. 32.

93   UN Security Council (1997), para. 38.

94   UN Office of the Iraq Programme, Statement by Benon V. Sevan, Executive Director of the Iraq Programme to the Security Council on 4 September 1998 (www.reliefweb.int).

95   As of 31 October 1998, a total of $8,399.2 million has been deposited in the UN escrow account. The following were the allocations of oil revenues since the inception of the programme:

Humanitarian supplies:	$ million
Allocation for Government of Iraq purchases	4,194.5
Allocation for UN programme in the north	1,028.2
UN Compensation Fund	2,492.1
UN operational expenses for implementation of oil-for-food programme	175.2
UNSCOM operating expenses	59.4
Costs of oil pipeline transportation (through Turkey)	370.7
Reimbursement of funds paid into the escrow account by states under Resolution 778 (1992) paragraph 6	79.1

Source: UN Security Council (1998ii), para. 7 and Annex, 'United Nations Iraq Account'

CHAPTER 8

The Impact of Aid Programmes

Aid workers in Iraq faced a variety of challenges, most of which were essentially political in nature. What could be done was constrained by the actions of the international community, Iraq's responses, and changes which occurred within the country. However, neither the UN nor NGOs were entirely without power. Their own decisions also influenced the impact, beneficial or otherwise, which their programmes had.

During the refugee crisis of 1991, international aid agencies had been able to act largely unfettered by government and UN bureaucratic constraints. But those agencies which remained in Iraq after the refugees' return faced increasing restrictions on their work. They had the choice of operating in two difficult environments. They could base themselves in Baghdad, working throughout the country under the aegis of a government which sought to control their access to the population, and the kinds of programme they could undertake. The second option was to work only in northern Iraq, with a Kurdish-controlled administration which had no international recognition, but a limited measure of continued protection from the international community. This administration soon fell victim to internal and regional political conflicts which influenced the lives and well-being of the population and aid agencies' ability to work effectively.

DIMINISHING RETURNS: AID AGENCIES IN GOVERNMENT-CONTROLLED IRAQ 1991–98

A number of aid agencies sent staff to Baghdad soon after the uprisings, when they had relatively free access to most parts of the country. But they faced a confusing and rapidly changing situation in which it was difficult to decide what assistance would be most effective. Reliable information on conditions in different parts of the country was in short supply, and few UN or NGO personnel were familiar with Iraqi society. Discovering where the most acute need was, and whether aid agencies could address it even if they could confirm its existence, continued to be difficult issues.

Many aid workers, especially those who were familiar with humanitarian emergencies in Africa, found the situation disconcerting. Here was a relatively rich nation whose people had suffered a dramatic decline in living conditions because of wars and sanctions. Their predicament was dire and, for the young and vulnerable, often life-threatening; but the situation bore little resemblance to the mass starvation and extreme poverty encountered in previous humanitarian crises, such as that in Ethiopia.

In Iraq, the main problem was the rapid fall in living standards, rather than extreme endemic poverty. Later experiences in Serbia and Bosnia were probably more comparable. The dilemma in assessing need in Iraq was between focusing on the poorest, or on those who had experienced the most dramatic fall in living standards and who were ill-equipped to deal with their practical needs and the psychological shock of sudden poverty.

The Iraqi authorities were unwilling to accept low-technology alternative solutions, because they saw these as indicating an acceptance of the embargo. This discouraged both UN and NGO staff from seeking cheaper or quicker ways of adapting to the new situation. For everyone concerned, the humanitarian crisis was a short-term problem created by war and sanctions. When it was unexpectedly prolonged, it became increasingly difficult to find a viable response.

The UN humanitarian agencies' work during 1991 remained focused primarily on the north. In Baghdad, UNICEF and WFP geared up slowly, with only limited staff in Iraq until the last quarter of the year. Although most of its staff were in the north, UNHCR at that time had the largest presence in Baghdad and also had personnel in Basra. UNICEF continued its distribution of basic drugs, in cooperation with WHO and its support for the water and sanitation systems, but at a low level because of shortage of funds. It also assisted the Ministry of Health in restoring immunisation programmes.

In the face of evident need – particularly as a result of looting of medical supplies and destruction of hospital facilities – some NGOs began by providing emergency assistance in Karbala, Najaf and Basra, where the extent of damage was greatest. However, only a few agencies were able to establish longer-term programmes in these areas.[1] Similarly it was possible to visit Mosul and Kirkuk to provide assistance, but no international NGOs were based there. By September 1991, free movement was hampered by increasing difficulties and delays in obtaining travel permissions from the authorities.

After the summer of 1992, the number of aid organisations present in government-controlled areas was dramatically reduced. Oxfam (UK), which signed the October 1992 Memorandum of Understanding (MoU) with the Government and the UN continued to work in the south on water projects and sanitation facilities in schools until it closed its programme in 1995. Care International/Care Australia, the other NGO signatory to the MoU, established school feeding programmes in several governorates, and cooperated with UNICEF on water projects.

By May 1992, WFP was envisaging withdrawing from Iraq within a short time, but lack of progress towards lifting sanctions and the internal embargo in the north meant that food aid was still regarded even after Resolution 986 came into effect in 1997. In 1994, the rapidly worsening economic and health conditions led the International Federation of Red Cross and Red Crescent Societies to launch a country-wide programme of food relief in cooperation with the Iraqi Red Crescent (IRC), whose branches around the country determined the beneficiaries. The Federation's work had taken a low profile in 1992–3 after difficulties with the IRC in 1991 (see below). In 1997, despite the implementation of Resolution 986 and its successors, the Federation still considered it necessary to provide high-protein, high-energy food to 46,000 malnourished children under five along with a general ration for their families.

Relief or rehabilitation?

The unexpectedly prolonged embargo meant a continued need for relief supplies, including water and sanitation equipment and chemicals as well as food, medical supplies and equipment.

Since 1992 most aid contributions to government areas have been in the form of deliveries of goods, primarily medicines, food and spare parts. Although clearance of such goods through the Sanctions Committee did not usually present problems for UN agencies or larger NGOs, it added to the time and paperwork entailed in filling orders. For smaller NGOs operating from the US, clearance for goods – especially for items other than medication and food – posed particular problems, since the US embargo against Iraq is particularly strict. Organisations applying to make such deliveries often experienced long delays in obtaining clearance, usually from US customs authorities rather than the Sanctions Committee.[2]

The Iraqi Government encouraged aid organisations to act as a channel for imports. One aid consultant noted in early 1992 that aid agencies were under pressure from local government departments with which they worked to 'increase the hardware they bring in, particularly spare parts for health, electric, water and sanitation facilities'.[3] At the same time, aid agencies, and in particular the UN humanitarian agencies, were expected to act as 'sanctions enforcers'. 'They have often been asked to interpose themselves between the Iraqi Government and the sanctions committee, making requests for spare parts and monitoring the distribution of dual purpose items', for example chlorine gas, distributed and supervised by UNICEF.[4]

The Iraqi authorities soon began to insist that NGOs use the IRC, which is closely aligned to the Government and the Ba'th Party, as the main channel for the delivery of aid.[5] During 1991, the IRC therefore underwent a very rapid expansion in its new and unfamiliar role of working with international NGOs and managing inflows of relief goods. At that time, one aid worker described its operation as 'chaotic', and there were reportedly serious problems with corruption. Subsequently new directors were appointed and the organisation was brought under tighter control.[6]

The volume of humanitarian goods arriving through NGOs and private organisations abroad was relatively small in relation to the scale of need, and there has been no way of tracking exactly who benefited or what impact the assistance had. For smaller NGOs which continued to import relief goods into Iraq, the IRC's approval was essential in order to gain access to hospitals, clinics and other institutions.

Some donors managed to develop relations with particular hospitals and clinics, which gave some continuity to their work and allowed them to keep some track of how their donations were used. By the mid-1990s, some external aid agencies had developed relations with locally-based relief organisations established in mosques and churches which receive donations or direct deliveries of goods, and have occasionally established small projects within communities. In a situation of scarcity, some religious and community leaders were able to use such supplies to increase their congregations or adherents.[7] Even more difficult to track were the periodic consignments of aid delivered clandestinely across the border by Iraqi groups in Iran.[8]

Targeting food aid was always a sensitive issue, and one where the Government wanted to keep the upper hand. Even large organisations delivering relief aid had a limited role in defining and choosing beneficiaries. The WFP conducted food monitoring, and no major crises over direct misappropriations of food aid have been reported since May 1991, when part of a WFP shipment of wheat from Jordan was 'diverted' by the Iraqi authorities into the government rationing system.[9]

However, the Iraqi Government began to challenge the autonomy of aid agencies in deciding whom to target in the latter part of 1991. It blocked attempts by UNICEF and the US agency Catholic Relief Services to start mother and child feeding programmes through health clinics, as well as food distribution through local institutions such as churches and mosques (for which CRS had signed an agreement with the Government in June 1991). Local authorities in provincial centres were reportedly willing to accept this food aid, but the central government adamantly opposed it. The media coverage of this incident, coming in November 1991 when there was a good deal of publicity over Iraq's refusal to accept Resolutions 706 and 712, did little to help the aid programme.[10]

In 1998, the UN again raised the issue of targeting vulnerable groups. Kofi Annan's February 1998 report suggested that the UN should assess the needs of vulnerable groups for special assistance but the Iraqi Government insisted that, under the oil-for-food resolutions, targeting of humanitarian supplies should remain under its control. The proposal, the Government asserted, was intended to 'serve political interests which have nothing to do with the humanitarian objectives underlying the "oil for food" plan'.[11] In practice, by mid-1998, the Government appeared willing to accept limited targeting of vulnerable groups by the UN.

Attempts to shift aid programmes to focus on rehabilitation have met with difficulties because the scale of the infrastructural damage far exceeded the capacities of NGOs – and indeed the UN programme, given its funding constraints – to import parts or to carry out repairs. Until the implementation of Resolution 986, very limited funding was available from donors to the FAO for agricultural rehabilitation and UNESCO for education. In these sectors, the aid effort has had only a marginal impact.

UNICEF and the International Committee of the Red Cross (ICRC) undoubtedly made a significant contribution to keeping water and sewerage systems running, though by no means at full capacity. Oxfam and Care also cooperated on this programme. ICRC resumed its work on the deteriorating water and sanitation services in 1994, alongside UNICEF and the local water authorities.

The work mostly involved basic maintenance rather than rehabilitation of the system. There have been two major problems: increasing shortages of trained staff, and the difficulties and delays in obtaining sufficient spare parts for treatment plants which depend on advanced technology only obtainable from companies in Europe or the US. As a UN official with experience of this sector pointed out, the relatively large sums of money expended to achieve even partial maintenance of the Iraqi water and sanitation system would be enough to completely renew a simpler, low-cost system.

Maintenance work was frequently hampered by delays in obtaining parts from abroad. For example, applications to the Sanctions Committee for spare parts through ICRC were never refused, but it was a 'long and cumbersome process', which ICRC described as follows. The first step was to call for tenders and place orders for the parts, many of which had to be custom-made. Then application had to be made to the Sanctions Committee for every single part imported. 'Approval, which is only valid for three months but often has to be obtained before manufacture can commence, may have run out by the time the part is ready and have to be reapplied for. The authorities of the countries where manufacture is taking place may have to give additional clearance, as may the Jordanian authorities, since all material for Iraq is shipped via Jordan.'[12] Delays caused by sanctions waivers, shipping problems and bureaucratic holdups had a particular impact on seasonal activities in agriculture. Pesticides are no use if they arrive after the pests have already attacked a growing crop, while seeds must arrive in time for the planting season.

Some debate took place in 1991 and 1992 within the NGO community on the prospects for doing any more than providing relief aid in response to 'shopping lists'. The kind of goals frequently set by NGOs in rehabilitation – of sustainability and promoting communities' self-sufficiency – were not easily realisable in government-controlled Iraq.[13] The 'top-down' nature of social service structures gives little or no scope for local or community-based organisations, and the present structure of Iraqi society certainly does not allow an autonomous community-based approach. For example, primary health-care initiatives were difficult to implement because the health service focused on curative rather than preventive medicine. There were also difficulties of access in some regions, and the effectiveness of local clinics was weakened by security problems and lack of medical supplies. One aid consultant from the West Bank who worked in Iraq in 1991 also noted, 'Agencies had difficulty mobilising Iraqi people to be involved in the restoration of basic services and economic recovery. The government discouraged community-based work. The majority of the population works for enterprises owned by the government.'[14]

NGOs which had staff and programmes in the country had to work with government departments – mainly the ministries of Education, Health, and Water and Sanitation, and their directorates at governorate level – as well as with UNICEF. This was a triangular relationship in which the UN agencies had their own views and priorities, which were not always the same as those of the NGOs. At times good relations were developed with individual directorates, but heads of department changed frequently, as did policies imposed by central government. This made for difficulties in achieving continuity of work, monitoring and evaluation. These constraints may also have discouraged NGO staff from taking initiatives. At times, the expectation that any attempt by an NGO to establish its own priorities would be rejected may have inhibited its staff from even trying to negotiate or pressing for a particular course of action.

In contrast to the UN, NGOs were able to have staff members based outside Baghdad. They had more freedom of movement than international staff based in Baghdad, though they were still expected to take counterparts from the local directorates with them when visiting projects. However, sometimes the counterparts did not have transport, and in the south were often reluctant to travel after dark or far from the cities, fearing for their security.

There were continuing doubts about the reconstruction priorities pursued by the Iraqi Government, which often emphasised restoration of the military and strategic infrastructure and prestige projects over those which would improve basic health conditions. NGOs which remained in government areas after October 1992 had some difficulty in finding projects acceptable to the Government which they had the capacity to implement and which they had confidence would benefit local communities. The Government steered them towards refurbishment and maintenance of water and sanitation systems in schools, as well as school feeding programmes.

There were also times when government policy, combined with chronic infrastructural problems, undermined the purpose of the assistance being given. For example, providing school sanitation could be effective only if there was a reliable water supply, which was not always the case. Activities such as water tankering could only be a stop-gap measure for chronic problems. Some of these – for example the salinity of the Euphrates waters – were of a long-term nature, while others were the result of government policies relating both to water management and political or security priorities.

By the end of 1995, only Care (which had withdrawn from northern Iraq because of security problems) had a base in Baghdad. Oxfam had closed its entire programme in Iraq in 1995. Changing conditions in northern Iraq, the implementation of Resolution 986 and the shift in the EU's funding priorities induced some European NGOs to shift the focus of their programmes from Iraqi Kurdistan to government areas during 1997.[15] Most of the work they undertook was in the healthcare field, including hospital rehabilitation. However, the scale of the NGO presence in Baghdad remained relatively small, and by mid-1998 tensions over the continuation of sanctions led the Iraqi Government to issue statements rejecting donations of goods and suggesting that NGOs would not be needed in future.

Humanitarian agencies in government-controlled areas have therefore encountered numerous frustrations, including diminishing access to the population and, until 1996, shrinking resources, reflecting the downward spiral of interest and commitment in the international community. Even if it was possible to accept the limitations imposed on programmes by economic sanctions and government controls, a major problem in the eyes of some programme managers was the impossibility of persuading either their own organisations or the UN to make any medium- or long-term commitment to assistance. Because of the political uncertainties, time horizons for projects and for the employment of staff remained short-term, a year at the most.

Since 1991, the presence of the UN and the few remaining NGOs in government-controlled areas has provided some salaries for local employees, probably raised some rents in Baghdad, and for a while provided some business for Baghdad's hotels where, for the first year or more, most agencies were obliged to locate their offices and staff accommodation. But unlike some other sites of UN operations, the impact of the UN's presence on the local economy has been marginal, far smaller than in Iraqi Kurdistan. From the point of view of most Iraqis, the Government remained the dominant provider of relief and welfare, a result which it undoubtedly sought to achieve. The implementation of Resolution 986 secured only marginal leverage for the UN in defining vulnerable groups or the character of goods and materials needed.

HOPE AND FRUSTRATION: HUMANITARIAN ASSISTANCE IN IRAQI KURDISTAN 1992–8

Short-term relief – the provision of food, fuel and medical supplies – remained the main feature of UN support in Iraqi Kurdistan, since the Kurdish administration was constantly short of funds, and food and fuel shortages occurred each winter. The UN and aid agencies also had to respond to the new crises which have arisen since 1991. In addition to winter needs, the Iraqi Government cut supplies of fuel and electrical power to the north from 1993 until 1996. The limited capacities of UN agencies and the need to keep the main roads across the north open throughout the year to ensure the transit of food and fuel led some of the larger NGOs to undertake infrastructural work – particularly road maintenance – which they would not normally have done. Health services in Iraqi Kurdistan suffered less dramatic declines than those in government-controlled areas, despite the power cuts, largely because of the large scale of UN and NGO inputs. A few organisations, for example Handicap International and German Emergency Doctors, have also worked to provide prostheses to the numerous victims of mine accidents.

But in contrast to the situation in areas under government control, this 'fire-fighting' role continued alongside major efforts to rehabilitate the rural economy, destroyed during more than a decade of conflict and repression. The majority of non-specialist NGOs focused their attention on the rural areas, where destroyed villages were being rebuilt, often from scratch, reconstructing housing, infrastructure and agriculture.

From 1992 until 1996, a substantial number of international NGOs – 30–60 organisations, both large and small – maintained a presence in Iraqi Kurdistan alongside UN organisations and OFDA. They had more freedom to shape their aid programmes without the constraining hand of the Baghdad authorities, although political conflict in the region increasingly hampered their activities. The majority of NGOs did not work directly or exclusively with the UN, and were not limited in what they could do by UN bureaucracy or UN fears about Baghdad's reaction to activities in Iraqi Kurdistan. There were a few large agencies with multi-sector programmes spread over large areas, and many smaller agencies working in one district or town, or in a single sector. Some had large expatriate staffs, while others had either a handful of expatriate workers, or worked entirely through local organisations.[16]

Donor agencies also had a stronger presence in the north. After its staff were withdrawn along with the coalition forces in mid-1991, OFDA's role was minimal until the winter of 1992, after which its involvement was revived, continuing until September 1996. OFDA, operating through the MCC, was effectively detailed to advise, identify needs and help supervise disbursement of Department of Defence funds. These mostly took the form of contributions in kind, procured through Incirlik base command. In 1993–4 OFDA's remit was extended beyond the security zone (covering most of Dohuk governorate) to the whole Kurdish-controlled region. From 1994, a number of factors diminished its role, including the rising level of internal conflict, the weakened position of the US on the MCC, and the end of annual congressional allocations to the Department of Defence for Iraqi Kurdistan after the 1995 financial year.[17] At the beginning of 1996, its personnel in Iraqi Kurdistan was cut and its offices reduced from four to one, based in Zakho.[18] Both British and US sources noted that by early 1996 officials working for MCC/OFDA scarcely left their 'bunker' in Zakho, in contrast to their active engagement in earlier years.

The other coalition partners did not have an equivalent arrangement for their official aid organisations, although ECHO had representatives in northern Iraq between 1993 and 1996. The British Overseas Developoment Agency had one project – sunnapest spraying – which it directly supervised, but aside from this it has worked through NGOs.

International NGOs and local organisations

The main indigenous organisations in Iraqi Kurdistan prior to the Gulf War were the Kurdish political and military groups, which had very limited contact with international NGOs of any kind. In 1988, after the Anfal operations, only a handful of international NGOs worked on the Iran-Iraq border.[19] After the establishment of the safe haven, Kurdish NGOs were established mainly in response to the inflow of funds from the UN and international NGOs.

The largest Kurdish NGOs – for example, the Kurdish Reconstruction Organisation, KSRO and KURDS – evolved as part labour contractors, part businesses and part humanitarian agencies, and focused mostly on the physical reconstruction of villages. Only the KRA had existed as an 'NGO-like' structure prior to 1991, mainly through its branches outside Iraq. Subsequently the local NGO sector diversified, sometimes with support from international NGOs, with the development of new groups working in agriculture, health, children's education, disability and human rights, in addition to physical reconstruction.

The presence of a large number of international NGOs during 1991, with a largely uncoordinated patchwork of activities and relatively large amounts of money, created high expectations both among Kurdish NGOs and in the population generally. Monitoring of funds disbursed in the early period was often weak or non-existent. Most of these new NGOs had some affiliation to one of the main political parties. The newness of local NGOs also made it difficult for international NGOs to assess which would be an effective local partner. Most choices were made by trial and error. It was, for example, difficult to apply a criterion such as the strength of their community or 'grass roots' support, because this barely existed.

The participation of local organisations in reconstruction was regarded as a practical necessity, but for those international NGOs which sought to build some form of civil society in Iraqi Kurdistan, the new Kurdish NGOs represented a step, however limited, towards that goal. Some of the Kurdish organisations did effective work and had high-calibre staff. But the political climate in Iraqi Kurdistan did not favour the development of politically independent organisations or of 'civil society' more generally.

The large international NGOs working in Iraqi Kurdistan had significant influence in deciding how money was to be spent, and the policies of rehabilitation to be followed. Even after the Kurdish administration was established in 1992, its weakness and lack of funds meant that international NGOs retained their autonomy of action and decision-making. Donors were reluctant to fund the administration directly, since this would imply some form of official recognition. Therefore Kurdish organisations as well as international NGOs were often used as channels for funds. As a consequence, local NGOs were often perceived as the administration's rivals. Fears were expressed in Kurdish circles of a 'parallel government', with local NGOs 'in essence becoming contractors sponsored by foreigners', with no overarching authority exercised either by the Kurdish administration or the UN.[20]

The administration's lack of leverage on the allocation of aid served to undermine its already weak grip on the allocation of funds, goods and the implementation of projects. Over time, this served to intensify party rivalries by creating a scramble for resources and bypassing the administration which, at least in theory, was bipartisan.

In 1993, the administration proposed a basic law to control NGOs and an overall development plan for the region within which all NGOs, local and international, were to work. Neither of these plans materialised. There was some opposition to the idea of an NGO law, with NGOs fearing it would be too restrictive. The development plan did not happen, partly because of the lack of funds and partly because the administration failed to sort out clear lines of responsibility for rehabilitation work between different ministries, which were riven by party rivalries.[21]

Some international NGOs did make efforts to work directly with the administration either with specific ministries (especially health, education and agriculture) or – more commonly – in a contracting role, for example in building and maintaining roads. In some cases good working relationships developed, especially on a local level. Before inter-party fighting hardened allegiances in each region, NGOs sometimes also worked through provincial governors. However, there were differing views of the Kurdish administration: some NGOs remained unwilling to become too closely involved, regarding it as a relic of Ba'thist rule.

Ironically, both donors and NGOs began to place more emphasis on working with the administration after it had split in two in 1995. By this time, many of its officials felt resentful of those NGOs which had ignored them in the past. Some of these officials, unable either to earn a reasonable living or to influence anything through the administration, had begun to set up their own NGOs or to become contractors. The oil-for-food deal led to the formation of a number of new NGOs, directly under party auspices whose main, if not sole purpose, was to get '986' contracts from the UN.

Restoring village life

The collaboration between international agencies, local NGOs and villagers themselves in restoring rural life produced some remarkable results, although this work has not been free of constraints and dilemmas. However, most NGO staff would probably still argue that rural rehabilitation was the right focus for international assistance, if only because in the peculiar economic and political circumstances of Iraqi Kurdistan, other conceivable rehabilitation or development targets would have been impractical. Many agencies and individuals also viewed this work as an act of solidarity with the Kurdish people who had survived such a violent overturning of their lives.

After the work of UNHCR and NGOs in the winter of 1991 to provide tempo-rary shelter for families who had returned to their villages, reconstruction began in earnest in 1992–3. An important priority was the clearance, or at least demarcation, of areas infested with anti-personnel mines, without which rural rehabilitation could be very dangerous. In fact the prevalence of mines on agricultural land precluded the resettlement of some villages.

Mine eradication, training local de-mining teams and creating mines awareness in the population is a painfully slow and laborious task. In Iraqi Kurdistan it has been carried out mainly by the UK-based Mines Advisory Group (MAG), with limited and tardy assistance from the UN.[22] MAG has worked mostly in Arbil and Sulaymaniya governorates, where mines pose most problems on arable lands. Aside from the scale of the problem (an estimated nine million mines laid in the three northern governorates), the agency has had numerous difficulties with the Turkish authorities in importing de-mining equipment into the area. They showed suspicion of all de-mining operations, particularly in areas close to their borders. MAG has also faced periodic interruptions to its work because of inter-Kurdish fighting.

Despite the scale of the work undertaken, the absence of coordinated planning in rural rehabilitation was a striking feature of the process. There was no overarching control over which agencies worked where, or the quality of work. Not only was there little coordination with the UN, but NGOs each decided where to work according to their own criteria of need, their contacts and degree of access. Criteria for choosing which villages to work in, and which individuals, families or groups to support varied from agency to agency. Needs assessments were often cursory or non-existent, leading to duplication or inappropriate use of resources. Some agencies chose where to work according to their personal contacts in Kurdistan.

There was, therefore, no overall rationale as to who received assistance and who did not. The weakness of the Kurdish administration's influence meant that it could not prevent duplication of projects.[23] Monitoring of the disbursement of funds and their impact depended entirely on the efficiency and commitment of the particular NGO and its staff, and the requirements of donors.

This was a recipe for confusion, manipulation and poor planning, with plenty of potential for political friction. 'At times, one village would be wholly reconstructed, while neighbouring villages were left to their own devices. This imbalance in recon-struction activities risked creating mutual jealousy and competition among potential beneficiaries, and carried the potential for further social instability and conflict.'[24] Villagers, not being very familiar with the concept of aid agencies, often had little idea which NGO they were working with, since some villages received visits from a succession of agencies. There were instances when an organisation which had stopped work for a period of time while awaiting materials or funds, was superseded by another one. Villagers might also hear that an NGO working in a neighbouring village provided assistance with building. Therefore if an agency working in their village insisted that the villagers had to contribute their own labour for building, con-siderable resentment could result.

For some aid agencies, rehabilitation meant mainly providing amenities: houses, water and sanitation infrastructure, and sometimes access roads. In some, but not all, cases, schools and clinics were included. Many agencies provided individual families returning to their villages with a package of support, consisting of a range of standard building materials, with the family contributing its own labour. These packages varied from one agency to another, and evolved over time. By 1994, SCF (UK), for example, had developed a more flexible system of vouchers, allowing returning villagers to choose which elements would suit particular families and communities. This differed from the earlier method in which the aid agency decided on distribution of particular inputs, agricultural or building, sometimes, but not always, after consultation with either villagers or local leaders.

Some NGOs came with an agenda which sought to move away from emergency aid towards food security, resettlement and regeneration of economic activity. The agricultural sector was identified as the key productive sector in Iraqi Kurdistan, and its restoration appeared feasible, with immediate benefits to the resettled population. They argued that restoring the infrastructure of village life, while important, was insufficient. Restored villages, they argued, needed to fit an economic context and develop a potential for economic sustainability. This entailed a greater emphasis on the long term, restoring agricultural production to create livelihoods for those whose vulnerability was the result of their dispossession.

International aid did make a significant contribution to restoring the agricultural infrastructure of Iraqi Kurdistan. Aid agencies began delivering seeds, fertilisers and pesticides to the north early in 1992. There were numerous projects to distribute goats, chickens and other livestock, and bees. Fruit trees which had been destroyed in large numbers during the Anfal were also replanted, though the problem has been for farmers to have the confidence in the future to set land aside for a crop which will take five years or more to come into production. The restoration of veterinary services and disease control and extension services followed, though these projects proved more difficult to implement.[25]

Helping the vulnerable?

While village rehabilitation, supported by a broader programme of agricultural reha-bilitation, undoubtedly represented a step forward from the previous 'top-down' emergency focus, a number of problems arose with its implementation. Some of the difficulties related to the general political and economic environment in which the programme was operating, while others were the result of Western NGO precon-ceptions which were not always in tune with the social and political conditions in which they were working.

The situation was unusually complex. Most aid workers had only a limited under-standing of how Kurdish society worked. International NGOs generally worked either with Kurdish NGOs or through local village committees which had remained in existence from Ba'thist rule before 1991. These committees were responsible to regional committees and finally to the provincial governor. Some of these structures were still in place. However, in practice village committees were frequently said to be dominated by, or embodied in, one person who took the role of village headman. Such positions were clearly influenced by political party links, especially as the poli-tical climate became increasingly polarised.

Pre-existing tribal loyalties, as well as party structures, reasserted themselves, particularly in the Badinan region where they had always been strongest. The patterns of landownership also allowed tribal leaders, absentee landowners, or those who had obtained control of village lands after their inhabitants had been pushed out to influence how much control villagers had over the products of agricultural work. Some aid agencies, including OFDA, stipulated that they would only support villages which were free of land tenure problems and disputes over water rights. This evidently excluded significant numbers of potential resettlements.

In many cases external aid for rebuilding created new opportunities for local tribal or party leaders, allowing them to corner political control and lucrative contracts. OFDA, which was involved in large-scale purchasing and transport of building materials and other goods conceded that control of contracts and purchases was very loosely monitored, so that it was not surprising to find sole-source and non-competitive contracting to be the norm. 'A few local vendors allegedly profited disproportionately because of such contracts.'[26]

Rivalry developed between powerful individuals for the contracting and trade opportunities which the rural aid programme generated, in turn fuelling the rivalry between the main parties. Their control over rural areas, either directly or through allies, facilitated recruitment of *peshmerga* into the military forces of both parties, a critical resource once inter-party fighting began in 1994. Local Kurdish NGOs involved in reconstruction could not avoid becoming drawn into this nexus, particularly since they already had party allegiances. Indeed, some local NGO directors themselves became rich and powerful private contractors.[27]

These factors could prevent resettled village communities from gaining any significant control over the assets which the aid agencies had put in or over the products of their own agricultural work. The model followed by many NGOs envisaged creating a smallholder sector which, by producing modest surpluses, would have a measure of economic independence. Returning villagers undoubtedly did benefit from the rebuilding of homes and infrastructure, but the rebuilt villages did not necessarily emerge as economically or politically self-sufficient communities.

Many agencies tried to focus assistance on the poorest or most vulnerable groups, particularly the 'Anfal' widows. There was little dispute within the Kurdish community and the main political parties about the needs of this group. However, for these women the decision to go back to villages was a difficult one which was not just a matter of personal preference. The political parties regarded them as the widows of martyrs and therefore as under party protection. The parties, or family groups, not the women themselves, frequently decided who was to resettle.

Aid agencies frequently distributed livestock – mainly goats and chickens – to help women get re-established. In fact it was found that many of the animals were sold. Either the women needed the cash, or because they had to pay for a goat-herd. Those with children in school who were not living full-time in the village would either have to find members of their family to look after the animal or pay a goat-herd. Another outcome was that male relatives took over the livestock. A critical difficulty for many female-headed households was the shortage of labour within the depleted family group, unless they were able to move in with relatives. These issues raised questions as to whether this strategy was actually supporting the women in attaining an independent livelihood.

The criteria for sustainability of projects were at times in conflict with support for the most vulnerable. An Italian agency attempted to implement a project which envisaged the creation of a revolving fund, with farmers contributing 25–30 percent of their crop yield as repayment for loans to improve productivity. It stipulated that all participating villagers must have four dunums of land, so excluding tenants, sharecroppers and those who owned only very small amounts of land because they could not be expected reliably to pay enough into the fund to keep it going in the longer term.[28]

It gradually became clear that a key element in the calculations of many returnees was whether their children could go to school. Some kept a foot in the collective settlements, both to collect rations and to keep children in school. Some agencies went so far as to insist that families left collective towns completely if they were to be supported. However, not all the aid packages for village rehabilitation included school rebuilding, and even when they did there was no guarantee that the local authorities could supply, or pay, a teacher or teachers and provide educational materials. Sometimes the numbers of children in one village would not warrant a school, but it was not always easy to persuade neighbouring villages to pool resources and share one.

A further weak link in the process of rural rehabilitation was the Kurdish administration, which, as constituted after 1992, was not able to oversee effectively the process of resettlement, nor to support and service these resettled communities – providing teachers, educational materials, health care, veterinary and other extension services – on a consistent basis.

Finally, the external constraints imposed by the two embargoes made the future uncertain even for villagers who succeeded in growing their own food and even producing for the market. The peculiar and unstable version of the 'free market' in Iraqi Kurdistan produced rapid fluctuations of prices which made it difficult to predict, for a small farmer, what he might expect to make from selling his crop. The destruction caused by sunnapest, despite the efforts of the eradication programme, created a further hazard for wheat growers which would not have existed under 'normal' circumstances.[29]

Thus the sustainability of the return to the villages remains in question. Many of these restored rural communities could be characterised as fragile, physically, economically and socially. Their future viability will depend on a less volatile security situation and the economic and social policies of whatever authority controls the area in the future.

TARGETING AID 1992–6

This unusual rehabilitation of village life focused on a relatively a small proportion of the population of Iraqi Kurdistan, where the majority lives in towns, large or small, or in *mujamma'at*. With the exception of assistance to displaced persons, the humanitarian assistance programme has had a much more limited impact on urban life. 'There was a relative neglect of reconstruction aid in the cities, where the majority of the population was now living. There have been relatively few concerted efforts at, for example, creating new employment opportunities and seeking other ways of reducing the urban population's dependence on state support.'[30]

In the first years after the refugee crisis of 1991, aside from village resettlement international efforts focused on providing relief assistance for the long-term displaced, primarily the estimated 140,000 people who remain displaced from Kirkuk and other areas under Iraqi government control. Shelter for the displaced remained both a major need and an unsolved problem. Until 1995, some remained in a prefabricated camp at Shanandary in Sulaymaniya governorate, but the majority continued to live in overcrowded and sub-standard conditions in abandoned public buildings in Arbil and Sulaymaniya – up to 100,000 displaced people in Sulaymaniya alone. The Kurdish administration was reluctant to house the displaced in collective settlements whose inhabitants had returned to their villages.

From 1995 onwards, the fighting in Iraqi Kurdistan added to the numbers of people who had become homeless, creating new priorities for emergency aid. Since the advent of UNSC Resolution 986, the UN organisation Habitat has been developing a programme to re-house the growing numbers of displaced people throughout the region.

It was more difficult to identify and target groups in need in urban areas. Targeting aid has always been politically controversial and obviously became more so as internal tensions grew within the region. During 1993 and 1994 debates centred on whether the focus of assistance on the displaced Kirkukis was excluding the growing numbers of urban poor. There were also arguments over the UN estimates of the overall numbers in need during the winter, and then in 1993–4 whether those in need were effectively targeted by WFP food distributions.[31]

The food aid provided was generally regarded as inadequate and poorly targeted, partly out of lack of solid information on vulnerable groups. A study in 1994 found that the poor in urban areas had been particularly ill-served by the food distribution programme. Although some 52 percent of the poor lived in towns and cities, one third of them had not received assistance.[32] There was also some evidence of problems characteristic of food aid programmes, with out-of-date ration lists and people claiming the rations of relatives who had died or moved on.[33]

In general, the targeting of displaced groups for food assistance seemed justifiable, though given the lack of assistance for other impoverished urban groups, it led to popular resentment, especially in Sulaymaniya, where the majority of the displaced were housed. Collective settlements also seemed a logical target for food assistance because their residents had previously been heavily dependent on government rations and had few possibilities of employment. One problem was that control of these distributions remained in the hands of *mustashars* in the settlements, further strengthening their position.[34] The provision of food aid in the collective settlements also perpetuated their highly dependent situation.

By 1994 and 1995 some NGOs which had previously worked mainly in rural areas began to shift the focus of their concern to urban areas. They supported building and equipping schools and housing the displaced. Some initiatives were taken to combat what appeared to be an increasing rate of school dropouts by providing education for out-of-school children, and skills training for women, but the scale of this work is small. The most serious problems – unemployment, low wages and high inflation – NGOs could not effectively address.

The inflow of goods under the oil-for-food programme in 1997 and 1998, and the lifting of the Iraqi internal embargo, took some of the pressure off the urban poor by reducing prices of basic goods, increasing stocks of food and medicine. But this has not resolved the problem of the region's dependence on external assistance, whether from the Iraqi Government or from external donors.

POLITICAL AND SECURITY CONSTRAINTS

Humanitarian programmes have been increasingly constrained by political conflict. Security problems for the UN and NGOs did not reach the scale experienced in Bosnia or Somalia, but security incidents in the north became increasingly common between 1991 and 1994. While there was rarely direct proof of Iraqi government involvement, there is little doubt that the Iraqi Government viewed aid workers as hostile agents who had 'sided' with the Kurdish administration. It reportedly offered financial rewards to those who carried out attacks on foreigners.

Among the most lethal incidents was a bomb explosion near Sulaymaniya in early July 1992 which killed several Kurdish guards escorting Danielle Mitterand, who was visiting France Liberté's projects in northern Iraq. In early 1993, two NGO workers were shot dead in roadside ambushes: Stuart Cameron of Care International in January, and Vincent Tollet of Handicap International in March.[35] Two Kurdish workers in a school supported by Equilibre in Sulaymaniya governorate were killed in a bomb explosion in May 1993. In 1994 a German journalist, Lissy Schmidt, who worked for Agence France Presse and was the only Western journalist permanently based in Iraqi Kurdistan, was shot dead in an ambush.

Agencies with staff involved in food and fuel distribution also suffered periodic threats and harassment from people seeking to divert stocks for political or commercial reasons. In January 1995, a Care convoy was ambushed near Dokkan, resulting in the death of one local CARE worker and the injury of six others. Care decided to withdraw from northern Iraq after this incident, citing security problems, but continued to work in government areas.

In addition to the bombs planted on aid convoys during the winters of 1992–3 and 1993–4, there were also bomb attacks in public places, targeting the local population and attacks on members of Kurdish opposition parties. In these latter cases, the perpetrators may have been either Kurds or government agents. Several UN Guards have been killed and injured since 1991.

Security problems also resulted from Iraqi raids and incursions across the *de facto* border, Turkish raids (including aerial bombing, shelling and several major ground attacks) against PKK targets, PKK military activities, sporadic Iranian shelling across the border into Sulaymaniya governorate, and clashes between rival Kurdish factions. While these attacks did not prevent NGOs working, except for short periods, some international NGOs recruited large guard contingents to protect property and staff when travelling. Some aid workers were made uneasy by the need to go everywhere in convoy with *peshmergas* riding shotgun.[36]

The unstable political environment made it difficult to plan ahead, and local communities themselves sometimes had difficulty in taking long-term decisions, preferring activities which had immediate and tangible benefits.[37] But until 1994, there was a belief – both among expatriate workers and Kurds involved in rehabilitation work – that what had been achieved could be further built upon. However, from 1994 onwards several pressures combined to reduce aid agencies' freedom of action.

Turkish influence

Turkey's control over access to the region has had a major impact on the aid pro-gramme in Iraqi Kurdistan. Most of the humanitarian aid destined for the north came across this border.[38] An assessment in 1996 of OFDA's programme noted: 'Deference to Turkey and its problems with its own Kurdish population seems to lie at the heart of much of the aid policy on external assistance to the Iraqi Kurds'.[39] Experience during the 1992–3 winter programme highlighted numerous bureaucratic obstacles and a good deal of corruption, especially at a local level, in the border region. Aid officials claimed that a good deal of money was made in Turkey through the aid programme, which one source described as a 'gold mine'. Turkish officials and businessmen would probably argue that they were simply trying to recoup what they had lost from the interruption of regular trade by the international trade embargo. From 1994 onwards, the Turkish authorities imposed more rules and red tape on the import of goods by NGOs and the UN.[40] By the mid-1990s, the Turkish army, the PKK and the local Kurdish authorities had become involved in competition to control the traffic in aid, smuggled goods and people to and from Iraqi Kurdistan.

As Turkish involvement in the MCC increased from 1993 onwards, its officials intervened more directly in the aid programme. An important part of their agenda was to monitor how humanitarian aid was distributed, their particular concern being to prevent it falling into PKK hands. Although the Turkish Red Crescent developed a role in providing relief aid in northern Iraq, the Turkish authorities have tried to prevent Western donors from providing assistance which might make Kurdish autonomy 'permanent'.[41] From 1993 onwards Turkish aid was given to both the north and government-controlled areas. There was no direct coordination with the UN programme, though the DHA was informed what the TRC was distributing. Turcoman groups in Iraqi Kurdistan have also received substantial funds from Turkey for charitable or humanitarian work.

Further efforts to increase Turkish influence inside Iraqi Kurdistan followed the arrival in Dohuk governorate in 1994 of 12,000–14,000 Turkish Kurdish refugees. The Turkish authorities regarded these refugees as part of the PKK. While it was evi-dent that the PKK had relations with some of the refugees and was active in their camp, the majority were women and children.[42] Turkish suspicions about the role of NGOs as well as journalists focused on whether they were in any way assisting or contacting these Turkish refugees. The authorities accused aid agencies of supporting or assisting the PKK, though only a handful of NGOs worked with UNHCR in Atrush camp, where the refugees were living, and this scarcely made them PKK supporters. After strong pressure from the Turkish Government, UNHCR finally closed Atrush camp in December 1996.[43]

Another result of Turkish concerns about PKK influence was the increasing control they imposed on the movement of international NGO staff, who had pre-viously moved quite freely across the border. From September 1994 onwards NGOs had to name of all staff working in Iraq, and the list was held at the border. From September 1995, individual applications for visas had to be made, and each agency had to supply additional information on its work, including annual reports and details of its aid programme. At this point, several agencies found their work disrupted when staff who had been going in and out of the area without problems suddenly could not get visas.[44] From September 1996 the Turkish authorities indicated that no visas would be issued until 'all NGOs' had complied with requirements for information and visa applications. As of mid-1998, the Turkish border remained closed to NGOs.

Finally, Turkish military activities inside the borders of northern Iraq created a precarious security situation for people living in rebuilt villages in those regions, jeopardising the work of both villagers and aid agencies to restore the rural economy. There were instances of rebuilt homes and facilities being destroyed and the inhabitants displaced.[45] Once the PUK–KDP conflict began in 1994, and the cross-border Turkish–PKK fighting intensified in the following year, security problems overtook other concerns for those resettled in proximity to the Turkish border. The area affected by both the PKK and Turkish army activities has expanded since 1995. Subsequently, many have left because of the increased presence of the PKK in the area and frequent incursions of Turkish forces. Some, sadly, have ended up returning to collective towns, having nowhere else to go.

The inter-Kurdish conflict

From 1994, the number of apparently Iraqi Government-inspired attacks on aid workers declined but the political climate in which the agencies had to work deteriorated. The inter-Kurdish fighting did not directly threaten aid organisations but hampered daily work. In some instances local commanders made life difficult for aid workers, though at a formal level the Kurdish leadership continued to welcome NGOs and urged them to stay, regarding them, like the UN Guards and the no-fly zone, as a token of international support.[46]

The more influential NGOs expressed their concern to the Kurdish leaders at the damage being done to the population, and warned that if the fighting continued they might have to stop their work. They joined Western governments in pointing out that the Kurds were damaging their international image and jeopardising their chances of continued funding from an international community faced with many other pressing demands for aid. However, at least until 1998 these messages largely fell on deaf ears.

Meanwhile, the acute humanitarian problems caused by new population displacements, the interruption of payments to public employees and further weakening of public services hampered economic and social recovery. Most ministries were divided into separate PUK and KDP components, creating difficulties for NGOs. Some agencies tried to work with both sides; others, because of the geographical location of their programmes, had to deal with one side or the other. Efforts were made to bring officials from the two sides together to deal with practical issues – for example in preparing public examinations – but each round of fighting halted such initiatives.

Aid agencies experienced intensified pressure from the political parties to create political 'balance' by working on both sides of the KDP–PUK divide, regardless of whether they had identified a particular need. Some donors, including ECHO, reportedly also began to press for an 'even-handed' approach.

From 1994, the significant numbers of Kurdish staff working for international NGOs began to feel the pressure of party rivalries. Employees who were identified with one party found it difficult to continue working for an NGO with a programme in the territory of the other. The fact that the international NGOs disposed of large amounts of money meant local staff were sometimes subject to pressures to ensure that those funds were used in ways favourable to the party in control. There seems to have been relatively little overt violence, but even international NGOs found it increasingly difficult to maintain neutrality and even-handedness between the parties while at the same time protecting their own staff members.

The inter-Kurdish conflict weakened not just the administration, but all local civil structures not directly related to the PUK and KDP. Most local NGOs had some party allegiance or were under the patronage of a powerful individual with party ties. International NGOs which already had clear political allegiances accepted this situation. Those which had hoped to support local NGOs in achieving a more independent position, 'left that concept behind', as it simply could not work in that climate of polarisation.

The US withdrawal

The Iraqi incursion into Arbil in September 1996, and the subsequent growth of Iraqi government influence in parts of northern Iraq further increased the potential difficulties for international NGOs and their local staff. The US Government's decision to pull out all US nationals and local staff who had any connection with US organisations also had repercussions for the rest of the international aid community.[47]

Soon after the attack on Arbil, over 2000 local staff who worked directly for the MCC and OFDA were taken via Turkey to Guam to be resettled in the US. Then some 600 Iraqis who had been associated with the CIA were evacuated, after waiting in hiding for more than a month. The Iraqi Kurdish parties responded 'very reluctantly to the US request to help with the evacuation.[48] Finally, in late November, at the urging of NGOs in the US, some 4000 local people who had worked for American NGOs and for US-funded organisations in Iraqi Kurdistan were given the opportunity to leave with their families.[49]

No other country withdrew its aid workers *en masse*. At the time when the KDP took Sulaymaniya, some local employees of international aid organisations fled to Iran, fearing that Iraqi agents would regard them as traitors. However, most returned once the PUK retook Sulaymaniya. Other donors and NGOs were critical of the manner in which the US exodus was conducted, describing it as 'excessive' and 'an overreaction'. The British Government argued that it sent the wrong message to Saddam Hussein about the West's commitment to protect the Kurdish region.[50] British officials argued that a better course would have been to withdraw temporarily and see how the situation developed, rather than effectively to remove US NGOs from the region for the duration.

Apparently some State Department officials had doubts about withdrawing the whole US aid operation. But with a presidential election near, the administration insisted. There was also pressure from US organisations. The US Committee for Refugees, and InterAction, a coordinating body for US NGOs, argued that US agencies and their local employees were particularly vulnerable because of the CIA's presence in the north, and because of the US role vis-à-vis Iraq since 1991. There were fears that the Iraqis would return to the area in full force, with unknown consequences for local employees of 'illegal' international NGOs. The Iraqi Government protested the evacuations and emphasised that aid organisations should not send international staff or hired local employees without the approval of the Government.[51] A few US aid organisations which did not concur with their Government's action argued, however, that the act of withdrawal made NGOs appear to have too close an association with the US Government and its policies.

The US action reduced donor funding, as funds channelled via OFDA interrupted and depleted the capacities of NGOs in the north as a group, at the time when Resolution 986 was coming into operation. It also contributed to the outflow of skilled and well-educated people. Both State Department officials and those in the US NGO community who advocated the withdrawals admit that these were drawbacks.

In earlier years, a concern in the back of the minds of aid agency managers was how to get staff out of Iraqi Kurdistan if there was a crisis. Since September 1996, with Turkey effectively closing its border to aid personnel, the headache became how to guarantee that staff could get into the region at all. Aid agencies were obliged to enter Iraqi Kurdistan from Syria, whose commitment to keeping this border open as a transit route for aid workers in future was not assured.[52] Some agencies have also had staff refused entry because their activities do not meet with the approval of the KDP, which controls entry into the Kurdish region via Syria. Efforts by the EU and member states to persuade Turkey to reopen its borders to aid organisations had, as of early 1998, been unsuccessful.

Resolution 986 and the changing status of NGOs

By 1997, the 'age of the NGO' in Iraqi Kurdistan seemed to be over. It was certainly due for a rethink. The aid community was unable to prevent the burgeoning black economy of smuggling and party-based monopolies from expanding. It did not have the capacity to combat the structures of patronage which, in the absence of a state structure, has helped people to survive. Aid agencies could become players as patrons, but had not found ways to break the cycle. This could only be done by establishing a more viable economy which promoted employment and self-sufficiency, and by offering support – both in funds and capacity building – to a credible form of regional administration.

Aside from the impact of aid programmes, the inflows of funds with the UN and NGOs have, as is characteristic, contributed to the local economy: to employment for those with certain skills, to high rents on housing and storage facilities, to the transport sector and probably to considerable profits for merchants and middlemen reselling aid goods. In early 1995, the total number of Iraqis employed by the aid programme was estimated at 3899, of whom 3683 were employed by NGOs, the vast majority in the north. Hence in employment terms as in most other ways, the north benefitted more from the presence of aid agencies than Government areas.[53] Resolution 986 has put significant amounts of money into the local economy and has increased local employment by the UN, though only on short-term contracts.

The inflow of food, medicines and basic goods under Resolution 986 improved the humanitarian situation, particularly in urban areas. It has resulted in the restoration of a ration for the whole population, compared with the WFP's previous target vulnerable group of some 750,000. The *de facto* lifting of the Iraqi embargo on the north (on most, though not all, movement of goods) also eased the economic situation. However, all this does nothing to deal with the causes of poverty: low or non-existent salaries for those in work, and large numbers of people with no form of employment. The UN Secretary General's report of 1 February 1998 emphasised that the humanitarian situation in the north remained 'precarious, with shortages in electricity having a critical impact on virtually all other sectors, including hospitals, pumps for water and sewerage, and irrigation for agriculture'.[54]

There are a variety of conflicting interests in determining the use of these funds (see box). The main interest of the UN is its role in delivering supplies. Some NGOs have been critical of its planning for the use of these funds in the north, arguing that its approach is 'top down' and does not sufficiently involve either NGOs or the local administrations.

Resolution 986 and food aid

Imported food aid has been criticised strongly by NGOs in Iraqi Kurdistan because it tended to discourage or undermine the revival of local agriculture. In the summer of 1993, WFP launched a harvest buy-back scheme, mainly as an attempt to prevent the big Kurdish landowners from exporting their grain harvest to government-controlled areas. However, some NGOs felt that the scheme was primarily intended to benefit WFP, which was running out of food, by building up stocks locally instead of having to import from Turkey. The buy-back did not reach the target volume of grain, and WFP claimed that there were problems with local milling capacity and the variable quality of the flour. It seems that the scheme also brought objections from the Baghdad Government, and it was discontinued in 1994.

The clashes of interest between the needs of the agricultural sector and the urban population resurfaced once Resolution 986 was implemented. The resolution allowed the Iraqi Government to act as food purchaser for the whole country, and its control over all flour milling has been criticised as giving a stranglehold over Iraqi Kurdistan.

The inflow of food has improved the living conditions of the urban population and lessened the danger of malnutrition. However, some critics have again argued that importing grains and pulses brings down local agricultural prices, thus undermining efforts to re-establish the region's rural economy. Since agriculture is the only economic sector aside from smuggling in which there is significant activity, it seems important to support the local market. For the large-scale cereal-producing farmers the most likely option is to sell their produce in other markets – whether direct to government-controlled Iraq, to Turkey or Iran; to reduce the acreage they plant; or to switch to other crops. Some of these large landowners also have significant non-agricultural sources of income.

However, small farmers have fewer alternatives and aid agencies have suggested that the low prices have discouraged many from planting cereal crops. The restoration of the ration has also led to a decline in trade, both in locally produced food and some agricultural inputs. On the more positive side, since the implementation of Resolution 986 in the north, the FAO has reported improved animal health, higher yields, greater crop protection and lower prices for agricultural inputs.[55]

By mid-1998, the UN admitted that there was an oversupply of food in the north, suggesting that it would be better to rely more on local production than to continue importing food. However, the terms of the oil-for-food resolutions and the MoU between the Iraqi Government and the UN do not allow local purchase of goods with oil funds. Hence, under the scheme, foodstuffs have to be purchased outside the country. Any exception made for Iraqi Kurdistan would meet resistance from the Government, or demands that it too should be allowed to use the oil funds for local purchases.

The Kurdish administrations had achieved some degree of cooperation in humanitarian matters by mid-1998, and given the growing discontent of their own followers with the problems caused by inter-party conflict, welcomed the improvements in conditions. Local administration officials, meanwhile, needed the money to pay salaries. The administrations did not appear to have any long-term strategies of their own, and considered themselves in a weak position vis-à-vis the UN, which only had limited consultations with them. Although import taxes are not charged on goods imported under Resolution 986, and hence party coffers (mostly those of the KDP) are not swelled by this new inflow of goods, control over their distribution (including lucrative transport contracts and contracts for building and infrastructural work) was undoubtedly a significant consideration. UN officials, meanwhile, saw the administrations as demanding excessive control over who got the contracts.

The implementation of Resolution 986 reversed the situation in the pre-1996 period, when international and local NGOs served as the channel for most of the funds coming into the region. Now these are under UN auspices, with NGOs in some cases sub-contracted to do certain tasks. In this sense, many agencies working in the north regarded Resolution 986 as firstly a threat and only secondarily as an opportunity.

There has been a marked decline in the number of international NGOs which still work in Iraqi Kurdistan, mainly because some of the main donors have either dramatically reduced their funding (OFDA), or have switched most of their funding to government-controlled areas (ECHO). For those which remain, the options have been to play the role of subcontractors for the UN in the disbursement of oil-for-food funds, which does not allow them to be involved in the planning, implementation and evaluation of programmes. If they operate outside the framework of Resolution 986, working in areas which the UN does not cover, they are constrained by lack of funding, difficulties of access to the region, and staffing problems as increasing numbers of trained and professional people try to leave the region.

The political uncertainties relating to the future of sanctions overshadow the programme. It is clear that the Iraqi Government is reluctant to continue with limited oil sales, and hopes to see sanctions lifted. The international community remains divided on the issue. In Iraqi Kurdistan, as the benefits of funds from the oil sale begin to make a difference to living standards, there is more inclination to support the continuation of limited sales. The leadership fears the freedom of action which the lifting of sanctions would give to the Iraqi Government, while there appears to be no guarantee of any continuing form of external protection for the Kurds. Faced with this scenario, the continuation of limited oil sales seems a more attractive option.

INFORMATION AND ITS USES: ASSESSING THE IMPACT OF SANCTIONS

With economic sanctions in place, aid agencies could in theory have provided the data which would show incontrovertibly whether unacceptable damage was being done to the civilian population of the sanctioned state. In Iraq, this role has not proved easy to fulfil. All humanitarian agencies operating in Iraq have been constrained by the limits on their freedom of movement and the absence of bases outside Baghdad from which they could systematically observe the welfare of the population, or track possible diversions of goods.

Furthermore, as already noted, there has been no system of independent monitoring to track the impact of sanctions on the population, with the result that the aid
available has not necessarily been targeted in the most effective way. Both the Iraqi
Government and the warring Kurdish political parties played their part in trying to
direct aid to suit their political goals rather than the welfare of the population.

The mixture of secrecy and political manipulation of information by all sides has
added to the difficulties for independent researchers. Furthermore, most of the
research concentrated on mortality, morbidity and malnutrition. Very little detailed
research has been done on other, more long-term, social indicators.

In post-war conditions in Iraq, a number of problems have arisen in measuring
the impact on morbidity, mortality and malnutrition. First, it is unclear which baseline data from the 1980s is reliable. Although no-one contests that infant and child
mortality levels fell rapidly in Iraq during the 1980s, aggregate nationwide figures
may not reflect major variations between different regions of the country, or different
sections of society.[56] A second problem relates to the difficulty of conducting nationwide sample surveys of the population since 1991, or doing regular surveys of the
same areas which would give a measure of change over time. The earliest studies
alerted the world to the fact that war and sanctions were adversely affecting the
population, but each had considerable limitations, using small samples or partial
statistics.[57] The first rapid survey of health conditions and medical supplies was
conducted by a joint WHO/UNICEF team in the midst of the war, for the most part
in the Baghdad metropolitan area.[58] The Harvard Study Team, visiting Iraq in April
and May 1991, used hospital statistics from a number of centres to project likely
under-five mortality for the whole country.[59]

In addition to some studies of Kurdish refugees in the north returning to the safe
haven area, there were three small-scale studies on child malnutrition in southern
Iraq between May and August 1991.[60] These had the advantage of examining conditions in areas hard hit by wars and sanctions – Basra and Amara governorates – but
they were based on small sample surveys supplemented by hospital or clinic records.

One of these studies, commissioned by UNICEF and Tufts University, was an
example of how nutritional data could become part of the political debate. The team
noted that the stunting they found among both urban and rural children in Basra
governorate (suggesting chronic malnutrition) meant that not all the malnutritional
problems were linked to sanctions. The press release issued by Tufts University in
early July – when the first post-war debates were taking place in the Security Council
and in the media on the future of sanctions – emphasised that there were no signs of
imminent famine, and that pre-existing malnutrition was the fault of the Iraqi
Government. Thus, it argued, there was no justification for lifting sanctions. The
report's authors, on the other hand, while stating that famine conditions did not exist
at that time in Iraq, stressed that they could easily emerge, and that the longer the
embargo continued, the more young children, already prone to malnutrition, would
be at risk.[61]

The first nationwide survey was conducted in August 1991 by the International
Study Team (IST). The IST study was a community-based sample survey in all Iraq's
governorates, based on the 1987 census. It suffered from the drawbacks of working
in what was still a crisis situation. Large numbers of people had been displaced since
1987, so that the census figures were seriously outdated. The samples covered women
between the ages of fifteen and forty-nine who had given birth in the previous six

years. However, this missed out a significant number of orphans, children separated from their parents and women or children who were away from home through illness or other reasons.

Despite the limitations of the IST survey, it did represent a country-wide sample, and unimpeded access was gained to most areas. However, when the initial findings were published in late 1991 their impact was diminished by the political backwash caused by Iraq's refusal to accept Resolutions 706 and 712. There were also criticisms of the results, particularly of the initial findings on infant mortality. After re-analysis, the researchers concluded that there had been some 46,900 excess deaths of children under-five in the eight months from the beginning of 1991, representing more than a three-fold increase on the pre-war period.[62]

Further analysis suggested that the main causes of infant and under-five mortality were probably diarrhoeal disease (mainly water-related), acute respiratory infections and refugee accidents, with a smaller impact from nutritional factors than might initially have been expected. It has been pointed out that many children whose systems were accustomed to clean water and living conditions initially had no immunity to water-borne bugs.[63]

Despite their various limitations, all these studies suggested that malnutrition had sharply increased. There were several key reasons. First, the collapse of water and sanitation facilities led to widespread diarrhoeal disease among young children. Second, actual shortages of food in the country were probably less significant than its escalating cost in relation to incomes. The Tufts/UNICEF study also noted that doctors frequently did not identify or record 'malnutrition' in their medical notes as a condition, but rather recorded the symptoms they treated. Hence the use of medical records in some of these surveys would have created some distortions.[64]

All surveys had to rely on the Government's census data to generate samples, and researchers have usually worked with the state-run National Research Institute and the Central Statistical Organisation. The main source of health data is obviously the Ministry of Health, the quality of whose data is thought to have declined significantly since 1990. It has always relied heavily on hospital-based statistics. But during the period 1991–7, diminishing numbers of people attended hospitals because medicine and treatment were in short supply. Consequently, rates of illness and mortality would be less accurately reflected by hospital records. In addition, many deaths attributed to 'sanctions' could be the result of other problems, or it could be that the cause of death remained unknown because laboratory and diagnostic equipment was lacking.[65]

In 1993, a team conducting the WFP/FAO nutritional survey commented that much of the data provided by the Ministry of Health was inadequate to reach any clear conclusions. There were no longitudinal studies on nutrition in government-controlled areas, on which a reliable estimate of nutritional status in different areas could be based. The 1995 FAO report mentioned the Ministry of Health's estimate of 109,720 deaths annually between August 1990 and March 1994 as a result of the effects of sanctions. 'The Mission was unable to confirm these numbers', though it conceded they were 'plausible'.[66]

Subsequent nutritional studies – for example those commissioned by the FAO in 1993 and 1995, and a study sponsored by the Centre for Economic and Social Rights (New York) in 1996 – were based on sample surveys in neighbourhoods of Baghdad, with a particular focus on Saddam City, one of the poorest areas. These had the benefit of returning to the same areas for comparison but the disadvantages of being conducted over very short time periods, being limited to one part of the country, and surveying a very small sample.

The 1993 survey in Saddam City of 506 persons, some of whom had been included in the International Study Team survey in 1991, concluded that 'the nutritional situation, particularly among children under the age of five, has deteriorated among underprivileged urban dwellers'.[67] These sample surveys also indicated that children of illiterate mothers – likely to be among the poorest families – were faring almost three times worse than those with mothers with high levels of education, with an eight-fold increase in mortality compared with a three-fold one. This certainly conforms with other findings on child health and mothers' education in poor countries.

In Iraqi Kurdistan, it was easier to conduct social, nutritional and health surveys and to evaluate the outcomes of aid programmes, but in practice agencies tended to gather information which only covered their specific area of work. For the most part, these data were for internal use, and not shared with other agencies. From 1994 onwards, survey work was sometimes interrupted by fighting and problems of access. By 1998, the absence of any coordinated databases on the region was still evident.

In 1996, UNICEF and the Government's Central Statistical Office conducted cluster surveys in all eighteen governorates. This was the first country-wide survey since the IST survey in 1991, and its authors claimed that it gave a better picture of the differences between regions than the IST had been able to provide. Recent research which attempts to use a variety of sources to estimate mortality rates for under-fives (considered the most vulnerable group under sanctions conditions) came up with an estimate of 88 per 1000 country-wide. However, broken down regionally, there is a variation from 76 for greater Baghdad, to 81 for the three northern governorates and 83 for the central governorates, but 102 for the southern governorates.[68]

The Western media have tended to give more attention to scenarios of famine and death than to the observations of aid agencies, which emphasised the structural problems in the health, water and sanitation sectors. Some observers, including UN officials, accept that in the years since the Gulf War the cry of imminent famine in Iraq has been raised too often. For the purposes of raising funds in a hostile environment it might have seemed appropriate, but it conjures up images of an Ethiopian or Somali-type situation which are not substantiated. Whatever the criticisms of the Iraqi government ration system, it does appear to have prevented this happening. But in combination with a major decline in environmental health and medical services, moderate-to-acute levels of malnutrition and vulnerability to disease among the most vulnerable groups has resulted in excess deaths.

Longer-term effects of sanctions which are not measurable at present may include the impact on the growth and development of children and an increase in illness and death from stress-related diseases. The long-term impact of inadequate nutrition on the health of poorer women, especially during their child-bearing years, may also become evident. When food is short it is usually women in the family who get least to eat and who therefore tend to bear the brunt of deprivation and strain of overwork.

The experience of aid agencies also led to questions about the effectiveness of the system of humanitarian exceptions put in place after April 1991. Suggestions have been made for criteria to regulate the humanitarian impact of economic embargoes, setting a level below which living standards – based on indicators of infant mortality, public health and food supply – should not decline.[69]

The impact of sanctions has to be seen as a sequence: from the immediate shocks imposed by the interruption of trade, and government responses, to the intermediate effects on health and food security, and finally to the long-term effects on social support systems and the results of chronic economic decline. To be meaningful, therefore, an assessment of impact when an embargo is in place over a number of years would need to go beyond the national statistics of per capita GDP, infant mortality rates, or output indicators. Less easily measurable forms of 'collateral damage' need to be considered in assessing the longer-term impact of sanctions: for example, the impact of sanctions not only on basic civilian infrastructure and the health of the population, but also on education and employment structures.

Another issue about which little hard information exists is the differential impact of economic sanctions on various sections of the population, by region and across social classes, or how the power structures within the country have adapted and whether they have gained new forms of control over the population. Recently, some researchers have stressed that the household is the most effective unit for analysis of impact, particularly on the most vulnerable, who include children, the chronically sick and the elderly. Data at this level is thought to be much more sensitive to impacts than aggregate regional or national data.[70]

In political situations like that of Iraq, a major question is how these indicators would be monitored, even if the international community could agree on the relevant criteria. So far everyone agrees that in Iraq effective monitoring has been weak and in some sectors non-existent. Furthermore, the UN humanitarian agencies do not see their mandates as including monitoring of this kind, which can appear as 'intelligence' work for the Security Council.

NOTES ON CHAPTER 8

1   Among those which did continue to have a presence in the south until mid-1992 were Oxfam (UK) in Amara and Nasariya, SCF (US) in Basra, and a German agency, Action Directe Hilfe, in Nasariya. Oxfam continued to work in the south until 1995.

2   This applied even to highly reputable organisations such as the American Friends Service Committee and Church World Service. A good deal of time and energy could be taken up in organising such deliveries from the US. The US Treasury Office of Foreign Assets Control had to licence even the transfer of funds to a third party. One source said it took at least six months to get authorisation. The US Treasury Department reportedly tended to blame the UN Secretariat (Sanctions Committee) and the latter blamed the Treasury Department. When obtained, licences for Iraq were for a limited time period.

3   Kuttab (1992), p 38.

4   Hoskins (1997), p 135.

5   The other major social organisation in the country is the General Federation of Iraqi Women which, like the Iraqi Red Crescent, works from regional offices and is closely tied to government and party.

6   Jim Fine, interview with the author, 23 May 1997.

7   Some observers have argued, however, that in Christian communities the involvement of the laity in distribution of aid since the Gulf crisis seemed to have brought some changes within traditionally hierarchical church structures.

8   Some donors, including the British Overseas Development Agency, channelled small

amounts of assistance to some Iraqi humanitarian organisations in Iran which were also involved in smuggling aid (both goods and money) into southern Iraq.

9   *The Times*, 7 June 1991, 'Saddam Food Pilfering Halts UN Aid Shipments'; *The Times*, 1 July, 'UN Food Aid' (letter from WFP).

10 *Guardian*, 4 November 1991, 'Baghdad Blocks Direct Relief to Children'.

11 Letter dated 15 February 1998 form the Deputy Prime Minister and Acting Minister for Foreign Affairs of the Republic of Iraq to the UN Secretary General, S/1998/125.

12 ICRC, *Water in Iraq*, Special Brochure, Geneva, July 1996.

13 The American Friends Service Committee and Quaker Peace and Service in the UK had a particularly intense debate on the advisability of becoming involved in development work in Iraq. The focus on rehabilitation work, it was argued, was consistent with the original reasons for becoming involved in Iraq: as recognition of Western governments' responsibility in destroying Iraqi infrastructure; as opposition to the continuation of non-military sanctions against post-war Iraq; and more appropriate for a country of Iraq's (potential) wealth. For them to undertake development work effectively and responsibly would require a long-term commitment to work in the country which was not felt to be appropriate. It was felt by QPS that to begin a development project and withdraw after a few years would probably cause more damage than benefit.

14 Kuttab (1992), p 38.

15 *Le Monde*, 14 May 1997, 'Les difficiles relations entre Baghdad et les ONG'. Some seven agencies were based in Baghdad as of late 1998, most of them French.

16 On the whole, the NGOs did not have large staffs, but a few agencies, such as Care and SCF UK, had substantial numbers of employees including guards, drivers and cleaners. In 1994, Care International/Care Australia had approximately 1400 national staff in Iraq.

17 The military and the Department of Defence reportedly 'did not want to be in the humanitarian business' (Cuny [1995], p 39).

18 OFDA (1996), p 13.

19 For example, Medico International and Aide Médicale International.

20 De Boer and Leezenberg (eds) (1993), p 84, Group Session 2: NGOs in Kurdistan and the Regional Authority – Coordination, Planning and Policies.

21 Netherlands Kurdistan Society (1996), p 38.

22 Keen (1993), p 39. It was not until money became available under Resolution 986 that UN mines work got underway.

23 Hama (1997), p 18.

24 Netherlands Kurdistan Society (1996), p 38.

25 A major improvement was the annual sunnapest spraying campaign, mainly funded by the ODA. Previously aerial spraying had been carried out by the Iraqi Ministry of Agriculture, but political complications with the no-fly zone prevented this. For 1993–4 the sunnapest programme was run by SCF and funded by the ODA. Between 1994 and 1997, the ODA gave contracts to experts who ran the programme in the field, with the ODA paying for equipment.

26 OFDA (1996), p 9.

27 Netherlands Kurdistan Society (1996), p 38.

28 Hama (1997), pp 20–22.

29 *Ibid.*, pp 27–28.

30 Netherlands Kurdistan Society (1996), p 8.

31 The World Food Programme used the system of food agents established by the Iraqi Government but targeted only specific groups: those displaced from Kirkuk, residents of collective settlements, hospitals and other institutions, and, as salaries of civil servants slipped below subsistence, teachers and civil servants. There have been occasional 'general distributions' within cities and periodic distributions to rural communities. Between 1992 and 1995, Care International/Care Australia did the distribution of goods.

32   Ward and Rimmer (1995), p 30.

33   OFDA (1996), p 5.

34   Netherlands Kurdistan Society (1996), p 21.

35   Handicap International did not send in any further permanent international staff after Vincent Tollet's death. Since that time, local staff have continued the programme in Sulaymaniya, but in December 1993 one HI local staff member was killed and several injured in a bomb attack during the first round of inter-Kurdish fighting in Sulaymaniya. The remaining local staff, however, requested further external support and training.

36   Médecins sans Frontières withdrew from the region in 1993, arguing that for an organisation which focuses on emergency medical care, the needs at that time did not justify remaining if this scale of security provision was necessary.

37   Hama (1997), p 17.

38   Turkey was also the single largest source for the purchase of humanitarian goods (excluding food aid), though the authorities often complained that the UN did not purchase sufficient amounts there (Cuny [1995], p 21).

39   OFDA (1996), p 4.

40   In 1996 the operation of the UNDHA's Silopi transportation office had to be transferred to WFP after the Turkish authorities reportedly tried to interfere in the DHA's appointment of a director.

41   Cuny (1995), p 21.

42   Human Rights Watch, *World Report* 1996, p 286 noted that these refugees were at risk during the 1995 Turkish incursion, during which UNHCR sought to protect them by moving them further from the border. According to Human Rights Watch/Middle East, '... Turkey stated it only targeted PKK rebels, however, Kurdish civilians from both Turkey and Iraq were casualties in the fighting'.

43   The refugees from the camp dispersed, with about 1000 reportedly returning to Turkey. About half the remaining refugees relocated to the KDP-controlled areas of northern Iraq. However, 6800 refugees moved south, to the border between KDP- and government-controlled areas at Sheykhan, south of Ain Sifni (43kms from Mosul), and reportedly requested help from the Iraqi Government. UNHCR was reportedly working with the Iraqi Red Crescent to improve sanitary conditions, and WFP was providing food rations.

44   For example, staff from Christian Aid and the International Catholic Migration Commission were refused visas. The ostensible reason given by the Turkish Government was the Christian orientation of these agencies, which were thought to be 'proselytising', something which is not in their mandates. There was no apparent logic to the accusation, except for the agencies' names.

45   For example, the UN reported that in April 1996, military operations in the border area displaced about 1000 families from villages around Zakho and Amadiya (UN Consolidated Inter-Agency Humanitarian Assistance Programme to Iraq, *Implementation Report for the period 1 April 1996-31 August 1996* [September 1996], p 2. In March/April 1995 OFDA reported a similar number of families displaced by Turkish incursions, and reduced access for NGOs in areas under Turkish military occupation. US Agency for International Development, Office of US Foreign Disaster Assistance (OFDA), *Situation Report: Northern Iraq – Displaced Persons*, No. 3 (FY 1995) (April 26 1995), p 1.

46   See, for example, UN Department of Humanitarian Affairs, Note on 'The Humanitarian Situation in North Iraq', 18 September 1996.

47   In 1991, a dispute had arisen between military commanders of Operation Provide Comfort and the State Department over whether to offer asylum to a small group of Kurds who were regarded as being at risk after OPC forces left because they had worked very closely with US forces. After much bureaucratic shuffling and resistance from the

State Department, the military took the decision to fly the group to Turkey, having secured the Turkish Government's agreement to give them temporary asylum while their cases were processed. For a detailed account of this incident, see Brilliant *et al* (1995), pp 36–38.

48 *New York Times*, 'Aid Workers: US Exit From Northern Iraq Will Cripple Efforts', 16 September 1996; *al-Hayat* (London), 2 August 1998, 'Robert Pelletreau, the Kurdish Negotiations'.

49 *Washington Post*, 'US to Help More Kurds Flee Iraq', 26 November 1996. These were known as 'quick transit' categories. The last category (QT3) consisted of three sub-groups: anyone working for a US NGO with an OFDA contract, for example ICMC, IRC and Shelter Now International; second, those working for other US NGOs. This included small organisations – for example, Wells of Life and Concern for Kids – some of which were local religious groups in the US; third, staff of local Kurdish NGOs which had worked under OFDA contracts (Bill Frelick, interview with the author, 15 May 1997).

50 *Guardian*, 11 December 1996, 'Saddam Fails to Hit Right Button to Satisfy West'.

51 BBC Summary of World Broadcasts, 8 November 1996, 'Iraq accuses USA of providing "illegal protection" to NGO employees', quoting INA news agency (Baghdad), 7 November 1996.

52 Travel permissions have not been formalised. Syria gives entry visas, but not exit or re-entry visas at Syria-Iraq border, and visas have to be renewed in Damascus.

53 UNDHA Cooperation Programme, *Implementation Report 1994–5*, p 108.

54 United Nations Security Council (1998i), paras 41–2.

55 Majid (forthcoming).

56 A recent survey of data, examining a number of sources, estimated the infant mortality rate (IMR – children under one year) in 1990 as 32–34 per 1000, and under-five mortality as 38–41 per 1000 (Garfield [1999]). However, other sources using demographic estimates of long-term trends, give higher figures. The World Bank gave IMR for Iraq as 67 per 1000 live births in 1989 (119 in 1965) (*World Development Report* 1991) and UNICEF gave an IMR of 70 per 1000 in 1987 (139 in 1960), with under-five mortality at 96 per 1000 (222 in 1960) (*Health of the World's Children* 1989). A UNICEF study published in the late 1980s gave IMR in 1980 as 89 per 1000 falling to 40 per 1000 or less in 1989, dropping faster in rural areas where it had been higher than average. It seems the improvement was due at least in part to a greater emphasis in the latter years of the war on child survival policies which fitted with the pro-natalist strategy of the Government. Urban-rural discrepancies were lessened but not eliminated, and those areas closest to the war zones probably saw least improvement (Sayigh [1992], pp 49, 57).

57 *Independent*, 2 March 1991, 'UN Warns of Human "Catastrophe"'; Press Release for Harvard Study Team Report, 22 May 1991, '170,000 Iraqi Children to Die From Delayed Effects of Gulf Crisis'.

58 WHO/UNICEF, *Special Mission to Iraq*, February 1991.

59 Harvard Study Team (1991).

60 Helen Keller International (1991); Field and Russell (1992), pp 41–46; Sato, Obeid and Brun (1991), p 1202.

61 Field and Russell (1992), p 46; House of Representatives, Select Committee on Hunger, Humanitarian Dilemma in Iraq: Challenge for US Policy: Hearing before the International Task Force of the Select Committee on Hunger, 102nd Congress, 1st session, August 1, 1991, pp 33–34.

62 Ascherio, *et al* (1992), p 933.

63 Sarah Zaidy, interview with the author, May 1997.

64 Smith and Zaidy (1993), p 77; Field and Russell, pp 43–44.

65 Garfield (1999).

66 FAO 1995, Section IV, General Health and Nutrition Background.
67 Quoted in *Gulf Newsletter*, March 1994, no. 9, 'Food and Nutrition in Iraq', p 4.
68 Garfield (1999).
69 This approach was suggested by Eric Hoskins, who was part of the International Study Team in 1991, in subsequent work for UNICEF, based on the experience of the prolonged embargo against Iraq (Weiss *et al* [1997], p 38).
70 *Ibid.*

PART III
OVERVIEW

THE DILEMMAS OF HUMANITARIAN ACTION IN IRAQ

The experience of protracted humanitarian crises in the 1990s, in Iraq and elsewhere, have undermined the idea that 'emergencies' are, of their nature, short-lived and will be followed by the restoration of 'normality'.[1] The causes of these crises – in Iraq, Somalia and Rwanda – have been essentially political, and conflict has been perpetuated by the inability of either the protagonists or the external powers involved to find solutions. In the case of Iraq, the initial conflict was triggered by an event with international dimensions – the invasion of Kuwait. However, a second, internal, crisis followed Iraq's defeat in that war. The international crisis was prolonged because Iraq refused over the course of more than seven years to comply with all aspects of the post-war ceasefire terms. Meanwhile, conflicts between different elements in Iraq's population have remained unresolved and large sections of the population remain vulnerable, both as a result of economic deprivation and human rights abuses.

For aid agencies, one challenge was to find an effective role in mitigating the impact of international sanctions and their consequences, intended and unintended, for the civilian population. Another was to address the continuing infringement of basic civil and political rights – in particular the rights of minorities and groups who are disempowered by the state – while at the same time dealing with the economic and social costs of sanctions. Finally, there was the problem of planning and implementing coherent strategies for rehabilitation in a situation of conflict which was played out at regional, national and local levels.

The serious failures of international intervention and humanitarian action in crises in the former Yugoslavia and Rwanda have led to a measure of self-criticism among aid agencies. The Iraq case has produced less soul-searching, but in fact it has confronted NGOs quite starkly with the issue of access versus effectiveness, and raised the question of their ability to speak out about conditions in the country. It is probably fair to say that after the initial emergency, most agencies' responses were reactive rather than strategic, and few had a clear sense of goals. This was partly the result of the peculiar conditions created by sanctions and the highly politicised climate. But it also raised questions about the ethos of aid agency operations: for example, what are the acceptable limits of agency autonomy – for each to choose its goals, its staff (local and international) and its way of operating? At what point does this concern with autonomy become a reluctance to cooperate, an over-emphasis on competition with other agencies, for money and areas to work? What are the benefits of this way of working to the local communities and organisations with which the NGOs work?

AID AND ECONOMIC SANCTIONS

After the [Gulf] war, the United Nations found itself in an unprecedented role. It implemented and tried to enforce the economic embargo which, whatever its broader political objectives, was generally recognised as being a primary cause of widespread disease and malnutrition. At the same time the United Nations humanitarian agencies tried to alleviate the same crisis.[2]

Under the conditions created by sanctions, the humanitarian role of the international community, according to one analyst, is compensatory: 'To protect civilians, aid organisations are obliged to mount additional assistance efforts, sometimes on a triage basis, until the sanctions impasse ends'.[3] Most humanitarian agencies did not feel comfortable with this role. Many regard the prolonged use of a comprehensive economic embargo as unjust in that it causes disproportionate suffering to the vulnerable groups upon whose behalf they aim to act. As one aid worker put it, 'We break their legs and give them crutches'. However, as long as the UN Security Council 'leg-breaking' continues, vulnerable people in Iraq continue to need the 'crutches' in the form of assistance from the UN and other humanitarian agencies.

Interviews have highlighted the great difficulties faced by those who wish to 'de-politicise' aid in such a highly polarised and conflictive atmosphere. As one analysis noted, 'attempts by humanitarian staff to keep their distance from the political aspects of the UN were as unsuccessful as attempts by the UN's political organs to accommodate humanitarian concerns'.[4]

The dual role of the UN as enforcer of the embargo and provider of humanitarian aid challenged the neutrality of its humanitarian agencies. Their response – to put as much distance as possible between themselves and the decisions of the Security Council – was neither easy to sustain nor, in the view of many observers, satisfactory. Sadruddin Aga Khan, the UN Secretary General's Executive Delegate to Iraq who negotiated the April 1991 Memorandum of Understanding, was convinced of the need to establish this distance, arguing that the consent of the Iraqi Government for an aid programme was necessary and that humanitarian aid had to be separated from the political concerns of the Security Council. He saw concessions to induce Iraq to accept the UN Guards and the UN/NGO humanitarian programme as necessary face-saving measures to achieve a minimum of agreement.[5] Some Western observers regarded Sadruddin as naive in his dealings with the Iraqi Government. But it was also true that he was under pressure from coalition states to reach an agreement so that their troops could return home. They certainly did not want to sustain the cost or the political problems entailed in remaining in northern Iraq.

The DHA inherited the conviction that in order to work in Iraq at all, its actions must be clearly separated from those of the Security Council. Its staff were therefore reluctant to invoke Security Council assistance in its difficulties with the Iraqi Government. Furthermore, the Security Council showed no great enthusiasm for such intervention. The humanitarian programme was seen very much as an after-thought to the embargo, a way of avoiding criticism for harsh treatment of the civilian population of Iraq, and of asserting that 'protection' was being provided to the population of Iraqi Kurdistan.

The only way to have avoided this would have been to pursue more forcibly Iraq's compliance with the terms of Resolution 688 as regards humanitarian aid – for example, when the Government blocked the establishment of a UN humanitarian centre in Kirkuk, and free movement of aid workers in the south – as did UNSCOM inspectors when they felt their work was thwarted. However, not only was the Security Council consensus on action under Resolution 688 much weaker than on arms-control issues, but the UN humanitarian agencies did not believe aid pro-grammes could be delivered by coercion. Indeed it is very difficult to see how such a policy could be effective over a long period of time. Operation Provide Comfort/Safe Haven was an example of enforcing delivery of humanitarian aid, but it involved using more than 20,000 ground troops over a short period of three months. In the longer term it was an expensive and unattractive option. However, it has to be said that the Security Council did not use fully the leverage it had with the Iraqi Government, short of outright military action or a military presence, to back UN humanitarian agencies. Essentially, the DHA never had the political clout to summon up such backing, even had it wanted to.

NGOs on the whole have had hard words for the UN humanitarian agencies in their implementation of the assistance programme, but many shared the basic unease about working in such a politically polarised situation. The majority of aid agencies – although certainly not all of them – have an ethic of political neutrality in assisting civilians in a crisis. Yet most find that in complex political situations, this goal cannot be achieved in its entirety. Others have increasingly begun to question whether it is an achievable or even desirable goal in the first place.

The efforts of the Iraqi Government to pressure aid agencies into undertaking particular types of work, and to restrict their access to sections of the population, would have come as no surprise to aid workers who had worked in other countries with authoritarian regimes. What was unusual was that aid agencies had to operate in the context of international sanctions and a political battle of wills between the Iraqi Government and the international community. Perhaps inevitably, humanitarian aid was dragged into the resulting propaganda battle.

The fact that economic sanctions were so patently being used for a variety of political goals was troubling. Humanitarian assistance fell victim to political pressures in several ways. From the earliest days of the Gulf emergency, humanitarian priorities were subordinated, in the eyes of the Security Council, to political priorities. This, combined with UN organisations' predisposition to respect state sovereignty, created considerable tensions in the demands placed on aid organisations. The various parties to the conflict viewed decisions on where aid was given, and to whom, as political ones. The recipient authorities – the Government of Iraq and the Kurdish authorities – developed their own agendas in regard to aid. For the Iraqi Government, the main priority has been to control the way in which aid is distributed. In the Kurdish areas, aid funds certainly provided a measure of rehabilitation but also became part of the political competition between various contestants for power.

This highly politicised context made it difficult for NGOs to find a convincing space in which to lobby on the humanitarian effects of sanctions. Every statement could be seized as partisan to one camp or the other, limiting open discussion of the options. Quaker agencies have been particularly outspoken in criticising the UN Security Council's practice of using humanitarian measures to accomplish political objectives. Many of the solidarity groups which developed after the war have called for all non-military sanctions to be lifted. Few of the major NGOs wanted the economic embargo entirely or unconditionally lifted, but effective modifications to the embargo have been hard to agree upon. In Iraqi Kurdistan, many NGOs supported the Kurdish administration's unheeded call for the lifting of sanctions on this region, since it was outside the control of the Government of Iraq.

Most agencies did not wish to be seen as taking the Government's part, but did not necessarily want to be associated with the line taken by Western governments. A former director of OFDA has argued that the decision of aid agencies to work in Iraq to mitigate the effects of the economic embargo entailed in itself a political choice, since in effect it constituted support for the policy of sanctions. By mitigating their impact on the civilian population, aid agencies were also deflecting public concerns about the welfare of the population which might make the sanctions policy politically unpopular: '[ICRC, UNICEF and some NGOs] were furthering the foreign policy of the great powers by making sanctions more palatable to the international community'.[6] While not all agencies would agree with this view, there was deep unease in many NGOs, and among some UN staff, at having to assist people whose level of need was the direct or indirect result of the international embargo. Even if the government of the state concerned had provided mitigation and relief to the best of its ability, the problem would still have existed. As it was, humanitarian agencies alone were not in a position to change the Government's behaviour, any more than was most of the civilian population of Iraq.

It rapidly became evident that the humanitarian assistance available was quite inadequate to redress the deprivation of the civilian population. This dilemma led many agencies to support the implementation of Resolutions 706 and 712, although, as already mentioned, there were doubts about the scale of the assistance it would provide and the 'packaging' of humanitarian aid with war reparations and the expenses of UNSCOM.

By the time Resolution 986 was finally agreed, the scale of need, particularly for infrastructural repair, had greatly increased. Despite the higher value of the oil to be sold, the underlying damage caused by the events of the previous eight years and the long-term needs of the population – for employment, food security and public health and education – remained largely unaddressed. Yet again, aid agencies have been uncomfortable with the political agenda which underlies the oil-for-food resolutions, with their evident priority of keeping sanctions in place. Among officials of the UN humanitarian agencies there was a sense that the resolution was based on political not humanitarian considerations but the humanitarian agencies were left to it carry out.

One of the early advocates of 'le droit d'ingérence' has suggested that the oil-for-food resolutions, as a form of humanitarian mitigation of sanctions, could be considered as manifestations of the right to intervene – to force Iraq to provide for its people.[7] However, in practice this has not proved a simple procedure. The

Government retained a significant degree of leverage, first through its refusal to implement the scheme and, since 1997, by exercising some choice over how the funds are used. The relative enthusiasm shown by leading Security Council members to make the arrangement work sprang from their political interest in sustaining the arrangement, not in seeking the best way to address humanitarian needs.

WORKING IN A SITUATION OF CONFLICT

Aid agencies found themselves working in situations where conflict took a number of different forms. First there was the conflict between Iraq and members of the international community; second, there was dislocation between the areas under government control and those under Kurdish control; third, there was internal conflict. In Iraqi Kurdistan this took the form of inter-party fighting, and in the rest of the country, of a very low level of insurgency in parts of the south combined with repressive state policies, including extrajudicial killings, mutilation, collective punishments and disappearances.

In such a polarised situation, NGOs had to choose where to work and with whom. Even if these decisions were apparently made on 'technical' and practical grounds, they would be 'read' locally as political decisions. It was sometimes true that such choices strengthened the position of one group in relation to another. Those agencies which chose to work in the north, however good their reasons, were choosing to work with a minority of the population. For those whose *raison d'etre* was to support the Kurds, obviously there were no problems with this approach, but for agencies whose aim was to help the people of Iraq as a whole, it was more problematic. Clearly once this was the arena for their work, it also became the arena for their advocacy. They were nonetheless aware that there were other highly vulnerable groups in Iraq about whom little was said because so few aid agencies had any contact with them. There was also the little discussed but nonetheless significant problem that aid agencies, while working to assist and supposedly 'protect' the Kurds in Iraq, could say nothing about the conduct of the Turkish Government towards its Kurdish population. This was first because none of the NGOs could work there, and secondly because, until 1996, they had relied on Turkish cooperation to work in Iraqi Kurdistan.

The position of aid agencies in relation to their own governments cannot of course be completely neutral. Bilateral funds come from governments – the US, Britain, France and other EU members – which are in the forefront of the political conflict with Iraq. Politically, international NGOs which had close relations with their own governments were listened to and sometimes used as channels by the Kurdish authorities to communicate their views to Western governments. There are also different political cultures in the aid communities, and they have by no means spoken with one voice. Some agencies see their work as including advocacy and human rights as much as aid. Others are bound by national rules on their status or by their own mandates to confine political statements to issues directly related to their aid programmes.

Aid workers in Iraq acknowledge also that local perceptions of their work, even where they are welcomed, are never free from the assumption that they have some intelligence function: the lack of any tradition of civil society and non-governmental organisations in Iraq, and the history of Western political involvement in the region, make this attitude inevitable. In a sense, like it or not, NGOs did to some extent serve this function since governments with limited access and poor 'human intelligence' sources needed information on what was happening in Iraq. Aid agencies certainly became one of their sources of information.

NGOs have frequently criticised the UN agencies for their short-term perspective on the provision of humanitarian assistance. However, the question of how to plan in such a volatile situation is one which led to many hours of discussion but only limited results. While there have been plenty of examples from this and every other complex emergency of the futility of providing material aid without backup, training or thought for its longer-term uses, the difficulty of deciding what will be viable assistance to insecure communities, living in an area whose future status is uncertain, is immense.

Not only have there been few serious attempts to evaluate what has already been done, and what exactly the beneficiaries have gained, but with some exceptions consultation with those beneficiaries was limited, or non-existent, especially in the early phases of the crisis. NGOs working in Iraqi Kurdistan (the vast majority) have begun to evaluate what has been achieved since 1991 with rather less optimism than they felt in 1993–4. This is in part because they still have doubts about an end to the internal Kurdish party conflict and anticipate continued regional pressures, especially from Turkey. Thus little space remains to develop any aspects of 'civil society' as some had hoped to do. Rural rehabilitation is still regarded as a considerable achievement, but its sustainability is now acknowledged to be fragile without a political settlement and the restoration of a measure of economic prosperity.

The 'top-down' nature of most UN programmes, and many in the NGO sector, driven by political pressures and donor requirements, meant there was limited local consultation. In government areas, this was not permitted, and in the north it was made more difficult by increasing political polarisation. However, the Western perception of 'saving' people, both in the international legal approach to protection and in humanitarian aid, has been detrimental to involvement of communities in deciding their future.

AID AGENCIES AND HUMAN RIGHTS

Many NGOs have been critical of lack of real commitment by the international community to protection of the Iraqi population and to human rights concerns. In the north, aid agencies, whatever their views, were seen at least as a symbolic part of that protection, along with the UN Guards and the no-fly zone. Working closely with the military forces from coalition states during Operation Provide Comfort raised some initial questions about neutrality, but subsequently the problem became more complex. Humanitarian aid became a substitute for a political solution, and aid agencies working in the north were inevitably implicated in this project.

NGOs' role as 'whistleblower' on human rights has been diminished since 1992 by the difficulties of working in government areas. After that time there were so few agencies working in the field that any information passed on to external press or human rights workers could be easily traced back, exposing staff, including local employees, to danger as well as jeopardising both access to beneficiaries and the continuation of the programme. This little-discussed dilemma faced the handful of agencies which remained after 1992. From 1994 onwards this problem also applied to a lesser extent in Iraqi Kurdistan. NGOs found themselves trying to repair the damage to communities, whether caused by the actions of the Iraqi Government or the Kurdish political parties.

On the whole, the work of human rights organisations has remained separate from that of aid organisations despite informal contacts between staff members. Publicly the two categories of organisation have focused on different aspects of the problem according to their mandates: the aid agencies have emphasised the impact of the economic embargo while infrequently discussing abuse of political rights; human rights agencies have concentrated on gathering evidence on torture, forced displacement and victimisation of individuals and groups, while limiting their comments on the effects of sanctions. This may be an inevitable result of the division of labour and the constraints imposed by differing mandates. However, it has inhibited the development of an integrated analysis which would show how the absence of political rights has interacted with the undermining of economic and social rights by economic sanctions.

THE UN MEMBER STATES AND HUMANITARIAN AID

The operation of the humanitarian aid programme in Iraq has exposed serious weaknesses in the UN system, but it has also revealed ambiguous attitudes among member states. While Security Council members have criticised the UN humanitarian agencies for being supine towards the Iraqi Government, they did little to insist on access for humanitarian aid to all parts of Iraq. Diminishing freedom of movement hampered the aid programme by limiting assessment of vulnerable groups and making monitoring of the uses of aid funds very difficult.

The whole experience raises particularly difficult issues which subsequent emergencies have not resolved: how should UN humanitarian agencies, and indeed NGOs providing aid, deal with authoritarian governments which are known to abuse their citizens? The reluctance of leading Security Council states to put their full weight behind the provisions of Resolution 688 on access for humanitarian aid has a political dimension which has already been discussed. It also raises a fundamental question of how far coercion can or should be used to implement aid programmes.

The contradictory roles of different parts of the UN machinery has been starkly revealed in Iraq. The UN humanitarian agencies certainly did not perform well in many instances, and these organisations have their own bureaucratic and political dynamics which are undoubtedly difficult to change. But so far those countries which are most critical have yet to put their full weight behind reform. In particular, the fact that the US owes the UN many millions of dollars in contributions which Congress has refused to authorise despite pleas from the current administration, does not add conviction to its demands for change.

The fear that reforms would further increase Western and particularly US hegemony has also led to objections from states in the 'Group of 77'. For example, concerns over the formation of the DHA as an emergency coordinating body which would place the priorities of humanitarian intervention beyond the control of individual states and their sovereign rights – 'delivering gifts by coercion' as one delegate put it – led to objections in the General Assembly to its establishment.[8]

Two authors who have written extensively on the delivery of humanitarian aid have asked, 'Can humanitarian intervention be pursued in association with a political-military strategy without creating problems that the international community may lack the patience to resolve?' The authors go on to question how such a UN-orchestrated programme can effectively be insulated from political pressures, as some UN officials in the case of Iraq have wished but not achieved.[9] The international community has certainly shown more tenacity in dealing with Iraq than with other emergencies, because of the relatively strong strategic interests at stake in the region, but the policies pursued have led to an *impasse* rather than to a resolution of the underlying problems. Humanitarian agencies have had to deal with the consequences of these confusions of purpose. A US Congressman from Maryland observed in the course of a congressional hearing on humanitarian aid in Iraq in late 1991, 'Humanitarian aid versus sovereignty, somewhere along the line the gap needs to be bridged there'.[10] In the case of Iraq, the gap has remained.

As an observer who had worked with aid agencies in Iraq in 1991 and 1992 rightly predicted:

If Iraq remains indefinitely impoverished and unstable, with large numbers of Iraqis enjoying minimal physical and economic security, the credibility of the UN in the country and the region will continue to decline. In particular, unwillingess or inability to pursue a tough policy on humanitarian and human rights issues, as opposed to military and strategic ones, will jeopardise the status of the UN and give added weight to the charge that the UN is completely beholden to Northern interests... The Iraqi government has placed enormous obstacles in the way of the pursuit of humanitarian objectives in Iraq. At the same time there is little evidence that on this issue, unlike others, they were pushed very hard once the Kurdish refugee crisis disappeared from the screens. An opportunity was lost for upgrading the significance of humanitarian factors in international relations.[11]

NOTES ON PART III OVERVIEW

1   Mark Duffield (1994), pp 50–69.
2   Dammers (1994), p 407.
3   Weiss *et al* (1997), p 18.
4   Minear *et al* (1992), p 22.
5   *International Herald Tribune*, 13 June 1991, 'Give the United Nations Guards a Chance in Iraq' (by Sadruddin Aga Khan).
6   Natsios (1997), p 71.
7   Bettati (1996i), p 162.
8   *New York Times*, 13 November 1991, 'Disaster Relief Proposal Worries Third World'.
9   *International Herald Tribune*, 1 July 1992, 'Iraq Puts the "New Humanitarian Order" to the Test' (by Larry Minear and Thomas Weiss).
10   Representative Wayne T. Gilchrest at the hearing before the International Task Force of the Select Committee on Hunger, House of Representatives, November 13, 1991, p 31.
11   Dammers (1994), p 411.

CONCLUSION

THE LEGACY OF THE GULF CRISIS

In 1998 and early 1999, 'the least worst option' was a recurring phrase in discussions of policy options on Iraq, a far cry from the apparently clear-cut views expressed in 1991. This book has endeavoured to show that neither the choices, nor the decisions were ever that simple. But in the early years after the war, most observers would not have predicted that such a state of confusion would have prevailed eight years later, nor indeed that the same Iraqi Government would still be confronting the international community.

The end of the Cold War released international policy-making from the constraints imposed by superpower deadlock, and Iraq's invasion of Kuwait in 1990 was the first occasion on which the new possibilities of international action could be effectively tested. While the issue was Iraq's infringement of another state's sovereignty, there was broad support for action against it, despite differences of view about the methods: whether to resort to force or to let sanctions take their course. In the event, the occupation was not ended by economic sanctions but by military action.

The scale of international military action encouraged a belief in 'a quick fix', by which Iraq would simply succumb to overwhelming international pressure. However, the war did not remove Saddam Hussein's regime as some had hoped, but triggered a largely unforeseen internal conflict.

The dilemmas created by this second phase of the crisis, played out inside Iraq, had greater relevance for subsequent conflicts in which the international community has been involved. Given that this particular internal conflict was triggered by international military intervention, did the international community have a duty to step in?

The US had justified its decision not to advance further into Iraq by arguing first that this was beyond the scope of action envisaged by the Security Council, and secondly that it could result in coalition forces suffering higher casualties and getting 'bogged down' by internal political conflict. However, it seems there was a further choice: once it was obvious that the uprisings were in progress, the Coalition could have made more effective use of the leverage created by the presence of US forces in

332

southern Iraq to bring pressure on the regime. This would certainly not have been risk-free, but might have changed the course of events. But in the event, a variety of political calculations, already outlined, deterred both the US and the other leading coalition states from pursuing this option.

The military enforcement of cross-border international humanitarian assistance, the establishment of a safe haven within Iraq, and the use of no-fly zones, ostensibly for protective purposes, all seemed to be dramatic departures from previous international practice when civilian populations were at risk from internal conflict. But these measures masked serious doubts and hesitations even within leading coalition states on the wisdom of such intervention. This reluctance to intervene was far more evident in subsequent conflicts in Bosnia, Somalia, Rwanda and Kosovo.

Until at least 1996, the international responses to the Gulf crisis of 1990–91 – both the Gulf War itself and Operation Safe Haven – were still held up as examples of international action which 'worked', particularly when compared with subsequent UN endeavours. Yet eight years later, a longer-term assessment has to be less favourable. By early 1999, the goals of coercing Iraq into disarmament and 'peaceful intentions' were far from achieved, either by prolonged UN sanctions or by the periodic use of force. Meanwhile the country had become impoverished and suffered from severe social problems. No clear political alternative to the Ba'thist regime had emerged.

This called into question both the effectiveness of the various international instruments designed to coerce governments and protect the civilian population, and the collective political will of the international community – as distinct from the individual political goals of member states – to achieve these goals.

The unprecedentedly cohesive international action in the face of aggression against a neighbouring state was explained mainly by Kuwait's status as an oil producer and an ally of the Western powers. The willingness of leading Security Council members to deploy overwhelming military force made this an unusual case. Since then, however, decisions on whether or not to intervene in a particular conflict have been determined by the degree of commitment shown by leading Security Council members. US involvement has usually been critical to the mobilisation of international resources, whether military or humanitarian and logistical.

As often as not, the international community has not acted decisively. The long-running civil war and famine conditions in Sudan and the recent civil war in Algeria are stark examples of situations of intense violence and human misery. Yet the international community has not paid serious attention to their solution. This state of affairs calls into question the notion that UN resolutions such as UNSCR 688 might set a precedent for systematic international responses to civil war, massive repression and humanitarian crises.

Examples of the underlying reluctance to respond – as well as difficulties in deciding what to do – were to be found in the tardy and half-hearted international action in Rwanda, Bosnia and, until very recently, in Kosovo. Neither the permanent five Security Council members, nor indeed other states on the Council have responded consistently to infringements of international law or the abuse of civilian populations. The US, the 'hawk' on Iraq, vacillated for three years before finally putting its weight behind the commitment of NATO troops to Bosnia, ending the role of the UN protection force, UNPROFOR. The UK, another hawk on Iraq, took a much less confrontational position in regard to Serbia. In Rwanda, France played an interventionist role, while on Iraq it progressively retreated from the interventionist consensus of 1991. China, while opposing or demurring on military action against Iraq and actions infringing sovereignty and abstaining on Resolution 688, supported, along with African members of the council, the resolution establishing the UN Transitional Assistance Force (UNTAF) in Somalia. This allowed US troops, under UN auspices but with a US commander, to enter Somalia.

When the Security Council has been reluctant to act or deadlocked, it has sometimes been left to regional organisations to impose economic embargoes, mount humanitarian relief efforts or send in troops. In the European context, NATO, rather than the UN, eventually became the key military force in Bosnia and Kosovo, while monitoring activities in Kosovo are carried out under the auspices of the Organisation for Security and Cooperation in Europe (OSCE). The EU has so far proved unable to muster a sufficient consensus to act as a major diplomatic and political force in most recent crises. In Africa, where most Western powers have little or no interest in intervening, regional organisations have played a greater role, although the experiences of the economic embargo on Burundi and the West African peacekeeping forces in Liberia and Sierra Leone have not been altogether happy ones. In the Middle East, the dominant role of the US has left little room for organisations such as the Arab League to become involved, even supposing it could agree a strategy.

As a major study on the Rwandan crisis suggests, the experience of international intervention in internal conflict during this decade presents a conundrum: 'The rationale for UN peacekeeping is that it provides a neutral force, independent of partisan interest. However, partisan interests can provide motivation and energy to be directed at a problem when a commitment to conflict resolution per se is lacking'.[1] In the longer run, the Iraq case has demonstrated some of the drawbacks of a highly partisan approach. The US played a critical role in mobilising international action against Iraq in the first place, but the pursuit of its own policy goals though the UN Security Council has arguably undermined the credibility of UN collective action.

THE USE OF ECONOMIC SANCTIONS IN THE 1990s

Economic sanctions, whether imposed by the UN or individual states have been used more frequently in the 1990s than in previous decades. By the end of the decade, however, their effectiveness was increasingly being questioned. Comprehensive UN trade embargoes of the kind imposed on Iraq and the Former Republic of Yugoslavia (FRY, consisting of Serbia and Montenegro) raised some difficult political and humanitarian issues. One is how to weigh the social and economic costs of such embargoes against their value as tools of international coercion. Another is that when sanctions are imposed on authoritarian states whose citizens have no opportunity to alter government policies, they may be doubly victimised by economic decline and the absence of opportunities for political change.

Analyses of the outcomes of economic embargoes imposed prior to 1990 suggested that their success rate was not very high, in the region of 40 percent.[2] Among the characteristics identified by analysts as contributing to success were the degree of vulnerability of the target economy, the rigour of implementation, the existence of limited and clear-cut goals, rather than broad and general ones, and the possibility of offering the target state some incentives to comply.

By the first of these criteria, Iraq, as the only oil-producing state targeted for comprehensive trade sanctions, was highly vulnerable.[3] Compared to Rhodesia or FRY, the embargo has been enforced with some rigour. As one analyst noted, Iraq was initially a textbook case for the imposition of sanctions, which were implemented rapidly and with the clear goal of achieving its withdrawal from Kuwait. However, much more complex goals were set for sanctions in April 1991, and the criteria by which 'success' and compliance were judged became progressively muddied by diverging political goals within the Security Council.

From early 1991, the terms of Iraqi embargo had some novel dimensions. An economic embargo had never previously been used to enforce a ceasefire and an arms control regime. Furthermore, since 1991 they have been employed in conjunction with the threat of military force, not as an alternative to it. Few incentives to comply have been on offer, and the US has set its own additional goals for sanctions.

The sweeping coalition military victory of 1991 probably created a climate of excessive confidence that coercive sanctions against Iraq would achieve compliance over a whole range of post-conflict issues. A weakened state, it was thought, would be in no position to resist. But by 1994–5, the consensus had frayed as the results of the embargo proved patchy. For many states, Iraq's acceptance of Kuwait's sovereignty and borders was regarded as sufficient to justify some easing of sanctions. The US, however, led those states which not only wanted full compliance with all aspects of arms control but demanded that Iraq demonstrate its 'peaceful intentions' and comply with other UN resolutions, including Resolution 688. This became part of a strategy to keep sanctions in place. The US had never disguised the fact that it regarded sanctions not just as an instrument of international law to end Iraq's infringements, but also as a political tool.

Successive US administrations have not found any other strategy to deal with Iraq, so have opted to retain sanctions as a form of containment – 'the best failure we have', as one western diplomat was quoted as saying during the weapons crisis in early 1998.[4] Sanctions at this point cease to be an instrument to achieve certain specific goals, and become a generalised strategy of control.

However, other Security Council permanent members have drawn different conclusions from the difficulties in enforcing every detail of Resolution 687 and related resolutions. They have argued that pragmatically it appears impossible to guarantee that all weapons of mass destruction have been destroyed, and consider Iraq's peaceful intentions impossible to demonstrate. Hence they argue that such progress as has been made should be clearly acknowledged, and moves made toward lifting sanctions.

The dispute continues over what precise conditions Iraq must meet before sanctions are lifted. Each permanent member of the Council has a 'reverse veto', 'meaning the sanctions regime cannot be modified unless all five decide that the objectives of the resolution, as defined by each of them, have been met'.[5]

In the field of arms control, Iraq has been a one-off experiment in the use of a draconian arms inspection regime backed up by an embargo. It is one which, after eight years of Iraqi resistance, seems politically unsustainable in its present form. It would certainly suggest that any future exercise in disarmament would need to take account of the difficulties UNSCOM experienced, and ask whether a comprehensive economic embargo is an appropriate means of achieving it. A more directly political question is whether the focus on disarming a single state in a heavily armed region is really an effective solution.

Sanctions on FRY, on the other hand, were imposed in the absence of a clear strategy to end the war in former Yugoslavia, and were consequently 'fraught with complexity and confusion from the outset'.[6] A comprehensive UN economic embargo on Serbia and Montenegro, in theory more or less as draconian as that on Iraq, was not imposed until mid-1992. Resolution 757 of 30 May 1992 imposed a comprehensive trade ban, interdiction of air transport except for humanitarian aid, a ban on all financial transactions and the suspension of scientific, cultural and other exchanges. However, Serbia's geographical position, particularly on a network of land and river trade routes, made the embargo hard to enforce. There was massive cross-border leakage caused by pressure of transit trade, of which Serbia was able to take advantage. In November 1992, the Security Council approved naval interdiction in the Adriatic Sea, demanded that Serbia's neighbours clamp down on trans-shipment, and placed UN personnel on the ground to monitor enforcement in neighbouring states. Further restrictions were imposed in April 1993. In September 1994, sanctions were extended to the areas under Bosnian Serb control, but were partially lifted on Belgrade.[7]

The US, which had been the driving force behind the imposition and maintenance of sanctions on Iraq, did not put the same degree of pressure on FRY and accepted the feasibility of the staged lifting of sanctions. In terms of effectiveness, sanctions on FRY therefore resulted in limited compliance with the international community's demands, but only when combined with a number of other factors, including war weariness in Serbia itself as well as in Bosnia, and the US-supported counterattack in Bosnia by Croatian forces in 1995. However, some observers allege that Serbia did continue to give support the Bosnian Serbs for a period after the partial lifting of sanctions in 1994.[8] Furthermore, the 'subtext' of removing Milosevic from power faded once he had become a necessary prop to the Dayton accords. International concern over Serbian conduct in Kosovo since 1998 have brought only a very limited re-imposition of sanctions on FRY.

Impact on populations of sanctioned states

The complex politics associated with the disintegration of former Yugoslavia were very different from the situation in Iraq. However, the social and economic costs of comprehensive sanctions, though less prolonged in FRY, were strikingly similar.[9]

The following description of the impact of sanctions on the population in FRY echoes many aspects of the experience of Iraqis:

> ... economic hardship would require individuals to spend more time on daily survival and less on political action. It reinforced the informal economic networks of family, tribe, or crime at the popular level, and increased the power of the government and of Milosevic personally. The state gained greater authority in rationing goods and determining which goods would gain subsidies; which workers would therefore be employed; and whether farmers, veterans, pensioners and the army would have income. Finally, the sanctions encouraged the exodus of those most able to protest and organise independent political action: the professional middle class.[10]

Serbia's economy was more diversified than Iraq's, but the results of the economic pressure imposed by sanctions were similar: declining social services, the resort to printing money, high levels of inflation, and a burgeoning black market. As in Iraq, the most vulnerable groups – young children, the old and chronically ill, and refugees – suffered the most, while the middle class experienced the most dramatic fall in living standards. By 1994 more than a third of the population of FRY had reportedly fallen below the official poverty line, compared with 6.23 percent in 1990.[11]

In each case there are some difficulties in disentangling the impact of pre-existing economic problems from that of the embargo. In Serbia's case, the effects of sanctions overlaid the economic disruption caused by the collapse of the Soviet economic bloc. In both cases, there had also been serious economic mismanagement by the government, both before and during the embargo.

Despite the economic decline in both Iraq and FRY, their governments were able to maintain political control over the population and over elites which might have been expected to dissent from government policies. Neither the press nor political life in Serbia was subject to controls as severe as those in Iraq. However, analysts generally agree that one result of sanctions was further to limit the ability of opposition groups to challenge the regime, which was able to use the so-called 'rally round the flag' technique to good effect. After a short period following the imposition of UN sanctions, when there were large street demonstrations against the regime, the opposition was largely silenced until after sanctions were lifted.

Common issues arise from these two experiences of comprehensive embargoes. The key question is what level of economic and social deprivation is an acceptable consequence of an economic embargo. In Iraq and Serbia/Montenegro, a considerable number of excess deaths appear to have resulted from the imposition of the embargoes. The American Friends Service Committee has argued that the international community should be required to 'maintain proportionality'. This requires 'ensuring that basic survival needs are met'. 'A line must be drawn when deaths are knowingly inflicted.'[12]

Another issue arising out of these comprehensive trade embargoes relates to their administration and monitoring by the UN. Individual Sanctions Committees have been responsible for administering humanitarian exceptions and monitoring the impact of embargoes. The International Federation of Red Cross and Red Crescent Societies has described their work as a largely 'negative task inviting restrictive scrutiny of an item's humanitarian nature'.[13] Sanctions Committees have on the whole taken 'a minimal approach, reinforced by consensus decision-making, excluding humanitarian items that might have a dual function, such as pharmaceutical ingredients or water treatment chemicals, thereby excluding components that would prevent or alleviate ill-health'. Both the Iraq and FRY Committees worked with vague and ambiguously-worded definitions of 'humanitarian goods', and what constituted 'civilian need'. This allowed different interpretations by Committee members, and led to arguments based on political positions rather than some agreed form of evaluation.

The economic embargoes on both Iraq and FRY brought complaints about delays caused by Sanctions Committee procedures in obtaining humanitarian goods. Neither UN humanitarian agencies nor the ICRC nor any other aid agencies were exempted from these embargoes, thus slowing up the delivery of humanitarian goods.

In the Iraq case, efforts to mitigate the effects of sanctions, based on UN-controlled sales of oil, were more extensive than in FRY. This was partly because of the effects of war damage on the civilian infrastructure, and partly because of the length of time sanctions remained in place. However, no attempt has been made to rethink or re-target the sanctions themselves.

These experiences have raised serious doubts about the political value, as well as the morality of using comprehensive economic sanctions. Not only are they not necessarily very effective but, embarrassingly for the international community, they cause damage to civilian society. The Iraq and Yugoslav sanctions have created a groundswell of criticism within UN organisations. Those involved in delivering humanitarian aid have been particularly outspoken. 'Trying to implement a humanitarian program in a sanctions environment represents a fundamental contradiction', as one UNHCR official in Belgrade put it.[14]

In 1994, the ICRC, usually reticent in public statements, indicated its unease with the way embargoes were being used in an address by its President Cornelio Sommaruga to the UN General Assembly:

> I am convinced that all the humanitarian agencies wish to join me in inviting political leaders to take greater account of humanitarian criteria when taking decisions to impose economic and financial sanctions. Perhaps we should give special thought here to the grave effects on public health when water purification and pumping installations are paralysed. Is it not incongruous to impose debilitating sanctions on one hand while with the other bringing in humanitarian aid to restore supplies vital to the population's survival?[15]

In 1997, a subcommission of the UN Human Rights Commission asserted that the most serious effects of embargoes fell on the weak and poor in society, especially women and children, that these measures tended to aggravate existing imbalances in income distribution, and that they frequently gave rise to smuggling and trafficking, 'to the benefit of *mala fide* businessmen often close to the oppressive government authorities which are insensitive to the suffering of their people'.[16]

The extent to which the embargo on Iraq is now perceived as a tool of US foreign policy has also contributed to the decline in enthusiasm for sanctions within the UN. While some member states wish to retain sanctions as an instrument of international policy, they increasingly call for more clearly defined goals and a more targeted approach. They wish to avoid the problem which has arisen in both Iraq and FRY, when the populations rather than the regimes have proved to be the main victims. Many non-aligned states regard sanctions, as applied against Iraq, as a means by which powerful states can bully other nations.

As a consequence of these doubts and criticisms, some new strategies are being developed within the UN. It is now said to be accepted even within the Security Council that compliance with sanctions is not achieved through imposing hardship on the civilian population. The UN Office of Coordination of Humanitarian Affairs (UNOCHA, the successor to the Department of Humanitarian Affairs) has been charged with providing impact assessments on possible future targets of sanctions, with a view to minimising the humanitarian impact and creating the maximum political impact.

In a further move to challenge the future use of comprehensive sanctions, the Chairmen of all the eight Sanctions Committees[17] circulated a paper in October 1998, suggesting a careful analysis of the experience of targeted sanctions, as an alternative to comprehensive embargoes. They urged the Security Council to address 'the basic policy issue of flexibility and graduality in the imposition of sanctions'.[18] The question will be how seriously international decision-makers take these assessments when faced with future crises.

USING FORCE: TO WHAT PURPOSE?

The experience of using comprehensive economic sanctions to coerce recalcitrant states has revealed that there are serious difficulties in implementing this supposedly non-violent form of international pressure. However, the alternative of using UN-sanctioned military force has equally proved to have drawbacks.

Despite the reluctance of the US military to engage its troops in cross-border support for humanitarian aid to the Kurds, the immediate outcome was sufficiently positive to reassure many civilian policy-makers that such actions could be limited in time and low in casualties.

But the US experience of sending military forces to Somalia in late 1992 to enforce the distribution of food aid caused a revision of this view. The use of force had unforeseen political consequences. The military's favoured strategy of the 'quick exit' became messy and complicated. The Somali militias were not disarmed, and military confrontations with US and other UN troops merely compounded the UN's earlier political mistakes and misjudgment. UN contingents rapidly became viewed as partisans in an internal war.

During Operation Safe Haven, coalition military commanders were dealing with Iraqi military officers who observed a chain of command to the central authorities in Baghdad. In Somalia, there was no central interlocutor (since the state structure had dissolved) but rather a variety of military groups whose agendas were imperfectly understood by most of the American and other UN personnel.

The result was not only political damage in Somalia itself but a further diminution of American willingness to involve its ground troops in such ventures. From early in 1992, the US showed no wish to become militarily involved in the disintegrating Yugoslavia, and the Somalia debacle reinforced the reluctance to send ground troops into the Bosnian war. In Iraq too, the further use of ground forces – as opposed to air strikes – was effectively ruled out, despite repeated confrontations with the regime. This was still evident in US responses to Iraqi defiance of UNSCOM in 1998–9.

Other leading military powers, including Britain and France, have shown more readiness to use ground troops in certain circumstances, but the concern among both Western politicians and their military counterparts about casualty levels in this type of operation, as well as the expense of sustaining a military present on the ground, still represents a major limitation on the willingness to intervene.

The emphasis on air power has led to experiments with no-fly zones in Iraq and Bosnia to extend a measure of control over a region in which no ground troops are to be deployed. However, by 1993, US military officials were conceding that neither in Iraq nor in Bosnia did these zones significantly influence hostile action on the ground.[19] As part of intelligence surveillance, they may be felt to have some value, but as a means of demonstrating the political will to 'protect' civilian populations, air power has proved largely unconvincing.

The checkered history of the two no-fly zones in Iraq has already been described. Even in 1998–9 some politicians were still repeating that the southern no-fly zone was 'protecting the Shi'a', although this was little more than political rhetoric. Yet for other reasons already outlined, Iraq military challenges to the zones have almost always been met by force. In Bosnia, by contrast, there was less political will to maintain the no-fly zone strictly.

Experiments with safe havens

Despite the reluctance of most states to engage their troops in internal conflicts, there has been an increasing trend towards using troops to protect humanitarian aid deliveries. Safe havens offered one means of securing a limited area in which civilians could be helped or protected by military forces and aid agencies.

The idea of safe havens emerged from principles originally established by ICRC in its proposals for designated safe areas. Such a safe area, under ICRC's definition, is a region within a disputed territory which is neutral, free from belligerent forces and established with the consent of the parties to the conflict. Among recent initiatives of this kind, the Open Relief Centres in Sri Lanka established in 1990 have been described as 'relatively safe areas', and come closest to meeting these criteria.[20]

However, most recent efforts to establish 'protected areas' have departed from these principles. In northern Iraq, government troops and security services were partially but not fully withdrawn from the safe haven area. Kurdish forces were not disarmed. The short duration of the external military presence left unsolved the question of how to maintain security for refugees after the troops had withdrawn. The whole operation took place without Iraqi consent, and therefore force or the threat of force was needed to sustain protection. The answer was air cover provided by the no-fly zone, but this proved at best imperfect.

If the Iraqi Government had not decided to remove its forces from the three northern governorates at the end of 1991, the international community could have faced the problem of how to protect the civilian population while Iraqi officials, security services and probably troops remained in place. The remaining UN humanitarian agencies and the UN Guards might then have been faced with deteriorating security and human rights conditions and sporadic fighting, raising the question of whether further military intervention was required.

In the event, the Iraqi decision created an anomalous situation in which state power was withdrawn from one part of the country. However, no new *de jure* entity was created, whether a recognised autonomous zone, a federal province, an independent state, or even some kind of UN protectorate. This situation led to further conflict and suffering for the population, and difficulties for those who provided aid, or hoped to challenge human rights abuses.

To the extent that Operation Safe Haven was effective in the short run, that success was probably the result of the specific circumstances – it was imposed at the end of the war and mustered considerable military force against an already defeated army. A variety of political difficulties and human rights issues arose from securing, for a limited time, a safe area inside Iraq. However, it did avoid, for most of the refugees, a protracted period in exile, and some of the political problems which could have resulted.[21] Other attempts to create safe havens have been much less successful.

The notion of safe areas for displaced civilians was used again, though in very different circumstances, in Bosnia and Rwanda. In Bosnia six 'safe areas' were declared by the UN in the context of an ongoing conflict.[22] 'Cynically, they were not called safe havens because the Iraq precedent would have implied a similar western commitment to protect them with force.'[23] The policy ended in disaster, mainly because the UN did not deploy sufficient troops to hold them against the besieging Serbian forces. The Security Council decided at the outset to take the 'light option' of 7600 troops instead of the 34,000 asked for by the UN Secretary General.

None of the fighting forces within the enclave or entering it was disarmed. The meagre UN contingents could not prevent attacks on the enclaves, nor attacks launched by Bosnian army units from inside them. In the end UN troops as well as civilians were besieged and starving, since the UN was unable to deliver enough aid. The option of using air power to enforce UN access to the zones was not effective, and little used, primarily because UNPROFOR commanders felt such attacks would make peacekeeping operations on the ground impossible, and feared their troops and UN personnel might become hostages.

In Rwanda, Operation Turquoise was carried out by French forces in 1994. Although the action was supported by a Security Council resolution adopted under Chapter VII of the UN Charter, only French troops were involved. This once again signalled the reluctance of major powers to get involved unless their direct interests were at stake. At the same time, France's political involvement in this region led to doubts as to the neutrality of the intervention. It was designed to protect internally displaced persons, and prevent them crossing borders to become refugees. Like Operation Provide Comfort, it had a time-frame, in this case limited – by the Security Council rather than military commanders – to two months.

By the time the troops had established the safe area, the worst of the massacres were over, though their action undoubtedly saved some lives. However, the haven also protected Hutu forces fleeing the Rwandan Patriotic Front (RPF) advance. Furthermore, the way the RPF Government eventually 'reintegrated' displaced persons who remained in camps in the 'safe' zone resulted in a large number of deaths, despite the efforts of the UN and NGOs to develop a joint strategy to close down the camps peacefully.

In contrast to the Kurdish safe haven, Operation Turquoise did not create sufficient confidence to encourage refugees to return to other parts of Rwanda, and there was no mechanism to protect them if they did. Consequently a major refugee problem remained, particularly in the Zaire camps which became centres for extremist Hutu opponents of the RPF. This later had repercussions not just in Rwanda but in the whole region, leading to further human rights abuses and humanitarian crises.

Safe areas have not satisfactorily addressed situations where the civilians have remained at risk over a long period. So far, 'the international community has been cavalier with regard to nature and duration of safety in some of the safe havens it has created'.[24] Their usefulness in the short term has to be weighed against the changes in the political and military balance of power which may result (especially if no demilitarisation is achieved). The other major question is the political and military will of the international community to sustain such 'havens'.

HUMANITARIAN AID AS A POLITICAL TOOL

The promotion of a humanitarian 'solution' to the Iraqi refugee crisis in 1991 boosted the notion of humanitarian assistance as a way of responding to crises, regardless of the wishes of the state concerned. The process of challenging state sovereignty in regard to the delivery of humanitarian aid across borders had begun in the 1980s, with French NGOs playing a leading role in pushing their government to initiate action at the UN. A resolution in 1988 (GA 43/131) accepted that humanitarian NGOs should have free access to disaster victims on grounds of urgent need and threat to life. A number of NGOs were already working cross-border without government consent in Eritrea. A further General Assembly resolution adopted in 1990 at the initiative of the French (Resolution 45/100) called for the establishment of 'humanitarian corridors' to reach disaster victims.[25]

The post-Gulf War refugee crisis took the argument one step further by legitimising, under the rubric of a threat to international peace and security, the use of force to reverse a massive cross-border flow of refugees and the risk of large numbers of deaths among fleeing people. Subsequently, Security Council resolutions adopted under Chapter VII, again citing 'a threat to international peace and security' created by war and mass movements of population, were passed in relation to former Yugoslavia and Somalia.[26] These allowed military support for international humanitarian aid efforts.

However, these efforts were ultimately constrained by political circumstances, both international and internal to the region of conflict. For example, in former Yugoslavia 'humanitarian efforts were substitutes for effective decisions by governments and the international community to end the warfare and unconscionable violence'.[27]

The issue of access for humanitarian aid in both Somalia and former Yugoslavia was often a stark and violent one. Aid agencies became involved in confrontations with armed groups which had little regard for humanitarian principles and saw civilians as part of the battlefield. Would UN agencies or NGOs insist on their right of unfettered access to people in need, at the risk of being barred, or would they acquiesce in some of the extraneous demands of the belligerents to open the door to needy civilians?

In both Bosnia and Somalia, and in several situations of internal conflict in Africa – Rwanda, Liberia and Sierra Leone – humanitarian aid also became part of the material base of war, 'the currency of an internal conflict'. It is not only a matter of hijacked aid convoys and diverted food. Humanitarian aid can become a form of political leverage. In the absence of political solutions, aid programmes can become paralysed or compromised by the actions of the warring parties. 'If the political environment surrounding humanitarian operations is disregarded, there is a high risk that relief work by outsiders will intensify conflict or fall victim to manipulation by one or more parties to the conflict'.[28]

During the Bosnian war, UNPROFOR was unable to prevent humanitarian aid being used as a lever by the warring parties, while UNHCR faced the difficulty of deciding whether to move people in danger to places where they could be helped, or whether this risked in fact aiding and abetting ethnic cleansing.

In Iraq, aid delivery was never threatened on this scale. UN convoys to Iraqi Kurdistan were periodically attacked despite the presence of UN Guards, but these were relatively minor problems. However, strong constraints were imposed on the aid programme. As a former DHA official observed 'beneficiary governments tend to manipulate the delivery of aid for their own political purposes'.[29] This is regarded as a fact of life by UN agencies. Iraq was no exception, since, despite the economic embargo and the other constraints imposed on its freedom to manoeuvre, the Government was still in a position to block any aid agency work it did not approve of. The highly politicised context in which humanitarian assistance was given made the UN more than usually reluctant to challenge government decisions.

In Iraqi Kurdistan, there is evidence that aid deliveries and aid programmes did become entangled with competition between the PUK and KDP for control of economic resources, but this was on a small scale compared with other internal conflicts.

The substantial NGO presence in the north was mostly welcomed by the Kurds as symbolic of international commitment to their protection, but the UN was regarded with more ambivalence because of its links to Baghdad.

The provision of humanitarian assistance and protection to civilian populations has several different aspects. The immediate international response is usually the delivery of basic material goods – for example food, shelter materials and medicine – to save lives in a crisis. This is followed by longer-term efforts to build food security and restore, or create, economic and social stability. Another set of goals is to protect the population against abuses by the state or other parties, and to support efforts towards conflict resolution. In practice, these activities are often seen as separate and discrete operations, carried out by different organisations which have minimal overlap or coordination.

The emergency phase remains the area to which most funds and effort have been devoted, often without much thought as to the longer-term results of these interventions. More flexible responses to changing needs during a prolonged crisis or longer-term rehabilitation are not encouraged by rigid systems of donor funding for 'emergency' aid. Not only governments, as political actors and donors, but aid agencies too must bear some responsibility for the flaws in the prevailing 'crisis' approach to humanitarian aid, and its marked lack of strategic thinking.

In recent years, many aid agencies have tended to assume there is a continuum from relief, through rehabilitation, to development. In fact, in most situations of prolonged conflict, not only does the situation change from month to month, with setbacks as well as improvements, but needs often vary from one area to another. Initially one area may be barely touched by conflict, only to become a battleground later. Regions where there is no fighting may suffer a sudden economic crisis because they become host to a flood of displaced people from other regions. Regions with good trading links may recover faster than those which are isolated.

Between 1990 and 1996, the scale of emergency aid for 'humanitarian action' grew rapidly, creating systems of funding and bureaucracies to administer them – in the UN humanitarian agencies, multilateral and bilateral donor organisations and the larger NGOs. Dealing with complex emergencies became a growth industry to which increasing proportions of national and multilateral aid budgets were dedicated. In the NGO community, participation in such emergency work is not only regarded as intrinsically important but is driven by institutional considerations of profile and funding in the increasingly competitive aid environment.

This also encourages a 'depoliticised' view of emergency response, as a largely technical exercise. This approach sometimes obscures the political aspects of 'humanitarian action'. Aid agencies may not represent state interests, and may even seek to distance themselves from the policies of their own national governments. But whatever their intentions, their work may in fact serve the political interests of donor governments. Furthermore, the resources they bring to the region of conflict may alter, for better or worse, the internal balance of forces. Furthermore, much of the thinking so far on the protection of civilians in conflict has focused on the issue of how to gain access to those at risk, and what humanitarian aid can do 'for' the vulnerable. Money and assistance pour in for 'victims' of war, famine and conflict, but few think of the vulnerable also as actors with rights, needs and opinions. Aid agencies should be accountable not just to donors, but also to beneficiaries. As actors, these beneficiaries themselves often have to choose between unpalatable alternatives and allegiances. Failure to understand how and why these so-called victims make decisions affects the success or failure of aid programmes.

HUMAN RIGHTS AND CONFLICT

The notion that human rights abuses committed within a state's borders should be the proper concern of the international community and lead to action, rather than simply rhetoric, was put on the international agenda by Resolution 688. After 1991, the issue of protecting civilians from abuse has been raised in every major conflict. In practice, however, humanitarian responses have far outstripped actions to contest human rights abuses. Jan Eliasson, the first Under Secretary General for Humanitarian Affairs, concluded: 'Today there is an acceptance of humanitarian action – I prefer this term to humanitarian intervention – but there is no acceptance of international action crossing a border for human rights violations'.[30]

Doling out food and blankets, even in highly dangerous situations, is regarded as more 'do-able' than either confronting governments and other parties committing abuses, or seeking the difficult and complex changes which might end these abuses. Discussing the humanitarian emergencies in Iraq, Somalia and FRY, Human Rights Watch observed, 'While these humanitarian emergencies were the product of widespread human rights abuses, the UN has tended to proceed as if all that is at stake is the logistical problem of delivering relief supplies. UN officials remain fixated on the symptoms of humanitarian catastrophe while remaining blind to the cause – the abuses that disrupt the production, distribution and acquisition of food and other necessities.'

In cases where there is a predisposition to act, 'protecting human rights' is frequently included in the rationale for intervening, but so far these expressions of intention have rarely been matched in practice. In many instances, initiatives are too little, too late.

Rwanda was probably the worst failure of the international community in this respect. It has now been acknowledged that the US and other members of the international community, as well as UN organisations, by their inaction bear some responsibility for the scale and ferocity of the massacres in Rwanda.[31] In their reluctance to get more involved in the Yugoslav crisis in 1992, leading Western states are also alleged to have 'sat on' a growing body of evidence of Bosnian Serb concentration camps, as well as large-scale ethnic cleansing. US officials were reportedly still denying evidence of such camps on 4 August when ICRC had been providing information through diplomatic channels since mid-June.[32]

So far, effective ways to implement human rights monitoring have yet to be found in situations where no peace settlement has been agreed. The very limited powers of the UN's human rights institutions have been evident in both Iraq and Yugoslavia. The Special Rapporteurs appointed for both countries made energetic attempts to highlight abuses. The resolution to place human rights monitors in Iraq was not implemented, but it set a precedent for the introduction of monitors in Bosnia and Rwanda.

However, even where access is allowed for rapporteurs and monitors, questions remain as to their effectiveness. The government, political party or militia which controls a particular area can often limit or manipulate the information which is available. Obviously, the role of the rapporteurs and monitors in raising awareness of abuses is important, but in the case of former Yugoslavia, the abuses were not halted while the fighting continued, either by the presence of monitors or humanitarian agencies. While monitors may be an important first step, without some means of stopping the protagonists from carrying out abuses this is shown to be limited.

In 1998–9, international action in Kosovo – appointing unarmed monitors from the OSCE and bringing Serbian actions there within the scope of the International Tribunal on former Yugoslavia – also raises this issue. Aside from the very real difficulties facing the OSCE monitors in carrying out their mandate, the question remains as to how the international community will be able to prevent abuses continuing and convince the parties to the conflict to negotiate. Air-strikes have been threatened, but even if they take place they are unlikely to resolve the question of Kosovo's future status, which is at the root of the current conflict.

There have been significant developments over the past 20 years in the international instruments available for the prosecution for war crimes and crimes against humanity. The International Criminal Tribunals for the former Yugoslavia and for Rwanda have been criticised for their slow progress and the difficulty in bringing to trial the 'big fish' rather than minor actors. However, they did create a momentum for the vote to establish the International Criminal Court in 1998.[33]

States also have, in theory, universal jurisdiction in respect of crimes against humanity, genocide and war crimes. Some states now have national laws which formalise this jurisdiction. If implemented, these laws could allow cases to be brought in national courts against members of abusive governments who travel abroad. The threat of such action could restrict the movement of political leaders accused of such crimes, even if other international sanctions were not in place. The recent case brought in the Spanish courts against General Pinochet, and the subsequent Spanish request for his extradition from the UK, is the first high-profile case to test this process. However, in the final analysis, these options depend on individual states' political will to act.

Humanitarian interventions and the status of refugees

The 1991 Iraqi refuge crisis, combined with the collapse of the Soviet Union, marked a shift in international attitudes towards refugees. In Europe, the widening scope of EU harmonisation has created increasingly restrictive legislation relating to refugees.

More emphasis has been placed on 'containing' flows of refugees in 'safe or protected' zones in their own country as an alternative to asylum.[34] Ironically, the development of this idea has probably increased pressure for the international community to intervene in the territory and affairs of sovereign states, in order to prevent internally displaced people from crossing borders and becoming refugees.

During the war in former Yugoslavia, there was a general reluctance among European states to accept refugees (with the partial exception of Germany). In July 1992, a conference convened by UNHCR in Geneva called, among other things, for exploration of the creation of 'special protection zones' inside Bosnia as a possible alternative to quotas for their resettlement in other European countries. However, no effective safe areas were ever established in Bosnia, and housing refugees in other states of the former Yugoslav Republic – Serbia, subject to sanctions, and Croatia, still effectively at war – was also problematic.

European and US efforts to control the inflow of refugees to their shores have not been accompanied by any systematic effort at burden-sharing with states bordering regions of conflict, which still receive the bulk of the refugees. Turkey was supported in 1991 in its wish not to accept Kurdish refugees, but other states in that region did not receive similar concessions. Iran's hardening line on refugees since 1991, already described in relation to the Iraqi Kurds, was further exemplified by its handling of Azeri refugees. They were first helped on the Azerbaijan side of the border, then, when the fighting came close to the border and the refugees were forced across, were moved *en masse* through Iranian territory and back to a part of Azerbaijan away from the fighting and regarded as safe.[35]

There has been a marked increase in UNHCR's role in assisting displaced people (those who had fled their homes but not crossed an international border). It points out that support for the displaced is nothing new, but that since 1990 the scale and geographical scope of this work has greatly increased.[36]

In northern Iraq, UNHCR was initially faced with numbers of internally displaced people, some who had not left the country with the wave of refugees in March/April 1991, some who were returned refugees, but who could not return to their homes in areas under Iraqi government control, and others who were later displaced by fighting along the *de facto* border between government and Kurdish-controlled areas. Finally, there was a further round of internal displacements due to inter-Kurdish fighting and Turkish incursions from 1994 onwards. *De facto*, UNHCR assisted many of these people, but this was seen as less of an anomaly than in the past. In former Yugoslavia, the breakup of the state meant many became refugees inside what had been one country, but many more were displaced.

It may well be that changing circumstances make aspects of the 1951 Convention on Refugees out of date, but many of those who work with refugees fear that the current climate of opinion on refugee rights would lead to revisions which would further restrict the right to asylum. If the international community does not at the same time find more effective and long-term ways to support the rights of the internally displaced, the scale of vulnerability among those caught up in internal or regional conflicts – both in terms of loss of livelihood due to conflict, and danger of abuse of civil and political rights – will continue to grow.

ROLE OF THE UN

Since 1990, the role of the UN in conflict has clearly shifted from operations which predominantly focused on peacekeeping to various forms of peace enforcement. Peacekeeping depended on a political settlement of some kind having been reached, which the UN would monitor. This was a much more passive activity, though not without its dangers, as UNIFIL's role in Lebanon demonstrated. Peace enforcement – active intervention in a situation where no peace had been achieved – became characteristic of major UN actions in the 1990s. It is much more risky, in political and military terms, and requires large inputs of military personnel and funds, which major powers have rarely been willing to provide for more than a short period.

Whether the situation is one of low-level conflict or full-scale war, the UN's task includes protecting civilians from harm and meeting their needs for food, medical care and shelter. It is this UN role which has presented the most problems. In Bosnia,

UNPROFOR found itself acting under Chapter VII resolutions, but without suffi-cient forces, and with rules of engagement on the ground which were closer to a peacekeeping mandate, in that they stressed neutrality. Facing hostile road-blocks and frequent attacks, the troops guarding humanitarian aid convoys found them-selves ill-served by this confused formula.

As the number of enforcement actions and humanitarian rescue missions has increased, the position of national contingents and regional defence organisations in operations overseen by the UN Security Council has not been clarified. In Iraq, national contingents operating during the 1991 Gulf War and in Operation Provide Comfort/Safe Haven claimed UN endorsement for these actions. But the UN was not directly involved in the military command, which in both cases was dominated by the US. In Somalia, US forces in UNTAF were theoretically acting under UN control, but with a US commander.

In Bosnia a major problem was the mismatch between the tasks set by the Security Council and the political will to carry out the military actions provided for. The US was particularly loath to become militarily involved on the ground, and until 1995 blocked the use of NATO forces 'out of area', while the EU still struggled to frame a common policy on military action. UNPROFOR, and its national contin-gents, suffered from the contradictions between its mandate, the tasks it was expected to perform, and the resources at the commander's disposal.[37]

The UN's humanitarian agencies have also been challenged to expand their acti-vities or take on new roles. In 1991 the Iraq crisis revealed serious inadequacies in the responses of UN agencies, but the subsequent establishment of the Department of Humanitarian Affairs as a body to coordinate the UN response to humanitarian crises achieved only very limited improvements. It became evident that the political will vital to the success of such an organisation was lacking at all levels.

The UN's multiple functions have made it not only cumbersome but often self-contradictory. Its difficulties in this respect were particularly obvious in relation to economic sanctions on Iraq and FRY, where the role of UN agencies in delivering aid and protecting civilians has been at odds with the Security Council's implemen-tation of comprehensive embargoes. In Yugoslavia:

> UN humanitarian organisations were caught in a no-win situation. They were tarnished by association with Security Council decisions that failed to achieve their stated objectives. They were also faulted for not having found a way of extracting cooperation from the same belligerents who had ignored the expressed wishes and established standards of the inter-national community.[38]

There have also been contradictory pressures on UN humanitarian agencies. They need the cooperation of governments to deliver assistance and implement aid programmes, but in order to do so, sometimes turn a blind eye to human rights abuses which are wit-nessed by their staff, making no protest either to the government concerned or through diplomatic channels. Although neutrality may be a valued characteristic of humani-tarian aid organisations, if this is reduced to mere passivity it loses its significance.

UN humanitarian agencies rarely have much input into policy-making at Security Council level. Certainly in the case of Iraq these agencies have frequently tried to distance themselves from actions taken by the Council, and more especially those ini-tiated by the US and UK. However, there are still few mechanisms for their concerns to be represented to the Council. In former Yugoslavia, the DHA was unable to raise the profile of humanitarian issues with the Security Council and the Sanctions Committee, nor to exert a coordinating influence on other agencies, whose heads outranked the DHA's coordinator and were not directly answerable to the Secretary General.[39]

LESSONS FROM IRAQ

Since 1990, there have been major changes in the international community's response to civil wars and protracted conflicts. The military and political power of a handful of states in the Security Council has allowed them to chose whether or not, and how, to intervene in conflicts. On the whole, these judgements still appear to be based primarily on national foreign policy priorities, and sometimes on the domestic concerns of the government.

The key problem so far has been that, having decided to intervene, to use sanctions and provide humanitarian aid, the international community – both collectively and its leading members – have shown little sense of strategic direction in resolving the underlying problems which caused the conflicts.

The main lesson of the international community's policies on Iraq are, in sum, that 'quick fixes' do not work. Economic sanctions, military force or humanitarian aid will not resolve the range of complex national and regional problems, of which the current Iraqi Government is one, if there is no clear and agreed sense of what longer-term outcomes are desirable. These would include longer-term peace and stability and, hopefully, a more open style of government.

The other major problem clearly revealed in dealings with Iraq is that the international community's political will to act is still driven primarily by powerful states' internal agendas. While numerous political speeches and many column inches in the media may be devoted to the suffering of the 'victim' population, and the abuses committed by their government, these are not the concerns which drive policy. In the case of Iraq, this disjunction between rhetoric and reality has been particularly evident.

NOTES ON CONCLUSION

1   Eriksson *et al* (1996), p 22.
2   Patterson (1995), p 94.
3   UN sanctions against Libya, also heavily dependent on oil revenues, did not prohibit the sale of its oil.
4   *Guardian*, 3 March 1998, 'Saddam's elite rides high despite UN sanctions'; *New York Times*, 8 November 1998, 'US to Give Up Arms Inspections for Curbing Iraq', which suggested that the US Government had given up on full enforcement of arms controls in favour of using sanctions to sustain containment of Iraq, described by a senior official: 'Given the Security Council and the state of the Arab world, this is a least worst policy'.
5   Johnstone (1994), p 65.
6   Doxey (1996), p 39.
7   Weiss *et al* (1997), p 157.
8   Ed Vulliamy quotes General Philippe Morillon, a former UNPROFOR commander in Sarajevo and later commander of NATO's Rapid Reaction Force, as saying that

President Milosevic admitted to him that Serbian army troops remained in Bosnia until May 1995 (*Guardian*, 12 January 1996, "'Only passivity is dishonorable'").

9   Although analysts have differed in their views of the effectiveness of sanctions on former Yugoslavia, and whether or not they should have been sustained, most agree on their impact on Serbian society, economically and politically. See Woodward (1995), pp 141–151; Bojicic and Dyker (1993); Dimitrijevic and Pejic (1995), pp 142–53.

10   Woodward (1995), p 148.

11   Dyker and Vejvoda (1996), p 188.

12   Patterson (1995), p 91.

13   International Federation of Red Cross and Red Cross and Red Crescent Societies (1995), p 21–2.

14   Minear *et al* (1994), p 97, quoting Judith Kumin, UNHCR Chief of Mission in Belgrade.

15   International Committee of the Red Cross (1994), 'Strengthening the Coordination of Emergency Humanitarian Assistance', address by Mr Cornelio Sommaruga, President of the ICRC at the United Nations General Assembly, 49th session, 23 November 1994.

16   Human Rights Commission, Sub-Commission on Prevention of Discrimination and Protection of Minorities, 'Adverse consequences of economic sanctions on the enjoyment of human rights', Sub-Commission resolution 1997/35, 37th meeting, 28 August 1997.

17   Angola, FRY, Iraq, Liberia, Libya, Rwanda, Sierra Leone and Somalia.

18   It recommended the harmonisation of guidelines between the committees, more transparency in the committees' work and better channels of communication. It also stressed the need to develop indicators for systematic monitoring of the impact of sanctions on vulnerable groups ('Issue paper concerning the sanctions imposed by the Security Council', 30 October 1998).

19   It was argued that even if the no-fly zone over Bosnia had been fully enforced, this would have had no appreciable military effect.

20   Landgren (1995), p 441.

21   This point was argued strongly by the US Agency for International Development, Office of US Foreign Disaster Assistance (1991ii), Section on Operational Lessons, p 1.

22   First Srebrenica (under UNSC Resolution 819 on 16 April 1993); then Sarajevo, Tuzla, Zepa, Gorazde and Bihac (under UNSC Resolution 824 of 6 May 1993).

23   Halverson (1996), p 18.

24   Landgren (1995), p 438.

25   Bettati (1996ii), pp 102–4.

26   For example, UNSC Resolution 794 (3 December 1992) on Somalia, authorising action under Chapter VII 'to establish a secure environment for humanitarian relief operations'.

27   Minear *et al* (1994), p ix.

28   Smith (1993), p 98–9.

29   Dedring (1996), p 44.

30   Loehr and Wong (1995), p 504.

31   Press briefing by Ambassador Bill Richardson, US Permanent Representative to the United Nations, Palais des Nations, Geneva, 26 March 1998.

32   *Guardian*, 22 June 1996, 'Hard truths swept under red carpets'.

33   The US was among the group of states which refused to endorse the treaty establishing the ICC, along with China, Iraq, Israel, Libya, Qatar and Yemen (Lawyers Committee for Human Rights, *Advisor*, Fall 1998, vol. 2, no. 3, p 1, 'The US and the War Crimes Court').

34   UNHCR (1997), p 48.

35   Frelick (1994), pp 598–9.

36   UNHCR (1997), p 120.

37   General Francois Briquement, a former UNPROFOR commander in Sarajevo, has argued

that in former Yugoslavia, and in Bosnia in particular, the international community claimed 'a dual right of interference', seeking first to secure recognition for the Bosnian state, and second a humanitarian right of interference because it could not countenance the scale of human rights abuses. In this situation, he argued the only strategy could be one of force, or at least duress, but the resources allocated to the military command were never commensurate with the Security Council resolutions passed (Liaison Committee [1994], p 10).

38   Minear *et al* (1994), p 8.
39   Dedring (1996), p 39; Minear *et al* (1994), pp 108–9.

APPENDIX
The Use and Threat of Force Against Iraq, July 1991–February 1999

1991

25 July: Iraq failed to meet a July 25 deadline for disclosure of its nuclear capabilities. Earlier in the month the US had threatened to bomb Iraq's remaining nuclear weapons plants and numerous other targets if it did not disclose its nuclear programme.

23–28 September: 44 UN weapons inspectors were detained in Baghdad after finding evidence of Iraqi nuclear programmes; Iraq also refused to allow use of German rather than Iraqi helicopters to visit missile sites. On 25 September The US Department of Defense announced the dispatch of 96 Patriot missiles and 1380 troops to Saudi Arabia. Action was constrained by the reluctance of Turkey, and to a lesser extent Saudi Arabia, to allow the US to use their territory as a base for strikes on Iraq.

1992

14 April: The US, UK and France warned Iraq to halt all threatening military activity and withdraw missile batteries from the de facto border with the Kurdish-controlled areas or face 'serious consequences'.

5–22 July: UNSCOM chemical weapons inspectors were refused entry to a Ministry of Agriculture building in Baghdad. On 6 July the Security Council ordered Iraq to grant immediate access, calling the refusal a 'material and unacceptable breach' of Resolution 687. A compromise was subsequently reached with the UN involving the appointment of a new team of 'impartial' inspectors. The US and UK indicated that they were willing to take military action to enforce Iraqi compliance. However, later reports suggested that President Bush and his advisers had been reluctant to renew air attacks.

26 August: Air exclusion zone below 32nd parallel announced by President Bush, banning the use of helicopters and fixed wing aircraft.

27 December: Iraqi MIG was shot down by a US F-16 in the southern no-fly zone. On 28 December another two fighters crossed and were chased by US aircraft. The US aircraft carrier Kittyhawk was redeployed from Somali coastal waters.

1993

First week January: The allies reported that Iraq was moving surface-to-air missiles into the southern no-fly zone, and Kuwait reported a clash with Iraqi soldiers in the border zone.

6 January: US, UK and French UN Ambassadors demanded the removal of the missiles from the no fly zone within 48 hours. Hours before the ultimatum expired, the US reported that the missiles had been moved.

9 January: UN weapons inspectors were refused permission to fly to Baghdad from Bahrain: the Iraqis said they should use Iraqi planes. The Security Council warned Iraq of 'serious consequences' of this 'material breach of UN resolutions'.

10–13 January: Series of Iraqi incursions into the demilitarised Iraq-Kuwait border zone to collect equipment. Security Council again warned of 'serious consequences'. Iraqis said they would stop moving equipment and allow UN inspectors to fly. 114 US, British and French planes bombed sites at Nasariya, Amara, Samawa, Basra and Najaf. Only about half the targets were reportedly hit.

14 January: The US demanded that Iraq remove police posts in the demilitarised border area, due to be handed to Kuwait on 15 January.

15 January: 1200 US troops arrived in Kuwait; Iraq said it would guarantee the safety of the weapons inspectors' flight 'except when hostile actions are being carried out against Iraq'.

17 January: Raid by 40 US Tomahawk missiles destroyed a factory alleged to be part of the nuclear programme; the Rashid Hotel in central Baghdad was hit. Iraq removed its police posts on the Kuwait border.

18 January: 75 US, British and French aircraft hit four sites below the 32nd parallel; the Iraqis reported 21 people killed.

17–19 January: Clashes in the northern no-fly zone.

19 January: The Iraqis announced a unilateral ceasefire from 20 January to coincide with the inauguration of President Clinton.

21–25 January: Further clashes in both air exclusion zones.

9 April: US planes in the northern no-fly zone drop cluster bombs, claiming they came under Iraqi anti-aircraft fire.

27 June: US missiles launched against Baghdad intelligence headquarters on basis of 'compelling evidence' against Iraqi suspects in the attempted assassination of ex-President Bush in Kuwait (in April 1993).

19 August: US planes attacked an air defence battery near Mosul after allegedly being fired on.

1994

8 October: A Security Council meeting expressed 'grave concern' over the deployment of Iraqi troops near the Kuwaiti border, urging 'redoubled vigilance' to guard against 'any potentially hostile act' that might endanger the sovereignty of Kuwait.

9–10 October: US troops began to arrive in Kuwait. On 9 October, France despatched one frigate to the Gulf, and on 10 October, the UK ordered 1000 Royal Marines to join US ground forces in Kuwait. At this time the US asserted that some 80,000 Iraqi troops were moving towards the Kuwait border. By mid-October, the US had mobilised some 40,000 troops, 350 additional aircraft and a naval task force.

10 October: Foreign Minister Sahhaf announced Iraqi troops were withdrawing from the Kuwait border area after pressure from 'friendly countries', including Russia, Pakistan, China and Belgium. The US nonetheless continued its troop build-up.

1996

31 August: Iraqi troops entered Arbil (12 miles inside no fly zone) in alliance with KDP.

2–3 September: Iraqi troops reported to be withdrawing.
3 September: President Clinton announced extension of southern no-fly zone to 33rd parallel.

3–4 September: 44 US cruise missiles (fired from ships in the Gulf and B52s despatched from Far East) attacked Iraqi air defences south of Baghdad.

1997

29 October: The Iraqi Government demanded that all US members of UNSCOM inspection teams leave Iraq after the Security Council adopts Resolution 1134 (23 October 1997) calling on Iraq to cease obstructing inspectors' access to sites.

3 November: Iraq threatened to shoot down US U-2 surveillance planes used by the UN.

6 November: UNSCOM alleged that the Iraqis moved arms-related equipment out of sight of monitoring equipment.

12 November: Security Council imposed travel ban on Iraqi officials responsible for Iraq's failure to cooperate with UNSCOM (UNSC Resolution 1137).

13 November: UNSCOM inspectors were withdrawn from Iraq and a US military build-up began, but opposition encountered in Arab world.

21 November: Iraq announced that UNSCOM inspectors were to return after reaching an understanding brokered by Russia.

14–15 December: At meetings with Richard Butler, Executive Chairman of UNSCOM, the Iraqi Deputy Prime Minister asserted that UNSCOM could not be granted access to what Iraq defined as 'presidential and sovereign' sites.

1998

13 January: Iraq announced that it was 'suspending the activity' of an UNSCOM inspection team lead by a US national, Scott Ritter.

Early February: Large-scale build up of American and British naval and air forces in the Gulf, but little support for military action from the Arab world, or in the Security Council. Russia in particular issued strong warnings against such action but failed to broker a diplomatic solution.

22 February: UN Secretary General, on a mission to Baghdad, agreed a formula with President Saddam Hussein to end the crisis. This was embodied in a Memorandum of Understanding of 23 February.

2 March: The Security Council adopted Resolution 1154 endorsing the MoU signed by the Secretary General, threatening 'the severest consequences' if Iraq did not comply.

1 November: Iraq halted all cooperation with UN weapons inspectors, all of whom were withdrawn from the country on 7 November.

11 November: The US began deploying additional military forces in the Gulf, with President Clinton declaring that the US must be 'prepared to act forcefully' to end Iraq's defiance of the UN.

15 November: The US launched and then aborted a missile strike on Iraq after its Government agreed to cooperate with UNSCOM. The US and the UK said if Baghdad defied the UN again, their forces would strike without warning.

17 November: The weapons inspectors returned to Baghdad.

16 December: UNSCOM Chairman Richard Butler reported to the Security Council that Iraq had not fully cooperated with the inspectors.

17–20 December: US and UK forces launched four nights of air-strikes again targets throughout Iraq, called Operation Desert Fox. The Iraqi Government subsequently announced that the weapons inspectors were barred from returning to the country.

28 December 1998–3 February 1999 (time of writing): Iraq embarked on a series of challenges to the US and UK in the northern and southern no-fly zones (France having withdrawn from the southern no-fly zone after the bombing), leading to missile attacks on Iraqi planes and ground control and radar facilities.

BIBLIOGRAPHY

Sources are arranged under headings which relate to each part of the book, so that sources which relate to similar subject matter are grouped together. If a source is cited in more than one part of the book, it will be mentioned under each of the parts in which it appears. If two books by the same author appeared in the same year, this is indicated by a number next to the date.

INTRODUCTION

Claude Angeli and Stephanie Mesnier (1992), *Notre Allié Saddam* (Paris, Olivier Orban)

Naseer Aruri (1992), 'Human Rights and the Gulf Crisis: The Verbal Strategy of George Bush' in Phyllis Bennis and Michel Moushabeck (eds), *Beyond the Storm: A Gulf Crisis Reader* (Edinburgh, Canongate Press), pp 305–324

Aspen Institute (1995), *Managing Conflict in the Post-Cold War World: the Role of Intervention*, Report of The Aspen Institute Conference, 2–6 August, Aspen, Colorado

Les Aspin (1991), *The Aspin Papers: Sanctions, Diplomacy and War in the Persian Gulf*, Significant Issues Series, vol. XIII, no. 2 (Washington DC, Centre for Strategic and International Studies)

James A. Baker III with Thomas M. DeFrank (1995), *The Politics of Diplomacy: Revolution, War and Peace 1989–1992* (New York, G.P. Putnam's Sons)

Shaul Bakhash (1993) 'Iranian Politics since the Gulf War' in R.B. Satloff, *The Politics of Change in the Middle East* (Boulder CO, Westview Press), pp 63–84

G. Barzilai, A. Klieman and G. Shidlo (eds) (1993), *The Gulf Crisis and its Global Aftermath* (London and New York, Routledge)

Phyllis Bennis (1992), 'False Consensus: George Bush's United Nations' in Phyllis Bennis and Michel Moushabeck (eds), *Beyond the Storm: A Gulf Crisis Reader* (Edinburgh, Canongate Press), pp 112–125

Campaign Against the Arms Trade (1991), *Arming Saddam: The Supply of British Military Equipment to Iraq 1979–1990* (London)

Shahram Chubin (1987), 'Iran and its Neighbours: the Impact of the Gulf War', *Conflict Studies*, no. 204, Centre for Security and Conflict Studies (London)

Shahram Chubin and Charles Tripp (1988), *Iran and Iraq at War* (London, I.B. Tauris)

Jack Colhoun (1992), 'How Bush Backed Iraq', *Middle East Report*, no. 176, (May–June), pp 35–37

Chris Dammers (1994), 'Post War Iraq and the Politics of Humanitarianism' in Herbert H. Blumberg and Christopher C. French (eds), *The Persian Gulf War: Views from the Social-Behavioural Studies* (Lanham MD, University Press of America), pp 399–411

Richard Falk (1994), 'Reflections on the Gulf War Experience in the UN System' in T.Y. Ismael and J.S. Ismael (eds), *The Gulf War and the New World Order: International Relations in the Middle East* (Gainsville, University Press of Florida), pp 25–39

Thomas M. Francke and Georg Nolte (1993), 'The Good Offices Function of the UN

Secretary General' in Adam Roberts and Benedict Kingsbury (eds), *United Nations, Divided World: the UN's Roles in International Relations* (2nd edition) (Oxford, Oxford University Press), pp 143–182

Lawrence Freedman and Efraim Karsh (1993), *The Gulf Conflict 1990–1991: Diplomacy and War in the New World Order*, (London and Boston, Faber & Faber)

Graham E. Fuller (1991), 'Moscow and the Gulf War', *Foreign Affairs*, vol. 70, no. 3, Summer, pp 55–76

Galia Golan (1992i), 'Gorbachev's Difficult Time in the Gulf', *Political Science Quarterly*, vol. 107, no. 2, pp 213–230

Michael Gordon and Bernard C. Trainor, *The General's War*, (Boston, Little Brown)

J. Gow (ed.) (1993), *Iraq, the Gulf Conflict and the World Community*, Centre for Defence Studies (London and New York, Brasseys)

Francois Heisbourg (1992), 'France and the Gulf Crisis' in Nicole Gnesotto and John Roper (eds), *Western Europe and the Gulf: a Study of West European Reactions to the Gulf War*, Institute of Security Studies (Paris, Western European Union)

Richard K. Herrman (1991), 'The Middle East and the new world order: rethinking US political strategy after the Gulf war', *International Security*, vol. 16, no.2, Fall, pp 42–75

Helmut Hubel (1994), 'Western Europe and Iraq: the cases of France and West Germany' in A. Baram and B. Rubin (eds.), *Iraq's Road to War* (Basingstoke, Macmillan), pp 272–285

Robert C. Johansen (1991), 'The United Nations after the Gulf war: Lessons for Collective Security', *World Policy Journal*, Summer, pp 561–574

Efraim Karsh and Inari Rautsi (1991), *Saddam Hussein, a Political Biography* (London, Brasseys)

Chris Kutschera (1997), *Le défi kurde, ou le rêve fou de l'indépendance* (Paris, Bayard Editions)

Anthony Parsons (1991), 'The United Nations after the Gulf War', *The Round Table*, no. 319, pp 265–273

Evgueni Primakov (1991), *Missions à Baghdad: Histoire d'une negociation secrete* (Paris, Editions du Seuil)

Philip Robins (1991), *Turkey and the Middle East* (London, Royal Institute of International Affairs/Pinter)

Barry Rubin (1994), 'The United States and Iraq: from appeasement to war' in A. Baram and B. Rubin (eds), *Iraq's Road to War* (Basingstoke, Macmillan), pp 255–272

Oscar Schachter (1991), 'United Nations Law in the Gulf Conflict', *American Journal of International Law*, vol. 85, no. 3, pp 452–473

Richard Schofield (1991), *Kuwait and Iraq: Historical Claims and Territorial Disputes*, Middle East Programme Paper, Royal Institute of International Affairs, London

Sir Richard Scott (1996), *Report of the Inquiry into the Export of Defence Equipment and Dual-Use Goods to Iraq and Related Prosecutions*, vols 1 and 2; ordered by the House of Commons to be printed 15 February 1996 (London, HMSO)

Edwin M. Smith (1994), 'Collective Security and Collective Defense: Changing Concepts and Institutions' in Edwin M. Smith and Michael G. Schechter, *The United Nations in a New World Order*, Monograph no. 6. Claremont McKenna College (Claremont CA, The Keck Center for International Strategic Studies), pp 1–47

Oles M. Smolansky with Bettie M. Smolansky (1991), *The USSR and Iraq: the Soviet Quest for Influence* (Durham NC and London, Duke University Press)

Robert Springborg (1994), 'The United Nations in the Gulf War' in T.Y. Ismael and J.S. Ismael (eds), *The Gulf War and the New World Order: International Relations in the Middle East* (Gainsville, University Press of Florida), pp 40–51

Strobe Talbott (1992), 'Post victory blues', *Foreign Affairs*, vol. 71, no.1 pp 53–69

Paul Taylor and A.J.R. Groom (1992), *The United Nations and the Gulf War 1990–1991: Back to the Future?* Royal Institute of International Affairs, Discussion Paper 38 (London, Royal Institute of International Affairs)

UN Commission on Human Rights (1989), *Report on the 45th Session*, 30 January–March 10

1989, Economic and Social Council, Official Records 1989, Supplement 2, E/1989/20; E/CN.4/1989/86

Brian Urquhart (1993), 'The UN and International Security after the Cold War' in Adam Roberts and Benedict Kingsbury (eds), *United Nations, Divided World: the UN's Roles in International Relations* (2nd edition) (Oxford, Oxford University Press), pp 81–103

US General Accounting Office (1994), *Iraq: US Military Items Exported or Transfered to Iraq in the 1980s*, Report to the Chairman, Committee on Foreign Affairs, House of Representatives, Washington DC, February

Jim Wurst (1991), 'The United Nations after the Gulf war: A Promise Betrayed' Stephen Lewis, interviewed by Jim Wurst, *World Policy Journal* (Summer), pp 539–549

PART I

Howard Adelman (1992), 'Humanitarian Intervention: The Case of the Kurds', *International Journal of Refugee Law*, vol. 4, no. 1, pp 4–38

H.J. Agha and A.S. Khalidi (1995), *Syria and Iran: Rivalry and Cooperation*, Chatham House Papers, Royal Institute of International Affairs (London. Pinter Publishers)

Jose E. Alvarez (1995), 'The Once and Future Security Council', *The Washington Quarterly*, vol. 18, no. 2 (Spring), pp 5–20

Amnesty International (1991), *Iraq: Human Rights Violations Since the Uprisings* (London)

Amnesty International (1994), *Saudi Arabia: Unwelcome 'guests': the plight of Iraqi refugees* (London)

Mahmut Bali Aykan (1996), 'Turkey's Policy in Northern Iraq 1991–5', *Middle East Studies* vol. 32, no. 4 (October), pp 343–366

Kathleen C. Bailey (1995), *The UN Inspections in Iraq: Lessons for On-Site Verification* (Boulder CO, Westview Press)

James A. Baker III (1995), *The Politics of Diplomacy: Revolution, War and Peace* (New York, G.P. Putnam's Sons)

Shaul Bakhash (1993) 'Iranian Politics Since the Gulf War' in R.B. Satloff (ed.), *The Politics of Change in the Middle East* (Boulder CO, Westview Press), pp 63–84

Henri J. Barkey, 'Turkey and the New Middle East: A Geopolitical Exploration' in Henri J. Barkey (ed.), *Reluctant Neighbour: Turkey's Role in the Middle East* (Washington DC, US Institute of Peace Press), pp 25–43

Alon Ben Meir, (1996) 'The Dual Containment Strategy is No Longer Viable', *Middle East Policy*, vol. 4, no.3 (March), pp 58–71

D.L. Bethlehem (ed.) (1991), *The Kuwait Crisis: Sanctions and their Economic Consequences*, 2 vols, Cambridge International Documents Series (Cambridge, Grotius Publications)

Mario Bettati (1996i), *Le droit d'ingérence: mutation de l'ordre international* (Paris, Editions Odile Jacob)

Laurie A. Brand (1994), *Jordan's Inter-Arab Relations: The Political Economy of Alliance Making* (New York, Columbia University Press)

Claudia von Braunmuhl and Manfred Kulessa (1995), *The Impact of UN Sanctions on Humanitarian Assistance Activities: Report on a Study Commissioned by the United Nations Department of Humanitarian Affairs*, December, Gesellschaft fur Communication Management Interkultur Training mbH – COMIT

Franca Brilliant, Frederick C. Cuny and Victor Tanner (1995), *Humanitarian Intervention: A Study of Operation Provide Comfort* (ed. Pat Reed) (Dallas, Intertect)

R.J. Brown (1995), *With the Marines in Operation Provide Comfort: Humanitarian Operations in Northern Iraq, 1991* (Washington DC, History and Museums Division, Headquarters, US Marine Corps)

Zbigniew Brzezinski and Brent Scowcroft (1997), *Differentiated Containment: US Policy Toward Iran and Iraq: Report of an Independent Task Force* (New York, Council on Foreign Relations)

Michel Chatelus (1997), 'Pétrole et gaz dans les relations franco-arabes et euro-arabes: order du marché et faiblesse de la politique', *Confluences Méditerranée*, no 22 (Été), pp 37–47

S. Chubin (1994), *Iran's National Security Policy: Capabilities, Institutions and Impact* (Washington DC, Carnegie Endowment for International Peace)

Patrick Clawson (1993i), *Iran's Challenge to the West: How, When and Why*, Policy Paper no. 33 (Washington DC, The Washington Institute for Near East Policy)

Lois B. McHugh and Susan Epstein (1991), *Kurdish Refugee Relief and Other Humanitarian Aid Issues in Iraq*, updated 31 May (Washington DC, Congressional Research Service)

Paul Conlon (1995), 'Lessons from Iraq: the Functions of the Iraq Sanctions Committee as a Source of Sanctions Implementation Authority and Practice', *Virginia Journal of International Law*, vol. 35, no. 633, pp 633–668

Paul Conlon (1996), 'How Legal are Jordan's Oil Imports from Iraq?' *Middle East Economic Survey*, vol. 39, no. 22, 26 February

Paul Conlon (1997), 'The Humanitarian Mitigation of UN Sanctions', *German Yearbook of International Law 1996*, vol. 39, pp 249–284

Helena Cook (1995), *The Safe Haven in Northern Iraq: International Responsibility for Iraqi Kurdistan* (Colchester and London: University of Essex Human Rights Centre/Kurdistan Human Rights Project)

Anthony H. Cordesman and Ahmed S. Hashim (1997), *Iraq: Sanctions and Beyond* (Boulder, CO, Westview Press)

Frederick C. Cuny, (1995), *The Political, Military, Economic and Humanitarian Situation in Iraqi Kurdistan: An Assessment*, January (Carnegie Endowment for International Peace)

Chris Dammers (1994), 'Post War Iraq and the Politics of Humanitarianism', in Herbert H. Blumberg and Christopher C. French (eds.), *The Persian Gulf War: Views from the Social-Behavioural Studies* (Lanham MD, University Press of America), pp 399–411

Lori Fisler Damrosch (1993), 'The Civilian Impact of Economic Sanctions' in Damrosch (ed.) *Enforcing Restraint: Collective Intervention in Internal Conflicts* (New York, Council on Foreign Relations Press), pp 274–315

Roland Danreuther (1991), *The Gulf Conflict: A Political and Strategic Analysis*, Adelphi Papers, no. 264 (London, Brasseys for the International Institute of Strategic Studies)

Alan Dowty (1994), 'Sanctioning Iraq: the Limits of the New World Order', *Washington Quarterly*, vol. 17, no. 3 (Summer), pp 179–198

William J. Durch (1993), 'The Iraq-Kuwait Observation Mission' in Durch (ed.), *The Evolution of United Nations Peace Keeping* (New York, St Martins' Press), pp 258–271

John Ellicott (1996), 'An Overview of US Sanctions Programs Targeting Particular Countries and Parties, as They Existed at May 15 1996', *International Quarterly*, vol. 8 (July), pp 554–567

James Fine (1992), 'The Iraq Sanctions Catastrophe', *Middle East Report*, no. 174 (January–February 1992), pp 36, 39

Lawrence Freedman and David Boren (1992), 'Safe havens for Kurds in Post-War Iraq' in Nigel Rodley (ed.), *To Loose the Bonds of Wickedness: International Intervention and Defence of Human Rights* (London and New York, Brassey's), pp 43–92

Lawrence Freedman and Efraim Karsh (1993), *The Gulf Conflict 1990–1991: Diplomacy and War in the New World Order* (London and Boston, Faber & Faber)

Bill Frelick (1992), 'The False Promise of Operation Provide Comfort: Protecting Refugees or Protecting State Power?' *Middle East Report*, no. 176 (May–June), pp 22–27

Graham E. Fuller (1993), 'Turkey's New Eastern Orientation' in Graham E. Fuller and Ian O. Lessor (eds.), *Turkey's New Geopolitics: from the Balkans to Western China* (Boulder CO, Westview Press), pp 37–95

Richard Garfield (1999), 'Morbidity and Mortality in Iraq, 1990–1998', Occasional Paper, Fourth Freedom Forum, Indiana

E. Gregory Gause III (1997), 'Arms Supplies and Military Spending in the Gulf', *Middle East Report*, no. 204 (July–September), pp 12–14

Michael Gordon and Bernard C. Trainor (1995), *The General's War* (Boston, Little Brown)

Sarah Graham-Brown (1995), 'Intervention, Sovereignty and Responsibility: the Iraq Sanctions Dilemma', *Middle East Report*, no. 193 (March–April), pp 2–12, 32

Alain Gresh (1998), 'Intérêts nationaux divergent et coopération obligée: de Washington à Moscou, regards croisés sur le Golfe', *Le Monde Diplomatique*, June

Ahmed Hashim (1996), 'Iraq: Fin de Regime?' *Current History*, vol. 95, no. 597 (January), pp 10–15

Gary Clyde Hufbauer, Jeffrey J.Schott, Kimberly Ann Elliott (1990), *Economic Sanctions Reconsidered: History and Current Policy*, 2nd Edition, (Washington DC, Institute for International Economics)

Human Rights Watch (1993), *The Lost Agenda: Human Rights and UN Field Operations*, June (New York)

Human Rights Watch, *World Report* 1996, (New York etc)

Human Rights Watch, *World Report* 1997, (New York etc)

Human Rights Watch, *World Report* 1998, (New York etc)

Human Rights Watch/Middle East (1995i), *Iraq's Crime of Genocide: the Anfal campaign against the Kurds* (New Haven and London, Yale University Press)

Human Rights Watch/Middle East (1995ii), *Iraq's Brutal Decrees – Amputation, Branding and the Death Penalty*, June (New York)

George Jacovy (1992), 'The Middle East and the Peace Agenda: has UNSCOM set a precedent?' in Steven Mataija and J. Marshall Beier (eds), *Multilateral Verification and the Post Gulf War Environment: Learning form the UNSCOM Experience*, symposium proceedings, Centre for International and Strategic Studies, December (Toronto, York University)

Ian Johnstone (1994), *Aftermath of the Gulf War: An Assessment of UN Action*, International Peace Academy, Occasional Paper Series (Boulder CO and London, Lynne Rienner)

David Keen (1993), *The Kurds in Iraq: How Safe is Their Haven Now?* (London, Save the Children Fund)

Kemal Kirisci (1993), '"Provide Comfort" and Turkey: Decision Making for Refugee Assistance', *Low Intensity Conflict and Law Enforcement*, vol. 2, no. 2 (Autumn), pp 227–253

Bernard Kouchner (1991), *Le Malheur des Autres* (Paris, Editions Odile Jacob)

Chris Kutschera (1997), *Le défi kurde, ou le rêve fou de l'indépendance* (Paris, Bayard Editions)

Anthony Lake (1994), 'Confronting Backlash States', *Foreign Affairs*, vol. 73, no. 2 (March/April), pp 45–55

Karin Landgren (1995), 'Safety Zones and International Protection: A Dark Grey Area', *International Journal of Refugee Law*, vol.7, no.3 (July), pp 436–458

Lawyers Committee for Human Rights (1992), *Asylum under attack: a report on the protection of Iraqi refugees and displaced persons one year after the humanitarian emergency in Iraq*, April (New York)

Phebe Marr (1996), 'Turkey and Iraq' in Henri J. Barkey (ed.), *Reluctant Neighbour: Turkey's Role in the Middle East* (Washington DC, US Institute of Peace Press), pp 45–69

James Mayall (1991), 'Non-Intervention, Self-Determination and the "New World Order"', *International Affairs*, vol. 67, no. 3 (July), pp 421–29

David McDowall (1992), *The Kurds: a nation denied* (London, Minority Rights Group)

David McDowall (1997), *A Modern History of the Kurds* (London, I.B. Tauris)

Middle East Watch[1] (1992), *Endless Torment: The 1991 Uprising in Iraq and its Aftermath*, June (New York)

Larry Minear *et al* (1992), *United Nations Coordination of the International Humanitarian Response to the Gulf Crisis, 1990–1992*, The Thomas J. Watson Jr Institute for International Studies, Occasional Paper no. 13 (Providence RI, Brown University)

Fareed Mohamedi (1997), 'Oil, Gas and the Future of Arab Gulf Countries', *Middle East Report*, no. 204 (July–September), pp 26

Eric E. Morris (nd), 'The Limits of Mercy: Ethnopolitical Conflict and Humanitarian Action', (Boston, Center for International Studies, MIT)

Alan Munro (1996), *An Arabian Affair: Politics and Diplomacy behind the Gulf War* (London, Brasseys)

John F. Murphy (1995), 'Force and Arms' in Oscar Schachter and Christopher C. Joyner (eds), *United Nations Legal Order*, vol. 1, The American Society of International Law/Grotius Publications (Cambridge, Cambridge University Press), pp 247–318

New Zealand, Ministry of Foreign Affairs and Trade (1995), 'New Zealand in the Security Council 1993-4', *Information Bulletin*, no. 52

Roger Normand (1996), 'Iraqi Sanctions, Human Rights and Humanitarian Law', *Middle East Report*, no. 200 (July–September), pp 40–43, 46

Soli Ozel (1995), 'Of Not Being a Lone Wolf: Geography, Domestic Plays, and Turkish Foreign Policy in the Middle East' in Geoffrey Kemp and Janice Gross Stein (eds), *Powder Keg in the Middle East: The Struggle for Gulf Security* (London, Rowman & Littlefield), pp 161–194

Jack T. Patterson (1995), 'The Political and Moral Appropriateness of Sanctions' in David Cortright and George A. Lopez (eds), *Economic Sanctions: Panacea or Peacebuilding in a post-Cold War World?* (Boulder CO, Westview Press), pp 89–96

William J. Perry (1995), 'Gulf Security and US Policy', *Middle East Policy*, vol. 3, no.4 (April), pp 7–14

Jean-Christophe Ploquin et Abderrahim Lamchichi (1997), 'La "fibre pro-arabe" de Jacques Chirac', *Confluences Méditerranée*, no. 22 (Été), pp 9–12

Rene Provost (1992), 'Starvation as a weapon: legal implications of the United Nations food blockade against Iraq and Kuwait', *Columbia Journal of Transnational Law*, vol. 30, pp 577–640

Jonathan C. Randal (1997), *After Such Knowledge, What Forgiveness? My Encounters with Kurdistan* (New York, Farrar, Straus and Giroux)

Bruce O. Riedel (1997), 'The Future of Iraq' in John Calabrese (ed.), *The Future of Iraq* (Washington DC, Middle East Institute), pp 127–31

Philip Robins (1991), *Turkey and the Middle East* (London, Royal Institute of International Affairs/Pinter)

Philip Robins (1993), 'The overlord state: Turkish policy and the Kurdish issue', *International Affairs*, vol. 69, no. 4, pp 657–676

Robin Ross (1991), 'Some early lessons from Operation Haven', *RUSI Journal*, vol. 136/4 (Winter), pp 19–25

Eric Rouleau (1995), 'America's Unyielding Policy Toward Iraq', *Foreign Affairs*, vol. 74, no. 1 (January/February), pp 59–72

Gordon William Rudd (1993), 'Operation Provide Comfort: Humanitarian Intervention in Northern Iraq, 1991', PhD Thesis, Duke University

Oscar Schachter (1991), 'United Nations Law in the Gulf Conflict', *American Journal of International Law*, vol. 85, no. 3, pp 452–473

H. Norman Schwarzkopf (1992), *It doesn't take a hero: General H. Norman Schwarzkopf, the autobiography* (New York, Bantam Books)

Chris Seiple (1996), *The US Military/NGO Relationship in Humanitarian Interventions Peacekeeping Institute* (Center for Strategic Leadership, US Army War College, Pennsylvania)

Stockholm International Peace Research Institute (1997), *SIPRI Yearbook 1997: Armaments, Disarmament and International Security* (Stockholm, SIPRI and Oxford, Oxford University Press)

Jane E. Stromseth (1993), 'Iraq's Repression of Its Civilian Population: Collective Responses and Continuing Challenges' in Damrosch (ed.), *Enforcing Restraint: Collective Intervention in Internal Conflicts* (New York, Council on Foreign Relations Press), pp 77–117

Serge Sur (1992), *Security Council Resolution 687 of 3 April 1991 in the Gulf Affair: Problems of restoring and safeguarding peace*, Research Paper no. 12 (New York, UN Institute for Disarmament Research)

'Symposium on dual containment' (1994) (Martin Indyk, Graham Fuller, Anthony Cordesman and Phebe Marr), *Middle East Policy*, vol. 3, no. 1, pp 1–26

'Symposium: US Policy toward Iran' (1995), *Middle East Policy*, vol. 4, nos 1/2, pp 1–21

Strobe Talbott (1992), 'Post victory blues', *Foreign Affairs*, vol. 71, no. 1, pp 53–69

Victor Tanner (1991), 'Operation Provide Comfort, Iraq 1991: A Unique Operation, Lessons Learned' (August) (Texas, Intertect)

Paul Taylor and A.J.R. Groom (1992), *The United Nations and the Gulf War 1990–1991: Back to the Future?* Royal Institute of International Affairs Discussion Paper 38 (London, Royal Institute of International Affairs)

Charles Tripp (1995), 'The Future of Iraq and of Regional Security' in Geoffrey Kemp and Janice Gross Stein (eds), *Powder Keg in the Middle East: The Struggle for Gulf Security* (London, Rowman & Littlefield), pp 133–159

United Nations (1991i) *Report on humanitarian needs in Iraq in the immediate post-crisis environment by a Mission to the area led by the Under-Secretary-General for Administration and Management 10–17 March 1991*, extract published in United Nations (1996i), Document 31

United Nations (1991ii) *Report to the Secretary-General on Humanitarian Needs in Iraq* by a Mission led by Sadruddin Aga Khan, Executive Delegate of the Secretary General, 15 July 1991

United Nations (1996i), *The United Nations and the Iraq-Kuwait Conflict 1990–1996*, UN Blue Books Series, vol. IX E.96.3 92-1-100596-5 (New York, UN Publications)

United Nations (1996ii), *Report of the Security Council Committee established by Resolution 661 (1990) concerning the situation between Iraq and Kuwait*, S/1996/700, 26 August 1996

United Nations Economic and Social Council, Commission on Human Rights (1992), *Report on the Situation of Human Rights in Iraq prepared by Mr Max van der Stoel, Special Rapporteur on Human Rights, in accordance with Commission 1991/74*, 18 February 1992, E/CN.4/1992/31

United Nations Economic and Social Council, Commission on Human Rights (1994), *Report on the situation of human rights in Iraq, submitted by Mr Max van der Stoel, Special Rapporteur of the Commission on Human Rights in accordance with Commission resolution 1993/74*, Commission on Human Rights, Geneva, 50th session, agenda item 12, 25 February 1994, E/CN.4/1994/58

United Nations Economic and Social Council, Commission on Human Rights (1998), *Report on the situation of human rights in Iraq, submitted by the Special Rapporteur, Mr Max van der Stoel, in accordance with Commission resolution 1997/60*, 10 March 1998

United Nations General Assembly (1992), *The Situation of Human Rights in Iraq*, 47th session, Agenda item 97 (c), 13 November 1992, A/47/367/Add 1

UNHCR (1992i), *Report on Northern Iraq April 1991–May 1992*, Geneva, September

UNHCR (1992ii), *Review of UNHCR Emergency Preparedness and Response in the Persian Gulf Crisis*, March

UNHCR (1997), *The State of the World's Refugees 1997-98: A Humanitarian Agenda* (Oxford, Oxford University Press)

United Nations Security Council (1992), *Interim report on the situation of human rights in Iraq prepared by Mr Max van der Stoel, Special Rapporteur of the Commission on Human Rights*, 5 August 1992, S/24386

US Agency for International Development, Office of US Foreign Disaster Assistance (1991), *Kurdish Relief and Repatriation: DOD-AID/OFDA Partnership. The Kurdish Response After-Action Report*, Washington DC, December

US Committee for Refugees (1994), *World Refugee Survey 1994*, Washington DC

US Committee for Refugees (1995), *World Refugee Survey 1995*, Washington DC

US Committee for Refugees (1997), *World Refugee Survey 1997*, Washington DC

US Congress, House of Representatives, Committee on Appropriations, *Foreign Operations, Export Financing, and Related Programs Appropriations for 1997 and Supplemental for 1996, Hearings before a Subcommittee of the House Appropriations Committee*, 104th Congress, 2nd session, March 6, 1996.

US Congress, House of Representatives, Committee on Armed Services, *Options for Dealing with Iraq: Hearings before the Defense Policy Panel of the Committee on Armed Services*, 102nd Congress, 2nd session, August 10 and 11, 1992

US Congress, House of Representatives, Committee on Foreign Affairs, *United States Policy Toward the Middle East and Persian Gulf: Hearings before the Subcommittee on Europe and the Middle East of the Committee on Foreign Affairs*, 102nd Congress, 1st session, June 17 and 26, 1991

US Congress, House of Representatives, Committee on Foreign Affairs, *UN Role in the Persian Gulf and Iraqi Compliance with UN Resolutions: Hearing before the Subcommittees on Europe and the Middle East and on Human Rights and International Organizations of the Committee on Foreign Affairs*, 102nd Congress, 1st session, April 23, July 18 and October 21, 1991

US Congress, House of Representatives, Committee on Foreign Affairs, *Developments in the Middle East, November 1991: Hearing before the Subcommittee on Europe and the Middle East of the Committee on Foreign Affairs*, 102nd Congress, 1st session, November 20, 1991

US Congress, House of Representatives, Committee on Foreign Affairs, *Developments in the Middle East: Hearing before the Subcommittee on Europe and the Middle East of the Committee on Foreign Affairs*, 102nd Congress, 2nd session, March 17, 1992

US Congress, House of Representatives, Committee on Foreign Affairs, *Iraq's Nuclear Weapons Capability and IAEA Inspections in Iraq: Joint Hearing of the Subcommittees on Europe and the Middle East and International Security, International Organizations and Human Rights of the Committee on Foreign Affairs*, 103rd Congress, 1st session June 29, 1993

US Congress, House of Representatives, Committee on Foreign Affairs, *Developments in the Middle East October 1993: Hearing before the Subcommittee on Europe and the Middle East of the Committee on Foreign Affairs*, 103rd Congress, 1st session, October 21, 1993

US Congress, House of Representatives, Committee on Foreign Affairs, *US Policy toward Iraq 3 Years after the Gulf War: Hearing before the Subcommittee on Europe and the Middle East of the Committee on Foreign Affairs*, 103rd Congress, 2nd session, February 23, 1994

US Congress, House of Representatives, Committee on Foreign Affairs, *Developments in the Middle East March 1994: Hearing before the Sub-Committee on Europe and the Middle East of the Committee on Foreign Affairs*, 103rd Congress, 2nd session, March 1, 1994

US Congress, House of Representatives, Committee on Foreign Affairs, *Developments in the Middle East June 1994: Hearing before the Subcommittee on Europe and the Middle East of the Foreign Affairs Committee*, 103rd Congress, 2nd session, June 14, 1994

US Congress, House of Representatives, Committee on International Affairs, *Developments in the Middle East: Hearing before the Committee on International Relations*, 104th Congress, 2nd session, June 12, 1996

US Congress, House of Representatives, Committee on International Affairs, *US Policy in the Persian Gulf: Hearing before the Committee on International Relations*, 104th Congress 2nd session, September 25, 1996

US Congress, House of Representatives, Select Committee on Hunger, *Humanitarian Dilemma in Iraq: Challenge for U.S. Policy: Hearing before the International Task Force of the Select Committee on Hunger*, 102nd Congress, 1st session, August 1, 1991

US Congress, House of Representatives, Select Committee on Hunger, *Humanitarian Crisis in Iraq: Challenge for U.S. Policy: Hearing before the International Task Force of the Select Committee on Hunger*, 102nd Congress, 1st session, November 13, 1991

US Congress, Senate, Committee on Armed Services, *The Situation in Iraq: Hearing before the Committee on Armed Services*, 104th Congress, 2nd session, September 12, 1996

US Congress, Senate, Committee on Foreign Relations, *Persian Gulf: the Question of War Crimes: Hearing before the Committee on Foreign Relations*, 102nd Congress, 1st session, April 9, 1991

US Congress, Senate, Committee on Foreign Relations, *Civil War in Iraq: A Staff Report to the Committee on Foreign Relations*, May 1991

US Congress, Senate, Committee on Foreign Relations, *Middle East Arms Transfer Policy: Hearing before the Committee on Foreign Relations*, 102nd Congress, 1st session, June 6, 1991

US Congress, Senate, Foreign Relations Committee, *US Policy Toward Iran and Iraq: Hearing before the Subcommittee on Near Eastern and South Asian Affairs*, 104th Congress, 1st session, March 2, 1995

US Congress, Senate, Foreign Relations Committee, Subcommittee on Near East and South Asia Affairs, Washington DC, March 11, 1998 (electronic copy: http://www.state.gov)

US Congress, Senate, Foreign Relations Committee, Subcommittee on Near East and South Asia Affairs, Washington DC, May 21, 1998 (electronic copy: http://www.state.gov)

US Congress, Senate, Committee on the Judiciary, *Refugee Crisis in the Persian Gulf: Hearings before the Subcommittee on Immigration and Refugee Affairs of the Committee of the Judiciary*, 102nd Congress, 1st session, April 15–May 20, 1991

US Department of State (1995), *Report on Human Rights Practices for 1994: Iraq* (Washington DC, US Government Printing Office)

US Department of State (1997), *Report on Human Rights Practices for 1996: Iraq* (Washington DC, US Government Printing Office)

US Department of State (1998i), *Report on Human Rights Practices for 1997: Turkey* (Washington DC, US Government Printing Office)

Thomas G. Weiss, David Cortright, George A. Lopez and Larry Minear (eds) (1997), *Political Gain and Civilian Pain: Humanitarian Aspects of Economic Sanctions* (Lanham MD and New York, Rowman and Littlefield)

Marc Weller (ed.) (1993), *Iraq and Kuwait: the hostilities and their aftermath*, Cambridge International Documents Series, vol. 3 (Cambridge, Research Centre for International Law/Grotius Publications)

Paul Wolfowitz (1997), 'The United States and Iraq' in John Calabrese (ed.) *The Future of Iraq* (Washington DC, Middle East Institute), pp 107–113

Marjoleine Zieck (1997), *UNHCR and Voluntary Repatriation of Refugees: a legal analysis* (The Hague and London, Martinus Nijhoff)

Sami Zubaida (1992), 'Introduction' in P. Kreyenbroek and S. Sperl (eds), *The Kurds: A contemporary overview* (London and New York, Routledge), pp 1–9

PART II
General sources on Iraq
(for material on the Kurds, see section below)

Hassan Mohammed Ali (1955), *Land Reclamation and Settlement in Iraq* (Baghdad, Baghdad Printing Press)

Amnesty International (1991), *Iraq: Human Rights Violations Since the Uprisings*, (London)

Amnesty International (1993), *'Disappearance' of Shi'a clerics and students*, (London)

Amnesty International (1996), *Iraq – State cruelty: branding amputation and the death penalty*, (London)

Amnesty International (1998), *Annual Report* 1998 (London)

I. Ascherio *et al* (1992), 'Effects of the Gulf War on Infant and Child Mortality in Iraq' (by members of the International Study Team), *The New England Journal of Medicine*, vol. 327, no. 13 (24 September), pp 931–936

Sultan Barakat (1993), *Post war reconstruction in Iraq: the case study of Basrah and Fao*, (York, Institute of Advanced Architectural Studies, University of York)

Amatzia Baram (1991), *Culture, History and Ideology in the Formation of Ba'thist Iraq 1968–89* (Basingstoke, Macmillan/Oxford, St Antony's College)

Amatzia Baram (1993), 'The Future of Ba'thist Iraq: Power Structure, Challenges, and Prospects' in R.B. Satloff (ed.), *The Politics of Change in the Middle East* (Boulder CO, Westview Press), pp 31–62

Amatzia Baram (1994), 'Two Roads to Revolutionary Shi'ite Fundamentalism in Iraq' in M.E. Marty and R. Scottt Appleby (eds), *Accounting for Fundamentalisms: the Dynamic Character of Movements* (Chicago and London, University of Chicago Press), pp 531–588

Amatzia Baram (1997), 'Neo-Tribalism in Iraq: Saddam Hussein's Tribal Policies 1991–96', *International Journal of Middle East Studies*, vol. 29, pp 1–31

Hanna Batatu (1978), *The Old Social Classes and the Revolutionary Movements of Iraq* (Princeton NJ, Princeton University Press)

Hanna Batatu (1989), 'Iraq's Shi'a: their political role and the process of their integration into society' in B. Stowasser (ed.), *The Islamic Impulse* (Washington DC, Georgetown University Centre for Contemporary Arab Studies), pp 204–13

Peter Beaumont (1993), 'Iraq: Environmental, Resource and Development Issues' in D. Hopwood, H. Ishow and T. Koszinowski (eds.), *Iraq: Power and Society* (Reading, Ithaca Press, for St Antony's College, Oxford), pp 117–40

Bela Bhatia, Mary Kawar and Mariam Shahin (1992), *Unheard Voices: Iraqi women on war and Sanctions*, Change International Reports: Women and Society, London

Peter Boone, Haris Gazdar and Athar Hussain (1997), *Sanctions against Iraq: costs of failure*, report prepared for the Center of Economic and Social Rights on the impact of United Nations-imposed economic sanctions on the economic well-being of the civilian population of Iraq, London

Claudia von Braunmuhl and Manfred Kulessa (1995), *The Impact of UN Sanctions on Humanitarian Assistance Activities: Report on a Study Commissioned by the United Nations Department of Humanitarian Affairs*, Gesellschaft fur Communication Management Interkultur Training mbH – COMIT, December

Center for Economic and Social Rights (1996), *Unsanctioned suffering: a human rights assessment of UN sanctions on Iraq*, May, New York

Kiren Aziz Chaudry (1991), 'On the Way to Market: Economic Liberalisation and Iraq's Invasion of Kuwait', *Middle East Report*, no. 170 (May–June), pp 14–23

Shahram Chubin and Charles Tripp (1988), *Iran and Iraq at War* (London, I.B. Tauris)

Patrick Clawson (1993ii), *How Has Saddam Hussein Survived?* McNair Paper 22, Insitute for National Strategic Studies, August (Washington DC, National Defense University)

Jean Dreze and Haris Gazdar (1991), *Hunger and Poverty in Iraq* (International Study Team) Development Economics Research Programme, London School of Economics, September

Mary C. Smith Fawzi, Walid Aldoori, W.W. Fawzi and Nagib Armijo-Hussein (1997), 'The Gulf War, Child Nutrition and Feeding Practices in Iraq', *Nutrition Research*, vol. 17, no. 5, pp 775–784

Robert A. Fernea (1970), *Shaykh and Effendi: Changing Patterns of Authority Among the El Shabana of Southern Iraq* (Cambridge, Harvard University Press)

Lawrence Freedman and David Boren (1992), 'Safe havens for Kurds in Post-War Iraq' in Nigel Rodley (ed.), *To loose the bonds of wickedness: international intervention and defence of human rights* (London and New York, Brassey's), pp 43–92

Lawrence Freedman and Efraim Karsh (1993), *The Gulf Conflict 1990–1991: Diplomacy and War in the New World Order* (London and Boston, Faber & Faber)

Clifford Geertz (1973), *The Interpretation of Cultures: Selected Essays* (New York, Basic Books)

Michael Gordon and Bernard C. Trainor (1995), *The General's War* (Boston, Little Brown)

Sarah Graham-Brown (1995), 'Intervention, Sovereignty and Responsibility: the Iraq Sanctions Dilemma', *Middle East Report*, no. 193 (March–April), pp 2–12, 32

Joost R. Hilterman (1993), 'Diverting Water: Displacing Iraq's Marsh People', *Middle East Report*, no. 181 (March–April), pp 36–37

Eric Hoskins (1993), *Iraq: Children, War and Sanctions*, report prepared for UNICEF, Baghdad

Eric Hoskins (1997), 'The Humanitarian Impacts of Economic Sanctions and War in Iraq' in Thomas G. Weiss, David Cortright, George A. Lopez and Larry Minear (eds), *Political Gain and Civilian Pain: Humanitarian Aspects of Economic Sanctions* (Lanham MD, New York, Rowman and Littlefield), pp 91–147

Human Rights Watch (1998), *World Report* 1998 (New York etc)

Human Rights Watch/Middle East (1995), *Iraq's Brutal Decrees – Amputation, Branding and the Death Penalty*, June, New York

Shireen Hunter (1993), 'Two years after the Gulf War: a status report on Iraq and the region', *Security Dialogue*, vol. 24, no. 1, pp 21–36

Faleh 'Abd al-Jabbar (1994), 'Why the uprisings failed' in Fran Hazelton (ed.), *Iraq since the Gulf War: prospects for democracy* (London, Zed Books), pp 97–117

Faleh A. Jabbar (1998), 'L'hégémonie des Etats-Unis à l'épreuve: comment Washington voudrait renverser le pouvoir irakien', *Le Monde Diplomatique*, March

Suad Joseph, 'The Mobilisation of Iraqi Women into the Wage Labour force', *Studies in Third World Societies*, no. 16

Efraim Karsh and Inari Rautsi (1991), *Saddam Hussein, a political biography* (London, Brassey's)

Isam al-Khafaji (1986), 'State Incubation of Iraqi Capitalism', *Middle East Report* (September –October), pp 4–9, 12

Isam al-Khafaji (1994) 'State Terror and the Degradation of Politics' in Fran Hazleton (ed.), *Iraq since the Gulf War: prospects for democracy* (London, Zed Books), pp 20–31

Isam al-Khafaji (1995), *War as a Vehicle for the Rise and Demise of a State-controlled Society: the Case of Ba'thist Iraq*, Middle East Paper, no. 4 (Amsterdam, University of Amsterdam, Research Centre for International Political Economy and Foreign Policy Analysis)

Samih al-Khalil (1991), *Republic of Fear*, new edition (London, Hutchinson Radius)

Tariq al-Khudayri (1997) 'The Manufacturing Industry of Iraq: Status and Future Prospects', paper presented at the Conference on 'Frustrated Development: The Iraqi Economy in War and Peace', Centre for Arab Gulf Studies, Exeter University, July 1997

Pierre Kopp (1996), 'Embargo et criminalisation de l'economie' in François Jean and Jean-Christophe Rufin (eds), *Economie des guerres civiles* (Paris, Hachette/Pluriel), pp 425–465

Atallah Kuttab (1992), 'Dilemmas of Relief Work in Iraq', *Middle East Report*, no. 174 (January/February), pp 37–8

The Lancet (1995), 'Health of Baghdad's Children', vol. 346 (2 December), p 1485

Pierre-Jean Luizard (1994), 'Baghdad: une métropole moderne et tribale, siège de gouverne-ments assiégés', *Monde arabe Maghreb-Machrek*, numéro spéciale (1er trimestre), pp 225–242

Pierre-Jean Luizard (1995), 'The Iraq Question from the Inside', *Middle East Report*, no. 193 (March–April), pp 18–22

Kamil Mahdi (1995), 'The Political Economy of Iraq's Agriculture' in Eric Watkins (ed.), *The Middle Eastern Environment: selected papers of the 1995 conference of the British Society for Middle East Studies* (Cambridge, St Malo Press), pp 192–208

Edward Maltby (ed.) (1994), *An Environmental and Ecological Study of the Marshlands of Mesopotamia*, draft consultative bulletin, May 1994, Wetlands Ecosystems Research Group, University of Exeter/Amar Appeal

Phebe Marr (1995), *The Modern History of Iraq* (Boulder CO, Westview Press and London, Longman)

Middle East Watch[1] (1992), *Endless Torment: The 1991 Uprising in Iraq and its Aftermath*, June (New York)

Minority Rights Group (1993), *The Marsh Arabs of Iraq*, updated edition, June (London)

Yitzhak Nakash (1994), *The Shi'is of Iraq* (Princeton NJ, Princeton University Press)

Abbas Alnasrawi (1994), *The Economy of Iraq: oil wars, destruction of development and prospects 1950–2010* (Westport CT and London, Greenwood Press)

Suha Omar (1994), 'Women: Honour, Shame and Dictatorship' in Fran Hazleton (ed.), *Iraq since the Gulf War: prospects for democracy* (London, Zed Books), pp 60–71

Eric Rouleau (1994), 'Le peuple irakien: première victime de l'ordre americain', *Le Monde Diplomatique*, November

S.M. Salim (1962), *Marsh Dwellers of the Euphrates Delta* (London, University of London/Athlone Press)

Juliette Sayegh (1992) *Child Survival in Wartime: a Case Study from Iraq, 1983–1989* (Baltimore MD, Department of Population Dynamics, Johns Hopkins School of Hygiene and Public Health)

Sinan al-Shabibi (1997), 'Prospects for Iraq's Economy: Facing the New Reality' in John Calabrese (ed.), *The Future of Iraq* (Washington DC, Middle East Institute), pp 54–80

Marion Farouk-Sluglett and Peter Sluglett (1983), 'The Transformation of Land Tenure and Rural Social Structure in Central and Southern Iraq c 1870–1958', *International Journal of Middle East Studies*, vol. 15, pp 491–505

Peter Sluglett and Marion Farouk-Sluglett (1990i), *Iraq since 1958: from revolution to dictatorship* (London and New York, I.B. Tauris)

Peter Sluglett and Marion Farouk-Sluglett (1990ii), 'Iraq Since 1986: the strengthening of Saddam', *Middle East Report*, no. 167 (November-December), pp 19–24

Robert Springborg (1987), 'Iraq's Agrarian Infitah', *Middle East Report*, no. 145 (March–April), pp 16–21

Barbara Stapleton (1993), *The Shi'as of Iraq: a historical perspective on the present human rights situation*, report to the Parliamentary Human Rights Group (London)

Joe Stork (1989), 'Class, State and Politics in Iraq' in B. Berberoglu (ed.), *Power and Stability in the Middle East* (London, Zed Books), pp 31–54

'Symposium on dual containment' (1994) (Martin Indyk, Graham Fuller, Anthony Cordesman and Phebe Marr), *Middle East Policy*, vol. 3, no. 1, pp 1–26

Charles Tripp (1995) 'The Future of Iraq and of Regional Security' in Geoffrey Kemp and Janice Gross Stein (eds), *Powder Keg in the Middle East: The Struggle for Gulf Security* (London, Rowman & Littlefield), pp 133–159

United Nations (1991ii), *Report to the Secretary-General on Humanitarian Needs in Iraq*, by a Mission led by Sadruddin Aga Khan, Executive Delegate of the Secretary General, 15 July 1991

United Nations Children's Fund (UNICEF, 1995), *The Status of Children and Women in Iraq: A Situation Report*, September

United Nations Food and Agriculture Organisation (1993), *Report of the Nutritional Status Assessment Mission to Iraq*, December, Rome

United Nations Food and Agriculture Organisation, Technical Cooperation Programme (FAO, 1995), *Evaluation of Food and Nutrition Situation in Iraq: Terminal Statement Prepared for the Government of Iraq*, Rome

United Nations Security Council (1997), *Report of the Secretary General pursuant to Paragraph 3 of Resolution 1111*, S/1997/685, 8 September 1997

United Nations Security Council (1998i) *Report of the Secretary General pursuant to Paragraph 7 of Resolution 1143*, S/1998/90, 1 February 1998

United Nations Security Council (1998ii), *Report of the Secretary General pursuant to Paragraph 10 of Resolution 1153*, S/1998/1100, 19 November 1998

United Nations Special Rapporteur on Human Rights in Iraq:

    United Nations Economic and Social Council Commission on Human Rights (1992), *Report on the Situation of Human Rights in Iraq prepared by Mr Max van der Stoel, Special Rapporteur on Human Rights, in accordance with Commission 1991/74*, 18 February 1992, E/CN.4/1992/31

    United Nations Economic and Social Council Commission on Human Rights (1993), *Report on the Situation of Human Rights in Iraq prepared by Mr Max van der Stoel, Special Rapporteur on Human Rights, in accordance with Commission 1992/71*, 19 February 1993, E/CN.4/1993/45

    United Nations Economic and Social Council, Commission on Human Rights (1994), *Report on the situation of human rights in Iraq, submitted by Mr Max van der Stoel, Special Rapporteur of the Commission on Human Rights in accordance with Commission resolution 1993/74*, 25 February 1994, E/CN.4/1994/58

    United Nations Economic and Social Council, Commission on Human Rights (1995), *Report on the situation of human rights in Iraq, submitted by Mr Max van der Stoel, Special Rapporteur of the Commission on Human Rights in accordance with Commission resolution 1994/74*, 15 February 1995, E/CN.4/1995/56

United Nations Economic and Social Council, Commission on Human Rights (1996), *Report on the situation of human rights in Iraq, submitted by Mr Max van der Stoel, Special Rapporteur of the Commission on Human Rights in accordance with Commission resolution 1995/76*, 4 March 1996, E/CN.4/1996/61

United Nations Economic and Social Council, Commission on Human Rights (1998), *Report on the situation of human rights in Iraq, submitted by the Special Rapporteur, Mr Max van der Stoel, in accordance with Commission resolution 1997/60*, 10 March 1998

United Nations General Assembly (1994), *The Situation of Human Rights in Iraq*, 49th session, Agenda item 100 (c). A/49/651, 8 November 1994

United Nations General Assembly (1995), *The Situation of Human Rights in Iraq*, 50th session, Agenda item 112 (c), A/50/734, 8 November 1995

United Nations General Assembly (1996), *The Situation of Human Rights in Iraq*, 51st session, Agenda item 110 (c), A/51/496, 15 October 1996

United Nations General Assembly (1997), *The Situation of Human Rights in Iraq*, 52nd session, Agenda item 11 (c), A/52/476, 15 October 1997

US Committee for Refugees (1994), *World Refugee Survey* 1994, Washington DC

US Committee for Refugees (1995), *World Refugee Survey* 1995, Washington DC

US Congress, House of Representatives, Committee on Foreign Affairs, *Iraq Rebuilds Its Military Industries: A Staff Report to the Subcommittee on International Security, International Organisations and Human Rights*, Committee on Foreign Affairs, 103rd Congress, June 29, 1993

US Congress, House of Representatives, Committee on Foreign Affairs, *Iraq's Nuclear Weapons Capability and IAEA Inspections in Iraq: Joint Hearing of the Subcommittees on Europe and the Middle East and International Security, International Organisations and Human Rights of the Committee on Foreign Affairs*, 103rd Congress, 1st session, June 29, 1993

US Congress, Senate, Foreign Relations Committee, *US Policy Toward Iran and Iraq: Hearing before the Subcommittee on Near Eastern and South Asian Affairs*, 104th Congress, 1st session, March 2, 1995

US Department of State (1994), *Country Reports on Human Rights Practices for 1993: Iraq* (Washington DC, Government Printing Office)

US Department of State (1995), *Country Reports on Human Rights Practices for 1994: Iraq* (Washington DC, Government Printing Office)

US Department of State (1998ii), *Country Reports on Human Rights Practices 1997: Iraq* (Washington DC, Government Printing Office)

Sarah Zaidy (1994), 'War, Sanctions and Humanitarian Assistance: The Case of Iraq 1990–93', *Medicine and Global Survival*, vol. 1, no. 3, September

Sami Zubaida (1991), 'Community, Class and Minorities in Iraqi Politics' in Robert A. Fernea and William Roger Louis (eds), *The Iraqi Revolution of 1958: The Old Social Classes Revisited* (London and New York, I.B. Tauris), pp 197–210

Sources on the Kurds

Rizgar Amin and Kerim Yildiz (1996), *The Internal Conflict and Human Rights in Iraqi Kurdistan: Report of KHRP Delegations to Iraqi Kurdistan, June 1995 and December 1995*, March (London, Kurdish Human Rights Project)

Amnesty International (1995), *Iraq: Human rights abuses in Iraqi Kurdistan since 1991* (London)

Hamit Bozarslan (1996) 'Kurdistan: economie de guerre, economie dans la guerre' in Francois Jean and Jean-Christophe Rufin (eds), *Economie des guerres civiles Paris*, (Paris, Hachette/Pluriel), pp 105–146

Hamit Bozarslan (1997), *La question kurde: Etats et minorités au Moyen Orient* (Paris, Presses de Sciences PO)

Martin van Bruinessen (1992), *Agha, Shaikh and State: the Social and Political Structures of Kurdistan* (London and New Jersey, Zed Books)

Martin van Bruinessen (1994), 'Nationalisme Kurde et Ethnicités intra-Kurdes', *Peuples Méditerranéens*, no. 68–69 (July–December), pp 11–37

Helena Cook (1995), *The Safe Haven in Northern Iraq: International Responsibility for Iraqi Kurdistan* (Colchester and London, University of Essex Human Rights Centre/Kurdistan Human Rights Project)

Chris Dammers (1994), 'Post War Iraq and the Politics of Humanitarianism', in Herbert H. Blumberg and Christopher C. French (eds), *The Persian Gulf War: Views from the Social-Behavioural Studies* (Lanham MD, University Press of America), pp 399–411

Nader Entessar (1992), *Kurdish Ethnonationalism* (Boulder CO, Lynne Reinner Publishers)

Rend Rahim Francke (1994), 'The Opposition' in Fran Hazleton (ed.), *Iraq since the Gulf War: prospects for democracy* (London, Zed Books), pp 153–177

Sarah Graham-Brown (1995), 'Intervention, Sovereignty and Responsibility: the Iraq Sanctions Dilemma', *Middle East Report*, no. 193 (March–April), pp 2–12, 32

Michael M. Gunter (1993), 'A de facto Kurdish state in northern Iraq', *Third World Quarterly*, vol. 14, no. 2, pp 295–319

Salahaddin al-Haffid (1992), *The Economic Conditions of Iraqi Kurdistan: its outstanding problems*, vol. I, Sulaymaniya Governorate (Arbil)

Ruud Hoff, Michiel Leezenberg, Pieter Muller (1992), *Elections in Iraqi Kurdistan (May 19, 1992): An Experiment in Democracy*, Report of a Delegation Sponsored by: Pax Christi International, Brussels, Interchurch Peace Council, The Hague, and Netherlands Kurdistan Society, Amsterdam (August)

Human Rights Watch/Middle East (1994), *Human Rights Conditions in the Middle East in 1993*, January (New York)

Human Rights Watch/Middle East (1995), *Iraq's Crime of Genocide: the Anfal campaign against the Kurds* (New Haven and London, Yale University Press)

Keen, David (1993), *The Kurds in Iraq: how safe is their haven now?* June (London, Save the Children Fund)

Isam al-Khafaji (1996), 'The Destruction of Iraqi Kurdistan', *Middle East Report*, no. 201 (October–December), pp 35–38, 42

Philip Kreyenbroek and Stefan Sperl (eds) (1992), *The Kurds: A contemporary overview* (London and New York, Routledge)

Chris Kutschera (1997), *Le défi kurde, ou le rêve fou de l'independance* (Paris, Bayard Editions)

Lawyers Committee for Human Rights (1992), *Asylum under attack: a report on the protection of Iraqi refugees and displaced persons one year after the humanitarian emergency in Iraq*, April (New York)

Michiel Leezenberg (1997), 'Iraqi Kurdistan since the second Gulf War' (unpublished English translation by the author). Published in German in C. Borck, S. Hajo and E Savelsberg (eds) (1997), *Ethnizitat, Nationalismus, Religion und Politik in Kurdistan*, Kurdologie, Band 1 (Munster, LIT Verlag), pp 45–78

Nisar Majid (forthcoming), 'Northern Iraq, Sanctions and UNSCR 986', for Save the Children Fund (UK), (London)

Phebe Marr (1996), 'Turkey and Iraq' in Henri J. Barkey (ed.), *Reluctant Neighbour: Turkey's Role in the Middle East* (Washington DC, US Institute of Peace Press)

David McDowall (1992), *The Kurds: a nation denied* (London, Minority Rights Group)

David McDowall (1995) 'Addressing the Kurdish Issue' in Geoffrey Kemp and Janice Gross Stein (eds), *Powder Keg in the Middle East: The Struggle for Gulf Security* (London, Rowman & Littlefield), pp 211–236

David McDowall (1997), *A Modern History of the Kurds* (London, I.B. Tauris)

Michael Meadowcroft and Martin Lunn (1992), *Kurdistan: Elections for the Iraqi Kurdish National Assembly and Leader of the Kurdistan Liberation Movement, Tuesday 19th May 1992: Monitoring Report* (London, Electoral Reform Society, Consultancy Services)

Middle East Watch[1] (1992), *Hidden Death: Land Mines and Civilian Casualties in Iraqi Kurdistan* (New York)

Pieter Muller (1992), *Report on the situation in Free Kurdistan (Liberated Zone of Iraqi Kurdistan)*, May (Amsterdam, Netherlands Kurdistan Friendship Society)

Netherlands Kurdistan Society (1996), *Iraqi Kurdistan 1991–1996: Political Crisis and Humanitarian Aid* (Amsterdam)

Jonathan C. Randal (1997), *After Such Knowledge, What Forgiveness? My Encounters with Kurdistan* (New York, Farrar, Straus and Giroux)

Philip Robins (1993), 'The overlord state: Turkish policy and the Kurdish issue', *International Affairs*, vol. 69, no. 4, pp 657–676

Irma Silva-Barbeau, Guy Templer, Patrick Ward (1994), *Methodology for Measuring Basic Needs Requirements and Identifying Vulnerable Groups: Kurdistan, Northern Iraq*, Report Prepared for the Office of Foreign Disaster Assistance (Washington DC, United States Agency for International Development)

Peter Sluglett and Marion Farouk-Sluglett (1990i), *Iraq since 1958: from revolution to dictatorship* (London and New York, I.B. Tauris)

United Nations General Assembly (1996), *The Situation of Human Rights in Iraq*, 51st session, Agenda item 110 (c), A/51/496, 15 October 1996

UNHCR (1992i) *Report on Northern Iraq April 1991–May 1992*, September (Geneva)

United Nations Security Council (1997), *Report of the Secretary-General Pursuant to Paragraph 3 of Resolution 1111* (1997) S/1997/685, 8 September 1997

US Department of State (1995), *Country Reports on Human Rights Practices for 1994: Iraq* (Washington DC, US Government Printing Office)

US Department of State (1998ii), *Country Reports on Human Rights Practices for 1997: Iraq*, (Washington DC, US Government Printing Office)

Patrick Ward and Martin Rimmer (1995), *Targeting the Poor in Northern Iraq: The Role of Formal and Informal Research Methods in Relief Operations*, Relief and Rehabilitation Network, Paper no. 8, April (London, Overseas Development Institute)

PART III

I. Ascherio *et al* (1992), 'Effects of the Gulf War on Infant and Child Mortality in Iraq' (by members of the International Study Team), *The New England Journal of Medicine*, vol. 327, no. 13 (24 September), pp 931–936

A. de Boer and M. Leezenberg (eds) (1993), *Iraqi Kurdistan: The Need for Durable Development*, proceedings of the International Conference: 'Iraqi Kurdistan: The need for continuing support and development', Brussels, October 10–12

Franca Brilliant, Frederick C. Cuny, Victor Tanner (1995), *Humanitarian Intervention: A Study of Operation Provide Comfort* (ed. Pat Reed) (Dallas, Intertect)

Paul Conlon (1997), 'The Humanitarian Mitigation of UN Sanctions', *German Yearbook of International Law 1996*, vol. 39, pp 249–284

Frederick C. Cuny, (1995), *The Political, Military, Economic and Humanitarian Situation in Iraqi Kurdistan: An Assessment*, January (Carnegie Endowment for International Peace)

Chris Dammers (1994), 'Post War Iraq and the Politics of Humanitarianism' in Herbert H. Blumberg and Christopher C. French (eds), *The Persian Gulf War: Views from the Social-Behavioural Studies* (Lanham MD, University Press of America), pp 399–411

John Osgood Field and Robert M. Russell (1992), 'Nutrition Mission to Iraq for UNICEF', *Nutrition Reviews*, vol. 50, no. 2 (February), pp 41–46

Richard Garfield (1999), 'Morbidity and Mortality in Iraq, 1990–1998', Occasional Paper, Indiana, Fourth Freedom Forum

Azad Hama (1997), *A community-based approach for the evaluation of a development-oriented project in Southern Kurdistan* (Venice, Istituto Universitario di Architettura di Venezia)

Harvard Study Team (1991), 'The Effect of the Gulf Crisis on the Children of Iraq', *New England Journal of Medicine*, vol. 325, no. 13, 26 September, pp 977–980

Helen Keller International (1991), *Vitamin A Deficiency and Other Nutritional Problems in Southern Iraq 14-26 May 1991*

Eric Hoskins (1997), 'The Humanitarian Impacts of Economic Sanctions and War in Iraq' in Thomas G. Weiss, David Cortright, George A. Lopez and Larry Minear (eds), *Political Gain and Civilian Pain: Humanitarian Aspects of Economic Sanctions* (Lanham MD and New York, Rowman and Littlefield), pp 91–147

Francois Jean (ed.) (1993), *Life, Death and Aid: the Médecins Sans Frontières Report on World Crisis Intervention* (London and New York, MSF/Routledge)

Atallah Kuttab (1992), 'Dilemmas of Relief Work in Iraq', *Middle East Report*, no. 174 (January/February), pp 37–8

Lawyers Committee for Human Rights (1992), *Asylum under attack: a report on the protection of Iraqi refugees and displaced persons one year after the humanitarian emergency in Iraq* (New York)

Nisar Majid (forthcoming), 'Northern Iraq, Sanctions and UNSCR 986', for Save the Children Fund (UK), (London)

Larry Minear *et al* (1992), *United Nations Coordination of the International Humanitarian Response to the Gulf Crisis, 1990–1992*, The Thomas J. Watson Jr Institute for International Studies, Occasional Paper no. 13 (Providence RI, Brown University)

Larry Minear, Colin Scott and Thomas G. Weiss (1996), *News Media, Civil War, and Humanitarian Action* (Boulder CO and London, Lynne Reinner)

Andrew S. Natsios (1997), *US Foreign Policy and the Four Horsemen of the Apocalypse: Humanitarian Relief in Complex Emergencies*, The Washington Papers 170 (Westport CT and London, Praeger/Center for Strategic and International Studies)

Netherlands Kurdistan Society (1996), *Iraqi Kurdistan 1991–1996: Political Crisis and Humanitarian Aid*, (Amsterdam)

Noriko Sato, Omar Obeid and Thierry Brun (1991), 'Malnutrition in southern Iraq', *The Lancet*, vol. 338 (November 9, 1991), p 1202

Juliette Sayegh (1992), *Child Survival in Wartime: a Case Study from Iraq, 1983–1989* (Baltimore MD, Department of Population Dynamics, Johns Hopkins School of Hygiene and Public Health)

Mary C. Smith and Sarah Zaidy (1993), 'Malnutrition in Iraqi Children Following the Gulf War: Results of a National Survey', *Nutrition Reviews*, vol. 51, no.3, pp 74–78.

United Nations Food and Agriculture Organisation (1993), *Report of the nutritional status assessment mission to Iraq* (Rome)

United Nations Food and Agriculture Organisation, Technical Cooperation Programme (1995), *Evaluation of Food and Nutrition Situation in Iraq: Terminal Statement Prepared for the Government of Iraq* (Rome)

UNHCR (1992i) *Report on Northern Iraq April 1991–May 1992*, Geneva (September)

UNHCR (1992ii), *Review of UNHCR Emergency Preparedness and Response in the Persian Gulf Crisis* (March)

United Nations Security Council (1997), *Report of the Secretary General pursuant to Paragraph 3 of Resolution 1111*, S/1997/685, 8 September 1997

United Nations Security Council (1998i), *Report of the Secretary General pursuant to Paragraph 7 of Resolution 1143*, S/1998/90, 1 February 1998

United Nations Security Council (1998ii), *Report of the Secretary General pursuant to Paragraph 10 of Resolution 1153*, S/1998/1100, 19 November 1998

US Congress, House of Representatives, Select Committee on Hunger, *Humanitarian Crisis in Iraq: Challenge for US Policy: Hearing before the International Task Force of the Select Committee on Hunger*, 102nd Congress, 1st session, November 13, 1991

US Congress, House of Representatives, Select Committee on Hunger, *Humanitarian Dilemma in Iraq: Challenge for US Policy: Hearing before the International Task Force of the Select Committee on Hunger*, 102nd Congress, 1st session, August 1, 1991

US Congress, Senate, Committee on Foreign Relations, *Mass Killings in Iraq: Hearing before the Committee on Foreign Relations*, 102nd Congress, 1st session, March 19, 1992

US Office of Foreign Disaster Assistance, United States Agency for International Development (1996), *Stategic Evaluation of the US Government Humanitarian Assistance Program in Northern Iraq*, Final Draft Report

Patrick Ward and Martin Rimmer (1995), *Targeting the Poor in Northern Iraq: The Role of Formal and Informal Research Methods in Relief Operations*, Relief and Rehabilitation Network Paper No 8 (London, Overseas Development Institute)

Thomas G. Weiss, David Cortright, George A. Lopez and Larry Minear (eds) (1997), *Political Gain and Civilian Pain: Humanitarian Aspects of Economic Sanctions* (Lanham MD and New York, Rowman and Littlefield)

CONCLUSION

Mario Bettati (1996ii), 'The International Community and Limitations of Sovereignty' *Diogenes*, vol. 44/4, no. 176, Winter 1996, pp 91–109

Vesna Bojicic and David Dyker (1993), *Sanctions on Serbia: sledgehammer or scalpel?* Working papers in Contemporary European Studies, Sussex University European Institute

Juergen Dedring (1996), 'Humanitarian Coordination' in Jim Whitman and David Pocock (eds), *After Rwanda: The Coordination of United Nations Humanitarian Assistance* (Basingstoke, Macmillan)

Julia Devin and Jaleh Dashti-Gibson (1997), 'Sanctions in the Former Yugoslavia: Convoluted Goals and Complicated Consequences' in Thomas G. Weiss, David Cortright, George A. Lopez and Larry Minear (eds), *Political Gain and Civilian Pain: Humanitarian Aspects of Economic Sanctions* (Lanham MD and New York, Rowman and Littlefield), pp 149–187

Vojin Dimitrijevic and Jelena Pejic (1995), 'UN Sanctions Against Yugoslavia: Two Years Later' in Dimitris Bourantonis and Jarrod Wiener (eds), *The United Nations in the New World Order: The World Organisation at Fifty* (Basingstoke, Macmillan), pp 124–153

Alan Dowty (1994), 'Sanctioning Iraq: the Limits of the New World Order', *Washington Quarterly*, vol. 17, no. 3 (Summer), pp 179–198

Margaret P. Doxey (1996), *International Sanctions in Contemporary Perspective*, 2nd ed. (Basingstoke, Macmillan)

Mark Duffield (1994i), 'Complex Emergencies and the Crisis of Developmentalism', *IDS Bulletin*, vol. 25, no. 4 (October), pp 37–45

Mark Duffield (1994ii), 'The Political Economy of Internal War: Asset Transfer, Complex Emergencies and International Aid' in Joanna MacRae and Anthony Zwi (eds), *War and Hunger: Rethinking International Responses to Complex Emergencies* (London, Zed Books with Save the Children [UK]), pp 50–69

David A. Dyker and Ivan Vejvoda (eds) (1996), *Yugoslavia and After: a Study in Fragmentation, Despair and Rebirth* (London, Longman)

John Eriksson *et al* (1996), *The International Response to Conflict and Genocide: Lessons from the Rwanda Experience*, Synthesis Report Joint Evaluation of Emergency Assistance to Rwanda (London)

Bill Frelick (1994), 'Faultlines of Nationality Conflict: Refugees and Displaced Persons from Armenia and Azerbaijan', *International Journal of Refugee Law*, vol. 6, no. 4, pp 598–99

John Harriss (ed.) (1995), *The Politics of Humanitarian Intervention* (London and New York, Save the Children/Pinter)

Thomas Halverson (1996), 'American Perspectives' in Alex Danchev and Thomas Halverson (eds), *International Perspectives on the Yugoslav Conflict* (Basingstoke, Macmillan/Oxford, St Antony's College), pp 1–28

Human Rights Watch (1993), *The Lost Agenda: Human Rights and UN Field Operations*, June (New York)

International Federation of Red Cross and Red Crescent Societies (1995), *World Disasters Report* (Geneva)

Francois Jean (ed.) (1993), *Life, Death and Aid: The Médecins Sans Frontières Report on World Crisis Intervention* (London and New York, MSF/Routledge)

Karin Landgren (1995), 'Safety Zones and International Protection: a Dark Grey Area', *International Journal of Refugee Law*, vol. 7, no. 3 (July), pp 436–458

Liaison Committee of Development NGOs to the European Union (1994), *Conflict, Development and Military Intervention: the role, position and experience of NGOs*, Report of the European Conference, Brussels, 8/9 April 1994 (NGDO-EU Liaison Committee, Brussels)

Robert C. Loehr and Eric M. Wong (1995), 'Interview: The UN and Humanitarian Assistance: Ambassador Jan Eliasson', *Journal of International Affairs*, vol. 48, no. 2 (Winter), pp 491–505

Larry Minear *et al* (1994), *Humanitarian Action in the former Yugoslavia: the UN's role 1991–1993*, Occasional Paper no. 18, Thomas J. Watson Jr Institute for International Studies and Refugee Policy Group (Providence RI, Brown University)

Oliver Ramsbotham (1997), 'International intervention 1990–5: a need to reconceptualise?' *Review of International Studies* (1997), vol. 23, pp 445–468

Adam Roberts (1996), *Humanitarian Action in War: Aid, Protection and Impartiality in a Policy Vacuum*, Adelphi Paper 305 (Oxford, Oxford University Press)

Francois Jean and Jean-Christophe Rufin (1996), *Economie des guerres civiles* (Paris, Hachette/Pluriel)

Hugo Slim and Angela Penrose (1994), 'UN Reform in a Changing World: Responding to Complex Emergencies' in Joanna MacRae and Anthony Zwi (eds), *War and Hunger: Rethinking International Responses to Complex Emergencies* (London, Zed Books with Save the Children [UK]), pp 194-208

Gayle E. Smith (1993), 'Relief Operations and Military Strategy' in T.G. Weiss and Larry Minear (eds), *Humanitarianism Across Borders: Sustaining Civilians in Times of War* (Lynne Reiner, Boulder CO), pp 97–116

Katerina Tomasevski (1994), 'Human Rights and Wars of Starvation' in Joanna MacRae and Anthony Zwi (eds), *War and Hunger: Rethinking International Responses to Complex Emergencies* (London, Zed Books with Save the Children [UK]), pp 70–90

UNHCR (1997), *The State of the World's Refugees 1997–98: A Humanitarian Agenda* (Oxford, Oxford University Press)

Alex de Waal (1994), 'Dangerous Precendents? Famine Relief in Somalia 1991–3' in Joanna MacRae and Anthony Zwi (eds), *War and Hunger: Rethinking International Responses to Complex Emergencies* (London, Zed Books with Save the Children [UK]), pp 139–59

Alex de Waal (1997), 'Democratising the aid encounter in Africa', *International Affairs*, vol. 73, no. 4 (October), pp 623–639

Susan L. Woodward (1995), 'The Use of Sanctions in Former Yugoslavia: Misunderstanding Political Realities' in David Cortright and George A. Lopez (eds), *Economic Sanctions: Panacea or Peacebuilding in a Post-Cold War World?* (Boulder CO, Westview), pp 141–51.

NOTES ON BIBLIOGRAPHY

1   Middle East Watch has changed its name. It is now the Middle East Division of Human Rights Watch.

INDEX

Main entry under acronym or full name of an organisation follows main text usage, but cross references are provided where necessary. References to a note are followed with an 'n', references to boxed text with a 'b'.